Webster's
Dictionary of
American Writers

Webster's Dictionary of American Writers

Created in cooperation with the Editors of
MERRIAM-WEBSTER

**BARNES
& NOBLE
BOOKS**
NEW YORK

2004 Barnes & Noble Books

ISBN 0-7607-5544-2

Printed and bound in the United States of America

04 05 06 07 08 09 MC 9 8 7 6 5 4 3 2 1

Contents

Introduction

This volume surveys the entire history of literature in the area of the present-day United States from its first settlement by European colonists to the dawn of the new millennium. It embraces the writings of the entire American spectrum, including those of numerous American Indians, former slaves, and immigrants from every corner of the earth. It deals not only with the authors of fiction, poetry, and drama but also with a range of historians, essayists, biographers, diarists, and philosophers, as well as a number of journalists (though only those who also wrote important books) and screenwriters (though only those who also wrote important plays or fiction). Lengthy appendixes are devoted to some 500 individual literary works and to over 70 literary groups, movements, and periodicals.

Browsing the volume's entries will lead the reader down sometimes surprising byways. It introduces such figures as the writer who gave both Buffalo Bill and Wild Bill Hickok their nicknames, and had both of them perform a starring role in his own play (p. 225); the man who created over 15 young-people's series that included the *Bobbsey Twins, Hardy Boys, Tom Swift,* and *Nancy Drew* series (p. 388); the U.S. president who found time to write not only numerous books and 2,000 articles but also 150,000 personal letters (p. 349); the largely forgotten novelist who was probably the best-selling American writer of the 20th century's first two decades (p. 81); the three women whose works became perhaps the three most socially influential American books of the 19th and 20th centuries (pp. 73, 149, and 387); the unsuccessful novelist who would write the screenplay adaptation of the work of a successful fellow novelist, then go on to win the Nobel Prize several years before him (p. 137); the man who, after serving seven years in prison for armed robbery, would write several highly regarded serious novels and a classic series of murder mysteries (p. 198); the writer and editor who emigrated from Russia at 14 by himself, never finished high school, and became one of the most influential of the New York Intellectuals (p. 336); and the dramatist, born Frederick August Kittel, who would become the most celebrated African-American playwright of all time (p. 439).

Most of the entries were adapted from *Merriam-Webster's Encyclopedia of Literature,* whose own entries were largely redacted from *Encyclopaedia Britannica* by Mary Rose McCudden, Anita Wolff, and others under the direction of Kathleen Kuiper. New editorial work was carried out by Francesca M. Forrest, Jocelyn White Franklin, C. Roger Davis, and Mark A. Stevens. Additional pronunciations were contributed by Joshua S. Guenter. Lynn Stowe Tomb served as art coordinator. Robert D. Copeland provided technical assistance. Further assistance was provided by Michael L. Belanger, Deanna Stathis, Penny L. Couillard, G. James Kossuth, Frederick C. Mish, and Thomas F. Pitoniak.

Photograph Credits

Explanatory Notes

As in most dictionaries, the entries are alphabetized letter-by-letter; spaces between words are ignored. Diacritics, apostrophes, and hyphens are ignored in alphabetization.

Boldface type is used for entry headwords, as well as for alternative names by which a person may have been widely known; alternative names not commonly used appear in ordinary roman type. The label *known as* or *pseudonym* precedes the writer's usual authorial name (in boldface):

> **Doolittle, Hilda** *known as* **H.D.**
> **Geisel, Theodor Seuss** *pseudonym* **Dr. Seuss**

The label *originally* precedes the birth name of a person who is entered under a name that was adopted or acquired subsequently:

> **Ayn Rand** *originally* Alisa Zinovievna Rosenbaum

When used within parentheses, *originally* applies only to the first name or names, not the surname:

> **Chayefsky, Paddy** (*originally* Sidney)

Parentheses enclose portions of the name of a person or work that are rarely used:

> **Lewis, (Harry) Sinclair**
> **Donleavy, J(ames) P(atrick)**
> **Look Homeward, Angel(: A Story of the Buried Life)**

The label *in full*, generally used where parentheses might be awkward, precedes a fully spelled-out version of a name usually encountered in its shorter form:

> **Carver, Raymond** *in full* Raymond Clevie Carver, Jr.

A label consisting of a language name precedes a native version or spelling of a name or term:

> **Gibran, Khalil** *Arabic* Jubran Khalil Jubran

Pronunciations are supplied for all entry names whose pronunciation might not be obvious. A key to the pronunciation symbols appears on page xi.

Cross-references to other entries are indicated by SMALL CAPITALS. In the main biographical section, cross-references are provided to works by the entry author that receive their own entries in the "Literary Works" section. In the "Literary Works" section itself, cross-references are provided to authors and to other works. In the "Groups, Movements, and Periodicals" section, cross-references are provided to authors, works, and other groups, movements, or periodicals. However, where an individual or entity is not of central importance, it is not indicated as a cross-reference.

Pronunciation Symbols

ə	banana, collide, abut, humdrum
ᵊ	immediately preceding \n\ as in mitten, eaten
ər	further, merger, bird
a	mat, gag
ā	day, fade, aorta
ä	bother, cot, father, cart
à	father as pronounced by speakers who do not rhyme it with *bother*; French patte
au̇	now, loud, out
b	baby, rib
ch	chin, nature \ˈnā-chər\
d	did, adder
e	bet, bed, peck
ē	beat, easy
f	fifty, cuff
g	go, big
h	hat, ahead
i	tip, banish
ī	site, buy
j	gem, judge
k	kin, cook, ache
k̲	German ich, Buch
l	lily, pool
m	murmur, dim
n	no, own
ŋ	sing \ˈsiŋ\, singer \ˈsiŋ-ər\, finger \ˈfiŋ-gər\, ink \ˈiŋk\
ō	bone, know, beau
ȯ	saw, all, caught
œ	French boeuf, German Hölle
ȯi	coin, destroy
p	pepper, lip
r	red, car, rarity
s	source, less

sh	shy, mission, machine, special
t	tie, attack, late, later, latter
th	thin, ether
th̲	then, either, this
ü	rule, youth, union \ˈyün-yən\, few \ˈfyü\
u̇	pull, wood, book
u̅e̅	French rue, German fühlen
v	vivid, give
w	we, away
y	yard, cue \ˈkyü\, union \ˈyün-yən\
z	zone, raise
zh	vision, azure \ ˈa-zhər\
ˈ	precedes a syllable with primary (strongest) stress: \ˈpen-mən-ˌship\
ˌ	precedes a syllable with secondary (medium) stress: \ˈpen-mən-ˌship\
-	marks syllable division
( )	indicate that what is enclosed is pronounced by some but not by others: *factory* \ˈfak-t(ə-)rē\
Engl	indicates a familiar anglicization of a name of foreign origin

Dictionary of
American Writers

Abbey, Edward (b. Jan. 29, 1927, Home, Pa.—d. March 14, 1989, Oracle, Ariz.) Novelist and essayist whose works, set primarily in the Southwest, reflect an uncompromising environmentalist philosophy.

The son of a Pennsylvania farmer, Abbey earned bachelor's and master's degrees at the University of New Mexico in the 1950s. He subsequently worked as a park ranger and fire lookout for the National Park Service, an experience that gave him insight into the relationship between man and the environment, especially as he observed the remnants of ancient Indian cultures and the encroachment of consumer civilization. *Desert Solitaire* (1968) is an extended meditation on Utah's sublime and forbidding wilderness. That work, with the novel *The Monkey Wrench Gang* (1975), which recounts the exploits of a band of guerrilla environmentalists, became virtual handbooks of the environmental movement. *Hayduke Lives!*, a sequel to *The Monkey Wrench Gang*, was published posthumously in 1990.

Abbott, Jacob (b. Nov. 14, 1803, Hallowell, Maine—d. Oct. 31, 1879, Farmington, Maine) Clergyman, teacher, and writer, best known as a writer of children's books.

The second of seven children, Abbott attended Bowdoin College and studied at Andover Newton Theological School. In 1829 he moved to Boston, where with a brother he founded the Mount Vernon School for girls. Abbott was sole author of 180 books and coauthor or editor of 31 others, notably the instructive 28-volume "Rollo" series, considered the first fictional series for children. Though now chiefly noted for their picture of 19th-century rural American life, the Rollo books were written to entertain, edify, and help children learn to think and read. Abbott also wrote 22 volumes of biographical histories and 10 volumes of *Franconia Stories*. He was the father of the clergyman, author, and editor Lyman Abbott (1835–1922).

Abish \\'ab-ish\\, **Walter** (b. Dec. 24, 1931, Vienna) Writer whose experimental novels and short stories take language itself as their subject.

Abish spent his childhood in Shanghai, where his family were refugees from Nazi-occupied Europe. In 1949 they moved to Israel, where Abish served in the army and developed strong interests in architecture and writing. He moved to the United States in 1957. From 1975 he taught English at several eastern colleges and universities.

In *Alphabetical Africa* (1974), the first of the 52 chapters consists solely of words beginning with "A," the second chapter adds words beginning with "B," and so forth through the alphabet and back again. *Minds Meet* (1975) contains short stories in which language is used symbolically rather than to relay specific information. In *In the Future Perfect* (1977), a collection of short stories, words are juxtaposed in unusual patterns. *How German Is It / Wie deutsch ist es* (1980, PEN/Faulkner Award), often considered Abish's best work, is a multilayered

A

novel about postwar Germany and its past. Other works include a collection of poems, *Duel Site* (1970); *99: The New Meaning* (1990), a group of narratives; and the novel *Eclipse Fever* (1993).

Abrams, M(eyer) H(oward) (b. July 23, 1912, Long Branch, N.J.) Literary critic known for his analysis of the Romantic period.

After receiving his doctorate from Harvard, Abrams joined the faculty of Cornell University in 1945, where he became professor emeritus in 1983.

He wrote his first book, *The Milk of Paradise,* which dealt with the effects of opium on the visions of the English Romantics (1934), while an undergraduate. With his second work, *The Mirror and the Lamp* (1953), he joined the front rank of scholars of Romantic literature. The book's title denotes the two metaphors by which Abrams characterized 18th- and 19th-century English literature, respectively—the former as a cool, intellectual reflection of outward reality and the latter as an illumination shed by artists on their inner and outer worlds. *Natural Supernaturalism* (1971) explores a broader reach of the Romantic sensibility, including its religious implications and its influence on modern literature. Abrams was also general editor of the much-used *Norton Anthology of English Literature.*

Acker, Kathy (b. 1948? New York City—d. Dec. 3? 1997, Tijuana, Mexico) Novelist whose writing style and subject matter reflect the "punk" sensibility that emerged in the 1970s.

Acker studied classics at Brandeis University and UC–San Diego. Her early employment ranged from clerical work to performing in pornographic films. In 1972 she began publishing willfully crude, disjointed prose that drew heavily on her personal experience and constituted a literary analogue to contemporary developments in music, fashion, and the visual arts. From the outset, Acker blatantly lifted material from other writers, manipulating it for her own often unsettling purposes. In the early novel *The Childlike Life of the Black Tarantula* (1973), this process of appropriation is central to the narrator's quest for identity. Themes of alienation and objectified sexuality recur in such later novels as *Great Expectations* (1982), *Blood and Guts in High School* (1984), *Don Quixote* (1986), and *Empire of the Senseless* (1988). *My Mother: Demonology* (1993) consists of seven love stories. Acker died at an alternative cancer-treatment center after a double mastectomy failed to stop the spread of breast cancer.

Ackerman, Diane *originally* Diane Fink (b. Oct. 7, 1948, Waukegan, Ill.) Writer whose works reflect her interest in natural science.

Ackerman graduated from Pennsylvania State University and received advanced degrees from Cornell. In 1975 she wrote a series of nine radio programs for the Canadian Broadcasting Corporation under the title "Ideas into the

Universe." She has directed the writers' program at Washington University, and from 1988 she has been a staff writer at the *New Yorker*.

Ackerman's memoir *On Extended Wings* (1985) was adapted for the stage in 1987, and in 1988 she published the play *Reverse Thunder*. Her later books include the acclaimed *A Natural History of the Senses* (1990), *The Moon by Whale Light* (1991), *A Natural History of Love* (1994), and *Cultivating Delight* (2001). Her poetry, which incorporates such subject matter as viruses, quasars, and blood cells, includes *The Planets* (1976) and *Jaguar of Sweet Laughter* (1991). In 1995 she hosted *Mystery of the Senses,* a five-hour PBS television series.

Adamic \ˌä-ˈdäm-ich, *Engl* ˈad-ə-mik, ə-ˈdam-ik\, **Louis** (b. March 23, 1899, Blato, Slovenia, Austria-Hungary—d. Sept. 4, 1951, near Riegelsville, N.J.) Novelist and journalist who wrote about the experiences of American minorities, especially immigrants, in the early 1900s.

Adamic immigrated to the United States from Carniola (now in Slovenia) at 14 and was naturalized in 1918. He wrote about what he called the failure of the American melting pot in the nonfictional *Laughing in the Jungle* (1932). He returned to Slovenia on a Guggenheim Fellowship and used that journey as the basis for *The Native's Return* (1934). Two successful sequels, *Grandsons* (1935) and *Cradle of Life* (1936), were followed by publication of his first novel, *The House in Antigua* (1937). *My America* (1938), a mixture of memoir and social philosophy, outlines his dream of a unified American people. He was deeply distressed by the breakup of Yugoslavia during World War II and became a supporter of Marshal Tito. His death from a gunshot wound was ruled a suicide.

Adams, Abigail *originally* Abigail Smith (b. Nov. 11 [Nov. 22, New Style], 1744, Weymouth, Mass.—d. Oct. 28, 1818, Quincy, Mass.) Prolific letter writer whose correspondence gives an intimate and vivid portrayal of life in the young American republic.

Though her formal education was meager, she was an avid reader of history, and she became a supporter of women's rights and a vigorous opponent of slavery. Several enforced separations from her husband, the future president John Adams—including a 10-year period when he was at the Continental Congress in Philadelphia—prompted streams of letters. Her artless spontaneity brings the times to life in a charming blend of comments on minutiae of the day and observations on the momentous events of the Revolutionary period.

Following the peace treaty of 1783, Mrs. Adams joined her husband abroad in Paris, The Hague, and London. Her letters to friends and family at home again provide a colorful commentary on manners and customs, and her correspondence continued when they returned to the United States. Successive printings of the letters have periodically revived public appreciation of her contribution to the original source material of the early American period.

Adams, Alice (b. Aug. 14, 1926, Fredericksburg, Va.—d. May 27, 1999, San Francisco) Novelist and short-story writer.

After graduating from Radcliffe College, Adams married and moved to San Francisco; she began writing after her divorce in 1958. Her first novel, *Careless Love* (1966), received mixed reviews, and she turned to writing short stories. Beginning in 1969, over 25 of her stories—many of which were particularly praised for their treatment of the complex relations between men and women—appeared in the *New Yorker.* The novels *Families and Survivors* (1975), *Listening to Billie* (1978), and *Rich Rewards* (1980) preceded the best-selling *Superior Women* (1984), about the lives of five Radcliffe women after they leave college. Adams's later works include the story collections *To See You Again* (1982), *Return Trips* (1985), *After You've Gone* (1989), and *The Last Lovely City* (1999), and the novels *Second Chances* (1988), *Caroline's Daughters* (1991), *Almost Perfect* (1993), *A Southern Exposure* (1995), and *Medicine Men* (1997).

Adams, Brooks (b. June 24, 1848, Quincy, Mass.—d. Feb. 13, 1927, Boston) Historian who questioned the success of democracy in the United States.

The grandson of John Quincy Adams, he practiced law in Boston until 1881 and traveled extensively in Europe, the Middle East, and India. In correspondence with his brother Henry Adams, he developed the idea that by its nature and substance U.S. democracy was foreordained to degradation and decay. In *The Law of Civilization and Decay* (1895) he held that the center of trade corresponded to the westward movement of population, shifting from ancient population centers of the Far East to Constantinople, Venice, and finally London. In *America's Economic Supremacy* (1900) he foresaw that within 50 years there would be only two world powers, Russia and the United States. In 1913 he published *The Theory of Social Revolutions,* a study of defects in the American form of government.

Adams, Charles Follen (b. April 21, 1842, Dorchester, Mass.—d. March 8, 1918, Roxbury, Mass.) Regional poet.

As a teenager, Adams was employed by a dry-goods firm; after serving in the army during the Civil War, he returned to Boston, where he established himself as a "dealer in dry and fancy goods." In 1872 he began writing humorous verses for periodicals and newspapers in a Pennsylvania German dialect. He collected his verses in *Leedle Yawcob Strauss, and Other Poems* (1877) and *Dialect Ballads* (1888). His complete poetical writings, *Yawcob Strauss, and Other Poems*, with illustrations by "Boz," were published in 1910.

Adams, Franklin Pierce *known as* **F. P. A.** (b. Nov. 15, 1881, Chicago—d. March 23, 1960, New York City) Newspaper columnist, translator, poet, and radio personality.

Adams's newspaper career began in 1903 at the *Chicago Journal*. The next year he went to New York, where he wrote for several newspapers. His column "The Conning Tower" appeared in the *Herald Tribune* and other New York newspapers from 1913 to 1937, with interruptions during World War I (when he wrote a column for *Stars and Stripes*) and from 1923 to 1931 (when he worked for the *New York World*). Witty and well-written, his columns offered informal yet careful critiques of the contemporary American scene, including commentary on such contemporaries as Somerset Maugham, Sinclair Lewis, and Dorothy Parker. His Saturday columns imitated the language and style of Samuel Pepys's diary, and Adams is credited with a renewal of interest in Pepys. Reprints were collected in *The Diary of Our Own Samuel Pepys* (1935). Adams's poetry is light and conventionally rhymed. *The Melancholy Lute* (1936) is a selection from 30 years of his writing. In 1938 Adams became one of the panel of experts on the long-running radio show "Information, Please."

Adams, Henry (Brooks) (b. Feb. 16, 1838, Boston—d. March 27, 1918, Washington, D.C.) Historian and man of letters.

Adams was the great-grandson of John Adams and the grandson of John Quincy Adams. He graduated from Harvard in 1858 and embarked on a grand tour of Europe. From 1861 to 1868 he acted as his father's private secretary in London, where his father was serving as a diplomat.

Returning to the United States, Adams traveled to Washington, D.C., as a correspondent for the *Nation* and other leading journals. He wrote numerous essays exposing political corruption and continued his reformist activities as editor of the *North American Review* (1870–76). The failure of Horace Greeley's campaign for the presidency led to his disillusionment with a world he felt was devoid of principle. His anonymously published *Democracy, an American Novel* (1880) reflected that loss of faith in Americans.

Henry Adams

In 1870 Adams was appointed professor of medieval history at Harvard, where he was the first American to employ the seminar—as contrasted with the lecture—method in teaching history. He resigned in 1877 and soon completed two biographies, *The Life of Albert Gallatin* (1879) and *John Randolph* (1882). His study of American democracy culminated in his nine-volume *History of the United States of America During the Administrations of Thomas Jefferson and James Madison* (1889–91), which received immediate acclaim. In 1884 Adams wrote (under a pseudonym) another novel, *Esther*. His wife's suicide the following year stunned him and led to a period of restless wandering abroad.

From the 1870s until his last years, intellectuals gravitated to his home to discuss art, science, politics, and literature. His closest friends were the geologist Clarence King, with whom he maintained a rich and illuminating correspondence, and the diplomat and writer John Hay.

On several trips to France, Adams examined medieval Christendom, and in the much-admired MONT-SAINT-MICHEL AND CHARTRES (1913) he described the medieval worldview as reflected in its cathedrals. THE EDUCATION OF HENRY

ADAMS (1918) remains Adams's best-known work and one of the most distinguished of all autobiographies; it was awarded a posthumous Pulitzer Prize in 1919, and in 2000 a distinguished panel named it the greatest American work of nonfiction of the 20th century. In 1908 Adams published his edition of John Hay's letters and diary. His last work, *The Life of George Cabot Lodge*, appeared in 1911.

Adams, James Truslow (b. Oct. 18, 1878, Brooklyn, N.Y.—d. May 18, 1949, Southport, Conn.) Writer of popular books on American history.

After a career in business and as a Wall Street broker, Adams amassed enough money to retire in 1912. He turned to the study of American history, writing the successful *The Founding of New England* (1921, Pulitzer Prize) and two other books on early New England.

He lived in London from 1927 to 1935, where he wrote *The Adams Family* (1930), about the Massachusetts Adamses. In *The Epic of America* (1931), his most popular book, he surveyed the "American dream" of a better life for all. His other books included the Civil War history *America's Tragedy* (1934) and a history of the British empire (2 vols., 1938, 1940). He was also the editor of the five-volume *Dictionary of American History* (1940).

John Adams

Adams, John (b. Oct. 30, 1735, Braintree, Mass.—d. July 4, 1826, Quincy, Mass.) Statesman, political theorist, and president of the United States.

Adams attended Harvard, established a law practice, and in 1764 married Abigail Smith. He joined the American colonists protesting British tax acts, and from 1765 wrote frequent articles for the *Boston Gazette*. Elected to the Continental Congress (1774–76), Adams helped Thomas Jefferson and others draft the Declaration of Independence. From 1778 to 1788 he served as a diplomat in France, the Netherlands, and England. In the new country's first presidential election, he ran a distant second to George Washington and served as vice president from 1789 to 1797, when he was narrowly elected to succeed Washington. His single term was marked by controversy over his signing the Alien and Sedition Acts in 1798 and his alliance with the conservative Federalist Party. After losing his bid for reelection to Jefferson in 1801, he retired to his home in Quincy, Mass. There he devoted much of his time to correspondence, including after 1812 a long exchange of erudite, incisive, and humorous letters with his former rival Jefferson, later published in many editions. These letters were the long coda to an extensive series of distinguished philosophical pamphlets on political issues that Adams had produced in the decades following 1768. His grandson Charles Francis Adams edited his major writings in 10 volumes (1850–56).

Adams, Léonie (Fuller) (b. Dec. 9, 1899, Brooklyn—d. June 27, 1988, New Milford, Conn.) Poet and educator.

After graduating from Barnard College, she became editor of the *Measure*, a literary publication, in 1924. She was persuaded to publish a volume of poetry, *Those Not Elect*, in 1925. She spent two years (1928–30) in France, and her second collection of lyric poetry in largely traditional forms, *High Falcon*, was published during that period. On her return she began to teach the writing of poetry in New York and in 1932 edited *Lyrics of François Villon*. She published rarely after 1933, but lectured at various colleges and universities over the years and served as poetry consultant for the Library of Congress (1948–49). Her selected poems (1954) won the Bollingen Prize.

Adams, Samuel (b. Sept. 27, 1722, Boston—d. Oct. 2, 1803, Boston) American Revolutionary leader.

A cousin of John Adams, he attended Harvard College. After several business failures, he served as Boston's tax collector (1740–56). From 1764 he became a strong opponent of British taxation measures, and from 1769 he was the leader of the Massachusetts radicals, writing innumerable newspaper letters and essays, including many powerful polemical pieces, over various signatures. He was a founder of the Committees of Correspondence, which kept other towns and colonies informed of growing opposition to the British. By now passionately committed to independence, he helped plan the Boston Tea Party (1773). He was an influential delegate to the Continental Congress (1774–1781) and a signer of the Declaration of Independence. In 1780 he helped draft the Massachusetts constitution, and he later served as the state's governor (1794–97). His *Writings* were edited by H. A. Cushing in four volumes (1904–8).

Samuel Adams

Adams, Samuel Hopkins (b. Jan. 26, 1871, Dunkirk, N.Y.—d. Nov. 15, 1958, Beaufort, S.C.) Journalist and author of more than 50 books of fiction, biography, and exposé.

Adams graduated from Hamilton College in 1891 and worked for the *New York Sun* until 1900. From 1901 to 1905 he was associated with McClure's syndicate and *McClure's Magazine*. One of the so-called muckrakers of the period, Adams contributed to *Collier's* a series of articles exposing quack patent medicines (1905). *The Great American Fraud* (1906) aided the passage of the Pure Food and Drug Act that year. In articles appearing in 1915–16 in the *New York Tribune*, he exposed dishonorable practices in advertising. The novel *Revelry* (1926) and a biography of Warren G. Harding, *Incredible Era* (1939), chronicled the scandals of Harding's administration. Adams also wrote biographies of Daniel Webster (*The Godlike Daniel*, 1930) and Alexander Woollcott (1945). His novels and stories included "Night Bus" (1933; film, *It Happened One Night*, 1934) and *The Harvey Girls* (1942; film, 1946).

Adams, William Taylor *pseudonym* **Oliver Optic** (b. July 30, 1822, Medway, Mass.—d. March 27, 1897, Boston) Teacher and author known for his children's magazine and a series of adventure books.

Though he never graduated from college, Adams was a teacher and principal in Boston elementary schools for more than 20 years. Under the name Oliver Optic, he began writing stories for boys, and in 1865 he resigned his position to pursue his writing full-time. Soon after that he began *Oliver Optic's Magazine for Boys and Girls* (1867–75), which enjoyed great popularity.

Immensely prolific, he produced about a thousand magazine and newspaper stories and well over a hundred full-length books, which take their young heroes through exotic and educational adventures. His well-traveled characters are athletic and patriotic, and the stories always have a strong moral. Like the books of his rival Horatio Alger, Adams's works were dime novels with far more entertainment value than literary merit, but their popularity was phenomenal.

Addams, Jane (b. Sept. 6, 1860, Cedarville, Ill.—d. May 21, 1935, Chicago) Social reformer and founder of Hull House social settlement.

After graduating from college in 1881, Addams traveled extensively in Europe and visited the Toynbee Hall settlement house in London's industrial district. On her return to the United States, she determined to create a similar social settlement; in 1889 she founded Hull House in Chicago to provide practical services and educational opportunities for the poor. She worked with reform groups for justice for immigrants and blacks and for women's suffrage. In 1910 she became the first female president of the National Conference of Social Work. An ardent pacifist, Addams chaired the International Congress of Women held at The Hague in 1915.

Her books included *Democracy and Social Ethics* (1902), *Newer Ideals of Peace* (1907), the classic *Twenty Years at Hull House* (1910), and *The Second Twenty Years at Hull House* (1930). In 1931 she shared the Nobel Peace Prize with Nicholas Murray Butler.

Ade \'ād\, **George** (b. Feb. 9, 1866, Kentland, Ind.—d. May 16, 1944, Brook, Ind.) Playwright and humorist known for his *Fables in Slang*.

After graduating from Purdue University, Ade worked for the *Chicago Record* from 1890 to 1900. Characters introduced in his widely acclaimed editorial-page column, "Stories of the Streets and of the Town," became the subjects of his early books, *Artie* (1896), *Pink Marsh* (1897), and *Doc Horne* (1899). His greatest recognition came with *Fables in Slang* (1899), a national best-seller that was followed by 11 other books of fables that poked gentle fun at his fellow countrymen.

In 1902 Ade's *The Sultan of Sulu*, a comic opera with an anti-imperialist theme, began a long New York run; it was followed by such successful comedies as *The County Chairman* (1903) and *The College Widow* (1904). One of the most successful playwrights of his time, he also wrote many film scripts and, during the Prohibition era, the humorous *The Old Time Saloon* (1931).

Adler, Renata (b. Oct. 19, 1938, Milan) Italian-born journalist, experimental novelist, and film critic best known for her analytical essays and reviews.

Educated at Bryn Mawr, the Sorbonne, and Harvard, Adler earned a law degree from Yale. Since 1962 she has worked principally for the *New Yorker*. Essays and reviews she wrote there were collected and published as *Toward a Radical Middle* (1969). A year as film critic for the *New York Times* resulted in the collection *A Year in the Dark* (1970). *Speedboat* (1976), her first novel, consists of a series of disparate sketches and vignettes set mainly in New York; a second novel, *Pitch Dark* (1983), was also episodic and nonlinear. Critical response to both was mixed. Her nonfiction includes *Reckless Disregard* (1986), an investigation into libel suits brought by American and Israeli generals against American news organizations, and the essay collections *Politics and Media* (1988) and *Canaries in the Mineshaft* (2001). In 1999 she published *Gone: The Last Days of the New Yorker*, in which she lambasted fellow *New Yorker* staffers.

Agee \ˈā-jē\, (Rufus) James (b. Nov. 27, 1909, Knoxville, Tenn.—d. May 16, 1955, New York City) Poet, novelist, and one of the most influential film critics of the 1930s and '40s.

Agee grew up in Tennessee's Cumberland Mountain area, attended Harvard University, and wrote for *Fortune* and *Time* after he graduated in 1932. *Permit Me Voyage*, a volume of poems, appeared in 1934. For a proposed article in *Fortune*, Agee and the photographer Walker Evans lived for six weeks among poverty-stricken sharecroppers in Alabama in 1936. The article never appeared, but the social injustice witnessed became the widely admired LET US NOW PRAISE FAMOUS MEN (1941).

As film critic for the *Nation* (1941–48), Agee brought an almost unprecedented seriousness to American film criticism. From 1948 until his death, he worked mainly as a screenwriter, notably for *The African Queen* (1951) and *The Night of the Hunter* (1955). His novella *The Morning Watch* (1951) and the novel A DEATH IN THE FAMILY (1957, Pulitzer Prize), published after his death from a heart attack at 45, are both autobiographical.

James Agee

Aiken \ˈā-kən\, Conrad (Potter) (b. Aug. 5, 1889, Savannah, Ga.—d. Aug. 17, 1973, Savannah) Poet, short-story writer, novelist, and critic whose works were influenced by early psychoanalytic theory.

At 11 Aiken discovered the bodies of his parents after his father had killed his mother and committed suicide. Taken to live with relatives in Massachusetts, he was educated at private schools and at Harvard, where he met T. S. Eliot, whose poetry was to influence his own. He divided his life almost equally

Conrad Aiken

between England and the United States until 1947, when he settled in Massachusetts, and he played a significant role in introducing American poets to the British.

After three early collections of verse, he wrote five poetry "symphonies" (1915–20) in which he tried to duplicate music's ability to express several levels of meaning simultaneously. Broad in stylistic scope, he also wrote narrative poems, lyrics, and meditations. His *Selected Poems* (1929) received a Pulitzer Prize; his *Collected Poems* (1953, National Book Award) includes the admired long sequence "Preludes to Definition," as well as "Morning Song of Senlin." Most of his fiction was written in the 1920s and '30s. Generally more successful than his novels of this period were his short stories, notably "Strange Moonlight" from *Bring! Bring!* (1925) and "Silent Snow, Secret Snow" and "Mr. Arcularis" from *Among the Lost People* (1934). His autobiography, *Ushant*, appeared in 1952. His daughter, Joan Aiken (b. 1924), is a successful children's novelist.

Albee \\'ȯl-bē\\, **Edward (Franklin)** (b. March 12, 1928, Virginia) Dramatist and theatrical producer.

Adopted as a child by the son of a prominent vaudeville producer whose name he was given, Albee grew up in affluence in New York City and nearby Westchester County, briefly attended Trinity College, and moved to Greenwich Village to begin writing plays in the late 1950s. Among his early one-act plays, THE ZOO STORY, THE AMERICAN DREAM, *The Death of Bessie Smith,* and THE SANDBOX (all published 1959) were the most successful, and established Albee as a harsh satirist of American values and a practitioner of the theater of the absurd. Many critics consider his first full-length play, WHO'S AFRAID OF VIRGINIA WOOLF? (1962, Tony Award; film, 1966), to be his most important work. It was followed by a number of full-length works, including *Tiny Alice* (1964), A DELICATE BALANCE (1966, Pulitzer Prize, Tony Award), *Seascape* (1975, Pulitzer Prize), *The Lady from Dubuque* (1979), *The Play About the Baby* (1998), and *The Goat or Who is Sylvia* (2002, Tony Award). The main character of *Three Tall Women* (1991, Pulitzer Prize), a domineering woman shown at three stages of her life, resembles Albee's adoptive mother. His stage adaptations of other writers' work include *The Ballad of the Sad Café* (1963), *Malcolm* (1966), and *Lolita* (1979).

Alcott \\'ȯl-kət, 'al-, -ˌkät\\, **Bronson** *originally* Amos Bronson Alcox (b. Nov. 29, 1799, Wolcott, Conn.—d. March 4, 1888, Concord, Mass.) Philosopher, teacher, reformer, and member of the New England Transcendentalists.

The self-educated son of a poor farmer, Alcott traveled in the South as a peddler before establishing a series of innovative schools for children. His aim as an educator, set forth in several books, was to stimulate thought and "awaken the soul." His innovations were not widely accepted, however, and before he was 40 he was forced to close his last school, the famous Temple School in Boston, after admitting a black student. He contributed a series of "Orphic Sayings" and other pieces to the *Dial.* In 1842 he visited England, where a similar school founded near London was named Alcott House in his honor. He returned with a kindred spirit, the mystic Charles Lane, and together they founded a short-lived utopian community, Fruitlands, outside Boston. Living principally in Concord, the home of his friends R. W. Emerson and H. D. Thoreau, he lectured widely and successfully, but did not become financially secure until his daughter Louisa May established herself as a writer.

Alcott, Louisa May (b. Nov. 29, 1832, Germantown, Pa.—d. March 6, 1888, Boston) Author known for her children's books, especially LITTLE WOMEN.

Louisa May Alcott

Daughter of Bronson Alcott, she spent most of her life in Boston and Concord, Mass., where she grew up in the company of R. W. Emerson, Theodore Parker, and H. D. Thoreau. Recognizing that her father was too impractical to provide for his wife and four daughters, Alcott set about trying to meet the family's financial needs. She taught briefly, worked as a domestic, and finally began to write, producing potboilers at first, and eventually more serious works. An ardent abolitionist, she volunteered as a nurse during the Civil War, only to contract typhoid and be sent home. She was never completely well again, but the publication of her letters in book form, *Hospital Sketches* (1863), brought her the first taste of fame.

Alcott's stories then began to appear in the *Atlantic Monthly.* She wrote the autobiographical *Little Women* (1868–69) under the pressure of serious financial need. An immediate success, it allowed her to settle the family's debts at last. *An Old-Fashioned Girl* (1870), *Aunt Jo's Scrap Bag* (6 vols., 1872–82), *Little Men* (1871), *Eight Cousins* (1875), and *Jo's Boys and How They Turned Out* (1886) all drew on her personal experiences.

Publication in 1995 of *A Long Fatal Love Chase*, a gothic romance, and *Behind a Mask,* a collection of Alcott's "blood and thunder" tales, sparked a reevaluation of her early gothic novels.

Aldrich \\'ȯl-drich, 'ȯl-drij\\, **Thomas Bailey** (b. Nov. 11, 1836, Portsmouth, N.H.— d. March 19, 1907, Boston) Poet, short-story writer, and editor whose use of the surprise ending influenced the development of the short story in America.

Aldrich left school at 13 to work as a merchant's clerk in New York, and soon began to contribute to various newspapers and magazines. After publication of his first book of verse, *The Bells* (1855), he became a literary critic on the *New York Evening Mirror,* and he later served as an editor of the *Home Journal* and *Every Saturday.* He drew on his childhood experiences in New Hampshire in his popular classic THE STORY OF A BAD BOY (1870). From 1881 to 1890 he was editor of the *Atlantic Monthly,* succeeding William Dean Howells.

Several collections of his poems were published—the long poems *Judith and Holofernes* and *Friar Jerome's Beautiful Book* (both 1862) were especially successful—but his short-story collection *Marjorie Daw and Other People* (1873) proved that his true talents lay with short fiction. He also wrote a number of other novels.

Alexie \ə-ˈlek-sē\, **Sherman** *originally* Sherman Joseph Alexie, Jr. (b. Oct. 7, 1966, Spokane, Wash.) Novelist, poet, and short-story writer.

Alexie grew up on the Spokane Indian reservation of his mother's tribe—where he has continued to live—and graduated from Washington State University. In 1992 he published the verse collection *I Would Steal Horses*. His first major work, the story-and-poem collection *The Business of Fancydancing* (1992), was followed by the story collection *The Lone Ranger and Tonto Fistfight in Heaven* (1994), on part of which he based his screenplay for the acclaimed film *Smoke Signals* (1998). Like his later work, they focus unsentimentally on American Indians making their way in the contemporary world, and their frequently poignant or painful stories are often underlined or undercut by quirky humor. His subsequent fiction includes the novels *Reservation Blues* (1995) and *Indian Killer* (1996) and the story collection *The Toughest Indian in the World* (2000), and he has published several more poetry collections, including *The First Indian on the Moon* (1993).

Alger \ˈal-jər\, **Horatio, Jr.** (b. Jan. 13, 1832, Chelsea, Mass.—d. July 18, 1899, Natick, Mass.) One of America's most popular late 19th-century authors and perhaps the most socially influential American writer of his generation.

The son of a Unitarian minister, Alger distinguished himself in the classics at Harvard University, graduating with Phi Beta Kappa honors. After leaving Harvard, he worked as a schoolteacher and contributed to magazines. He enrolled in Harvard Divinity School in 1857 and was ordained in 1864.

He accepted the pulpit of a church in Brewster, Mass., but was forced to leave in 1866 following allegations of "unnatural familiarity" with local boys. In that year he moved to New York, and with the publication and sensational success of RAGGED DICK (1868), the story of a poor shoeshine boy who rises to wealth, he found the vein in which he was to write more than 100 volumes.

In a steady succession of books with a standard plot and negligible literary quality, Alger's characters rise from rags to riches, thanks to honesty, cheerful perseverance, hard work, and a stroke of deserved good luck. His most popular books were the *Ragged Dick, Luck and Pluck,* and *Tattered Tom* series. Before his death he chose Edward Stratemeyer, who would go on to write the *Hardy Boys* series, to complete his unfinished works. Alger's books sold more than 20 million copies despite—or perhaps because of—the predictability of their formulaic stories.

Algren \'ȯl-grən\, **Nelson** *originally* Nelson Ahlgren Abraham (b. March 28, 1909, Detroit, Mich.—d. May 9, 1981, Sag Harbor, N.Y.) Writer whose novels of the poor are lifted from routine naturalism by his characters' pride, humor, and unquenchable yearnings.

Nelson Algren

The son of a machinist, Algren grew up in Chicago, where his parents moved when he was 3. He worked his way through the University of Illinois, graduating in journalism in the depths of the Depression. He undertook a variety of jobs, including editing the *New Anvil*, a radical periodical, with the proletarian writer Jack Conroy.

Somebody in Boots (1935), his first novel, chronicles the Depression-era driftings of a poor young Texan who ends up among the down-and-outs of Chicago. *Never Come Morning* (1942) tells of a Polish petty criminal who dreams of escaping his squalid Chicago environment by becoming a prizefighter. The short-story collection *The Neon Wilderness* (1947) followed a wartime stint as an army medical corpsman and contains some of his best writing. His first popular success was THE MAN WITH THE GOLDEN ARM (1949, National Book Award; film, 1956); its hero's golden arm as a poker dealer is threatened by shakiness brought on by drug addiction. A WALK ON THE WILD SIDE (1956; film, 1962) is a picaresque novel of New Orleans bohemian life in the 1930s. Algren's nonfiction includes the prose poem *Chicago, City on the Make* (1951) and sketches collected as *Who Lost an American?* (1963) and *Notes from a Sea Diary* (1965).

Allen, Frederick Lewis (b. July 5, 1890, Boston—d. Feb. 13, 1954, New York City) Writer and editor.

After receiving his master's degree from Harvard University, Allen worked in journalism, first as assistant editor of the *Atlantic Monthly* (1914–16). He joined *Harper's* in 1923 and served as its editor in chief from 1941 to 1953. He wrote several lively and highly readable books on American social history: *Only Yesterday* (1931), an account of the 1920s before the Crash of 1929, sold over a million copies; *Since Yesterday* (1940) treated the Depression decade of the 1930s; and *The Big Change* (1952) surveyed science and technology in 20th-century America.

Allen, Hervey *originally* William Hervey Allen, Jr. (b. Dec. 8, 1889, Pittsburgh—d. Dec. 28, 1949, Coconut Grove, Fla.) Poet, biographer, and novelist who made his mark on popular literature with ANTHONY ADVERSE.

Allen's first published work was a book of poetry, *Ballads of the Border* (1916). During the 1920s he established a reputation as a poet, publishing several more volumes of verse. Following service in World War I, he published *Toward the Flame* (1926), a novel inspired by his wartime experience. That same year also saw publication of his *Israfel,* a biography of Edgar Allan Poe. In 1933 he published *Anthony Adverse*, which was a huge success. Set in the Napoleonic era, its considerable length and undisguised passages about sex introduced a new standard for popular fiction. Allen's later novels were less successful.

Ambrose \\'am-₁brōs\\, **Stephen E(dward)** (b. Jan. 10, 1936, Decatur, Ill.—d. Oct. 14, 2002, Bay St. Louis, Miss.) History educator and writer.

After earning a Ph.D. from the University of Wisconsin (1963), Ambrose taught history at Johns Hopkins before joining the faculty at the University of New Orleans in 1971, where he taught until retiring in 1995.

His most important early books were *Eisenhower and Berlin 1945* (1967) and the durable text *Rise to Globalism: American Foreign Policy 1938–70* (1970; with Douglas Brinkley). He came to wider attention with the major presidential biographies *Eisenhower* (2 vols., 1983–84) and *Nixon* (3 vols., 1987–90). His later books were broader histories, many about World War II. *D-Day June 6, 1944* appeared in 1994. *Undaunted Courage* (1996), the story of the Lewis and Clark expedition, became a major best-seller. *Citizen Soldiers* (1997) deals with the U.S. Army in the last year of World War II; *The Victors* (1998) discusses Gen. Eisenhower and his subordinates; and *Nothing Like It in the World* (2000) is a history of the Transcontinental Railroad. Ambrose also wrote many television documentaries, including *Eisenhower: The Commander*.

Ammons \\'am-ənz\\, **A(rchie) R(andolph)** (b. Feb. 18, 1926, Whiteville, N.C.—d. Feb. 25, 2001, Ithaca, N.Y.) Poet, a late exponent of the Transcendentalist tradition.

A graduate of Wake Forest College, Ammons worked as an elementary-school principal and a glass-company executive before turning his full attention to literature. From 1964 he taught creative writing at Cornell University. In his first collection of poems, *Ommateum: With Doxology* (1955), he wrote about nature and the self, themes that remained his central focus. Subsequent collections, such as *Tape for the Turn of the Year* (1965; composed on adding-machine tape), *Uplands* (1970), *Collected Poems 1951–1971* (1972, National Book Award), and *Sphere* (1974, Bollingen Prize), continued his investigation into the relationship between the knowable and the unknowable. His poetry is both cerebral and conversational, reflecting the influences of Robert Frost, Wallace Stevens, and William Carlos Williams. His later work—notably *A Coast of Trees* (1981), *Sumerian Vistas* (1988), and the book-length poem *Garbage* (1993, National Book Award)—exhibit a mature command of imagery and ideas, balancing a scientific approach to the universe with a subjective, even romantic one.

Anaya \\ä-'nī-ə\\, **Rudolfo A(lfonso)** (b. Oct. 30, 1937, Pastura, N.M.) Novelist often called the founder of modern Chicano literature.

Anaya graduated from the University of New Mexico and taught in public schools from 1963 to 1970. From 1974 he has taught at the University of New Mexico.

Bless Me, Ultima (1972), his acclaimed first novel and perhaps the most celebrated Chicano novel of its century, concerns a young boy growing up in New Mexico in the late 1940s. *Heart of Aztlán* (1976) follows a family's move from rural to urban surroundings and confronts some of the problems of Chicano laborers. In *Tortuga* (1979), a boy encased in a body cast stays at a hospital for paralyzed children. La Malinche, the Indian slave who became Hernán Cortés's consort, is the protagonist of *The Legend of La Llorona* (1984). Anaya has also published short-story collections, the nonfictional *A Chicano in China* (1986), and *Zia Summer* (2000), a mystery.

Anderson, Margaret (Caroline) (b. Nov. 24, 1886?, Indianapolis—d. Oct. 18, 1973, Le Cannet, France) Founder and editor of the LITTLE REVIEW.

Raised in a conventional Midwestern home, Anderson renounced the values of her middle-class upbringing at an early age and moved to Chicago. There she joined the staff of the *Dial*, a literary review. In 1914 she founded the *Little Review*, a magazine that reflected her interest in avant-garde art, philosophy, feminism, and psychoanalysis. Ezra Pound, whom she engaged as her European editor, attracted eminent European and expatriate American writers to the magazine; contributors included Carl Sandburg, William Carlos Williams, W. B. Yeats, and T. S. Eliot. When her financial backers abandoned the *Little Review*, she lost her home and offices and was forced to camp with family and staff members on the shores of Lake Michigan for six months (1914).

When Anderson began serializing James Joyce's *Ulysses* in 1918, the U.S. Post Office seized and burned four issues of the magazine, and Anderson was convicted on obscenity charges and fined $50. In 1924 she moved to Paris, where she continued to publish the *Little Review* until 1929. Her own writings include her three-volume autobiography, consisting of *My Thirty Years' War* (1930), *The Fiery Fountains* (1951), and *The Strange Necessity* (1962).

Anderson, Maxwell (b. Dec. 15, 1888, Atlantic, Pa.—d. Feb. 28, 1959, Stamford, Conn.) Playwright who attempted to popularize verse tragedy.

Educated at the University of North Dakota and Stanford University, Anderson taught school and worked as a journalist before the success of his first play, *White Desert,* let him pursue a career as a playwright. The comedy *What Price Glory?* (1924; films, 1926, 1952), a collaboration with Laurence Stallings, was a ribald and profane view of World War I. Anderson then composed two ambitious historical dramas in verse—*Elizabeth the Queen* (1930; film, 1939) and *Mary of Scotland* (1933; film, 1963)—and his humorous prose satire, *Both Your Houses* (1933, Pulitzer Prize), an attack on venality in the U.S. Congress. He reached the peak of his career with *Winterset* (1935; film, 1936), a poetic drama inspired by the Sacco–Vanzetti case. He collaborated with the composer Kurt Weill (1900–1950) on the musical plays *Knickerbocker Holiday* (1938), based on early New York history, and *Lost in the Stars* (1949), a dramatization of

Alan Paton's South African novel *Cry, the Beloved Country*. His stage adaptation (1954) of William March's *The Bad Seed* was itself adapted as a screenplay (1957). His other plays include *Key Largo* (1939; film, 1949) and *Anne of the Thousand Days* (1948; film, 1969).

Anderson, Poul (William) (b. Nov. 25, 1926, Bristol, Pa.—d. July 31, 2001, Orinda, Cal.) Prolific science-fiction and fantasy writer praised for his scrupulous attention to scientific detail.

Anderson published his first science-fiction story while at the University of Minnesota and became a freelance writer following his graduation with a degree in physics in 1948. He published his first novel, *Vault of the Ages*, in 1952 and thereafter worked at the rate of several books per year. A number of his works concern the "future history" of what he calls the Technic Civilization, an age of human history lasting from the year 2100 to 7100. Much of these books' sociological, political, and economic content derives from patterns associated with the European Age of Exploration. In *Tau Zero* (1970), considered by some his best work, travelers inside a spaceship traveling at near light speed experience time as they have always known it while witnessing through the portholes the collapse and rebirth of the universe. Among Anderson's later works are the epic *The Boat of a Million Years* (1989), *Harvest the Stars* (1993), and *Genesis* (2000). He has written over 100 books in all.

Anderson, Regina M. *later* **Regina Andrews** (b. May 21, 1901, Chicago—d. 1993?) Librarian, playwright, and arts patron whose New York City home was a Harlem Renaissance salon.

As a librarian in the New York Public Library system, Anderson produced lecture and drama series and arts exhibitions from the early 1920s to 1967. Her Harlem apartment became an important meeting place for black artists and intellectuals in the early 1920s. In 1924 she helped organize a dinner at the Civic Club, attended by such notable authors as W. E. B. Du Bois, Jean Toomer, Countee Cullen, and Langston Hughes, that helped launch the Harlem Renaissance. Later that year she helped Du Bois found the Krigwa Players, a company of black actors performing plays by black authors. This evolved into the Negro (or Harlem) Experimental Theatre, which in 1931 produced Anderson's one-act play *Climbing Jacob's Ladder* (written under the pseudonym Ursala Trelling), about a lynching that happened while people prayed in church. The next year it produced her one-act play *Underground*, about the Underground Railroad. The group inspired little theater groups around the country and encouraged black playwrights. Anderson later coedited the *Chronology of African-Americans in New York, 1621–1966* (1971).

Anderson, Sherwood (b. Sept. 13, 1876, Camden, Ohio—d. March 8, 1941, Colón, Panama) Author who strongly influenced American short-story writing between World Wars I and II.

Anderson grew up in poverty and left school at 14 to find work. He held a number of jobs, served in the National Guard, and founded a paint factory, which he ran for five years before abandoning it, along with his wife and children, for a literary life. In Chicago he associated with Carl Sandburg and Theodore Dreiser and began publishing in Margaret Anderson's *Little Review*. His first novels, *Windy McPherson's Son* (1916) and *Marching Men* (1917), were written while he was still a manufacturer. WINESBURG, OHIO (1919), a collection of interrelated short stories and sketches linked by the characters' connections to a newspaper reporter to whom they bare their souls, made his reputation. His other novels include *Poor White* (1920), which describes the effects of the shift from an agrarian to an industrial society, *Dark Laughter* (1925), and *Beyond Desire* (1932), a novel that draws on labor struggles at Southern textile mills. Other short-story collections include *The Triumph of the Egg* (1921), *Horses and Men* (1923), and *Death in the Woods* (1933). Anderson influenced other American writers, including William Faulkner and Ernest Hemingway, both of whom he helped with the publication of their first books.

Sherwood Anderson

Angelou \\'an-jə-ˌlō, *commonly* 'an-jə-ˌlü\\, **Maya** *originally* Marguerite Annie Johnson (b. April 4, 1928, St. Louis, Mo.) Poet whose several volumes of autobiography explore the themes of economic, racial, and sexual oppression.

Raped at the age of 7 by her mother's boyfriend, Angelou went through a five-year period of muteness. She began her career as an actress and dancer. Marriage to a South African freedom fighter took her to Africa; in Cairo she edited the *African Observer,* an English-language newspaper. She later taught at the University of Ghana and edited the *African Review.* In the 1960s she was asked by Martin Luther King to be the northern coordinator of the Southern Christian Leadership Conference, and in the 1970s she was appointed to special commissions by Presidents Gerald Ford and Jimmy Carter.

Maya Angelou

Her early life is the focus of her first autobiographical work, *I Know Why the Caged Bird Sings* (1970), which became widely popular. Her subsequent volumes include *Gather Together in My Name* (1974), *The Heart of a Woman* (1981), and *All God's Children Need Traveling Shoes* (1986). She wrote the admired television documentary *Afro-Americans in the Arts,* and her screenplay *Georgia, Georgia* (1972) was the first by a black woman to be filmed. Her poetry, collected in such volumes as *Just Give Me a Cool Drink of Water 'fore I Diiie* (1971) and *And Still I Rise* (1978), draws heavily on her personal history but employs the points of view of various personae. In 1981 she received a lifetime faculty appointment in American studies at Wake Forest University. She became nationally famous after delivering a poem, "On the Pulse of Morning," at the inauguration of President Bill Clinton in 1993.

Anthony, Katharine (Susan) (b. Nov. 27, 1877, Roseville, Ark.—d. Nov. 20, 1965, New York City) Biographer.

Initially a geometry teacher, Anthony early conceived an interest in psychiatry. This would influence the biographies she undertook of famous women, to whose psychological development and motivation she would give increasing prominence. Her early biographies include *Margaret Fuller* (1920), *Catherine the Great* (1925), and *Louisa May Alcott* (1938). Her readers were scandalized by *The Lambs* (1945), in which she theorized that incestuous feelings were reflected in the lives and literary collaborations of Charles Lamb and his sister, Mary. Her later works included *Dolley Madison* (1949) and *Susan B. Anthony* (1954).

Anthony, Susan B(rownell) (b. Feb. 15, 1820, Adams, Mass.—d. March 13, 1906, Rochester, N.Y.) Pioneer in the women's-suffrage movement.

From her Quaker parents, Anthony acquired a stern moral rectitude. After teaching at a female academy in upstate New York (1846–49), she returned to her parents' home near Rochester, N.Y., and joined the abolitionist group that met at their house, also meeting the women—including Elizabeth Cady Stanton, Lucretia Mott, and Amelia Bloomer—who would be her principal allies in the suffrage movement. When her attempt to involve herself in the temperance movement was rebuffed because of her sex, she organized a women's temperance group. In 1856 she became an agent for the American Anti-Slavery Society.

From 1868 to 1870 she and Stanton copublished the New York weekly *The Revolution*. In 1872, demanding voting rights for women, she twice led a group of women to the polls and was arrested. A founding officer of the National Woman Suffrage Association (from 1869), she served as president (1892–1900) of the larger consolidated group that replaced it. In the face of intense opposition, she wrote and lectured tirelessly throughout the country and in the western territories on behalf of her cause.

Her autobiography, *Eighty Years and More*, appeared in 1898. She conceived, coauthored (with Stanton and Matilda Gage), and published the first four volumes of *The History of Woman Suffrage* (1881–1902).

Antin \\'ant-ən\\, **David** (b. Feb. 1, 1932, New York City) Poet, translator, and art critic who championed primitive art and poetry and the use of clichés and pop vernacular.

After receiving a B.A. from CCNY and an M.A. from NYU, Antin worked as an editor, translator, and researcher. From 1968 he taught visual arts at UC–San Diego. His early poetry collections include *Definitions* (1967) and *Code of Flag Behavior* (1968). He is perhaps best known for his improvisational "talk poems," first published in *Talking* (1972); such poems also appear in *After the War (A Long Novel with Few Words)* (1973), *Talking at the Boundaries* (1976), and *Tuning* (1984). Antin improvised his talk poems in public places, tape-recording his performances. Considering the resulting poems to be "adapted notations" of his performances, he later published those he thought had merit. His later works include *What It Means to Be Avant Garde* (1993).

Antin, Mary (b. 1881, Polotsk, Russia—d. May 15, 1949, Suffern, N.Y.)
Author of books on immigrant life in the United States.

Antin immigrated to the United States in 1894 and attended Columbia University's Teachers College and Barnard College. She wrote in Yiddish about her voyage to the United States in her first book, *From Polotsk to Boston* (Eng. trans., 1899). *The Promised Land* (1912) contrasts the experiences of European Jews in Europe with their experiences after arrival in the United States. A third book on immigrants, *They Who Knock at Our Gates*, was published in 1914. Antin would later spend many years campaigning effectively against restrictive immigration legislation.

Apess \\'ā-pes, 'āps\\, **William** *or* **William Apes** (b. Jan. 31, 1798, Colrain, Massachusetts—d. April, 1839, New York City) Minister and writer.

Born to a Pequot mother and a half-blooded descendant of King Philip (Metacom), he became an indentured servant; introduced to Christianity by his master, by 20 he was proselytizing in Connecticut and New York. In 1829 he was ordained a Methodist minister.

His autobiography, *A Son of the Forest,* published in 1829, was the first ever written by an American Indian. He was arrested in 1833 for his part in the Mashpee Revolt. *The Experiences of Five Christian Indians of the Pequot Tribe* (1833) described racism against the Pequots, which he saw as incompatible with Christianity, and the need for Indian self-government. His long *Eulogy on King Philip* (published 1836) extolled the 17th-century Wampanoag chief who died defending his people. Apess's writings, edited by Barry O'Connell, have been republished as *On Our Own Ground* (1992) and *A Son of the Forest and Other Writings* (1997).

Apple, Max (Isaac) (b. Oct. 22, 1941, Grand Rapids, Mich.) Writer whose stories chronicle pop culture and other aspects of American life.

Apple received his doctorate from the University of Michigan in 1970, and has taught at Rice University since 1972. His satire is distinguished by its gentle spoofing. His cast of characters often includes a mix of historical figures and fictional creations. *The Oranging of America* (1976) consists of stories about materialism that feature such historical figures as C. W. Post, Howard Johnson, and Norman Mailer; J. Edgar Hoover, Fidel Castro, and Jane Fonda make brief appearances in *Zip: A Novel of the Left and the Right* (1978). Apple's later works include *The Propheteers* (1987), *Roommates: My Grandfather's Story* (1994), and *I Love Gootie: My Grandmother's Story* (1998).

Arp, Bill *pseudonym of* Charles Henry Smith (b. June 15, 1826, Lawrenceville, Ga.—d. Aug. 24, 1903, Cartersville, Ga.) Humorist and writer.

Smith practiced law in Rome, Ga., from 1851 to 1877, interrupted only by the Civil War. Beginning in 1861 he contributed weekly letters to Rome's newspaper, the *Southern Confederacy* (and later to such larger papers as the *Atlanta*

Constitution), from "Bill Arp," a Northerner who sympathized with Yankee aims but whose foolishness served to satirize Northern views on such issues as blacks, women's rights, agricultural policies, and the income tax. Over time Arp evolved into a benign cracker-barrel philosopher. His columns were compiled in several books, including *Bill Arp's Peace Papers* (1873), *Bill Arp's Scrap Book* (1884), *The Farm and Fireside* (1891) and *Bill Arp: From the Uncivil War to Date* (1903).

Asch \ˈåsh, *Engl* ˈash\, **Sholem** (b. Nov. 1, 1880, Kutno, Poland, Russian Empire—d. Aug. 10, 1957, London) Novelist and playwright, one of the most widely known writers in modern Yiddish literature.

Asch was educated at Kutno's Hebrew school. In 1899 he went to Warsaw, and in 1900 published his highly praised first story—written, as was a cycle that followed, in Hebrew. On the advice of the Yiddish writer and leader I. L. Peretz, he decided to write only in Yiddish, and with *The Little Town* (1904) he began a career outstanding for both output and impact.

Asch's work falls into three periods. Works of the first are set in small Eastern European Jewish villages and depict the conflict between devotion to Orthodox Jewry and the urge toward emancipation. To this period belong the novels *Mottke the Thief* (1916) and *Kidesh hashem* (1919) and the play *The God of Vengeance* (1907). After immigrating to America in 1914 he produced *Uncle Moses* (1918), *Judge Not* (1926), *Chaim Lederer's Return* (1927), and *Three Cities* (1933), which all deal with the cultural and economic conflicts experienced by Eastern European Jewish immigrants in America. In his last, most controversial period, he produced the works best known to Americans—*The Nazarene* (1943), *The Apostle* (1943), and *Mary* (1949)—in which he tried to unite Judaism and Christianity, stressing their historical, theological, and ethical continuity. His attempt angered some American Jews, and he moved to Israel in 1956.

Ashbery \ˈash-ber-ē\, **John** (**Lawrence**) (b. July 28, 1927, Rochester, N.Y.) Poet noted for his work's elegance, originality, and obscurity.

Ashbery studied at Harvard University and Columbia (M.A. 1951), then worked as a copywriter in New York (1951–55) and as an art critic in Paris. Returning to New York, he served as executive editor of *Art News* (1965–72) before taking a teaching post at Brooklyn College. He has since taught principally at Bard College.

His first published poetry collection, *Turandot* (1953), was followed by *Some Trees* (1956), *The Tennis Court Oath* (1962), *Rivers and Mountains* (1966), and *The Double Dream of Spring* (1970). *Self-Portrait in a Convex Mirror* (1975) won the Pulitzer Prize, National Book Award, and National Book Critics Circle Award. Subsequent titles include *A Wave* (1984, Bollingen Prize), *Flow Chart* (1991), and *Your Name Here* (2000), his 20th collection.

Ashbery's poetry has often been greeted with puzzlement and even hostility owing to its extreme difficulty. His poems are characterized by arresting images and exquisite rhythms, an intricate form, sudden shifts in tone and subject, and frequent humor.

Asimov \\'az-i-ˌmóf\\, **Isaac** (b. Jan. 2, 1920, Petrovichi, Russia—d. April 6, 1992, New York City) Prolific writer and biochemist.

Isaac Asimov

Asimov was taken to America at 3, grew up in Brooklyn, graduated from Columbia University, and earned his Ph.D. in biochemistry there in 1948. He taught at Boston University for most of his subsequent career.

He began contributing stories to science-fiction magazines in 1939 and in 1950 published his first book, *Pebble in the Sky*. His classic trilogy consisting of *Foundation*, *Foundation and Empire*, and *Second Foundation* (1951–53, Hugo Award) recounts the collapse of an empire in the universe of the future. Other novels, stories, and story collections include the influential *I, Robot* (1950); *The Gods Themselves* (1972, Hugo and Nebula Awards), Asimov's personal favorite; "Bicentennial Man" (1972, Hugo and Nebula Awards); *The Robots of Dawn* (1983); and the posthumously published *Forward the Foundation* (1993). His "Nightfall" (1941) is thought by many the finest science-fiction short story ever written. Asimov claimed to have coined the word "robotics"; his concept of robots and his Three Laws of Robotics profoundly influenced subsequent portrayals of robots in fiction. His nonfiction was written with lucidity and humor; Carl Sagan called him "the greatest explainer of the age." Astonishingly prolific, he published more than 400 books, including many science books for the general public but also works on religion, social sciences, language, and history.

Atherton \\'ath-ər-tən\\, **Gertrude (Franklin)** *originally* Gertrude Franklin Horn (b. Oct. 30, 1857, San Francisco—d. June 14, 1948, San Francisco) Novelist noted for her fictional biography and history.

Atherton began her prolific writing career to escape the restrictions of a stifling marriage. Her first work, *The Randolphs of Redwoods* (c.1882), was published anonymously in *The Argonaut* and republished as a book, *A Daughter of the Vine* (1899). Based on a local story of a well-bred girl turned alcoholic, its publication offended her husband's prominent family.

After her husband's death Atherton traveled extensively; her travels would lend vividness to her writing. Her work generally drew mixed reviews, with the notable exception of *The Conqueror* (1902), a fictional biography of Alexander Hamilton. Her controversial novel *Black Oxen* (1923), the semiautobiographical story of a woman rejuvenated by hormone treatments, was her biggest popular success. She wrote more than 40 novels and many nonfiction works in her long career.

Auchincloss \ˈȯk-in-ˌklȯs\, **Louis (Stanton)** (b. Sept. 27, 1917, Lawrence, N.Y.) Novelist, short-story writer, and critic known for his novels of manners set in upper-class New York City.

Born into a wealthy family, Auchincloss obtained a law degree after graduating from Yale University and was admitted to the New York State bar in 1941, beginning a legal career that lasted until 1986. He found time to write more than 50 books, often taking a writing notebook with him to court.

He wrote his first novel, *The Indifferent Children* (1947) under the pseudonym Andrew Lee, but by 1950 he was publishing stories under his own name. Noted for his stylistic clarity and skill at characterization, he became the prolific chronicler of life in the rarefied world of corporate boardrooms and brownstone mansions. Several of his best novels, including *The House of Five Talents* (1960) and *Portrait in Brownstone* (1962), examine family relationships over a period of decades. Others, notably *The Rector of Justin* (1964) and *Diary of a Yuppie* (1987), are studies of a single character, often from many points of view. His many short-story collections frequently are organized around a given theme or a geographic locale. He has also published critical works on Edith Wharton, Henry James, and other writers.

W. H. Auden

Auden \ˈȯd-ən\, **W(ystan) H(ugh)** (b. Feb. 21, 1907, York, England—d. Sept. 28, 1973, Vienna, Austria) British-American poet.

Auden took a degree at Oxford in 1928 and published his first book of poems the same year. From the beginning his varied works would deal with intellectual and moral issues of public concern as well as the inner world of fantasy and dream. In the 1930s, when his work became notably politically engaged and the influence of Freudianism and aspects of Marxism became visible, he published such collections as *Poems* (1930) and *Look, Stranger!* (1936), and collaborated with Christopher Isherwood on the verse plays *The Dog Beneath the Skin* (1935), *The Ascent of F6* (1936), and *On the Frontier* (1938). He reported on the Spanish Civil War in *Spain* (1937) and on the Sino–Japanese War in *Journey to a War* (1939; with Isherwood). In 1939 he moved to the United States, and he became a U.S. citizen in 1946. *Another Time* (1940) contains such well-known poems as "In Memory of W. B. Yeats" and "September 1, 1939."

Influenced by Kierkegaard, Auden converted to Anglicanism in the 1940s, and his later poetry addresses religious and existential themes. His postwar works include the long poem *The Age of Anxiety* (1947, Pulitzer Prize) and the collections *The Shield of Achilles* (1955, National Book Award), *Homage to Clio* (1960), and *City Without Walls* (1970). With his longtime companion Chester Kallman, he wrote opera librettos for Benjamin Britten, Igor Stravinsky (*The Rake's Progress,* 1951), and H. W. Henze. From 1956 to 1961 he was professor of poetry at Oxford. He returned to England in 1972, and later settled with Kallman in Austria. Distinguished by his intellectual brilliance and superb technical mastery, Auden was widely considered, after the death of T. S. Eliot, to be the foremost poet writing in English.

Auster \\'ȯs-tər\\, **Paul** (b. Feb. 3, 1947, Newark, N.J.) Novelist, poet, and screenwriter.

Nephew of the translator Allen Mandelbaum, Auster did graduate work in Renaissance literature at Columbia University and spent his early career in France, translating French writers and pursuing his own writing while working odd jobs. He gained serious attention with his "New York trilogy," the experimental detective stories *City of Glass* (1985), *Ghosts* (1986), and *The Locked Room* (1986), all of which feature characters whose identities shift and change. In *The Country of Last Things* (1986), he used the science-fiction genre as the vehicle for his musings. It was followed by *Moon Palace* (1989), *The Music of Chance* (1990), *Leviathan* (1992), which features characters with multiple identities, and *Mr. Vertigo* (1994), which employs elements of magic realism.

Drawn into screenwriting by the director Wayne Wang, Auster has written the well-received *Smoke* (1995), *Blue in the Face* (1995; codirected with Wang), and *Lulu on the Bridge* (1998; directed by himself).

Austin \\'ȯs-tən, 'äs-tən\\, **Mary** *originally* Mary Hunter (b. Sept. 9, 1868, Carlinville, Ill.—d. Aug. 13, 1934, Santa Fe, N.M.) Novelist and essayist who wrote on American Indian culture and social problems.

Austin spent 14 years in an unhappy marriage, teaching, writing, and observing nature in California, where they had settled. After separating from her husband, she became the friend and chronicler of Indians. Her first book, *The Land of Little Rain* (1903), a description of desert life in the West, won her immediate fame, and was followed by two story collections, *The Basket Woman* (1904) and *Lost Borders* (1909), and a play, *The Arrow Maker* (1911). After traveling in Europe, she joined the radical artistic circle of Mabel Dodge in New York, where she published her best novel, *A Woman of Genius* (1912). In 1924 she settled near Dodge in Santa Fe. Her nature writing, imbued with personal spiritualism, followed in the tradition of Thoreau and John Muir. Her other causes included feminism and socialism. A prolific writer, she published 32 volumes and about 200 articles in her lifetime.

B

Babbitt, Irving (b. Aug. 2, 1865, Dayton, Ohio—d. July 15, 1933, Cambridge, Mass.) Critic and teacher, leader of the movement in literary criticism known as NEW HUMANISM, or Neohumanism.

Educated at Harvard and the Sorbonne, Babbitt taught French literature and comparative literature at Harvard from 1894 until his death. A vigorous teacher, lecturer, and essayist, he was the unrestrained foe of Romanticism and its off-shoots, realism and naturalism, championing instead the classical virtues of restraint and moderation. His early followers included T. S. Eliot and George Santayana, who later criticized him; his major opponent was H. L. Mencken.

Babbitt extended his views beyond literary criticism: *Literature and the American College* (1908) calls for a return to the study of classical literatures; *The New Laokoön* (1910) deplores the confusion in the arts created by Romanticism; *Rousseau and Romanticism* (1919) criticizes the effects of Rousseau's thought in the 20th century; *On Being Creative* (1932) adversely compares the Romantic concept of spontaneity to classic theories of imitation.

Bacheller \\'bach-ə-lər\\, **Irving (Addison)** (b. Sept. 26, 1859, Pierpont, N.Y.—d. Feb. 24, 1950, White Plains, N.Y.) Journalist and novelist who chronicled life in upstate New York.

Bacheller began his career as a journalist, founding the first modern newspaper syndicate in 1883 in Brooklyn. He serialized Stephen Crane's *Red Badge of Courage* and introduced the works of Arthur Conan Doyle and Rudyard Kipling to the American public. He sold the syndicate in 1896, and was briefly editor of the *New York World*.

He first tried his hand at creative writing in the 1890s, publishing a ballad, a short story, and a couple of unsuccessful novels. His first success, *Eben Holden* (1900), which provided an authentic picture of 19th-century farm life in upstate New York, sold more than a million copies. *D'ri and I* (1901), a novel about the Battle of Lake Erie in the War of 1812, was also popular. Bacheller's own favorites were *The Light in the Clearing* (1917) and *A Man for the Ages* (1919), about Abraham Lincoln. *Opinions of a Cheerful Yankee* (1926), *Coming up the Road* (1928), and *From Stores of Memory* (1938) were autobiographical.

Baker, Carlos (Heard) (b. May 5, 1909, Biddeford, Maine—d. April 18, 1987, Princeton, N.J.) Teacher, novelist, and critic.

Baker taught at Princeton University from 1951 to 1977. His early scholarship includes *Shelley's Major Poetry* (1948), but he devoted most of his career to work on Ernest Hemingway. His acclaimed *Hemingway: The Writer as Artist* (1952) was the first full-length study of the author; along with a portrait of an artist and his generation, it provides a critique of his novels in moral and aesthetic terms. In 1961 he published a collection of Hemingway's letters to such figures as Gertrude Stein and F. Scott Fitzgerald. *Ernest Hemingway: A Life Story* (1969), the authorized biography, is highly regarded.

Baker, George Pierce (b. April 4, 1866, Providence, R.I.—d. Jan. 6, 1935, New York City) Teacher of some of America's most notable dramatists.

Baker graduated from Harvard University in 1887 and subsequently taught there until 1925. In 1905 he started his class for playwrights, 47 Workshop (named after its course number), the first of its kind to be part of a university curriculum. He concerned himself not only with writing but also with stage design, lighting, costuming, and dramatic criticism. His students over the years included Eugene O'Neill, Philip Barry, Sidney Coe Howard, and S. N. Behrman. Baker's university productions pioneered advanced staging techniques, and his annual lecture tours introduced the American public to European ideas of theater art.

From 1925 until 1933 Baker taught at Yale University, where he founded a drama department and directing the university theater. Of his writings, the best known are *The Development of Shakespeare as a Dramatist* (1907) and *Dramatic Technique* (1919).

Baker, Houston A(lfred), Jr. (b. March 22, 1943, Louisville, Ky.) Educator and critic.

Baker attended Howard University, the University of Edinburgh, and UCLA (Ph.D., 1968) and has taught at Yale and Cornell universities, Haverford College, the University of Virginia, and the University of Pennsylvania. In addition to editing collections of poetry and essays, he has written poetry as well as scholarly works, including *Black Literature in America* (1971), *Modernism and the Harlem Renaissance* (1987), *Blues, Ideology, and Afro-American Literature* (1987), and *Black Studies, Rap, and the Academy* (1993). He has questioned the traditional literary canon's bias toward established "greats," speaking out for greater inclusion of minority voices in studies of English literature.

Baker, Nicholson (b. Jan. 7, 1957, Rochester, N.Y.) Novelist.

After graduating from Haverford College, Baker worked on Wall Street as an oil analyst, and later took jobs as a word processor and technical writer. From 1987 he has devoted himself to writing full-time.

Several short stories appeared in the *New Yorker* and the *Atlantic* before he published his admired first novel, *The Mezzanine* (1988), a heavily footnoted work that takes place largely during a lunch hour. *Room Temperature* (1990) takes place while a man is giving his infant daughter her bottle; *Vox* (1992) concerns telephone sex; the protagonist of *The Fermata* (1995) can stop time at will. Many of his works show a fascination with everyday technologies that are usually overlooked. His nonfiction includes *U and I* (1991), about his obsession with John Updike; *Double Fold* (2001), about the disappearance of newspaper files; and *The Size of Thoughts* (1997), an essay collection.

Baker, Ray Stannard *pseudonym* David Grayson (b. April 17, 1870, Lansing, Mich.—d. July 12, 1946, Amherst, Mass.) Journalist, essayist, and literary crusader for the League of Nations.

Raised in frontier Wisconsin, he studied agriculture and law before becoming a reporter for the *Chicago Record* (1892–98), then joining the staff of *McClure's* magazine, where he celebrated American imperialism, only to be called a muckraker when he came out in favor of striking coal miners in 1903. In 1906, with Ida Tarbell, Lincoln Steffens, and others, he helped establish and edit *American Magazine*, in which, as David Grayson, he published highly popular optimistic philosophical essays, which he later published as *Adventures in Contentment* (1907). He explored the plight of black Americans in *Following the Color Line* (1908). In 1910 he met Woodrow Wilson, whom he came increasingly to admire and about whom he would write numerous books. At Wilson's request, he served as head of the American Press Bureau at the Paris Peace Conference (1919–20), where the two were in close and constant association. Despite prolonged ill health, Baker wrote the authorized biography *Woodrow Wilson: Life and Letters* (8 vols., 1927–39), which received a Pulitzer Prize.

Baker, Russell (Wayne) (b. Aug. 14, 1925, Loudoun County, Va.) Newspaper columnist, author, and humorist.

After graduating from Johns Hopkins University in 1947, Baker worked as a journalist for the *Baltimore Sun* (1947–54), becoming its London bureau chief in 1953. In London he wrote a lively weekly column, "From a Window on Fleet Street." At the Washington bureau of the *New York Times* (1954–62), he covered the White House, State Department, and Congress. In the early 1960s he began writing the *Times'* "Observer" column, a syndicated humor column initially focused on political satire, which broadened to comment on such topics as Norman Rockwell, inflation, and fear. In 1979 he won the Pulitzer Prize for commentary. He published several collections of his columns. The engaging memoir *Growing Up* (1982) won him another Pulitzer Prize, and a sequel, *The Good Times*, was published in 1989. In 1993 he succeeded Alistair Cooke as host of the television program *Masterpiece Theatre*.

Baldwin, James (Arthur) (b. Aug. 2, 1924, New York City—d. Dec. 1, 1987, Saint-Paul, France) Essayist, novelist, and playwright noted for his eloquence and passion on the subject of race in America.

Baldwin grew up in poverty in Harlem. From 14 to 16 he was active as a preacher in a small revivalist church, a period he would write about in his semi-autobiographical first and finest novel, GO TELL IT ON THE MOUNTAIN (1953) and in the play *The Amen Corner* (performed 1965), about a woman evangelist.

After high school he began a restless period of ill-paid jobs, self-study, and literary apprenticeship in New York City. Disgusted with America's racial injustice, he left in 1948 for Paris, where he lived in poverty for eight years, during which he wrote the essay collection *Notes of a Native Son* (1955) and his second novel, GIOVANNI'S ROOM (1956), which dealt explicitly with homosexuality. After 1969 he divided his time between the south of France, New York, and New England.

In 1957 Baldwin became an active participant in the civil-rights struggle. A book of essays, *Nobody Knows My Name* (1961), explores black-white relations, a theme also central to his novel ANOTHER COUNTRY (1962). In the impassioned THE FIRE NEXT TIME (1963), perhaps his most powerful civil-rights statement, he said that blacks and whites must come to terms with the past and make a future together or face destruction. Baldwin's later works include the bitter play about racist oppression BLUES FOR MISTER CHARLIE (produced 1964), the story collection *Going to Meet the Man* (1965), the novel *Tell Me How Long the Train's Been Gone* (1968), and the essay collection *No Name in the Street* (1972). Ranked with Richard Wright and Ralph Ellison as a spokesman for his generation of black writers, he has been acknowledged for his support and inspiration by such figures as Maya Angelou, Toni Morrison, and Amiri Baraka.

James Baldwin

Baldwin, Joseph G. (b. Jan. 1815, Winchester, Va.—d. Sept. 30, 1864) Lawyer and humorist.

Baldwin practiced law from 1839 in Alabama, where he also served in the state legislature (1844–49). From notes on his experiences, he wrote *Flush Times in Alabama and Mississippi* (1853), a humorous view of life in the frontier South. His more serious *Party Leaders* (1855) consists of portraits of contemporary political figures.

In 1854 he moved to San Francisco, where he helped establish standards of legal practice in the almost lawless city. After serving on the California Supreme Court (1858–62), he returned to private practice.

Bambara \bäm-'bar-ə\, **Toni Cade** *originally* Toni Cade (b. March 25, 1939, New York City—d. Dec. 9, 1995, Philadelphia) Writer, civil-rights activist, and teacher.

Bambara (a surname she adopted in 1970) was educated at Queens College and CCNY, and subsequently became a frequent lecturer and teacher at universities, as well as a political activist.

Her fiction, set in the rural South as well as the urban North, is written in black street dialect and presents sharply drawn characters whom she portrays with affection. It includes the short-story collections *Gorilla, My Love* (1972) and *The Sea Birds Are Still Alive* (1977) as well as the novels *The Salt Eaters* (1980) and *If Blessing Comes* (1987). She collaborated on documentary films on the bombing of the MOVE group in Philadelphia and on W. E. B. Du Bois. *Those Bones Are Not My Child* (1999), published posthumously under the supervision of Toni Morrison, deals with the serial murders of black children in Atlanta between 1979 and 1981.

Bancroft, George (b. Oct. 3, 1800, Worcester, Mass.—d. Jan. 17, 1891, Washington, D.C.) Historian and diplomat, the "father of American history."

After graduating from Harvard University, Bancroft studied in Germany and in 1820 received a Ph.D. from the University of Göttingen. In 1823 he cofounded a school in Northampton, Mass., and he taught there eight years while embarking on the writing of his magnum opus, *History of the United States.* The first three volumes (1834, 1837, 1840), written in florid prose and with a marked democratic and nationalist bias, established him as the country's leading historian.

Having gained influence in the Democratic Party, he was appointed secretary of the navy in 1845, and used his office to promote the establishment of the U.S. Naval Academy. As acting secretary of war (1845), he issued the order that effectively started the Mexican-American War. As U.S. minister to Great Britain (1846–49), he continued his research on the *History*, whose final seven volumes he would publish in the years 1852–74. In 1867 he became U.S. minister to Prussia, and in 1871 minister to Germany. Returning to the United States in 1874, he continued to write articles and books, including *The History of the Formation of the Federal Constitution* (2 vols., 1882).

Banks, Russell (b. March 28, 1940, Newton, Mass.) Novelist known for his portrayals of the interior lives of characters trapped by economic and social forces beyond their understanding.

Banks was raised in a working-class family in New Hampshire and worked as a plumber before attending the University of North Carolina. From 1966 he was associated with Lillabulero Press, which published his first novel, *Waiting to Freeze*, in 1967. Other early works include *Snow* (1975), *Family Life* (1975), and the collection of stories *The New World* (1978). The novel *Hamilton Stark* (1978) and the story collection *Trailerpark* (1981) explore a hardscrabble New Hampshire existence. Like many of Banks's stories, these early works generally concern men whose lives have been shaped by violence. A stint in Jamaica produced the novels *The Book of Jamaica* (1980) and *Continental Drift* (1985). *The Relation of My Imprisonment* (1984) is a novel of 17th-century New England. The novels *Affliction* (1989) and *The Sweet Hereafter* (1991) were both made into successful films. *Rule of the Bone* (1995) concerns a 14-year-old runaway. *Cloudsplitter* (1998) is a historical novel about John Brown. Banks's collected stories were published as *The Angel on the Roof* (2000).

Baraka \bə-'räk-ə\, **Amiri** *originally* **(Everett) LeRoi Jones** (b. Oct. 7, 1934, Newark, N.J.) Playwright, poet, novelist, essayist, and activist.

During his childhood, Baraka became a prolific cartoonist. Offered scholarships to a number of colleges, he transferred from Rutgers University to the predominantly black Howard University. Initially he enjoyed his classes, but, oppressed by the university's atmosphere, he eventually flunked out. He joined the air force (1954), where he excelled for three years only to be discharged for suspected communist sympathies. He studied German literature at Columbia and the New School for Social Research (where he would later teach), became involved with the Beat movement, founded a literary magazine with his first wife, Hettie Jones, and brought out his first poetry collection, *Preface to a Twenty-Volume Suicide Note* (1961).

In 1964 he published the poetry collection *The Dead Lecturer*. Three angry, confrontational, obscenity-laden plays produced in 1964—DUTCHMAN, *The Slave,* and *The Toilet*—brought him fame. In the mid-1960s he became a black nationalist and changed his name to Imamu Amiri Baraka. He founded the Black Arts Repertory Theater in Harlem in 1965. His only novel, *The System of Dante's Hell,* appeared in 1966. He also published a number of works on jazz and blues, including the well-known *Blues People* (1963) and *Black Music* (1968). Active with the Black Muslims, in 1968 he helped found a Muslim group to affirm black culture and promote black political power. His writings of the 1970s show a shift from black nationalism to Marxism. He continued to compose poetry in the 1990s; collections include *Wise, Why's, Y's* (1995) and *Funk Lore* (1996). He is a professor emeritus at SUNY–Stony Brook. Apparent anti-Semitism in a poem about the Sept. 11 attacks led to his removal from the post of poet laureate of New Jersey in 2003.

Barlow, Joel (b. March 24, 1754, Redding, Connecticut Colony—d. Dec. 24, 1812, Zarnowiec, Poland) Writer and poet primarily remembered for the mock-heroic poem *The Hasty Pudding* (1796).

A graduate of Yale University, Barlow was a chaplain for three years in the Revolutionary Army, and was later admitted to the bar. In 1784 he established a weekly paper, the *American Mercury*, at Hartford, Conn., and he became a member of the group of young writers known as the Hartford (or Connecticut) wits, whose patriotism led them to attempt to create a national literature. Barlow's *Vision of Columbus* (1787), a poetic paean to America in nine books, brought him immediate fame; in 1807 he would publish a revised and expanded version as *The Columbiad*.

In 1788 Barlow sailed to France and England, where he lived periodically for the next 17 years. He was made a French citizen in 1792 after writing his radically democratic *Advice to the Privileged Orders* in response to Edmund Burke's tract on the French Revolution. *The Hasty-Pudding* (1793), his best-remembered poetical work, is a humorous pastoral evocation of New England. He returned to the United States in 1805, but left when he was named U.S. plenipotentiary to France in 1811. Caught up in Napoleon's disastrous retreat from Russia, he died of exposure in Poland.

Barnes, Djuna (b. June 12, 1892, Cornwall-on-Hudson, N.Y.—d. June 18?, 1982, New York City) Avant-garde writer, a well-known figure in the Parisian literary scene of the 1920s and '30s.

Barnes attended the Pratt Institute and Art Students League and worked as an artist and journalist. In 1915 she published an eccentric chapbook entitled *The*

Book of Repulsive Women: 8 Rhythms and 5 Drawings; four years later three of her plays were produced by the Provincetown Players. She moved to Paris in 1920; there she interviewed expatriate writers and artists for several magazines and became an established figure. She wrote and illustrated a collection of plays, short stories, and poems titled *A Book* (1923), which she expanded as *A Night Among the Horses* (1929) and much later revised as *Spillway* (1962). She also published *Ladies Almanack* (1928) and the novel *Ryder* (1928), about "a female *Tom Jones*." Her second novel, *Nightwood* (1936), about the doomed homosexual and heterosexual loves of five extraordinary people, is her masterpiece. After her return to New York in 1940, Barnes wrote little and lived reclusively; her verse drama *The Antiphon* (1958) was a later work.

Barry, Philip (b. June 18, 1896, Rochester, N.Y.—d. Dec. 3, 1949, New York City) Dramatist known for his comedies of life and manners among the socially privileged.

An avid reader, Barry started writing at 9. He was educated at Yale and in 1919 entered George Pierce Baker's theater workshop at Harvard. Barry's *A Punch for Judy* was produced by the workshop in 1920. *You and I*, also written at Harvard, played 170 performances on Broadway in 1923. The next 20 years saw a succession of plays, including such very successful comedies as *Paris Bound* (1927), *Holiday* (1928; films, 1930, 1938), *The Animal Kingdom* (1932; film, 1932), and *The Philadelphia Story* (1939; film, 1940).

White Wings (1926), a fantasy, is often considered Barry's best play. Other serious works include *John* (1927), a drama about John the Baptist; *Hotel Universe* (1930); *Here Come the Clowns* (1938), an allegory of good and evil; and his final play, *Second Threshold* (1951; completed by Robert E. Sherwood).

Barth, John *originally* John Simmons Barth, Jr. (b. May 27, 1930, Cambridge, Md.) Writer known for novels that combine philosophical depth with biting satire and boisterous, often bawdy humor.

Barth grew up on Maryland's eastern shore, the site of much of his fiction, and studied at Johns Hopkins University, where he principally taught (1973–1995). His first two novels, *The Floating Opera* (1956) and *The End of the Road* (1958; film, 1970), describe characters burdened by a sense of futility. THE SOT-WEED FACTOR (1960) is a picaresque tale that burlesques the early history of Maryland; GILES GOAT-BOY (1966) is a bizarre tale of the career of a mythical hero and religious prophet. These novels, distinguished by their 18th-century narrative style and their rich, antic, and erudite language, exerted notable influence on later writers. *Lost in the Funhouse* (1968) consists of short experimental pieces interspersed with stories based on Barth's childhood. It was followed by *Chimera* (1972, National Book Award), a volume of three novellas; *Letters* (1979), an experimental novel; and *Coming Soon!!!* (2001).

Barthelme \ˈbärt-əl-mē\, **Donald** (b. April 7, 1931, Philadelphia—d. July 23, 1989, Houston) Short-story writer and novelist.

Son of an architect, he attended the University of Houston and, after serving in the Korean War, settled in Houston, where he became managing editor of the review *Location* and was briefly director of the Contemporary Arts Museum. He moved permanently to New York in 1962, though he subsequently held a professorship at his alma mater. Known for his influential modernist "collages" marked by technical experimentation and melancholy gaiety, he has been labeled a minimalist and an absurdist and is regarded as a seminal figure in postmodernist fiction. His first collection of short stories, *Come Back, Dr. Caligari*, was published in 1964. His novella *Snow White* (1967), a gloss on Walt Disney's film, initially appeared in the *New Yorker*, with which he was long associated. His story collections include *Unspeakable Practices, Unnatural Acts* (1968), *City Life* (1970), *Sadness* (1972), the celebrated *Sixty Stories* (1981), and *Overnight to Many Distant Cities* (1983). He wrote three additional novels: *The Dead Father* (1975), *Paradise* (1986), and *The King* (1990). Frederick Barthelme is his brother.

Barthelme, Frederick (b. Oct. 10, 1943, Houston) Short-story writer and novelist.

Brother of Donald Barthelme, he attended Tulane University and the University of Houston. In the 1960s, after studies at Houston's Museum of Fine Arts, he had his artworks displayed in Houston and Seattle galleries and at New York's Museum of Modern Art. He obtained a master's degree in English from Johns Hopkins University and joined the faculty of the University of Southern Mississippi. Much of his gently ironic and disorienting work is set in the suburban world of shopping malls and fast-food franchises. *Rangoon*, his first story collection, appeared in 1970; his later collections include *Moon Deluxe* (1983) and *The Law of Averages* (2000). His novels include *Second Marriage* (1984), *Natural Selection* (1989), *The Brothers* (1993), and *Bob, the Gambler* (1997), reflecting his own disastrous gambling habit. He edits the *Mississippi Review*.

Bartram, William (b. Feb. 9, 1739, Kingsessing, Pa.—d. July 22, 1823, Kingsessing) Naturalist and writer.

In his early years Bartram worked with his father, the botanist John Bartram, tending the family's important collection of rare plants. In the 1780s he traveled in the Southeast, cataloging and describing the animals and plants he encountered in the primeval river swamps. His journal, published as *Travels Through North and South Carolina, Georgia, East and West Florida* in 1791, not only contributed to scientific knowledge but was later read for its description of wild scenery, influencing such English Romantics as William Wordsworth and Samuel Coleridge.

Barzun \\'bär-zən\\, **Jacques (Martin)** (b. Nov. 30, 1907, Créteil, France) Historian and educator.

Son of a poet, Barzun immigrated with his family to the United States in 1919, settling in New York City. In 1932 he obtained his doctorate from Columbia University, where he remained to teach history for decades. In 1958 he was named dean of faculties and provost; he retired in 1967.

A tireless advocate of the liberal arts and of adherence to traditional standards of language and scholarship, Barzun influenced American higher education by his insistence that undergraduates be given broad instruction in the humanities. His numerous books on education include *Teacher in America* (1945), *The House of Intellect* (1959), and *The American University* (1969). *The Modern Researcher* (1957), several times revised, has remained a standard text for researchers in the social sciences. *Berlioz and the Romantic Century* (2 vols., 1950, 1969) was instrumental in restoring Berlioz's diminished reputation. Barzun completed Wilson Follett's *Modern American Usage* (1966). His other books include *The Energies of Art* (1956), *Science: The Glorious Entertainment* (1964), *On Writing, Editing, and Publishing* (1971), and *The Use and Abuse of Art* (1974). *From Dawn to Decadence: 500 Years of Western Cultural Life, 1500 to the Present* (2000), published when he was 92, was an unexpected best-seller.

Bate, Walter Jackson (b. May 23, 1918, Mankato, Minn.—d. July 26, 1999, Boston) Scholar known for his studies of John Keats and Samuel Johnson.

Educated at Harvard University, Bate taught history and literature there from 1946 to 1986. In 1945 he published his *Stylistic Development of Keats*. His *John Keats* (1963) was awarded the Pulitzer Prize. *Samuel Johnson* (1977) won the acclaim of scholars and critics and received a second Pulitzer Prize and the National Book Award. Bate's other works include *From Classic to Romantic* (1946), *The Achievement of Samuel Johnson* (1955), and *Coleridge* (1968).

Bates, Katharine Lee (b. Aug. 12, 1859, Falmouth, Mass.—d. March 28, 1929, Wellesley, Mass.) Author and educator who wrote the text of "America the Beautiful."

Bates was educated at Wellesley College. Upon graduation she taught public and private school until 1885, when she returned to Wellesley to teach English for 40 years. Several collections of her poetry were published, but she is only remembered today for the national hymn "America the Beautiful," the first draft of which she penciled after a journey west in 1893. She rewrote it in 1904. She also published two travel books and scholarly works on English religious drama, American literature, and Shakespeare.

Baum \\'bäm, 'bȯm\\, **L(yman) Frank** (b. May 15, 1856, Chittenango—d. May 6, 1919, Hollywood, Calif.) Author of the highly popular Oz series for children.

A shy child with a weak heart, Baum cultivated his imagination throughout his youth. At 15 he started publishing a paper, the *Rose Lawn Home Journal,* which he followed with similar ventures. In 1880 he took over management of a string of opera houses owned by his father, and soon he was writing for the theater. His play *The Maid of Arran,* in which he took a starring role, was a success. He married in 1882, and in 1888 the family moved West, where he ran a general store for 10 years.

He collaborated with the illustrator Maxfield Parrish to produce *Mother Goose in Prose* (1897), which he followed with the highly successful *Father Goose* (1899). *The Wonderful Wizard of Oz* (1900) was even more popular; the story of a girl from a drab Kansas farm lifted by a tornado into a fantastical world of colors and remarkable characters, it was embraced immediately as a characteristically American fairy tale and captivated a huge audience. Baum adapted it as a musical stage play in 1902; it would be adapted for stage and screen many more times, most notably in the 1939 film *The Wizard of Oz.* Baum went on to write 13 sequels, and after his death the series was continued by Ruth Plumly Thompson.

L. Frank Baum

Baum, Vicki (*originally* Hedwig) (b. Jan. 24, 1888, Vienna—d. Aug. 29, 1960, Hollywood) Austrian-American novelist whose fame rests on *Menschen im Hotel* (1929; "People at the Hotel").

Originally a harpist, Baum began working as an editor in 1906. Though she began writing in her teens, her first book, *Frühe Schatten* (1919), was not published until she was 31. *Menschen im Hotel* first appeared serially in *Berliner Illustrierte Zeitung,* where Baum was an editor. It achieved immediate success in Germany. She rewrote it as a play, and it enjoyed a great success on Broadway as *Grand Hotel.* Baum moved to the United States in 1931 and became a Hollywood screenwriter. A highly successful film adaptation appeared that same year.

Baum's later novels include *Men Never Know* (1935), *Shanghai '37* (1939), *Grand Opera* (1942), *Hotel Berlin '43* (1944), *Mortgage on Life* (1946), *Danger from Deer* (1951), *The Mustard Seed* (1953), *Written on Water* (1956), and *Theme for Ballet* (1958).

Bausch \\'bȯsh, 'baùsh\\, **Richard (Carl)** (b. April 18, 1945, Ft. Benning, Ga.) Novelist and short-story writer.

Bausch earned an M.F.A. from the University of Iowa in 1975 and has taught at George Mason University since 1980. His fiction is characterized by its poignant and often painful probing of his subjects' lives and relationships. His novels include *Real Presence* (1980), *Take Me Back* (1981), *The Last Good Time* (1984; film, 1994), *Mr. Field's Daughter* (1989), *Violence* (1992), *Rebel Powers* (1993), *Good Morning Mr. and Mrs. America and All the Ships at Sea* (1996), and the psychological thriller *In the Night Season* (1999). His collections of short stories include *Spirits* (1987), *Fireman's Wife* (1990), *Rare and Endangered Species* (1994), *Aren't You Happy for Me?* (1995), and *Someone to Watch Over Me* (1999).

Beard, Charles A(ustin) (b. Nov. 27, 1874, Knightstown, Ind.—d. Sept. 1, 1948, New Haven, Conn.) Historian.

After graduating from DePauw University, Beard traveled and studied in Europe before obtaining his Ph.D. from Columbia University in 1904. He taught history and politics at Columbia from 1904 to 1917 while writing the first of his iconoclastic studies of U.S. political institutions, which emphasize the dynamics of socioeconomic conflict and change and analyze motivational factors in the founding of institutions. His highly influential *An Economic Interpretation of the Constitution of the United States* (1913) claimed that the Constitution was formulated to serve the economic interests of the founders and established Beard as a leading progressive historian and a founder of economic determinism. *The Economic Origins of Jeffersonian Democracy* (1915) pursued similar themes. It would be followed by many more works, principally on political policy. In 1919 he helped found the New School for Social Research.

His wife, Mary Ritter Beard (1876–1958), was active in the women's-suffrage movement. Her books include *A Short History of the American Labor Movement* (1920) and *On Understanding Women* (1930). The Beards collaborated on the monumental four-volume *Rise of American Civilization* (1927–44). Their *Basic History of the United States* (1921) was long a standard textbook.

Beattie \\'bē-tē\\, **Ann** (b. Sept. 8, 1947, Washington, D.C.) Novelist and short-story writer.

Beattie graduated from American University and received a master's degree from the University of Connecticut in 1970, and her stories began to appear in the *New Yorker* and elsewhere in the early 1970s. In 1976 she published her first story collection, *Distortions*, and her first novel, *Chilly Scenes of Winter* (film, 1979).

Beattie's stories chronicle the lives of people who came of age in the 1960s and find themselves trapped, in later decades, in unsatisfying careers and lives. Her style is detached and unemotional; there is little examination of motivation, and historical background is usually absent. Though some critics found the style off-putting, it resonated strongly with many readers. Later collections of her stories include *Secrets and Surprises* (1978), *The Burning House* (1982), *What Was Mine* (1991), *Where You'll Find Me* (1995), *Convergences* (1998), and *Park City* (1998), and her later novels include *Falling in Place* (1980) and *Picturing Will* (1989).

Behrman \\'ber-mən\\, **S(amuel) N(athaniel)** (b. June 9, 1893, Worcester, Mass.—d. Sept. 9, 1973, New York City) Short-story writer and playwright best known for his popular Broadway plays.

Behrman studied drama at Harvard and Columbia, and as a young man contributed to leading newspapers and magazines, including the *New Republic* and the *New Yorker*. His play *The Second Man* (1927) was the first in a string of successes that included *Meteor* (1929), *Brief Moment* (1931), and *Biography* (1932). He tackled the subject of fascism in *Rain from Heaven* (1934). In 1938 he helped found the Playwrights' Company. Criticized for letting his characters speak for him, he wrote *No Time for Comedy* (1939), in which an author of light comedy criticizes himself for his failure to address serious contemporary problems. He later collaborated on *Jacobowsky and The Colonel* (1944; with Franz Werfel) and *Fanny* (1954; with Joshua Logan; film, 1961). Of more than two dozen comedies written during a 40-year career, nearly all were hits. Behrman also wrote many short stories, two biographies, the novel *The Burning Glass* (1968), and a number of screenplays, including *Anna Karenina* (1935).

Belasco, David (b. July 25, 1853, San Francisco—d. May 14, 1931, New York City) Theatrical producer and playwright.

Belasco acted from his childhood with traveling theater companies before becoming a theater manager, first in San Francisco and, from 1880, in New York. In 1890 he became an independent producer, and in 1906 he built the Belasco Theater.

He gained a reputation for minute attention to detail, sensational realism, lavish settings, astonishing mechanical effects, and experiments in lighting that led to the virtual elimination of footlights and to the first lensed spotlights. As a result, he was the first American producer whose name, regardless of star actor or play, attracted patrons to the theater. His austere dress and personal manner won him the epithet "the bishop of Broadway."

Belasco wrote or collaborated on numerous plays, including *Hearts of Oak* (1879); *The Heart of Maryland* (1895); *Madame Butterfly* (1900) and *The Girl of the Golden West* (1905), both of which were turned into operas by Giacomo Puccini; *Du Barry* (1901); *The Music Master* (1904); and *Lulu Belle* (1926). *The Theatre Through Its Stage Door* (1919) is his autobiography.

Bellamy \\'bel-ə-mē\\, **Edward** (b. March 26, 1850, Chicopee Falls, Mass.—d. May 22, 1898, Chicopee Falls) Writer known chiefly for his utopian novel *Looking Backward, 2000–1887*.

Bellamy first became aware of the plight of the urban poor at 18 while studying in Germany. He studied law and was admitted to the bar in 1871, but he soon turned to journalism, becoming an editorial writer for the *New York Evening Post*.

In *Looking Backward* (1888), set in Boston in the year 2000, he described the United States under an ideal socialist system that featured cooperation, brotherhood, and an industry geared to human need. It sold more than a million copies. Bellamy became an active propagandist for the nationalization of public services; Nationalist clubs devoted to the realization of his vision sprang up across the nation, and political groups inspired by his works also appeared in Europe. A sequel, *Equality* (1897), was less successful. Additional writings, published posthumously, included *Edward Bellamy Speaks Again!* (1937) and *Talks on Nationalism* (1938).

Saul Bellow

Bellow, Saul (b. June 10, 1915, Lachine, near Montreal) Novelist.

Bellow's parents emigrated in 1913 from Russia to Montreal, and he grew up speaking Yiddish. When he was 9 the family moved to Chicago, and he attended the University of Chicago and Northwestern University. Following wartime service in the Merchant Marine, he embarked on a career in writing and teaching, first in New York and then for many years in Chicago.

His first two novels, *Dangling Man* (1944) and *The Victim* (1947), were admired by a small readership. THE ADVENTURES OF AUGIE MARCH (1953, National Book Award), a wide-ranging bildungsroman begun while Bellow was in Paris on a Guggenheim fellowship, brought much wider acclaim, and made Bellow a standard-bearer for the Jewish-American writers whose works became central to postwar American literature. HENDERSON THE RAIN KING (1959), also picaresque in structure, is the tale of an eccentric American millionaire on a quest in Africa. The novella SEIZE THE DAY (1956) deals with a man who is a failure in a society that values only success. In 1967 Bellow served as a war correspondent in Israel for *Newsday*. The following year he published a volume of short stories, *Mosby's Memoirs*.

His most celebrated novels of the 1960s and '70s were HERZOG (1964, National Book Award, International Literary Prize), MR. SAMMLER'S PLANET (1970, National Book Award), and HUMBOLDT'S GIFT (1975, Pulitzer Prize). Three short plays were produced on Broadway in 1966, collectively entitled *Under the Weather.* In 1976 Bellow was awarded the Nobel Prize for Literature. His later fiction includes *The Dean's December* (1982), the story collection *Him with His Foot in His Mouth* (1984), *More Die of Heartbreak* (1987), *A Theft* (1989), *The Bellarosa Connection* (1989), and *The Actual* (1997); *Ravelstein* (2000) concerns a man closely resembling the scholar Allan Bloom. Most of Bellow's fiction deals with the modern urban dweller, disaffected by society but not destroyed in spirit, in a voice that distinctively combines cultural sophistication and street wisdom.

Benchley, Robert (Charles) (b. Sept. 15, 1889, Worcester, Mass.—d. Nov. 21, 1945, New York City) Drama critic and actor noted for his humorous short films and essays.

A graduate of Harvard University, Benchley joined the staff of the humor magazine *Life* in 1920 as drama critic, and became a founding member of the Algonquin Round Table. His monologue "The Treasurer's Report," delivered as a skit in an amateur revue in 1922, became the basis for one of the first all-talking film shorts. He subsequently wrote and acted in 46 shorts; his *How to Sleep* (1934) won an Academy Award. Benchley was drama critic for the *New Yorker* (1929–40), for which (as Guy Fawkes) he also wrote "The Wayward Press" column.

Benchley's essays were illustrated by Gluyas Williams's caricatures and collected in more than 10 books, including *My Ten Years in a Quandary, and How They Grew* (1936) and *Benchley Beside Himself* (1943). His writing is characterized by warmth and the humor of the non sequitur; his satire, though sharp, was never cruel.

In the late 1930s he was writing three syndicated magazine columns simultaneously. From 1938 to 1940 he starred on his own radio show; he also made guest appearances on other radio shows, including *Amos 'n' Andy* and *The Fred Allen Show. The Benchley Roundup* (1954) was a selection from his writings edited by his son Nathaniel, who also wrote his biography (1955).

Benét \bə-'nā\, **Stephen Vincent** (b. July 22, 1898, Bethlehem, Pa.—d. March 13, 1943, New York City) Poet, novelist, and writer of short stories.

Benét published his first collection of poems at 17. Civilian service during World War I interrupted his education at Yale, but he received his master's degree after the war, submitting his third volume of poems instead of a thesis.

After publishing the much-admired *Ballad of William Sycamore 1790–1880* (1923), three novels, and a number of short stories, he wrote JOHN BROWN'S BODY (1928). A book-length poem of the Civil War, it was widely read and received a Pulitzer Prize; dramatized by Charles Laughton in 1953, it was performed across the country.

A Book of Americans (1933), poems written with his wife, the former Rosemary Carr, brought many historical characters to life for American schoolchildren. Benét's preoccupation with historical themes was also the basis for *Western Star*, an ambitious story of America left uncompleted at his death; Book I, complete in itself, was published posthumously and won a Pulitzer Prize. His best-known short story, THE DEVIL AND DANIEL WEBSTER (1937), was the basis for a popular play, an opera by Douglas Moore, and a film (*All That Money Can Buy,* 1941).

His brother, William Rose Benét (1886–1950), was a poet, novelist, and longtime editor at the *Saturday Review of Literature* (1924–50). His best-known verse collection is *The Dust Which Is God* (1941, Pulitzer Prize); his novels include *The First Person Singular* (1922). He married the poet Eleanor Wylie in 1923.

Bennett, Gwendolyn B(ennetta) (b. July 8, 1902, Giddings, Texas—d. May 30, 1981, Reading, Pa.) Poet, essayist, short-story writer, and artist of the Harlem Renaissance.

After her parents' divorce, Bennett lived with her father, a lawyer, in Brooklyn and later studied art at Columbia University and the Pratt Institute. In the early 1920s she had poems published in *Opportunity, Crisis,* and *Gypsy,* and she designed covers for *Crisis* and other journals. As an editor at *Opportunity* she wrote its popular literary news column (1926–28). Most of her published work, including two short stories, appeared 1923–28; it has not yet been collected. Her best-known poem is the sensual "To a Dark Girl." She directed the Harlem Community Arts Center 1939–44.

Berger \\'bər-gər\\, **Thomas (Louis)** (b. July 20, 1924, Cincinnati) Novelist whose darkly comic fiction probes and satirizes the American experience.

Berger graduated from the University of Cincinnati. His first novel, *Crazy in Berlin* (1958), inaugurated a tetralogy about Carlo Reinhart, who in the first novel is an adolescent American soldier in Germany. His story continues in *Reinhart in Love* (1962), *Vital Parts* (1970), and *Reinhart's Women* (1981). In his best-known novel, *Little Big Man* (1964; film, 1970), the only white survivor of the Battle of the Little Big Horn, the 111-year-old Jack Crabb, tells his life story. A sequel, *Return of Little Big Man,* appeared in 1999.

Berger's other novels include *Killing Time* (1967), *Regiment of Women* (1973), *Who Is Teddy Villanova?* (1977), *Arthur Rex: A Legendary Novel* (1978), *Neighbors* (1980; film, 1981), *Nowhere* (1985), *The Houseguest* (1988), *Orrie's Story* (1990), *Meeting Evil* (1992), *Robert Crews* (1994), and *Suspects* (1996).

Berrigan \\'ber-i-gən\\, **Daniel** (b. May 9, 1921, Virginia, Minn.) Priest whose poems and essays reflect his commitment to social, political, and economic change.

Berrigan grew up in Syracuse, N.Y., joined the Jesuit order in 1939, and was ordained a priest in 1952. He published his first collection of poems, *Time Without Number*, in 1957, and later taught literature at Le Moyne College (1957–62).

Influenced by his brother Philip (then also a priest), he became active in the antiwar movement. He went to North Vietnam to help obtain the release of three American pilots, an experience he recorded in *Night Flight to Hanoi* (1968). His best-known work, *The Trial of the Catonsville Nine* (1970), is a courtroom drama based on his conviction in a federal court for destroying draft records, an offense for which he served 18 months in prison. Some of his most eloquent poetry was published in *Prison Poems* (1973). *We Die Before We Live* (1980) was based on his experiences working in a cancer ward. Throughout the 1980s he took part in Plowshares raids, protests at the sites of weapons manufacturers and military bases. He appeared in *In the King of Prussia* (1982), a documentary on the raids, and as an 18th-century Jesuit priest in the film *The Mission* (1986).

Berry, Wendell (Erdman) (b. Aug. 5, 1934, Port Royal, Ky.) Poet, novelist, and essayist whose sensitivity to nature, rural life, and the need for ecological responsibility stem from his experiences as a farmer.

Berry obtained a master's degree from the University of Kentucky. Though he has taught at Stanford and New York universities, his base since 1964 has been Kentucky. He taught at the University of Kentucky until 1977, when he left to concentrate on his writing and farming.

From his first collection, *The Broken Ground* (1964), to more recent collections such as *Sabbaths* (1987), Berry's poetry reveals a steadily growing concern with the abuse of the land and the need to restore the balance of nature. The theme of human responsibility to the earth is also present in his novels, including *The Memory of Old Jack* (1974). Among his nonfiction works, *The Hidden Wound* (1970) explores racism, while *The Unsettling of America* (1977) discusses the late-20th-century crises of culture and morality. His essays in *The Gift of Good Land* (1981), *What Are People For?* (1990), *Sex, Economy, Freedom, and Community* (1993), and *Another Turn of the Crank* (1995) expand on his themes of ecology and human responsibility; *Life Is a Miracle* (2000) is his rebuttal to Edward O. Wilson's assertion that science will one day supply the answers to all life's questions.

Berryman, John (b. Oct. 25, 1914, McAlester, Okla.—d. Jan. 7, 1972, Minneapolis) Poet noted for his confessional poetry laced with humor.

When Berryman was 12, his father shot himself outside his window, a tragedy that was to haunt him. At Columbia University he was influenced by the poet Mark Van Doren. After study at Cambridge University (1938), he returned to America to teach at Wayne State University, beginning a career that would include posts at Harvard, Princeton, and the University of Minnesota.

Five Young American Poets (1940) contained 20 of his poems, and two of his own collections—*Poems* (1942) and *The Dispossessed* (1948)—soon followed. He also wrote short fiction: "The Lovers" appeared in *The Best American Short Stories of 1946*, and his story "The Imaginary Jew" (1945) is often anthologized.

John Berryman

HOMAGE TO MISTRESS BRADSTREET (1956) was one of Berryman's first experimental poems. His new technical daring was also evident in 77 *Dream Songs* (1964, Pulitzer Prize), which was augmented to form a sequence of 385 DREAM SONGS by *His Toy, His Dream, His Rest* (1968, National Book Award). *Berryman's Sonnets*, a richly erotic autobiographical sequence about a love affair, appeared in 1967. *Love & Fame* (1970), like much of his poetry, had a confessional tone.

Subject to deep depressions, he committed suicide by jumping from a bridge onto the ice of the Mississippi River. *Recovery*, an account of his alcoholism, was published posthumously in 1973.

Bester, Alfred (b. Dec. 18, 1913, New York City—d. Oct. 20?, 1987, Doylestown, Pa) Innovative science-fiction writer whose output was small but influential.

Bester attended the University of Pennsylvania, and from 1939 to 1942 he published 14 short stories in science-fiction magazines, including "Hell Is Forever" (1942), which in its fast pacing and obsessive characters anticipated the style of his major novels. He wrote scenarios for superhero comic books and scripts for radio and television, and he created English-language librettos for operas by Verdi and Moussorgsky. His first novel was the satirical, non-science-fiction work *Who He?* (1953).

Bester's first major work, the novel *The Demolished Man* (1953), won the first Hugo Award and became a cult favorite. It was followed by *The Stars My Destination* (1955), a tale of revenge acknowledged as a science-fiction masterpiece. His fiction often employed narrative techniques—such as interior monologue—that were new to science fiction. His several short-story collections include *Starburst* (1958) and *The Dark Side of the Earth* (1964). After a long stint as literary editor at *Holiday* magazine, he published such later works as *The Computer Connection* (1975; also published as *Extro*), followed by *Golem 100* (1980) and *The Deceivers* (1982), none of which matched the popularity of his early works.

Beverley, Robert (b. c.1673, Middlesex County, Va.—d. 1722, King and Queen County, Va.) Historian.

Educated in England, Beverley returned to Virginia and by 1696 held important posts as clerk of the colony's general court and general assembly. From 1699 to 1706 he served intermittently in the House of Burgesses. His *History and Present State of Virginia* (1705) describes the colony, its people, and its administrators, often with critical humor and sarcasm. The *History* (revised and softened in 1722) has remained a valuable source of contemporary colonial life.

Bidart \bi-'därt\, **Frank** (b. 1939, Bakersfield, Calif.) Poet whose introspective verse, notably dramatic monologues by troubled characters, deals with personal guilt, family life, and madness.

Bidart graduated from UC–Riverside and later studied at Harvard University; he has taught at Wellesley College since 1972. His first volume of verse was *Golden State* (1973), whose title poem is an autobiographical account of a father-and-son relationship. *The Book of the Body* (1977) features the dramatic monologues of an amputee and of a suicidal anorexic.

Critical acclaim greeted *The Sacrifice* (1983), a collection of five long poems about guilt. It was followed by the collected-poems volume *In the Western Night* (1990) and *Desire* (1997).

Bierce \'birs\, **Ambrose (Gwinnett)** (b. June 24, 1842, Meigs County, Ohio—d. 1914, Mexico?) Newspaperman, wit, satirist, and author of sardonic short stories with themes of death and horror.

Reared in Indiana, Bierce became an apprentice on a local antislavery paper after about a year of high school. In 1861 he enlisted in the army and fought in a number of Civil War battles, being seriously wounded in 1864. Resettling in San Francisco, he began contributing to periodicals, particularly the *News Letter*, of which he became editor in 1868. He was soon the principal literary arbiter of the West Coast. "The Haunted Valley" (1871) was his first story. From 1872 to 1875 he lived in England, where he wrote for London magazines, edited the *Lantern*, and published *The Fiend's Delight* (1872), *Nuggets and Dust Panned Out in California* (1872), and *Cobwebs from an Empty Skull* (1874).

In 1877 he joined the *San Francisco Argonaut,* but he left it for an unsuccessful try at mining in the Dakota Territory (1879–80). Thereafter he spent five years as editor of the *San Francisco Wasp.* In 1887 he joined the staff of the *San Francisco Examiner*, for which he wrote the "Prattler" column. In 1891 he published *Tales of Soldiers and Civilians,* which included some of his finest stories, such as AN OCCURRENCE AT OWL CREEK BRIDGE, "The Eyes of the Panther," and "The Boarded Window." THE DEVIL'S DICTIONARY (1906) was a volume of ironic, even bitter, definitions. In 1896 he moved to Washington, D.C., and there continued newspaper and magazine writing. In 1913 he went to Mexico, then in the middle of a revolution led by Pancho Villa. His end is a mystery, but he was likely killed in the siege of Ojinaga in January 1914. Carlos Fuentes's *The Old Gringo* (1985; film, 1989) is a fictional account of Bierce's last days.

Biggers, Earl Derr (b. Aug. 26, 1884, Warren, Ohio—d. April 5, 1933, Pasadena, Calif.) Novelist and journalist remembered for the popular character Charlie Chan.

Biggers graduated from Harvard University and became a journalist for the *Boston Traveler*. His successful mystery novel *Seven Keys to Baldpate* (1913) was adapted into a well-received play and a film. He moved to New York and from 1914 to 1919 wrote many successful plays, including *Inside the Lines* (1915), a war play. Having moved to California, he wrote his six novels featuring Charlie Chan, an aphorism-spouting Chinese-American detective on the Honolulu police force. Initially serialized in the *Saturday Evening Post,* the novels spawned numerous feature films, radio dramas, and comic strips.

Billings, Josh *pseudonym of* Henry Wheeler Shaw (b. April 21, 1818, Lanesboro, Mass.—d. Oct. 14, 1885, Monterey, Calif.) Popular humorist known for his rustic aphorisms and droll delineations of animal life.

Son of a Congressman, Shaw was expelled from Hamilton College for a prank, and lived an unsettled life in the West and Midwest before settling in Poughkeepsie, N.Y., in 1858 as an auctioneer and land dealer. He began writing his comic pieces at 45, but became successful only when he adopted the misspelling vogue. His "Essa on the Muel" made him famous, and after joining the *New York Weekly* in 1867 he became a national figure, partly through his popular deadpan lectures. Some of his best work is in the 10-year series *Josh Billings' Farmer's Allminax* (1869–80), a burlesque of *The Old Farmer's Almanac*. His other books were hasty collections of his newspaper writings, the most comprehensive being *Everybody's Friend* (1874). As Uncle Esek, he also made contributions to the *Century* magazine.

Bird, Robert Montgomery (b. Feb. 5, 1806, New Castle, Del.—d. Jan. 23, 1854, Philadelphia) Novelist and dramatist.

Bird obtained a medical degree from the University of Pennsylvania but practiced only a year. He wrote several unproduced plays before seeing his first drama staged. *The Gladiator* (1831), which dealt with a slave revolt in Rome in 73 BC, was intended as an oblique attack on American slavery. Later plays included *Oralloossa* (1832) and *The Broker of Bogota* (1834), both set in South America. He turned to writing novels, beginning with *Calavar* (1834), about the Spanish conquistadores, and its sequel, *The Infidel* (1835). His remaining novels were frontier stories; the most popular was *Nick of the Woods* (1837), notable for its realistic portrayals of American Indians. Unable to make a living from his writing, he tried his hand at farming; at his death he was literary editor and part owner of a newspaper.

Though immensely popular in its day, his work is now principally of interest to the literary historian. In the 1990s hitherto unknown collections of his experimental photography and his sketches revealed his interest in the visual arts.

Elizabeth Bishop

Bishop, Elizabeth (b. Feb. 8, 1911, Worcester, Mass.—d. Oct. 6, 1979, Boston) Poet known for her subtle, profound, and formally superb descriptive verse.

Brought up largely by her grandparents in Nova Scotia after her father died and her mother was institutionalized, Bishop attended Vassar College, where she met the poet Marianne Moore, who became a lifelong friend and mentor. After graduating, she traveled widely and lived in Key West and Mexico. She subsequently lived 16 years near Rio de Janeiro with the aristocratic Brazilian woman she loved, later dividing her time between Brazil and San Francisco.

The poems in her first collection, *North & South* (1946), displayed a close attention to nature and physical reality, as well as the formal brilliance for which Bishop would be celebrated. Reprinted with additions as *North & South: A Cold Spring* (1955), they received the Pulitzer Prize.

Bishop served as consultant in poetry at the Library of Congress 1949–50. Her *Complete Poems* was published in 1969. *Geography III* (1976) won the National Book Critics Circle Award. She taught writing at Harvard from 1970 to 1977. Her Portuguese translations include Alice Brant's Brazilian classic *The Diary of Helena Morley* (1957), and she later edited and translated *An Anthology of Twentieth-Century Brazilian Poetry* (1972).

Esteemed by her fellow poets during her lifetime, Bishop only began to be widely read after her death, and she is now widely acknowledged as one of the finest poets of her era. Posthumous collections include her *Collected Prose* (1984) and a much-admired edition of her letters, *One Art* (1994).

Bishop, John Peale (b. May 21, 1892, Charles Town, W.Va.—d. April 4, 1944, Hyannis, Mass.) Poet, novelist, and critic.

A temporary loss of eyesight made the young Bishop abandon plans to become an artist, and during his convalescence he became interested in poetry. At Princeton he formed lifelong friendships with Edmund Wilson and with F. Scott Fitzgerald, who would depict Bishop as the highbrow writer Tom D'Invilliers in *This Side of Paradise*.

He published his first volume of verse, *Green Fruit*, in 1917. After military service in World War I, he became an editor at *Vanity Fair* magazine (1920–22). He married into wealth and traveled throughout Europe. Living in France from 1926 to 1933, he acquired a deep admiration for French culture and became good friends with the expatriates Archibald MacLeish and Allen Tate. A collection of stories about his native South, *Many Thousands Gone* (1931), was followed with a volume of poetry, *Now with His Love* (1933). The novel *Act of Darkness* and the verse collection *Minute Particulars* appeared in 1935. During the 1930s Bishop also wrote critical pieces on Hemingway and Thomas Wolfe and on poetry and painting. He became chief poetry reviewer for the *Nation* in 1940, the year he published perhaps his finest poem, "The Hours," an elegy for Fitzgerald. His *Collected Poems* and *Collected Essays* appeared in 1948.

Bissell \ˈbis-əl\, Richard (Pike) (b. June 27, 1913, Dubuque, Iowa—d. May 4, 1977, Dubuque) Novelist and playwright whose works provide fresh and witty images of Midwestern speech and folkways.

Bissell graduated from Harvard in 1936. From his experiences as a river pilot in the 1940s came the novels *A Stretch on the River* (1950) and *The Monongahela* (1952). His first successful novel was *7 1/2 Cents* (1953), based on his experiences as a supervisor in a Dubuque pajama factory; with George Abbott, Richard Adler, and Jerry Ross, he turned it into the hit musical *The Pajama Game* (1954; film, 1957). His experiences in the theater led to the novel *Say, Darling* (1957), which with his wife and Abe Burrows he also adapted as a musical (1958). His later books include the novels *Good Bye, Ava* (1960), *Still Circling Moose Jaw* (1965), and *New Light on 1776 and All That* (1975).

Black Elk (b. December 1863?, Little Powder River, Wyo.—d. Aug. 17, 1950) Oglala Lakota Sioux spiritual leader.

Born to a medicine man who followed Crazy Horse, Black Elk witnessed the Battle of Little Big Horn in 1876 and the upheaval that followed the tribe's flight to Canada to join Sitting Bull. In 1886 he joined Buffalo Bill's Wild West Show. In 1889 he returned to the Pine Ridge Reservation, where, as a spiritual authority, he supported the Ghost Dance movement. The movement, built on the belief that ritual observances would cause the white people to leave and the buffalo to return, declined after it failed to protect its followers at the Battle of Wounded Knee.

In 1904 he was converted by a priest to the Catholic faith and took the name Nicholas Black Elk. As a member of the Society of St. Joseph, he helped sponsor the annual Catholic Sioux Congress and was active in converting others to Catholicism.

In BLACK ELK SPEAKS (1932), edited by John G. Neihardt, he describes his childhood and early adult life and the spiritual life of the Sioux. In *The Sacred Pipe* (1953), edited by Joseph E. Brown, he describes Sioux ritual and spiritual practices.

Blackmur \\'blak-mər\\, **R(ichard) P(almer)** (b. Jan. 21, 1904, Springfield, Mass.—d. Feb. 2, 1965, Princeton, N.J.) Critic and poet.

Blackmur's formal education largely ended with high school, after which he worked in bookstores in Cambridge, Mass. Through friendship with the publishers, he was appointed editor of the little magazine *Hound and Horn* (1928–30). His essays there began to establish his reputation as a literary critic.

His influential books of literary criticism and analysis of aesthetics were noted for their difficulty. His first book was *The Art of the Novel* (1934). His second, *The Double Agent* (1935), is often regarded as the founding document of New Criticism, which emphasized the meticulously close analysis of literary texts without regard for any larger sociocultural context. At Allen Tate's invitation, he began teaching at Princeton University in 1940, the year he published *The Expense of Greatness*. In later works such as *Language as Gesture* (1952), *The Lion and the Honeycomb* (1954), and *Primer of Ignorance* (1967), he turned decisively away from the critical school he had helped establish. His poems were collected in *From Jordan's Delight* (1937), *The Second World* (1942), and *The Good European* (1947).

Blitzstein \\'blit-,stīn\\, **Marc** (b. Mar. 2, 1905, Philadelphia—d. Jan. 22, 1964, Fort-de-France, Martinique) Composer and playwright.

A musical prodigy as a child, Blitzstein appeared as a piano soloist with the Philadelphia Orchestra at 15. In the 1920s he studied in Europe with Nadia Boulanger and Arnold Schoenberg. His early works, including the ballet *Jig Saw* (1927), *The Condemned* (1933), and *Children's Cantata* (1935), were noted by the avant-garde. The circumstances of the premiere of his first opera, *The Cradle Will Rock* (1937), notorious for its anticapitalist theme, became a theatrical legend when it was almost aborted by the public authorities. His texted *Airborne*

Symphony (1946) was inspired by his air-corps service in World War II. His greatest success came with his translation of Kurt Weill's and Bertolt Brecht's *Threepenny Opera* (1952), which ran off-Broadway for a record-breaking six years. His other works included the successful operas *Regina* (1949), based on Lillian Hellman's *The Little Foxes*, and *Reuben, Reuben* (1951). He was at work on an opera based on the Sacco-Vanzetti case—for which, as for virtually all his musical works, he wrote the text—when he was beaten to death in Martinique.

Bloom, Harold (b. July 11, 1930, New York City) Literary critic known for his innovative interpretations of literary history and the creation of literature.

A scholar from the start, Bloom taught himself to read Yiddish at 3, Hebrew at 4, and English at 5. He attended Cornell and Yale universities and began teaching at Yale in 1955. His early books, *The Visionary Company* (1961) and *The Ringers in the Tower* (1971), explored the Romantic tradition and its influence on 20th-century poets. He also wrote extensively on Shakespeare, on whom he is considered a leading authority.

In his most influential works, *The Anxiety of Influence* (1973) and *A Map of Misreading* (1975), Bloom proposed that poets deliberately misread the works that influence them. *Figures of Capable Imagination* (1976) expands on this theme. In his later years Bloom became the most famous critic in America, and his books—increasingly written for a general audience—became reliable best-sellers. In *The Book of J* (1990), he speculated that the earliest known biblical texts were written by a woman and were less religious than literary. *The Western Canon* (1994), *Shakespeare: The Invention of the Human* (1998), and *How to Read and Why* (2000) are eloquent defenses of the traditional literary classics.

Blume, Judy *originally* Judy Sussman (b. Feb. 12, 1938, Elizabeth, N.J.) Novelist and children's and young adult fiction writer.

After graduating from NYU in 1960, she married and reared two children. In the 1970s she began writing her best-selling books for children and especially adolescents, which confront forthrightly—to a degree that appalled many adults and led to campaigns for their removal from libraries—such sensitive issues as bodily development and losing one's virginity. They include *Iggy's House* (1970), *Are You There God? It's Me, Margaret* (1970), *Tales of a Fourth Grade Nothing* (1972), *Blubber* (1974), *Forever* (1976), *Superfudge* (1980), *Fudge-a-mania* (1990), and *Here's to You Rachel Robinson* (1993). Her popular adult novels include *Wifey* (1977), *Smart Women* (1984), and *Summer Sisters* (1998).

Bly, Nellie *pseudonym of* Elizabeth Cochrane (b. May 5, 1867, Cochrane's Mills, Pa.—d. Jan. 27, 1922, New York City) Journalist.

At 18 Cochrane began work as a feature writer for the *Pittsburgh Dispatch*, writing sensational articles on slum life and poor working girls under the pen name "Nellie Bly" (taken from Stephen Foster's song). She traveled through

Mexico in 1887, sending back reports to the newspaper which were later compiled in *Six Months in Mexico*. In 1888 she moved to New York to work for Joseph Pulitzer's *New York World*. For an exposé of conditions among the patients, she feigned insanity to be committed to Blackwells Island; her articles (collected as *Ten Days in a Mad House* in 1887) brought about needed reforms.

She attained worldwide celebrity when, in 1889–90, seeking to beat the fictional record in Jules Verne's *Around the World in Eighty Days*, she circled the globe in 72 days, 6 hours, 11 minutes. The much-publicized trip, which she recounted in *Nellie Bly's Book: Around the World in Seventy-two Days* (1890), made "Nellie Bly" a synonym for a female star reporter.

In 1895 she married the steel manufacturer Robert L. Seaman. After his death in 1904 she attended to his business interests before eventually returning to journalism in 1920.

Bly, Robert (Elwood) (b. Dec. 23, 1926, Madison, Minn.) Poet, translator, and editor.

Bly studied at St. Olaf College, Harvard University, and the University of Iowa. In 1958 he cofounded the magazine *The Fifties* (its name changed with the decades), which published other important young poets and Bly's own translations and serene nature poems. In 1966 he cofounded American Writers Against the Vietnam War; when *The Light Around the Body* (1967) won a National Book Award, he donated the prize money to a draft resisters' organization. His later poems and "prose poems," including those in *Sleepers Joining Hands* (1973) and *This Tree Will Be Here for a Thousand Years* (1979), returned to personal and pastoral themes. Throughout his career he has also translated the work of German, Scandinavian, Spanish, Latin American, and Indian writers.

In the 1980s Bly became best known as the father of the "men's movement," which urged men to investigate the primitive wellsprings of their psyches communally, in a spirit not antagonistic to women. *The Man in the Black Coat Turns* (1981) explored themes of male grief and the father-son connection, as did his best-selling *Iron John* (1990), which drew on myth, legend, folklore, fairy tales, and Jungian psychology.

Bodenheim \\'bō-dən-ˌhīm\\, **Maxwell** *originally* Maxwell Bodenheimer (b. May 26, 1893, Hermanville, Miss.—d. Feb. 6, 1954, New York City) Poet of the American modernist movement.

Bodenheim received little or no formal schooling. He moved to Chicago around 1913, during the period of the Chicago literary renaissance. He wrote plays with Ben Hecht, with whom he edited the short-lived *Chicago Literary Times* (1923–24). Later the two conducted a much-publicized feud, featuring each other as characters in their novels. His often cynical and grotesque poems were first published in *Poetry* magazine in 1914. His earliest collection was *Minna and Myself* (1918); in this and later collections, he employed many of the striking visual techniques of the Imagists. He settled in New York's Greenwich Village in the late 1920s. Though his novels and poetry appeared regularly during that decade and the next, his last years were spent in alcoholism and poverty. He had been reduced to peddling his poems in bars when he and his third wife were murdered in their temporary lodgings by a former mental patient. His unfinished autobiography, *My Life and Loves in Greenwich Village*, appeared in 1954. His largely forgotten novels include *Blackguard* (1923), *Crazy Man* (1924), *Replenishing Jessica* (1925), *Georgia Man* (1927), and *Naked on Roller Skates* (1931).

Bogan \\'bō-ˌgan\\, **Louise (Marie)** (b. Aug. 11, 1897, Livermore Falls, Maine—d. Feb. 4, 1970, New York City) Poet and literary critic whose verse resembles that of the English Metaphysical poets.

Bogan attended college for only a year. Widowed early, she moved to New York and became a protégée of Edmund Wilson. Bogan's poems first appeared in the *New Republic*. Her first collection, *Body of This Death*, was published in 1923. She later wrote verse and literary criticism for the *New Yorker*, the *Atlantic Monthly*, and the *Nation*. As a critic and as poetry editor of the *New Yorker* for 38 years, Bogan became known for her fairness and generosity, and she focused on her subjects' strengths in such works as *Achievement in American Poetry 1900–1950* (1951) and *Selected Criticism: Prose, Poetry* (1955). Her own poetry was often compared to the Metaphysical poets for its compressed diction and imagery. Her *Collected Poems 1923–1953* (1954) received the Bollingen Prize. Her other collections include *Dark Summer* (1929), *The Sleeping Fury* (1937), and *The Blue Estuaries: Poems 1923–1968* (1968), and she also published translations of Goethe and Jules Renard.

Bok \\'bäk\\, **Edward (William)** (b. Oct. 9, 1863, Den Helder, the Netherlands—d. Jan. 9, 1930, Lake Wales, Fla.) Editor and writer.

Born to a distinguished Dutch family, Bok was brought to Brooklyn, N.Y., in 1870. He worked as an office boy to help his family while attending night school. In 1882 he began working for publishing companies, also editing a magazine for Henry Ward Beecher's Plymouth Church. To distribute Beecher's sermons, he established a newspaper syndicate in 1886. With it he soon began distributing the "Bok page" of women's features and the book-notes pages "Bok's Literary Leaves." The syndicate's success led to his being named editor of *Ladies' Home Journal* in 1889. Soliciting ideas from his female readers, he devised numerous popular features on personal advice, child care, health (breaking the taboo on printed mention of venereal disease), and religion, while soliciting contributions from the leading literary figures of the time. He crusaded for wildlife conservation, public health, civic reform, beautification, women's suffrage, and truth in advertising. After retiring in 1919 he wrote his famous and highly popular autobiography, *The Americanization of Edward Bok* (1920,

Pulitzer Prize). He devoted the rest of his life to the causes of civic improvement and world peace.

Boker \'bō-kər\, **George Henry** (b. Oct. 6, 1823, Philadelphia—d. Jan. 2, 1890, Philadelphia) Playwright and diplomat.

In 1862 Boker was a founder of the Union League of Philadelphia, one of the associations formed to support the Union in the Civil War. He later served as U.S. minister to Turkey (1871–75) and to Russia (1875–78).

Of his 11 plays, the blank-verse tragedies were most admired; though not immediately successful, they have been called the most original romantic heroic tragedies of 19th-century America. They include *Calaynos* (1848), *Leonor de Guzman* (1853), and the moving *Francesca da Rimini* (1855), the finest of his works. His collections of poetry included *A Lesson of Life* (1848), *Poems of the War* (1864), and *Königsmark* (1869).

Bolton, Guy (Reginald) (b. Nov. 23, 1884, Broxbourne, Hertfordshire, England—d. Sept. 5, 1979, London) Playwright and librettist.

Born to American parents in England, Bolton moved to America early and saw his first play mounted on Broadway in 1911. His career took off in the 1920s when he shifted his energies to musicals. With his collaborators, he turned out scripts that were enhanced with music by the best composers on Broadway. Among his finer works are *Oh, Boy!* (1917; with P. G. Wodehouse and Jerome Kern), *Sally* (1920; with Kern), *Lady, Be Good!* (1924; with Fred Thompson and George and Ira Gershwin), *Oh, Kay!* (1926; with Wodehouse, the Gershwins, and Howard Dietz), *Girl Crazy* (1930; with John McGowan and the Gershwins), and *Anything Goes* (1934; with Wodehouse, Howard Lindsay, Russel Crouse, and Cole Porter). In his later years he turned away from musicals; the drama *Anastasia* (1954) was a Broadway hit.

Bontemps \bän-'täm\, **Arna (Wendell)** (b. Oct. 13, 1902, Alexandria, La.—d. June 4, 1973, Nashville, Tenn.) Writer who depicted the lives and struggles of black Americans.

Having graduated from Pacific Union College at 17, Bontemps began submitting his poetry, including "A Black Man Talks of Reaping," to the influential black magazines *Opportunity* and *Crisis* in the mid-1920s. His first novel, *God Sends Sunday* (1931), is considered the final work of the Harlem Renaissance; with Countee Cullen, he dramatized it as *St. Louis Woman* (1946). His next two novels, *Black Thunder* (1936) and *Drums at Dusk* (1939), were about slave revolts in Virginia and Haiti.

After obtaining a graduate degree from the University of Chicago, Bontemps worked as a librarian at Fisk University from 1943 to 1966. Among the important anthologies he edited are *The Poetry of the Negro* (1949) and *The Book of Negro Folklore* (1958), both with Langston Hughes; *American Negro Poetry*

(1963); and *Great Slave Narratives* (1969). The father of six, he also wrote many nonfiction children's books, including *The Story of the Negro* (1948), *Frederick Douglass* (1959), *One Hundred Years of Negro Freedom* (1961), and *Famous Negro Athletes* (1964).

Booth, Wayne C(layson) (b. Feb. 22, 1921, American Fork, Utah) Critic and teacher associated with the Chicago school of literary criticism.

Booth graduated from Brigham Young University in 1944, and became devoted to Neo-Aristotelian critical methods while studying with R. S. Crane at the University of Chicago (Ph.D., 1950). He taught at Haverford College and Earlham College, then at Chicago until his retirement in 1992.

In his influential first book, *The Rhetoric of Fiction* (1961), he argued that rhetoric can enhance communication between author and reader as opposed to simply manipulating the reader's response. His other books include *Now Don't Try to Reason with Me* (1970), *A Rhetoric of Irony* (1974), and *Critical Understanding* (1979). In 1974 he cofounded the quarterly *Critical Inquiry*, which he coedited until 1985. His passion for cello playing led to *For the Love of It* (1999), on the meaning of the word amateur.

Boucicault \'bü-sē-ˌkō**, Dion** *originally* Dionysius Lardner Boursiquot (b. Dec. 26, 1820/22, Dublin—d. Sept. 18, 1890, New York City) Playwright and actor.

Educated in England, Boucicault began acting in 1837. His second play, *London Assurance* (1841), which foreshadowed the modern social drama, was a huge success. Other notable early plays were *Old Heads and Young Hearts* (1844) and *The Corsican Brothers* (1852). In 1853 he and his second wife, the actress Agnes Robertson, came to New York City, where his plays and adaptations were long popular. He led a playwrights' movement that produced the first U.S. copyright law for drama in 1856. *The Poor of New York* had a long run in 1857 and was adapted for presentation elsewhere (as, for example, *The Poor of Liverpool*). *The Octoroon* (1859) caused a sensation with its implied attack on slavery.

Boucicault and his wife joined Laura Keene's theater in 1860, and he began a series of his highly popular Irish plays—*The Colleen Bawn* (1860), *Arrah-na-Pogue* (1864), *The O'Dowd* (1873), and *The Shaughraun* (1874). Returning to London in 1862, he provided Joseph Jefferson with a successful adaptation of *Rip Van Winkle* (1865). In 1872 he returned to America. About 150 plays are credited to Boucicault, who, as both writer and actor, raised the stage Irishman from caricature to character.

Bourne \'bůrn, *commonly* 'bȯrn**, Randolph (Silliman)** (b. May 30, 1886, Bloomfield, N.J.—d. Dec. 22, 1918, New York City) Literary critic and essayist whose polemical articles made him a spokesman for young radicals.

Though afflicted with a serious physical deformity, Bourne held a variety of odd jobs before winning a scholarship at 23 to Columbia University. He graduated in 1913, the same year a collection of his essays (originally published in the *Atlantic Monthly*), asserting that the youth of his day would sweep away much that was antiquated and unworthy in American life, appeared as *Youth and Life*. A year in Europe resulted in "Impressions of Europe: 1913–14" (1914). He then turned his attention to the progressive educational theories of John Dewey, his teacher at Columbia; the outcome was two books, *The Gary Schools* (1916) and *Education and Living* (1917). The coming of the European war led to his increasingly passionate radicalism. He died at 32 in the influenza epidemic of 1918–19. The essay collections *Untimely Papers* (1919) and *The History of a Literary Radical and Other Essays* (1920) appeared posthumously, and many of his writings analyzing culture, power, and the modern state were later edited by Olaf Hansen as *The Radical Will* (1977).

Bowen \\'bō-ən\\, **Catherine Drinker** *originally* Catherine Shober Drinker (b. Jan. 1, 1897, Haverford, Pa.—d. Nov. 1, 1973, Haverford) Historical biographer known for her partly fictionalized biographies.

After attending the Peabody Institute and the Juilliard School of Music, she took up writing, her earliest works being inspired by the lives of musicians. Over the years she produced a long series of admired and best-selling works, including *Beloved Friend* (1937), about Tchaikovsky and his patroness; *Yankee from Olympus* (1944), about Oliver Wendell Holmes, Jr.; *John Adams and the American Revolution* (1950); *The Lion and the Throne* (1957, National Book Award), about Sir Edward Coke; and *Miracle at Philadelphia* (1966), about the Constitutional Convention of 1787.

Bowles \\'bōlz\\, **Jane** *originally* Jane Sydney Auer (b. Feb. 22, 1917, New York City—d. May 4, 1973, Málaga, Spain) Writer whose reputation rests on a small body of highly individualistic work.

Auer married the composer and author Paul Bowles in 1938. They lived in Costa Rica, France, Mexico, and the United States, where she began writing her only published novel, *Two Serious Ladies* (1943), a plotless narrative about two women, one weak and sinful, the other virtuous and domineering. In the late 1940s the couple settled in Tangier, Morocco, where she fell in love with a Moroccan woman. In 1953 her play *In the Summer House* was staged in New York. She also published seven short stories, dark, compelling works which won her a small but devoted following. A series of cerebral hemorrhages beginning in 1957 left her unable to read or write in her later years. Her *Collected Works* (1966) was expanded after her death as *My Sister's Hand in Mine* (1978).

Bowles, Paul (Frederick) (b. Dec. 30, 1910, New York City—d. Nov. 18, 1999, Tangier, Morocco) Composer, translator, and author of novels and short stories that recount violence and psychological collapse in a detached and elegant style.

Bowles began publishing Surrealist poetry in the journal *transition* at 16. In Paris he studied musical composition under Virgil Thomson and Aaron Copland, and he would eventually compose music for more than 30 theatrical productions and films. He was inspired to take up writing after reading a draft of the novel *Two Serious Ladies* (1943) by his wife, Jane Bowles. In the late 1940s the couple moved to Tangier, Morocco, which would become Bowles's most potent source of inspiration and where he would spend more than 50 years. There he wrote his first and best-known novel, THE SHELTERING SKY (1948; film, 1990), a harsh tale of death, rape, and sexual obsession.

His later novels include *Let It Come Down* (1952), *The Spider's House* (1955), *Up Above the World* (1966), and *In the Red Room* (1981). His *Collected Stories* (1979) and his subsequent short-story collections, including *Midnight Mass* (1981) and *Call at Corazón* (1988), similarly depict depravity amid exotic settings. He also recorded Moroccan folk music for the Library of Congress, wrote travel essays, translated works from several European and Middle Eastern languages, and recorded and translated oral tales from Arabic. *Without Stopping* (1972) and *Days* (1990) are autobiographical.

Boyle, Kay (b. Feb. 19, 1902, St. Paul, Minn.—d. Dec. 27, 1992, Mill Valley, Calif.) Novelist, poet, essayist, and short-story writer noted for her elegant style.

Boyle grew up mainly in Europe, and studied architecture and music there and in the United States. During World War I she raised funds for the families of conscientious objectors. She moved to France in 1923 after marrying a French student; they lived there and in England and Austria until 1941. Two of her finely wrought short stories from that period, "The White Horses of Vienna" (1935) and "Defeat" (1941), won O. Henry awards. From 1946 to 1953 she served as a foreign correspondent in France and West Germany for the *New Yorker*. During the 1960s she was arrested at a protest against the Vietnam War; her novel *The Underground Woman* (1975) featured a woman jailed for her antiwar stance. After the death of her third husband, a baron, in 1963, she taught literature at San Francisco State University, and she continued writing until her death, publishing her *Collected Poems* in 1991. In all she wrote 18 novels, including *Plagued by the Nightingale* (1931) and *A Frenchman Must Die* (1946), and some 60 short stories, published in such collections as *A Smoking Mountain* (1951) and *Nothing Ever Breaks but the Heart* (1966).

Boyle, T(homas) Coraghessan *originally* Thomas John Boyle (b. Dec. 2, 1948, Peekskill, N.Y.) Novelist and short-story writer.

Boyle turned to writing short stories in college, later obtained a Ph.D. from the University of Iowa in 1977, and has since taught at USC. His first novel, *Water Music* (1981), won him critical notice, and such later works as *Budding Prospects* (1984) and the story collection *Greasy Lake* (1985) confirmed him as one of the most gifted young American writers. His other works, all of which display vivid imagination and a sharp comic edge, include the story collections *The Descent of Man* (1979), *If the River Was Whiskey* (1990), *Without a Hero* (1994), and *After the Plague* (2001); and the novels *Worlds End* (1987, PEN/Faulkner Award), *East Is East* (1991), *The Road to Wellville* (1993; film, 1994), *The Tortilla Curtain* (1995), *Riven Rock* (1998), *A Friend of the Earth* (2000), and *Drop City* (2003).

Brackenridge, Hugh Henry (b. 1748, Kintyre, Argyll, Scotland—d. June 25, 1816, Carlisle, Pa.) Author and judge.

After his family immigrated to America in 1753, Brackenridge studied at the College of New Jersey (now Princeton), joined George Washington's army as a chaplain, and published two verse dramas on Revolutionary themes, *The Battle of Bunkers-Hill* (1776) and *The Death of General Montgomery at the Siege of Quebec* (1777). In an attempt to promote a national American literature, he established and edited the *United States Magazine* in 1779, but it failed within the year. He became a lawyer and settled in the frontier village of Pittsburgh in 1781, where he helped start the *Pittsburgh Gazette*, the first newspaper in what was then the Far West. After he was elected to the Pennsylvania Assembly in 1786, he obtained funds to found the academy that became the University of Pittsburgh. In 1795 he published an account of the Whiskey Rebellion. He served on the Pennsylvania Supreme Court from 1799 until his death. Between 1792 and 1815 he published the satirical six-part novel *Modern Chivalry,* the first novel to portray frontier life after the Revolutionary War.

Bradbury, Ray (Douglas) (b. Aug. 22, 1920, Waukegan, Ill.) Science-fiction writer whose stories and novels blend social criticism with an awareness of the hazards of runaway technology.

By the time he graduated from high school, Bradbury was committed to writing. His first short story was published in 1941, and by 1943 he was supporting himself by writing. His first story collection, *Dark Carnival* (1947), was followed by his best-known work, *The Martian Chronicles* (1950; film, 1966), a science-fiction classic that addressed such social issues as racism, cultural imperialism, and the threat of nuclear war. The novel *Fahrenheit 451* (1953; film, 1966) deals with the suppression of the written word in a future totalitarian state. *Dandelion Wine* (1957) is a magically evocative story of youth; *Something Wicked This Way Comes* (1962; film, 1983) involves a carnival where the audience's wishes are fulfilled. His other story collections include *The Illustrated Man* (1951), *The Golden Apples of the Sun* (1953), and *I Sing the Body Electric* (1969). Bradbury has also written stage plays and screenplays, including *Moby Dick* (1956; with John Huston), as well as poetry and children's stories, and has produced a cable-television series, *The Ray Bradbury Theater*. He won a lifetime achievement award from the National Book Foundation in 2000.

Bradford, Roark (Whitney Wickliffe) (b. Aug. 21, 1896, Lauderdale County, Tenn.—d. Nov. 13, 1948, New Orleans) Novelist and short-story writer.

The son of a plantation owner, Bradford was from childhood interested in black storytelling and folklore. He began work as a reporter in 1920 and became reacquainted with the musicians, preachers, and storytellers familiar from his youth. In 1927 his story "Gild of God" was awarded the first O. Henry prize. A series of stories for the *New York World* were collected in his popular first book, *Ol' Man Adam an' His Chillun* (1928), biblical stories as related by unlettered blacks which were later adapted by Marc Connelly into the hit play *The Green Pastures* (1930, Pulitzer Prize; film, 1936). Though popular in their time, his stories were criticized in later decades for their sentimentality and their condescending portraits of blacks.

Bradford, William (b. March, 1590, Yorkshire, England—d. May 9, 1657, Plymouth, Mass.) Governor of the Plymouth colony.

As a member of the Separatist movement within Puritanism, Bradford migrated to Holland in 1609 in search of religious freedom and lived 11 years in Leiden. In 1620 he helped organize the *Mayflower*'s expedition to the New World.

To bind the group into a political body, Bradford helped draft the important Mayflower Compact en route to America. Once on land, he helped select the site for the new colony. In 1621, after the colony's first, disastrous winter, he was unanimously elected governor, and he served in that position for some 30 years between 1621 and 1656. His remarkable tact, honesty, and political ability proved indispensable in assuring the colony's survival, and he helped avert numerous potential disasters. He was instrumental in establishing and fostering the principles of self-government and religious freedom that characterized later American colonial government.

Though lacking in formal education, Bradford possessed native literary ability. His vivid account of the early settlement, *History of Plimoth Plantation, 1620–1647,* not published in full until 200 years after his death (1856), has been a unique source of information about the Puritans' voyage and the challenges that faced the settlers.

Bradstreet, Anne *originally* Anne Dudley (b. c.1612, Northampton?, Northamptonshire, England—d. Sept. 16, 1672, Andover, Massachusetts Bay Colony) One of the first poets to write English verse in the American colonies.

Anne married Simon Bradstreet at 16, and two years later they sailed with other Puritans to become the first settlers on Massachusetts Bay, where both her father, Thomas Dudley, and her husband would serve as governor. She wrote her poems while rearing eight children. Her brother-in-law, without her knowledge, took her poems to England, where they were published as *The Tenth Muse Lately Sprung Up in America* (1650). The first American edition was published in revised and expanded form as *Several Poems Compiled with Great Variety of Wit and Learning* (1678).

Her later poems, written for her family, show spiritual growth but also a warm and frank humanity. The sequence "Contemplations," contained graceful and pleasant verse in welcome contrast to the Puritan stereotype; not published until the 19th century, it won her critical acceptance in the 20th century. She also wrote personal poems about such subjects as her thoughts before childbirth and her response to the death of a grandchild. Her prose works include "Meditations," a collection of succinct and pithy aphorisms. *The Works of Anne Bradstreet* was published in 1981.

Brand, Max *pseudonym of* **Frederick (Schiller) Faust** (b. May 29, 1892, Seattle—d. May 12?, 1944, Santa Maria Infante, Italy) Writer of pulp-fiction novels.

After dropping out of the University of California, Faust discovered his facility for rapid writing and action-filled plotting, and began writing western stories for popular pulp magazines. As Max Brand he wrote about 100 novels, including *The Untamed* (1918; films 1929, 1940), *The Night Horseman* (1920), and *Dead or Alive* (1938); *Destry Rides Again* (1930; films, 1939, 1954; musical, 1997) is perhaps the best known. His novels, with simple plots and characters and much "blazing-guns" action, were underresearched and undistinguished but became vastly popular. Faust also created the Dr. Kildare movie character (based on his best friend) in the 1930s, from which he derived a series of novels. In all, some 80 movies have been made from his works.

Faust also wrote under about 20 other pen names, including Evan Evans, Frank Austin, and Walter C. Butler. Astonishingly prolific, he apparently produced some 500 full-length books (along with innumerable short stories) in his lifetime, or about one for every two weeks of his writing life; his productivity earned him the title "King of the Pulp Writers." He lived in Italy until World War II; as a correspondent for *Harper's* magazine, he joined U.S. troops attacking Santa Maria Infante and was killed there by German artillery.

Brautigan \\'brȯt-i-gən\\, **Richard (Gary)** (b. Jan. 30, 1933, Tacoma, Wash.—d. September?, 1984, Bolinas, Calif.) Writer whose fiction and poetry was especially popular among 1960s and '70s counterculture readers.

Brautigan refused to discuss his early life, but he became involved with the Beats in San Francisco in the late 1950s. His whimsically humorous but dark novels feature passive protagonists whose innocence shields them from the moral consequences of their actions. His first novel, *A Confederate General from Big Sur*, was published in 1964. His second, *Trout Fishing in America* (1967), a commentary on the state of nature in contemporary America, sold two million copies, and its title was adopted as the name of several communes. His later novels include *In Watermelon Sugar* (1968), *The Abortion: An Historical Romance, 1966* (1971), *The Hawkline Monster: A Gothic Western* (1974), and *The Tokyo-Montana Express* (1979). He also published a short-story collection, *Revenge of the Lawn* (1971), and several poetry collections. A gradual decline in his readership may have been one of the factors that led to his suicide.

Brinnin, John Malcolm (b. Sept. 13, 1916, Halifax, Nova Scotia, Canada— d. June 26, 1998) Poet, editor, and social historian, also known for his biographies of other poets.

Brinnin moved to Detroit in his childhood and graduated from the University of Michigan. His first volume of poetry, *The Garden Is Political* (1942), was highly praised. His five subsequent collections, which increasingly displayed his interest in and experiments with form, were *The Lincoln Lyrics* (1942), *No Arch, No Triumph* (1945), *The Sorrows of Cold Stone* (1951), *Selected Poems* (1963), and *Skin Diving in the Virgins* (1970).

A close friend of Dylan Thomas and a witness to Thomas's mental and physical deterioration and eventual death, Brinnin accompanied Thomas on his American tours in the early 1950s and later wrote the detailed account *Dylan Thomas in America* (1955). He also wrote biographies of Gertrude Stein (1959), William Carlos Williams (1963), and Truman Capote (1986) as well as the memoir *Sextet* (1981). Among the books he edited were three anthologies of 20th-century American and British poetry. He also wrote three histories of North Atlantic steamships.

Brodkey \'bräd-kē\, **Harold** *originally* Harold Roy Weintraub (b. Oct. 25, 1930, Staunton, Ill.—d. Jan. 26, 1996, New York City) Novelist and short-story writer whose near-autobiographical fiction concentrated on careful, close description of feeling.

Brodkey had a grim childhood. His mother died when he was 2, and his father was alcoholic; he was adopted by relatives who also soon died. He graduated from Harvard University in 1952 and was soon publishing short stories in magazines. His first collection, *First Love and Other Sorrows* (1957), contained stories of youthful romance and marriage, using incidents from his own life. Around this time he began writing a large autobiographical novel, *The Runaway Soul*, which was to occupy him for most of the next 30 years; it was finally published in 1991 to mixed reviews. Excerpts had been published earlier as *Women and Angels* (1985). Wiley Silenowicz, its protagonist, is also featured in 12 of the 18 tales in *Stories in an Almost Classical Mode* (1988). In 1994 Brodkey published another novel—*Profane Friendship*, about a homosexual affair in Venice— shortly after his dramatic announcement in the *New Yorker* that he had AIDS. He intimately recorded his struggle with the disease in *This Wild Darkness* (1996).

Harold Brodkey

Brodsky \'bròd-skē, *Engl* 'brōēd-skē, 'bräd-skē\, **Joseph** *originally* Iosip Aleksandrovich Brodsky (b. May 24, 1940, Leningrad [now St. Petersburg]— d. Jan. 28, 1996, New York City) Russian-American poet.

Brodsky was part of the circle around the older Anna Akhmatova, and his early poetry had begun to earn him a reputation in the Leningrad literary scene when his independent spirit and irregular work record resulted in five years of hard labor for "social parasitism." The sentence was commuted in 1965 after prominent Soviet literary figures protested. Exiled in 1972, he settled in New York's Greenwich Village and taught principally at Columbia University and (from 1981) Mount Holyoke College. He served as poet laureate of the United States in 1991–92.

Brodsky's lyric and elegiac poems treat the universal concerns of life, death, and the meaning of existence in a powerful, meditative fashion. His earlier works include *Verses and Poems* (1965) and *A Halt in the Wasteland* (1970); these and other works were translated in *Selected Poems* (1973). His important later works include the verse collections *A Part of Speech* (1980), *History of the Twentieth Century* (1986), and *To Urania* (1988) and the essay collections *Less Than One* (1986) and *On Grief and Reason* (1996). In 1987 he was awarded the Nobel Prize.

Bromfield, Louis (b. Dec. 27, 1896, Mansfield, Ohio—d. March 18, 1956, Columbus, Ohio) Novelist and essayist.

Bromfield grew up on a farm and attended Cornell and Columbia universities. He was awarded the Croix de Guerre for his service in France in World War I. He went on to serve as a critic for several periodicals, including the *Bookman* and *Time* magazine. The success of his first published novel, *The Green Bay Tree* (1924), freed him to write full-time. After the publication of *Possession* (1925), he and his family moved to France, where they lived for 14 years. *Early Autumn* (1926, Pulitzer Prize) is regarded as his best novel. The fourth novel of the admired tetralogy, *A Good Woman,* appeared in 1927. Later works include the story collection *Awake and Rehearse* (1929) and the novel *The Man Who Had Everything* (1935).

With the onset of World War II, he returned to the United States, where he continued to write. Though several of his later novels, including *Mrs. Parkington* (1943), were made into films, they garnered less critical acclaim. Having bought a farm in his native Ohio, realizing a childhood dream, he introduced new farming techniques there and wrote about farming in several well-received nonfiction books, including *Pleasant Valley* (1945).

Brooks, Cleanth (b. Oct. 16, 1906, Murray, Ky.—d. May 10, 1994, New Haven, Conn.) Teacher and critic whose work was important in establishing the New Criticism, which stressed close reading and structural analysis of literature.

Brooks was educated at Vanderbilt and Tulane universities. At Vanderbilt he became acquainted with the Southern Agrarian writers J. C. Ransom, R. P. Warren, and Donald Davidson. From 1932 he taught at several universities, including Louisiana State and Baton Rouge, but he spent most of his later career at Yale. From 1935 to 1942, with Warren and Charles W. Pipkin, he edited the *Southern Review*, a journal that advanced the New Criticism and published such Southern writers as Randall Jarrell, Eudora Welty, and Katherine Anne Porter. His critical works *Modern Poetry and the Tradition* (1939) and *The Well-Wrought Urn* (1947) became required reading in many university English departments. He also wrote several books on Faulkner. He witnessed the decline of the New Criticism with equanimity, remarking that no theory is influential for long, but poetry endures.

Brooks, Gwendolyn (Elizabeth) (b. June 7, 1917, Topeka, Kan.—d. Dec. 3, 2000) Poet whose works dealt with the everyday life of urban blacks.

Brooks grew up in Chicago. Her father used to recite poetry, and she began composing poetry at 7. At 16 she received encouragement from Langston Hughes, who told her she would publish one day. Her first published collection, *A Street in Bronzeville* (1945), reveals her talent for making the ordinary life of her neighbors extraordinary. Her second collection, *Annie Allen* (1949), a loosely connected series of poems about a black girl growing up in Chicago, won the Pulitzer Prize, making her the first black to win a Pulitzer in any category. Her autobiographical novel *Maud Martha* appeared in 1953.

The Bean Eaters (1960) contains some of her best verse. Her *Selected Poems* (1963) was followed in 1968 by *In the Mecca*, half of which is a long narrative poem about people in the Mecca, a vast apartment building on Chicago's South Side. The autobiographical *Report from Part One* (1972) and *Report from Part Two* (1995) were assemblages of personal memoirs, interviews, and letters. Later works include *Blacks* (1987), *Winnie* (1988), and *Children Coming Home* (1991).

Brooks, Van Wyck (b. Feb. 16, 1886, Plainfield, N.J.—d. May 2, 1963, Bridgewater, Conn.) Critic, biographer, and literary historian.

Educated at Harvard, Brooks thereafter devoted virtually his entire life to writing. In 1918 he published his first book, *The Wine of the Puritans*, in which he blamed America's cultural shortcomings on its Puritan heritage. He expanded on this theme in his first major work, *America's Coming-of-Age* (1915), in which he theorized that the Puritan duality separating the spiritual from the material had resulted in a corresponding split in contemporary American culture between "highbrow" and "lowbrow."

The Ordeal of Mark Twain (1920) was a psychological study (one of the first of its kind) that presented Twain as a failed artist, attempting to show that Twain had repressed his natural artistic bent for the sake of his Calvinist upbringing. Over the years Brooks revised it substantially, eventually repudiating much of his main thesis. After completing *The Pilgrimage of Henry James* (1925), he suffered a nervous breakdown; he reemerged with the publication of *The Life of Emerson* (1932).

Brooks's major literary accomplishment was his *Finders and Makers* series. It began with *The Flowering of New England, 1815–1865* (1936, Pulitzer Prize) and continued with *New England: Indian Summer, 1865–1915* (1940), *The World of Washington Irving* (1944), *The Times of Melville and Whitman* (1947), and *The Confident Years: 1885–1915* (1952).

Brougham \\'brům, 'brōm, 'brüm, 'brō-əm, 'brü-əm\\, **John** (b. May 9, 1814, Dublin—d. June 7, 1880, New York City) Irish-born theater manager, comic actor, and author of more than 75 popular plays.

Brougham made his acting debut in 1830, playing six parts in *Tom and Jerry*. A year later he wrote his first play, a burlesque, which was followed by a number of other works. In 1840 he became manager of the Lyceum Theatre, for which he wrote such works as *Life in the Clouds*, *Love's Livery*, *Enthusiasm*, *Tom Thumb the Second*, and *The Demon Gift* (with Mark Lemon). In 1842 he immigrated to the United States, where he managed theaters in New York and wrote numerous comedies and dramas. A trip to London in 1860 led to a five-year stay in England. His last stage performance came less than a year before his death.

Brown, Charles Brockden (b. Jan. 17, 1771, Philadelphia—d. Feb. 22, 1810, Philadelphia) Writer known as the "father of the American novel."

Born to Quaker parents, Brown was apprenticed to a Philadelphia lawyer in 1787, but his strong interest in writing led him to help found a literary society. In 1793 he gave up the law entirely to pursue a literary career. After publishing a treatise on women's rights, he produced the four gothic novels that would constitute his finest work. The first, WIELAND (1798), is a minor masterpiece that features murder, insanity, and spontaneous combustion as an apparent consequence of breaking an oath. The others were *Ormond* (1799), *Edgar Huntly* (1799), and *Arthur Mervyn* (2 vols., 1799–1800). Though these works established him as the first professional novelist in America, Brown had less success with his later works and was forced to enter business to support his family.

Brown, Claude (b. Feb. 23, 1937, New York City—d. Feb. 2, 2002, New York City) Novelist.

Brown grew up in New York's Harlem, where he began a life of crime at an early age. After several periods in reform school and a near-fatal shooting, he was influenced to break away from the ghetto and resume his education. Admitted to Howard University, where he studied with Toni Morrison, he graduated in 1965.

After writing an article on Harlem for *Dissent* magazine, he was encouraged to write his autobiography, which became the autobiographical novel MANCHILD IN THE PROMISED LAND (1965). The book was one of the first to detail the life of young blacks in urban America; with its stark recounting of gang life, it was an instant success, and has gone on to sell over 4 million copies. His novel *The Children of Ham* (1975) continued the same theme.

Brown, Sterling (Allen) (b. May 1, 1901, Washington, D.C.—d. Jan. 17, 1989, Washington, D.C.) Teacher and literary critic whose poetry was rooted in folklore sources and black dialect.

The son of a former slave who rose to become a professor of theology, Brown was educated at Williams College and Harvard University. He went on to teach at several schools in the South, where he began collecting black folk songs and stories. In 1929 he began a 40-year teaching career at Howard University, where he and his wife opened their home to students and teachers. In 1932 his first volume of poetry, *Southern Road*, was published. His poetry captured the rhythms of black speech and reflected the influence of ballads, work songs, spirituals, and the blues.

Though *Southern Road* was widely praised, Brown found no publisher for his second collection, *No Hiding Place*, which he eventually incorporated into his *Collected Poems* (1980). As critic, essayist, and columnist for *Opportunity*, he supported realistic writing and harshly attacked literature that distorted black life. In 1937 he published the pioneering studies *Negro Poetry and Drama* and *The Negro in American Fiction*, and in 1941 he coedited *The Negro Caravan*, a major anthology of black writing.

Brown, William Hill (b. Nov. 1765, Boston—d. Sept. 2, 1793, Murfreesboro, N.C.) Novelist and dramatist.

Brown's romantic tale "Harriot" (1789) was published in the first issue of *Massachusetts Magazine*. His anonymously published *The Power of Sympathy* (1789), long falsely attributed to Sarah W. Morton, was advertised as the first American novel. He agitated for the opening of a theater in Massachusetts, and wrote the comedy *Penelope* in anticipation of its opening. His play *West Point Preserved* was published posthumously in 1797. Brown also wrote a series of verse fables, essays, and a short second novel about incest and seduction, *Ira and Isabella* (1807). He moved south to study law, but succumbed to a fever at 28.

Brown, William Wells (b. 1814?, near Lexington, Ky.—d. Nov. 6, 1884, Chelsea, Mass.) Novelist, historian, and abolitionist.

Born a slave, Brown escaped in 1834 and adopted the name of Wells Brown, the Quaker who aided him. In 1847 his popular autobiography *Narrative of William W. Brown, A Fugitive Slave* was published. Having educated himself, Brown began lecturing on abolitionism and temperance reform. His antislavery lectures in Europe inspired *Three Years in Europe* (1852), which was expanded as *The American Fugitive in Europe* (1855).

His only novel, CLOTEL (1853), tells the story of the daughters and granddaughters of Thomas Jefferson and his slave Currer. His only published play was *The Escape* (1858). Brown's historical writings include *The Black Man* (1863), *The Negro in the American Rebellion* (1867), and *The Rising Son* (1873). His final book, *My Southern Home* (1880), contains miscellanea about slave life, abolitionism, and racism.

Brownell \braủ-'nel\, **W(illiam) C(rary)** (b. Aug. 30, 1851, New York City—d. July 22, 1928, Williamstown, Mass.) Critic who sought to expand the scope of American literary criticism.

After graduating from Amherst College, Brownell worked for the *New York World* and the *Nation*. He married in 1878 and lived three years overseas. On his return he worked for the *Philadelphia Press* before taking a position as editor and literary adviser at Charles Scribner's Sons (1888), where he remained the rest of his life. His first two books, *French Traits* (1889) and *French Art* (1892), established a new and high standard for the American critic, one that Brownell maintained in his succeeding books: *Victorian Prose Masters* (1901), *American Prose Masters* (1909), *Criticism* (1914), *Standards* (1917), *The Genius of Style* (1924), and *Democratic Distinction in America* (1927).

Brownson, Orestes A(ugustus) (b. Sept. 16, 1803, Stockbridge, Vt.—d. April 17, 1876, Detroit) Clergyman and writer.

Completely self-educated, Brownson was a voracious reader from childhood. He was ordained a Universalist minister in 1826, but his increasing liberalism led him to adopt an independent ministry while working for socialist causes. His intellectual influences came to include the positivist Auguste Comte and particularly the British reformer Robert Owen. He became a Unitarian minister in 1832, but again broke away to found his own Boston church and organization, the Society for Christian Union and Progress, in 1836, the year he founded the *Boston Quarterly Review*.

He became associated with the Transcendentalists, but was too intellectually restless to stay with them. In 1844 he converted very publicly to Roman Catholicism. That same year he founded *Brownson's Quarterly Review,* a highly personal journal of opinion; apart from a seven-year interruption (1865–72), it would continue to appear until 1875. Brownson's versatility was expressed in his mystical poetry and his interest in philosophy and social amelioration. The novel *Charles Elwood* (1840) is an autobiographical romance; *The Convert* (1857) is an autobiography. In *The American Republic* (1865) he based government on ethics, declaring the national existence to be a moral and even a theocratic entity, not depending for validity upon the sovereignty of the people. After his death, his son collected and published his *Works* in 20 volumes (1882–1907).

Bryant, William Cullen (b. Nov. 3, 1794, Cummington, Mass.—d. June 12, 1878, New York City) Poet and longtime editor of the *New York Evening Post*.

Bryant entered the sophomore class of Williams College at 16, but financial hardship prevented him from graduating. At 21 he was admitted to the bar, and he spent nearly 10 years as an attorney, a profession he hated. During that time he published the first version of what would become his most famous poem, THANATOPSIS (1817), in the *North American Review;* it won him instant recognition. His *Poems* (1821) contained TO A WATERFOWL and other lyrics. In 1825 he moved to New York to become coeditor of the *New York Review.* Two years later he became an editor of the *New York Evening Post;* in 1829 he became editor in chief and part owner, and he would spend the next 50 years with the paper. His poetic output dropped thereafter, but he did publish three other slim collections.

Under Bryant the *Post* became one of the country's leading Democratic journals, supporting free trade, workers' rights, free speech, and abolition of slavery. In 1856 he left the Democratic Party to help found the abolitionist Republican Party.

William Cullen Bryant

Buck, Pearl S(ydenstricker) *originally* Pearl Comfort Sydenstricker (b. June 26, 1892, Hillsboro, W.Va.—d. March 6, 1973, Danby, Vt.) Author noted for her novels of life in China.

She spent her youth in China, where her parents were Presbyterian missionaries. After graduating from Randolph-Macon Woman's College, she returned to China and later became a university teacher in Nanjing.

Her stories about Chinese life first appeared in American magazines in 1923, but she first reached a wide audience with the hugely successful THE GOOD EARTH (1931, Pulitzer Prize), which would be translated into 30 languages and made into a celebrated film (1932). The novel *Sons* followed (1932); *A House Divided* (1935) was the third in the trilogy, which was issued complete as *The House of Earth* (1935). She turned to biography with lives of her father (*Fighting Angel*, 1936) and mother (*The Exile,* 1936). In 1938 she became the third American, and the first American woman, to be awarded the Nobel Prize for Literature.

Her concern for children's welfare led her to found the Welcome House (1947) for the Asian children of U.S. servicemen, and the Pearl S. Buck Foundation (1964), also for Asian-American children. She continued to write novels set in China, including *Dragon Seed* (1942; film, 1944), and *Letter from Peking* (1946), as well as two autobiographies, *My Several Worlds* (1954) and *A Bridge for Passing* (1962), and several novels under the pseudonym John Sedges.

Pearl Buck

Buckley, William F(rank), Jr. (b. Nov. 24, 1925, New York City) Writer and editor, a major intellectual figure in conservative politics.

Born to a wealthy family, Buckley was schooled in France, England, and Mexico as well as the United States. He served in the army in World War II before entering Yale University, where he taught Spanish, distinguished himself in debate, and was chairman of the *Yale Daily News.* The year after graduating he published *God and Man at Yale* (1951), deploring the secularism of higher education. *McCarthy and His Enemies* (1954; with L. Brent Bozell) defended Senator Joseph McCarthy's anticommunist crusade.

In 1955 Buckley founded the conservative weekly *National Review.* Its circulation grew rapidly under Buckley's editorship (until 1990), and it soon became the country's leading conservative journal. He began writing a syndicated political column in 1962; renamed "On the Right," it would eventually appear in over 200 newspapers. From 1966 to 1999 he hosted the widely viewed television interview program *Firing Line*. His many books on politics and public affairs include *Up from Liberalism* (1959) and *Rumbles Left and Right* (1963). He has also written several accounts of his sailing voyages, and since the late 1970s he has produced a successful series of spy novels featuring the CIA agent Blackford Oates. In 1991 he received the Presidential Medal of Freedom.

Bukowski \byü-ˈkaů-skē\, **Charles** (b. Aug. 16, 1920, Andernach, Germany—d. March 9, 1994, San Pedro, Calif.) Writer whose poetry and fiction describe an existence of drinking, gambling, and womanizing.

Bukowski's family moved to Los Angeles when he was a toddler, and he began drinking at 13 to escape the misery of abuse at his father's hands. He briefly attended Los Angeles City College and worked at menial jobs while writing short stories, the first of which were published in the mid-1940s. Beginning with *Flower, Fist and Bestial Wail* (1959), volumes of his poetry appeared almost annually. By 1963, the year he published *It Catches My Heart in Its Hands*—a collection of poetry about alcoholics, prostitutes, losing gamblers, and others among the down-and-out—Bukowski had a loyal following.

His short stories were unsparingly realistic and most often comic. Collections of his stories include *Notes of a Dirty Old Man* (1969) and *Erections, Ejaculations, Exhibitions, and General Tales of Ordinary Madness* (1972; film, 1983). Fourteen years' employment with the post office inspired the novel *Post Office* (1971); *Factotum* (1975) chronicled his earlier hobo days. He wrote the screenplay for the film *Barfly* (1987), a semiautobiographical comedy about alcoholic lovers on skid row. The novel *Hollywood* (1989) dealt with its filming. The novel *Pulp* was published posthumously in 1994.

Bullins \ˈbůl-inz\, **Ed** (b. July 2, 1935, Philadelphia) Playwright, novelist, poet, and journalist.

Bullins left high school in 1952 and served three years in the navy. In 1958 he moved to California, where he continued his self-education. He began writing fiction, essays, and poetry, but shifted to writing plays to reach a large black audience. In 1965 his one-act plays *How Do You Do?*, *Dialect Determinism*, and *Clara's Ole Man* were produced. In 1967 he began creating plays for Harlem's New Lafayette Theater; over six years he had a hand in almost a dozen productions. His first full-length play, *In the Wine Time* (produced 1968), examines the scarcity of options available to the black urban poor. It was the first in his proposed Twentieth-Century Cycle, about a group of young friends who grew up in the 1950s. In 1975 he received acclaim for *The Taking of Miss Janie*, about the failed alliance of an interracial group of political idealists in the 1960s. He earned his B.A. from Antioch University in 1989, and an M.F.A. from San Francisco State University in 1994; in 1995 he joined the Northeastern University theater faculty. Though his output declined in the 1980s and '90s, he remains an active playwright, with over 50 plays to his credit.

Bunner, Henry Cuyler (b. Aug. 3, 1855, Oswego, N.Y.—d. May 11, 1896, Nutley, N.J.) Poet, novelist, and editor whose verse and fiction primarily depict New York scenes and people.

Educated in New York City, Bunner served on the staff of the *Arcadian*. At 22 he became assistant editor of the new humorous weekly *Puck*; he would later be named its editor, a position he would hold until his death, developing the magazine into a powerful social and political organ. His short fiction, particularly the collection *"Made in France"; French Tales Retold with a United States Twist* (1893), reflects the influence of Guy de Maupassant and other French writers. His several novels are considered inferior to his stories and sketches. As a playwright he is known chiefly for *Tower of Babel* (1883). Collections of his verse include *Airs from Arcady and Elsewhere* (1884), *Rowen* (1892), and *Poems* (1896).

Buntline, Ned See **E. Z. C. Judson**

Burgess, (Frank) Gelett (b. Jan. 30, 1866, Boston—d. Sept. 17, 1951, Carmel, Calif.) Humorist and illustrator.

Burgess graduated from MIT in 1887 and became a draftsman for the Southern Pacific Railroad, after which he taught topographical drawing at the University of California. In 1894 he changed professions, becoming associate editor of *Wave* magazine. In 1895 he became the founding editor of the humor magazine *Lark*, and in 1897 he began to publish books of his self-illustrated whimsical writings. Among his best-known works are *Goops and How to Be Them* (1900), on bad-mannered children, and *Are You a Bromide?* (1906), the origin of *bromide* as meaning "a boring person." Burgess also coined the word *blurb* to describe the praise printed on book jackets. He is best known for the quatrain "I never saw a purple cow, / I never hope to see one; / But I can tell you, anyhow, I'd rather see than be one."

Burke, Kenneth (Duva) (b. May 5, 1897, Pittsburgh—d. Nov. 19, 1993, Andover, N.J.) Literary critic known for his psychologically based analyses of the nature of knowledge.

Burke attended several universities but never took a degree. In his early years he wrote poems, a novel, and short stories and translated the works of many German writers. After serving as music critic of the *Dial* (1927–29) and the *Nation* (1934–36), he turned to literary criticism, lecturing at the University of Chicago, Bennington College, and other schools. An important early publication was *The Philosophy of Literary Form* (1941). Believing that language was what made people capable of moral and ethical action, he elaborated on his theory in *A Grammar of Motives* (1945), *A Rhetoric of Motives* (1950), and *Language as Symbolic Action* (1966). Though not widely known to the general public, he was influential in scholarly circles.

Burnett \bər-'net, 'bər-nət\, **Frances Hodgson** *originally* Frances Eliza Hodgson (b. Nov. 24, 1849, Manchester, England—d. Oct. 29, 1924, Plandome, N.Y.) Anglo-American playwright and children's novelist.

After her father's death, her childhood was spent in the tenements of Manchester. In her adolescence she moved with her mother to Tennessee, where she began writing, paying for writing paper by gathering and selling wild grapes. Her first success was *That Lass o' Lowrie's* (1877), a tale of the Lancashire coal mines. *Little Lord Fauntleroy* (1886), a huge success, was the story of a poor American boy who inherits an English earldom. It was dramatized, and Burnett turned to writing plays, all of which were successful; *A Lady of Quality* (1896) is judged her best. *Sarah Crewe* (1888), another children's novel, was dramatized as *A Little Princess* in 1905; film versions appeared in 1917, 1937, and 1995. THE SECRET GARDEN (1911), the most famous and perhaps the best of her novels, is considered a children's classic; it has been dramatized many times, filmed twice, and adapted as a musical. Though she also wrote novels for adults, it is for her children's novels that Burnett is remembered.

Burroughs, Edgar Rice (b. Sept. 1, 1875, Chicago—d. March 19, 1950, Encino, Calif.) Novelist whose Tarzan stories created a folk hero known around the world.

After leaving a military academy, Burroughs served with the cavalry until he was discovered to be underage. He drifted from job to job before publishing his first story, "Under the Moons of Mars," in the adventure magazine *All-Story* in 1911. It was so successful that he began writing full-time. His first Tarzan story appeared in 1912; it was followed in 1914 by the novel *Tarzan of the Apes*, the first of 25 such books about the son of an English nobleman abandoned in the African jungle during infancy and brought up by apes. Hugely successful, they led to a long series of films over several decades.

Of his 43 other novels, many were science fiction, including a series set on Mars. During World War II Burroughs was a correspondent for the *Los Angeles Times*, becoming, at 66, the oldest war correspondent in the South Pacific.

Burroughs, John (b. April 3, 1837, near Roxbury, N.Y.—d. March 29, 1921, en route from California to New York) Essayist and naturalist who lived and wrote after the manner of Thoreau.

In his earlier years Burroughs worked as a teacher and farmer and for nine years as a clerk in the U.S. Treasury Department. In 1867 he paid tribute to his friend Walt Whitman in *Notes on Walt Whitman as Poet and Person,* which would be followed in 1896 by *Whitman: A Study*. In 1871 *Wake-Robin*, the first of his books on birds, flowers, and rural scenes, was published. Two years later he moved to a farm in the Hudson River valley and, from various retreats, wrote for half a century on nature subjects. He traveled around the United States and Europe, and camped out with his fellow nature-lovers Theodore Roosevelt and John Muir. His other important nature books, in which he developed the nature essay into a finely wrought literary form, are *Birds and Poets* (1877), *Locusts and Wild Honey* (1879), *Signs and Seasons* (1886), and *Ways of Nature* (1905). Burroughs also published a volume of poems, *Bird and Bough* (1906), and collections of essays and travel sketches.

Burroughs, William S(eward) (b. Feb. 5, 1914, St. Louis, Mo.—d. Aug. 2, 1997, St. Louis) Experimental novelist, an icon of the Beat generation.

William Burroughs

Grandson of the inventor of the adding machine, Burroughs was born into wealth and graduated from Harvard University in 1936. While living in New York, he met Allen Ginsberg and Jack Kerouac and became one of the early core members of the group that would become known as the Beats. He became addicted to heroin around 1945 and would remain a junkie for almost 15 years. While living in Mexico in 1951, he killed his second wife in an attempt to shoot a glass off her head at a party. He fled Mexico and wandered through the Amazon region, continuing his experiments with drugs, experiences described in *The Yage Letters* (1963), his 1953 correspondence with Allen Ginsberg.

He published his first book, *Junkie* (1953), under the pen name William Lee. *Queer*, about his homosexual life, remained unpublished until 1985. His most famous book, THE NAKED LUNCH, published in Paris in 1959 but kept from U.S. publication until 1962 due to obscenity charges, satirizes the grotesquerie of the drug addict's world and also deals with homosexuality and police persecution. Burroughs continued to experiment with the structure of the novel in his later works, including *The Soft Machine* (1961), *The Ticket That Exploded* (1962), and *Nova Express* (1964). His late works include *Cities of the Red Night* (1981), *The Place of Dead Roads* (1983), and *Interzone* (1989). Filled with paranoia, sometimes violent homosexual fantasies, the detritus of American popular culture, and lyrically beautiful evocations of landscape, Burroughs's novels have horrified many readers while attracting a loyal cult following.

Busch, Frederick (Matthew) (b. Aug. 1, 1941, Brooklyn, N.Y.) Critic, editor, novelist, and short-story writer.

Busch received his master's degree from Columbia University in 1967, and has taught literature at Colgate University ever since. He has written more than 20 books, many revolving around familial relations. They include *Manual Labor* (1974), *Rounds* (1979), *The Mutual Friend* (1978), an imaginative account of Charles Dickens's last years, *Girls* (1997), *The Night Inspector* (1999), *Don't Tell Anyone* (2000), and *A Memory of War* (2003).

Butler, Octavia E(stelle) (b. June 22, 1947, Pasadena, Calif.) Science-fiction writer.

A shy only child, Butler spent much of her childhood in libraries. Having begun writing at 12, she received encouragement from Harlan Ellison, and in 1976 she published her first novel, *Patternmaster*. It launched her five-volume Patternist series about an elite group of mentally linked telepaths, which eventually included *Mind of My Mind* (1977), *Survivor* (1978), *Wild Seed* (1980), and *Clay's Ark* (1984). Her short story "Bloodchild" (1984), about human male slaves who incubate their alien masters' eggs, won several awards. Her later novels include the Xenogenesis trilogy, which also deals with human-alien interbreeding, *The Parable of the Sower* (1993), and *The Parable of the Talents* (1999, Nebula Award). As a black woman, she has remained a notable anomaly in the field of science fiction.

Byrd, William (b. March 28, 1674, Virginia Colony—d. Aug. 26, 1744, Westover, Va.) Virginia planter, satirist, and diarist who portrayed colonial plantation life.

Born at his family's James River plantation home, Byrd studied law in London. He returned to Virginia after being admitted to the bar in 1695, but two years later was back in London as colonial agent. In 1705, after his father died, he returned to Virginia to manage the large family estate. He spent the years 1715–26 largely in England before returning to the colony for good to lead the busy life of a planter and a member of Virginia's ruling clique. His accomplishments include founding the city of Richmond and amassing the largest private library in the colonies.

His diaries illuminate the domestic economy of the great plantations. His "History of the Dividing Line," a witty, satirical account of a 1728 survey of the North Carolina–Virginia boundary, is among the earliest colonial literary works. His accounts of similar expeditions, "A Journey to the Land of Eden" and "A Progress to the Mines," were published in 1841 in *The Westover Manuscripts*. He also kept a more revealing personal diary in shorthand, published in 1941 as *The Secret Diary of William Byrd of Westover, 1709–12*.

Cabell \\ˈkab-əl\\, **James Branch** (b. April 14, 1879, Richmond, Va.—d. May 5, 1958, Richmond) Writer known chiefly for his novel JURGEN.

Born into a prominent Virginia family, Cabell graduated from the College of William and Mary with high honors and worked as a journalist, genealogist, and freelance writer while also producing his early novels. In 1919 he published *Jurgen* (1919), the fourth of the 19-novel series *Biography of Manuel*. An elaborate allegory set in the mythical French province of Poictesme, through which Cabell satirized Southern idealism, ancestor worship, and philistinism and expressed his skeptical view of human experience, it also included *The Cream of the Jest* (1917), *Beyond Life* (1919), *Figures of Earth* (1921), and *The High Place* (1923). *Jurgen*'s suppression on charges of indecency for its sexual symbolism led to phenomenal publicity, success, and extravagant praise for Cabell. In the 1930s and '40s he published three trilogies, including the set *Smirt* (1934), *Smith* (1935), and *Smire* (1937), but already his ornate and mannered style and disillusioned romanticism had cost him popularity, and by the end of his life he was largely forgotten.

Here Let Me Lie (1947) consists of essays about Virginia, *Quiet Please* (1952) of autobiographical essays.

Cable, George W(ashington) (b. Oct. 12, 1844, New Orleans—d. Jan. 31, 1925, St. Petersburg, Fla.) Author and reformer.

George W. Cable

The son of slaveholders, Cable fought in the Confederate cavalry, but came to believe that slavery and attempts to deny freed slaves full public rights were wrong. His best-known works are the early story collection *Old Creole Days* (1879) and the novel *The Grandissimes* (1880), which capture the picturesque life of New Orleans with a new realism, while their handling of caste and class and sanctioned oppression contain overtones of moral condemnation. In the face of violent abuse in the Southern press, Cable used essays and public lectures to urge the cause of black rights. In 1885, having found the South too unfriendly to his views, he settled in Northampton, Mass., and soon published two collections of social essays, *The Silent South* (1885) and *The Negro Question* (1888). He continued to write novels, many still set in the South, until he was past 70, but, despite their superior construction, they lack the freshness, charm, and moral conviction of his early work.

Cahan \\ˈkä-hȧn, *Engl* ˈkä-ˌhan, kə-ˈhän, ˈkän\\, **Abraham** (b. July 7, 1860, Vilna, Russian Empire [now Vilnius, Lithuania]—d. Aug. 31, 1951, New York City) Reformer, novelist, and editor of New York's Yiddish-language daily FORVERTS (*Jewish Daily Forward*).

Cahan immigrated to the United States in 1882. While working in a cigar factory, he learned enough English in six years to lecture and write. In the 1880s he helped organize trade unions in the garment industry, and in 1891 he was a delegate to the Second Congress of the Socialist Second International. In 1897 he helped found *Forverts*, which became one of the most important institutions upholding the interests of immigrants. During World War I it brought Jewish immigrants news of their kin in the war zone; in the 1920s it was distributed to cities across the country. Cahan would remain its editor for over 40 years.

Cahan's own fiction is largely unremarkable except for *The Rise of David Levinsky* (1917), one of the first books about the Jewish immigrant experience. Its value is historical rather than literary; its strength lies chiefly in its vivid re-creation of life in New York's Lower East Side. More influential as a mentor than as an author, Cahan provided writers such as Sholem Asch, I. J. Singer, and I. B. Singer with a Yiddish-language forum.

Cain, James M(allahan) (b. July 1, 1892, Annapolis, Md.—d. Oct. 27, 1977, University Park, Md.) Novelist whose works epitomized the hard-boiled fiction of the 1930s and '40s.

Cain served in World War I and afterward worked as an editorial writer for the *New York World* (1924–31) and briefly as managing editor of the *New Yorker.* His first novel, *The Postman Always Rings Twice* (1934; films, 1946, 1981) was a spectacular success, and its sordid milieu, its characters who seek to gain their ends through violence, and its taut, fast-paced prose and deftly rendered dialogue set the pattern for most of his later books. *Serenade* (1937) was daring in its presentation of a bisexual hero. *Mildred Pierce* (1941) was also adapted to the screen (1945). *Three of a Kind* (1943) contained the short novels *Sinful Woman*, *Double Indemnity* (first published 1936; film, 1944), and *The Embezzler*. Cain's postwar books, including *The Butterfly* (1947), *The Moth* (1948), *The Root of His Evil* (1954), *The Magician's Wife* (1965), and *Rainbow's End* (1975), were less successful.

Caldwell, Erskine (Preston) (b. Dec. 17, 1903, Coweta County, Ga.—d. April 11, 1987, Paradise Valley, Ariz.) Author whose unadorned novels and stories about the rural poor of the South mix violence and sex in grotesque tragi-comedy.

Caldwell's deep familiarity with Georgia's impoverished sharecroppers was acquired while traveling with his father, an itinerant preacher. At 14 he struck out on his own, later attending several colleges but never graduating. In 1926 he moved to Maine to pursue a career as a novelist.

Fame arrived with TOBACCO ROAD (1932; film, 1941), a controversial novel whose title became a byword for rural squalor and degradation. A dramatization ran for an unprecedented seven and a half years on Broadway. Caldwell's reputation as a novelist largely rests on *Tobacco Road* and on *God's Little Acre* (1933), another best-selling novel featuring a cast of hopelessly poor and degenerate whites in the rural South. Among his other works are *Trouble in July* (1940) and the episodic narrative *Georgia Boy* (1943), similarly written with a frankness bordering on sensationalism. He also wrote several short-story collections and several screenplays.

Caldwell provided the text and Margaret Bourke-White (later briefly one of his four wives) provided the photographs for a powerful documentary book on the rural South, *You Have Seen Their Faces* (1937). They later collaborated on similar books about Czechoslovakia and the Soviet Union. During World War II Caldwell was a correspondent for *Life* and CBS in China, Mongolia, and the Soviet Union. He continued to write prolifically after the war, publishing 55 books in all, but fell from popularity as literary tastes changed.

Caldwell, (Janet) Taylor (b. Sept. 7, 1900, Manchester, England—d. Aug. 30, 1985, Greenwich, Conn.) Novelist known for her family sagas and historical fiction.

Caldwell's family moved to the United States in 1907 and settled in Buffalo, N.Y. She worked in government offices (1923–31) while attending the University of Buffalo, from which she graduated in 1931. Her first novel, *Dynasty of Death* (1938), created a minor sensation with its portrayal of a family of munitions makers; the saga was continued in *The Eagles Gather* (1940) and *The Final Hour* (1944). Her other books, typically dramatic tales set in the past and nearly all very popular, included *The Arm and the Darkness* (1943), *This Side of Innocence* (1946), *The Devil's Advocate* (1952), *Tender Victory* (1956), *A Prologue to Love* (1961), *Testimony of Two Men* (1968), *The Captains and the Kings* (1972), *Ceremony of the Innocent* (1976), and *Bright Flows the River* (1978); *Answer as a Man* (1981) was ranked as a best-seller before its official publication date. Many of her books were dramatized for television.

Calhoun \kal-'hün\, **John C(aldwell)** (b. Mar. 18, 1782, Abbeville County, S.C.—d. Mar. 31, 1850, Washington, D.C.) Political leader and political theorist.

An ardent Jeffersonian, Calhoun was elected to the state legislature in 1808 and to the U.S. House of Representatives in 1811, where as leader of the War Hawks he introduced the declaration of war against Britain in 1812. After serving as secretary of war (1817–25), he was twice elected vice president, serving under both John Quincy Adams and Andrew Jackson (1825–32). In the 1830s he became extreme in his support of states' rights, slavery, and strict interpretation of the U.S. Constitution. He resigned the vice presidency in 1832 and was elected to the U.S. Senate, where he served until 1850 except for two years as secretary of state (1843–45).

He introduced legislation anonymously through the South Carolina legislature that advocated nullification (the right of a state to nullify an act of the federal government). He employed his famous debating skills effectively on behalf of many regional causes, including opposition to tariffs. Though he was devoted to the Union, his exuberant defense of slavery as a "positive good" aroused strong anti-Southern feeling in the free states. His speeches were later used by Southern politicians to buttress their arguments for secession.

His two posthumously published books, *Disquisition on Government* and *Discourse on the Constitution and Government of the United States,* and his many cogent speeches have gained him a reputation as one of the country's foremost original political theorists.

Calisher \\'kal-ish-ər\\, **Hortense** (b. Dec. 20, 1911, New York City) Novelist and short-story writer.

The daughter of a German immigrant father and an uprooted Southern mother, Calisher had a middle-class upbringing in New York City. She graduated from Barnard College in 1932 and later taught there and elsewhere.

The recipient of four O. Henry short-story awards, Calisher excels in well-plotted, psychologically perceptive short fiction peopled by well-drawn characters. Her story collection *In the Absence of Angels* (1951) and her *Collected Stories* (1975) feature her alter ego, Hester Elkins, a Jewish child living in New York with her extended family. Her other collections include *Tale for the Mirror: A Novella and Other Stories* (1962), *Extreme Magic: A Novella and Other Stories* (1964), and *Saratoga, Hot* (1985). Her first novel, *False Entry* (1961), contains characters who are reintroduced in a radically different setting in *The New Yorkers* (1969), in which a 12-year-old girl kills her father's unfaithful wife. Other novels include *Queenie* (1971), *On Keeping Women* (1977), *Mysteries of Motion* (1983), *Age* (1987), *In the Palace of the Movie King* (1993), and *In the Slammer with Carol Smith* (1997).

Calverton, V(ictor) F(rancis) *originally* George Goetz (b. June 25, 1900, Baltimore—d. Nov. 29, 1940, New York City) Writer, editor, and Marxist literary critic.

Goetz began teaching in Baltimore public schools in 1922. A socialist, he was influenced by the Communist Party but did not become a member. In 1923 he founded the radical *Modern Quarterly* (later the *Modern Monthly*) and served as its editor under the pen name V. F. Calverton, adopted to protect his teaching job. He applied Marxist theory to American thought in such books as *The Newer Spirit* (1925), *The Liberation of American Literature* (1932), *The Passing of the Gods* (1934), and *The Awakening of America* (1939). In the 1930s, on lecture tours in the United States and Europe, he criticized the Communists for their totalitarian ideas, while retaining his own radical ideology. His last book, *Where Angels Fear to Tread* (1941), was a history of utopian groups in America.

Campbell \\'kam-bəl\\, **John W.** *originally* John Wood Campbell, Jr. (b. June 8, 1910, Newark, N.J.—d. July 11, 1971, Mountainside, N.J.) Science-fiction writer, considered a father of modern science fiction.

Campbell began writing science fiction while obtaining a degree in physics from Duke University. His first published story, "When the Atoms Failed" (1930), contained one of science fiction's earliest depictions of computers.

Through the early 1930s, while continuing with stories of outer space, he adopted the pseudonym Don A. Stuart for a new kind of story in which technology is secondary to the development of characterization and mood. In "Twilight" (1934), machines work on incessantly long after humans are gone. His popular works of this era prompted much imitation. Campbell continued to exert influence on other writers when he turned in 1937 to editing *Astounding Stories* (later titled *Astounding Science Fiction*, then *Analog*). The magazine's contributors, including Isaac Asimov and Robert A. Heinlein, would dominate the field in mid-century, and it would earn nine best-magazine Hugo Awards under Campbell's editorship. His uncannily accurate predictions about nuclear weaponry led to his investigation by the FBI. The John W. Campbell Award for the year's best science-fiction novel has been presented since 1973,

---

Campbell, Joseph (b. March 26, 1904, New York City—d. Oct. 31, 1987, Honolulu) Mythologist who examined mythology's universal functions in human cultures and examined the mythic figure in a range of literatures.

A reader of American Indian folklore as a child, Campbell later revived his interest in the subject while working on a master's degree in English literature. Discovering that many themes in Arthurian legend resembled the basic motifs in American Indian folklore, he began pursuing the problem of mythological archetypes. Told that mythology was an unacceptable discipline, he dropped out of graduate school and devoted five years to intensive self-study, after which he was offered a teaching post at Sarah Lawrence College, where he would teach mythology for almost 30 years. *The Hero with a Thousand Faces* (1949), his most famous work, examined the archetype of the hero. Other works include the huge study of world mythology *The Masks of God* (4 vols., 1959–67); the essay collection *Flight of the Wild Gander* (1969); *Myths to Live By* (1972); and *The Way of the Animal Powers*, vol. 1 (1983), a historical atlas of world mythology (the next installment in the series, *The Way of the Seeded Earth*, was published posthumously). He was also the editor of *Myths, Dreams, and Religion* (1971).

Canfield, Dorothy See **Dorothy Canfield Fisher**

Capote \kə-ˈpō-tē\, **Truman** *originally* Truman Streckfus Persons (b. Sept. 30, 1924, New Orleans—d. Aug. 25, 1984, Los Angeles) Novelist, short-story writer, and playwright.

Capote spent his childhood in small towns in Louisiana and Alabama, which he fled at the first opportunity, and he ceased his education after attending high schools in Connecticut and New York. His first novel, *Other Voices, Other Rooms* (1948), about a 13-year-old boy's search for his father and his own identity, was followed by the story collection *A Tree of Night* (1949) and the novel *The Grass Harp* (1951). All three are written in an elegant but dark Southern

Truman Capote

Gothic style. In 1954 he collaborated with Harold Arlen on *House of Flowers*, a musical set in a West Indies bordello. *Local Color* (1950) is a collection of travel sketches. His travels accompanying a tour of *Porgy and Bess* in the Soviet Union resulted in *The Muses Are Heard* (1956). *Breakfast at Tiffany's* (1958; film, 1961) is a novella about a young, fey Manhattan call girl. Capote also wrote screenplays for his own works as well as such films as *Beat the Devil* (1956) and *The Innocents* (1961).

Capote's later journalistic style emerged in the best-selling "nonfiction novel" *In Cold Blood* (1966; film, 1967), an account of a multiple murder. Other later works include the collections *The Dogs Bark* (1973) and *Music for Chameleons* (1980). He became a notable social figure in the 1960s, but his productivity suffered subsequently. His novel *Answered Prayers* (published posthumously in 1986) was unfinished at his death.

Carr, John Dickson (b. Nov. 30, 1906, Uniontown, Pa.—d. Feb. 27, 1977, Greenville, S.C.) Detective-fiction writer.

Carr studied at Haverford College and the Sorbonne. His first novel, *It Walks by Night* (1930), won favor that endured as he continued to create well-researched "locked-room" puzzles of historical England, where he settled in 1933. Called back to America in 1942 to answer a draft notice, he was assigned to England, where he worked for the BBC. His expatriate existence continued until 1967, when he settled in North Carolina. Among his later works are *The Witch of the Low-Tide* (1961), *Dark of the Moon* (1967), and *The Hungry Goblin* (1972). Fifty of his mysteries feature one of his three detectives—Henri Bencolin, Dr. Gideon Fell, and Sir Henry Merrivale. His other successful works include *The Life of Sir Arthur Conan Doyle* (1949) and *The Exploits of Sherlock Holmes* (1954; cowritten with Doyle's son Adrian).

Carruth \kə-'rüth**, Hayden** (b. Aug. 3, 1921, Waterbury, Conn.) Poet and literary critic.

Carruth was educated at the University of North Carolina and the University of Chicago; during World War II he served in the air force and spent time in Italy. During hospitalization for psychiatric illness and alcoholism in 1953, he began a long poem later published as *The Bloomingdale Papers* (1975). *Brothers, I Loved You All* (1978), considered by some his best work, uses jazz imagery. Recent collections include *Sonnets* (1989) and *Scrambled Eggs and Whiskey* (1996, National Book Award). His books of criticism include *After "The Stranger": Imaginary Dialogues with Camus* (1965) and *Effluences from the Sacred Caves* (1983). He collaborated with the poet and publisher James Laughlin on *A New Directions Reader* (1964), edited Laughlin's *Collected Poems* (1994), and published a memoir of their friendship, *The Shadblow Tree* (1999).

Carson, Rachel (Louise) (b. May 27, 1907, Springdale, Pa.—d. April 14, 1964, Silver Spring, Md.) Biologist known for her natural history of the sea and the influential SILENT SPRING.

Carson entered Pennsylvania College for Women intending to become a writer but soon changed her major to biology. After receiving her master's degree from Johns Hopkins, she taught at the University of Maryland (1931–36). In 1936 she took a position as aquatic biologist with the U.S. Bureau of Fisheries, where she would remain until 1952, the last three years as editor in chief of the service's publications. An article in the *Atlantic* in 1937 served as the basis for her first book, *Under the Sea-Wind* (1941). It was widely praised, as her later books would be, for its combination of scientific accuracy and thoroughness with an elegant and lyrical prose style. *The Sea Around Us* (1951, National Book Award) became a national best-seller and was eventually translated into 30 languages. Her third book, *The Edge of the Sea*, was published in 1955.

Her prophetic *Silent Spring* (1962) created a sensation when it was serialized in the *New Yorker*; credited with sparking a worldwide awareness of the dangers of environmental pollution, it ranks as one of the most influential books of the century. Carson died before she could see any substantive results from her work.

Carver, Raymond *originally* Raymond Clevie Carver, Jr. (b. May 25, 1938, Clatskanie, Ore.—d. Aug. 2, 1988, Port Angeles, Wash.) Short-story writer noted for his spare, unadorned tales about the wrenching lives of working-class people.

The son of a sawmill worker, Carver married a year after finishing high school and supported his wife and two children by working as a janitor, gas-station attendant, and delivery boy. He became interested in writing after taking a creative-writing course and went on to study at Humboldt State College.

He taught several years in universities throughout the United States before the appearance of his first short-story collection, *Put Yourself in My Shoes* (1974). It was followed in 1976 by the highly successful *Will You Please Be Quiet, Please?*, which established his reputation. His later collections include *What We Talk About When We Talk About Love* (1981), *Cathedral* (1983), *Where I'm Calling From* (1988), and *Elephant and Other Stories* (1988). His stories, which often center on sudden, harsh, life-changing violence that invades the meager lives of unremarkable working-class people, are told in a minimalist style that often suggests affectlessness. Carver is credited as a major force in revitalizing the short story in the late 20th century.

Cary, Alice and Phoebe (b. April 26, 1820, Mount Healthy, near Cincinnati—d. Feb. 12, 1871, New York City; b. Sept. 4, 1824, Mount Healthy—d. July 31, 1871, Newport, R.I.) Writers whose work was both moralistic and idealistic.

Self-educated and never married, the Cary sisters wrote in unbroken companionship throughout their lives. After moving to New York City, they wrote to support themselves. Their poems, which appeared in *Harper's* and other magazines, were first collected in *Poems of Alice and Phoebe Cary* (1849). Alice, much the more prolific writer, also wrote prose sketches (including *Clovernook Papers,* 1852–53) and novels (including *Hagar,* 1852), the best of which treat the difficult lives of the neighbors and friends of her girlhood. Phoebe published only two individual volumes—*Poems and Parodies* (1854) and *Poems of Faith, Hope, and Love* (1868); she is best known for the hymn "Nearer Home." Both supported the women's rights movement, and Phoebe was briefly an assistant editor on Susan B. Anthony's paper *Revolution.*

Willa Cather

Cather \\'kath̲-ər\\, **Willa** *originally* Willela (Sibert) (b. Dec. 7, 1873, Winchester, Va.—d. April 24, 1947, New York City) Novelist known for her portrayals of frontier life on the American plains.

In 1883 Cather moved with her family from Virginia to the Nebraska village of Red Cloud, where she grew up among the immigrants from Europe—Swedes, Bohemians, Russians, Germans—who were establishing homesteads on the Great Plains. After graduating from the University of Nebraska in 1895, she obtained a position in Pittsburgh on a family magazine. Later she worked as copy editor and music and drama editor of the *Pittsburgh Leader*. In 1903 she published her first book of verses, *April Twilights*. In 1905, after publishing her first collection of short stories, THE TROLL GARDEN, she was appointed managing editor of *McClure's*. She left in 1912 to devote herself wholly to writing novels.

After her first novel, *Alexander's Bridge* (1912), set in Boston and London, Cather turned to her familiar Nebraska for material. With O PIONEERS! (1913) and MY ÁNTONIA (1918), often called her finest achievement, she found her characteristic themes—the spirit and courage of the frontier she had known in her youth. ONE OF OURS (1922, Pulitzer Prize) and A LOST LADY (1923) mourned the passing of the pioneer spirit.

SONG OF THE LARK (1915) and the tales assembled in *Youth and the Bright Medusa* (1920), including the much-anthologized PAUL'S CASE, described the other side of prairie life: the struggle of a talent to emerge from the stifling environment of the small town. A mature statement of both themes can be found in *Obscure Destinies* (1932), a group of three stories. With success and middle age, Cather experienced disillusionment, reflected in THE PROFESSOR'S HOUSE (1925) and her essays *Not Under Forty* (1936). Her solution was to write of the pioneer spirit of earlier eras, that of the French Catholic missionaries in the Southwest in DEATH COMES FOR THE ARCHBISHOP (1927) and of the French Canadians at Quebec in SHADOWS ON THE ROCK (1931). Her last novel, SAPPHIRA AND THE SLAVE GIRL (1940), marked a return to the Virginia of her ancestors.

Catton, (Charles) Bruce (b. Oct. 9, 1899, Petoskey, Mich.—d. Aug. 28, 1978, Frankfort, Mich.) Journalist and historian of the Civil War.

As a child in a small town in Michigan, Catton was stimulated by the reminiscences of local Civil War veterans, and while working as a reporter for the *Boston American*, the *Cleveland News*, and the *Cleveland Plain Dealer* (1920–26), he continued his lifelong study of the period. In 1954 he joined the staff of *American Heritage* magazine, and from 1959 was its senior editor.

A commission to write a centennial history of the Civil War evolved into Catton's celebrated trilogy on the Army of the Potomac: *Mr. Lincoln's Army* (1951), *Glory Road* (1952), and *A Stillness at Appomattox* (1953, Pulitzer Prize, National Book Award). The trilogy displayed his brilliance at bringing to historical narrative the immediacy of reportage. A second trilogy consisted of *The Coming Fury* (1961), *Terrible Swift Sword* (1963), and *Never Call Retreat* (1965). His other works include *The War Lords of Washington* (1948) and *U. S. Grant and the American Military Tradition* (1954).

Chambers, (David) Whittaker *originally* Jay Vivian Chambers (b. April 1, 1901, Philadelphia—d. July 9, 1961, Westminster, Md.) Journalist and principal figure in the Alger Hiss spy case.

Chambers's family suffered severe financial privation in his early years. In 1925, after attending Columbia University, Chambers was inspired by Lenin's writings to join the Communist Party, and he subsequently worked as an editor of the *New Masses* and the *Daily Worker*. In 1932 he was recruited as a spy by the Soviet Union. In the late 1930s, disillusioned with Stalin's purges, he underwent a radical change in ideology, becoming fervently right-wing, and joined the staff of *Time* magazine. In 1948, before the House Un-American Activities Committee, he identified Alger Hiss, a distinguished diplomat and administrator, as a fellow member of his spy ring in Washington, D.C., during the 1930s. He produced copies of State Department documents typed on Hiss's typewriter, and led federal agents to the "pumpkin papers"—microfilms of government documents, allegedly supplied by Hiss, hidden in a pumpkin on Chambers's Maryland farm. Hiss's subsequent investigation and trials were among the most sensational of the century and brought Richard Nixon to national prominence.

Chambers's autobiography, *Witness* (1952), became a best-seller. Intense in tone and extreme in its opinions, it resonated strongly with the anticommunist fervor sweeping the country. In his last years Chambers largely abandoned his conservative ideology.

Chandler, Raymond (Thornton) (b. July 23, 1888, Chicago—d. March 26, 1959, La Jolla, Calif.) Detective-fiction writer.

Chandler spent his youth in England with his Irish mother and served in the Royal Flying Corps during World War I. After the war he lived in California and prospered as an oil-company executive until the Great Depression, when he turned to writing for a living. His first published short story appeared in the pulp magazine *Black Mask* in 1933.

He completed seven novels featuring the detective hero Philip Marlowe and set in the Los Angeles area: *The Big Sleep* (1939; film, 1946), *Farewell, My Lovely* (1940; film, 1945), *The High Window* (1942), *The Lady in the Lake* (1943; film, 1946), *The Little Sister* (1949; film, *Marlowe,* 1969), *The Long Good-Bye*

(1953; film, 1973), and *Playback* (1958). Among his numerous short-story collections are *Five Murderers* (1944) and *The Midnight Raymond Chandler* (1971). From 1943 he was a Hollywood screenwriter; *Double Indemnity* (1944), *The Blue Dahlia* (1946), and *Strangers on a Train* (1951; with Czenzi Ormonde) are his best-known film scripts. Regarded as Dashiell Hammett's principal successor, Chandler is also esteemed as an outstanding regional writer for his depictions of Los Angeles life.

Channing, Edward (Perkins) (b. June 15, 1856, Dorchester, Mass.—d. Jan. 7, 1931, Cambridge, Mass.) Historian.

Son of the poet and biographer Ellery Channing (1817–1901), he was associated throughout his career with Harvard University, where he earned his doctorate and later taught for many years (1883–1929). He wrote several historical works in preparation for his magnum opus, the *History of the United States* (6 vols., 1905–25), a monumental study of America's development from AD 1000 through the Civil War which ranks as one of the major accomplishments of American historical writing. Its sixth volume, *The War for Southern Independence,* received the Pulitzer Prize; a seventh volume was left unfinished at Channing's death. Opinionated and iconoclastic, and influenced by social Darwinism, Channing stressed the forces of union over those of particularism (though he was sometimes chided for a New England bias) as the dominant theme in U.S. history, and his intensive research into original sources convincingly supported his claims for the unique contribution of each section to the whole. In emphasizing the significance of urbanization and of improvements in transportation, he challenged the frontier thesis of his illustrious colleague Frederick Jackson Turner.

Channing, William Ellery (b. April 7, 1780, Newport, R.I.—d. Oct. 2, 1842, Bennington, Vt.) Clergyman and writer known as "the apostle of Unitarianism."

Channing studied theology at Harvard and thereafter worked two years in the South as a tutor, an experience that confirmed him in his strong opposition to slavery. Once back in Boston, he quickly established a large reputation as a preacher of broad liberal sympathies; from 1803 until his death, he preached in Boston's Federal Street (Congregational) Church. Denounced by the Calvinist Jedidiah Morse as a "Unitarian" rather than a Christian, he eventually adopted the label, delivering his famous sermon "Unitarian Christianity" in 1819 and publishing his historic "Moral Argument against Calvinism" the next year. The conference of liberal Congregational ministers he formed in 1820 was reorganized in 1825 as the American Unitarian Association. Channing contributed greatly to the development of New England Transcendentalism—influencing Emerson, Longfellow, and O. W. Holmes, among others—and he spoke out against slavery, drunkenness, poverty, and war in a steady stream of sermons and essays. Though he published such books as *Remarks on a National Literature* (1830), *Slavery* (1835), *The Abolitionist* (1836), and *Duty of the Free States*

(1842), his reputation as a man of letters rests principally on several long essay-reviews, including one on Milton's "Treatise on Christian Doctrine" and another on Walter Scott's biography of Napoleon. Edward Channing was his son.

Chapman, John Jay (b. March 2, 1862, New York City—d. Nov. 4, 1933, Poughkeepsie, N.Y.) Poet, dramatist, and critic who attacked the get-rich-quick morality of the post–Civil War "Gilded Age."

Chapman graduated from Harvard and Harvard Law School. A man of intense religious morality, he lost his left hand in 1887 after plunging it into a fire out of remorse for having assaulted a man for his insulting attentions to Chapman's future wife. Admitted to the New York bar in 1888, he practiced for 10 years. As editor and publisher of *The Political Nursery* (1897–1901), he took a leading part in the movement against the machine politics of Tammany Hall. *Causes and Consequences* (1898) and *Practical Agitation* (1900) stressed his belief that individuals should take a moral stand on issues troubling the nation. His play *The Treason and Death of Benedict Arnold* appeared in 1910. In 1912, on the anniversary of a lynching, he made a memorial speech, burning with indignation, that became a classic and was reprinted in the collection *Memories and Milestones* (1915). His many other works include a biography of William Lloyd Garrison (1913), collected *Songs and Poems* (1919), and volumes of criticism on Emerson, Dante, Shakespeare, and ancient Greek culture.

Chappell \\'cha-pəl\\, **Fred (Davis)** (b. May 28, 1936, Canton, N.C.) Poet and educator.

Since 1964 Chappell has taught at the University of North Carolina at Greensboro. His fiction includes four short-story collections and an autobiographical quartet of novels (1985–1999). He is the author of many volumes of poetry, including *It Is Time, Lord* (1963), *Dagon* (1968), *The Gaudy Place* (1972), *Midquest* (1981), *Source* (1985), *First and Last Words* (1989), *Plow Naked* (1993), and *A Way of Happening* (1998). In 1985 he shared the Bollingen Prize with John Ashbery.

Chase, Mary Ellen (b. Feb. 24, 1887, Blue Hill, Maine—d. July 28, 1973, Northampton, Mass.) Scholar and novelist.

Chase earned a Ph.D. from the University of Minnesota and joined the faculty of Smith College in 1926, where she would teach until 1955. She began her writing career with books for children such as *The Girl from the Big Horn Country* (1916) and *Mary Christmas* (1926). Her first novel, *Uplands* (1927), was followed by *Mary Peters* (1934), *Silas Crockett* (1935), *Windswept* (1941), and other works set on the Maine coast that contain sharply drawn portraits of its people. She commemorated time spent in England in a book of essays, *This England* (1936). *Dawn in Lyonesse* (1938) is a retelling of the Tristan and Isolde story. She also wrote literary criticism, biblical studies, and essays. Three autobiographical works describe her Maine childhood: *A Goodly Heritage* (1932), *A Goodly Fellowship* (1939), and *The White Gate* (1954).

Chayefsky \chä-ʹyef-skē\, **Paddy** (*originally* Sidney) (b. Jan. 29, 1923, New York City—d. Aug. 1, 1981, New York City) Playwright and screenwriter.

Chayefsky worked as a printer's apprentice before beginning to write radio adaptations and television mystery dramas. His first full-length television play was *Holiday Song* (1952). His greatest success was *Marty* (1953; film, 1955, Academy Award). Two other successful television plays were made into motion pictures—*The Bachelor Party* (1954; film, 1957) and *The Catered Affair* (1955; film, 1956). The television drama *The Middle of the Night* (1954; film, 1959) became his first stage play (1956). His other stage plays include *The Tenth Man* (1959), *Gideon* (1961), *The Passion of Josef D.* (1964), and *The Latent Heterosexual* (1967). Other acclaimed screenplays included *The Hospital* (1971, Academy Award) and *Network* (1976, Academy Award). The Paddy Chayefsky Laurel Award is the Writers Guild's highest award for television writing.

Cheever, John (b. May 27, 1912, Quincy, Mass.—d. June 18, 1982, Ossining, N.Y.) Short-story writer and novelist.

Cheever's first published story appeared in the *New Republic* in 1930, shortly after he was expelled from private school. Encouraged, he moved to New York City to write, and he was soon supporting himself by writing. Beginning in 1945, he would remain closely associated with the *New Yorker* for two decades, though his works also appeared in other magazines. His first collection, *The Way Some People Live* (1943), was followed by many others, including *The Enormous Radio* (1953) and *The Brigadier and the Golf Widow* (1964), which included THE SWIMMER. In them he delineates, in clear, elegant, and frequently lyrical prose, the drama and sadness of life in comfortable suburban America, often through fantasy and ironic comedy and satire. His first novel, THE WAPSHOT CHRONICLE (1957), won a National Book Award for its often comic depiction of an old New England family; later novels include *The Wapshot Scandal* (1964), *Falconer* (1977), and *Oh What a Paradise It Seems* (1982). *The Stories of John Cheever* (1978) won the Pulitzer Prize. His son's edition of his letters was published in 1988, and his revealing journals in 1991.

Chesnut, Mary *originally* Mary Boykin Miller (b. March 31, 1823, Pleasant Hill, S.C.—d. Nov. 22, 1886, Camden, S.C.) Author of an important contemporary account of the Civil War from a Confederate viewpoint.

The daughter of a prominent South Carolina political leader, in 1840 she married James Chesnut, Jr., a lawyer, who later served as a U.S. senator from South Carolina, resigning to take an important role in the secession movement and the Confederacy. She had kept a journal since her school days; with the advent of secession, she determined to record events both great and small for the use of future historians. Accompanying her husband, now a staff officer, on his military missions, Chesnut began her conscientious record of her views and observations on Feb. 15, 1861, and closed it on Aug. 2, 1865. An ardent but not blind Southern patriot, she was also a longtime opponent of slavery. Placed in close proximity to most of the military and political leaders of the Confederacy, she employed her intelligence and native writing ability to produce a skillful and vivid account of the war from a unique perspective. A portion of her journals was published as *A Diary from Dixie* in 1905, and a larger edition in 1949. Though not a day-by-day account, it is highly regarded by historians for its perceptive views of the Confederacy's leaders and its insight into wartime Southern society.

Chesnutt, Charles (Waddell) (b. June 20, 1858, Cleveland—d. Nov. 15, 1932, Cleveland) First important black novelist in America.

Chesnutt was the son of free blacks who had left their native North Carolina before the Civil War but returned after the war. By the time he was 25, he was married and a successful school principal, but the treatment of blacks in the South so distressed him that he moved his new family back to Cleveland. Admitted to the bar there in 1887, he would go on to pursue a distinguished legal career.

Between 1885 and 1905 he published more than 50 tales, short stories, and essays, as well as a biography of Frederick Douglass and three novels. His "The Goophered Grapevine" (1887), the first work by a black accepted by the *Atlantic Monthly*, was so subtle in its refutation of the romantic view of plantation life that most readers missed its irony. This and similarly authentic, psychologically realistic stories of folk life among North Carolina blacks were collected in THE CONJURE WOMAN (1899). The collection *The Wife of His Youth* (1899) examines color prejudice among blacks as well as between the races in a manner reminiscent of George W. Cable. His third novel, *The Colonel's Dream* (1905), deals trenchantly with problems of the freed slave.

Chester, Alfred (b. Sept. 7, 1928, Brooklyn, N.Y.—d. Aug. 1, 1971, Jerusalem, Israel) Novelist and short-story writer.

As a child Chester was traumatized by the loss of his body hair caused by x-ray treatments for a childhood disease. He graduated from NYU and in 1951 he moved to Paris, where he would live for nine years. His reputation among a coterie of the avant-garde was established with his first books, the story collection *Here Be Dragons* (1955) and the novel *Jamie Is My Heart's Desire* (1956), and his stories and reviews began to appear in such magazines as the *New Yorker, Commentary, Partisan Review,* and the *New York Review of Books.* Stress and increasing mental fatigue, partly consequences of his dissipated life, took a toll on his health. In 1963 he moved to Tangier, where he suffered several psychotic episodes. In 1964 he published the story collection *Behold, Goliath.* He later returned to the United States, but left after his novel *The Exquisite Corpse* (1967) received unenthusiastic reviews. He settled in Israel, cutting off contact with most of his friends, and died under mysterious circumstances at 42.

Child, Lydia Maria *originally* Lydia Maria Francis (b. Feb. 11, 1802, Medford, Mass.—d. Oct. 20, 1880, Wayland, Mass.) Influential abolitionist author.

Born into an abolitionist family, in the 1820s she taught, wrote historical novels, and founded the country's first monthly periodical for children, *Juvenile Miscellany* (1826). She married David Lee Child in 1828; through him she met William Lloyd Garrison in 1831, and she thereafter would devote her life to the abolitionist cause. The Childs' best-known work, *An Appeal in Favor of That Class of Americans Called Africans* (1833), recounts the history of slavery and denounces the inequality of education and employment for blacks; it was the first such work published in book form. Though Child was ostracized socially and her magazine failed in 1834, she succeeded in inducing many people to join the abolitionist movement. Her further abolitionist efforts included coediting the *National Anti-Slavery Standard* (1840–44) and later transcribing the recollections of freed slaves, and making her home a stop on the Underground Railroad that aided escaping slaves.

Child's early work includes popular volumes of advice for women, such as *The Frugal Housewife* (1829), and she later wrote books promoting the cause of American Indians and lectured widely against capital punishment.

Childress \'chil-drəs\, **Alice** (b. Oct. 12, 1916, Charleston, S.C.—d. Aug. 14, 1994, New York City) Playwright, novelist, and actress, known for her realistic stories about the enduring optimism of black Americans.

Childress grew up in Harlem and studied drama with the American Negro Theater in the 1940s. There she wrote, directed, and starred in her first play, *Florence* (1949). In 1950, with the support of Paul Robeson, she opened and ran her own theater for several years. Of her plays, *Trouble in Mind* (1955), *Wedding Band* (1966), *String* (1969), and *Wine in the Wilderness* (1969) all examine racial and social issues. *Just a Little Simple* (1950; based on Langston Hughes's *Simple Speaks His Mind*), *Gold Through the Trees* (1952), *The African Garden* (1971), *Gullah* (1984; based on her 1977 play *Sea Island Song*), and *Moms* (1987) were other successful plays.

Childress was wrote successful novels for young people. The protagonist of the best-selling *A Hero Ain't Nothin' but a Sandwich* (1973; film, 1978) is a teenage drug addict; *Rainbow Jordan* (1981) also deals with the struggles of poor black urban youth. Her other novels include *A Short Walk* (1979), *Many Closets* (1987), and *Those Other People* (1989).

Chopin \shō-'pan; 'shō-pan, 'shō-pən\, **Kate** *originally* Katherine O'Flaherty (b. Feb. 8, 1851, St. Louis—d. Aug. 22, 1904, St. Louis) Novelist and short-story writer known as an interpreter of New Orleans culture.

Chopin lived in Louisiana after her marriage in 1870 to Oscar Chopin. After his death she began to write about the Creole and Cajun people she had observed in the South. Her first novel, *At Fault* (1890), was undistinguished, but she was later acclaimed for her finely crafted short stories, of which she would write more than 100. Collected in *Bayou Folk* (1894) and *A Night in Acadie* (1897), the stories would be recognized as major additions to the local-color genre, and two of them, DÉSIRÉE'S BABY and "Madame Celestin's Divorce," continue to be widely anthologized.

In 1899 Chopin published what is today her best-known work, THE AWAKENING, about the sexual and aesthetic awakening of a young mother. Roundly condemned for its sexual frankness, it later received critical approval for the beauty of its writing and its modern sensibility.

Christian, Barbara (b. Dec. 12, 1943, St. Thomas, U.S. Virgin Islands—d. June 25, 2000, Berkeley, Calif.) Educator and feminist critic who attempted to define a black feminist philosophy.

Christian entered Marquette University at 15, and earned a Ph.D. at Columbia University in 1970. She taught at CCNY (1965–72) and later in the African-American Studies department at UC–Berkeley (1971–2000). Her works include *Black Feminist Criticism* (1985), which emphasizes literary, textual analysis of fiction by black women; *Black Women Novelists* (1980); and *Teaching Guide to Accompany Black Foremothers* (1980). She frequently contributed to the journals *Black Scholar* and *Journal of Ethnic Studies*.

Churchill, Winston (b. Nov. 10, 1871, St. Louis—d. March 12, 1947, Winter Park, Fla.) Writer of popular historical novels.

After graduating from the U.S. Naval Academy, Churchill married the daughter of a wealthy manufacturer in 1895 and thereafter devoted himself to writing. His first novel, *The Celebrity*, appeared in 1898. His next, *Richard Carvel* (1899), a novel of Revolutionary Maryland in which the hero serves under John Paul Jones, sold nearly a million copies. There followed a succession of huge successes—many chiefly dealing with political, religious, or social problems—that made Churchill perhaps the most successful American writer of the first two decades of the 20th century: *The Crisis* (1901), a Civil War novel whose heroine is a descendant of Richard Carvel; *The Crossing* (1904), about Kentucky pioneers during the American Revolution; *Coniston* (1906); *Mr. Crewe's Career* (1908); *A Modern Chronicle* (1910); *The Inside of the Cup* (1913); and *A Far Country* (1915).

Ciardi \\'chär-dē, 'chyär-dē\\, John (Anthony) (b. June 24, 1916, Boston, Mass.—d. March 30, 1986, Edison, N.J.) Poet, critic, and translator.

Educated at Bates College, Tufts University, and the University of Michigan (M.A., 1939), Ciardi served in the Army Air Corps (1942–45) and then taught at universities until 1961. He served as poetry editor of the *Saturday Review* from 1956 to 1972, where he generated continuous controversy with his critical reviews.

His first volume of poetry, *Homeward to America*, appeared in 1940. His *How Does a Poem Mean?* (1960) found wide use as a poetry textbook in high schools and colleges. Later poetry collections include *Person to Person* (1964), *The Little That Is All* (1974), and *For Instance* (1979). He also wrote many books of prose and verse for children. His highly acclaimed translation of Dante's *Divine Comedy,* rather than following Dante's rhyme scheme, attempted to capture the feeling of the original in a terse and economical modern verse idiom. His later works include *Limericks, Too Gross* (1978) and *A Grossery of Limericks* (1981), both written with Isaac Asimov; *A Browser's Dictionary and Native's Guide to the Unknown American Language* (1980); and *A Second Browser's Dictionary . . .* (1983).

Cisneros \sis-ʼner-ōs\, **Sandra** (b. Dec. 20, 1954, Chicago) Short-story writer and poet known for her evocation of Mexican-American life in Chicago.

Despite the poverty of her childhood, which was partly spent in Mexico, Cisneros was always an avid reader. After graduating from Chicago's Loyola University, she obtained a master's degree from the University of Iowa Writers' Workshop, where she began to identify herself as a Hispanic woman and to write in a distinctive voice.

Her first book of fiction, *The House on Mango Street* (1983), was a collection of semiautobiographical tales that recall a girlhood spent trying to be a creative writer in an antagonistic environment. *Woman Hollering Creek* (1991) contained tales of beleaguered girls and women. *Caramelo* (2002) is a generational saga of conflicting cultures. Her volumes of poetry include *My Wicked, Wicked Ways* (1987) and *Loose Woman* (1994).

Clampitt, Amy (b. June 15, 1920, New Providence, Iowa—d. Sept. 10, 1994, Lenox, Mass.) Poet whose work won critical acclaim for its evocation of the natural world.

After graduating from Grinnell College, Clampitt worked as an editor and reference librarian, meanwhile writing several novels that were not accepted for publication. *Multitudes, Multitudes* (1973), her first book of poetry, was not published until she was in her fifties, and then at her own expense, but soon afterward her poems started to appear in the *New Yorker.* Her first full-length collection was *The Kingfisher* (1983), which won her fame. It was especially noted for its gracefully elaborate syntax and vocabulary and its subject matter drawn from the natural world. *What the Light Was Like* (1985) was also highly praised; critics commented on the ease and certainty with which she employed literary allusions and on her ornamented, sometimes eccentric style. Later collections included *Archaic Figure* (1987), *Westward* (1990), and *A Silence Opens* (1994).

Clancy, Tom *originally* Thomas L. Clancy, Jr. (b. April 12, 1947, Baltimore) Popular novelist.

Clancy attended Baltimore's Loyola College and worked as an insurance agent before beginning his writing career. His first novel was the surprise best-seller *The Hunt for Red October* (1984; film, 1990), which virtually created the "technothriller" genre, novels of suspense that display extensive knowledge of military technology and espionage. Clancy's later novels, most of which feature the CIA agent Jack Ryan, and almost all of which were hugely successful if not critically admired, include *Red Storm Rising* (1986; with Larry Bond), *Patriot Games* (1987; film, 1992), *Clear and Present Danger* (1989; film, 1994), *Sum of All Fears* (1991; film, 2000), *Debt of Honor* (1994), *Executive Orders* (1996), *The Bear and the Dragon* (2000), and *The Teeth of the Tiger* (2003).

Clark, Mary Higgins *originally* Mary Higgins (b. Dec. 24, 1929, New York City) Novelist and mystery writer.

Clark attended secretarial school and later worked as a flight attendant. She began writing while rearing five children. After her husband's death in 1964, she worked as a radio scriptwriter and producer to support her family (1965–70). Her first mystery-suspense novel was *Where Are the Children* (1975; film 1986). She finally earned her bachelor's degree (Fordham University, 1979) after publishing *A Stranger Is Watching* (1978; film, 1982). She won ever greater success with her subsequent suspense novels, including *The Cradle Will Fall* (1980), *A Cry in the Night* (1982; film, 1985), *Stillwatch* (1984), *Weep No More, My Lady* (1987), *Loves Music, Loves to Dance* (1991), and *Pretend You Don't See Her* (1997), sometimes collaborating with her daughter, Carol Higgins Clark.

Clark, Walter van Tilburg (b. Aug. 3, 1909, East Orland, Maine—d. Nov. 10, 1971, Reno, Nev.) Novelist and short-story writer.

From the age of 9 Clark's childhood was spent in Reno, which forms the background for his novel *The City of Trembling Leaves* (1945), the story of a sensitive adolescent boy's development. His best-known work is THE OX-BOW INCIDENT (1940; film, 1943); the story of a lynching in 1885 of three suspected cattle rustlers, it conveys powerful and dramatic insight into mob psychology. *The Track of the Cat* (1949; film, 1954), about a hunt for a black panther during a blizzard, is also a moral parable. *The Watchful Gods* (1950) is a collection of short stories. Clark taught at the University of Nevada from 1962 until his death.

Clemens, Samuel Langhorne See **Mark Twain**

Clement, Hal *originally* Harry Clement Stubbs (b. May 30, 1922, Somerville, Mass.—d. Oct. 29, 2003, Milton, Mass.) Science-fiction writer and novelist.

Stubbs earned degrees in astronomy, education, and chemistry from Harvard, Boston University, and Simmons College. He served as a bomber pilot in World War II, and subsequently rose to the rank of colonel. From 1949 to 1987 he taught science at Milton (Mass.) Academy. In 1942 he began to have his stories published in science-fiction magazines, and his first novel, *Needle* (1951), was originally serialized in *Astounding Science Fiction* (now *Analog*) magazine. His novels often depicted highly imagined alien worlds; the most famous was *Mission of Gravity* (1954). Later novels include *Close to Critical* (1964), *Star Light* (1971), *Left of Africa* (1976), *The Nitrogen Fix* (1982), *Still River* (1987), *Fossil* (1993), *Half Life* (1999), and *Noise* (2003).

Clifton, Lucille *originally* Thelma Lucille Sayles (b. June 27, 1936, Depew, N.Y.) Poet and children's author who employs black vernacular to examine family relationships and life in the urban ghetto.

Clifton grew up in a largely Polish community, where she recalls hers was the only black family. She graduated from high school at 16 and studied mathematics at Howard University but did not graduate. She married in 1958 and had six children in seven years; the oldest was seven when her first poetry collection, *Good Times* (1969), was published. Over the years she has published many more collections; the most recent include *The Book of Light* (1993), *The Terrible Stories* (1996), and *Blessing the Boats* (2000, National Book Award). She has also written many children's books, generally with a black audience in mind, including *All Us Come Cross the Water* (1973) and *My Friend Jacob* (1980), as well as the Everett Anderson series, poems about the adventures of a young boy. Though she has battled breast cancer, received a kidney transplant, and had a tumor in the stomach removed, she continues to write and teach at St. Mary's College of Maryland.

Clurman \\'klùr-mən\\, **Harold** (b. Sept. 18, 1901, New York City—d. Sept. 9, 1980, New York City) Theater director and drama critic.

Clurman attended Columbia University and later the Sorbonne, when he shared his Paris apartment with Aaron Copland. He made his stage debut at the Greenwich Village Theatre, and in 1931 he became a founding member of the experimental Group Theatre, for which he directed several plays, notably Clifford Odets's *Awake and Sing!* (1935). He later directed the American premieres of such wide-ranging works as Carson McCullers's *A Member of the Wedding* (1950), Jean Giraudoux's *Tiger at the Gates* (1955), Jean Anouilh's *Waltz of the*

Toreadors (1957), Eugene O'Neill's *Touch of the Poet* (1957), and Arthur Miller's *Incident at Vichy* (1965).

Clurman's influence was felt most widely through his highly respected reviews when he served as drama critic for the *New Republic* (1948–52) and the *Nation* (1953–80). His books include *On Directing* (1972), *The Divine Pastime* (1974), and the memoir *All People Are Famous* (1974).

Cobb, Irvin S(hrewsbury) (b. June 23, 1876, Paducah, Ky.—d. March 10, 1944, New York City) Journalist and humorist.

Forced to quit school at 16 to support his family, Cobb became a reporter for his town's newspaper and rose to managing editor in three years, while also serving as a correspondent for several larger papers, including the *Chicago Tribune.* In 1904 he moved to New York, where the quality of his writing prompted Joseph Pulitzer to hire him for the *Evening World* and *Sunday World* as a humorist. First through syndicated newspaper features and later in magazines, he became widely known for such articles as "Speaking of Operations," which in book form sold more than 500,000 copies, and for his short stories. His first collection of regional tales, *Back Home* (1912), featured Judge Priest, a shrewd and kindly Confederate veteran who would later figure in such subsequent collections as *J. Poindexter, Colored* (1922), as well as the films *Judge Priest* (1934) and *The Sun Shines Bright* (1953). Cobb collaborated on many plays and musicals, and in 1934 moved to Hollywood, where he worked as a screenwriter and actor.

Codrescu \kə-'dres-kyü, kō-'dres-kyü\, **Andrei** (b. Dec. 20, 1946, Sibiu, Romania) Poet, editor, journalist, and social critic.

Codrescu immigrated to the United States in 1966. Since 1984 he has taught English at Louisiana State University. He edits the literary monthly *Exquisite Corpse*. His many publications include the poetry collections *License to Carry a Gun* (1970), *Belligerence* (1993), and *Alien Candor* (1996), the memoirs *The Life and Times of an Involuntary Genius* (1974) and *In America's Shoes* (1983), and the novels *The Repentance of Lorraine* (1994) and *The Blood Countess* (1995); most exhibit a darkly comic surrealism. Several of his books, including *Disappearance of the Outside* (1990) and *The Hole in the Flag* (1991), deal with the countries of the former Soviet bloc. He has gained a wide following with his incisive deadpan commentary on National Public Radio.

Coffin \'kȯf-ən, 'käf-ən\, **R(obert) P(eter) Tristram** (b. March 18, 1892, Brunswick, Maine—d. Jan. 20, 1955, Portland, Maine) Poet of New England farm and seafaring life.

Born into a distinguished New England family, Coffin spent his earliest years on remote island farms in Maine. He graduated from Bowdoin College, earned an M.A. at Princeton, and studied at Oxford as a Rhodes scholar. After

World War I he took a teaching position at Wells College, and within a few years had published several poetry collections. In 1934 he began teaching at Bowdoin. His verse collection *Strange Holiness* (1935) won the Pulitzer Prize. Like his poetry, his novels *Red Sky in the Morning* (1935) and *John Dawn* (1936) depict life on the Maine coast. He also published essay collections as well as several biographies.

George M. Cohan

Cohan \\'kō-ˌhan, ˌkō-'han\\, **George M(ichael)** (b. July 3, 1878, Providence, R.I.—d. Nov. 5, 1942, New York City) Actor, songwriter, playwright, and producer.

Having received little formal education, Cohan performed from an early age with his parents and sister as The Four Cohans, and he moved on to comedy roles in vaudeville and on the legitimate stage. By 1893 he was writing vaudeville skits and popular songs. His first full-length play opened in New York in 1901. His first major hit, *Little Johnny Jones* (1904; film, 1930), is regarded as a milestone in the history of the musical. Among his later musicals, most of which he also produced and appeared in, were *The Governor's Son* (1901), *Forty-five Minutes from Broadway* (1906), *The Talk of New York* (1907), *Hello, Broadway* (1914), and *The Song and Dance Man* (1923). His nonmusical plays include *Broadway Jones* (1912) and *Seven Keys to Baldpate* (1913).

Notable among his 500 songs are "You're a Grand Old Flag," "Mary's a Grand Old Name," "Give My Regards to Broadway," "I'm a Yankee Doodle Dandy," and "Over There," the great World War I recruiting song for which Congress authorized him a special medal in 1940. Cohan's most famous acting roles include those in *Ah, Wilderness!* (1933) and *I'd Rather Be Right* (1937). *Twenty Years on Broadway and the Years It Took to Get There* (1925) is an autobiography. His career has also been the subject of a film, *Yankee Doodle Dandy* (1942), and a Broadway musical, *George M!* (1968).

Colby, Frank Moore (b. Feb. 10, 1865, Washington, D.C.—d. March 3, 1925, New York City) Encyclopedia editor and essayist.

Colby taught history and economics at three colleges before becoming editor of the *International Year Book* in 1898. His *Outlines of General History* (1899) became a popular and durable textbook. He coedited the *New International Encyclopedia* (1900–3) and later helped supervise its second edition (1913–15). He contributed to many magazines, including *Bookman,* the *New Republic*, and *Vanity Fair*, and his witty essays were widely read. After his death, his popularity rose with the publication of *The Colby Essays* (1926), edited by Clarence Day, Jr.

Coles, Robert (b. Oct. 12, 1929, Boston) Child psychiatrist, educator, and writer.
After earning his M.D. from Columbia University in 1954, Coles was asso-

ciated with several psychiatric clinics. Since 1963 he has been associated with Harvard University, where he teaches psychiatry and social ethics.

Coles has published some 60 books and over 1,300 articles and reviews. His books on children and their mental health include the widely praised *Children of Crisis* (5 vols., 1963–78; Pulitzer Prize), *Dead End School* (1968), *Teachers and the Children of Poverty* (1970), *The Darkness and the Light* (1974), *The Political Life of Children* (1986), and *The Spiritual Life of Children* (1990). He is a founder and coeditor of *DoubleTake* magazine and contributing editor to the *New Republic*, *New Oxford Review*, *Poetry Review*, and *Literature and Medicine*.

Commager \\'kä-mi-jər\\, **Henry Steele** (b. Oct. 25, 1902, Pittsburgh, Pa.—d. March 2, 1998, Amherst, Mass.) Historian and educator.

Commager earned his doctorate from the University of Chicago in 1928, and subsequently taught history at NYU (1929–38), Columbia, (1938–56), and Amherst College (1956–92). He first gained attention in 1930 as coauthor (with S. E. Morison) of *The Growth of the American Republic*, where he first displayed his clear, cogent narrative style; the book became a perennial textbook. With Allan Nevins he edited *The Heritage of America* (1939) and wrote *America: The Story of a Free People* (1942). Among his many later books were *The Story of the Second World War* (1945), *The American Mind* (1951), often considered his finest work; *Freedom, Loyalty, Dissent* (1954); and *The Empire of Reason* (1977). Rejecting economic determinism as an explanation of American history, Commager portrayed the United States as the best example of a nation based on a system of rational law, in the form of the U.S. Constitution, which he held to be a perfect blueprint for a political system. In 1972 he received the National Academy of Arts and Letters gold medal for history.

Connell \\'kän-əl\\, **Evan S.** *originally* Evan Shelby Connell, Jr. (b. Aug. 17, 1924, Kansas City, Mo.) Writer whose works explore philosophical and cultural facets of the American experience.

Connell's first published work, *The Anatomy Lesson* (1957), was an admired collection of stories whose subject matter ranges from the near-mythic to the mundane. He is best known for a linked pair of novels: *Mrs. Bridge* (1959) dissects the life of a conventional upper-middle-class Kansas City matron who lacks a sense of purpose and conforms blindly to social expectations; *Mr. Bridge* (1969) relates the same story from her husband's point of view. *Son of the Morning Star* (1984), a revisionist biography of George Armstrong Custer, was a critical and popular success. Connell's other novels include the disturbing *Diary of a Rapist* (1966); *The Connoisseur* (1974); *Double Honeymoon* (1976); an experimental fictional biography of Paracelsus, *The Alchymist's Journal* (1991); and *Deus Lo Volt!* (2000), a panoramic novel of the Crusades. He has also written two books of historical essays, two book-length poems, and further collections of short stories.

Marc Connelly

Connelly, Marc(us Cook) (b. Dec. 13, 1890, McKeesport, Pa.—d. Dec. 21, 1980, New York City) Playwright, journalist, teacher, actor, and director.

Connelly worked as a reporter in Pittsburgh until 1917, when he joined the *New York Morning Telegraph*, covering theatrical news. He soon met George S. Kaufman, with whom he would enjoy a notable collaboration; both men would become members of the Algonquin Round Table. Their first successful comedy, *Dulcy* (1921), was quickly followed by *To the Ladies* (1922), *The '49ers* (1922), the Hollywood satire *Merton of the Movies* (1922), and *Beggar on Horseback* (1924). They also collaborated on the musicals *Helen of Troy, New York* (1923) and *Be Yourself* (1924).

Green Pastures (1930, Pulitzer Prize), based on Roark Bradford's *Ol' Man Adam an' His Chillun*, was extremely popular both on the stage and in its film version (1936), but when revived in 1951 it was criticized for perpetuating unacceptable stereotypes of blacks. Connelly's last Broadway success, *The Farmer Takes a Wife* (1934; film, 1935), was written with Frank Elser. His novel *A Souvenir from Qam* was published in 1965. His screenplays include *Captains Courageous* (1937).

Conroy, Jack (Wesley) (b. Dec. 5, 1899, near Moberly, Mo.—d. Feb. 28, 1990, Moberly) Writer of proletarian fiction.

Conroy was born and raised in a mining camp, where his father and two brothers lost their lives in accidents. He first became known in 1933 with his acclaimed novel *The Disinherited*, a largely autobiographical tale of a young man's search for work during the Depression. From 1931 to 1941 he founded and edited successively the magazines *Rebel Poet*, *Anvil*, and *New Anvil*, which published the writings of Erskine Caldwell, Langston Hughes, and William Carlos Williams. He would later coedit a collection from these journals, *Writers in Revolt* (1973).

In 1938 he began to work with the WPA Federal Writers' Project. With Arna Bontemps he wrote the juvenile book *The Fast-Sooner Hound* (1942) and *They Seek a City* (1945), a history of black migration and settlement, later updated and expanded as *Anyplace But Here* (1966). *The Jack Conroy Reader* was published in 1980.

Conroy, (Donald) Pat(rick) (b. Oct. 26, 1945, Atlanta, Ga.) Novelist and playwright.

Conroy graduated from The Citadel in 1967 and published his first novel, *The Boo,* in 1970. His next novel, *The Water Is Wide* (1972), dealt with his experiences as a teacher in an isolated black community; it was adapted as the film

Conrack (1973) and as a stage musical (1987). His later books, most of them similarly based on his own life, include *The Great Santini* (1976; film, 1979), *The Lords of Discipline* (1980; film, 1983), *The Prince of Tides* (1986; film, 1991), and *Beach Music* (1995; film, 1997).

Conway, Moncure Daniel (b. March 17, 1832, Stafford County, Va.—d. Nov. 15, 1907, Paris) Clergyman, author, and abolitionist.

Born to slaveholding parents, Conway converted to Unitarianism while serving in the Methodist ministry, but because of his outspoken abolitionist views he was dismissed from his first Unitarian pastorate in 1856. He moved to Cincinnati and became active in abolitionist causes, even establishing a colony of fugitive slaves at Yellow Springs, Ohio. In 1862 he became coeditor of the *Commonwealth*, a Boston antislavery paper. During the Civil War he lectured in England on behalf of the North. He contributed to journals in England and America and wrote more than 70 books and pamphlets on a great variety of subjects, including *Demonology and Devil Lore* (1878), *The Wandering Jew* (1881), and scholarly works on Thomas Paine. His *Autobiography* (1904) is valuable for its sketches of important 19th-century figures.

Cook, George Cram (b. Oct. 7, 1873, Davenport, Iowa—d. Jan. 14, 1924, Delphi, Greece) Novelist, poet, and playwright, cofounder of the Provincetown Players.

After completing his degree at Harvard, Cook studied at the Universities of Heidelberg and Geneva. After teaching at the University of Iowa and at Stanford University, he began working as a small farmer. Nietzsche's influence is reflected in his first novel, *Roderick Taliaferro* (1903), a historical romance set in the Mexico of Emperor Maximilian. One of Cook's hired workers, Floyd Dell, who later became a novelist, converted him to socialism, a change reflected in *The Chasm* (1911), in which the protagonist is torn between Nietzschean aristocratic individualism and socialist ideas, with the latter eventually winning. Soon after joining Dell at the *Chicago Evening Post*, Cook married Susan Glaspell, and in 1915 they launched the Provincetown Players in Provincetown, Mass., initially to perform their play *Suppressed Desires* (1915), a satire on psychoanalysis. He continued with the group when it moved to Greenwich Village and formed the Playwrights' Theatre, performing plays written by American authors. In 1922 the couple settled in Greece, where Cook wrote the verse collection *Greek Coins* (1925) and the plays *The Spring* (1925) and *The Athenian Women* (1926).

Cooper, James Fenimore (b. Sept. 15, 1789, Burlington, N.J.—d. Sept. 14, 1851, Cooperstown, N.Y.) First major American novelist.

Cooper was a year old when his father, a U.S. Congressman, moved his family to the frontier settlement (now Cooperstown) he had founded in upstate New York. He attended Yale but was expelled in his junior year because of a prank. He then joined the navy as a midshipman, but left in 1809 when his father's death made him financially independent.

For 10 years he led the life of a dilettante. His first fiction, reputedly written on a challenge from his wife, was *Precaution* (1820), a plodding imitation of Jane Austen's novels of English gentry manners. His second novel, *The Spy* (1821), was based on Walter Scott's Waverley novels but used a Revolutionary War setting and introduced several distinctively American character types. It soon brought him international fame and even wealth, which was fortunate, as he had become the sole support of his brothers' families (upon their deaths) as well as his own.

The first of the renowned LEATHERSTOCKING TALES, *The Pioneers* (1823), introduced the wilderness scout Natty Bumppo. Public fascination with the character led Cooper to write a series of sequels in which Bumppo's entire life was gradually unfolded: *The Last of the Mohicans* (1826), *The Prairie* (1827), *The Pathfinder* (1840), and *The Deerslayer* (1841). The series, which contained the finest of all his books, won him a great reputation in Europe, where he lived from 1826 to 1833.

His fourth novel, THE PILOT (1823), inaugurated a series of popular and influential sea novels that included *The Red Rover* (1827) and *The Sea Lions* (1849). As developed by Cooper, the genre became a powerful vehicle for spiritual and moral exploration. He also wrote a meticulously researched but highly readable *History of the Navy of the United States of America* (1839).

Between 1822 and 1826 Cooper lived in New York City and participated in its intellectual life, founding the Bread and Cheese Club, which had many influential members. He then returned to his estate in Cooperstown, where he was troubled by lawsuits—mostly the result of later books he wrote deploring Jacksonian democracy—and agrarian unrest. Though he wrote some of his most popular works late in life, profits from publishing had so diminished that he was unable to retire from writing.

Coover \\'kü-vər\\, **Robert (Lowell)** (b. Feb. 4, 1932, Charles City, Iowa) Avant-garde writer.

Coover attended Southern Illinois University, Indiana University, and the University of Chicago (M.A. 1965). From 1979 he has taught at Brown University. His first and most conventional novel, the admired *The Origin of the Brunists* (1966), tells of the rise and eventual disintegration of a religious cult. His best-known work, *The Public Burning* (1976), called by Coover a "factional account" of the trial and execution of Julius and Ethel Rosenberg, uses Richard Nixon as its narrator and satirizes the national mood of the early 1950s; it was extravagantly praised by many critics. His short-story collections include *Pricksongs and Descants* (1969) and *A Night at the Movies* (1987); his more recent works include *Pinocchio in Venice* (1991), *Briar Rose* (1997), and *Ghost Town* (1998), a "metafiction" on the topic of westerns. Several of his short stories, including "The Baby Sitter" and "Spanking the Maid," have been adapted for the theater. Coover has supported and taught the writing of hypertext novels, novels for the computer in which clicking on words sends the reader to different portions of the text.

Corn, Alfred *in full* Alfred Dewitt Corn III (b. Aug. 14, 1943, Bainbridge, Ga.) Poet.

Corn attended Emory and Columbia universities and has taught at several institutions. He earned acclaim for his first poetry collection, *All Roads at Once* (1976). *Notes from a Child of Paradise* (1984), one of his best-known works, is a long semiautobiographical poem modeled on Dante's *Paradiso*. Other verse collections, characterized by a mild-mannered, meditative lyricism that belies considerable sophistication, include *The West Door* (1988), *Autobiographies* (1992), and *Present* (1997). The novel *Part of His Story* (1997) deals with the specter of AIDS.

Corso \\'kȯr-sō\\, Gregory (Nunzio) (b. March 26, 1930, New York City– d. Jan. 17, 2001, New York City) Beat poet.

Abandoned by his mother when he was a year old, Corso grew up in orphanages and foster homes. At 17 he was sentenced to three years in prison for theft, and there began writing poetry. In Greenwich Village, shortly after his release in 1950, he met Allen Ginsberg, who encouraged him and promoted his work, and Corso's first volume of verse, *The Vestal Lady on Brattle*, appeared in 1955. In 1956 he moved to San Francisco, where Ginsberg was residing and the Beat movement was gaining momentum. With Ginsberg, Jack Kerouac, and others of the Beats, he thereafter traveled widely and gave unconventional readings.

Corso's poetry is appreciated for his light touch and humor. Later collections include *Gasoline* (1958), *The Happy Birthday of Death* (1960), *The American Express* (1961), *Elegiac Feelings American* (1970), *Herald of the Autochthonic Spirit* (1981), and *Mindfield* (1989).

Cortez \\kȯr-'tez\\, Jayne (b. May 10, 1936, Arizona) Poet noted for her poetry performances, often accompanied by jazz.

Cortez grew up in California and New York. From 1964 to 1970 she was artistic director of the Watts Repertory Theater Company. Unfulfilled love, unromantic sex, and jazz greats—including Cortez's ex-husband Ornette Coleman— are subjects of her first collection of poems, *Pissstained Stairs and The Monkey Man's Wares* (1969). With the poems of *Festivals and Funerals* (1971) she turned to larger social issues, including the place of the artist in revolutionary politics. In *Scarifications* (1973) she confronted the Vietnam War and wrote with a new-found romanticism about a journey to Africa.

Cortez often performs with her band of jazz improvisers, the Firespitters; they have released many recordings, including *Taking the Blues Back Home* (1996). Among her later poetry collections are *Everywhere Drums* (1990), *Poetic Magnetic* (1991), and *Somewhere in Advance of Nowhere* (1996).

Costain \\'käs-ˌtän\\, **Thomas B(ertram)** (b. May 8, 1885, Brantford, Ontario, Canada—d. Oct. 8, 1965, New York City) Historical novelist.

A journalist for many years on Canadian newspapers and an editor at *Saturday Evening Post* from 1920 to 1934, Costain was 57 when he published his first romance, *For My Great Folly* (1942), about the 17th-century rivalry between England and Spain. An immediate success, it was followed almost yearly by meticulously researched historical adventure tales, the best-known of which are *The Black Rose* (1945), a tale of a Mongolian warrior, which sold a million copies in six months, and *The Silver Chalice* (1952), about the early Christians in Rome.

Cotton, John (b. Dec. 4, 1585, Derby, England—d. Dec. 23, 1652, Boston) Puritan leader.

Educated at Cambridge University, Cotton became vicar of a parish church in Lincolnshire in 1612. He remained in the post for 21 years, during which he gradually became more Puritan in his outlook and ceased to observe certain Anglican rituals. In 1632 legal action was taken against him for his Nonconformism, and in 1633 he emigrated to the Massachusetts Bay Colony; there he became "teacher" of the First Church of Boston, where he would remain until his death. His popularity in the colony was unbounded, and his influence in both civil and ecclesiastical affairs was probably greater than that of any other minister in New England. Impressively learned, he staunchly defended established Puritan institutions against Anne Hutchinson and Roger Williams.

He wrote several works that constitute an invaluable exposition of New England Congregationalism, including *The Way of the Churches of Christ in New England* (1645) and *The Way of Congregational Churches Cleared* (1648). His catechism *Milk for Babes, Drawn out of the Breasts of Both Testaments* (1646) was widely used for many years for the religious instruction of children.

Cousins, Norman (b. June 24, 1912, Union Hill, N.J.—d. Nov. 30, 1990, Los Angeles) Editor, essayist and humanitarian.

Cousins studied to be a teacher at Columbia University but began an editorial career in 1934. As the longtime editor of the *Saturday Review* (1942–72), he introduced essays that drew connections between literature and current events. *The Good Inheritance* (1942) expressed his strong belief in America's unique potential for greatness. His other wide-ranging books included a biography of Albert Schweitzer and a book of reflections on humanity in the atomic age, *Modern Man Is Obsolete* (1945). He served as a diplomatic emissary for Pope John XXIII and for Presidents Eisenhower, Kennedy, and Johnson; his negotiations with Nikita Khrushchev helped lead to a limited nuclear test-ban treaty. He supported world federalism and a strengthened United Nations. His best-selling *Anatomy of an Illness* (1979), which explores the healing ability of the human mind, was based on his experience with a life-threatening illness; *The Healing*

Heart (1983) and *Head First* (1989) further explored the mind-body connection. In 1990 Cousins was awarded the Albert Schweitzer Prize for Humanitarianism.

Cowl \\'kaù(ə)l\\, **Jane** *originally* Grace Bailey (b. Dec. 14, 1883, Boston—d. June 22, 1950, Santa Monica, Calif.) Playwright and actress.

After attending public schools in Brooklyn, Bailey made her acting debut in New York in 1903, using the stage name Jane Cowl, at the theater of her mentor, David Belasco, in *Sweet Kitty Bellairs*. Among her many successful roles were in *Lilac Time* (1917) and in *Smilin' Through* (1919–22), which ran for 1,170 performances; both were written by Cowl and Jane Murfin (*Smilin' Through* under a male pseudonym) and produced by Cowl's husband, the *New York Times* drama critic Adolph Klauber. With Murfin she also wrote *Daybreak* (1917) and *Information Please* (1918); she collaborated with Theodore Charles on *The Jealous Moon* (1928) and with Reginald Lawrence on *Hervey House* (1935).

Cowley \\'kaù-lē, 'kü-lē\\, **Malcolm** (b. Aug. 24, 1898, Belsano, Pa.—d. March 27, 1989, New Milford, Conn.) Critic and social historian who chronicled the writers of the Lost Generation of the 1920s and their successors.

Cowley was educated at Harvard University and in France at the University of Montpellier. He helped publish the little magazines *Secession* and *Broom* in Paris, where he joined the American expatriate community. In 1929 he published a collection of poems, *Blue Juniata*. From 1929 to 1944 he served as literary editor of the *New Republic,* to which he brought a leftish political slant.

Exile's Return (1934) was a social and literary history of the Lost Generation. *The Portable Faulkner* (1946), a paperback selection edited by Cowley, revived William Faulkner's literary reputation when his books had fallen out of print, and paved the way for his Nobel Prize. Cowley's other works include *The Literary Situation* (1954), *Think Back on Us* (1967), and *A Many-Windowed House* (1970). His correspondence with Faulkner appeared in 1966 in *The Faulkner-Cowley File.* Among the many books he edited are *After the Genteel Tradition* (1937) and *Books That Changed Our Minds* (1939). *And I Worked at the Writer's Trade* (1976) combines literary history and autobiography.

Coxe \\'käks\\, **Tench** (b. May 22, 1755, Philadelphia—d. July 16, 1824, Philadelphia) Political economist and pamphleteer.

Coxe joined the family's financial business in 1776. A member of the Continental Congress, he wrote one of the first pamphlets to advocate ratification, *An Examination of the Constitution of the United States* (1788). A political pragmatist, he was consecutively a Whig, a Federalist, and a Republican, and won federal appointments as assistant secretary of the treasury (1789–92), commissioner of revenue (1792–97), and purveyor of public supplies (1803–12). To promote prosperity in the new nation, he encouraged manufacturing and served as president of the Pennsylvania Society for the Encouragement of Manufactures and the Useful Arts. He was one of the first to promote the cultivation of cotton in the South and the development of cotton manufacture. In his major work, the popular *View of the United States* (1794), he described the future importance of coal reserves in Pennsylvania.

Cozzens \\'kəz-ənz\\, **James Gould** (b. Aug. 19, 1903, Chicago—d. Aug. 9, 1978, Stuart, Fla.) Novelist whose writings dealt with life in middle-class America.

Cozzens grew up on Staten Island, N.Y., and attended Harvard University but left after two years, following publication of his first novel, *Confusion* (1924). A year of teaching in Cuba provided background material for the short novels *Cockpit* (1928) and *The Son of Perdition* (1929). He gained critical attention in 1931 with his novella *S.S. San Pedro*. Thereafter he published increasingly complex novels, most of which focus on professional people. In *The Last Adam* (1933; film, *Doctor Bull,* 1933) the protagonist is a doctor; *Men and Brethren* (1936) depicts the life of an Episcopalian minister; *The Just and the Unjust* (1942) is about lawyers; the acclaimed *Guard of Honor* (1948, Pulitzer Prize) concerns air-force officers and men; and the highly successful *By Love Possessed* (1957) again deals with lawyers. His last novel, *Morning, Noon, and Night* (1968), reflected most strongly his trend toward an increasingly convoluted style and plot.

Craddock \\'krad-ək\\, **Charles Egbert** *pseudonym of* Mary Noailles Murfree (b. Jan. 24, 1850, near Murfreesboro, Tenn.—d. July 31, 1922, Murfreesboro) Regional writer who depicted Tennessee mountain life in her short stories.

For her stories published in *Appleton's Journal* and the *Atlantic,* Murfree employed the pen name Charles Egbert Craddock; her robust writing style and bold handwriting deceived the *Atlantic's* editor, Thomas Bailey Aldrich, into believing her to be a man, and her identity was not disclosed until after publication of her first volume of short stories, *In the Tennessee Mountains* (1884), and earned her much valuable publicity. She subsequently wrote prolifically; her many novels include *Where the Battle Was Fought* (1884) and *Down the Ravine* (1885), and her story collections include *Phantoms of the Footbridge* (1895). Most of her stories present the narrow, stern life of the mountaineers who were left behind in the advance of modern civilization.

Crane, (Harold) Hart (b. July 21, 1899, Garrettsville, Ohio—d. April 27, 1932, at sea, Caribbean Sea) Poet who celebrated the richness of life in lyrics of visionary intensity.

Crane's family broke up during his unhappy childhood, and he left high school during his last year to work at a variety of insignificant jobs in New York and Cleveland while reading and writing poetry. He settled in New York in 1923.

His first published book, *White Buildings* (1926), contains the long poem "For the Marriage of Faustus and Helen," which he described as "symphonic" in form. His greatest work, THE BRIDGE (1930), had begun gestating while he was still in Cleveland. He intended it as a refutation of the pessimism of his generation's intellectuals as expressed in T. S. Eliot's *Waste Land.* Its poetic language, though convoluted and difficult, is often rhapsodic and almost mystical in its fervor. Its mixed reception deeply disappointed him. In later years, though it was deemed a failure as a coherent whole, many of its individual lyrics were judged among the finest American poems of the century.

Granted a Guggenheim Fellowship, Crane traveled to Mexico City, where he wrote "The Broken Tower" (1932). Alcoholic, blocked in his writing, and despondent over his homosexuality, on his return journey he jumped from the ship into the Caribbean and drowned. His *Collected Poems* appeared in 1933; *The Complete Poems and Selected Letters and Prose* (1966) incorporated previously uncollected writings.

Crane, R(onald S(almon) (b. Jan. 5, 1886, Tecumseh, Mich.—d. July 12, 1967, Chicago) Critic and leading figure of the Chicago school.

Educated at the Universities of Michigan and Pennsylvania, Crane later taught at Northwestern University and then for many years at the University of Chicago (1935–52). His landmark book *The Languages of Criticism and the Structure of Poetry* (1953) formed the theoretical basis of the Chicago school of criticism. Though Crane was an outspoken opponent of the New Criticism, he argued persuasively for a humanistic pluralism that values separate, even contradictory, critical schools. In addition to publishing many journal articles, he edited the influential *Critics and Criticism: Ancient and Modern* (1952). Much of his writing was collected in *The Idea of the Humanities* (1967) and *Critical and Historical Principles of Literary History* (1971).

Crane, Stephen (b. Nov. 1, 1871, Newark, N.J.—d. June 5, 1900, Badenweiler, Baden, Germany) Author most famous for THE RED BADGE OF COURAGE.

Crane had finished only one full year of college before he moved to New York City, where his exploration of the slums led to *Maggie: A Girl of the Streets* (1893), a sympathetic, uncompromisingly realistic study of a slum girl's descent into prostitution and eventual suicide. Its subject was so shocking that Crane published it under a pseudonym and at his own expense. He struggled as a poor and unknown freelance journalist until he was befriended by Hamlin Garland and William Dean Howells, with whose encouragement he wrote and published *The Red Badge of Courage* (1895), a subtle, impressionistic study of a young Civil War soldier, which brought him international fame.

Crane's first attempt, in 1897, to report on the insurrection in Cuba ended in near-disaster when the ship on which he was traveling sank, and Crane—reported drowned—finally rowed into shore in a dinghy with the captain, cook, and oiler. The result was one of the world's great short stories, THE OPEN BOAT (1898). He was soon traveling to Greece to report on the Greco-Turkish War for the *New York Journal*, and later to Cuba to report on the Spanish-American War for the *New York World* and later the *Journal*. Afterwards he settled in Sussex, England, married an older woman, and entertained extravagantly. He died at 28 of tuberculosis exacerbated by recurrent malarial fever contracted in Cuba.

For his collections *The Monster* (1988) and *Whilomville Stories* (1900), Crane is acknowledged as a master of the short story. THE BLUE HOTEL shows his skill with a reportorial style, while THE BRIDE COMES TO YELLOW SKY shows his lighter side. His poetry, particularly the volume *The Black Riders* (1895), is notable for its stark imagery and free form.

***

Crawford, F(rancis) Marion (b. Aug. 2, 1854, Bagni de Lucca, Grand Duchy of Tuscany [Italy]—d. April 9, 1909, Sorrento, Italy) Novelist.

Born to American expatriates in Italy, Crawford spent his youth being shuttled between Italy and America. Though he later chose to live in Italy, he remained a U.S. citizen. While attending several European universities, he became acquainted with their countries. A stay in India provided the inspiration for *Mr. Isaacs* (1882); the tale of a diamond merchant whose sale of a unique stone brings protest from Britain, it marked the beginning of Crawford's prosperous career. Dismissive of the serious instruction often presented in realistic fiction, he preferred to write romantic entertainment. In spite of its lack of depth, his work is noted for its versatile portrayals of European settings in all their richness and color. His best works are set in Italy; they include *Saracinesca* (1887), *Sant' Ilario* (1889), and *Don Orsino* (1892), part of a series about the effect of social change on an Italian family in the late 19th century.

***

Creeley, Robert (White) (b. May 21, 1926, Arlington, Mass.) Poet and founder of the Black Mountain poets.

Creeley attended Harvard University and later earned a master's degree from the University of New Mexico. He lived in Europe in the early 1950s, publishing his early poems in small magazines. In Majorca, Spain, he started the Divers Press. In 1955 he was invited onto the faculty of the experimental Black Mountain College and became the founding editor of the important but short-lived *Black Mountain Review*.

In *For Love* (1962), Creeley emerged as a master technician. Extremely prolific, he has since published over 60 verse collections; his later volumes include *Windows* (1990), *So There* (1998), and *Life and Death* (1998). His verse is noted for its emotional directness expressed in natural speech rhythms. In 1999 he was awarded the Bollingen Prize. For some 30 years (from 1964) he taught at SUNY–Buffalo.

***

Crèvecoeur \krev-'kœr\, **Michel-Guillaume-Saint-Jean de** *pseudonym*
J. Hector St. John de Crèvecoeur (b. Jan. 31, 1735, Caen, France—d. Nov. 12,
1813, Sarcelles, France) French-American author and naturalist whose work provides a broad picture of 18th-century life in the New World.

After spending four years as an officer and mapmaker in Canada, Crèvecoeur began wandering the Ohio and Great Lakes region. He took out citizenship
papers in New York in 1765 and became a farmer in Orange County. Torn
between the two factions in the American Revolution, he languished for months
in an English army prison before sailing for Europe in 1780. In London he published 12 essays as *Letters from an American Farmer* (1782); the book became
very popular and went through many editions.

Returning to America as French consul to three of the new American states,
he found his home burned, his wife dead, and his daughter and second son with
strangers in Boston. After reuniting with his children, he set about organizing a
packet service between the United States and France. Recalled from his consulship in 1790, he wrote *Travels in Upper Pennsylvania and New York* (1801), and
thereafter lived quietly in France and Germany until his death.

Crèvecoeur was for a time the most widely read commentator on America.
His reputation increased in the 1920s when a bundle of his unpublished English
essays discovered in an attic in France was brought out as *Sketches of Eighteenth
Century America* (1925).

Crews, Frederick C(ampbell) (b. Feb. 20, 1933, Philadelphia) Literary critic
who first supported and then turned against psychoanalytic principles.

Crews attended Yale and Princeton universities (Ph.D. 1958), and thereafter taught at UC–Berkeley for his entire career. He first attracted notice in academic circles with a controversial book of criticism, *The Sins of the Fathers*
(1966), in which he claimed that Nathaniel Hawthorne's work has little value
unless read on a Freudian level. Over the next two decades his doubts about psychoanalysis and Freud grew; *Out of My System* (1975) was a witty defense of the
psychoanalytic method that acknowledged its shortcomings, but *Skeptical
Engagements* (1986) was a salvo against psychoanalysis and a stinging indictment of Freud as little more than a charlatan. *Memory Wars* (1995) and *Unauthorized Freud* (1998) took the "psychoanalysis wars" even further. His less
contentious works include *The Pooh Perplex* (1963), a collection of parodic
scholarly journal articles, its sequel *Postmodern Pooh* (2001), and *The Random
House Handbook* (1974), a perennial text on rhetoric and grammar.

Crichton \'krī-t°n\, **(John) Michael** (b. Oct. 23, 1942, Chicago) Science-
fiction writer, screenwriter, and film director.

Crichton graduated from Harvard University and earned his medical degree
there in 1969, the year his first novel, *The Andromeda Strain,* was published
(film, 1971). His subsequent books, most of them runaway best-sellers, include

The Terminal Man (1972; film, 1974), *The Great Train Robbery* (1975; film, 1979), *Eaters of the Dead* (1976; film, 1999), *Congo* (1980; film, 1995), *Sphere* (1987; film, 1998), *Jurassic Park* (1990; film 1993), *Rising Sun* (1992; film, 1993), *Disclosure* (1994; film, 1994), *The Lost World* (1995; film, 1997), *Airframe* (1996), and *Timeline* (1999). He was the screenwriter and director of the films *Westworld* (1973), *Coma* (1978), *The Great Train Robbery* (1979), *Looker* (1981), and *Runaway* (1984). His greatly popular television series *ER* premiered in 1994. Crichton also writes under the pseudonyms Jeffery Hudson, John Lange, and (with his brother Douglas) Michael Douglas.

Davy Crockett

Crockett, Davy (*originally* David) (b. Aug. 17, 1786, eastern Tennessee—d. March 6, 1836, San Antonio, Texas) Frontiersman and politician.

Crockett grew up in the backwoods of Tennessee and fought ably in the Creek War (1813–15). In 1821 he was elected to the Tennessee legislature, winning popularity with campaign speeches larded with yarns and homespun metaphors. He later twice served in the U.S. House of Representatives (1827–31, 1833–35). Attempting to offset Andrew Jackson's popularity, the Whig Party promoted Crockett as a "coonskin" politician and sent him on a speaking tour of the East. The many stories about him in books and newspapers led to the legend of an eccentric but shrewd "b'ar hunter" and Indian fighter, though Crockett actually delivered his speeches in fairly conventional English and engaged in several business ventures. His *Autobiography* (1834; with Thomas Chilton), which emphasized his backwoods years and said little about politics, helped introduce a new style of vigorous, realistic writing into American literature.

In 1835 he headed west to Texas to join the American forces in the war against Mexico and was killed at the Alamo.

Croly \\'krō-lē\\, **Herbert (David)** (b. Jan. 23, 1869, New York City—d. May 17, 1930, New York City) Author, editor, and political philosopher, founder of the *New Republic*.

The son of well-known journalists, Croly was educated intermittently at Harvard University (finally receiving his B.A. in 1910) and spent his early adult years editing and contributing to architectural journals. His books *The Promise of American Life* (1909) and *Progressive Democracy* (1914) strongly influenced Theodore Roosevelt and the Woodrow Wilson administration. In 1914 he founded the liberal *New Republic*, "A Journal of Opinion" which he would edit until his death. In its pages he attacked American complacency and argued that democratic institutions must constantly be revised to suit changing situations. His opposition to the Treaty of Versailles for its vindictiveness cost the *New Republic* half its circulation, but was later seen to be vindicated in the rise of Nazi Germany.

Crosby, Harry (Grew) (b. June 4, 1898, Boston—d. Dec. 10, 1929, New York City) Poet who, as an expatriate in Paris in the 1920s, established the Black Sun Press.

Born into a wealthy Boston family, the nephew of J. P. Morgan, he barely escaped death as an ambulance-corps volunteer in World War I, and received the Croix de Guerre. After attending Harvard, he married and settled in Paris, joining the circle of American literary expatriates and pursuing a dilettantish and dissolute but literary life. In 1927 he and his wife, Caresse, began publishing their own poetry under the imprint Éditions Narcisse, later renamed the Black Sun Press. The following year they started printing books by other writers, including Archibald MacLeish, D. H. Lawrence, and James Joyce. Crosby's poetry, which unconsciously traced literary tradition from 19th-century Romanticism to automatic writing, is not highly regarded. The collection *Chariot of the Sun* (1928) and his unusual diaries, *Shadows of the Sun* (1928–30), demonstrate his obsessive, mystical sun worship. Often morbid and rebellious, and long known for bizarre behavior, he took his own life, with one of his many lovers, in an apparent double suicide pact.

Cross, Amanda See **Carolyn Heilbrun**

Crothers \ˈkrəth-ərz\, **Rachel** (b. Dec. 12, 1878, Bloomington, Ill.—d. July 5, 1958, Danbury, Conn.) Playwright who dramatized the position of women in American society more accurately than any of her contemporaries.

After graduating from the Illinois State Normal School, Crothers studied dramatic art in Boston and New York, where she also began acting. Her career as a playwright began in 1906 with the success of *The Three of Us*. For the next three decades, until *Susan and God* (1937; film, 1940), Broadway saw an average of one new Crothers play each year, most of them popular and critical successes, an achievement unequaled by any other woman.

Crothers chronicled, sometimes seriously but more often humorously, such issues as the double standard (*A Man's World*, 1909), trial marriage (*Young Wisdom*, 1914), the problems of the younger generation (*Nice People*, 1921), Freudianism (*Expressing Willie*, 1924), and divorce (*As Husbands Go*, 1931; *When Ladies Meet*, 1932, films, 1933, 1941). These and other successes were marked by simple plots, happy endings, and expert dialogue. She consistently advocated rationality and moderation. She took full responsibility for the entire production of almost all her plays, casting and directing many of the leading stars of the time. Her dramatic theory is stated best in the essay "The Construction of a Play," collected in *The Art of Playwriting* (1928).

Crumley, James (b. Oct. 12, 1939, Three Rivers, Texas) Detective novelist.

Crumley attended Georgia Institute of Technology and the University of Iowa Writers' Workshop. His experiences in the army (1958–61) are reflected in the Vietnam War novel *One to Count Cadence* (1969). After 1969, apart from occasional pieces of journalism and the short stories collected in *The Muddy Fork and Other Things* (1991), he has devoted himself to detective novels.

His down-and-out detectives, Milo Milodragovitch and C. W. Sughrue, work in the fictional mountain city of Meriwether, Montana. His first detective novel, *The Wrong Case* (1975), featured Milodragovitch; *The Last Good Kiss* (1978) introduced Sughrue. Milodragovitch returned in *Dancing Bear* (1983) and *The Final Country* (2001), while Sughrue was at the center of *The Mexican Tree Duck* (1993). The two team up for a road trip in *Bordersnakes* (1996). While the plots of Crumley's novels are conventional, the quality of his writing, his recurring comedy, and his emphasis on cataclysmic climaxes are distinctive.

Cullen \\ˈkəl-ən\\, **Countee** *originally* Countee Porter (b. May 30, 1903, Louisville, Ky.?—d. Jan. 9, 1946, New York City) Poet of the Harlem Renaissance.

Reared in New York City, he was unofficially adopted at 15 by the Reverend F. A. Cullen, minister of one of Harlem's largest congregations. Academic honors came easily to him, and he won a citywide poetry contest as a schoolboy. Major literary magazines began accepting his poems regularly, and his first collection, *Color* (1925), which includes the powerful YET DO I MARVEL, was published to critical acclaim before he finished his studies at NYU. After receiving an M.A. from Harvard, he worked as an editor for *Opportunity* magazine. The collection *The Black Christ* (1929) was criticized by blacks for not giving race the attention it had in *Color*. Most notable among Cullen's other works are the collections *Copper Sun* (1927), *The Ballad of the Brown Girl* (1928), with its famous title poem, and *The Medea and Some Poems* (1935). The play *St. Louis Woman* (1946) was written with Arna Bontemps. *One Way to Heaven* (1932) is a novel about Harlem. Cullen also wrote two volumes of children's stories. From 1934 until the end of his life, he taught in the New York City public schools.

Cummings, E(dward) E(stlin) (b. Oct. 14, 1894, Cambridge, Mass.—d. Sept. 3, 1962, North Conway, N.H.) Poet and painter.

After earning bachelor's and master's degrees from Harvard, Cummings served with an ambulance corps in wartime France, where he was interned six months in a detention camp over a misunderstanding with French authorities, an experience which formed the basis for his first book, the admired prose work *The Enormous Room* (1922). In the 1920s and '30s he divided his time between Paris, where he studied art, and New York. His first book of verse, *Tulips and Chimneys* (1923), was soon followed by *XLI Poems* (1925), *&* (1925), and *Is 5* (1926), all signed with the lowercase "e. e. cummings." Unorthodox in their capitalization and punctuation, and highly experimental in their style and diction, most of the poems were celebrations of the possibilities of life and love in the truly vital individual, while others savaged the soulless and conformist "unman."

In 1927 Cummings's play *him* was produced by the Provincetown Players. Though he exhibited his paintings and drawings, they failed to attract as much critical interest as his writings. His experimental prose work *Eimi* (1933) recorded a visit to the Soviet Union that confirmed his repugnance for collectivism. The lectures he delivered as the Charles Eliot Norton lecturer on poetry at Harvard were published as *i: six nonlectures* (1953). He received the Bollingen Prize in 1957.

Cummings's 12 volumes of verse, reprinted in his *Complete Poems* (2 vols., 1968), exhibit moods alternately satirical and tough or tender and whimsical; the erotic poetry and love lyrics have a childlike candor and freshness.

Cunningham, J(ames) V(incent) (b. Aug. 23, 1911, Cumberland, Md.— d. March 30, 1985, Waltham, Mass.) Poet and antimodernist literary critic.

Cunningham studied poetry with Yvor Winters at Stanford University and taught at several colleges before settling at Brandeis University in 1953. *The Helmsman* (1942) and *The Judge Is Fury* (1947) offer a mix of his early and mature poetry. In *The Quest of the Opal* (1950) he explains why he came to reject the modernism of his early verse.

In the 1950s he wrote two volumes of epigrams, *Doctor Drink* (1950) and *Trivial, Vulgar and Exalted* (1957). *To What Strangers, What Welcome* (1964) is a sequence of short poems about his travels through the West. Among his other verse collections are *The Exclusions of a Rhyme* (1960), *Some Salt* (1967), and *Collected Poems and Epigrams* (1971); he also published a volume of *Collected Essays* (1976).

Cunningham, Michael (b. Nov. 6, 1952, Cincinnati) Novelist and short-story writer.

Cunningham attended Stanford University and received an M.F.A. from the University of Iowa. From 1986 he worked for the Carnegie Corporation in New York. His first short story appeared in the *Atlantic* in 1981. His first novel, *Golden States,* was published in 1984. With his second novel, *A Home at the End of the World* (1990), whose gay characters appear within a context of family life, he became noted as a major gay writer. His later novels are *Flesh and Blood* (1995) and *The Hours* (1998, Pulitzer Prize). His short stories and essays have appeared in such magazines as the *New Yorker, Redbook,* and the *Paris Review.*

Curtis, George William (b. Feb. 24, 1824, Providence, R.I.—d. Aug. 31, 1892, Staten Island, N.Y.) Author, editor, and leader in civil-service reform.

Early in life Curtis spent two years at the Brook Farm community and school, and he later traveled in Europe, Egypt, and Palestine. In 1850 he joined the *New York Tribune.* As a result of his travels, he became a popular lecturer and published *Nile Notes of a Howadji* (1851) and *The Howadji in Syria* (1852). As an editor of *Putnam's Monthly Magazine* and author of the "Lounger" column in *Harper's Weekly* and the "Easy Chair" column in *Harper's Magazine*, he wrote prolifically. Collections of his essays include *The Potiphar Papers* (1853) and *Prue and I* (1856). In 1863 he became political editor of *Harper's Weekly*, and from 1871 until his death he led the movement for civil-service reform, force-fully denouncing the evils of the political patronage system. In 1890 he became Chancellor of the University of New York.

Daly \\'dā-lē\\, **(John) Augustin** (b. July 20, 1838, Plymouth, N.C.—d. June 7, 1899, Paris) Playwright and theatrical manager.

From 1859 Daly was drama critic for several New York newspapers. *Leah the Forsaken*, adapted from a German play in 1862, was his first success as a playwright. His first important original play, *Under the Gaslight* (1867), was the first to feature a character bound to railroad tracks in the face of an oncoming train. In 1869 he formed his own company, and he later developed such outstanding actresses as Fanny Davenport and Maude Adams. His best play, *Horizon* (1871), drew heavily on the Western-type characters of Bret Harte and fostered the development of a drama based on American themes and characters rather than on European models. *Divorce* (1871) ran for 200 performances. After Daly's Theatre opened in New York in 1879, with a company headed by John Drew and Ada Rehan, Daly confined himself to adaptations and management. In 1893 he opened Daly's Theatre in London.

D

Dana, Richard Henry (b. Aug. 1, 1815, Cambridge, Mass.—d. Jan. 6, 1882, Rome, Italy) Lawyer and author of TWO YEARS BEFORE THE MAST.

Richard Henry Dana

Dana withdrew from Harvard College when measles weakened his eyesight, and he shipped to California as a sailor in 1834 to regain his health. After voyaging among California's ports, he rounded Cape Horn, returned home in 1836, and reentered Harvard. In 1840, the year of his admission to the bar, he published *Two Years Before the Mast*, a personal narrative that revealed the abuses endured by sailors. In 1841 he published *The Seaman's Friend*, an authoritative guide to the legal rights and duties of seamen. Against vigorous opposition in Boston, he gave free legal aid to blacks captured under the Fugitive Slave Law. In 1863, as U.S. attorney for Massachusetts, he won before the U.S. Supreme Court the case of the *Amy Warwick*, securing the right of Union forces to blockade Southern ports without giving the Confederate states international status as belligerents. His scholarly edition of Henry Wheaton's *Elements of International Law* (1866) precipitated a lawsuit by an earlier editor. Charges of plagiarism contributed to Dana's defeat in the 1868 congressional election and caused the Senate to refuse his confirmation when President Grant nominated him as minister to Britain in 1876. Among Dana's other works are *To Cuba and Back* (1859), *Speeches in Stirring Times* (1910), and *An Autobiographical Sketch* (1953), the last two published posthumously.

Davenport, Guy *originally* Guy Mattison Davenport, Jr. (b. Nov. 23, 1927, Anderson, S.C.) Writer, scholar, and illustrator.

Davenport graduated from Duke University, studied at Oxford as a Rhodes scholar, and received his doctorate from Harvard. He spent 27 years on the faculty at the University of Kentucky, retiring in 1991. He established himself early as a writer of great erudition, and he tends to weave copious recondite allusions into his fiction with an elegant lightness of touch and considerable humor. His first and best-received story collection, *Tatlin!* (1974), was heavily influenced by the works of Ezra Pound, on whom Davenport is an authority. His short stories, many of them homoerotic, have appeared in such collections as *Da Vinci's Bicycle* (1979), *Eclogues* (1981), *Apples and Pears* (1984), *A Table of Green Fields* (1993), and *The Cardiff Team* (1996). The essays and reviews collected in *The Geography of the Imagination* (1981) cover a wide variety of subjects; the essay collection *Objects on a Table* (1998) is devoted to still-life painting. Davenport has made many admired translations of the poets of ancient Greece and has illustrated several books, including Hugh Kenner's *Stoic Comedians* and his own *Apples and Pears*. Though greatly admired by many critics, his work has never been embraced by a large audience.

Davidson, Donald (Grady) (b. Aug. 18, 1893, Campbellsville, Tenn.—d. April 25, 1968, Nashville, Tenn.) Poet, essayist, and teacher.

While attending Vanderbilt University (M.A., 1922), Davidson joined the Fugitives, a group of Southern writers determined to preserve their region's distinctive literature and rural economy, and joined them in publishing the journal *The Fugitive* (1922–25) and the essay collection *I'll Take My Stand* (1930). In time his fellow Fugitives—including Robert Penn Warren, Allen Tate, and John Crowe Ransom—altered their views, but Davidson, who taught many years at Vanderbilt, remained passionately devoted to his early ideals. In his verse collections, including *The Tall Men* (1927) and *Lee in the Mountains* (1938), and his prose, including *The Attack on Leviathan* (1938), *Why the Modern South Has a Great Literature* (1951), and *Still Rebels, Still Yankees, and Other Essays* (1957), he praised historic Southern heroes, defended racial segregation, and warned against the evils of industrialism, which he saw as the enemy of spiritual values. *The Tennessee* (2 vols., 1946, 1948) is a history of the Tennessee River valley.

Davis, H(arold) L(enoir) (b. Oct. 18, 1896, Yoncalla, Ore.—d. Oct. 31, 1960, San Antonio, Texas) Novelist and poet whose realistic portraits of the West rejected the stereotype of the cowboy as hero.

Davis worked as a cowboy, a typesetter, and a surveyor before being noticed for his writing. He first received recognition for his poems, written in the style of the 19th-century German Detlev von Liliencron. Later he was encouraged by H. L. Mencken to try prose, and the results appeared in *American Mercury*. In 1932 a Guggenheim Fellowship made it possible for him to go to Mexico, where he remained to write the novel *Honey in the Horn* (1935, Pulitzer Prize), which secured his reputation. His later books include *Beulah Land* (1949) and *The Distant Music* (1957). Mistrustful of heroics, Davis instead wrote realistically of the problems facing frontier men and women.

Davis, Richard Harding (b. April 18, 1864, Philadelphia—d. April 11, 1916, Mount Kisco, N.Y.) Author of romantic novels and short stories, and the best-known reporter of his generation.

Davis studied at Lehigh and Johns Hopkins universities and in 1886 became a reporter on the *Philadelphia Record*. His colorful and sensational reporting earned him jobs with other newspapers in Philadelphia and New York, and in 1890 he became managing editor of *Harper's Weekly*. On assignments for *Harper's*, he toured various parts of the globe; his impressions of the American West, Europe, and South America led to a series of books from 1892 to 1896. As a war correspondent he reported on every war from the Greco-Turkish war of 1897 to World War I. He defied rules in order to join in the Battle of San Juan Hill in the Spanish-American War and was nearly shot as a spy in World War I. His early collections of stories achieved immediate success, particularly *Gallegher* (1891), *Van Bibber and Others* (1892), and *Ranson's Folly* (1902). Many of his works were illustrated by Charles Dana Gibson. He produced seven novels between 1897 and 1909, all of which met with success. Several of his 25 plays were also very successful, notably *Ranson's Folly* (1904), *The Dictator* (1904), and *Miss Civilization* (1906).

Day, Clarence *originally* Clarence Shepard Day, Jr. (b. Nov. 18, 1874, New York City—d. Dec. 28, 1935, New York City) Writer, author of the autobiographical *Life with Father*.

Educated at Yale, Day joined his father's brokerage firm as a partner. He enlisted in the navy the following year but was stricken by arthritis, which left him an invalid the rest of his life. In 1920 he published his first book, *This Simian World*, a collection of humorous essays and illustrations; it was followed by *The Crow's Nest* (1921) and *Thoughts Without Words* (1928). For many years Day was a regular contributor to the *New Yorker*. He achieved his greatest success with *God and My Father* (1932) and *Life with Father* (1935), pleasant and gently satirical portraits (drawn from his own family experiences) of a late-Victorian household dominated by a gruff, opinionated father and a warm, charming mother. Dramatized by Howard Lindsay and Russel Crouse in 1939 (film, 1947), *Life with Father* enjoyed the longest Broadway run of any play up to its time. *Life with Mother* (1937) and *Father and I* (1940) were published posthumously.

Clarence Day

---

de Camp \də-'kamp\, **L(yon) Sprague** (b. 1907, New York City—d. Nov. 6, 2000, Plano, Texas) Science-fiction and fantasy writer.

De Camp attended the California Institute of Technology, received a master's degree from Stevens Institute of Technology, and served in World War II before beginning to write full-time. He wrote some 120 books, a number of them with other authors such as Fletcher Pratt, and influenced the science-fiction genre by including ordinary people and settings in his stories. *Lest Darkness Fall*

(1941), about time travel, is perhaps his best-known work. His later novels include *The Wheels of If* (1948), *Rogue Queen* (1951), *Cosmic Manhunt* (1954), *The Glory That Was* (1960), *The Arrow of Hercules* (1965), *Tales Beyond Time* (1973), *The Great Fetish* (1978), *The Prisoner of Zhamanak* (1982), and *Rivers of Time* (1993). With Robert E. Howard and others, he wrote a series of books featuring the swashbuckling Conan, beginning with *Tales of Conan* (1955). From the 1960s, he cowrote some of his books with his wife, Catherine Crook de Camp. *Time and Chance* (1996) is an autobiography.

DeForest, John William (b. May 31, 1826, Humphreysville, Conn.—d. July 17, 1906, New Haven, Conn.) Novelist, memoirist, and travel writer.

DeForest's travels in the Middle East (1848–49) inspired the travel book *Oriental Acquaintance* (1856), and a sojourn in Europe (1851–54) resulted in *European Acquaintance* (1858). When the Civil War broke out, he organized a company of volunteers and served as captain in several Union campaigns. After the war, he was district commander of the Freedmen's Bureau in Greenville, S.C. (1866–67). His records of those experiences were published decades after his death as *A Volunteer's Adventures* (1946) and *A Union Officer in the Reconstruction* (1948).

DeForest is best known for *Miss Ravenel's Conversion from Secession to Loyalty* (1867), a major novel of the Civil War. His other novels include *Kate Beaumont* (1872), which depicts South Carolina's prewar social life; *The Bloody Chasm* (1881), which deals with postwar social life; *Honest John Vane* (1875) and *Playing the Mischief* (1875), which deal with the corruption of President Grant's administration; and *A Lover's Revolt* (1898), a romance of the American Revolution.

Margaret Deland

Deland \di-ˈland\, **Margaret** *originally* Margaretta Wade Campbell (b. Feb. 23, 1857, Allegheny, Pa.—d. Jan. 13, 1945, Boston) Novelist and short-story writer.

She studied design and in 1876 became a drawing instructor at the Female Normal College of New York. She married in 1880 and thereafter lived with her husband in Boston. The couple took up the cause of unwed mothers, taking in some 60 women and infants in four years. In 1886 Deland published the verse collection *The Old Garden*. Her first novel, *John Ward, Preacher* (1888), depicts the irreconcilable conflict between a Calvinist minister and his wife, who cannot accept the doctrine of eternal damnation. Deland's most popular works were a nostalgic series of stories set in the fictional small town of Old Chester (based on the town where she was raised), collected in *Old Chester Tales* (1898), *Dr. Lavendar's People* (1903), *Around Old Chester* (1915), and *New Friends in Old Chester* (1924). Several other works dealt with such issues as divorce, feminism, and adultery. She also wrote a volume of childhood memories, *If This Be I* (1935), and an autobiography, *Golden Yesterdays* (1941).

Delany \də-ˈlā-nē\, **Martin R(obinson)** (b. May 6, 1812, Charles Town, Va. [now W.Va.]—d. Jan. 24, 1885, Xenia, Ohio) Writer and activist whose dedication to the cause of black nationalism in the pre–Civil War era marked him as a thinker ahead of his time.

Born to free parents, Delany was educated illegally during a period when black literacy was prohibited by law. He began the study of medicine in Philadelphia, where he first formed the Pan-Africanist views that confused and angered many of his contemporaries, including fellow blacks. In 1843 he began publishing a small paper, the *Mystery*. From 1847 until 1849, he was a coeditor with Frederick Douglass of the antislavery newspaper *North Star*.

In his most important work, *The Condition, Elevation, Emigration, and Destiny of the Colored People of the United States* (1852), Delany urged blacks to be financially and intellectually self-reliant. In 1859 he traveled to the Niger River valley, the homeland of his maternal grandfather, as well as London and Liverpool. *Blake; or, The Huts of America* (1861–62), his only novel, was one of the first novels by a black American to be published in the United States. Though it received little critical attention, it was revived in the 1960s and hailed as an early model for black consciousness and activism. During the Civil War Delany served as a major in the Union army; after the war he worked variously as a custom-house inspector, a trial justice, and in the Freedmen's Bureau. He published a treatise on race in 1879, and in his last years conducted business in Central America.

Delany, Samuel R(ay, Jr.) (b. April 1, 1942, New York City) Science-fiction novelist and critic whose highly imaginative works address racial and sexual issues and the nature of language.

A descendant of Martin Delany, he grew up in Harlem, attended CCNY, and published his first novel, *The Jewels of Aptor* (1962), when he was 19. *Babel-17* (1966, Nebula Award), which secured his reputation, explores the nature of language and its ability to give structure to experience. *The Einstein Intersection* (1967, Nebula Award) addresses issues of cultural development and sexual identity. It was followed by the novellas *The Star-Pit* (1967, Hugo Award) and *Lines of Power* (1968, Hugo and Nebula Awards) and the novel *Nova* (1968, Hugo Award). In *Dhalgren* (1974, Nebula Award), a young bisexual man searches for identity in a large, decaying city. In 1979 Delany began his elaborate *Return to Nevèryön* series, set in a magical past at the beginning of civilization. Later works include *Triton* (1976, Nebula Award), *Stars in My Pocket Like Grains of Sand* (1984), *The Mad Man* (1994), and *Atlantis* (1995). Delany's nonfiction works include *The Jewel-Hinged Jaw* (1977), *The American Shore* (1978), and *The Motion of Light in Water* (1988, Hugo Award). He has also written scripts for film, radio, and *Wonder Woman* comic books.

DeLillo \di-ˈlil-ō\, **Don** (b. Nov. 20, 1936, New York City) Postmodernist novelist.

Born in the Bronx to immigrant parents, DeLillo graduated from Fordham University and worked in advertising until the early 1960s, when he quit to devote his time to writing. His first novel, *Americana* (1971), is the story of a network television executive in search of the "real" America. It was followed by *End Zone* (1972) and *Great Jones Street* (1973). *Ratner's Star* (1976) attracted critical attention with its baroque comic sense and verbal facility.

His vision later turned darker and his characters more willful in their destructiveness and ignorance. Critics found little to like in the protagonists of *Players* (1977), *Running Dog* (1978), and *The Names* (1982), but much to admire in DeLillo's elliptic prose. *White Noise* (1985, American Book Award) tells of a professor of Hitler Studies who is exposed to an "airborne toxic event"; discovering that his wife is taking an experimental substance to combat the fear of death, he vows to obtain the drug for himself. *Libra* (1988) is a fictional portrayal of Lee Harvey Oswald. Later novels include *Mao II* (1991, PEN/Faulkner Award), about a writer enmeshed in political violence, *Underworld* (1997), about 1950s America, and *The Body Artist* (2001). In 1999 DeLillo became the first American to win the prestigious Jerusalem Prize.

Dell, Floyd (b. June 28, 1887, Barry, Ill.—d. July 23, 1969, Bethesda, Md.) Novelist and radical journalist whose fiction examined the political and sexual mores of American bohemians before and after World War I.

Dell moved to Chicago in 1908, where he worked as a newspaperman and soon became a leader of the city's literary movement. From 1909 he edited the *Friday Literary Review* of the *Evening Post*, making it one of the country's most noted literary supplements. As a critic, he furthered the careers of Sherwood Anderson and Theodore Dreiser.

A socialist from his youth, he moved to New York in 1914 to become associate editor of the *Masses* until 1917, thereafter working for its successor, the *Liberator*, until 1924. In 1918 he was indicted for conspiring to obstruct military recruiting, but two trials ended with hung juries.

His first and best novel, the autobiographical *Moon-Calf*, appeared in 1920, and a sequel, *The Briary-Bush*, in 1921. His other novels of life among the unconventional include *Janet March* (1923), *Runaway* (1925), and *Love in Greenwich Village* (1926). His nonfiction works include *Were You Ever a Child?* (1919), on child rearing; a biography of Upton Sinclair; *Love in the Machine Age* (1930), about sex; and his autobiography, *Homecoming* (1933).

Dennie, Joseph (b. Aug. 30, 1768, Boston—d. Jan. 7, 1812, Philadelphia) Essayist and editor.

Dennie graduated from Harvard and together with Royall Tyler formed a literary partnership; under the pseudonyms Colon and Spondee, they began contributing satirical pieces to local newspapers. Between 1792 and 1802 Dennie wrote his "Farrago" essays in various periodicals. He edited the *Farmer's Weekly*

Museum from 1796 to 1798, contributing the series of graceful, moralizing "Lay Preacher" essays that established his literary reputation.

He was personal secretary to Secretary of State Timothy Pickering in 1799–1800. In 1801, with Asbury Dickins, he founded the *Port Folio*, which became the most distinguished American literary weekly of its time; he himself contributed "Lay Preacher" essays while commissioning work from other prominent writers. As founder of the Tuesday Club, he was at the center of Philadelphia's aristocratic literary circle and for a time the nation's leading literary arbiter. He derided American rusticity and crudity, praised English literature, manners, and sophistication, advocated sound critical standards, and encouraged talented younger writers, such as Washington Irving.

Denton, Daniel (d. c.1696) Public official and historian.

Denton's father emigrated to Massachusetts in 1630, then moved to Long Island, where Daniel presumably grew up. He inherited land around New York City and became a magistrate of the town of Jamaica (now a borough of New York). After the English took New York from the Dutch in 1664, he became justice of Long Island (1666–86). His *Brief Description of New York* (1670), written to explain colonizing opportunities to Englishmen, gives an accurate description of contemporary New York and of the customs of the Indians and is the first work in English to praise America as a land of economic promise.

Deutsch \'dȯich\, **Babette** (b. Sept. 22, 1895, New York City—d. Nov. 13, 1982, New York City) Poet, critic, translator, and novelist.

Deutsch began publishing poems in such magazines as the *North American Review* and *New Republic* while a student at Barnard College, and she would subsequently teach at Columbia from 1944 until 1971. She first attracted critical notice for her poetry with *Banners* (1919), whose title poem celebrated the Russian Revolution of 1917. Her later poetry collections include *Honey Out of the Rock* (1925), Imagist verse on marriage, motherhood, and the arts; *Fire for the Night* (1930); *One Part Love* (1939); and *Take Them, Stranger* (1944) and *Animal, Vegetable, Mineral* (1954), both of which contain antiwar poetry. Her literary collaboration with her husband, Avraham Yarmolinsky, produced acclaimed translations of Russian and German poetry, many of them the first English translations of important works. Her novels include *A Brittle Heaven* (1926), *In Such a Night* (1927), *Mask of Silenus* (1933), and *Rogue's Legacy* (1942), and she produced nonfiction books on Whitman, Shakespeare, and the Finnish *Kalevala*.

De Voto \di-'vō-tō\, **Bernard (Augustine)** (b. Jan. 11, 1897, Ogden, Utah—d. Nov. 13, 1955, New York City) Novelist, journalist, historian, and critic.

After attending the University of Utah and Harvard University, De Voto taught at Northwestern University and then at Harvard (1929–36) and served briefly as editor of the *Saturday Review of Literature* (1936–38) before resigning to return to Cambridge, where he would spend the rest of his life. He wrote a number of novels, some serious (under his own name) and some potboilers (under the pseudonym John August), but he probably found his largest audience through his "Easy Chair" column for *Harper's Magazine*, which he wrote from 1935 until his death. His vigorous, outspoken style combined with sound scholarship made him one of the most widely read critics and historians of his day. His strong opinions and admitted prejudices for American life and culture put him at the center of many critical controversies.

His works on Mark Twain include *Mark Twain's America* (1932), *Mark Twain at Work* (1942), and *Mark Twain in Eruption* (1940). *Across the Wide Missouri* (1948, Pulitzer Prize) was a history of the fur trade in its peak years; it was the second in an acclaimed historical trilogy that began with *The Year of Decision: 1846* (1943) and concluded with *The Course of Empire* (1952, National Book Award). His edition of the journals of Lewis and Clark appeared in 1953.

De Vries \də-'vrēs, də-'vrēz\, **Peter** (b. Feb. 27, 1910, Chicago—d. Sept. 28, 1993, Norwalk, Conn.) Satirist, linguist, and novelist.

The son of Dutch immigrants, De Vries was reared in a Calvinist environment. He graduated from Calvin College during the Depression and worked at odd jobs until landing a position with *Poetry* magazine in Chicago in 1938. From 1944 until 1986 he was on the staff of the *New Yorker*, where he started out producing ideas for its cartoons.

His first novel, *But Who Wakes the Bugler?* (1940), was most notable for having been illustrated by Charles Addams, and his next two novels were hardly noticed at all. His first book of short stories, *No But I Saw the Movie* (1952), won critical acclaim, and his subsequent novel, *The Tunnel of Love* (1954), became a best-seller and was successfully adapted to stage and screen (1958). His novels, which also include *Comfort Me with Apples* (1956), *The Tents of Wickedness* (1959), *Reuben, Reuben* (1964), *Madder Music* (1977), and *Slouching Towards Kalamazoo* (1983), were appreciated for their imaginative wordplay and ironic vision beneath which lay a concern for morality that sprang from his upbringing.

Dewey \'dü-ē, 'dyü-ē\, **John** (b. Oct. 20, 1859, Burlington, Vt.—d. June 1, 1952, New York City) Philosopher, psychologist, and educator.

After receiving his Ph.D. from Johns Hopkins University, Dewey taught at the Universities of Minnesota and Michigan. At the University of Chicago (1894–1904) he taught philosophy, psychology, and pedagogy, and established a laboratory school to test his educational theories, described in *The Child and Society* (1899) and *The Child and the Curriculum* (1902). From 1904 to 1930 he taught at Columbia University, whose Teachers College he led to preeminence in its field.

A principal developer (with William James and C. S. Peirce) of the philosophy of Pragmatism, Dewey became one of the most influential American philosophers of the 20th century. As the leading theorist of the progressive edu-

John Dewey

cation movement, he greatly influenced American educational practice with his antiauthoritarian emphasis on the interests of the child and the use of the classroom to cultivate the interplay between thought and experience. His belief in democracy as a primary ethical value led to his active involvement in such progressive causes as women's suffrage. He was a founder of the American Association of University Professors (1915) and of the New School for Social Research (1919). His many books include *How We Think* (1910); *Democracy and Education* (1916); *Reconstruction in Philosophy* (1920); *Experience and Nature* (1925), considered his magnum opus; *Art as Experience* (1934); *Freedom and Culture* (1939); and *Problems of Men* (1946).

Dick, Philip K(indred) (b. Dec. 16, 1928, Chicago—d. March 2, 1982, Santa Ana, Calif.) Science-fiction writer.

Dick worked briefly in radio after studying at UC–Berkeley for a year. The publication of his first story, "Beyond Lies the Wub," in 1952 launched his full-time writing career. He published his first novel, *Solar Lottery*, three years later. The nature of reality was one of his central preoccupations. In several of his more than 35 novels, including *Time Out of Joint* (1959), the widely admired *The Man in the High Castle* (1962, Hugo Award), and *The Three Stigmata of Palmer Eldritch* (1965), he creates an alternate reality; beginning with *The Simulacra* (1964) and culminating in *Do Androids Dream of Electric Sheep?* (1968; film, *Blade Runner*, 1982), the illusion centers on artificial creatures at large in a real world of the future.

His story collections include *A Handful of Darkness* (1955), *The Variable Man* (1957), *The Preserving Machine* (1969), and the posthumously published *I Hope I Shall Arrive Soon* (1985).

Dickey, James (Lafayette) (b. Feb. 2, 1923, Atlanta, Ga.—d. Jan. 19, 1997, Columbia, S.C.) Poet, novelist, and critic.

Dickey served as a fighter-bomber pilot in the Army Air Forces during World War II. After the war he earned degrees from Vanderbilt University, where he excelled at sports. He subsequently worked as an advertising executive, and from 1968 until his death he taught at the University of South Carolina. He considered himself a man of action, and his poems reflect his interests in hunting, sports, and war. His first poetry collection, *Into the Stone* (1960), was followed by such volumes as *Drowning with Others* (1962), *Helmets* (1964), and *Buckdancer's Choice* (1965). He is best remembered for the immensely successful DELIVERANCE (1970; film, 1972), a novel of survival. Two subsequent novels did less well.

James Dickey

Dickinson, Emily (Elizabeth) (b. Dec. 10, 1830, Amherst, Mass.—d. May 15, 1886, Amherst) Lyric poet noted for her eloquent, concise, and deceptively simple verses.

Granddaughter of a founder of Amherst College and daughter of a respected lawyer and one-term congressman, Dickinson was educated at Amherst Academy and Mount Holyoke Female Seminary. Though she began to write verse around 1850, only a handful of her 1,775 poems can be dated before 1858, when she began to collect them into small, hand-sewn booklets. In the 1850s she began significant literary correspondences with Josiah G. Holland and Samuel Bowles, editors of the local *Springfield Republican* newspaper.

Dickinson's poems of the 1850s are fairly conventional in sentiment and form, but from about 1860 she began to experiment with both language and prosody. She lent complexity to even simple measures by constantly altering the hymnlike metrical beat to fit her thought. She broke new ground in her wide use of off-rhymes. Striving for epigrammatic conciseness, she stripped her language of superfluous words. She also tampered freely with syntax, often placing a familiar word in an extraordinary context. Her letters, some of them equal in artistry to her poems, classicize daily experience in an epigrammatic style.

In 1862 she wrote to Thomas Wentworth Higginson asking his opinion of her work. Though he advised her not to publish, Higginson recognized her originality and remained her "preceptor" for the rest of her life. Only seven poems would be published during her lifetime, five in the *Springfield Republican*.

In 1864 and 1865 persistent eye trouble caused her to seek treatment in Cambridge. Once back in Amherst she never traveled again and after the late 1860s never left the narrow boundaries of the family's property. After the Civil War, she sought increasingly to regulate her life by the rules of art. By 1870 she was dressing only in white and saw few of the callers who came to the homestead, her seclusion being fiercely guarded by her sister.

After Dickinson's death her sister determined to have her poems published. In 1890 *Poems by Emily Dickinson*, edited by Higginson and Mabel Loomis Todd, appeared; further volumes were published between 1891 and 1957. Thomas H. Johnson's 1955 edition of all the surviving poems and their variant versions sparked a major reconsideration of Dickinson's work, and she is today universally regarded as one of the two or three greatest of all American poets.

Dickinson, John (b. Nov. 8, 1732, Talbot County, Md.—d. Feb. 14, 1808, Wilmington, Del.) Colonial leader.

After studying law in London, Dickinson practiced in Philadelphia (1757–60) before entering public life. He represented Pennsylvania in the Stamp Act Congress (1765) and drafted its declaration of rights and grievances. In 1767 he wrote the *Letters from a Farmer in Pennsylvania, to the Inhabitants of the British Colonies*, which helped turn colonial opinion against the Townshend Acts (1767), a new tax to pay the salaries of royal officials in the colonies.

Dickinson was a delegate to the Continental Congress (1774–76) and the principal author of the "Declaration . . . Setting Forth the Causes and Necessity of Their Taking Up Arms." He helped prepare the first draft of the Articles of

Confederation (1776–77) but voted against the Declaration of Independence (1776) because he still hoped for conciliation with the British. Though he was accused of being a Loyalist, he later served in the patriot militia. As a delegate to the Constitutional Convention (1787), he signed the U.S. Constitution and later defended it in a series of letters signed "Fabius."

Didion \\'did-ē-ən\\, **Joan** (b. Dec. 5, 1934, Sacramento, Calif.) Novelist and essayist.

Didion graduated from UC–Berkeley (1956) and worked for *Vogue* magazine from 1956 to 1963, first as a copywriter and later as an editor. Her first novel, *Run River* (1963), examines the disintegration of a California family. In 1964 she met and married the writer John Gregory DUNNE. A collection of magazine columns published as *Slouching Towards Bethlehem* (1968) established her reputation as an essayist and confirmed her preoccupation with the forces of disorder. Didion's fiction, also centering on personal and social unrest, includes the short novels *Play It as It Lays* (1970; film, 1972), *A Book of Common Prayer* (1977), *Democracy* (1984), and *The Last Thing He Wanted* (1996). *The White Album* (1979) is another essay collection. With her husband she has collaborated on numerous screenplays, including *A Star Is Born* (1976) and *True Confessions* (1981).

Dillard \\'dil-ərd\\, **Annie** *originally* Annie Doak (b. April 30, 1945, Pittsburgh) Writer best known for her meditative essays on the natural world.

Dillard received two degrees from Hollins College. Her first book, the poetry collection *Tickets for a Prayer Wheel* (1974), was quickly overshadowed by the highly praised essay collection *Pilgrim at Tinker Creek* (1974, Pulitzer Prize), keen observations of her own habitat that inform and are informed by a questing religious mysticism. *Holy the Firm* (1977) examined the metaphysical aspect of pain, and *Teaching a Stone to Talk* (1982) included further explorations of nature and religion. *Living by Fiction* (1982), *Encounters with Chinese Writers* (1984), and *The Writing Life* (1989) discuss the art of writing. In 1987 she published a best-selling autobiography, *An American Childhood*. Her first novel, *The Living* (1992), is set in the Pacific Northwest at the start of the 20th century. The poems in *Mornings Like This* (1995) were compiled from individual lines of prose from diverse sources. Dillard has taught at Wesleyan University since 1979.

Di Prima \\di-'prē-mə\\, **Diane** (b. Aug. 6, 1934, New York City) Beat poet, one of the few women in the movement to attain prominence.

Di Prima dropped out of Swarthmore College, where she had been studying physics, to participate in the bohemian life of New York's Greenwich Village. Her first book of poetry, *This Kind of Bird Flies Backward*, was published in

1958. In 1961 she and LeRoi Jones (now Amiri Baraka) founded a monthly poetry journal, *Floating Bear*, that would feature the work of such writers as Jack Kerouac and William Burroughs. She later founded two publishing houses that specialized in avant-garde poetry, The Poets Press and Eidolon Editions. In 1974 she helped establish the Naropa Institute in Boulder, Colo.

Despite the social and political turbulence of the era in which she began her career, Di Prima's writing has tended toward the personal, focusing on relationships, her children, and the experiences of everyday life. Much of her later writing has reflected her interests in Eastern religions, alchemy, and female archetypes. Her later collections of poetry include *Loba, Parts 1–8* (1978) and *Pieces of a Song* (1990). She has also published the story collection *Dinners and Nightmares* (1961), the autobiographical *Memoirs of a Beatnik* (1969), and a number of plays, collected in *ZipCode* (1992). In 1983 she founded the Institute of Magical and Healing Arts.

Dixon, Thomas (b. Jan. 11, 1864, Shelby, N.C.—d. April 3, 1946, Raleigh, N.C.) Novelist, dramatist, and legislator who vigorously propagated ideas of white supremacy.

Dixon grew up in straitened circumstances during Reconstruction, fearing black domination and admiring the Ku Klux Klan. He was admitted to the bar in 1886. After a year in the North Carolina legislature, he resigned to become a Baptist minister, and subsequently served in Raleigh, Boston, and New York. In 1899 he retired to a large estate, where he began writing historical novels. His first was *The Leopard's Spots* (1902), but he is chiefly remembered for its sequel, *The Clansman* (1905), a sympathetic picture of the Ku Klux Klan on which D. W. Griffith would later base his landmark film *The Birth of a Nation* (1915). *The Traitor* (1907) completed the trilogy. All three books became best-sellers and enflamed racial hostility. Dixon continued to write novels and plays; as late as 1939 he would publish yet another fictional account of black–white relations, *The Flaming Sword*.

Dobie \\'dō-bē\\, **James Frank** (b. Sept. 26, 1888, Live Oak County, Texas—d. Sept. 18, 1964, Austin, Texas) Folklorist and educator.

Dobie grew up on a ranch and early developed a love for the land and lore of the Southwest. He graduated from Southwestern University and earned an M.A. from Columbia University. He returned from World War I to teach at the University of Texas, where he would remain until his retirement in 1947.

In the 1920s he began collecting the legends and stories of Texas and the Southwest, in what would become a lifelong project. He published over 30 books chronicling the region's history, including *A Vaquero of the Brush Country* (1929), *Coronado's Children* (1931), *Apache Gold and Yaqui Silver* (1939), *The Longhorns* (1941), *Voice of the Coyote* (1949), *Up the Trail from Texas* (1955), and *Cow People* (1964). His weekly column appeared in many Texas newspapers, and he was a leading spokesman for progressivism in the state. In 1964 he was awarded the Presidential Medal of Freedom.

Dobyns \\'däb-inz\\, **Stephen** (b. Feb. 19, 1941, Orange, N.J.) Poet and crime novelist.

Dobyns attended Wayne State University and the University of Iowa, and became a reporter for the *Detroit News* in 1969. From 1973, while writing fiction and poetry, he taught at several colleges and universities. His first collection of poetry, *Concurring Beasts*, appeared in 1971. The next year he published the novel *A Man of Little Evils*, and from then on he alternated between poetry and crime fiction, publishing roughly a book a year. Recent poetry collections include *Cemetery Nights* (1987) and *Velocities* (1994); recent novels include *The Church of Dead Girls* (1997), *Saratoga Strongbox* (1998), and *Boy in the Water* (1999).

Doctorow \\'däk-tə-,rō\\, **E(dgar) L(aurence)** (b. Jan. 6, 1931, New York City) Author of historical novels.

Doctorow graduated from Kenyon College and later attended Columbia University. In 1959 he joined the editorial staff of New American Library, leaving that post five years later to become editor in chief at Dial Press. He subsequently taught at several colleges and universities, including Sarah Lawrence College and NYU.

Most of Doctorow's novels have been major best-sellers. His first, *Welcome to Hard Times* (1960; film, 1967), was a philosophical turn on the western. His next, *Big As Life* (1966), used science fiction to explore the human response to crisis. *The Book of Daniel* (1971; film, *Daniel*, 1983) is a fictionalized treatment of the Rosenberg spy case. *Ragtime* (1975; film, 1981), his most commercially successful work, incorporates actual figures of early-20th-century America. *Loon Lake* (1980), *World's Fair* (1985), and *Billy Bathgate* (1989; film, 1991) examine the Great Depression and its aftermath, and *The Waterworks* (1994) is set in 19th-century New York. In *The City of God* (2000), Einstein and Wittgenstein offer theological opinions as the story unfolds around a cross stolen from a church. Doctorow's books generally illuminate aspects of American social history from a politically progressive perspective.

Dodge, Mary Mapes *originally* Mary Elizabeth Mapes (b. Jan. 26, 1831, New York City—d. Aug. 21, 1905, Onteora Park, N.Y.) Children's author and first editor of *St. Nicholas* magazine.

At 20 she married William Dodge, a lawyer, and they had two sons. To maintain her independence after she was suddenly widowed seven years later, Dodge started writing children's stories. Her first collection, *Irvington Stories* (1864), centered on the American colonial family. The following year she produced the beloved classic HANS BRINKER.

In 1873, in the middle of an economic depression, she was asked to become editor of the new children's magazine *St. Nicholas*. Its subsequent success owed largely to Dodge's high standards, which enabled *St. Nicholas* to attract such contributors as Mark Twain, Bret Harte, Lucretia Peabody Hale, Louisa May Alcott, Robert Louis Stevenson, and Rudyard Kipling.

Dodson, Owen (Vincent) (b. Nov. 28, 1914, Brooklyn, N.Y.—d. June 21, 1983, New York City) Poet, teacher, director, and playwright.

The son of a journalist, Dodson began writing poetry and directing plays while attending Bates College and Yale University. In the navy during World War II he wrote naval-history plays for black seamen; the verse chorale *The Ballad of Dorie Miller* (1943), about a black Navy hero; and the poem "Black Mother Praying in the Summer of 1943," a plea for racial integration. His black-history pageant *New World A-Coming* was performed at Madison Square Garden in 1944. His first poetry collection, *Powerful Long Ladder* (1946), was widely praised. The next year he began teaching at Howard University, where he would remain 20 years. His other works include the novels *Boy at the Window* (1951) and *Come Home Early, Child* (1977) and more than 35 plays and opera librettos; his verse dramas *Divine Comedy* (1938) and *Bayou Legend* (1948) are especially notable. He himself considered *The Confession Stone* (1970), a song cycle about Jesus often performed as an Easter play, to be his masterpiece.

Donleavy \ˌdən-ˈlē-vē, ˈdən-ˌle-vē, ˈdän-ˌle-vē\, **J(ames) P(atrick)** (b. April 23, 1926, Brooklyn, N.Y.) American-Irish author of the lusty comic novel *The Ginger Man*.

Donleavy served with the navy during World War II, after which he studied microbiology at Trinity College, Dublin. His experiences there inspired him to write *The Ginger Man*, which was first published as pornography in Paris. Considered iconoclastic, it became an international bestseller and has never gone out of print. Donleavy became an Irish citizen in 1967; his subsequent novels, including *A Singular Man* (1963), *The Saddest Summer of Samuel S.* (1966), and *The Beastly Beatitudes of Balthasar B* (1968), continued to develop the prose style of *The Ginger Man*, which is distinguished by alliteration and an original treatment of voice. Action occurs in the third person while thoughts are conveyed in the first, allowing the character to speak both as observer and observed. Later works include *The Destinies of Darcy Dancer, Gentleman* (1977), *Leila* (1983), *That Darcy, That Dancer, That Gentleman* (1990), and *Wrong Information Is Being Given Out at Princeton* (1997).

Donnelly, Ignatius (b. Nov. 3, 1831, Philadelphia—d. Jan. 1, 1901, Minneapolis) Novelist, orator, and social reformer.

Donnelly grew up in Philadelphia, where he became a lawyer. In 1856 he moved to Minnesota, where, with John Nininger, he founded Nininger City, intended as a cultural and industrial center. There he edited the erudite *Emigrant Aid Journal*, published in both English and German, to attract settlers. After initial success, a panic in 1857 caused abandonment of the town. He later served as lieutenant governor of Minnesota and as a U.S. congressman (1863–69).

His first and most popular book was *Atlantis* (1882), which traced the origin of civilization to the legendary submerged continent of Atlantis. It was followed in 1883 by another work of speculation, *Ragnarok*, which attempted to relate certain gravel and till deposits to an ancient near-collision of the earth and a huge comet. In *The Great Cryptogram* (1888) and *The Cipher in the Plays and on the Tombstone* (1899), he tried to prove that Francis Bacon was the author of the Shakespeare plays by deciphering a code he discovered in the plays. He also ascribed the plays of Marlowe and the essays of Montaigne to Bacon. His dystopian novel *Caesar's Column* (1891) portrays the United States in 1988 as ruled by a ruthless financial oligarchy and peopled by an abject working class; it also predicted such developments as radio, television, and poison gas. The book made him popular with the voting base of the Populist Party, and at the time of his death he was a vice-presidential candidate of a splinter party, the Middle Road Populists.

Dooley, Mr. See **Finley Peter Dunne**

Doolittle, Hilda *known as* **H. D.** (b. Sept. 10, 1886, Bethlehem, Pa.—d. Sept. 27, 1961, Zurich, Switzerland) Modernist poet, translator, novelist, and playwright.

While attending Bryn Mawr College in 1905–6, Doolittle was briefly engaged to Ezra Pound, who would deeply influence her work. In 1911 she moved to Europe, where she would spend the rest of her life. She was married to the English writer Richard Aldington from 1913 to 1938, and her friends included such literary figures as D. H. Lawrence and T. S. Eliot.

H. D. was one of the first Imagists, poets who used concrete language and avoided romantic or mystical themes. Her verse in such early collections as *Sea Garden* (1916) and *Hymen* (1921) was clear, impersonal, and sensual; her later work was somewhat looser and more passionate, with religious and mystic overtones. She won additional acclaim for her translations from the Greek, her verse drama, and her prose works.

Dos Passos \däs-ˈpas-əs, dəs-ˈpas-əs\, **John (Roderigo)** (b. Jan. 14, 1896, Chicago—d. Sept. 28, 1970, Baltimore) Major novelist of the post–World War I "lost generation."

John Dos Passos

The son of a wealthy lawyer, Dos Passos graduated from Harvard University and served as an ambulance driver in World War I. *Three Soldiers* (1921), an early novel, expressed his horror at the brutality of war. Extensive travel as a newspaper correspondent in the postwar years enlarged his sense of history, sharpened his social perception, and confirmed his radical sympathies.

The execution of Sacco and Vanzetti in 1927 crystallized for Dos Passos an image of the United States as "two nations"—one of the rich and privileged and one of the poor and powerless. His celebrated trilogy U.S.A. (1930–36) is a portrait of these two nations that makes use of actual newspaper headlines and popular songs, along with biographies of contemporary figures and brief personal reminiscences.

U.S.A. was followed by a less ambitious trilogy, *District of Columbia*—comprising *Adventures of a Young Man* (1939), *Number One* (1943), and *The Grand Design* (1949)—which chronicles Dos Passos's disillusion with the labor movement, radical politics, and New Deal liberalism. His subsequent, more conservative works received little attention.

Douglas, Lloyd C(assel) (b. Aug. 27, 1877, Columbia City, Ind.—d. Feb. 13, 1951, Los Angeles) Clergyman and novelist.

Douglas received a divinity degree in 1903 and was ordained in the Lutheran church. He was the pastor of churches in the Midwest and director of religious work at the University of Illinois (1911–15), then held Congregational pastorates in Michigan, Ohio, and California as well as Canada.

In the 1920s he began writing religious essays. To reach a wider audience, he wrote his first religious novel, *Magnificent Obsession* (1929; films, 1935, 1954), which became a great success. His later books, most of which similarly convey an optimistic religious message, included *Forgive Us Our Trespasses* (1932), *Precious Jeopardy* (1933), *Green Light* (1935), *White Banners* (1936), *Dr. Hudson's Secret Journal* (1939), and *Invitation to Live* (1940). His greatest success, the biblical novel *The Robe* (1942; film, 1953), sold over three million copies; his last book, *The Big Fisherman* (1948), sold over a million.

Douglass, Frederick *originally* Frederick Augustus Washington Bailey (b. Feb. 7, 1817, Tuckahoe, Md.—d. Feb. 20, 1895, Washington, D.C.) Orator and abolitionist.

The son of a slave mother (from whom he was early separated) and a white father he never knew, he lived with his grandmother on a Maryland plantation until the age of 8. He worked as a house servant (during which time he learned to read and write), field hand, and ship's caulker before managing to flee in 1838 to New York and then New Bedford, Mass., where he worked as a laborer for three years, eluding slave hunters by changing his name to Douglass.

At an antislavery convention in 1841, he was asked to speak extemporaneously about his own experiences; his remarks were so poignant and naturally eloquent that he was catapulted into a new career as an agent for the Massachusetts

Anti-Slavery Society. To counter skeptics who doubted he could ever have been a slave, he wrote his autobiography in 1845, revised and completed in 1882 as *Life and Times of Frederick Douglass*. It became a classic of American literature as well as a primary source about slavery from the bondsman's viewpoint. After a two-year speaking tour of Britain and Ireland, he returned with funds to purchase his freedom and to start his own antislavery newspaper, the *North Star* (later *Frederick Douglass's Paper*), which he published from 1847 to 1860 in Rochester, N.Y. He broke with William Lloyd Garrison over the need for a separate, black-oriented press and the need for political action in addition to moral suasion, and from 1851 he allied himself with James Birney's abolitionist faction.

Frederick Douglass

During the Civil War, Douglass was a consultant to Abraham Lincoln. Throughout Reconstruction he fought for full civil rights for freedmen and vigorously supported the women's-rights movement. He later held several government positions, including minister to Haiti (1889–91).

Dove, Rita (Frances) (b. Aug. 28, 1952, Akron, Ohio) Poet, short-story writer, and teacher.

Dove graduated from Miami University in Ohio and studied subsequently at Tübingen University in Germany. She studied creative writing at the University of Iowa and published the first of several chapbooks of her poetry in 1977. From 1981 to 1989 she taught at Arizona State University, leaving that post to teach at the University of Virginia.

In such poetry collections as *The Yellow House on the Corner* (1980) and *Museum* (1983), as well as in her short stories, Dove has focused on family life and personal struggle, addressing the larger social and political dimensions of black experience primarily by indirection. *Thomas and Beulah* (1986, Pulitzer Prize) is a cycle of poems chronicling the lives of Dove's maternal grandparents, born in the Deep South at the turn of the century. Subsequent works include the collections *The Other Side of the House* (1988), *Grace Notes* (1989), *Mother Love* (1995), and *On the Bus With Rosa Parks* (1999) and the novel *Through the Ivory Gate* (1992). Dove served as U.S. Poet Laureate from 1993 to 1995.

Drake, Joseph Rodman (b. Aug. 7, 1795, New York City—d. Sept. 21, 1820, New York City) Romantic poet.

After graduating from medical school in New York in 1816, Drake married an heiress and opened a pharmacy in New York. While a student, he had become friends with the poet Fitz-Greene Halleck, with whom he began collaborating in 1819 on topical satirical verses; the resulting "Croaker Papers," lampoons of public figures, were published under a pseudonym in the *New York Evening Post*, and were eventually collected in book form in 1860.

Drake died of tuberculosis at 25. Though he had asked his wife to destroy his unpublished poems, she kept them, and his daughter saw to the publication of 19 of them in 1835 as *The Culprit Fay*. The title poem, considered his best, takes the theme of the fairy lover and gives it a Hudson River setting. The volume also contains the fine nature poems "Niagara" and "Bronx." Drake's *Life and Works,* edited by F. L. Pleadwell, was published in 1935.

Theodore Dreiser

Dreiser \\'drīz-ər, *commonly* 'drīs-ər\\, **Theodore** (b. Aug. 27, 1871, Terre Haute, Ind.—d. Dec. 28, 1945, Hollywood, Calif.) Preeminent novelist of American naturalism.

The son of a German immigrant, Dreiser was the ninth of 10 children and grew up in poverty. He spent a year at Indiana University before becoming a newspaper reporter in 1892. His reading (especially of T. H. Huxley, John Tyndall, and Herbert Spencer) and personal experiences led him to a pessimistic view of human helplessness in the face of instinct and social forces.

The initial failure of his first novel, SISTER CARRIE (1900), the story of a kept woman whose behavior goes unpunished, plunged him into depression, but he recovered and achieved financial success as editor in chief of several women's magazines until he was forced to resign in 1910 because of his involvement with an assistant's daughter.

In 1911 his second novel, JENNIE GERHARDT, was published. It was followed in 1912 by THE FINANCIER, and in 1914 by *The Titan,* two volumes in a projected trilogy based on the life of the transportation magnate Charles T. Yerkes. *The 'Genius'* (1915), a sprawling semiautobiographical chronicle of Dreiser's numerous love affairs, was censured by the New York Society for the Suppression of Vice. Its sequel, *The Bulwark,* appeared posthumously in 1946.

In 1925 he published his first novel in a decade, AN AMERICAN TRAGEDY. Based on a celebrated murder case, it brought him a degree of critical and commercial success he had never before attained. Its highly critical view of the American legal system made him the adopted champion of social reformers. Though a visit to the Soviet Union had left him skeptical about communism, the Great Depression caused him to reconsider his opposition. His autobiographical *Dawn* (1931) is one of the most candid self-revelations by any major writer. He completed most of *The Stoic*, the long-postponed third volume of his trilogy on Yerkes, in the weeks before his death. His other works include short stories, plays, and essays.

Drury, Allen (Stuart) (b. Sept. 2, 1918, Houston, Texas—d. Sept. 2, 1998, San Francisco) Journalist and writer.

After graduating from Stanford University in 1939, Drury became a journalist for newspapers in California (1940–42). He later was a Washington (D.C.) correspondent for *The New York Times* (1954–59) and a contributing editor for *Reader's Digest* (1959–62).

His first and most famous novel, *Advise and Consent* (1959), was a story of corruption and scandal in the U.S. Senate; it won a Pulitzer Prize and became a Broadway play in 1960 and a movie in 1962. He wrote 19 additional novels, including *Capable of Honor* (1966), *Preserve and Protect* (1968), *The Throne of Saturn* (1971), *The Promise of Joy* (1975), *The Hill of Summer* (1981), and *A Thing of State* (1995), as well as five nonfiction books.

Du Bois \dü-'bȯis, dyü-'bȯis\, **W(illiam) E(dward) B(urghardt)** (b. Feb. 23, 1868, Great Barrington, Mass.—d. Aug. 27, 1963, Accra, Ghana) Sociologist and black-rights leader.

W. E. B. Du Bois

Of African, French, and Dutch ancestry, Du Bois graduated from Fisk University and received his Ph.D. from Harvard in 1895. From 1897 to 1910 he taught at Atlanta University. There he devoted himself to sociological investigations of the condition of American blacks, producing 16 research monographs and *The Philadelphia Negro* (1899), the first case study of an American black community.

The intolerable racism that continued to oppress African-Americans led Du Bois to support change through agitation and protest, a position that put him at odds with the period's most influential black leader, Booker T. Washington, who favored accepting the status quo while working to win the respect of whites. Du Bois's landmark work THE SOULS OF BLACK FOLK (1903) expressed the view that such a strategy would merely perpetuate oppression. In 1905 he founded the Niagara Movement, which in 1909 merged with the new National Association for the Advancement of Colored People. From 1910 to 1934 he served as editor of the NAACP's magazine, the *Crisis,* which he used to encourage the development of black literature and art. At five Pan-African Conferences (1900–27), he called for independence for African colonies. He resigned from the NAACP for ideological reasons and returned to Atlanta University to teach sociology (1934–44), during which time he also edited the *Encyclopedia of the Negro.* In 1940 he founded the magazine *Phylon*, the university's "Review of Race and Culture." During this period he also produced two major books: *Black Reconstruction* (1935), a Marxist interpretation of the post–Civil War era, and *Dusk at Dawn* (1940), in which he viewed his own career as a case study illuminating the complexity of black-white conflict.

Du Bois later returned to the NAACP (1944–48), but following a second bitter quarrel he severed his connection and thereafter moved steadily leftward politically. He joined the Communist Party in 1961 and moved to Ghana, where he renounced his American citizenship. His *Autobiography* was published posthumously in 1968.

---

du Bois \dü-'bwä, dᵫ-'bwä\, **William Pène (Sherman)** (b. May 9, 1916, Nutley, N.J.—d. Feb. 5, 1993, Nice, France) Author and illustrator of children's books.

Born into a family of artists, du Bois studied art in France and began publishing children's books in the mid-1930s. He served in World War II as a correspondent for *Yank* and other magazines, and in 1953 became the first art director of the *Paris Review*. *The Twenty-One Balloons* (1947, Newbery Medal) tells of a retired math teacher's fantastic escape by balloon from the eruption of Krakatau. *Lion* (1956) is a charming picture book about an angel's design for the first lion and the helpful criticism he receives. In an uncompleted series about the seven deadly sins, du Bois profiled sloth in *Lazy Tommy Pumpkinhead* (1966), pride in *Pretty Pretty Peggy Moffitt* (1968), gluttony in *Porko von Popbutton* (1969), and avarice in *Call Me Bandicoot* (1970). *The Alligator Case* (1965) and *The Horse in the Camel Suit* (1967) parody the detective novels of Raymond Chandler. Other works included *The Flying Locomotive* (1941), *Bear Party* (1951), and *The Forbidden Forest* (1978). He also illustrated the works of such well-known authors as Edward Lear, Jules Verne, Arthur Conan Doyle, Isaac Bashevis Singer, and Roald Dahl.

Dubus \də-'byüs\, **Andre** (b. Aug. 11, 1936, Lake Charles, La.—d. Feb. 24, 1999, Haverhill, Mass.) Short-story writer.

Dubus grew up in Lafayette, La., and graduated from McNeese State College. After six years in the Marine Corps, he took an M.F.A. degree from the University of Iowa, and he taught at Bradford (Mass.) College from 1966 to 1984. His first book, *The Lieutenant* (1967), was a novel, but he is better known for his short stories. His first collection, *Separate Flights* (1975), was followed by *Adultery and Other Choices* (1977). Many of his characters suffer compulsions or addictions; the setting for their struggles with life's vagaries is usually the working-class towns north of Boston. Many of his memorable characters are women; Dubus himself was married three times. Struck by a car on the highway in 1986, he lost one leg and was wheelchair-bound the rest of his life. In his essay collection *Broken Vessels* (1992), he maintained that those with whole and sound bodies often suffered from crippled hearts; in *Meditations from a Movable Chair* (1998), he documented the grief and self-pity he fought with after his accident. He has frequently been confused with his son, Andre Dubus III, author of the best-selling *House of Sand and Fog* (1998).

Dugan, Alan (b. Feb. 12, 1923, New York City—d. Sept. 3, 2003, Hyannis, Mass.) Poet.

Dugan served in World War II and graduated from Mexico City College. His acclaimed *Poems* (1961) won the Pulitzer Prize and the National Book Award. He taught at Sarah Lawrence College before joining the faculty at the Fine Arts Work Center in Provincetown, Mass., in 1971.

Dugan's poetry examines the triviality of war, the bleakness of ordinary life, the ignorance of humanity, and the nature of beauty and love. His terse cadences, ironic detachment, and colloquial style lend his works an understated humor. His ninth and last book of poems was *Poems Seven* (2001, National Book Award).

Dumas \dü-'mä\, **Henry** (b. July 20, 1934, Sweet Home, Ark.—d. May 23, 1968, New York City) Poet and short-story writer who examined the clash between black and white cultures.

Dumas grew up in Arkansas and in New York's Harlem. While in the Air Force (1953–57) he won awards for his contributions to Air Force periodicals. He was active in the civil-rights movement. In 1967 he began teaching in an experimental program at Southern Illinois University, where he met the poet Eugene Redmond, with whom he cofounded the Black River Writers Publishing Company.

The vulnerability of black children to the Southern white lynch-mob mentality, a young sharecropper encountering a civil-rights worker, and whites experiencing the mystical force of black music are among the subjects Dumas examined in his short stories, many of which were collected in *Ark of Bones* (1970) and *Rope of Wind* (1979). Nature, revolutionary politics, and music are frequent subjects of his poetry, which is noted for its faithfulness to the language and cadence of black speech. *Poetry for My People* (1970) contains blues-influenced verse. Dumas was shot and killed at 34 by a New York subway policeman, leaving an unfinished novel, *Jonoah and the Green Stone* (1976). Redmond has continued to publish collections of his work, such as *Goodbye Sweetwater* (1988), as well as a biography.

Dunbar, Paul Laurence (b. June 27, 1872, Dayton, Ohio—d. Feb. 9, 1906, Dayton) Poet, short-story writer, and novelist, the first black American to attempt to support himself by writing and one of the first to attain national prominence.

The son of former slaves, Dunbar excelled in high school (where the Wright brothers were his classmates), editing the school paper and heading its literary society. He published his first volume of poetry, *Oak and Ivy* (1893), at his own expense while working as an elevator operator and sold copies to his passengers. His second volume, *Majors and Minors* (1895), attracted favorable notice from William Dean Howells, who would furnish an introduction to his next collection, *Lyrics of Lowly Life* (1896), containing some of the finest verses of the first two volumes.

Dunbar's poems gained a large popular audience, and he read to audiences in the United States and England. Writing for a largely white audience, he depicted the pre–Civil War South in pastoral, idyllic tones. Only in a few later stories did a suggestion of racial disquiet appear. His first three novels—including *The Uncalled* (1898), which reflected his own spiritual problems—were about white characters. His last and perhaps best novel was *The Sport of the Gods* (1902), concerning an uprooted black family in the urban North. He died of tuberculosis at 33.

Dunbar Nelson, Alice *originally* Alice Ruth Moore (b. July 19, 1875, New Orleans—d. Sept. 18, 1935, Philadelphia) Novelist, poet, essayist, and critic associated with the early Harlem Renaissance.

The daughter of a Creole seaman and a black seamstress, Moore completed a two-year teacher-training program at Straight University at 17, and continued her studies at Cornell University, the Pennsylvania School of Industrial Art, and the University of Pennsylvania. She taught at the elementary, secondary, and college levels until 1931.

Her first collection of stories, poems, and essays, *Violets,* was published in 1895. She later moved to New York, where she taught and helped establish the White Rose Mission in Harlem. In 1898 she married Paul Laurence Dunbar. Her short-story collection *The Goodness of St. Rocque* was published as a companion piece to his *Poems of Cabin and Field* in 1899. She moved to Delaware after their separation in 1902. In 1916 she married the journalist Robert J. Nelson. While not considered a major figure in the Harlem Renaissance for her own literary contributions, Dunbar Nelson's precise, incisive literary style and her numerous reviews had a large influence on the work of other black writers.

Duncan, Robert (*originally* Edward Howard) (b. Jan. 7, 1919, Oakland, Calif.—d. Feb. 3, 1988, San Francisco) Poet, a leader of the Black Mountain poets of the 1950s.

Duncan's mother died in childbirth, and his adoptive parents named him Robert Edward Symmes. He attended UC–Berkeley, where he edited the *Experimental Review* (1938–40), served in the army but was given a psychiatric discharge in 1941, and graduated from Berkeley in 1950. He traveled widely thereafter, lecturing on poetry in the United States and Canada throughout the 1950s. He taught at Black Mountain College in 1956, and later moved to San Francisco and became active in that city's poetry community.

Duncan's poetry—evocative, highly musical, and sometimes obscure—reflects his belief that poetry is the source, rather than an expression of, feeling and thought. *The Opening of the Field* (1960), *Roots and Branches* (1964), *Bending the Bow* (1968), and *Ground Work* (1984) contain perhaps his finest poems; his other collections include *The Years as Catches* (1966) and *Derivations* (1968). He also wrote plays, including *Medea at Kolchis* (1965).

Dunlap, William (b. Feb. 19, 1766, Perth Amboy, N.J.—d. Sept. 28, 1839, New York City) Playwright, painter, and historian.

Dunlap was working as a professional portraitist by 1782. In 1784 he went to London to study with Benjamin West but became interested in the theater. On his return to New York in 1787 he began writing plays; his first was *The Father of an Only Child* (1789). After buying an interest in Lewis Hallam's American Company, he managed it from 1798 and produced his own works and foreign adaptations. His plays, also including *Leicester* (1794), *Fountainville Abbey* (1795), and *Andre* (1798), were the first significant body of dramatic writing produced in the United States.

After the theater went bankrupt in 1805, he returned to portrait painting. He helped found the National Academy of Design in 1826 and later served as its vice president (1831–38). He wrote several historical studies, including *History of the American Theatre* (1832) and *A History of the Rise and Progress of the Arts of Design in the United States* (1834).

Dunne, Finley Peter (b. July 10, 1867, Chicago—d. April 24, 1936, New York City) Journalist and humorist who created the homely philosopher Mr. Dooley.

The son of Irish immigrants, Dunne began working for various Chicago newspapers in 1884, specializing eventually in political reporting and editorial writing. In 1892 he began contributing Irish-dialect sketches to the *Chicago Evening Post* and five years later to the *Chicago Journal*. In these he introduced Martin Dooley, a saloonkeeper who commented incisively in a rich Irish brogue on politics and society. Dunne's witty penetration of shams and hypocrisies that victimized the disadvantaged gained Mr. Dooley an audience of millions and made him a force for clear thinking and tolerance in public affairs. Many of Mr. Dooley's remarks, such as "Thrust ivrybody, but cut th' ca-ards," became part of American lore. Many of Dunne's 700-odd dialect essays were republished in eight volumes, including *Mr. Dooley in Peace and War* and *Mr. Dooley's Philosophy,* from 1898 to 1919. Closely associated with the leading muckrakers, he joined Ida Tarbell, Lincoln Steffens, and others to purchase *American Magazine* in 1906.

Dunne, John Gregory (b. May 25, 1932, Hartford, Conn.—d. Dec. 30, 2003, New York City) Writer known for his works of social satire and personal analysis.

After graduating from Princeton University, Dunne joined the staff of *Time* magazine. He married JOAN DIDION in 1964 and moved to California, where they wrote screenplays (including *Panic in Needle Park*, 1971, and *A Star Is Born*, 1976) and contributed to such magazines as the *Saturday Evening Post,* for which they wrote a joint column (1967–69). His first book, *Delano* (1967), examined the labor and social issues surrounding the Delano grape-pickers' strike of the mid-1960s. *The Studio* (1969) is a telling portrait of the film industry. He examined Irish-American communities in a gritty trilogy of novels: *True Confessions* (1977; film, 1981), *Dutch Shea, Jr.* (1982), and *The Red White and Blue* (1987). *Playland* (1994) examined Hollywood from the 1930s through the 1950s. Dunne's other works include the autobiographical *Harp* (1988) and the essay collections *Quintana & Friends* (1978) and *Crooning* (1990).

His brother Dominick has written magazine journalism and numerous best-selling novels, mostly set in glamorous milieus, including *The Two Mrs. Grenvilles* (1985), *People Like Us* (1988), and *An Inconvenient Woman* (1990).

Durant \dù-ˈrant, dyù-ˈrant\, **Will(iam James)** (b. Nov. 5, 1885, North Adams, Mass.—d. Nov. 7, 1981, Los Angeles) Writer of popular philosophy and history.

A graduate of St. Peter's College, he taught Latin and French at Seton Hall College while studying for the priesthood. In 1911 he moved to New York City, where he joined radical circles and taught at an anarchist school. In 1913 he married his pupil Ada Kaufman (1898–1981), whom he called Ariel; she later adopted the name legally. He directed the Labor Temple School from 1914 to 1927, meanwhile obtaining his Ph.D. from Columbia University (1917). His writing career began with publication of *Philosophy and the Social Problem* (1917). His second book, *The Story of Philosophy* (1926), sold over two million copies and was translated into several languages. Several other books followed.

Having long planned a comprehensive history of civilization, in 1935 he published the first volume of what would be the 11-volume *The Story of Civilization* (1935–75). Though Ariel had been involved in the writing of every volume, she was not given formal recognition as his collaborator until 1961, with publication of the seventh volume, *The Age of Reason Begins*. She continued as coauthor of the subsequent volumes in the series, including the Pulitzer Prize–winning 10th volume, *Rousseau and Revolution* (1967). Admired for their rich, lively, and vivid writing, all the volumes of the series sold in large numbers. The Durants described their work together in *A Dual Autobiography* (1977).

Dwight, Timothy (b. May 14, 1752, Northampton, Mass.—d. Jan. 11, 1817, New Haven, Conn.) Educator, theologian, and poet.

Educated by his mother, a daughter of Jonathan Edwards, Dwight entered Yale at 13. After graduating, he worked as a tutor at Yale, a school principal, a Massachusetts legislator, and a chaplain with the Continental Army before founding a successful school in Greenfield Hill, Conn., where he became pastor of the Congregational Church and began to write poetry. His works include *Greenfield Hill* (1794), a popular history of and tribute to the village, and epics such as *The Conquest of Canaan* (1785), a biblical allegory of the taking of Connecticut from the British, which some critics regard as the first American epic poem. With John Trumbull and Joel Barlow, he was a leader of the Hartford wits, who sought to create a national literature. He served as president of Yale from 1795 to 1817.

Eastman, Max (Forrester) (b. Jan. 12, 1883, Canandaigua, N.Y.—d. March 25, 1969, Bridgetown, Barbados) Poet, editor, and prominent radical.

Eastman graduated from Williams College and taught four years at Columbia University. A leader of Greenwich Village's bohemian society, in 1910 he founded the first men's league for women's suffrage. In 1913 he cofounded the *Masses*, a radical political and literary periodical which he would serve as editor until it was suppressed by the government in 1918, when he was twice tried for its opposition to U.S. entry into World War I. In 1919 he helped found the *Liberator*, a similar magazine. In 1923 he traveled to Russia to study the Soviet regime; there he married the sister of the Soviet minister of justice, but he returned to the United States believing that the original purpose of the 1917 October Revolution had been subverted by corrupt leaders. In the 1920s and '30s he wrote several books perceptively attacking developments in the Soviet Union, including *Since Lenin Died* (1925), *The End of Socialism in Russia* (1937), and *Stalin's Russia and the Crisis in Socialism* (1939). A close friend of Leon Trotsky, he translated many of his writings.

From 1941 he was a roving editor for *Reader's Digest*. His literary books include the perennial and influential *Enjoyment of Poetry* (23 eds., 1913–48), *The Literary Mind* (1931), and *Enjoyment of Laughter* (1936). His several memoirs include *Enjoyment of Living* (1948) and *Love and Revolution* (1965).

Eberhart \'eb-ər-ˌhärt\, **Richard** (b. April 5, 1904, Austin, Minn.) Poet and teacher.

Educated at Dartmouth College, Cambridge, and Harvard, Eberhart published his first book of poems, *A Bravery of Earth*, in 1930. In the 1930s he tutored the son of King Prajadhipok of Siam (now Thailand), and he later taught at several American colleges, including Dartmouth (1956–70). He served as consultant in poetry at the Library of Congress (1959–61). His poetry has been called Transcendentalist in spirit. In 1962 he received the Bollingen Prize, in 1966 the Pulitzer Prize, and in 1977 the National Book Award. His *Collected Poems, 1930–1986* appeared in 1988, and *Maine Poems* in 1989.

Edel \ˌā-'del, 'ā-ˌdəl, 'ā-ˌdel, 'e-dəl\, **(Joseph) Leon** (b. Sept. 9, 1907, Pittsburgh—d. Sept. 5, 1997, Honolulu) Literary critic and biographer, notably of Henry James.

Reared in Saskatchewan, Canada, Edel received a master's degree from McGill University and a doctorate from the University of Paris, writing his thesis on Henry James. He held a variety of jobs in the 1930s, and served in the U.S. Army from 1943 to 1947. He later taught English at NYU (1950–72) and the University of Hawaii (1972–78). A bachelor most of his life, he married in 1980.

Edel's definitive biography of Henry James (5 vols., 1953–72) won the Pulitzer Prize for its second volume and the National Book Award for its third. He also edited James's *Complete Plays* (1949), his *Complete Tales* (12 vols.,

E

1963–65), and his letters (4 vols., 1974–84). His other books include *Willa Cather* (1953; with E. K. Brown); *The Psychological Novel, 1900–1950* (1955); *Literary Biography* (1957); *Bloomsbury: A House of Lions* (1979), a psychological portrait of the Bloomsbury group; and *Writing Lives* (1984).

Jonathan Edwards

Edwards, Jonathan (b. Oct. 5, 1703, East Windsor, Conn.—d. March 22, 1758, Princeton, N.J.) Greatest theologian and philosopher of Puritanism.

Edwards's father and grandfather were ministers. He entered Yale College at 12 and received his M.A. in 1723. In 1726 he joined his grandfather in the important Congregational church at Northampton, Mass., and on his grandfather's death in 1729 he became sole occupant of the pulpit. In his first published sermon, *God Glorified in the Work of Redemption*, Edwards blamed New England's moral ills on its assumption of religious and moral self-sufficiency.

In 1734 he delivered a series of sermons on "Justification by Faith Alone." The result was a great revival in the winter and spring of 1734–35. His subsequent report, *A Faithful Narrative of the Surprising Work of God* (1737), made a profound impression in America and Europe, particularly through his description of the types and stages of conversion experience.

In 1740–42 George Whitefield's preaching tour sparked the Great Awakening throughout the colonies. Edwards's sermon "Sinners in the Hands of an Angry God" (1741), with its arresting image of the unredeemed, like loathsome insects, deserving to be flung into the fires of hell, dates from this period. He wrote several treatises in defense and criticism of the Awakening, which produced not only conversions but also excesses and disorders.

In 1750 he was dismissed from his Northampton parish over a disagreement on who was eligible to receive communion and accepted the position of pastor of the frontier church at Stockbridge, Mass. Hampered by many difficulties, he nevertheless discharged his pastoral duties, including ministering to the Indians, and found time to write his famous work *Freedom of Will* (1754).

Two months after assuming the presidency of the College of New Jersey (later Princeton University), he died of smallpox contracted from a primitive attempt at inoculation.

Eggleston, Edward (b. Dec. 10, 1837, Vevay, Ind.—d. Sept. 4, 1902, Lake George, N.Y.) Clergyman, novelist, and historian.

By the age of 19 Eggleston had become an itinerant preacher, but the taxing activity broke his health. He held various pastorates, serving from 1874 to 1879 in Brooklyn, while also serving as an editor of the juvenile paper *Little Corporal* (1866–67), the *National Sunday School Teacher* (1867–73), and other periodicals.

In all his fiction he sought to write with "photographic exactness" of the real West. His most popular novel for adults was THE HOOSIER SCHOOL-MASTER (1871), a vivid study of the backwoods Indiana of his boyhood. His later novels, considered less significant, include *The End of the World* (1872), *The Mystery of Metropolisville* (1873), *Roxy* (1878), and *The Graysons* (1888). After a trip to Europe in 1879 he turned to the writing of history. His *Beginners of a Nation* (1896) and *Transit of Civilization from England to America* (1900) contributed to the growth of the study of social history. In 1900 he was elected president of the American Historical Association.

Eiseley, Loren (Corey) (b. Sept. 3, 1907, Lincoln, Neb.—d. July 9, 1977, Philadelphia) Anthropologist, educator, and writer.

Eiseley received his Ph.D. from the University of Pennsylvania in 1937 and began his academic career at the University of Kansas (1937–44) and Oberlin College (1944–47). In his subsequent long association with the University of Pennsylvania, he served not only as a professor but as a curator at the University Museum and university provost.

His writings dealt with evolution and its implications for humanity in a philosophically meditative prose that often approached poetry. His first book, *The Immense Journey* (1957), a narrative of the course of evolution, was widely acclaimed for its eloquent simplicity. His books *Darwin's Century* (1958) and *The Firmament of Time* (1960) also won high praise and several awards. His later works include *The Unexpected Universe* (1969), *The Invisible Pyramid* (1970), *The Night Country* (1971), the autobiography *All the Strange Hours* (1975), and the poetry collection *Another Kind of Autumn* (1977).

Eliot, T(homas) S(tearns) (b. Sept. 26, 1888, St. Louis, Mo.—d. Jan. 4, 1965, London) Modernist poet, playwright, and literary critic.

Born into a patrician family, Eliot studied at Harvard, spent a year studying in France under Henri Bergson and Alain-Fournier, then returned to Harvard to read Indian philosophy and study Sanskrit (1911–14). In 1914 he met Ezra Pound and moved to England. In 1915 he married his first wife; she soon declined into mental illness, and Eliot's distress would eventually lead to his leaving her in 1933. In 1957 he would remarry happily.

His first important publication, and the first masterpiece of modernism in English, was the radically experimental LOVE SONG OF J. ALFRED PRUFROCK (1915). With Pound, he sought to create new verse rhythms and poetic language that was "neither pedantic nor vulgar." While supporting himself as a bank clerk (1917–25), in 1919 he published *Poems*, containing the unique "Gerontion," a meditative interior monologue in blank verse. The 1922 publication of THE WASTE LAND, which expressed with startling power the disillusionment of the postwar years, secured his international reputation.

T. S. Eliot

Eliot's work as a critic is well represented by his first critical volume, THE SACRED WOOD (1920), which introduced two phrases—"objective correlative" (use of an external object, event, or situation to evoke emotion in the reader) and "dissociation of sensibility" (loss of the union between thought and feeling in poetry that occurred after the Metaphysical poets)—that became much discussed in later critical theory. From 1922 until 1939 he edited the important quarterly *Criterion* review. From the mid-1920s until his death, he was a director of the publishing firm Faber & Faber. In 1927 he was confirmed in the Church of England; his growing interest in theology and sociology resulted in *Thoughts After Lambeth* (1931), *The Idea of a Christian Society* (1939), and NOTES TOWARDS THE DEFINITION OF CULTURE (1948), and strongly affected all his subsequent poetry, including the philosophical FOUR QUARTETS (1936–42), regarded by some as his finest work. The light-verse collection *Old Possum's Book of Practical Cats* (1939) would inspire the hugely successful musical *Cats* (1981).

Though Eliot regarded drama as the highest form of poetry, his plays, including SWEENEY AGONISTES (1932), *The Family Reunion* (1939), THE COCKTAIL PARTY (1950), *The Confidential Clerk* (1953), and *The Elder Statesman* (1958), are inferior to his lyric and meditative poetry. The great exception is MURDER IN THE CATHEDRAL (1935), the story of St. Thomas Becket's martyrdom.

In 1948 Eliot was awarded the Nobel Prize. From then until his death he achieved public adulation unequaled by any other 20th-century poet.

Elkin, Stanley (Lawrence) (b. May 11, 1930, New York City—d. May 31, 1995, St. Louis, Mo.) Novelist and short-story writer.

Elkin grew up in Chicago. He was educated at the University of Illinois, completing a dissertation on William Faulkner in 1961, and he taught at Washington University in St. Louis from 1960 until his death. His first novel, *Boswell, A Modern Comedy* (1964), tells of an ordinary man who founds a club for famous individuals, hoping like his namesake to bask in reflected glory. *Criers and Kibitzers, Kibitzers and Criers* (1966) was a collection of comic short stories on Jewish themes and characters; like much of his later work, it exhibits outlandish humor and imagination.

In 1972 Elkin was diagnosed with multiple sclerosis; his subsequent works increasingly featured characters beset by helplessness, powerlessness, and disease. Ben Flesh, the protagonist in *The Franchiser* (1976), is adopted into a family in which all the offspring suffer from rare and incurable diseases; Ben himself suffers from multiple sclerosis. In *Stanley Elkin's The Magic Kingdom* (1985), seven terminally ill children are taken on a trip to Disney World. His last novel, published posthumously, was *Mrs. Ted Bliss* (1995).

Ellison, Harlan (Jay) (b. May 27, 1934, Cleveland, Ohio) Science-fiction writer.

Ellison endured a lonely childhood, left Ohio State University during his sophomore year, and moved to New York, where he infiltrated a gang, passing for 17 although he was actually 21. While serving in the army (1957–59), he wrote *Web of the City* (1958), a novel based on his gang experience. In 1962 he moved to California, where he became a prolific contributor to science-fiction, crime, and horror magazines.

Ellison's reputation rests principally on short stories such as "A Boy and His Dog" (1969; film, 1975), first collected in *The Beast That Shouted Love at the Heart of the World* (1969). The collection *I Have No Mouth and I Must Scream* (1967) helped cement his reputation. In the 1960s he was politically active, marching for civil rights and against the Vietnam War. He has edited several important anthologies; for each story he commissioned for *Dangerous Visions* (1967) and *Again, Dangerous Visions* (1972), he added an introductory essay that revealed as much about himself as about the story. He has written for numerous television programs and acted as conceptual consultant for *Babylon 5,* a successful science-fiction television series. Among his other numerous works are *Spider Kiss* (1961), *Deathbird Stories* (1975), *All the Lies That Are My Life* (1980), and *The Harlan Ellison Hornbook* (1990). His 70 books and 1,700 shorter works have won eight Hugo Awards and three Nebula Awards.

Ellison, Ralph (Waldo) (b. March 1, 1914, Oklahoma City, Okla.—d. April 16, 1994, New York City) Teacher and writer who won eminence with his first and only published novel, INVISIBLE MAN (1952), about race relations in the United States in the 20th century.

Initially drawn to music, Ellison won a scholarship to Tuskegee Institute, but left after three years to join the Federal Writers' Project in New York, where he met Langston Hughes and Richard Wright, who encouraged him in his writing. He began submitting short stories, reviews, and essays to various periodicals. He served in the Merchant Marine during World War II, but was forced to leave in 1944 due to illness.

Invisible Man (1952, National Book Award) appeared to great acclaim; it is still regarded as one of the greatest novels in English of the 20th century. Ellison's only subsequent publications were two collections of essays, *Shadow and Act* (1964) and *Going to the Territory* (1986). He lectured widely on black culture, folklore, music, and creative writing and taught at various colleges; from 1970 until his death he was affiliated with NYU. His second novel, *Juneteenth,* was left unfinished after decades of work; edited posthumously from a vast welter of manuscript, it was published to mixed reviews in 1999.

Ellmann, Richard (David) (b. March 15, 1918, Highland Park, Mich.—d. May 13, 1987, Oxford, Oxfordshire, England) Literary critic and scholar.

Ellmann graduated from Yale University and subsequently taught at Northwestern (1951–68), Yale (1968–70), and Oxford (1970–84). His book *Yeats: The Man and the Masks* (1948) is a study of one of Yeats's intense conflicts, the dichotomy between the self of everyday life and the self of fantasy, which revealed the timidity and confusion that lay behind the poet's arrogant facade.

The Identity of Yeats (1954) focused on his poems, and *Eminent Domain* (1967) on Yeats's relationships with several contemporary writers. The definitive biography *James Joyce* (1959) led to Ellmann's publishing an unexpurgated edition of Joyce's letters (1966). He also edited several books, including *The Artist as Critic* (1969), on Oscar Wilde, and *The New Oxford Book of American Verse* (1976). The admired biography *Oscar Wilde*, published posthumously in 1988, won the Pulitzer Prize.

Ellroy, James (*originally* Lee Earle) (b. March 4, 1948, Los Angeles) Crime novelist and screenwriter.

Ellroy's mother was murdered when he was 10, and he grew up on the streets of Los Angeles, living a life of petty crime. In 1977 he sought help for his alcoholism and obtained a job at a country club. In many hours spent at public libraries, he had read widely in the literature of crime, and in 1979 he began writing his own crime stories. His first novel, *Brown's Requiem* (1981; film, 1998), was soon followed by *Clandestine* (1982), *Blood on the Moon* (1984; film, *Cop*, 1987), and several others. In 1987 he wrote *The Black Dahlia*; it initiated his "L.A. Quartet," which was completed by *The Big Nowhere* (1988), *L.A. Confidential* (1990; film, 1997), and *White Jazz* (1992). His later books include *American Tabloid* (1995) and *L.A. Noir* (1998). *My Dark Places* (1996) is a memoir of Ellroy's attempt to solve the mystery of his mother's murder.

Emerson, Ralph Waldo (b. May 25, 1803, Boston—d. April 27, 1882, Concord, Mass.) Poet, essayist, and lecturer, the leading exponent of New England Transcendentalism.

Emerson graduated from Harvard College in 1821 and was ordained to the Unitarian ministry in 1829, the year he married. His preaching soon won him fame, but his doubts about traditional doctrine, which intensified after his wife's death in 1831, led to his resignation in 1832.

Ralph Waldo Emerson

His spiritual quest took him to England, where he met Coleridge, Wordsworth, and Carlyle. He returned to settle in Concord, Mass., the home of H. D. Thoreau, who would become his philosophical ally. In 1835 he married a second time. His anonymously published NATURE (1836) stated his belief that one could transcend the materialistic world of sense experience and become conscious of the all-pervading spirit of the universe, and that God could best be found by looking into one's own soul. The essay helped initiate Transcendentalism.

In the lecture "The American Scholar" (1837), he warned against pedantry, imitation, traditionalism, and scholarship unrelated to life. His "Address at Divinity College" (1838) was another challenge, directed against a lifeless Christian tradition; it alienated many and resulted in his being ostracized by Harvard for many years. Young disciples, however, joined the informal Transcendental Club (founded in 1836) and encouraged him in his activities.

In 1840 he helped launch the DIAL, which became the chief organ of the Transcendentalists; he succeeded Margaret Fuller as its editor. He continued to lecture, publishing two volumes of *Essays* (1841; 1844); these contained the well-known SELF-RELIANCE, which made him internationally famous.

His *Representative Men* (dated 1850) contains biographies of Plato, Swedenborg, Montaigne, Shakespeare, Napoleon, and Goethe. *The Conduct of Life* (1860), his most mature work, reveals a developed humanism together with a full awareness of human limitations. Emerson's collected *Poems* (dated 1847) were supplemented by others in *May-Day* (1867), and the two volumes established his reputation as a major American poet.

Erdrich \'er-drik\, **(Karen) Louise** (b. June 7, 1954, Little Falls, Minn.) Novelist whose principal subject is the Chippewa Indians in the northern Midwest.

Erdrich grew up in North Dakota, where her parents taught at an Indian boarding school. She attended Dartmouth College and received an M.A. from Johns Hopkins. In 1981 she married the writer Michael Dorris (founder of Dartmouth's Native American Studies Project); throughout their marriage, which ended with his suicide in 1995, the two were deeply involved in each other's writing. Her prize-winning short story "The World's Greatest Fisherman" became the basis of her celebrated first novel, *Love Medicine* (1984), the beginning of a tetralogy about the families on and around a Chippewa reservation that would comprise *The Beet Queen* (1986), *Tracks* (1988), and *The Bingo Palace* (1994). Her later novels include *Tales of Burning Love* (1996) and *The Antelope Wife* (1998).

Erdrich's novels are noted for their depth of characterization; they are inhabited by a variety of characters, some of which later reappear in other novels. White culture—with its alcohol, Roman Catholicism, and government policies—acts to destroy the Indian community; tradition and loyalty to family and heritage work to keep it intact.

Erskine \'ər-skin\, **John** (b. Oct. 5, 1879, New York City—d. June 2, 1951, New York City) Educator, novelist, and musician.

At Columbia University, Erskine studied music and literature; after earning his Ph.D. in 1903, he taught at Columbia from 1909 to 1937, earning a reputation as a learned, witty lecturer specializing in Elizabethan literature.

In the 1920s he appeared as a piano soloist with the New York Philharmonic, beginning a distinguished career as a concert pianist, during which he would serve as president of the Juilliard School of Music and director of the Metropolitan Opera Association.

Erskine wrote more than 45 books. His early satirical novels, legends retold with updated views on morality and society, were particularly successful. These include *The Private Life of Helen of Troy* (1925) and *Adam and Eve* (1927), the story of how Adam adjusts to life with women (in the novel, first Lilith and then Eve). He coedited the *Cambridge History of American Literature* (3 vols., 1917–19). *The Memory of Certain Persons* (1947), *My Life as a Teacher* (1948), and *My Life in Music* (1950) are memoirs.

Evans, Mari (b. July 16, 1923, Toledo, Ohio) Poet, children's writer, and playwright.

Evans attended the University of Toledo and later taught at several schools in the Midwest and East. She began five years of writing, producing, and directing the Indianapolis television program "The Black Experience" in 1968, the same year her first poetry collection, *Where Is All the Music?*, was published. With her second collection, *I Am a Black Woman* (1970), including the poem "Who Can Be Born Black," she was recognized as an important new poet.

Her later collections include *Nightstar* (1981), whose poems praise blues artists and community heroes and heroines, and *A Dark and Splendid Mass* (1992). She has also written works for juvenile readers and several plays, including *River of My Song* (1977) and the musical *Eyes* (1979), an adaptation of Zora Neale Hurston's *Their Eyes Were Watching God*. In 1984 she published the anthology *Black Women Writers (1950–1980)*.

Everett, Edward (b. April 11, 1794, Dorchester, Mass.—d. Jan. 15, 1865, Boston) Clergyman, statesman, and orator.

After graduating from Harvard College, Everett received his doctorate from the University of Göttingen (Germany). An outstanding scholar, he served as Harvard's first professor of Greek (1819–25). Elected to the U.S. House of Representatives (1825–35), he became known for his oratory. He later served as governor of Massachusetts (1835–39), U.S. minister to Britain (1841–45), and president of Harvard (1846–49). After a brief term in the U.S. Senate (1853–54), he devoted himself to a successful career as a lecturer. Throughout the Civil War, he traveled widely speaking in support of the Union. In 1863, at the dedication of the national cemetery at Gettysburg, he delivered the principal address, an outstanding two-hour oration. However, it was overshadowed by Abraham Lincoln's subsequent two-minute address. He wrote to Lincoln the next day, "I should be glad if . . . I came as near to the central idea of the occasion in two hours as you did in two minutes." Everett's speeches were published as *Orations and Speeches on Various Occasions* (1853–68).

Everson, William (Oliver) *known as* **Brother Antoninus** (b. Sept. 10, 1912, Sacramento, Calif.—d. June 3, 1994, Santa Cruz, Calif.) Poet whose works record a personal search for religious vision in a violent, corrupt world.

Raised as a Christian Scientist, Everson became an agnostic in his teens. His first book of poetry, *These Are the Ravens*, appeared in 1935. During World

War II he served at a work camp for conscientious objectors in Oregon, where he cofounded the Untide Press and printed his own poetry. His conversion to Catholicism and his decision to become a Dominican lay brother (1951) meant the dissolution of his second marriage; for seven years he lived in monastic withdrawal. His literary silence was broken in 1957 with his long poem *River-Root* (published 1976), which depicts sexual love as a form of religious contemplation. As Brother Antoninus, he became identified with the San Francisco poetry renaissance of the Beat movement. The Church eventually objected to his poetry's eroticism, and he left the order in 1969 to marry a woman 35 years his junior. He taught poetry and hand-set printing at UC–Santa Cruz until 1982, when he retired to a rustic cabin. Everson considered his life's work to form a trilogy, *The Crooked Lines of God*. This comprised *The Residual Years* (1968), his early nature poetry; *The Veritable Years* (1978), his religious poetry; and *The Integral Years* (1999), his post-1966 poetry.

William Everson

Fadiman \\'fa-də-mən\\, **Clifton (Paul)** (b. May 15, 1904, Brooklyn, N.Y.—d. June 20, 1999, Sanibel Island, Fla.) Editor, anthologist, and writer.

After college Fadiman taught school, was an editor at Simon & Schuster, and served as book editor of the *New Yorker* (1933–43). From 1938 to 1948 he was master of ceremonies of the popular radio program *Information Please!*, on which he and such panelists as Franklin P. Adams and John Kieran used questions from listeners as occasions for entertaining displays of wit and erudition. He was a long-time member of the editorial board of the Book-of-the-Month Club (1944–93) and of the board of editors of Encyclopædia Britannica (1959–98). At various times he was a magazine columnist, host of several television shows, and essayist, but he made his most lasting contributions as an anthologist. Among his volumes aimed at introducing readers of all ages to the joys of literature were *Reading I've Liked* (1941), *The American Treasury* (1955), *Fantasia Mathematica* (1958), *Gateway to the Great Books* (10 vols., 1963), *The World Treasury of Children's Literature* (1984–85), and *Treasury of the Encyclopædia Britannica* (1992).

Fariña \\fä-'rēn-yə\\, **Richard** (b. April 30, 1936?, Brooklyn, N.Y.—d. April 30, 1966, Carmel, Calif.) Folksinger, songwriter, and novelist.

Fariña studied engineering and literature at Cornell University, where he became a close friend of Thomas Pynchon; he served with the Irish Republican Army in the mid-1950s, and later briefly joined Fidel Castro's guerrillas in Cuba. In 1963 he married Mimi Baez, younger sister of Joan Baez, and the two recorded a number of successful albums.

Among the folk songs he composed were "Pack Up Your Sorrows" and "Hard Lovin' Loser." His first novel, *Been Down So Long It Looks Like Up to Me* (1966; film, 1971), written in an anarchic style, is a comic semiautobiographical work about the meaning of life that provides a portrait of the late-1950s counter-culture. Just after its publication Fariña was killed in a motorcycle accident. His novel *Long Time Coming and a Long Time Gone* was published in 1969.

Farrell \\'far-əl\\, **James T(homas)** (b. Feb. 27, 1904, Chicago—d. Aug. 22, 1979, New York City) Novelist and short-story writer known for his realistic portraits of Irish-Americans in Chicago, drawn from his own experiences.

Farrell grew up in an Irish neighborhood on Chicago's South Side, attended the University of Chicago, worked at a variety of jobs, and moved to New York City in 1932, the year he published the first volume of his celebrated STUDS LONIGAN trilogy, *Young Lonigan*, which was followed by *The Young Manhood of Studs Lonigan* (1934) and *Judgment Day* (1935). These works combined the naturalism of Theodore Dreiser with the stream-of-consciousness interior narrative of James Joyce with powerful effect.

The trilogy was followed by an admired five-novel series (1936–53), whose protagonist, Danny O'Neill, was a minor character in the *Studs Lonigan* series; its final volume, *The Face of Time* (1953), was particularly praised. Farrell published another trilogy in the years 1946–52, and a tetralogy in the years 1963–68. After 1958 he worked on what he intended to be a 25-volume cycle, *A Universe of Time*, of which he completed 10 volumes. His complete works include 25 novels, 17 collections of short stories, and such nonfiction works as *A Note on Literary Criticism* (1936) and *Reflections at Fifty* (1954).

Fast, Howard M(elvin) (b. Nov. 11, 1914, New York City—d. March 12, 2003, Greenwich, Conn.) Writer best known for his popular historical novels.

Fast grew up in poverty and from age 11 worked to help support his family, never finishing high school. He sold his first short story to a pulp magazine when he was 17, and published his first novel, *Two Valleys* (1933), when he was 18. His first best-seller was *The Last Frontier* (1941; film, *Cheyenne Autumn,* 1964); it was soon followed by such novels as *The Unvanquished* (1942), *Citizen Tom Paine* (1943), *Freedom Road* (1944), and *The American* (1946). Fast joined the Communist Party in 1943, and in 1950 he served three months in prison for refusing to name other party members. His books, many of them popular in schools, were purged from school libraries across the country. He left the party in 1956, explaining his disillusionment in *The Naked God* (1957), but was blacklisted until 1960.

His subsequent books include *Spartacus* (1958; film, 1960), *April Morning* (1961), and *Power* (1963). His highly successful six-novel "Immigrants saga" began with *The Immigrants* (1977) and concluded with *An Independent Woman* (1997). *Being Red* (1990) is a second memoir. Many of his works were made into films, including television films. Fast also wrote detective stories under the pen name E. V. Cunningham, and he wrote in a variety of other genres as well, producing more than 75 books; sales topped 80 million copies.

Faulkner \\'fȯk-nər\\, **William** *originally* William Cuthbert Falkner (b. Sept. 25, 1897, New Albany, Miss.—d. July 6, 1962, near Oxford, Miss.) Novelist and short-story writer best known for his epic Yoknapatawpha cycle.

Faulkner dropped out of high school in his second year, joined the Royal Air Force–Canada in World War I (but did not fly), and later endured a brief stint at the University of Mississippi before working at a series of odd jobs, including university postmaster (1921–24). A neighbor helped fund publication of his first book, the cycle of pastoral poems *The Marble Faun* (1924). His first novel, *Soldier's Pay* (1926), told of the return to Georgia of a fatally wounded aviator. SARTORIS (1929) was the first of his Yoknapatawpha novels; THE SOUND AND THE FURY (1929), his first masterwork, continued the cycle.

William Faulkner

In the years 1930–42 Faulkner published two collections of stories, a second book of poems (*A Green Bough*, 1933), and nine novels—AS I LAY DYING (1930), SANCTUARY (1931), LIGHT IN AUGUST (1932), *Pylon* (1935), ABSALOM, ABSALOM! (1936), *The Unvanquished* (1938), *The Wild Palms* (1939), THE HAMLET (1940), and GO DOWN, MOSES (1942), which includes the story THE BEAR. By 1945, however, his novels were effectively out of print. From 1932 until 1955 he worked intermittently writing screenplays in Hollywood to supplement his meager income from book royalties; his film scripts include *To Have and Have Not* (1944) and *The Big Sleep* (1946).

His long-delayed ascent to international fame began with the publication in 1946 of the paperback *Portable Faulkner*, edited by Malcolm Cowley, which introduced his Yoknapatawpha cycle as a whole. INTRUDER IN THE DUST appeared in 1948. In 1949 Faulkner was awarded the Nobel Prize; his acceptance speech became the most quoted of all Nobel Prize speeches.

Faulkner's *Collected Stories*, published in 1950, won the National Book Award. *Requiem for a Nun,* a sequel to *Sanctuary* in the form of a three-act play with a narrative prologue to each act, appeared in 1951. He worked nearly 10 years on his longest novel, *A Fable* (1954, Pulitzer Prize), and he rounded out the Yoknapatawpha story with THE TOWN (1957), THE MANSION (1959), and *The Reivers* (1962, Pulitzer Prize).

Jessie Redmon Fauset

Fauset \\'fȯs-ət\\, Jessie Redmon (b. April 27, 1882, Fredericksville, N.J.— d. April 30, 1961, Philadelphia) Novelist, critic, poet, and editor of the Harlem Renaissance.

Fauset was the first black woman admitted to Cornell University; in 1919 she earned a master's degree in French from the University of Pennsylvania. While teaching French in an all-black secondary school in Washington, D.C., she published articles in the *Crisis*, the journal of the NAACP. Its editor, W. E. B. Du Bois, persuaded her to move to New York to become its literary editor. In that capacity, from 1919 to 1926, she published the works of such writers as Langston Hughes, Countee Cullen, Claude McKay, and Jean Toomer. She also edited and wrote for the *Brownies' Book*, a short-lived periodical for black children.

In Fauset's own work, middle-class black characters deal with self-hate as well as racial prejudice. In her best-known novel, *Comedy: American Style* (1933), the protagonist is a black woman who longs to be white, while her son and husband take pride in their cultural heritage. Her other novels include *There Is Confusion* (1924), *Plum Bun* (1928), and *The Chinaberry Tree* (1931).

Faust, Frederick See **Max Brand**

Fearing, Kenneth (Flexner) (b. July 28, 1902, Oak Park, Ill.—d. June 26, 1961, New York City) Poet and novelist.

After graduating from the University of Wisconsin, Fearing moved to New York, where he worked as a commercial freelance writer the rest of his life. His early work appeared in *New Masses, Partisan Review,* and *Menorah Journal,* publications allied with the Communist Party, and his poetry for them was described as "proletarian." He also succeeded in having his work published in *Poetry* magazine and the *New Yorker*. His books include *Stranger at Coney Island* (1948) and *New and Selected Poems* (1956).

During the 1940s Fearing's readership shifted from his poetry to his psychological thrillers. His most successful book, *The Big Clock* (1946; film, 1948), is a satire about a magazine publisher who commits murder and then sets his top reporter to hunt down a suspect, who is the reporter himself.

Ferber, Edna (b. Aug. 15, 1885, Kalamazoo, Mich.—d. April 16, 1968, New York City) Novelist and short-story writer who wrote with compassion and curiosity of middle-class Midwestern life.

Edna Ferber

Ferber began her career at 17 as a reporter in Wisconsin. Her early stories introduced a traveling petticoat saleswoman named Emma McChesney, whose adventures would be collected in several books, including *Emma McChesney & Co.* (1915). In these and her later fiction, Ferber's careful attention to exterior detail comes at the expense of profound ideas, but her books offer a lively and accurate portrait of America through several decades. SO BIG (1924, Pulitzer Prize; films, 1932, 1953) became a major best-seller. SHOW BOAT (1926), likewise a huge best-seller, became a landmark musical that was filmed three times. By now critics were hailing Ferber as the greatest woman novelist of the period, and she had been admitted to the coterie of the Algonquin Round Table. Her successes continued with *Cimarron* (1929; films, 1931, 1960), *Come and Get It* (1936; film, 1936), *Saratoga Trunk* (1941; film, 1945), GIANT (1952; film, 1956), and *Ice Palace* (1958). With George S. Kaufman she wrote the plays *The Royal Family* (1930; film, 1930), *Dinner at Eight* (1933; film, 1933), *Stage Door* (1938; film, 1937), *The Land Is Bright* (1941), and *Bravo* (1949). Her autobiography, *A Peculiar Treasure* (1939), evinces her genuine and encompassing love for her country.

Ferlinghetti \ˌfer-liŋ-ˈget-ē\, **Lawrence (Monsanto)** *originally* Lawrence Ferling (b. March 24, 1919, Yonkers, N.Y.) Poet and bookseller, a founder of the Beat movement.

Lawrence Ferlinghetti

Ferlinghetti was reared by a female relative in France and later on a Long Island, N.Y., estate where she worked as a governess. He was a naval officer during World War II, and he later attended the University of North Carolina, Columbia University, and the Sorbonne (Ph.D. 1951). In 1953 he opened his City Lights bookstore in San Francisco, which he would continue to run for the next five decades. It was an early gathering place of the Beats, and its publishing arm was the first to print the Beats' books of poetry.

Ferlinghetti composed his own poetry mainly to be read aloud. It became popular in coffeehouses and on college campuses, where it struck a responsive chord in disaffected youth. *Pictures of the Gone World* (1955) and *A Coney Island of the Mind* (1958), with its notable verse "Autobiography," became highly popular, as did the long poem *Tentative Description of a Dinner Given to Promote the Impeachment of President Eisenhower* (1958). His later poems continued to be politically oriented, as indicated by such titles as *One Thousand Fearful Words for Fidel Castro* (1961), *Where Is Vietnam?* (1965), *Tyrannus Nix?*

(1969), and *Who Are We Now?* (1976). His selected poems were printed in *Endless Love* (1981).

Fern, Fanny See **Sara Payson Willis Parton**

Fiedler, Leslie A(aron) (b. March 8, 1917, Newark, N.J.—d. Jan. 29, 2003, Buffalo, N.Y.) Critic who applied psychological and social theories to American literature.

Fiedler attended the University of Wisconsin (Ph.D., 1941), and, after wartime service in the naval reserve, did further research at Harvard University. From 1965 he taught at SUNY–Buffalo. He gained notoriety with "Come Back to the Raft Ag'in, Huck Honey!" (reprinted in *An End to Innocence,* 1955), which claimed implicit homosexuality in the relationship between Huckleberry Finn and Jim. His major work, *Love and Death in the American Novel* (1960), argued that much of American literature embodies themes of innocent (presexual), but often homoerotic, male bonding and escape from a domestic, female-dominated society. This idea, and other ingenious but controversial theories, are further explored in *Waiting for the End* (1964) and *The Return of the Vanishing American* (1968). Fiedler's later critical works include *The Stranger in Shakespeare* (1972), *The Inadvertent Epic* (1979), *What Was Literature?* (1982), and *Fiedler on the Roof* (1990).

Field, Eugene (b. Sept. 2, 1850, St. Louis, Mo.—d. Nov. 4, 1895, Chicago) Poet and journalist.

Field worked for a variety of newspapers, including the *Denver Tribune*. Comic paragraphs from his *Tribune* column, "Odds and Ends," formed his first book, *The Tribune Primer* (1882), journalistic joking in the tradition of Artemus Ward and Josh Billings. In his "Sharps and Flats" column in the *Chicago Morning News* (renamed the *Record* in 1890), he satirized the cultural pretensions of Chicago's newly rich. *A Little Book of Western Verse* (1889), drawn in part from his column, included poems in rural dialect, verses for children in an affected Old English dialect, translations of Horace, and the well-known "Little Boy Blue" and "Dutch Lullaby" ("Wynken, Blynken, and Nod"). Field's collected works in 10 volumes were published in1896, and two more volumes in 1900.

Fish, Stanley (Eugene) (b. April 19, 1938, Providence, R.I.) Literary critic.

Fish was educated at the University of Pennsylvania and Yale University. He has taught at Johns Hopkins (1974–85), Duke (1985–98), and the University of Illinois at Chicago (from 1999).

In *Surprised by Sin* (1967), Fish suggested that the subject of *Paradise Lost* is in fact the reader, who is forced to undergo spiritual self-examination when led by Milton down the path taken by Adam, Eve, and Satan. In the influential *Is There a Text in This Class?* (1980), he further developed reader-response criticism, which holds that the meaning of a text is created, rather than discovered, by the reader. His later works include *There's No Such Thing as Free Speech* (1993), *Professional Correctness* (1996), and *The Trouble with Principle* (1999).

Fisher, Dorothy Canfield *originally* Dorothea Frances Canfield, *pen name* **Dorothy Canfield** (b. Feb. 17, 1879, Lawrence, Kan.—d. Nov. 9, 1958, Arlington, Vt.) Prolific author of novels, short stories, children's books, educational works, and memoirs.

In 1904 Canfield received the first Ph.D. in Romance languages awarded by Columbia University to a woman. In 1907 she married John Redwood Fisher and published her first novel, *Gunhild*. In the same year she inherited her great-grandfather's farm in Arlington, Vt.; the town appears, lightly veiled, in many of her works, including *Hillsboro People* (1915; written with Sarah Cleghorn) and the novel *The Bent Twig* (1915).

In 1912 Fisher met Maria Montessori in Italy and was impressed by the educator's theories. *A Montessori Mother* (1912), *The Montessori Manual* (1913), and *Mothers and Children* (1914) were the results of their friendship. Fisher's experiences in French clinics and war camps during World War I resulted in three volumes of short stories, including *Home Fires in France* (1918). After returning to the United States, she produced a string of marriage-and-family stories and novels, including *The Brimming Cup* (1921). Her translation of Giovanni Papini's *The Life of Christ* (1923) became a huge best-seller. *Her Son's Wife* (1926) is one of her best-regarded longer works. In the 1940s and '50s she worked for environmental, children's, and educational causes (her Children's Crusade raised $130,000 in pennies) while writing historical children's books, including *Paul Revere and the Minute Men* (1950).

Fisher, M(ary) F(rances) K(ennedy) *originally* Mary Frances Kennedy (b. July 3, 1908, Albion, Mich.—d. June 22, 1992, Glen Ellen, Calif.) Writer who created the new genre of the food essay.

Reared in Whittier, Calif., Kennedy became accomplished in the kitchen early. She married in 1929 and moved to Dijon, France, where she reveled in French cooking and culture. Her first book of essays celebrating food, *Serve It Forth*, was published in 1937. Other early works include *Consider the Oyster* (1941) and *How to Cook a Wolf* (1942), in which she encourages readers to make the most of whatever they can afford.

While all Fisher's books were well received, critics point to *The Gastronomical Me* (1943) as one of her best early efforts. Her 1949 translation of Brillat-Savarin's *The Physiology of Taste* is regarded as the definitive English version. *An Alphabet for Gourmets* (1949) is superbly witty, and *A Cordiall Water* (1961), a discourse on folk remedies, became something of a cult classic. Her 1971 memoir, *Among Friends*, details her early years. *Sister Age* (1983) is a meditation on growing older.

Fisher, Rudolph (John Chauncey) (b. May 9, 1897, Washington, D.C.—d. Dec. 26, 1934, New York City) Writer and physician.

After receiving a master's degree from Brown University and a medical degree from Howard University (1924), Fisher settled in Harlem to become one of the few African-American radiologists of the 1920s and '30s. He had begun writing short stories while in medical school; his first, "The City of Refuge," appeared in the *Atlantic Monthly* in 1924, and "High Yaller" won a prize in 1926. He subsequently wrote two novels, *The Walls of Jericho* (1928) and *The Conjure-Man Dies* (1932); the latter has been called the first black detective novel ever published in book form. Fisher died at 37 following several operations for a stomach disorder, and was mourned by such figures as Langston Hughes and Zora Neale Hurston as one of the greatest talents of the Harlem Renaissance.

Fitch, (William) Clyde (b. May 2, 1865, Elmira, N.Y.—d. Sept. 4, 1909, Châlons-sur-Marne, France) Playwright best known for plays of social satire and character study.

Fitch began organizing neighborhood theatricals by age 10. He graduated from Amherst College in 1886 and began writing short stories for magazines in New York. A prolific writer, he would eventually produce a total of 33 original plays and 22 adaptations. His earlier plays were largely melodramas and historical plays of lesser significance; the more important later plays include *Beau Brummel* (1890), written for the actor Richard Mansfield, *The Climbers* (1901), *Captain Jinks of the Horse Marines* (1901), *The Girl with the Green Eyes* (1902), *The Woman in the Case* (1905), *The Truth* (1907), and *The City* (1909). His popularity was such that in 1901 four of his works were playing simultaneously to packed houses.

Fitts, Dudley (b. April 28, 1903, Boston—d. July 10, 1968, Lawrence, Mass.) Teacher, critic, and poet known for his translations of classical Greek works.

Fitts spent most of his career teaching at Phillips Academy in Andover, Mass. New Directions, founded by his former student James Laughlin, published his *Poems 1929–1936* (1937) and his translations *One Hundred Poems from the Palatine Anthology* (1938) and *More Poems from the Palatine Anthology in English Paraphrase* (1941). His most widely read translations were those from ancient Greek. With Robert Fitzgerald he translated Euripides' *Alcestis* (1936) and Sophocles' *Antigone* (1939) and *Oedipus Rex* (1949); his solo translations included Aristophanes' *Lysistrata* (1954), *The Frogs* (1955), *The Birds* (1957), and *Ladies' Day* (1959). He also translated Latin and Spanish-language writings. He edited anthologies of poetry translations and, from 1960 to 1968, the Yale Series of Younger Poets.

Fitzgerald, F(rancis) Scott (Key) (b. Sept. 24, 1896, St. Paul, Minn.—d. Dec. 21, 1940, Hollywood, Calif.) Short-story writer and novelist known for his depictions of the Jazz Age.

Fitzgerald attended Princeton University but was forced to withdraw in 1917 because of poor grades, and later that year joined the army. In 1918 he met Zelda Sayre, daughter of an Alabama Supreme Court judge. To prove himself and win her, he rewrote the novel he had begun at Princeton; in 1920 THIS SIDE OF PARADISE was published and the two were married.

Fitzgerald started writing for periodicals, publishing early stories such as THE DIAMOND AS BIG AS THE RITZ, later collected in TALES OF THE JAZZ AGE (1922). Fame and prosperity were both welcome and frightening; in THE BEAUTIFUL AND DAMNED (1922), he describes the life he and Zelda feared, a descent into ennui and dissipation.

F. Scott Fitzgerald

The Fitzgeralds moved in 1924 to the French Riviera, where they fell in with a group of American expatriates, described in his last completed novel, TENDER IS THE NIGHT (1934). Shortly after their arrival, he completed his greatest work, THE GREAT GATSBY (1925), which poignantly expresses his ambivalence about American life, at once vulgar and dazzlingly promising. Some of his finest short stories of this period, particularly "The Rich Boy" and "Absolution," appeared in *All the Sad Young Men* (1926).

The stresses of fame and prosperity led Fitzgerald to drink excessively; Zelda suffered mental breakdowns in 1930 and 1932 from which she never fully recovered, and she spent most of her remaining years in a sanitarium. By 1937 Fitzgerald had become a scriptwriter in Hollywood; there he met the gossip columnist Sheilah Graham, with whom he would spend the rest of his life. He told the story of his downward slide in THE CRACK-UP, published posthumously in 1945. His last work, the Hollywood novel THE LAST TYCOON (1941), was left unfinished at his death at 44 of alcohol-related causes.

Flanner, Janet *pseudonym* **Genêt** (b. March 13, 1892, Indianapolis—d. Nov. 7, 1978, New York City) Longtime correspondent for the *New Yorker*.

Flanner began a career in journalism as the *Indianapolis Star*'s first movie critic in 1916. In 1922, after a failed marriage, she settled in Paris, where she would live (except for the war years) until 1975. In 1925 she was hired by Harold Ross to write a periodic "Letter from Paris" for his new magazine, the *New Yorker*. Signed "Genêt," the articles contained her penetrating observations, written in elegant prose, on politics, art, theater, and the general quality of French life. In the 1930s Flanner also began writing an occasional "Letter from London." Her first novel, *The Cubical City*, appeared in 1926. Most of her essays were collected in *American in Paris* (1940), *Paris Journal, 1944–1965* (1966), *Paris Journal, 1965–1971* (1971), and *Janet Flanner's World* (1979).

Fletcher, John Gould (b. Jan 3, 1886, Little Rock, Ark.—d. May 20, 1950, Little Rock) Poet and critic.

While enrolled at Harvard University (1903–7), Fletcher developed an interest in poetry. His first commercially published poetry collection, *Fire and Wine,* appeared in 1913; it was followed by several more over the next two decades. Interested in Zen Buddhism and Chinese and Japanese poetry, his work showed a pronounced Asian influence. He contributed to Amy Lowell's three Imagist anthologies (1915–17), and his literary friends included Ezra Pound and Conrad Aiken. During the 1930s he became committed to Southern agrarianism and joined the circle of the Fugitive poets. His *Selected Poems* (1938) won a Pulitzer Prize. He organized the Arkansas Folklore Society and wrote a history of Arkansas (*Arkansas,* 1947).

Fodor \\'fō-ˌdȯr, 'fō-dər\\, **Eugene** (b. Oct. 14, 1905, Léva, Hungary [now Levice, Slovakia.]—d. Feb. 18, 1991, Torrington, Conn.) Travel writer who created a series of popular tourist guidebooks.

After a university education in Czechoslovakia, Fodor continued his studies in France and Germany. While working as an interpreter for a French shipping company, he wrote articles about exotic ports of call and life aboard ship, and he soon became a full-time travel correspondent and editor in Prague (1930–33) and London (1934–38). His first book, *1936—On the Continent*, was an international best-seller. He became a naturalized U.S. citizen in 1942 and served in an army intelligence unit. In 1949 he settled in Paris and founded Fodor's Modern Guides, Inc. His guidebooks provided historical background and cultural insights into the places and people described, as well as reliable, practical information for inexperienced travelers. He returned to the United States in 1964 and sold his company in 1968. At the time of his death, his now-innumerable guides were selling some 3 million copies each year.

Foote, (Albert) Horton (b. March 14, 1916, Wharton, Texas) Playwright and screenwriter.

Foote left home at 16 to study acting in California and New York, and appeared on the stage in New York (1939–42). Encouraged by Agnes de Mille, he began writing plays, beginning with *Texas Town* (1942). It was followed by such dramas as *Celebration* (1948), *The Trip to Bountiful* (1953; film, 1985), *The Traveling Lady* (1954; film, 1964), *Tomorrow* (1960; film, 1971), and the nine-play "Orphans' Home" cycle (1974–77), which includes *Lila Dale* and *The Widow Claire*. *The Young Man from Atlanta* (1994) was awarded the Pulitzer Prize. Most of Foote's plays, noted for their quiet, loving attention to small-town ways, take place in Harrison, a Texas Gulf Coast town much like his hometown.

His dozens of screenplays include those for *Hurry Sundown* (1966), *On Valentine's Day* (1985), and *Convicts* (1991); those for *To Kill a Mockingbird* (1962) and *Tender Mercies* (1983) won Academy Awards.

Foote, Shelby (b. Nov. 17, 1916, Greenville, Miss.) Historian, novelist, and short-story writer known for his works treating the Civil War and the South.

Foote attended the University of North Carolina for two years (1935–37) and served in the army during World War II. His first novel, *Tournament*, was published in 1949. Like many of his later novels, it is set in the fictional Bristol, Miss., modeled on his hometown. *Follow Me Down* (1950), considered by many his best novel, was based on an actual murder trial. *Love in a Dry Season* (1951) is set against the changing fortunes of the South from the 1920s to World War II. *Shiloh* (1952), Foote's first popular success, uses the monologues of six soldiers to recreate the Civil War battle of the title. His major work, *The Civil War: A Narrative* (1958–74), consists of three volumes—*Fort Sumter to Perryville* (1958), *Fredericksburg to Meridian* (1963), and *Red River to Appomattox* (1974). Considered a masterpiece by many critics, it has also been criticized by academics for its lack of footnoting and other scholarly conventions. Foote appeared as narrator and commentator in Ken Burns's 11-hour television documentary *The Civil War* (1990). His 50-year correspondence with the novelist Walker Percy was published in 1996.

Forché \fòr-'shā\, **Carolyn** *originally* Caroline Louise Sidlosky (b. April 28, 1950, Detroit) Poet whose writing reflects her concern for human rights.

Forché was educated at Michigan State and Bowling Green State universities (M.A. 1975). Her first collection of poetry, *Gathering the Tribes* (1976), evokes her childhood and Slovak ancestry and reflects on sexuality, family, and race. From 1978 to 1980, as a journalist in El Salvador, she acted as a human-rights advocate for Amnesty International and translated works by Salvadoran poets. The poems collected in *The Country Between Us* (1981) examine the events she witnessed there. The book-length poem *The Angel of History* (1994) is a compelling distillation of her intensely moral sensibility.

Forché has also edited several books, including *Against Forgetting: Twentieth-Century Poetry of Witness* (1993), and has taught creative writing at George Mason University.

Ford, Richard (b. Feb. 16, 1944, Jackson, Miss.) Novelist and short-story writer.

Ford attended Michigan State University, Washington University Law School, and UC–Irvine, and subsequently taught in several American colleges and universities. In his first novel, *A Piece of My Heart* (1976), critics noted the influence of Faulkner. In the early 1980s Ford worked for a sports magazine; the protagonist of the highly praised *The Sportswriter* (1986) and its sequel *Independence Day* (1995, Pulitzer Prize, PEN/Faulkner Award), is an alienated, middle-aged sportswriter.

Rock Springs (1987) contains short stories about lonely and damaged people in the American West. *Women with Men* (1997) is a set of three novellas.

Forrest, Leon (b. Jan. 8, 1937, Chicago—d. Nov. 6, 1997, Evanston, Ill.) Novelist and journalist.

From 1965 to 1973 Forrest worked as a journalist for various papers, including the Nation of Islam's weekly *Muhammad Speaks*. He also published portions of what would become his first novel, *There Is a Tree More Ancient than Eden* (1973). The novel portrays the tangled relationships between the illegitimate offspring of a onetime slave-owning family; several of its distinctive characters reappear in Forrest's later novels. Echoes of classical mythology are present in *The Bloodworth Orphans* (1977), about the search by three orphaned siblings for roots and understanding amid turmoil. In *Two Wings to Veil My Face* (1983) an ex-slave tells her life story to her great-grandson. Forrest's most ambitious novel, *Divine Days* (1992), concerns the efforts of a black playwright to investigate the disappearance of a fellow black. *Relocations of the Spirit* (1994) is a book of essays. Forrest taught at Northwestern University from 1973 until his death.

Foster, Hannah   *originally* Hannah Webster (b. Salisbury, Mass., Sept. 10, 1758—d. April 17, 1840, Montreal, Canada) Novelist.

Born into a wealthy family, Webster married the Rev. John Foster in 1785. In 1797 she published *The Coquette*, one of the first novels written by a native-born American woman. An early American example of the epistolary novel and strongly influenced by Samuel Richardson, it was based on a well-known event, the seduction of the author's cousin by the son of the great theologian Jonathan Edwards and her death in childbirth in an inn. It implicitly deplored the prevailing social restrictions on women. Though *The Coquette* sold in large numbers for many decades, her second novel, *The Boarding School* (1798), was unsuccessful.

Frank, Waldo (David) (b. Aug. 25, 1889, Long Branch, N.J.—d. Jan 9, 1967, White Plains, N.Y.) Journalist, educator, and writer.

After graduating from Yale, Frank served on the staff of the *New York Times* and the *New York Evening Post* (1911–13). He helped found the journal *Seven Arts,* which he edited for its brief life (1916–17). His *Our America* (1919) examined American society from a leftist perspective. A trip through the South with the black writer Jean Toomer led him to write on race relations, and he also interested himself deeply in South America, about which he wrote and lectured extensively. His major work, *The Re-discovery of America* (1929), was a critique of American culture. In the 1930s he supported the Communist Party's presidential candidates; in the postwar years his leftist politics would lead to government investigations. Among his other works are several novels and essay collections, a study of Simón Bolívar (*Birth of a World,* 1951), and *The Rediscovery of Man* (1958).

Franklin, Benjamin (b. Jan. 6 [Jan. 17, New Style], 1706, Boston—d. April 17, 1790, Philadelphia) Printer and publisher, author, scientist, inventor, and diplomat.

Benjamin Franklin

Franklin ended his formal education at 10, and at 12 he was apprenticed to his brother, a printer. His first enthusiasm was for poetry, but he soon turned to prose. He achieved much of what was to become his characteristic style from imitating the writing in Joseph Addison and Richard Steele's famous periodical *The Spectator*. Around 1729 he became the printer of paper currency for Pennsylvania and other American colonies. In 1729 he purchased the *Pennsylvania Gazette*, which would become generally acknowledged as among the best of the colonial newspapers, and in 1732 he founded POOR RICHARD'S ALMANACK, whose proverbs and aphorisms emphasizing prudence, industry, and honesty would become part of American lore for many decades thereafter. He became prosperous and devoted much energy to promoting public services in Philadelphia, including a library, fire department, hospital, and insurance company, as well as an academy that would later become the University of Pennsylvania. In 1748 he gave up management of his publications to devote himself to science and inventing; his inventions would include the Franklin stove and bifocal spectacles, and his famous experiments in electricity led to the invention of the lightning rod.

He served 15 years in the colonial legislature (1736–51). He spent the years 1757–62 in London representing Pennsylvania in a dispute over taxation of lands held by the Penn family. In 1764 he was sent back to London, where he helped secure repeal of the Stamp Act. His initial belief in a unified colonial government under British rule gradually changed over the issue of taxation. He remained in England until 1775, when he departed in anticipation of war. Back in Philadelphia he served as a delegate to the Second Continental Congress, where he helped draft the Declaration of Independence. In 1776 he traveled to France to seek military and financial aid for the colonies. There he became a hero to the French people, the personification of the unsophisticated nobility of the New World. At the close of the Revolutionary War, he was one of the diplomats chosen to negotiate peace with Britain. As a member of the 1787 Constitutional Convention, he was instrumental in achieving adoption of the U.S. Constitution. Through the years he wrote a large number of editorials, articles, pamphlets, and monographs, principally on political and scientific subjects. His celebrated *Autobiography* (written 1771–88) was published posthumously. Franklin is remembered as one of the most extraordinary, brilliant, and indispensable public servants in the country's history.

Franklin, John Hope (b. Jan. 2, 1915, Rentiesville, Okla.) Historian and educator.

Franklin graduated from Fisk University and earned a Ph.D. from Harvard University in 1941. He taught history at numerous institutions, principally Howard University (1947–56), Brooklyn College (1956–64), the University of Chicago (1964–82), and Duke University (1982–92).

He first gained international attention with *From Slavery to Freedom: A History of Negro Americans* (1947; 7th ed., 1994), which has enjoyed a long life as a textbook and remains his best-known work. His other works include *The Emancipation Proclamation* (1963), *The Militant South 1800–1860* (1956), *Reconstruction After the Civil War* (1961), *Land of the Free* (1966), *Racial Equality in America* (1976), *Race and History* (1990), and *Race and Color* (1993).

Franklin was the first black president of the American Historical Association (1978–79). He has received dozens of honorary degrees, and in 1995 he was awarded the Presidential Medal of Freedom.

Frederic \'fred-rik\, **Harold** (b. Aug. 19, 1856, Utica, N.Y.—d. Oct. 19, 1898, Henley-on-Thames, Oxfordshire, England) Journalist, foreign correspondent, and author of several historical novels.

At 14 Frederic found employment with the *Utica Observer,* and by 20 he was reporting for the paper. In 1882 he became editor of the *Albany Evening Journal.* In 1884 he went to London as a correspondent for the *New York Times,* and London would remain his base the rest of his life, though he would cover stories from as far afield as Italy (for an 1884 cholera outbreak) and Russia (where he investigated persecution of Jews in 1891).

His historical fiction ranges in setting from the American Revolution (*In the Valley*, 1890) to the Civil War (*The Copperhead*, 1893, and *Marsena and Other Stories*, 1894). Of his New York State novels, *The Damnation of Theron Ware* (1896), the story of the decline and fall of a Methodist minister, brought him his greatest fame. Three other novels, *March Hares* (1896), *Gloria Mundi* (1898), and *The Market Place* (1899), are about English life.

Freeman, Douglas Southall (b. May 16, 1886, Lynchburg, Va.—d. June 13, 1953, Westbourne, Hampton Gardens, near Richmond, Va.) Journalist and author noted for his writings on the Confederacy.

After receiving his Ph.D. from Johns Hopkins (1908), Freeman began a journalistic career with the *Richmond News Leader,* becoming chief editor in 1915. His career as a historian began with his compilation of a catalog of the papers in Richmond's Confederate Museum (1908) and his edition of Robert E. Lee's correspondence with Jefferson Davis and the Confederate war department (1915). The latter led to the monumental four-volume biography *R. E. Lee* (1934), which won the Pulitzer Prize.

His other works include *Virginia—A Gentle Dominion* (1924); *The Last Parade* (1932); *The South to Posterity* (1939); the highly praised *Lee's Lieutenants, A Study in Command* (3 vols., 1942–44); *John Steward Bryan* (1947); and the vast *George Washington* (7 vols., 1948–57, Pulitzer Prize), whose final volume he left incomplete at his death.

Freeman, Mary Wilkins *originally* Mary Eleanor Wilkins (b. Oct. 31, 1852, Randolph, Mass.—d. March 13, 1930, Metuchen, N.J.) Novelist and short-story writer.

In 1867 Wilkins's family moved to Brattleboro, Vt. She began writing stories and verse for children to help support them, and quickly became successful. She subsequently returned to Randolph, where she did her best writing in the 1880s and '90s. She married in 1902 and moved with her husband to New Jersey. She produced a dozen volumes of short stories and as many novels, most of which chronicle the somber lives of poor New England villagers. She is remembered chiefly for her first two story collections, *A Humble Romance* (1887) and *A New England Nun* (1891), and for the novel *Pembroke* (1894).

Freneau \fre-'nō\, **Philip (Morin)** (b. Jan. 2, 1752, New York City—d. Dec. 18, 1832, Monmouth County, N.J.) Poet, essayist, and editor, known as the "poet of the American Revolution."

At the outbreak of the Revolution, Freneau wrote vitriolic satire against the British and Tories. He spent two years in the Caribbean islands as secretary to a wealthy planter; there he produced some of his most ambitious poems, including "The Beauties of Santa Cruz," "The Jamaica Funeral," and "The House of Night," which foreshadowed English Romanticism. On his return he became an active participant in the war. Captaining his own ship as a privateer, he was captured and imprisoned by the British in 1780, an experience he bitterly recounted after his release in the poem *The British Prison-Ship* (1781).

During the next several years he contributed poems to the *Freeman's Journal* in Philadelphia. He worked as a sea captain until 1790, when he again entered partisan journalism, and in 1791 he founded the highly partisan Jeffersonian *National Gazette* in Philadelphia.

Well schooled in the classics and in Neoclassical English poetry, Freneau strove for a fresh idiom that would be unmistakably American. Though he failed to achieve it except in a few poems, he was an important precursor of the native nature poets.

Friedan \fri-'dan\, **Betty** *originally* Betty Naomi Goldstein (b. Feb. 4, 1921, Peoria, Ill.) Feminist social reformer and writer.

Goldstein graduated from Smith College in 1942 and worked for five years before marrying Carl Friedan (divorced 1969) and settling uncomfortably into the life of a housewife, mother, and occasional freelance writer. Discovering in 1957 that several of her college classmates were as dissatisfied with their lives as she was with her own, she began a series of studies that eventually resulted in the landmark work *The Feminine Mystique* (1963). The book's thesis was that women were victims of a pervasive system of delusions and false values that urged them to find their fulfillment and identity vicariously, through their husbands and children. An immediate and controversial best-seller, it is now regarded as one of the most influential American books of the 20th century.

In 1966 Friedan cofounded the National Organization for Women (NOW), which was dedicated to achieving equality of opportunity for women. A founding member of the National Women's Political Caucus (1971), she was a leader of the campaign for ratification of the Equal Rights Amendment. *The Second Stage* (1981) assessed the status of the women's movement. *The Fountain of Age* (1993) addresses the psychology of old age, seeking to counter the notion that aging means loss and depletion. Her memoir, *Life So Far,* appeared in 2000.

Friedman, Bruce Jay (b. April 26, 1930, New York City) Novelist and short-story writer whose principal subject has been American Jews.

Friedman worked in publishing for several years before achieving success with his first novel, *Stern* (1962). The title character is a luckless descendant of the biblical Job, unable to assimilate into mainstream American life. Though most of Friedman's characters are Jewish by birth, they feel marginal to both Jewish and American culture. His later works, almost all of which exhibit his dark, mocking humor, include the novels *A Mother's Kisses* (1964), *About Harry Towns* (1974), *Violencia* (1988), and *The Current Climate* (1989); the short-story collections *Black Angels* (1966), *Let's Hear It for a Beautiful Guy* (1984), and *The Slightly Older Guy* (1995); the essay collection *The Lonely Guy's Book of Life* (1978); the plays *Steambath* (1971) and *Have You Spoken To Any Jews Lately* (1995); and screenplays for such films as *Splash* (1984).

Friedman, Milton (b. July 31, 1912, Brooklyn, N.Y.) Economist and writer.

A graduate of Rutgers University, Friedman worked as an economist for government agencies (1935–43). After obtaining his Ph.D. from Columbia University in 1946, he began teaching at the University of Chicago, where he would remain until his retirement in 1983. At Chicago he became a leading figure among conservative economists (the "Chicago school"), who supported laissez-faire policies and a deregulated marketplace and opposed the dominant Keynesian approach. An adviser to Sen. Barry Goldwater and Pres. Richard Nixon, Friedman later saw his ideas taken up by Pres. Ronald Reagan and Britain's Margaret Thatcher.

His many books included the influential *Studies in the Quantity Theory of Money* (1956), the monumental *Monetary History of the United States 1867–1960* (1963; with Anna J. Schwartz), and *Tax Limitation, Inflation, and the Role of Government* (1978); he collaborated with his wife, Rose, on such works as *Theory of the Consumption Function* (1957) and *Capitalism and Freedom* (1962). As a columnist for *Newsweek* magazine (1966–84) and author and host of the public-television series *Free to Choose* (1980), he disseminated his ideas to a wide audience, becoming perhaps the country's most famous economist. In 1976 Friedman was awarded the Nobel Prize in economics; in 1988 he received the Presidential Medal of Freedom.

Frost, Robert (Lee) (b. March 26, 1874, San Francisco—d. Jan. 29, 1963, Boston) Poet.

Frost's family moved to New England when he was young, and he briefly attended Dartmouth and Harvard colleges before settling on a family farm in Derry, N.H., where he farmed and later also taught school (1906–12). Frustrated and financially strapped, he sold the farm and in 1912 went to England, where Ezra Pound helped him publish his first two collections of poems, *A Boy's Will* (1913) and *North of Boston* (1914). In 1915 he returned to find himself a poet of some reputation, and bought a farm in Franconia, N.H. The collection *Mountain Interval* (1916) enhanced his stature, and *New Hampshire* (1923) won him the Pulitzer Prize. He accepted visiting positions offered by colleges and universities, beginning a distinguished career as a teacher that would take him to the University of Michigan, Harvard, Dartmouth, and especially Amherst College.

Robert Frost

His poetry reveals his almost mystical attachment to the fields and farms of New England. An ardent naturalist and botanist, he acutely observed the details of rural nature and his neighbors and endowed them with universal, even metaphysical, meaning, using colloquial language, familiar rhythms, and symbols taken from common life to express both the pastoral ideals and the dark complexities of New England life. Generations of readers have been introduced to poetry through reading such poems as STOPPING BY WOODS ON A SNOWY EVENING, THE ROAD NOT TAKEN, THE DEATH OF THE HIRED MAN, and MENDING WALL.

Frost's later collections, all of them distinguished, include *West-Running Brook* (1928), *Collected Poems* (1930, Pulitzer Prize), *A Further Range* (1936, Pulitzer Prize), *A Witness Tree* (1942, Pulitzer Prize), *Steeple Bush* (1947), and *In the Clearing* (1962). He was unique among 20th-century American poets in simultaneously achieving true popularity and deep critical admiration, and in his last decades he was unrivaled as the country's unofficial poet laureate.

Fuller, Charles H(enry), Jr. (b. March 5, 1939, Philadelphia) Playwright best known for A SOLDIER'S PLAY.

After studies at Villanova University and LaSalle College (where he would later obtain his doctorate), Fuller cofounded the Afro-American Arts Theater in Philadelphia in 1967, and served as its codirector until 1971. His play *The Perfect Party* opened in 1969. In the 1970s he wrote plays for New York's Henry Street Settlement theater, and in 1974 the Negro Ensemble Company produced his *In the Deepest Part of Sleep*. He based *The Brownsville Raid* (1975) on an incident involving the dishonorable discharge in 1906 of an entire black army regiment. *Zooman and the Sign* (1980) deals with a father's search for his daughter's killer. *A Soldier's Play* (1981; film, *A Soldier's Story*, 1984) follows the investigation by a black army captain of the murder of a black soldier at a base in Louisiana; it earned Fuller the second Pulitzer Prize for drama ever awarded to an African-American.

Fuller, Henry Blake (b. Jan. 9, 1857, Chicago—d. July 28, 1929, Chicago) Novelist who wrote about his native Chicago.

Fuller came from a prosperous Chicago family. His first two novels, *The Chevalier of Pensieri-Vani* (1890, written under the name Stanton Page) and *The Chatelaine of La Trinité* (1892), were gracefully told, brief but unhurried tales about Europe.

He took a decidedly new turn with *The Cliff-Dwellers* (1893), a realistic novel about inhabitants of a Chicago skyscraper, sometimes called the first important American city novel. *With the Procession* (1895) dealt with a wealthy Chicago merchant family. Fuller's later Chicago fiction includes the short-story collection *Under the Skylights* (1901) and the novels *On the Stairs* (1918) and *Bertram Cope's Year* (1919), and his later European-based fiction includes the collection *Waldo Trench and Others* (1908) and *Gardens of This World* (1929), which extends the tale begun in his first book.

Margaret Fuller

Fuller, (Sarah) Margaret (b. May 23, 1810, Cambridgeport, Mass.—d. July 19, 1850, at sea off Long Island, N.Y.) Critic, teacher, and woman of letters.

Fuller taught in Bronson Alcott's Temple School in Boston (1836–37) and later in Providence, R.I. (1837–39). In 1839 she published a translation of J. P. Eckermann's *Conversations with Goethe*; her most cherished project, never completed, was a biography of Goethe. From 1839 to 1844 she held her "conversations," forums at which Boston women discussed intellectual matters. These provided the material and inspiration for *Woman in the Nineteenth Century* (1845), a tract on feminism that was both a demand for political equality and an ardent plea for women's emotional, intellectual, and spiritual fulfillment.

A close friend of Emerson and the Transcendentalists, Fuller edited their magazine, the DIAL, from 1840 to 1842, and published her own poetry, reviews, and critiques in its pages. In 1844 she became literary critic on Horace Greeley's *New York Tribune*. Before she sailed for Europe in 1846, some of her essays appeared as *Papers on Literature and Art*; these assured the cordial welcome she received in English and French circles, and she visited Carlyle, Wordsworth, and George Sand. As America's first woman foreign correspondent, she reported on her travels for the *Tribune*; the "letters" were later published in *At Home and Abroad* (1856).

In Italy she struck up an acquaintance with the revolutionary leader Giuseppe Mazzini. She soon married the radical Italian nobleman Giovanni Angelo, Marchese Ossoli, and they worked together for the Roman revolution. Following the suppression of the republic they sailed for America with their infant son; all three perished in a shipwreck off Fire Island.

Gaddis \\'gad-əs\\, **William (Thomas)** (b. Dec. 29, 1922, New York City—d. Dec. 16, 1998, East Hampton, N.Y.) Novelist known for his long, experimental, satirical works.

Gaddis studied at Harvard and traveled extensively before gaining attention with his controversial novel THE RECOGNITIONS (1955). Rich in language and imagery, it began as a parody of *Faust* but developed into a multileveled examination of spiritual bankruptcy. Discouraged by its harsh critical reception, Gaddis published nothing for 20 years and instead worked as a freelance writer for various corporations. His experiences provided material for his second novel, JR (1975; National Book Award); hailed by many as an ambitious masterpiece, it uses long stretches of cacophonous dialogue to depict the greed, hypocrisy, and banality of American business. *Carpenter's Gothic* (1985) is even more pessimistic in its depiction of moral chaos in American society. Gaddis's fourth novel, *A Frolic of His Own* (1994; National Book Award), attacks the legal profession. He completed a fifth novel, *Agape Agape,* before his death.

Gaddis's fiction, containing long and often scathingly funny dialogues and monologues related by a minimum of plot and structured by scant punctuation, shows the influence of James Joyce and in turn influenced the work of Thomas Pynchon, and his first two books are regarded by many as landmarks of 20th-century American fiction.

Gaines, Ernest J(ames) (b. Jan. 15, 1933, Oscar, La.) Novelist whose fiction has reflected the black oral tradition of his rural Louisiana childhood.

When Gaines was 15, his family moved to California, where he attended San Francisco State College and pursued graduate studies at Stanford University. He has since taught at several institutions, including Denison and Stanford. His novels are set in rural Louisiana, often in a fictional plantation area named Bayonne that some critics have compared to William Faulkner's imaginary Yoknapatawpha County. His most acclaimed works are THE AUTOBIOGRAPHY OF MISS JANE PITTMAN (1971) and *A Lesson Before Dying* (1993). His other novels include *Catherine Carmier* (1964), *Of Love and Dust* (1967), *In My Father's House* (1978), and *A Gathering of Old Men* (1983).

Galarza \\gä-'lär-sä\\, **Ernesto** (b. Aug. 7, 1905, Jalcocotán, Nayarit, Mexico—d. June 22, 1984, San Jose, Calif.) Writer and labor organizer.

As a child Galarza moved with his family to Sacramento, Calif., where he worked in the fields while attending school. After graduating from Occidental College and earning a master's degree from Stanford University and a Ph.D. from Columbia University, he became a labor organizer, serving as vice president of the National Farm Labor Union and later executive secretary of the National Agricultural Workers Union. He wrote several books and numerous articles on labor conditions for Mexican workers in the United States and other Mexican-American social and economic topics, including *Merchants of Labor*

(1964). His best-known work, the autobiography *Barrio Boy* (1971), is widely read in high schools and colleges.

Galbraith \\'gal-ˌbrāth\\, **John Kenneth** (b. Oct. 15, 1908, Iona Station, Ontario, Canada) Economist and writer.

After study at the University of Toronto and UC–Berkeley (Ph.D., 1934), Galbraith taught at Harvard and Princeton universities until 1942. He held a variety of governmental posts, holding principal responsibility for overseeing consumer prices during World War II, and in 1948 resumed his academic career at Harvard, where he established himself as a politically active, liberal academician with a talent for communicating with the reading public. A key adviser to John F. Kennedy, he served as ambassador to India (1961–63). He retired from Harvard in 1975.

Galbraith's major works began with *American Capitalism* (1951) and *The Great Crash, 1929* (1955). *The Affluent Society* (1958), which called for less emphasis on production and more attention to public service, became a best-seller and brought Galbraith's name to widespread public attention. The elegance, lucidity, and wit of his prose thereafter ensured him a general popularity rare among economists, and his works were also influential in the setting of public policy. *The New Industrial State* (1967) traced similarities between "managerial" capitalism and socialism. His many other works include *The Liberal Hour* (1960), *The Anatomy of Power* (1983), and *The Culture of Contentment* (1992).

Gale, Zona (b. Aug. 26, 1874, Portage, Wis.—d. Dec. 27, 1938, Chicago) Novelist and playwright whose *Miss Lulu Bett* (1920) established her as a chronicler of Midwestern village life.

Gale graduated from the University of Wisconsin and worked as a reporter, first for various Milwaukee newspapers and later for the *New York World*. After publication of her first short story in 1903, she gave her full time to writing.

Her books include *Friendship Village* (1908), *A Daughter of the Morning* (1917), *Birth* (1918), and *Preface to a Life* (1926). Her early writings were sentimental evocations of the virtues of small-town life and fall within the local-color tradition. Her later writings, however, reveal her interest in progressive causes and are increasingly critical of small-town provincialism. The dramatization of *Miss Lulu Bett*, a study of an unmarried woman's attempts at self-assertion in the face of a constricting social environment, won Gale the Pulitzer Prize for drama in 1921.

Gallagher, Tess *originally* Tess Bond (b. July 21, 1943, Port Angeles, Wash.) Poet known for her introspective verses about self-discovery, womanhood, and family life.

Gallagher studied at the Universities of Washington and Iowa. Her first full-length volume of verse, *Instructions to the Double* (1976), is a confessional work about her efforts to synthesize her past life with her future career as a poet.

In 1978 she published three collections of poems: *Portable Kisses*, *On Your Own*, and *Under Stars*. Several poems in *Willingly* (1984), including "Boat Ride" and "3 A.M. Kitchen: My Father Talking," eulogize her late father. The collections *Amplitude* (1987) and *Moon Crossing Bridge* (1992) focus on her third husband, the writer RAYMOND CARVER. She has also written several plays for film and television and two story collections, *The Lover of Horses* (1986) and *At the Owl Woman Saloon* (1997).

Gallant \ga-'lant\, **Mavis** *originally* Mavis de Trafford Young (b. Aug. 11, 1922, Montreal, Canada) Canadian-born writer of essays, novels, plays, and especially short stories.

Following graduation from high school in New York City, Gallant worked in Montreal at the National Film Board and as a newspaper reporter for the *Montreal Standard*. From 1950 she lived mostly in Europe, eventually settling in France. In the 1950s she became a regular contributor to the *New Yorker*, which through the years would publish more than 100 of her short stories (more than by any other writer in its history) and much of her nonfiction. In unsentimental prose and with trenchant wit she delineated the isolation, detachment, and fear that afflict rootless North American and European expatriates. Collections of her well-constructed, ironic, often bitingly humorous short stories include *My Heart Is Broken* (1964), *The Pegnitz Junction* (1973), *Home Truths* (1981), *Overhead in a Balloon* (1985), *In Transit* (1988), *Across the Bridge* (1993), and *Collected Stories* (1998).

Galloway \'gal-ə-wā\, **Joseph** (b. c. 1731, West River, Md.—d. Aug. 29, 1803, Watford, England) Colonial attorney and legislator.

Galloway entered law practice in Philadelphia in 1747 and became a leading colonial attorney. Elected to the provincial assembly in 1756, he occupied the powerful post of speaker from 1766 to 1775. In "A plan of a proposed Union between Great Britain and the Colonies" (1774) he provided for a president general to be appointed by the king and a colonial legislature to have rights and duties similar to the House of Commons. After a day's debate, his carefully conceived plan was rejected by the Continental Congress by a single vote. During the American Revolution, which he opposed, he left Philadelphia and joined Gen. William Howe's British army. In 1777 he returned to the city as a civil administrator during the British occupation. He drew up several more plans of union with the hope that they might be used when the rebels had been defeated. With the reentry of the Continental army into Philadelphia in 1778 he fled to England.

Gardner, Erle Stanley (b. July 17, 1889, Malden, Mass.—d. March 11, 1970, Temecula, Calif.) Prolific pulp novelist whose best-known works center on the lawyer-detective Perry Mason.

Erle Stanley Gardner

Gardner dropped out of Valparaiso University and settled in California, where he found work as a typist in a law firm; three years later he was admitted to the California bar. While practicing trial law in Ventura, he began writing for the pulp magazines, creating accurate courtroom scenes and brilliant legal maneuvers resembling his own legal tactics. With the successful publication of the first Perry Mason detective stories, *The Case of the Velvet Claws* (1933) and *The Case of the Sulky Girl* (1933), he gave up the law. Eighty Perry Mason novels followed. A series of Perry Mason films in the 1930s was followed by a long-running radio show (1943–55) and a highly popular television series (1957–66). The phenomenally prolific Gardner also wrote several other series of detective stories, including 29 "Lam & Cool" novels under the pseudonym A. A. Fair.

John Gardner

Gardner, John *in full* John Champlin Gardner, Jr. (b. July 21, 1933, Batavia, N.Y.—d. Sept. 14, 1982, near Susquehanna, Pa.) Novelist and poet of philosophical fiction.

Gardner attended Washington University and received his doctorate in medieval studies from the University of Iowa, then taught at various institutions, including Oberlin and Bennington colleges and the University of Rochester.

He published two novels, *The Resurrection* (1966) and *The Wreckage of Agathon* (1970), before his reputation was established with *Grendel* (1971), a retelling of the Beowulf story from the monster's point of view. *The Sunlight Dialogues* (1972) is an ambitious epic with a large cast of characters. Later novels include *October Light* (1976, National Book Critics Circle Award), *Freddy's Book* (1980), and *Mickelsson's Ghosts* (1982). Gardner was also a gifted poet and a critic who published several books on Old and Middle English poetry. He expressed his views on writing in *On Moral Fiction* (1978) and other books, in which he deplored the pessimistic tendency of many modern writers, believing that the goal of true art is a celebration of life. He died in a motorcycle crash.

Garland, (Hannibal) Hamlin (b. Sept. 14, 1860, West Salem, Wis.—d. March 4, 1940, Hollywood, Calif.) Fiction writer remembered for his short stories and his autobiographical "Middle Border" series of narratives.

As his farming family moved progressively westward from Wisconsin, Garland rebelled against the vicissitudes of pioneering and moved to Boston in 1884. There he gradually won a place for himself in the Boston and Cambridge literary set and was influenced by the novelist William Dean Howells. He began recording the physical oppression and economic frustrations of pioneer life on the Great Plains in the short stories collected in *Main-Travelled Roads* (1891), one of his best works. The short stories he published in *Prairie Folk* (1892) and *Wayside Courtships* (1897) were later combined in *Other Main-Travelled Roads* (1910). His novel *Rose of Dutcher's Coolly* (1895) tells the story of a sensitive young woman who rebels against the drudgery of farm life and goes to Chicago to pursue her talent for writing. After producing a series of mediocre novels that were serialized in the popular "slick magazines," he published the acclaimed autobiographical tale *A Son of the Middle Border* (1917). Its sequel *A Daughter of the Middle Border* (1921) won a Pulitzer Prize. His later novels were lesser efforts. Garland is considered one of the foremost representatives of Midwestern Regionalism.

Garrison, William Lloyd (b. Dec. 10/12, 1805, Newburyport, Mass.—d. May 24, 1879, New York City) Journalist and abolitionist.

    Though only slightly educated, he was apprenticed to a printer and began contributing anonymous columns to the local newspaper. At 25 Garrison joined the abolition movement and began editing the first of several local newspapers dedicated to moral reform. In 1829 he became coeditor of the Baltimore monthly *Genius of Universal Emancipation*. In 1831 he founded *The Liberator*, which under his editorship for the next 35 years would become the most radical of the antislavery journals. In 1833 he helped found the American Anti-Slavery Society, and after a split in 1840 over the admission of women (which he favored) he became president of a small group of radicals (1840–65).

William Lloyd Garrison

    A pacifist, he demanded in 1844 that the North secede peacefully from the South. In the decade before the Civil War, his influence waned as his radicalism increased; through *The Liberator* he denounced such measures as the Compromise of 1850 and the Kansas-Nebraska Act, and in 1954 he publicly burned a copy of the U.S. Constitution as a pro-slavery document. During the war he forswore pacifism to support Pres. Abraham Lincoln and hailed the Emancipation Proclamation. After his retirement in 1865 he continued to press for women's suffrage, temperance, Indian's rights, and free trade. An edition of his letters was published in 1971.

Gass, William (Howard) (b. July 30, 1924, Fargo, N.D.) Writer and critic noted for his experimentation with stylistic devices.

    Gass received his doctorate in philosophy from Cornell University and thereafter taught at Purdue University and (from 1968) Washington University. He has called his fiction works "experimental constructions," and each contains stylistic innovations. His first novel, *Omensetter's Luck* (1966), concerns a man falsely connected to a mysterious death; in it Gass creates levels of insight into character and setting by piecing together various viewpoints without the use of quotation marks to distinguish speakers. His novella *Willie Masters' Lonesome Wife* (1968) employs typographical and other visual devices. His major novel THE TUNNEL (1995), on which he worked over 30 years, evoked superlatives from critics.

    Gass's other work includes the admired short-story collection *In the Heart of the Heart of the Country* (1968) and *On Being Blue* (1976), imaginative interpretations of the color blue. He received National Book Critics Circle Awards for the essay collections *Habitations of the Word* (1985) and *Finding a Form* (1996).

Gates, Henry Louis, Jr. (b. Sept. 16, 1950, Keyser, W.Va.) Critic and scholar.

Gates visited Africa while attending Yale University and did advanced studies at Cambridge University, where his tutor was the Nigerian Wole Soyinka. Since 1991 he has taught at Harvard University, where he has headed the distinguished Afro-American Studies department.

Gates's theory of "signifyin'" traces black Caribbean and American culture back through the "talking book," the central method for recording slave narratives, and the early "signifying monkey" storyteller to Esu, the trickster figure of the West African Yoruba. He has claimed that black culture maintains an ongoing dialogue, often humorous, insulting, or provocative, with what has preceded it, and that all works of black writers must be seen in this context. In *Figures in Black* (1987) and *The Signifying Monkey* (1988) he applied his theory to the slave narratives and works by Frederick Douglass, Phillis Wheatley, and Soyinka. He has been at the forefront of the restoration of lost works by black writers, and has argued in *Loose Canons* (1992) and elsewhere for the inclusion of African-American literature in the Western canon. His many anthologies include *Reading Black, Reading Feminist* (1990) and the *Norton Anthology of African-American Writers* (1997). He writes frequently to the general public, notably in the *New Yorker*, and he wrote and hosted the television series *Wonders of the African World* (1999).

Geisel \\'gī-zəl\\, **Theodor Seuss** *pseudonym* **Dr. Seuss** (b. March 2, 1904, Springfield, Mass.—d. Sept. 24, 1991, La Jolla, Calif.) Writer and illustrator of immensely popular children's books.

Geisel studied at Dartmouth College and did graduate work in English at Oxford before beginning work in 1927 as a freelance cartoonist, illustrator, and writer. The first book he published under his pseudonym was *And To Think That I Saw It on Mulberry Street* (1937). His lively children's books, crowded with outlandish creatures and brimming with nonsense words and humorous situations, represented a major departure from mainstream writing for children. In 1957 he published his most famous work, *The Cat in the Hat*, a book designed for beginning readers. Among his many other popular works are *Horton Hatches the Egg* (1940), *How the Grinch Stole Christmas* (1957), *Yertle the Turtle* (1958), *Green Eggs and Ham* (1960), *Hop on Pop* (1963), and *Oh, the Places You'll Go!* (1993). Geisel also designed and produced animated cartoons for television, many of them based on his books. He remains the best-selling children's author in the world.

Gelber \\'gel-bər\\, **Jack** (b. April 12, 1932, Chicago—d. May 9, 2003, New York City) Playwright and teacher.

After graduating from the University of Illinois, Gelber began working with the struggling Living Theater group in New York. His first play, *The Connection*, historically important for its disregard of the traditional relationship between audience and actor, was a breakthrough for the innovative troupe, whose 1959 production received wide notice. Set in a slum apartment, it was staged to suggest a naturalistic scene, with actors already on stage as the audience arrived (as if the audience were seeing life, not a play, in progress). Other nontraditional techniques included presenting an actor as an audience member, using the theater aisles as a performance area, and having the actors (representing drug addicts) panhandle the audience during intermission.

Jack Gelber

The Apple (1961), Gelber's second play, was also written for The Living Theater. None of his later works matched *The Connection*'s popular or critical success.

Gellhorn, Martha (Ellis) (b. Nov. 8, 1908, St. Louis—d. Feb. 15, 1998, London) War correspondent and novelist.

Gellhorn left Bryn Mawr College to move to Paris in 1929. There she wrote for magazines such as *Vogue* and published her first novel before returning to America in 1934 to cover the Depression, work which would result in a long friendship with Eleanor Roosevelt and would provide material for the novella *The Trouble I've Seen* (1936). She met Ernest Hemingway in America, and the two became lovers while covering the Spanish Civil War (1937–39). She went on to report from Czechoslovakia (1939) and the Russo–Finnish War (1939–40) before marrying Hemingway in 1940; the stormy marriage ended in divorce in 1946. She covered the D-Day invasion by sneaking aboard a hospital ship and coming to shore carrying a stretcher; she was also among the first to report on the horrors of the Holocaust. Later she covered the war in Vietnam, the conflicts in El Salvador and Lebanon, and the U.S. invasion of Panama. Her journalism was collected in several books, including *The Face of War* (1959). Her later novels include *A Stricken Field* (1940) and *The Lowest Trees Have Tops* (1967); *The Weather in Africa* (1978) is a collection of novellas.

George, Henry (b. Sept. 2, 1839, Philadelphia—d. Oct. 29, 1897, New York City) Writer on economics and social reformer.

George left school at 13 and went to sea in 1855. He arrived in California in 1857 but lived in poverty despite the gold-mining boom. He read widely and contributed articles to San Francisco newspapers, working intermittently as a typesetter and editor. In the pamphlet *Our Land and Land Policy* (1871) he described his "single-tax" theory, prescribing that the entire tax burden should be laid on land, freeing industry from taxation and equalizing opportunity and the distribution of wealth. He expanded his theory in his most famous work, *Progress and Poverty* (1877–79). After several worldwide lecture tours, he moved to New York in 1890 and ran unsuccessfully for mayor. His later books included *The Irish Land Question* (1881), *Social Problems* (1883), and *The Science of Political Economy* (1897).

Gernsback \\'gərnz-ˌbak\\, **Hugo** (b. Aug. 16, 1884, Luxembourg—d. Aug. 19, 1967, New York City) Luxembourgian-American inventor and publisher who was largely responsible for the establishment of science fiction as an independent literary form.

After receiving a technical education in Luxembourg and Germany, Gernsback traveled to the United States in 1904 to market an improved dry battery he had invented. In 1905 he established the world's first radio supply house, and in 1908 he founded *Modern Electrics* (later absorbed by *Popular Science*), the first magazine for radio enthusiasts.

In 1926 he began publishing *Amazing Stories*, the first magazine devoted exclusively to what he called "scientifiction." Though its stories were often crudely written, the very existence of the magazine and Gernsback's later science-fiction magazines, including *Wonder Stories* (from 1930), encouraged the development and refinement of the genre. Though Gernsback published only a handful of his own stories, they anticipate such major inventions as radar and fluorescent lighting. He also founded several other scientific and technical magazines and secured over 80 patents. Gernsback's contribution was later recognized with the establishment in 1953 of the annual Hugo Award for the best science-fiction writing.

Ghose \\'gōz\\, **Zulfikar** (b. March 13, 1935, Sialkot, India [now Pakistan]) Pakistani-American author of novels, poetry, and criticism.

Ghose grew up a Muslim in Sialkot and in largely Hindu Bombay, then moved with his family to England. He graduated from the University of Keele in 1959 and married an artist from Brazil (later the setting for six of his novels). In 1969 he moved to the United States to teach at the University of Texas.

His first novel, *The Contradictions* (1966), explores differences between Western and Eastern attitudes and ways of life. In *The Murder of Aziz Khan* (1967) a small farmer tries to save his traditional land from greedy developers. The trilogy *The Incredible Brazilian*, comprising *The Native* (1972), *The Beautiful Empire* (1975), and *A Different World* (1978), presents the picaresque adventures, often violent or sexually perverse, of a man who goes through several reincarnations. Ghose's other novels include *Crump's Terms* (1975), *A New History of Torments* (1982), *Don Bueno* (1983), *Figures of Enchantment* (1986), and *The Triple Mirror of the Self* (1992). His poems, from those in *The Loss of India* (1964) to the *Selected Poems* (1991), are often about the travels and memories of a self-aware alien.

Gibran \\ji-'brän\\, **Khalil** *Arabic* Jubran Khalil Jubran (b. Jan. 6, 1883, Bsharri, Lebanon—d. April 10, 1931, New York City) Lebanese-American philosophical essayist, novelist, mystic poet, and artist.

Gibran immigrated with his parents to Boston in 1895. After studying in Beirut, he returned to Boston, and in 1912 he settled in New York, where he devoted himself to writing essays and short stories, both in Arabic and in English, and to painting.

His writings are full of lyrical outpourings and are expressive of his deeply religious and mystical nature. His principal works in Arabic are *A Tear and a Smile* (1914), *Spirits Rebellious* (1920), *The Broken Wings* (1922), and the poetry collection *The Procession* (1923). His principal works in English are *The Madman* (1918), *The Forerunner* (1920), the immensely popular THE PROPHET (1923), *Sand and Foam* (1926), and *Jesus, the Son of Man* (1928).

Khalil Gibran

Gibson, William (Ford) (b. March 17, 1948, Conway, S.C.) American-Canadian writer of science fiction, leader of the genre's cyberpunk movement.

Many of Gibson's early stories were published in *Omni* magazine. With the publication of his astonishing first novel, *Neuromancer* (1984, Hugo and Nebula awards), he emerged as a leading exponent of cyberpunk, a new school of science-fiction writing. His conception of "cyberspace," a surreal alternative reality produced by the aggregate of computer power and information, is considered a major contribution to the genre.

Count Zero (1986) is set on the same world as *Neuromancer* seven years later. The trilogy was completed by *Mona Lisa Overdrive* (1988), whose characters can "die" into computers, where they may support or sabotage outer reality. After collaborating with Bruce Sterling on *The Difference Engine* (1990), a novel about Charles Babbage's invention of a proto-computer, Gibson returned to the subject of cyberspace in *Virtual Light* (1993). Later novels included *Idoru* (1996) and *All Tomorrow's Parties* (1999). Two stories from his collection *Burning Chrome* (1986), "Johnny Mnemonic" and "New Rose Hotel," were made into films.

Gilchrist \\'gil-(ˌ)krist\\, **Ellen** (b. Feb. 20, 1935, Vicksburg, Miss.) Short-story writer and novelist.

After graduating from Millsaps College, Gilchrist worked as a journalist in New Orleans (1976–79). Her first collection of short stories, *In the Land of Dreamy Dreams,* was published to acclaim in 1981, when Gilchrist was 46. Her first novel, *The Annunciation* (1983), was followed by such other novels as *The Anna Papers* (1988), *Net of Jewels* (1992), *Starcarbon* (1994), *Anabasis* (1994), *Sarah Conley* (1997), and *The Cabal* (2000). Her stories, collected in *Victory over Japan* (1984, National Book Award), *Drunk with Love* (1986), *Light Can Be Both Wave and Particle* (1989), and *The Courts of Love* (1996), are vivid, often funny, and rich with dialogue; most are set in and around New Orleans.

Gilman, Charlotte Perkins *originally* Charlotte Anna Perkins (b. July 3, 1860, Hartford, Conn.—d. Aug. 17, 1935, Pasadena, Calif.) Leading theorist of the women's movement in the United States.

Gilman began her literary career in the 1890s with the publication of poetry, short stories, and essays of social analysis. She also gained worldwide fame as a lecturer, speaking on topics concerning women, ethics, labor, and society. In her important *Women and Economics* (1898), she proposed that the sexual and maternal roles of women had been overemphasized to the detriment of their social and economic potential and that only economic independence could bring true freedom.

Gilman's autobiography, *The Living of Charlotte Perkins Gilman*, appeared in 1935. Among her other publications were the frequently anthologized short story THE YELLOW WALLPAPER (1899), *The Home* (1903), *The Man-Made World* (1911), and *His Religion and Hers* (1923).

Gilroy, Frank D(aniel) (b. Oct. 13, 1925, Bronx, N.Y.) Playwright and screenwriter.

Gilroy graduated from Dartmouth College and attended the Yale University School of Drama. He worked as a television scriptwriter for many drama programs in the 1950s and originated the series *Burke's Law*. His off-Broadway play *Who'll Save the Plowboy* (1957) was followed by the Broadway hit *The Subject Was Roses* (1964, Pulitzer Prize, Tony Award; film, 1968), about an Irish family living in the Bronx. His other plays include *That Summer–That Fall* (1967), *The Only Game in Town* (1968; film, 1970), *The Next Contestant* (1978), *Last Licks* (1979), *Match Point* (1990), and *Any Given Day* (1993). He has also written novels and screenplays and has directed several films.

Ginsberg, (Irwin) Allen (b. June 3, 1926, Newark, N.J.—d. April 5, 1997, New York City) Poet and activist, and leader of the Beat movement.

Allen Ginsberg

The son of a poet, Ginsberg studied at Columbia University, where he became close friends with Jack Kerouac and William Burroughs, and they became the core of the group that would be known as the Beats. HOWL (1956), the epic poem that was his first published book, laments what Ginsberg saw as the destruction by insanity of the "best minds of my generation" and became the most famous poem to emerge from the Beat movement. In *Howl* and later works, which show the influence of Walt Whitman, William Blake, and Ezra Pound, he also celebrated psychotropic drugs, footloose wandering, and homosexuality. The long confessional poem KADDISH (1961) is one of his most important works. The collection *Empty Mirror* appeared in 1960, and *Reality Sandwiches* in 1963. Ginsberg's life was one of ceaseless travel, poetry readings, and left-wing political activity. An important harbinger of the gay liberation movement, he became an influential guru of the broader youth counterculture in the late 1960s and '70s. His involvement in Eastern religions is evident in much of his poetry from the late 1950s on. His later collections include *Planet News* (1969), *The Fall of America* (1972, National Book Award), *Mind Breaths* (1978), and *White Shroud* (1986). His *Journals* were published in 1977, and his *Collected Poems* in 1984.

Giovanni \ˌjē-ō-ˈvän-ē\, **Nikki** *originally* Yolande Cornelia Giovanni, Jr. (b. June 7, 1943, Knoxville, Tenn.) Poet whose writings have ranged from calls for violent revolution to poems for children.

Giovanni entered Fisk University in 1960. By her graduation in 1967 she was firmly committed to the civil-rights movement and the concept of black power. In her first three collections of poems, *Black Feeling, Black Talk* (1968), *Black Judgement* (1968), and *Re: Creation* (1970), her content is urgently revolutionary and suffused with deliberate interpretation of experience through a black consciousness.

Giovanni's experiences as a single mother then began to influence her poetry. *Spin a Soft Black Song* (1971), *Ego-Tripping* (1973), and *Vacation Time* (1980) were collections of poems for children. She returned to political concerns in *Those Who Ride the Night Winds* (1983), with dedications to black heroes and heroines. Later volumes include *Love. Poems* (1997) and *Blues for All the Changes* (1999). *Gemini* (1971) consists of autobiographical reminiscences, and *Sacred Cows . . . and Other Edibles* (1988) is a collection of essays.

Glasgow \\'glas-gō\\, **Ellen (Anderson Gholson)** (b. April 22, 1873, Richmond, Va.—d. Nov. 21, 1945, Richmond) Novelist whose realistic depiction of Virginia life helped direct Southern literature away from sentimentality and nostalgia.

Ellen A. Glasgow

Irregularly schooled because of delicate health, Glasgow lived the life of a Southern belle, except for her intense seriousness about becoming a novelist of stature. In *The Voice of the People* (1900) she began a planned social history of Virginia from 1850, a series which eventually comprised *The Battle-Ground* (1902), *The Deliverance* (1904), *The Romance of a Plain Man* (1909), and *Virginia* (1913).

She was past 50 when she first gained serious critical attention with *Barren Ground* (1925), a story of the Piedmont countryside of Virginia. She then published a trilogy of ironic novels of manners set in Richmond (disguised as "Queenborough"): *The Romantic Comedians* (1926), *They Stooped to Folly* (1929), and *The Sheltered Life* (1932), the last often cited with *Barren Ground* as her best work. *In This Our Life* (1941) won the Pulitzer Prize. Glasgow's memoirs, *The Woman Within* (1954), and her *Letters* (1958) were published after her death. Her *Collected Stories* appeared in 1963.

Glaspell \\'glas-pel\\, **Susan** (b. July 1, 1882, Davenport, Iowa—d. July 27, 1948, Provincetown, Mass.) Dramatist and novelist, cofounder of the influential Provincetown Players.

Glaspell's first novel was *The Glory of the Conquered* (1909), and some of her short stories were collected in *Lifted Masks* (1912). George Cram Cook, whom she married in 1913, interested her in socialist ideas, which figured in her next novel, *The Visioning* (1911). While summering in Provincetown in 1915, Glaspell and Cook launched the Provincetown Players, ostensibly to produce their one-act play *Suppressed Desires*, a satire on psychoanalysis. Two of Glaspell's full-length plays—*Inheritors* (1921) and *The Verge* (1922)—were also produced by the Provincetown group.

After Cook's death in 1924, Glaspell gave a romantic account of his life in *The Road to the Temple* (1926). Her last play, *Alison's House* (1931, Pulitzer Prize), details the impact of a great poet (said to be patterned on Emily Dickinson) on her family 18 years after her death. Her later novels include *The Fugitive's Return* (1929) and *The Morning Is Near Us* (1940).

Glück \\'glik\\, **Louise (Elisabeth)** (b. April 22, 1943, New York City) Poet known for her insights into the self and her severe lyricism.

After attending Sarah Lawrence College and Columbia University, from 1971 Glück taught poetry at numerous colleges and universities. Her first collection, *Firstborn* (1968), used a variety of first-person personae, all disaffected or angry; its tone disturbed many critics, but Glück's exquisitely controlled language and imaginative use of rhyme and meter delighted others. *The House on Marshland* (1975) showed a greater mastery of voice, though its outlook was equally grim. Her adoption of different perspectives became increasingly imaginative; in "The Sick Child," from *Descending Figure* (1980), her voice is that of a mother in a museum painting looking out at the bright gallery. The poems in *The Triumph of Achilles* (1985) address archetypal concerns of classic myth, fairy tales, and the Bible, concerns also evident in *Ararat* (1990). *The Wild Iris* (1992) won the Pulitzer Prize. *Vita Nova* appeared in 1999. A volume of essays, *Proofs and Theories*, was published in 1994. She was named U.S. Poet Laureate in 2003.

Godwin, Gail (Kathleen) (b. June 18, 1937, Birmingham, Ala.) Novelist who has written about women searching for a personal identity.

After graduating from the University of North Carolina, Godwin worked as a reporter for the *Miami Herald* and then worked at the U.S. embassy in London (1962–65) before earning her doctorate at the University of Iowa. She examined the experiences of women smothered by marriage in her violent novel *The Perfectionists* (1970), based on her own brief first marriage, and in *Glass People* (1972).

The protagonist of her widely admired *The Odd Woman* (1974) is a college teacher who attempts to come to terms with her family and her married lover. The three principal characters of *A Mother and Two Daughters* (1982) grow in separate ways to self-fulfillment. Her other novels include *Violet Clay* (1978), *The Finishing School* (1984), *A Southern Family* (1987), *Father Melancholy's Daughter* (1991), *The Good Husband* (1994), and *Evensong* (1999).

Gold, Michael *pseudonym* of Itzok Isaac (*later* Irwin) Granich (b. Apr. 12, 1893, New York City—d. May 14, 1967, San Francisco) Journalist and writer.

Born to Jewish immigrants, Granich left school at 12 and from 1914 was active in the radical movement, contributing poems to the *Masses* and other radical newspapers. He adopted the pen name Michael Gold during the "Red Scare" of 1919–20. A stalwart Communist, he became editor of the *Masses* in 1926 and a columnist for the *Daily Worker* in 1933, for which he wrote thousands of columns up until his death. His greatest success was the novel *Jews Without Money* (1930), which became a model for the "proletarian literature" that he believed would help bring the worker to class consciousness. His other works include the plays *Fiesta* (1925), *Hoboken Blues* (1928), and *Battle Hymn* (1936) and the essay collections *Change the World!* (1937) and *The Hollow Men* (1941). He retired to San Francisco in the late 1950s.

Goldbarth, Albert (b. Jan. 31, 1948, Chicago) Poet noted for his erudition and wit and a compulsive wordiness reminiscent of Walt Whitman.

Educated at the Universities of Illinois, Iowa, and Utah, Goldbarth has since taught principally at the University of Texas and Wichita State University. Highly prolific, he has often published one or more collections of poems annually. They include *Coprolites* (1973), a group of meditations on human leavings; *Opticks* (1974), a long poem about glass, light, and perception; *Comings Back* (1976); *Curve: Overlapping Narratives* (1977); *Different Fleshes: A Novel/Poem* (1979); *Ink, Blood, Semen* (1980); *Faith* (1981); *Heaven and Earth: A Cosmology* (1991, National Book Critics Circle Award); and *Beyond* (1998).

Golden, Harry *originally* Harry Lewis Goldhirsch (b. May 6, 1903, Mikulinsty, Galicia, Austria-Hungary—d. Oct. 2, 1981, Charlotte, N.C.) Editor and publisher.

Golden arrived at Ellis Island with his father and brother at age 2, and he left school at 14 to work at a hat factory. After earning his high-school diploma in night school, he joined his sister's brokerage firm, but spent three years in jail for participating in a scheme to defraud investors. Released in 1933, he continued working in New York until 1941, when he moved to Virginia and then North Carolina, changed his name from Goldhurst (as it had been recorded at Ellis Island) to Golden, and founded the *Carolina Israelite*. In its pages he addressed the touchy issue of desegregation with humor. A collection of his articles for the *Israelite* (which he continued to edit until 1968) was published as *Only in America* (1957) and became a best-seller. Among his many other books were *For 2 Cents Plain* (1959), a biography of Carl Sandburg, and the autobiography *The Right Time* (1969).

Goodrich, Samuel Griswold *pseudonym* **Peter Parley** (b. Aug. 19, 1793, Ridgefield, Conn.—d. May 9, 1860, New York City) Publisher and author of children's books.

With only an elementary education, Goodrich became a bookseller, publisher, and textbook author in Hartford (1816) and later Boston (1826). In 1827 he began, under the name Peter Parley, his series of books for the young, which embraced geography, biography, history, science, and miscellaneous tales. He

Samuel Griswold
Goodrich

was the sole author of comparatively few of these, but in his *Recollections of a Lifetime* (1856) he wrote that he was "the author and editor of about 170 volumes," of which some 7 million copies had been sold, including in his list the spurious works published under his name. He was widely imitated, especially in England. Beginning in 1828, he published for 15 years an illustrated annual, the *Token*, which accepted some of the earliest work of Hawthorne and Longfellow and to which Goodrich himself frequently contributed both prose and verse. In 1832 he founded *Peter Parley's Magazine,* and in 1844 he merged it into his *Merry's Museum*, founded in 1841 and for a time edited by Louisa May Alcott.

Gordon, Mary (Catherine) (b. Dec. 8, 1949, Far Rockaway, Long Island, N.Y.) Writer whose fiction deals with growing up Roman Catholic and with the nature of goodness and piety as expressed within that tradition.

Gordon was educated at Barnard College and Syracuse University, and later returned to Barnard to teach. Her first novel, *Final Payments* (1978), was a huge critical and popular success. Its Catholic protagonist, Isabel, is 30 before she leaves home, having cared for her domineering father for his last 11 years. Soon she has friends, a career, and several married lovers. Feeling the need to atone for her "self-indulgence," she becomes the caregiver to her father's former housekeeper, a woman she hates.

Gordon's later works include a collection of short stories, *Temporary Shelter* (1987), the three novellas in *The Rest of Life* (1993), and the novels *The Company of Women* (1981), *Men and Angels* (1985), *The Other Side* (1989), and *Spending* (1998). She also has written nonfiction, including *Spiritual Quests: The Art and Craft of Religious Writing* (1988), *Good Boys and Dead Girls* (1991), and *The Shadow Man* (1996), which delves into her father's fraudulent identity.

Gorey, Edward (St. John) (b. Feb. 22, 1925, Chicago—d. April 15, 2000) Writer, illustrator, and designer, noted for his arch humor and gothic sensibility.

After graduating from Harvard, Gorey immersed himself in the New York cultural scene. While producing book covers and illustrations for publishing houses (1953–63), he also began writing and illustrating short books. *The Doubtful Guest* (1957), his first book for children, featured a penguinlike creature that moved into a wealthy home: "It came 17 years ago—and to this day / It has shown no intention of going away."

Gorey drew a pen-and-ink world of beady-eyed, blank-faced individuals whose dignified Edwardian demeanor is undercut by silly and often macabre events. His nonsense rhymes recalled those of Edward Lear, and his mock-Victorian prose delighted readers with its ludicrous fustiness. Gorey's work evoked the cozy sensibilities of childhood reading while subverting that feeling with its often grisly humor. He published under several playful pseudonyms, mostly anagrams such as Ogdred Weary. Of his illustrated alphabets, the most celebrated was *The Gashlycrumb Tinies* (1962), which disposes of 26 children: "M is for Maud who was swept out to sea / N is for Neville who died of ennui." From 1970 he concentrated on adult works, while still writing children's stories. His anthologies *Amphigorey* (1972), *Amphigorey Too* (1975), and *Amphigorey Also* (1983) sold in large numbers. In all he wrote about 100 books, illustrated about 500 more, and also wrote about 25 works for the theater.

Gould \'güld\, **Stephen Jay** (b. Sept. 10, 1941, New York City—d. May 20, 2002, New York City) Paleontologist, evolutionary biologist, and science writer.

Gould attended Antioch College, received his Ph.D. in paleontology from Columbia University in 1967, and joined the faculty of Harvard University, where he has taught until his death. In 1972 he and Niles Eldredge developed the controversial theory of punctuated equilibria, a revision of Darwinian theory proposing that the creation of new species through evolutionary change occurs not at slow, constant rates over millions of years but rather in rapid bursts over periods as short as thousands of years.

He is best known as a popularizer of evolutionary theory and other topics in the life sciences. His monographic works include *Ontogeny and Phylogeny* (1977), *The Mismeasure of Man* (1981), *Time's Arrow, Time's Cycle* (1987), and *Wonderful Life* (1989). His admired essays appeared principally in "This View of Life," the column he wrote for *Natural History* magazine 1974–2001. These have been collected in numerous volumes, including *The Panda's Thumb* (1980), *Hen's Teeth and Horse's Toes* (1983), *The Flamingo's Smile* (1985), and *Bully for Brontosaurus* (1991). His final work was *The Structure of Evolutionary Theory* (2002). A gifted and energetic polemicist, Gould has insistently attacked the teaching of creationism and race-based theories of inherited intelligence. His graceful literary style and ability to treat complex concepts with absolute clarity have made him perhaps the best-known science writer in America.

Grafton, Sue (b. April 24, 1940, Louisville, Ky.) Mystery writer and television script writer.

After graduating from the University of Louisville, Grafton worked at various medical clerical jobs. Her first novel, *Keziah Dane* (1967), was followed by *The Lolly-Madonna War* (1969). She wrote several scripts for television in the 1970s. Beginning with *A Is for Alibi* (1982), she has produced a highly successful series of mystery novels featuring the detective heroine Kinsey Millhone. New titles in the series have appeared almost annually, each employing a letter of the alphabet (in proper sequence) in its title.

Graham \'grā-əm, 'gram\, **Jorie** (b. May 9, 1951, New York City) Poet whose abstract, intellectual verse is known for its visual imagery, complex metaphors, and philosophical content.

After studying philosophy at the Sorbonne and filmmaking at NYU, Graham began publishing poems in 1977. Her first volume of verse, *Hybrids of Plants and of Ghosts* (1980), features compact, intricate poems that explore death, beauty, and change. *Erosion* (1983) examines the connection between the body and the soul in such poems as "Reading Plato," "I Watched a Snake," and "The Sense of an Ending." In *The End of Beauty* (1987) Graham experimented with form, constructing subtle, sometimes inaccessible poems divided into series of short, numbered stanzas with missing words and lively enjambment. *Region of Unlikeness* (1991), which is annotated to explain textual obscurities, furthers her exploration of philosophy and religion in such poems as "The Tree of Knowledge," "The Holy Shroud," and "Chaos." It was followed by *Materialism* (1993), *The Dream of the Unified Field* (1994, Pulitzer Prize), *The Errancy* (1997), and *Swarm* (2000). After some years teaching at the University of Iowa, she was named Boylston Professor of Rhetoric and Oratory at Harvard in 1998.

Grau \'graủ\, **Shirley Ann** (b. July 8, 1929, New Orleans) Novelist and short-story writer noted for her examinations of evil and isolation set in the South.

Grau's first book, *The Black Prince, and Other Stories* (1955), had considerable success. Her first novel, *The Hard Blue Sky* (1958), about Cajun fishermen and their families, was followed by *The House on Coliseum Street* (1961). *The Keepers of the House* (1964, Pulitzer Prize) deals with three generations of the Howland family, a once-mighty Southern dynasty. Her later novels are *The Condor Passes* (1971), *Evidence of Love* (1977), and *Roadwalkers* (1994), and her other short-story collections include *The Wind Shifting West* (1973) and *Nine Women* (1985).

Horace Greeley

Greeley \'grē-lē\, **Horace** (b. Feb. 3, 1811, Amherst, N.H.—d. Nov. 29, 1872, New York City) Newspaper editor and political leader.

Greeley was a printer's apprentice in Vermont before moving to New York City, where he began editing a literary magazine and campaign weeklies for the Whig Party. In 1841 he founded the *New York Tribune,* which he would edit until his death. A daily Whig paper dedicated to reforms, economic progress, and the elevation of the masses, the *Tribune* became the foremost paper in the country and Greeley came to be considered the outstanding newspaper editor of his time. In the early 1850s, disenchanted with Whig ambivalence toward slavery, he transferred his allegiance to the newly emerging Republican Party. His newspaper fed the rising tide of antislavery feeling of the North. He also supported free homesteading as a cure for the social and industrial problems of the East; "Go West, young man," he was quoted as advising, "and grow up with the country."

After the onset of the Civil War, Greeley pursued a politically erratic course and his influence waned. He subsequently published a history of the war, *The American Conflict* (2 vols., 1866), but the conciliatory attitude he expressed toward the South in the postwar years ruined its sales. His autobiography, *Recol-*

lections of a Busy Life, appeared in 1868. In 1872 he joined a group of Republican dissenters to form the Liberal Republican Party and was nominated for president; his defeat ended a lifelong dream of holding high public office, and he died soon afterward.

Green, Anna Katharine (b. Nov. 11, 1846, Brooklyn, N.Y.—d. April 11, 1935, Buffalo, N.Y.) Writer of detective fiction who helped make the genre popular in America.

Inspired by her father's work as a lawyer, Green began her writing career with the detective story *The Leavenworth Case* (1878), which introduced the detective hero Ebenezer Gryce; it rapidly became popular, and was twice filmed (1923, 1936). Several of her approximately 35 mystery novels and novellas feature the female detective Violet Strange. Green's later works include *Lost Man's Lane* (1898), *The Filigree Ball* (1903), *The House of the Whispering Pines* (1910), and *The Step on the Stair* (1923). Her tendency to intersperse romantic characterizations and dialogue in her work gives her style an old-fashioned tinge, but her skillful plotting and legal and technical accuracy attracted such fans as Wilkie Collins and Arthur Conan Doyle.

Green, Paul (Eliot) (b. March 17, 1894, Lillington, N.C.—d. May 4, 1981, Chapel Hill, N.C.) Novelist and playwright whose works characteristically deal with North Carolina folklore and regional themes.

Green began writing plays for the Carolina Playmakers in 1919, becoming one of the first white playwrights to write perceptively about the problems of Southern blacks. His best-known play, *In Abraham's Bosom* (1926, Pulitzer Prize), concerns a man's attempt to establish a school for his fellow blacks. During the Great Depression, Green's work took on a stronger note of social protest; his plays from this period, many of them written for the Group Theatre, include *Hymn to the Rising Sun* (1936), about a chain gang, and *Johnny Johnson* (1936), an expressionistic, episodic antiwar play for which Kurt Weill wrote the music. In 1941 Green collaborated with Richard Wright in dramatizing Wright's *Native Son.* He also wrote more than a dozen "symphonic dramas" (historical pageants blending music, mime, dance, and other elements), including *The Stephen Foster Story* (1959), *Trumpet in the Land* (1970), and *The Lone Star* (1977), which won wide popularity. His screenplays included *State Fair* (1945), the Rodgers and Hammerstein musical based on Green's earlier play (1933).

Gregory, Horace (Victor) (b. April 10, 1898, Milwaukee, Wis.—d. March 11, 1982, Shelburne Falls, Mass.) Poet, critic, translator, and editor.

Gregory began to write poetry while studying Latin in college, and he first contributed to periodicals in the early 1920s. Finding formal verse inadequate, he tried to combine the idiom of modern life with literary influences, and his poetry also appeared in many avant-garde magazines in the 1920s and '30s. *Chelsea Rooming House* (1930) was his first success. Later volumes included *Selected Poems* (1951, National Book Award), *Medusa in Gramercy Park* (1961, National Book Award), and *Another Look* (1976).

He also wrote biographies of Amy Lowell (1958) and James McNeill Whistler (1959), and his *Pilgrim of the Apocalypse* (1933) was one of the first important critiques of D. H. Lawrence. He edited the works of many writers, and collaborated with his wife, Marya Zaturenska, on *A History of American Poetry, 1900–1940* (1946).

Zane Grey

Grey, Zane *original name* Pearl Grey (b. Jan. 31, 1872, Zanesville, Ohio—d. Oct. 23, 1939, Altadena, Calif.) Prolific writer whose romantic novels of the American West helped create a new literary genre, the WESTERN.

Trained as a dentist, Grey practiced in New York City from 1898 to 1904, when he published privately a novel of pioneer life, *Betty Zane*, based on an ancestor's journal. He published several more works before achieving success with *The Heritage of the Desert* (1910). More than 80 books followed (many published posthumously). The novel *Riders of the Purple Sage* (1912) was the most popular; others include *The Lone Star Ranger* (1915), *The Border Legion* (1916), *The U.P. Trail* (1918), *Call of the Canyon* (1924), and *Code of the West* (1934). He moved to California in 1918 to form a film production company. He eventually became the world's best-paid author, and over 100 films were made from his novels. As a fisherman he held many world records, and his *Tales of Fishing* (1925) is prominent among his nonfiction works.

Grimké \'grim-kē\, **Angelina Weld** (b. Feb. 27, 1880, Boston—d. June 10, 1958, New York City) Poet and playwright, an important forerunner of the Harlem Renaissance.

Grimké was born into a prominent biracial family of abolitionists and civil-rights activists; Angelina and Sarah Grimké were her great-aunts, and her father, the son of a wealthy white aristocrat and a slave, would become executive director of the NAACP. Her early articles and poems deal with racism. Her play *Rachel* (1916) concerns a young black woman so horrified by racism that she vows never to bring children into the world. Though considered sentimental and criticized for its defeatism, it was one of the first plays written by a black author about black issues. Grimké is best known for her small body of poetry, some of which was published in the important anthologies *Negro Poets and Their Poems* (1923), *Caroling Dusk* (1927), and *The Poetry of the Negro* (1949). Her poems are mainly personal lyrics that draw images from nature and express a sense of isolation or a yearning for love, especially from other women.

Grimké, Sarah (Moore) and Angelina (Emily) (respectively, b. Nov. 26, 1792, Charleston, S.C.—d. Dec. 23, 1873, Boston; b. Feb. 20, 1805, Charleston, S.C.—d. Oct. 26, 1879, Boston) Antislavery crusaders and women's-rights advocates.

The sisters early developed an antipathy toward both slavery and limitations on the rights of women. In the 1820s they became Quakers and moved to the North. In 1835 Angelina wrote a letter of approval to William Lloyd Garrison, which he published in his abolitionist newspaper, *The Liberator.* From that time on, the sisters were deeply involved in the abolitionist movement, Angelina always taking the lead. Her pamphlet *An Appeal to the Christian Women of the South* (1836) urged women to use their moral force against slavery; Sarah followed with *An Epistle to the Clergy of the Southern States.* Under the auspices of the American Anti-Slavery Society, they lectured throughout New England as its first female agents. Angelina's *Appeal to the Women of the Nominally Free States* appeared in 1837, and Sarah's *Letters on the Equality of the Sexes and the Condition of Woman* in 1838.

In 1838 Angelina married the abolitionist Theodore Dwight Weld, and both sisters soon retired from public activity. They assisted in Weld's school in New Jersey (1848–62) before moving to Massachusetts.

Grisham, John (b. Feb. 8, 1955, Jonesboro, Ark.) Novelist.

Grisham grew up in Mississippi, earned a law degree at the University of Mississippi (1981), and served several years in the Mississippi state legislature (1984–89) while practicing law. His first novel, *A Time to Kill* (1989; film, 1996), inspired by a trial he had attended, was followed by *The Firm* (1991; film, 1993), a great success that allowed him to give up his law practice and write full-time. His later books, all best-sellers, include *The Pelican Brief* (1992; film, 1993), *The Client* (1993; film, 1994), *The Chamber* (1994; film, 1996), *The Rainmaker* (1995; film, 1997), *The Partner* (1997), and *The Brethren* (2000). Grisham has been generally lauded for his fast-paced page-turners, which, despite their lack of sex and violence, have attracted readers by making heroes out of ordinary people fighting corrupt government, the underworld, and immoral businessmen.

Guare \'gwar\, John (b. Feb. 5, 1938, New York City) Playwright known for his innovative and often absurdist dramas.

Guare was educated at Georgetown and Yale universities. He then began staging short plays, primarily in New York. His first notable works—*Muzeeka* (1968), about soldiers in the Vietnam War who have television contracts, and *Cop-Out* (1968)—satirized the American media.

In 1971 Guare earned critical acclaim for *The House of Blue Leaves*, a farce about a zookeeper who murders his insane wife after failing as a songwriter. *Two Gentlemen of Verona* (1972; with Mel Shapiro), a rock-musical modernization of

Shakespeare's comedy, won the Tony and New York Drama Critics Circle awards. He has since dealt with such issues as success—in *Marco Polo Sings a Solo* (1977) and *Rich and Famous* (1977)—and parent-child relationships—in *Landscape of the Body* (1978) and *Bosoms and Neglect* (1980). *Lydie Breeze* (1982), *Gardenia* (1982), and *Women and Water* (1990) make up a family saga set in 19th-century Nantucket. Guare's screenplays include *Atlantic City* (1981). His highly popular *Six Degrees of Separation* (1990, New York Drama Critics Circle Award; film, 1993) was followed by *Four Baboons Adoring the Sun* (1993), *Chaucer in Rome* (1999), and *A Book of Judith* (1999).

Guest, Edgar (Albert) (b. Aug. 20, 1881, Birmingham, Warwickshire, England—d. Aug. 5, 1959, Detroit, Mich.) Writer of widely popular sentimental, didactic, and hortatory verses.

Guest's family moved to the United States in 1891. Four years later he went to work for the *Detroit Free Press* as an office boy, eventually becoming a reporter and then a writer of daily rhymes; he would remain at the *Free Press* for over 60 years. His poems became so popular that they were eventually syndicated to newspapers throughout the country and made his name a household word. His first book, *A Heap o'Livin'* (1916), became a huge best-seller and was followed by similar best-selling collections of his optimistic rhymes on such subjects as home, mother, and the virtue of hard work. Though ignored by literary critics, he was the most popular poet in America in the 1920s and '30s, and some of his 11,000 poems can still be seen on greeting cards and wall plaques today.

Gunn, Thom(son William) (b. Aug. 29, 1929, Gravesend, Kent, England) Anglo-American poet whose verse is notable for its adroit, terse language.

Gunn's father was the editor of London's *Evening Standard* newspaper; his mother committed suicide when Gunn was in his teens. After graduating from Trinity College, Cambridge, he moved to California in 1954. He studied and later taught at Stanford University, and he has since taught at UC–Berkeley.

His first volume of verse was *Fighting Terms* (1954). *The Sense of Movement* (1957) contains one of his best-known poems, "On the Move," a celebration of black-jacketed motorcyclists. Like much of his later work, the early poems employ colloquial language in rigorously controlled forms. In the late 1950s his poetry became more experimental, a tendency evident in *My Sad Captains* (1961). In the 1970s Gunn produced both a euphoric volume, *Moly* (1971), and a collection expressing disenchantment, *Jack Straw's Castle* (1976). His widely admired *The Man with Night Sweats* (1992) has AIDS as its subject. Recent volumes have included *Frontiers of Gossip* (1998) and *Boss Cupid* (2000). *The Occasion of Poetry* (1982) is a collection of essays.

Gunther \\'gən(t)-thər\\, **John** (b. Aug. 30, 1901, Chicago—d. May 29, 1970, New York City) Journalist and writer.

After graduating from the University of Chicago, Gunther joined the *Chicago Daily News.* Eager to work in Europe, he made his way to London in 1924. He again became a correspondent for the *Daily News* and worked in various European bureaus, including Vienna from 1930.

His first book, *Inside Europe,* appeared in 1936. With its success, he quit the newspaper business to devote all his time to book writing. For the next nine years he covered various European capitals, the Balkans, and the Middle East. From 1942 to 1945 he reported on World War II as an NBC radio commentator.

He is best known for the series of "Inside" books launched by *Inside Europe*, each of which describes and interprets a region of the world; they include *Inside Asia* (1939), *Inside Latin America* (1941), *Inside U.S.A.* (1947), *Inside Africa* (1955), *Inside Russia Today* (1958), *Inside Europe Today* (1961), and *Inside South America* (1967). Gunther's other works include *The High Cost of Hitler* (1939), *D-Day* (1944), and *Roosevelt in Retrospect* (1950).

Gurganus \\gər-'ga-nəs\\, **Allan** (b. June 11, 1947, Rocky Mount, N.C.) Novelist and short-story writer.

After serving in the navy (1966–70) and attending Sarah Lawrence College and the University of Iowa (M.F.A., 1974), Gurganus taught fiction writing at Sarah Lawrence (1978–86). His short stories have appeared in *Harper's* magazine, the *New Yorker*, and several collections of works by gay writers. He came to wide attention with the best-selling historical novel *Oldest Living Confederate Widow Tells All* (1989). It was followed by the admired short-story collection *White People* (1991), including the long story "Blessed Assurance"; the novel *Plays Well with Others* (1997), about the AIDS crisis in New York; and *The Practical Heart* (2001), a set of four novellas.

Guthrie, A. B. *in full* Alfred Bertram Guthrie, Jr. (b. Jan. 13, 1901, Bedford, Ind.—d. April 26, 1991, Choteau, Mont.) Novelist best known for his writing about the American West.

Guthrie earned a degree in journalism from the University of Montana and later went to work for the *Lexington Leader* newspaper in Kentucky, where between 1926 and 1947 he rose from cub reporter to executive editor. After writing a pulp murder mystery (1943), he produced his three most famous novels (often designated a trilogy)—*The Big Sky* (1947), *The Way West* (1949, Pulitzer Prize), and *These Thousand Hills* (1956)—all of which depict the lives of Americans settling along the upper Missouri and Columbia rivers with near-unprecedented realism. Guthrie returned permanently to Montana in 1953, where he later successfully blended the Western and detective genres in such books as *Wild Pitch* (1973), *The Genuine Article* (1977), and *No Second Wind*

(1980). *Fair Land, Fair Land* (1982) was a sequel to *The Big Sky*. He also published the story collection *The Big It* (1960), the autobiography *The Blue Hen's Chick* (1965), and *A Field Guide to Writing Fiction* (1991).

Guy, Rosa *originally* Rosa Cuthbert (b. Sept. 1, 1925, Trinidad, West Indies) Writer of fiction for adolescents that has usually concerned life in the urban American ghetto and in the West Indies.

After immigrating to the United States with her family in 1932, Guy grew up in Harlem, living in a series of foster homes and institutions after her parents died. She studied at New York University and in the late 1940s, with other young black writers, formed the Harlem Writers' Guild.

Her first novel, *Bird at My Window* (1966), was set in Harlem and dealt with the relationship between a black mother and her children and with the social forces that foster the demoralization of black men. *Children of Longing* (1970), which Guy edited, contained accounts of the experiences and aspirations of young blacks aged 13 to 23. She later traveled in the Caribbean, living in Haiti and Trinidad, and subsequent novels such as *The Friends* (1973) and *Ruby* (1976)—perhaps the first novel with a lesbian theme intended for teenage readers—reflect West Indian and Haitian cultures. Still later works include *The Disappearance* (1979), *A Measure of Time* (1983), *New Guys Around the Block* (1983), *Paris, Pee Wee, and Big Dog* (1984), *My Love, My Love; or, The Peasant Girl* (1985), and *And I Heard a Bird Sing* (1987).

Hacker, Marilyn (b. Nov. 27, 1942, New York City) Poet and editor.

After attending New York University, Hacker married the science-fiction writer SAMUEL DELANY in 1960. During their unconventional marriage, she lived alone in San Francisco (1967–70) and in London (1971–76); they separated after their daughter's birth in 1974. Hacker has worked as an editor of such literary magazines as *City* (1967–70) and *Kenyon Review* (1990–94).

Her first collection of poetry, *The Terrible Children,* appeared in 1967; later collections include *Presentation Piece* (1974), *Separations* (1976), *Taking Notice* (1980), *Assumptions* (1985), *Going Back to the River* (1990), *Winter Numbers* (1994), and *Squares and Courtyards* (2000). A leading lesbian poet, she has seen her poetry anthologized in numerous collections of gay and lesbian works.

Hagedorn \\ˈha-gə-ˌdȯrn\\, **Jessica** *originally* Jessica Tarahata (b. 1950, Philippines) Novelist, editor, and performance artist.

Hagedorn's family immigrated to the United States when she was 13. Living in San Francisco, she was encouraged in her writing by Kenneth Rexroth and published her first book of poetry, *Dangerous Music,* in 1975. In 1978 she moved to New York City, where several of her performance pieces, including *Mango Tango* (1978), were produced. Her novella *Pet Food and Tropical Apparitions* (1981) attracted favorable attention. Her best-known book is the surreal novella *Dogeaters* (1990), about corruption in the Philippines. *The Gangster of Love* (1996) concerns the dissolute lives of young Filipino-Americans. Her stylistically anarchic books, whose subject matter is often scabrous, exhibit a multicultural mix of pop cultures. She edited *Charlie Chan Is Dead* (1993), an anthology of short stories by Asian-Americans. She has also worked as a musician, actress, and filmmaker.

Halberstam \\ˈhal-bər-ˌstam\\, **David** (b. April 10, 1934, New York City) Journalist.

After graduating from Harvard University, Halberstam worked as a reporter for the *Nashville Tennessean* (1956–60). He joined the *New York Times* in 1960 and was a foreign correspondent in the Congo, Vietnam, and Poland, receiving a Pulitzer Prize in 1964. With *The Making of a Quagmire* (1965) and *Ho* (1971), he began a series of books about politics and international relations, focusing on the Vietnam War. *The Best and the Brightest* (1972), a highly critical study of the leading foreign-policy figures in the Kennedy and Johnson administrations, became enormously successful and made Halberstam's name widely known. It was followed by such books as *The Powers That Be* (1979), about the increasing power of the news media; *The Reckoning* (1986), about the Japanese and American auto industries; *The Fifties* (1993), about American culture through the decade; and *The Children* (1998), about Southern civil-rights advocates of the 1960s. His books about baseball and other sports include *Playing for Keeps* (1999), about Michael

H

Jordan, and *The Teammates* (2003). Halberstam's novels include *The Noblest Roman* (1961), *One Very Hot Day* (1968), and *Firehouse* (2002).

Edward Everett Hale

Hale, Edward Everett (b. April 3, 1822, Boston, Mass.—d. June 10, 1909, Roxbury, Mass.) Clergyman and author best remembered for his short story "The Man Without a Country."

Hale trained on his father's newspaper, the *Boston Daily Advertiser*, and early on turned to writing. His pieces appeared in such journals as the *North American Review*, *Atlantic Monthly*, and *Christian Examiner*. From 1870 to 1875 he published and edited the Unitarian journal *Old and New*.

"My Double and How He Undid Me" (1859) established the vein of realistic fantasy that was Hale's forte. It introduced a group of loosely related characters who would figure in *If, Yes, and Perhaps* (1868), *The Ingham Papers* (1869), *Sybaris and Other Homes* (1869), *His Level Best* (1872), and other collections. His most famous work, "The Man Without a Country," appeared in the *Atlantic* in 1863 and aroused patriotic fervor during the Civil War. *East and West* (1892) and *In His Name* (1873) were his most popular novels.

Hale's ministry began in 1846, and he ended his career as U.S. Senate chaplain. He was an early apostle of the liberal Social Gospel movement, and many of his 150 books and pamphlets were tracts for such causes as the education of blacks, workers' housing, and world peace. The reminiscent writings of his later years—*A New England Boyhood* (1893), *James Russell Lowell and His Friends* (1899), and *Memories of a Hundred Years* (1902)—are rich and colorful.

Hale, Lucretia Peabody (b. Sept. 2, 1820, Boston, Mass.—d. June 12, 1900, Belmont, Mass.) Novelist and writer of children's books.

The sister of Edward Everett Hale, she began publishing her stories and books around 1858. In 1868 her stories about the impractical but endearing Peterkin family began to appear in magazines. These were eventually gathered into *The Peterkin Papers* (1880) and *The Last of the Peterkins* (1886). Their success arose from Hale's skill in combining a realistic depiction of a contemporary Boston family, full of self-improving idealism, with a silliness that charmed youngsters.

Hale, Sarah Josepha *originally* Sarah Josepha Buell (b. Oct. 24, 1788, Newport, N.H.—d. April 30, 1879, Philadelphia) Writer who, as the first female editor of a magazine, shaped many of the attitudes of women of her period.

Hale turned to writing in 1822 as a widow trying to support her family. After publishing poems and a novel, she was invited to edit the *Ladies' Magazine* (1828–37), most of which she would actually write herself. When it was bought by Louis A. Godey in 1837, Hale was retained as editor for the new magazine entitled *Lady's Book*, later called *Godey's Lady's Book* (1837–77), which under her became the most influential and widely circulated women's magazine of its time.

One of Hale's important books is *The Ladies' Wreath* (1837), a collection of poetry by English and American women that sold widely. Her most significant work is the 36-volume *Woman's Record: or, Sketches of All Distinguished Women from "the Beginning" till A.D. 1850* (1853), whose 2,500 biographical entries contain valuable, orderly information. Hale is also remembered as the author of "Mary Had a Little Lamb" (1830).

Haley, Alex(ander Murray Palmer) (b. Aug. 11, 1921, Ithaca, N.Y.— d. Feb. 10, 1992, Seattle, Wash.) Writer whose works of historical fiction and reportage depicted the struggles of American blacks.

Alex Haley

Haley spent 20 years in the coast guard, where he began writing adventure stories, and he later worked as a freelance writer. His first major work, THE AUTO-BIOGRAPHY OF MALCOLM X (1965; film, 1992), a widely read narrative based on interviews with the Black Muslim spokesman, is recognized as a classic of black American autobiography. His greatest success was ROOTS (1976), a genealogy that purports to cover seven generations of Haley's ancestors, which won him a special Pulitzer Prize, led to a television serial of record-breaking popularity, and revived widespread interest in genealogy. *Different Kind of Christmas* (1988) is a novella about a plantation owner who rejects slavery. *Queen* (1993; completed by David Stevens), like *Roots*, is a genealogical epic based on Haley's family history.

Hall, Donald *in full* Donald Andrew Hall, Jr. (b. Sept. 20, 1928, New Haven, Conn.) Poet and critic.

Hall received bachelor's degrees from both Harvard and Oxford universities. He taught at the University of Michigan (1957–75) before moving to rural New Hampshire. His first volume of poetry, *Exiles and Marriages* (1955), exhibits the influence of his academic training. In *The Dark Houses* (1958) he showed a richer emotional range, presaging the intuitive, often idiosyncratic later work collected in *A Roof of Tiger Lilies* (1964), *The Alligator Bride* (1968), *The Yellow Room* (1971), and *The Town of Hill* (1975). Subsequent volumes include *Kicking the Leaves* (1978), *The One Day* (1988), *Old and New Poems* (1990), and *The Old Life* (1996). From 1972 to 1995 he was married to the poet Jane Kenyon (1947–1995), whose decline and death he mourns in *Without* (1998). His critical writings include *Marianne Moore* (1970), *Writing Well* (1973), *Goatfoot Milktongue Twinbird* (1978), *To Read Literature, Fiction, Poetry, Drama* (1981), and *The Weather for Poetry* (1982). He has also published the memoirs *String Too Short to Be Saved* (1961) and *Life Work* (1993), several books on baseball, notably *Fathers Playing Catch with Sons* (1985), and a biography of the sculptor Henry Moore, and has edited numerous anthologies and textbooks.

Hall, James (b. Aug. 19, 1793, Philadelphia—d. July 5, 1868, Cincinnati, Ohio) Writer of fiction and descriptive works, one of the earliest American authors to write of the American frontier.

In 1828 Hall, a prominent lawyer, compiled the first western literary annual, the *Western Souvenir*, and from 1830 he edited the *Illinois Monthly Magazine*, which he continued at Cincinnati as the *Western Monthly Magazine* (1832–36). His own works include the nonfiction *Letters from the West* (1828); one novel, *The Harpe's Head* (1833); a survey of western exploration, *The Romance of Western History* (1857); and several volumes of short stories, including *Legends of the West* (1832) and *Tales of the Border* (1835). Such tales as "Pete Featherton" and "A Legend of Carondelet" established Hall early on as a short-story writer of distinction, particularly successful at sketching life in the French settlements of the Illinois country and interpreting such authentic figures as the backwoodsman, voyageur, and Indian-hater.

Halleck \\'hal-ək\\, Fitz-Greene (b. July 8, 1790, Guilford, Conn.—d. Nov. 19, 1867, Guilford) Poet of the Knickerbocker school known for both his satirical and romantic verse.

Halleck was for many years secretary to John Jacob Astor. In collaboration with Joseph Rodman Drake, he contributed the satirical "Croaker Papers" to the *New York Evening Post* in 1819, and on the death of Drake he wrote the moving tribute beginning "Green be the turf above thee." *Fanny* (1819) is a long satire in the style of Byron. Other popular works were the feudal romance "Alnwick Castle" (1822), "Burns" (1827), the often recited "Marco Bozzaris" (1825), "Red Jacket" (1828), and "Young America" (1865).

Alexander Hamilton

Hamilton, Alexander (b. Jan. 11, 1755/57, Nevis, British West Indies—d. July 12, 1804, New York City) Statesman.

Hamilton's father deserted the family and his mother died when he was 13. Sent by relatives to America in 1772, he studied at King's College (later Columbia University) and later served in the American Revolution as an aide to George Washington (1777–81). After the war he practiced law in New York. He served in the Constitutional Convention of 1787; after the Constitution was drafted, Hamilton, with James Madison and John Jay, wrote a long series of articles that appeared in New York newspapers to persuade voters to support ratification. Compiled as *The Federalist* (1788), the essays (about two-thirds of them apparently written by Hamilton) were critical in winning ratification of the Constitution by New York and other states.

Regarded as one of the most brilliant minds of his time, Hamilton was appointed the new country's first secretary of the treasury (1789). He established strong national fiscal policies, insisting on full payment of the national debt, federal assumption of state war debts, and a system of taxation to pay for it, and proposing creation of a national bank and a system of protective tariffs to encourage domestic industry. Opposition to his policies led to the rise of political parties; Hamilton became leader of the Federalist Party. He was instrumental in scuttling Aaron Burr's bid for the presidency in 1800 and for the governorship of New York in 1804, fueling a deep hatred in Burr (now vice president), who challenged Hamilton to a duel over alleged remarks questioning Burr's character that resulted in Hamilton's death.

Hamilton, Edith (b. Aug. 12, 1867, Dresden, Saxony—d. May 31, 1963, Washington, D.C.) Educator and writer who popularized classical literature.

Hamilton was educated at Bryn Mawr (M.A. 1894) and pursued her studies at the University of Munich (1895–96), the first woman to do so. She became head of Bryn Mawr's preparatory school for girls in Baltimore in 1896 and remained there until 1922, when she retired to devote herself to classical studies and writing. Her first book, *The Greek Way* (1930), was an engaging treatment of ancient Greece for the student and layperson, and became a perennial fixture in classrooms across America. *The Roman Way* (1932) was its successor. Hamilton's famous *Mythology* (1948) has been read by millions of students over the decades. Her translations of Greek plays were among the first to approximate in English the austere diction of the originals. She also wrote several books on the Judeo-Christian tradition. At 90 she was made an honorary citizen of Athens.

Hammett \\'ham-et\\, **(Samuel) Dashiell** (b. May 27, 1894, St. Mary's County, Md.—d. Jan. 10, 1961, New York City) Writer who helped to create the hard-boiled school of detective fiction.

Hammett left school at age 13 and worked at a variety of low-paying jobs before working for several years as a detective for the Pinkerton agency. He began to publish short stories and novelettes in pulp magazines, and published two novels—*Red Harvest* and *The Dain Curse* (both 1929)—before writing THE MALTESE FALCON (1930; films, 1931, 1936, 1941), often considered his finest work. The novel introduced Sam Spade, who became the prototype of the hard-boiled detective. Though Spade never appeared in another Hammett novel, several radio series devoted to his adventures made his name a household word. *The Maltese Falcon* was quickly followed by *The Glass Key* (1931) and THE THIN MAN (1934), which initiated a series of films built around his detective couple Nick and Nora Charles. Nora was based on the playwright Lillian Hellman, with whom Hammett formed a romantic alliance in 1930 that lasted until his death. *The Continental Op* (1930) is a collection of short stories. His health undermined by tuberculosis and alcohol, Hammett wrote little in the succeeding decades. For refusing to testify against communists before Congress, he was imprisoned for five months in 1951.

Dashiell Hammett

Handlin, Oscar (b. Sept. 29, 1915, Brooklyn, N.Y.) Historian and educator.

Handlin obtained his Ph.D. from Harvard University in 1940 and joined its history faculty, where he held prestigious professorships and directed two of Harvard's research centers as well as the university library. His first book, adapted from his doctoral thesis, was the well-received *Boston's Immigrants, 1790–1865* (1941). His most important historical study, *The Uprooted* (1951), described the waves of immigration to the United States and examined the immigrants' psychological and cultural adjustments after settling there; its combination of engaging literary style, acute scholarship, and humane reportage typified Handlin's writing of social history and won him a Pulitzer Prize. He went on to write about many other aspects of American history in such books as *Race and Nationality in American Life* (1956), *Fire-Bell in the Night* (1964), *History of the United States* (2 vols., 1967–68), *Facing Life* (1971; with Mary F. Handlin), *Truth in History* (1979), and *Liberty in America, 1600 to the Present* (4 vols., 1986–94; with his second wife, Lilian Handlin).

Hannah, Barry (b. April 23, 1942, Meridian, Miss.) Author of darkly comic, often violent novels and short stories set in the Deep South.

Educated at Mississippi College and the University of Arkansas, Hannah has subsequently taught writing, since 1983 at the University of Mississippi. His first novel, *Geronimo Rex* (1972), was a raucous coming-of-age story addressing the theme of racism. In the less successful *Nightwatchmen* (1973), a secret killer and a hurricane are unleashed on a small college town.

Hannah's reputation as a daring stylist was secured with *Airships* (1978), a collection of short stories whose recurrent motif of Civil War valor was developed more fully in the short novel *Ray* (1980). His later works include *The Tennis Handsome* (1983), about the misadventures of a dissipated tennis pro; *Captain Maximus* (1985), containing short stories and the outline of an original screenplay; the novel *Hey Jack!* (1987); *Never Die* (1991), an offbeat treatment of the western genre; the story collections *Bats Out of Hell* (1993) and *High Lonesome* (1996); and the novel *Yonder Stands Your Orphan* (2001).

Lorraine Hansberry

Hansberry \\'hanz-bər-ē, 'hanz-ˌber-ē\\, **Lorraine** (b. May 19, 1930, Chicago—d. Jan. 12, 1965, New York City) Playwright whose A RAISIN IN THE SUN was the first drama by a black woman to be produced on Broadway.

The daughter of a prosperous real-estate broker, Hansberry spent much of her early life in Mexico. *A Raisin in the Sun* (1959; film, 1961) is an insightful study of the stresses that both divide and unite a working-class black family when it is presented with a chance for a better life. It won the New York Drama Critics' Circle Award. Hansberry's next play, *The Sign in Sidney Brustein's Window,* a drama of political questioning and affirmation set in New York's Greenwich Village, where she had long made her home, had only a modest Broadway run in 1964. Hansberry's promising career was cut short by her death from cancer at 34. *To Be Young, Gifted, and Black,* adapted by Robert Nemiroff from her writings, was produced Off-Broadway with great success in 1969.

Hansen, Joseph (b. July 19, 1923, Aberdeen, S.D.) Author of crime novels featuring the homosexual insurance investigator and detective Dave Brandstetter.

Hansen (who has also written under the pseudonyms Rose Brock and James Colton) began his career as editor, novelist, and journalist in the mid-1960s. He coedited the pioneering gay journal *Tangents* (1965–70). In *Fadeout* (1970), the first novel to feature Brandstetter, the detective falls in love with a man he clears of murder charges. *Death Claims* (1973) is about surviving the death of a lover. Brandstetter investigates the murder of the owner of a gay bar in *Troublemaker* (1975). In *Early Graves* (1987) he traces a serial killer who murders men with AIDS. Brandstetter also appears in seven other novels and in the story collection *Brandstetter and Others* (1984). In addition to the Brandstetter series, Hansen wrote the novels *A Smile in His Lifetime* (1981), *Job's Year* (1983), *Living Upstairs* (1993), and *Jack of Hearts* (1995), and the collections *The Dog and Other Stories* (1979), *Bohannon's Book* (1988), and *Bohannon's Country* (1993).

Hardwick, Elizabeth (b. July 27, 1916, Lexington, Ky.) Novelist, short-story writer, and essayist known for her eloquent literary and social criticism.

Hardwick attended the University of Kentucky and Columbia University. Her experience as a young Southern woman in Manhattan provided the backdrop for her somber, introspective first novel, *The Ghostly Lover* (1945). As a frequent contributor to the *Partisan Review* and other liberal intellectual journals, she developed the elegant, incisive analytical voice that became her trademark. During her marriage to the poet ROBERT LOWELL (1949–72), she wrote her second novel, *The Simple Truth* (1955), edited the letters of William James (1961), published the essay collection *A View of My Own* (1962), and helped found the *New York Review of Books*, a major intellectual periodical (1963). It became the principal outlet for her criticism, a second volume of which, *Seduction and Betrayal: Women and Literature*, appeared in 1974. She also edited the series *Rediscovered Fiction by American Women* (1977). The acclaimed novel *Sleepless Nights* (1979) is partly autobiographical.

Harjo \\'här-jō\\, **Joy** (b. May 9, 1951, Tulsa, Okla.) Poet, writer, and Native American activist.

Daughter of a Creek father and a Cherokee-French mother, and an enrolled member of the Creek tribe, Harjo earned degrees from the Universities of New Mexico and Iowa and has taught at several colleges and universities.

Harjo has used Native American symbolism, imagery, history, and ideas set within a universal context. Her poetry has also dealt with social and personal issues, notably feminism, and with music, particularly jazz (she plays saxophone with an Indian jazz group). Her poetry collections include *The Last Song* (1975), *What Moon Drove Me to This?* (1979), *She Had Some Horses* (1983), *In Mad Love and War* (1990), *Fishing* (1993), and *The Woman Who Fell from the Sky* (1994).

Harper, Frances E(llen) W(atkins) (b. Sept. 24, 1825, Baltimore—d. Feb. 22, 1911, Philadelphia) Poet, orator, and social reformer.

Born into a black family, Harper taught school before becoming a traveling lecturer for abolition and other reform movements. Her lyrical poetry, which she often recited during her lectures, echoed her reformist ideals. Generally written in conventional rhymed quatrains and simple rhythms, it employs biblical imagery and its narrative voice reflects the storytelling style of the oral tradition.

Forest Leaves (c.1845) was her first volume of verse. Her most popular collection, Poems on Miscellaneous Subjects (1854), contains the antislavery poem "Bury Me in a Free Land." *Moses: A Story of the Nile* (1869) is a blank-verse allegory of the aspirations of black Americans during Reconstruction. *Sketches of Southern Life* (1872) is a series of poems told in black vernacular by Aunt Chloe, a former slave. Harper's novel *Iola Leroy* was published in 1892. Three novels serialized in *The Christian Recorder—Minnie's Sacrifice, Sowing and Reaping,* and *Trial and Triumph*—were not published in book form until 1994.

Harper, Michael S(teven) (b. March 18, 1938, New York City) Poet whose verse is concerned with ancestral kinship, jazz and the blues, and the separation of the races in America.

Harper grew up in New York and in West Los Angeles, and did graduate work at the Writers' Workshop at the University of Iowa. He taught at several West Coast colleges before joining the faculty of Brown University in 1971.

His first book, *Dear John, Dear Coltrane* (1970), addresses the theme of redemption in compact poems based both on historical events and figures and on his travels and personal relationships. The poetry in *History Is Your Own Heartbeat* (1971) and *Song: I Want a Witness* (1972) stresses the significance of history to the individual, particularly to black Americans. *Nightmare Begins Responsibility* (1974), one of his most acclaimed and complex works, contains portraits of individual courage. His later works include *Images of Kin* (1977), *Rhode Island* (1981), *Healing Song for the Inner Ear* (1985), *Honorable Amendments* (1995), and *Songlines in Michaeltree* (2000). He edited the collected poetry of Sterling A. Brown (1980) and the anthology *Every Shut Eye Ain't Asleep* (1994; with Anthony Walton).

Harrington, (Edward) Michael (b. Feb. 24, 1928, St. Louis—d. July 31, 1989, Larchmont, N.Y.) Socialist leader and writer.

After attending Holy Cross College and the University of Chicago (M.A., 1949), Harrington worked as a social worker in St. Louis. Enflamed by a passion for social justice, he joined the Young Socialist League, a Marxist but anti-communist group, and became a lecturer and college campus organizer. Active in the civil-rights movement, he concentrated on social welfare issues.

His first book, *The Other America: Poverty in the United States* (1962), exerted a major influence on federal policy. Inspired by the book, Pres. John Kennedy proposed a social welfare program, which was expanded by Pres. Lyndon Johnson as the "War on Poverty." Harrington served as an adviser to the program, and his reasoned arguments and compassion influenced important political figures.

His later books include *The Accidental Century* (1965), *Toward a Democratic Left* (1968), *Socialism* (1972), *Decade of Decision* (1980), and *The New American Poverty* (1984). He taught at Queens College (from 1972), cofounded the Democratic Socialist Organizing Committee, and served as editor of *Democratic Left* (from 1973).

Harris, George Washington (b. March 20, 1814, Allegheny City, Pa.—d. Dec. 11, 1869, on a train en route to Knoxville, Tenn.) Humorist who combined the skill of an oral storyteller with a dramatic imagination.

Harris was a steamboat captain from an early age. From 1843 until his death, he wrote humorous tales for the New York *Spirit of the Times* and other publications, which were reprinted widely throughout the country. The best of them, introduced in colorful vernacular by his comic narrator, the young Sut Lovingood, were published in *Sut Lovingood: Yarns Spun by a "Natural Born Durn'd Fool"* (1867) and, according to a leading critic, surpassed anything before Mark Twain, who himself knew and liked the tales.

Harris, Joel Chandler (b. Dec. 9, 1848, Eatonton, Ga.—d. July 3, 1908, Atlanta, Ga.) Author and creator of the folk character Uncle Remus.

As apprentice on a weekly paper, *The Countryman*, Harris became familiar with the lore and dialects of the plantation slave. He established a reputation as a brilliant humorist and writer of dialect while employed on various Southern newspapers, notably on the *Atlanta Constitution* for 24 years. In 1879 "Tar-Baby" appeared in the *Atlanta Constitution* and created a vogue for a distinctive type of dialect literature. *Uncle Remus: His Songs and His Sayings* was published in book form in 1880; it was followed by other collections of his tales told by the elderly black Uncle Remus about such immortal characters as Brer Rabbit and Brer Fox. A series of children's books included *Little Mr. Thimblefinger and His Queer Country* (1894), *The Story of Aaron* (1896), and *Aaron in the Wildwoods* (1897).

Joel Chandler Harris

Mingo, and Other Sketches in Black and White (1884), *Free Joe and Other Georgian Sketches* (1887), *Sister Jane, Her Friends and Acquaintances* (1896), and *Gabriel Tolliver* (1902) reveal Harris's ability to vitalize other Southern types and to delve into issues faced by the South after Reconstruction. From 1907 until his death he edited *Uncle Remus's Magazine*.

Harrison, Jim (*originally* James Thomas) (b. Dec. 11, 1937, Grayling, Mich.) Novelist and poet known for his lyrical treatment of the human struggle between nature and domesticity.

Harrison attended Michigan State University and later taught at SUNY–Stony Brook. He began his writing career as a poet. *Plain Songs* (1965), *Locations* (1968), *Walking* (1967), and *Outlyer and Ghazals* (1969) exhibited a distinctive amalgam of earthy style, philosophical inquiry, and formal experimentation. His novels and novellas, many of them set in rural northern Michigan, are marked by a robustly masculine viewpoint and a near-mystical communion with the natural world. His first novel, *Wolf* (1971), concerns the efforts of a disaffected man to view a wolf in the wilderness, an experience he believes will cause his luck to change. *A Good Day to Die* (1973) treats the issue of the environment more cynically. Quandaries of love and work illumine *Farmer* (1976) but take on increasingly dark and obsessive overtones in his best-known work, *Legends of the Fall* (1979; film, 1994), *Warlock* (1981), and *Sundog* (1984). *Dalva* (1988) and *The Woman Lit by Fireflies* (1990) have female protagonists. His later fiction includes *The Road Home* (1998) and the three novellas in *The Beast God Forgot to Invent* (2000). His later books of poetry include *Letters to Yesenin* (1973), *Returning to Earth* (1977), and *The Theory & Practice of Rivers* (1985).

Hart, Albert Bushnell (b. July 1, 1854, Clarksville, Pa.—d. June 16, 1943, Boston) Historian and educator.

Hart graduated from Harvard University and earned a Ph.D. from the University of Freiburg in 1883, then taught at Harvard until his retirement in 1926, where he was known as a popular lecturer and inspiring teacher. A prominent Republican and Progressive, he was a close friend and adviser of Theodore Roosevelt.

He was the author, coauthor, or editor of over 100 works, most of them on American history. These included *Formation of the Union* (1892), *Guide to the Study of American History* (1896; with Edward Channing), *Foundations of American Foreign Policy* (1901), *The Monroe Doctrine* (1917), and *We and Our History* (1932). His biographies include *Samuel Portland Chase* (1899), *Abraham Lincoln* (1914), and *George Washington* (1927). He earned respect as an outstanding editor for such publications as *American History Told by Contemporaries* (5 vols., 1897–1929), *American Patriots and Statesmen* (5 vols., 1916), and the *American Nation* series (28 vols., 1904–18), and also edited the *Ameri-*

can Historical Review (1895–1909) and the *American Year Book* (1910–19, 1926–32).

Hart, Moss (b. Oct. 24, 1904, New York City—d. Dec. 20, 1961, Palm Springs, Calif.) One of the most successful American playwrights of the 20th century.

Hart left school at 15, and after taking work as an office boy for a theatrical producer he wrote his first play at 18. In 1929 he wrote *Once in a Lifetime*, a satire on Hollywood that became a hit the following year, after its exuberant humor had been tempered by the sardonic skill of George S. Kaufman. Until 1941 he continued to work with Kaufman, a notable collaboration that produced such popular comedies as *You Can't Take It with You* (1936, Pulitzer Prize) and *The Man Who Came to Dinner* (1939). He wrote books for musicals for Irving Berlin and Cole Porter (including *As Thousands Cheer*, 1933, and *Jubilee*, 1935), and he himself directed *Lady in the Dark* (1941), a collaboration with Kurt Weill. Among other musicals he directed were the long-running *My Fair Lady* (1956; Tony Award) and *Camelot* (1960). His screenplays included *Gentlemen's Agreement* (1947, Academy Award) and *A Star Is Born* (1954). In 1959 he published *Act One*, the story of his theatrical apprenticeship.

Harte \ˈhärt\, Bret *originally* Francis Brett Harte (b. Aug. 25, 1836, Albany, N.Y.—d. May 5, 1902, London, England) Writer who helped create the local-color school in American fiction.

Having left school at 13, in 1854 Harte left New York for California and went into mining country on a brief trip that legend has expanded into a lengthy participation in camp life. In 1857 he was employed by the *Northern Californian*, a weekly paper. Around 1860 he moved to San Francisco and began to write for the *Golden Era*, a newspaper, which published the first of his *Condensed Novels*, brilliant parodies of James Fenimore Cooper, Charles Dickens, Victor Hugo, and others. After 1864 he intermittently edited the *Californian*, for which he engaged Mark Twain to write weekly articles.

Bret Harte

In 1868, after publishing a series of Spanish legends akin to Washington Irving's *The Alhambra*, Harte was named editor of the new *Overland Monthly*, for which he wrote THE LUCK OF ROARING CAMP and THE OUTCASTS OF POKER FLAT. Publication of the collection *The Luck of Roaring Camp, and Other Sketches* (1870) and the poem "Plain Language from Truthful James," or "The Heathen Chinee" (1870), made him world-famous. His best play, *Ah Sin* (1877), a collaboration with Twain, would be based on the poem.

Flush with success, Harte in 1871 signed with the *Atlantic Monthly* for $10,000 for 12 stories a year, the highest figure offered an American writer up to that time. He moved east, where he was greeted as an equal by H. W. Longfellow, J. R. Lowell, O. W. Holmes, and W. D. Howells. But his work had begun to slump, and after publication of *Tales of the Argonauts* (1875) and several years of indifferent success on the lecture circuit, Harte accepted consulships in Germany and Scotland. In 1885 he retired to London, where he found a ready audience for his tales of a past or mythical California long after American readers had tired of the formula.

Hartman, Geoffrey H. (b. Aug. 11, 1929, Frankfurt-am-Main, Germany) Literary critic and theorist.

Born into a Jewish family in Germany, he was transported to safety in England in 1938 and came to the United States in 1946. After studying at Queens College, the University of Dijon (France), and Yale University, he embarked on a university teaching career, most of it spent at Yale. Romantic poetry has been a particular concern, and he has written several books on Wordsworth. In *The Unmediated Vision* (1954) he argued that poetry mediates between its readers and direct experience, much as religion had done in more religious eras. In *The Fate of Reading* (1975) he held that history, like literature, is open to many interpretations, and therefore is also a kind of "critical energy." In *Criticism in the Wilderness* (1980) he called for uniting the studies of literature, history, and philosophy and disputed the common notion of criticism as a form separate from and inferior to creative writing. His later writings include *Easy Pieces* (1985), *Minor Prophecies* (1991), *Saving the Text* (1995), and *Scars of the Spirit* (2002). Hartman is also well known for his major works on the Holocaust, extensive video documentation of the testimony of Holocaust survivors, and contributions to the formation of Jewish-studies programs in American colleges.

Hartog \\'här-tȯk\\, **Jan de** (b. April 22, 1914, Haarlem, Netherlands—d. Sept. 22, 2002, Houston, Texas) Dutch-American novelist and playwright who wrote adventure stories in both Dutch and English.

Hartog's first major novel, *Hollands glorie* (1947; *Captain Jan*), is a humorous tale of a young boy's career in the merchant navy; published in German-occupied Holland, it made Hartog a national hero. After the war he settled in the United States and wrote entertaining novels in English, many of which reflect his Quaker faith and his love of the sea. They include *A Sailor's Life* (1956), *Stella* (1950; film, *The Key,* 1958) *The Inspector* (1960), *The Hospital* (1964), the best-selling *The Captain* (1966), *The Spiral Road* (1957; film, 1962), *The Peaceable Kingdom* (1972), *The Lamb's War* (1980), *The Trail of the Serpent* (1983), *Star of Peace* (1984), and *The Centurion* (1990). Of his plays, the most popular is *The Fourposter* (1951), the basis for the 1966 musical *I Do! I Do!* He is also known for his children's story *The Little Ark* (1953; film, 1972).

Hass, Robert (b. 1941, San Francisco) Poet and educator.

After graduating from St. Mary's College in California, Hass earned a Ph.D. at Stanford University. He taught at SUNY–Buffalo (1967–71) and St. Mary's (1971–89) before joining the faculty at UC–Berkeley.

His first collection of poems, *Field Guide* (1973), was followed by *Praise* (1979), *Human Wishes* (1989), and *Sun Under Wood* (1996). He has edited the essay collection *Twentieth Century Pleasures* (1985) as well as *The Essential Haiku* (1994). With Czeslaw Milosz he has translated several volumes of Milosz's poetry.

As U.S. poet laureate (1995–97), Hass traveled throughout the United States to promote literacy, and he has also worked energetically for environmental causes.

Hawkes, John *in full* John Clendennin Burne Hawkes, Jr. (b. Aug. 17, 1925, Stamford, Conn.—d. May 15, 1998, Providence, R.I.) Author whose novels achieve a dreamlike (often nightmarish) intensity through the suspension of traditional narrative constraints.

Hawkes attended Harvard University and later taught for 30 years at Brown University. His first novel, *The Cannibal* (1949), depicts harbingers of a future apocalypse amid the rubble of postwar Germany. *The Beetle Leg* (1951) is a surreal parody of the pulp western. In 1954 he published two novellas, *The Goose on the Grave* and *The Owl*, both set in Italy. With *The Lime Twig* (1961), a dark thriller set in postwar London, Hawkes attracted the critical attention that would place him among the front rank of avant-garde American writers. His next novel, *Second Skin* (1964), is the first-person confessional of a retired naval officer. *The Blood Oranges* (1971), *Death, Sleep, and the Traveler* (1974), and *Travesty* (1976) explore marriage and freedom. *The Passion Artist* (1979) and *Virginie* (1982) are tales of sexual obsession. Later works include *Adventures in the Alaskan Skin Trade* (1985), *Whistlejacket* (1988), *Sweet William* (1993), *The Frog* (1996), and *An Irish Eye* (1997). *The Innocent Party* (1966) is a collection of short plays, and *Lunar Landscapes* (1969) is a volume of short stories and novellas.

Hawthorne, Nathaniel (b. July 4, 1804, Salem, Mass.—d. May 19, 1864, Plymouth, N.H.) Novelist and short-story writer, a master of the allegorical and symbolic tale and one of the greatest fiction writers in American literature.

Hawthorne grew up in Salem and in Raymond, Maine, on the shores of Sebago Lake. He returned to Salem in 1825 after four years at Bowdoin College. His first work was the amateurish novel *Fanshawe*, which he published in 1828 at his own expense, only to decide that it was unworthy of him and to try to destroy all copies. He soon found his own voice, style, and subjects in such impressive and distinctive stories as "The Hollow of the Three Hills" and "An Old Woman's Tale." By 1832, MY KINSMAN, MAJOR MOLINEUX and ROGER MALVIN'S BURIAL, two of his greatest tales, had appeared. YOUNG GOODMAN BROWN, perhaps the greatest tale of witchcraft ever written, appeared in 1835.

Even when his first signed book, TWICE-TOLD TALES, was published in 1837, it brought him little financial reward. By 1842, however, his writing was producing a sufficient income to allow him to marry Sophia Peabody; the couple rented

Nathaniel Hawthorne

the Old Manse in Concord and began a happy three-year period that he would later record in his essay "The Old Manse."

Hawthorne welcomed the companionship of his Transcendentalist neighbors—Emerson, Thoreau, Bronson Alcott—but in general he had little confidence in artists and intellectuals. At the Old Manse, he continued to write stories, with the same result as before: literary success, financial failure. His short-story collection MOSSES FROM AN OLD MANSE, which included such stories as RAPPACCINI'S DAUGHTER, was published in two volumes in 1846.

A growing family and mounting debts compelled the family's return in 1845 to Salem, where Hawthorne was appointed surveyor of the Custom House. Three years later he lost his job, but in a few months of concentrated effort he produced his masterpiece, THE SCARLET LETTER (1850), which made him famous and was eventually recognized as one of the greatest American novels.

After moving to Lenox in western Massachusetts, he began work on THE HOUSE OF THE SEVEN GABLES (1851), the story of the Pyncheon family, who for generations had lived under a curse until it was removed at last by love. In 1851 he moved his family to West Newton, and there quickly wrote THE BLITHEDALE ROMANCE (1852), based on his disenchantment with Brook Farm, the agricultural cooperative in West Roxbury where he had lived in 1841. His two delightful children's books—*A Wonder-Book for Girls and Boys* (1851) and *Tanglewood Tales for Girls and Boys* (1853)—date from this period.

In 1853 he was appointed to the consulship in Liverpool, England, by his old college friend, President Franklin Pierce. He spent most of 1857–58 sightseeing in Italy, an experience that resulted in THE MARBLE FAUN (1860). *Our Old Home* (1863) is based on his experiences in England.

Hawthorne's dark, brooding, richly symbolic works, reflecting his Puritan heritage and contrasting sharply with the optimism of his Transcendentalist neighbors, achieve a depth and power that make them one of the greatest legacies in American literature.

Hay, John (Milton) (b. Oct. 8, 1838, Salem, Ind.—d. July 1, 1905, Newbury, N.H.) U.S. secretary of state and author of both fiction and historical works.

Hay studied law in Springfield, Ill., where he met Abraham Lincoln. He served as a private secretary to President Lincoln (1861–65), and under succeeding Republican administrations he held various diplomatic posts. He spent five years (1870–75) as editorial writer for the *New York Tribune*. He became nationally prominent as secretary of state (1898–1905) under William McKinley and Theodore Roosevelt.

Throughout his life Hay found time to exercise his considerable literary talent, and his *Pike County Ballads and Other Pieces* (1871) and his novel *The Bread-Winners* (1883) were well received. In collaboration with John G. Nicolay, he was also responsible for two historical works that remained standard for many years: the 10-volume *Abraham Lincoln: A History* (1890) and an edition of Lincoln's *Complete Works* (1894).

Hayden, Robert (Earl) *originally* Asa Bundy Sheffey (b. Aug. 4, 1913, Detroit, Mich.—d. Feb. 25, 1980, Ann Arbor, Mich.) Poet whose chief subject was the black experience.

Robert Hayden

Hayden spent an unhappy childhood in a foster home. In 1936 he joined the Federal Writers' Project, researching black folklore and the history of the Underground Railroad in Michigan. His first collection of poems, *Heart-Shape in the Dust*, was published in 1940. He received his master's degree from the University of Michigan, where he studied with W. H. Auden. He later taught at Fisk University (1946–69) and thereafter at Michigan. He gained a public after *A Ballad of Remembrance* (1962) won a grand prize at the First World Festival of Negro Arts in 1966 in Dakar, Senegal. In 1976 he became the first African-American to be appointed poetry consultant to the Library of Congress.

Hayden's best-known poem dealing with black history is "Middle Passage," an alternately lyric, narrative, and dramatic view of the slave trade. His Baha'i beliefs were often reflected in his poetry, which confronted the brutality of racism. His other collections include *Words in the Mourning Time* (1970), including his tribute to Malcolm X, *The Night-Blooming Cereus* (1972), *Angle of Ascent* (1975), and *American Journal* (1980).

Hayne, Paul Hamilton (b. Jan. 1, 1830, Charleston, S.C.—d. July 6, 1886, Grovetown, Ga.) Poet and editor, one of the best-known poets of the Confederate cause.

Hayne wrote for the *Charleston Evening News* and Richmond's *Southern Literary Messenger* and was associate editor of the weekly *Southern Literary Gazette*. His first collected poems were published at his own expense in 1855. He was coeditor of the influential *Russell's Magazine* (1857–60). During the Civil War he contributed verse supporting the Southern cause—notably "The Battle of Charleston Harbor"—to the *Southern Illustrated News* of Richmond. His books include *Sonnets and Other Poems* (1857), *Legends and Lyrics* (1872), *The Mountain of the Lovers* (1875), and *The Broken Battalions* (1885).

Hazzard \ˈhaz-ərd\, Shirley (b. Jan. 30, 1931, Sydney, Australia) Australian-American writer of novels and short stories acclaimed for their refinement and emotional complexity.

Hazzard moved to the United States in 1951 and spent 10 years (1952–62) working at the United Nations. Her first collection of short stories, *Cliffs of Fall* (1963), won immediate critical praise. Her first two novels, *The Evening of the Holiday* (1966) and *The Bay of Noon* (1970), are elegiac love stories set in Italy. A collection of character sketches, *People in Glass Houses* (1967), satirizes the intricate play of idealism and cynicism at the United Nations. Though she had long enjoyed critical favor, her reputation swelled to fame with publication of *The Transit of Venus* (1980, National Book Critics Circle Award), a novel of international scope and rich psychological texture whose omniscient narrative voice constitutes a stylistic tour de force. The nonfiction *Defeat of an Ideal* (1973) and *Countenance of Truth* (1990) harshly condemn the corruption of the United Nations. Her romance *The Great Fire* (2003) won The National Book Award.

H.D. See **Hilda Doolittle**

Hearn, (Patricio) Lafcadio (Tessima Carlos) (b. June 27, 1850, Levkás, Ionian Islands, Greece—d. Sept. 26, 1904, Okubo, Japan) Writer, translator, and teacher who introduced the culture and literature of Japan to the West.

Hearn immigrated to the United States at 19 and settled in Cincinnati, where he worked as a reporter and translated stories by French authors. In 1877 he went to New Orleans to write a series of articles on Louisiana politics, while continuing his translations and producing original stories and sketches. Two early works—*Stray Leaves from Strange Literature* (1884) and *Some Chinese Ghosts* (1887)—were adapted from foreign literature. *Chita* (1889), an adventure novel about the only survivor of a tidal wave, dates from this time. An assignment for *Harper's Weekly* in the West Indies (1887–89) produced *Two Years in the French West Indies* (1890) and the novel *Youma* (1890), a highly original story of a slave insurrection.

In 1890 Hearn traveled to Japan for *Harper's Monthly*. He soon broke with the magazine and began working as a schoolteacher in Izumo. There he married a Japanese woman of high samurai rank in 1891. His articles on Japan began appearing in the *Atlantic Monthly* and were syndicated in several U.S. newspapers. These essays and others, reflecting Hearn's initial captivation with the Japanese, were subsequently published as *Glimpses of Unfamiliar Japan* (2 vols., 1894), the first of a series of brilliant books that gave Western readers their first studied, sympathetic view of Japanese culture. In 1895 he became a Japanese subject, taking the name Koizumi Yakumo. His most brilliant and prolific period was from 1896 to 1903 as professor of English literature at the Imperial University of Tokyo. In the books written during this time—including *Exotics and Retrospectives* (1898), *In Ghostly Japan* (1899), *Shadowings* (1900), and *A Japanese Miscellany* (1901)—he is informative about Japan's customs, religion, and literature. *Kwaidan* (1904) is a collection of stories of the supernatural and translations of haiku.

Hecht \\'hekt\\, **Anthony (Evan)** (b. Aug. 16, 1923, New York City) Poet.

After graduating from Bard College and doing graduate work at Columbia University, Hecht taught poetry at various colleges and universities, including the University of Rochester and Georgetown University. His poetry collections include *A Summoning of Stones* (1954), *The Hard Hours* (1967, Pulitzer Prize), *Millions of Strange Shadows* (1977), *The Venetian Vespers* (1979), *The Transparent Man* (1990), *Flight Among the Tombs* (1996), and *The Darkness and the Light* (2001). *The Hidden Law* (1993) is a critical study of W. H. Auden, and *On the Laws of Poetic Art* (1995) is a collection of lectures. He received the Bollingen Prize in 1983.

Hecht, Ben (b. Feb. 28, 1894, New York City—d. April 18, 1964, New York City) Journalist, novelist, playwright, and film writer.

The son of Russian-Jewish immigrants, he grew up in Racine, Wis., and moved to Chicago to work as a reporter for the *Chicago Journal* and later the *Chicago Daily News*, which sent him to Berlin during the revolutionary upheaval following World War I. From this experience came some of the material for the first of his 35 novels, *Erik Dorn* (1921). For the *Daily News* he developed a column that formed the basis of his collection of sketches *1001 Afternoons in Chicago* (1922). He also became associated with the city's flourishing literary movement, and lively reminiscences of these years are found in his *A Child of the Century* (1954), *Gaily, Gaily* (1963), and *Letters from Bohemia* (1964).

Hecht later divided his time between New York and Hollywood. Though his early attempts at writing for the stage had failed, in 1928 he began his famous collaboration with Charles MacArthur. Their first effort, *The Front Page*, was a huge hit on Broadway. *Twentieth Century* (1932) nearly matched its success. In Hollywood he wrote scripts in the 1930s and '40s, often with MacArthur, for some 70 motion pictures, including *Scarface* (1932), *Underworld* (1934, Academy Award), *The Scoundrel* (1935, Academy Award), *Spellbound* (1945), *Notorious* (1946), *Gunga Din* (1939), and *Wuthering Heights* (1939).

Hecht's last Broadway success was *Ladies and Gentlemen* (1939; also with MacArthur). Columns written for the New York newspaper *PM* appeared as *1001 Afternoons in New York* (1941). Among his other works are *A Guide for the Bedevilled* (1944), about the ongoing Holocaust in Germany; *Collected Stories* (1945); and *Perfidy* (1961).

Heilbrun \ˈhīl-ˌbrən\, **Carolyn** *originally* Carolyn Gold *pseudonym* **Amanda Cross** (b. Jan. 13, 1926, East Orange, N.J.) Scholar and feminist literary critic also known for the mystery novels written under her pseudonym.

Heilbrun attended Wellesley College and Columbia University, and in 1960 she joined the Columbia faculty. Among her scholarly works are *The Garnett Family* (1961), about the British literary family, and *Christopher Isherwood* (1970). She also edited *Lady Ottoline's Album* (1976) and coedited *The Representation of Women in Fiction* (1983). In *Toward a Recognition of Androgyny* (1973) and *Reinventing Womanhood* (1979) she examined the effects of rigid gender roles. *Hamlet's Mother and Other Women* (1990) is a collection of her feminist literary essays.

Not until Heilbrun received tenure from Columbia did she reveal that she was the author of the Amanda Cross mysteries, which feature the literate amateur detective Professor Kate Fansler and are typically set in academic surroundings. Fourteen Amanda Cross books appeared between 1964 and 2000.

Heinlein \\'hīn-līn\\, **Robert A(nson)** (b. July 7, 1907, Butler, Mo.—d. May 8, 1988, Carmel, Calif.) Prolific writer considered one of the most sophisticated of science-fiction writers.

Heinlein was an established professional writer from 1939. His first story, "Life-Line," was published in the pulp magazine *Astounding Science Fiction*, for which he wrote until 1942, when he began war work as an engineer. He returned to writing in 1947, with an eye toward a more sophisticated audience. His first book, *Rocket Ship Galileo* (1947), was followed by numerous novels and story collections, including works for children and adolescents. After the 1940s he largely avoided shorter fiction. His popularity reached its peak after the publication of his best-known work, *Stranger in a Strange Land* (1961), which attracted a cult audience. Among his more popular books are *The Green Hills of Earth* (1951), *Double Star* (1956), *The Door into Summer* (1957), *Citizen of the Galaxy* (1957), *Methuselah's Children* (1958), *Starship Troopers* (1959; film, 1997), *The Moon Is a Harsh Mistress* (1966), and *I Will Fear No Evil* (1970). Later works include *Friday* (1982) and *The Cat Who Walks Through Walls* (1985). Heinlein won an unprecedented four Hugo Awards.

Heller, Joseph (b. May 1, 1923, Brooklyn, N.Y.—d. Dec. 12, 1999, East Hampton, N.Y.) Writer whose satirical novel CATCH-22 (1961) was one of the most significant works of protest literature to appear after World War II.

Heller flew 60 combat missions as a bombardier with the Army Air Forces in Europe. He received an M.A. at Columbia University in 1949 and was a Fulbright scholar at Oxford (1949–50). After teaching briefly at Pennsylvania State University, he worked as an advertising copywriter for *Time* (1952–56) and *Look* (1956–58) and as promotion manager for *McCall's* (1958–61), meanwhile writing *Catch-22* in his spare time. Though lukewarmly received on its publication, the book slowly acquired an audience, and during the Vietnam War its satire resonated so strongly that it became ubiquitous on college campuses.

Though several of Heller's later novels—*Something Happened* (1974), *Good as Gold* (1979), *God Knows* (1984), and *Closing Time* (1994), a sequel to *Catch-22*—were best-sellers, none achieved the status of his first. His dramatic work includes the play *We Bombed in New Haven* (1968).

Hellman, Lillian (b. June 20, 1905, New Orleans—d. June 30, 1984, Vineyard Haven, Martha's Vineyard, Mass.) Playwright and screenwriter whose dramas bitterly attacked injustice and exploitation.

After studies at NYU and Columbia, she worked as a book reviewer and play reader. Her marriage to the playwright Arthur Kober ended in divorce in 1932, by which time she had begun an intimate friendship with the novelist Dashiell Hammett that would continue until his death in 1961.

Her dramas expose various forms in which evil appears—a malicious child's lies about two schoolteachers (in THE CHILDREN'S HOUR, 1934, her first success), a ruthless family's exploitation of fellow townspeople and of one another (THE LITTLE FOXES, 1939, and *Another Part of the Forest*, 1947), and the irresponsible selfishness of the post-World War I generation (WATCH ON THE RHINE, 1941, and *The Searching Wind*, 1944). In the 1950s she showed her skill in handling the more subtle structure of Chekhovian drama (*The Autumn Garden*, 1951) and in translation and adaptation (Jean Anouilh's *The Lark*, 1955, and Leonard Bernstein's musical version of Voltaire's *Candide*, 1957). Her play *Toys in the Attic* was produced in 1960. Several of her works became successful films, often with her own screenplays. She also edited Chekhov's *Selected Letters* (1955) and a collection of stories and short novels, *The Big Knockover* (1966), by Hammett. Her reminiscences, *An Unfinished Woman* (1969), were continued in *Pentimento* (1973) and *Maybe* (1980); though they sold well, their accuracy was impugned by Mary McCarthy and others. A longtime supporter of leftist causes, she detailed in *Scoundrel Time* (1976) her troubles and those of her friends during the anticommunist crusade of the postwar decade.

Lillian Hellman

Hemingway, Ernest (Miller) (b. July 21, 1899, Oak Park, Ill.—d. July 2, 1961, Ketchum, Idaho) Novelist and short-story writer, one of the principal figures of 20th-century American fiction.

On graduation from high school in 1917, Hemingway became a reporter for the *Kansas City Star*. During World War I he served as an ambulance driver for the American Red Cross; wounded on the Austro-Italian front, he was decorated for heroism.

After recuperating in the United States, he sailed for France as a foreign correspondent for the *Toronto Star*. In Paris he became part of the coterie of expatriate Americans that included Gertrude Stein, Ezra Pound, and F. Scott Fitzgerald. In 1925 his first important book, the superb story collection *In Our Time*, was published. The following year he published THE SUN ALSO RISES, the novel with which he scored his first solid success.

Ernest Hemingway

Based in Paris, he traveled widely for the skiing, bullfighting, fishing, and hunting that by then was forming the background for much of his writing. His position as a master of short fiction was advanced by *Men Without Women* (1927), with the story HILLS LIKE WHITE ELEPHANTS, and was confirmed by *Winner Take Nothing* (1933), which included A CLEAN, WELL-LIGHTED PLACE. The concentrated prose style of these early works would influence British and American writers for decades. Among the reading public, the novel A FAREWELL TO ARMS (1929), with its powerful fusion of love story with war story, overshadowed both collections.

Hemingway's love of Spain and his passion for bullfighting are evident in *Death in the Afternoon* (1932), a study of a spectacle he saw more as tragic ceremony than as sport. An African safari provided the subject for *Green Hills of Africa* (1935). *To Have and Have Not* (1937) reflected his growing concern with social issues and the worsening international situation.

As a correspondent he made four trips to Spain, then in the throes of civil war. He raised money for the Loyalists and wrote the play *The Fifth Column*, set in besieged Madrid, that was published with some of his best stories, including

THE SHORT HAPPY LIFE OF FRANCIS MACOMBER and THE SNOWS OF KILIMANJARO, in *The Fifth Column and the First Forty-Nine Stories* (1938). The harvest of his considerable experience of Spain was the novel FOR WHOM THE BELL TOLLS (1940), the best-selling of all his books.

After seeing action in World War II, he returned to his home (since about 1940) in Cuba. He received the Pulitzer Prize for the short novel THE OLD MAN AND THE SEA (1952), a book as enthusiastically praised as his previous novel, *Across the River and into the Trees* (1950), had been damned. In 1954 he was awarded the Nobel Prize for Literature.

By 1960 Fidel Castro's revolution had led Hemingway to leave Cuba and settle in Idaho. There, anxiety-ridden, depressed, and ill with cancer, he shot himself, leaving behind many manuscripts. Two of his posthumously published books are the admired memoir of his apprentice days in Paris *A Moveable Feast* (1964), and *Islands in the Stream* (1970), consisting of three closely related novellas.

Henley, Beth (*originally* Elizabeth Becker) (b. May 8, 1952, Jackson, Miss.) Playwright of regional dramas set in provincial Southern towns.

The daughter of an actress, Henley studied acting at Southern Methodist University but turned to writing because she felt the theater offered few good contemporary roles for Southern women. Her first play, the one-act *Am I Blue*, was produced while she was still an undergraduate. *Crimes of the Heart*, her first full-length play, was produced in 1979 (film, 1986) and won the Pulitzer Prize. Later plays include *The Miss Firecracker Contest* (1979; film, 1988), about the attempts of a small-town young woman of dubious reputation to gain respect by winning a beauty contest; *The Wake of Jamey Foster* (1983); *The Debutante Ball* (1985); *The Lucky Spot* (1986); *Abundance* (1990); and *Impossible Marriage* (1998). She has also written several screenplays.

Henry, O. *pseudonym of* William Sydney Porter (b. Sept. 11, 1862, Greensboro, N.C.—d. June 5, 1910, New York City) Short-story writer whose tales romanticized the commonplace, in particular the life of ordinary people in New York City.

Porter began writing sketches around 1887, and in 1894 he started a humorous weekly, *The Rolling Stone*. When the venture failed, he joined the *Houston Post* as reporter, columnist, and occasional cartoonist.

He was convicted of embezzling bank funds while working as a teller in Austin, Texas, and in 1898 he entered an Ohio penitentiary. While in prison he began writing stories to earn money to support his daughter. His stories of adventure in the Southwest and Central America were immediately popular with magazine readers, and by the time he emerged from prison W. S. Porter had become O. Henry.

In 1902 he arrived in New York City. From December 1903 to January 1906 he produced a story a week for the *New York World*, while writing also for magazines. His stories characteristically expressed the effect of coincidence on character through humor, grim or ironic, and often had surprise endings, a device that would become identified with his name and cost him critical favor when its vogue had passed. His first book, *Cabbages and Kings* (1904), depicted fantastic characters against exotic Honduran backgrounds. Both *The Four Million* (1906), with the well-known stories THE GIFT OF THE MAGI and THE FURNISHED ROOM, and *The Trimmed Lamp* (1907), with THE LAST LEAF, explored the lives of the multitudes of New York in their daily routines and searchings for romance and adventure. *Heart of the West* (1907) contained accurate and fascinating tales of the Texas range.

He then published, in rapid succession, *The Voice of the City* (1908), *The Gentle Grafter* (1908), *Roads of Destiny* (1909), *Options* (1909), *Strictly Business* (1910), and *Whirligigs* (1910), with perhaps his funniest story, THE RANSOM OF RED CHIEF.

Despite his success, his final years were marred by ill health, a desperate financial struggle, and alcoholism. After his death at 47, three more volumes appeared: *Sixes and Sevens* (1911), *Rolling Stones* (1912), and *Waifs and Strays* (1917).

Herbert, Frank (Patrick) (b. Oct. 8, 1920, Tacoma, Wash.—d. Feb. 11, 1986, Madison, Wis.) Science-fiction writer noted as the author of the best-selling *Dune* series.

Until 1972, when he began to write full-time, Herbert held a variety of adventurous jobs while writing socially engaged science fiction, including his acclaimed first novel, *Dragon in the Sea* (1956). His reputation was made with the publication of the epic *Dune* (1965, Hugo and Nebula awards), which has sold more than 12 million copies, and its sequels, *Dune Messiah* (1969), *Children of Dune* (1976), *God-Emperor of Dune* (1981), and *Chapterhouse: Dune* (1985), a group of highly complex works that explore such themes as ecology, human evolution, the consequences of genetic manipulation, and mystical and psychic possibilities. Also notable among his more than two dozen novels are *The Green Brain* (1966), *The Santaroga Barrier* (1968), *The Heaven Makers* (1968), *The God Makers* (1972), and *The Dosadi Experiment* (1977).

Herbst \ˈhərpst\, Josephine (Frey) (b. March 5, 1892, Sioux City, Iowa—d. Jan. 28, 1969, New York City) Journalist and novelist.

Born into a poor family, Herbst graduated from UC–Berkeley in 1918. She moved to New York City, where she joined the radical community, working on magazines and writing short stories. In 1922 she traveled to Europe, moving to Paris in 1924. She and her husband later settled in Pennsylvania; as members of literary and left-wing circles, they wrote for such radical magazines as *New Masses.* Her first novel, *Nothing Is Sacred* (1928), was followed by *Money for Love* (1929), but she is perhaps best known for a trilogy based on her own family history: *Pity Is Not Enough* (1933), the widely acclaimed *The Executioner Waits*

(1934), and *Rope of Gold* (1939). She covered the Spanish Civil War as a journalist. Her later works included *Satan's Sergeants* (1941), *Somewhere the Tempest Fell* (1947), and *New Green World* (1954), a biography of John and William Bartram.

Hergesheimer \\ˈhər-gə-ˌshī-mər\\, **Joseph** (b. Feb. 15, 1880, Philadelphia—d. April 25, 1954, Sea Isle City, N.J.) Author of novels typically concerned with the sophisticated decadence of the very wealthy.

After giving up the study of painting, Hergesheimer turned to writing. Beginning with *The Lay Anthony* (1914), he established himself as a popular and prolific writer of novels, short stories, biography, history, and criticism. His novels are noted for their lushly descriptive style and psychological penetration; the best are perhaps *The Three Black Pennys* (1917), the story of three generations of the wealthy, mine-owning Penny family; *Java Head* (1919); *Linda Condon* (1919); and *Balisand* (1924). In 1921 Henry King made a classic film from his short story "Tol' able David." Hergesheimer's high reputation went into eclipse in his later years.

Herne \\ˈhərn\\, **James A.** *originally* James Ahern (b. Feb. 1, 1839, Troy, N.Y.—d. June 2, 1901, New York City) Playwright who helped bridge the gap between 19th-century melodrama and the 20th-century drama of ideas.

After several years as a traveling actor, Herne scored an impressive success with his first play, *Hearts of Oak* (1879), written with the young David Belasco; it was noted, as his later works would be, for its sharp character delineation. The subsequent *Drifting Apart* (1885) and *The Minute Men* (1886) did not achieve the same popularity. *Margaret Fleming* (1890), a drama of marital infidelity, has been judged his major achievement. His most popular play, *Shore Acres*, was mounted in 1892.

Hersey \\ˈhər-sē\\, **John (Richard)** (b. June 17, 1914, Tianjin, China—d. March 24, 1993, Key West, Fla.) Novelist and journalist noted for his documentary fiction about catastrophic events in World War II.

The son of missionaries, Hersey lived in China until age 10, when his family returned to the United States. He graduated from Yale University in 1936, then served as a foreign correspondent in the Far East, Italy, and Russia for *Time* and *Life* magazines from 1937 to 1946. His early novel A BELL FOR ADANO (1944; film, 1945), depicting the Allied occupation of a Sicilian town during World War II, won the Pulitzer Prize. His next books demonstrated his gift for combining a reporter's skill for relaying facts with imaginative fictionalization. Both HIROSHIMA (1946), an objective account of the atomic bomb explosion as experienced by survivors, and THE WALL (1950), about the Warsaw Ghetto uprisings, are ambiguous hybrids of fact and fiction; *Hiroshima*, first published in a single issue of the *New Yorker*, stunned the reading public with its horrifying vision of nuclear devastation. Hersey's later novels, most of which center on moral issues, include *The Marmot Drive* (1953), *The War Lover* (1959; film, 1962), and *The Child Buyer* (1960).

Heyward, (Edwin) DuBose (b. Aug. 31, 1885, Charleston, S.C.—d. June 16, 1940, Tryon, N.C.) Novelist, dramatist, and poet.

Heyward left school at 14, and by 17 he was working on the waterfront, where he observed the Gullah-speaking blacks who would become the subjects of much of his writing. His poetry collections include *Carolina Chansons* (1922; with Hervey Allen), *Skylines and Horizons* (1924), and *Jasbo Brown* (1931). His first novel, PORGY (1925), a tragic story set in a black Charleston tenement, became a best-seller and the basis for a highly successful play. The landmark folk opera *Porgy and Bess,* with libretto and words by Heyward and Ira Gershwin and music by George Gershwin, was produced in 1935. Heyward's other novels include *Angel* (1926), about North Carolina mountain people; *Mamba's Daughters* (1929); *Peter Ashley* (1932), about pre-Civil War Charleston; and *Star-Spangled Virgin* (1939), about the Virgin Islands during the New Deal.

Hicks, Granville (b. Sept. 9, 1901, Exeter, N.H.—d. June 18, 1982, Franklin Park, N.J.) Critic, novelist, and teacher, one of the foremost practitioners of Marxist criticism in American literature.

After graduating from Harvard and studying two years for the ministry, Hicks joined the Communist Party in 1934. As literary editor of the *New Masses* (1934–39), he became one of the party's chief cultural spokesmen and an important advocate of proletarian literature. His best-known book, *The Great Tradition* (1933), evaluated American literature since the Civil War from a Marxist point of view.

Dismissed from his teaching position at Rensselaer Polytechnic Institute in 1935, he became the center of a storm of controversy over academic freedom. After the 1939 Nazi-Soviet pact he broke with the communists, citing the party's uncritical endorsement of Soviet policy in a letter to the *New Republic*. His later books include *Part of the Truth: An Autobiography* (1965).

Highsmith, Patricia *originally* Mary Patricia Plangman (b. Jan. 19, 1921, Fort Worth, Texas—d. Feb. 4, 1995, Locarno, Switzerland) Novelist and short-story writer best known for her admired psychological thrillers.

Highsmith graduated from Barnard College and worked as a comic-strip artist before publishing *Strangers on a Train* (1950; filmed by Alfred Hitchcock, 1951), an intriguing story of two men, one ostensibly good and the other ostensibly evil, who undergo character reversals. In 1952, under the pseudonym Claire Morgan, she published the very successful lesbian novel *The Price of Salt. The*

Talented Mr. Ripley (1955; films, 1960, 1999) was the first of several books—including *Ripley Under Ground* (1970), *Ripley's Game* (1974; filmed by Wim Wenders as *The American Friend*, 1977), *The Boy Who Followed Ripley* (1980), and *Ripley Under Water* (1991)—featuring the adventures of a likable murderer, Tom Ripley, who takes on his victims' identities. Her eight collections of short stories include *The Black House* (1981) and *Tales of Natural and Unnatural Catastrophes* (1987).

In *Plotting and Writing Suspense Fiction* (1966), Highsmith held that "art has nothing to do with morality, convention or moralizing." This stance, as reflected in her fiction, may have adversely affected its reception in America, and from 1963 she lived in Europe, where she enjoyed a high reputation.

Oscar Hijuelos

Hijuelos \ē-'kwā-lōs\, **Oscar** (b. Aug. 24, 1951, New York City) Novelist whose writing chronicles the pre-Castro Cuban immigrant experience, particularly in New York.

Born to Cuban-American parents, Hijuelos studied writing with Donald Barthelme in the City University system and became a full-time writer in 1984. He won acclaim for his first novel, *Our House in the Last World* (1983), which concerns members of the immigrant Santinio family who try to integrate into their Cuban identity and values the rhythms and culture of life in New York's Spanish Harlem, employing surreal effects suggestive of Latin-American fiction. For his second novel, *The Mambo Kings Play Songs of Love* (1989; film, 1992), he became the first Hispanic writer to be awarded the Pulitzer Prize. *Mambo Kings* likewise chronicles Cuban immigrants, their quest for the American dream, and their eventual disillusionment, while vividly recreating the musical and social environment of the 1950s. His later works include *The Fourteen Sisters of Emilio Montez O'Brien* (1993), *Mr Ives' Christmas* (1995), and *Empress of the Splendid Season* (1999).

Himes, Chester (Bomar) (b. July 29, 1909, Jefferson City, Mo.—d. Nov. 12, 1984, Moraira, Spain) Writer whose novels reflect his encounters with racism.

Born into a troubled middle-class black family, Himes attended Ohio State University for two years before being expelled for delinquency. From 1929 to 1936 he was incarcerated for armed robbery. In prison he began to write fiction, and a number of his stories appeared in *Esquire* and other magazines. After his release, he joined the Works Progress Administration, eventually serving as a writer with the Ohio Writers' Project. His first two novels, IF HE HOLLERS LET HIM GO (1945) and *Lonely Crusade* (1947), concern racism in the defense industry and labor movement. *Cast the First Stone* (1952) portrays prison life, and *The Third Generation* (1954) examines family life.

In the mid-1950s, still dismayed by American racism, Himes moved to Paris. There he wrote what would become a classic series of murder mysteries set in Harlem featuring the detectives Coffin Ed Johnson and Grave Digger Jones, beginning with *For Love of Imabelle* (1957; film, *A Rage in Harlem,* 1991) and including *The Crazy Kill* (1959), *Cotton Comes to Harlem* (1965; film, 1970), and *Blind Man with a Pistol* (1969). Among his other works are *Run Man, Run* (1966), a thriller; *Pinktoes* (1961), a satirical work of interracial erotica; and *Black on Black* (1973), a collection of stories. He also published the autobiographies *The Quality of Hurt* (1972) and *My Life as Absurdity* (1976).

Hinton, S(usan) E(loise) (b. 1948, Tulsa, Okla.) Writer of fiction for adolescents.

While growing up in Tulsa, Hinton decided at 16 to write a novel about teenage conflicts that portrayed her peers more realistically than the books she was given to read. *The Outsiders* (1967; film, 1983), about teenage alienation, received wide acclaim and numerous awards. Her later books include *That Was Then, This Is Now* (1971; film, 1985), *Rumble Fish* (1975; film, 1983), *Tex* (1979; film, 1982), *Taming the Star Runner* (1988), *Big David, Little David* (1994), and *The Puppy Sister* (1999).

Hoagland \\'hōg-lənd\\, Edward (b. Dec. 21, 1932, New York City) Novelist, travel writer, and essayist noted especially for his writings about nature and wildlife.

Hoagland sold his first novel, *Cat Man* (1956), before graduating from Harvard. *The Circle Home* (1960), set in a seedy boxing milieu, and *The Peacock's Tail* (1965) contained sympathetic portrayals of impoverished, struggling people. His fourth novel, *Seven Rivers West* (1986), tells of the cultural collision between railroad builders and Indians in Canada in the 1880s. *City Tales* (1986) and *The Final Fate of the Alligators* (1992) are short-story collections.

Hoagland turned a British Columbia diary into *Notes from the Century Before* (1969); *African Calliope: A Journey to the Sudan* (1979) was a later travel book. Perhaps his best work appears in his nature essays and editorials (in the *New York Times,* 1979–89), which combine depth of feeling with close observation. His essays have been collected in *The Courage of Turtles* (1971), *Walking the Dead Diamond River* (1973), *The Moose on the Wall* (1974), *Red Wolves and Black Bears* (1976), *Balancing Acts* (1992), and *Tigers and Ice* (1999).

Edward Hoagland

Hoban \\'hō-ˌban\\, Russell (Conwell) (b. Feb. 4, 1925, Lansdale, Pa.) American-British novelist and children's writer who has combined myth, fantasy, humor, and philosophy to explore issues of self-identity.

Hoban attended the Philadelphia Museum School before beginning his career as an advertising artist and copywriter. His first book, *What Does It Do and How Does It Work?* (1959), developed from his drawings of construction machinery. He then started writing fiction for children. One of his most enduring creations is the badger Frances, featured in a series of books beginning with *Bedtime for Frances* (1960). Fear and mortality intrude on the classic fantasy story *The Mouse and His Child* (1967; film, 1977). His other notable works for children include *The Sorely Trying Day* (1964), *Charlie the Tramp* (1967), *Emmet Otter's Jug-Band Christmas* (1971), and *Dinner at Alberta's* (1975).

Among Hoban's adult-oriented novels are *The Lion of Boaz-Jachin and Jachin-Boaz* (1973), *Kleinzeit* (1974), and *Turtle Diary* (1975; film, 1985). *Riddley Walker* (1980), his best-known novel, is set in the future in an England (where Hoban moved in 1969) devastated by nuclear war and is narrated in a futuristic form of English. Later writings include the novels *Pilgermann* (1983), *The Medusa Frequency* (1987), and *Angelica's Grotto* (1999). Though most of Hoban's works are fantastical, his overall oeuvre has resisted classification.

Hobson, Laura Z. *originally* Laura Kean Zametkin (b. June 18/19, 1900, New York City—d. Feb. 28, 1986, New York City) Novelist and short-story writer.

The daughter of Jewish socialist parents, she was educated at Cornell University. In the early 1930s she began writing advertising copy and short stories, and in 1934 she joined the promotional staff of the Henry Luce publications. After 1940 she devoted herself entirely to writing, producing nine novels and hundreds of short stories and magazine articles. She is best known for *Gentleman's Agreement* (1947; film, 1947), the best-selling story of a journalist who poses as a Jew in order to gain a firsthand experience of anti-Semitism, and a scathing depiction of anti-Semitism's subtle and insidious manifestations in American society. Hobson's other novels include *The Trespassers* (1943) and *Consenting Adult* (1975), about a son's revelation of his homosexuality. She also wrote a two-volume autobiography, *Laura Z.* (1983, 1986).

Hoffman \\'hȯf-mən\\, **Alice** (b. March 16, 1952, New York City) Novelist whose books about women in search of their identities have mixed realism and the supernatural.

Hoffman studied writing at Stanford University and contributed short stories to magazines before publishing her first novel, *Property Of* (1977); both gritty and romantic, it traces the relationship of a suburban girl and a gang leader. *The Drowning Season* (1979) is a modern fairy tale about a grandmother, Esther the White, and her granddaughter, Esther the Black. *Angel Landing* (1980) is a love story set near a nuclear power plant. *Fortune's Daughter* (1986) is a sentimental tale about the healing friendship between Rae, a pregnant young woman, and Lila, a middle-aged fortune-teller. In *Illumination Night* (1988), a young couple's marriage is challenged by a teenaged girl. In *At Risk* (1988) a young girl with AIDS sparks varied reactions from her family and community. Later novels include *Seventh Heaven* (1990), *Turtle Moon* (1992), *Second Nature* (1994), *Here on Earth* (1999; film, 2000), *Practical Magic* (1995; film, 1998), and *The River King* (2000).

Hofstadter \\'hōf-ˌsta-tər\\, **Richard** (b. Aug. 6, 1916, Buffalo, N.Y.—d. Oct. 24, 1970, New York City) Historian.

After graduating from the University of Buffalo and Columbia University (Ph.D., 1942), Hofstadter taught at the University of Maryland before returning to spend the rest of his professional life at Columbia (1946–70).

In his principal works, several of which were best-sellers, he used sociological concepts to interpret American history. His books include *The American Political Tradition* (1948), *The Age of Reform* (1955, Pulitzer Prize), *The Paranoid Style in American Politics* (1965), *The Idea of a Party System* (1969), and *American Violence* (1970). *Anti-Intellectualism in American Life* (1963, Pulitzer Prize) presented his controversial thesis that the egalitarian, populist sentiments of Jacksonian democracy, a recurrent theme in U.S. political history, produced in many Americans a deep-seated prejudice against intellectuals, who are perceived as representatives of an alien elite.

Holland, Josiah Gilbert (b. July 24, 1819, Belchertown, Mass.—d. Oct. 12, 1881, New York City) Writer and editor.

After studying medicine, Holland turned to teaching and then publishing. In 1849 he became an editor, under Samuel Bowles, of the *Springfield* (Mass.) *Republican*, and he helped to make the paper a literary center for the region. He and his wife enjoyed a correspondence with Emily Dickinson, but the newspaper declined to publish more than a handful of her poems. His numerous pieces for the paper were collected in many books, including *History of Western Massachusetts* (1855) and *The Bay-Path* (1857). As his popularity grew, he began publishing books of moral essays, including *Lessons in Life* (1861) and *Plain Talks on Familiar Subjects* (1865). His novels included *Miss Gilbert's Career* (1860), *Sevenoaks* (1875), and *Nicholas Minturn* (1877). In 1870 he helped found and became the first editor of *Scribner's Monthly* (later the *Century* magazine).

Hollander, John (b. Oct. 28, 1929, New York City) Poet and educator.

After graduating from Columbia University and earning a Ph.D. from Indiana University (1959), Hollander taught at Yale University (1959–66) and then at Hunter College (1966–77) before returning to Yale in 1977. His admired volumes of poetry include *A Crackling of Thorns* (1961), *A Beach Vision* (1962), *Types of Shape* (1969), *The Head of the Bed* (1974), *Powers of Thirteen* (1983, Bollingen Prize), *The Figurehead* (1999), and *Picture Window* (2003). His books of criticism include *The Untuning of the Sky* (1961), *Melodious Guile* (1988), and *The Work of Poetry* (1997). He has also edited anthologies of poetry, including anthologies of verse for children, and has written librettos for several operas.

Holmes \\'hōlmz, 'hōmz\\, **Oliver Wendell** (b. Aug. 29, 1809, Cambridge, Mass.—d. Oct. 7, 1894, Cambridge) Physician, poet, and humorist chiefly remembered for a few poems and for his "Breakfast-Table" series of essays.

Holmes received a degree from Harvard in 1836. He practiced medicine for 10 years, taught anatomy at Dartmouth College, and in 1847 became professor of anatomy and physiology at Harvard, where he served as dean of the medical school (1847–53).

He achieved fame as a humorist and poet. He won national attention with the publication of "Old Ironsides" (1830), which aroused public sentiment against destruction of the USS *Constitution*. Beginning in 1857, he contributed his witty, conversational "Breakfast-Table" essays to the *Atlantic Monthly,* and he subsequently published them in the collections *The Autocrat of the Breakfast-Table* (1858), *The Professor of the Breakfast-Table* (1860), *The Poet of the Breakfast-Table* (1872), and *Over the Teacups* (1891). Among his other works are the widely known poems THE CHAMBERED NAUTILUS (1858) and THE WONDERFUL "ONE-HOSS SHAY" (1858) and the psychological novel *Elsie Venner* (1861). The best-known and best-loved American man of letters of his time (with H. W. Longfellow), he came to enjoy a worldwide reputation. His son and namesake had a highly distinguished career on the U.S. Supreme Court.

Hooker, Thomas (b. probably July 7, 1586, Markfield, England—d. July 7, 1647, Hartford, Conn.) Colonial clergyman.

From about 1620 Hooker held pastorates in England, but in 1629 he came under attack for his Puritan leanings. In 1630 he fled to Holland, and in 1633 he immigrated to the Massachusetts Bay Colony. At New Towne (now Cambridge), he became pastor of a company of Puritans.

Becoming restive over issues of policy, in 1636 he led a group of followers to Connecticut to settle Hartford, where he served as pastor until his death. Critical of limiting suffrage to church members, he told the Connecticut General Court in 1638 that the people had the God-given right to choose their magistrates. Though his view was advanced for his time and has led many historians to call him "the father of American democracy," Hooker did not support separation of church and state, declaring instead that the privilege of voting should be exercised according to the will of God. He was active in formulating the Fundamental Orders for governing Connecticut (1639), favoring in church governance the more autonomous Congregational model to the hierarchical structure of Presbyterianism. He defended his views in *A Survey of the Summe of Church Discipline* (1648).

Hooper, Johnson Jones (b. June 9, 1815, Wilmington, N.C.—d. June 7, 1862, Richmond, Va.) Humorist and writer.

At age 15 Hooper began working on a newspaper in Charleston, S.C. In 1835 he began to travel throughout the Gulf states, settling in Lafayette, Ala., in 1840. He edited several newspapers and wrote humorous pieces featuring an invented character, Simon Suggs. He compiled his journals into the popular book *Some Adventures of Captain Simon Suggs, Late of the Tallapoosa Volunteers*

(1846); the first portrayal of early Southern frontiersmen, it established Hooper as a popular local-color writer.

His other books included *The Widow Rugby's Husband, A Night at the Ugly Man's and Other Tales of Alabama* (1851) and *Dog and Gun, A Few Loose Chapters on Shooting* (1858). In 1851 he moved to Montgomery, Ala.; there he founded a newspaper, the *Mail*, which he edited until 1861.

Hopkins, Pauline (Elizabeth) (b. 1859, Portland, Maine—d. Aug. 13, 1930, Cambridge, Mass.) Novelist, playwright, journalist, and editor who used the traditional romance novel to explore racial and social themes.

In 1880 Hopkins joined her mother and stepfather in performing her first work, the musical *Slaves' Escape* (or *Peculiar Sam*). She then spent several years touring with her family's singing group, Hopkins' Colored Troubadors. Her second play, *One Scene from the Drama of Early Days*, based on the biblical Daniel, was written about this time. The racist violence of post-Civil War America forms the background of her first novel, CONTENDING FORCES (1900). She also wrote short stories and biographical articles for the *Colored American Magazine*, of which she was women's editor and literary editor from about 1900 to 1904.

Hopkins's other novels are *Hagar's Daughter* (published serially in 1901–2 under the pseudonym Sarah A. Allen), *Winona* (published serially in 1902), and *Of One Blood* (published serially in 1902–3). Her final work was the novella *Topsy Templeton* (published serially in 1916). She was working as a stenographer when she died, her works having gone into eclipse; only in the 1980s were they brought back into print.

Hopkins, Sarah Winnemucca *also known as* **Sarah Hopkins Winnemucca** *or* **Thocmectony** ("shell flower") (b. c.1844, Humboldt Sink, Mexico [now in Nevada]—d. Oct. 16, 1891, Monida, Mont.) Educator, lecturer, tribal leader, and writer.

A granddaughter and daughter of Northern Paiute chiefs, she lived with a white family, learned fluent English, and attended a convent school in San Jose, Calif., until bigotry forced her removal. As an army interpreter and scout, Hopkins led a group of Paiutes, including her father, to safety during the Bannock War of 1878, and was awarded tribal honors for bravery.

To protest government policy toward Native Americans, she toured the East in the early 1880s, giving some 300 lectures and portraying the U.S. military as a fairer and abler manager of Indian matters than the corrupt and self-serving Bureau of Indian Affairs. In these years she wrote the book for which she is best known, *Life Among the Piutes* (1883). This and her other writings, valuable for their description of Northern Paiute life and their insights into the impact of white settlement, are among the few contemporary Native American works. She taught Indian children at an army post in Vancouver, Wash., and later returned to

Nevada to found an Indian school with private donations, but lack of money and ill health ended the endeavor.

Horgan, Paul (b. Aug. 1, 1903, Buffalo, N.Y.—d. March 8, 1995, Middletown, Conn.) Versatile author noted especially for histories and historical fiction about the Southwest.

Horgan moved with his family to New Mexico in 1915. His career as a novelist began with the satirical novel *The Fault of Angels* (1933), about a Russian emigré's attempt to bring high culture to an American city. His trilogy *Mountain Standard Time*, consisting of *Main Line West* (1936), *Far From Cibola* (1938), and *The Common Heart* (1942), depicts life in the Southwest in the early 1900s. *A Distant Trumpet* (1960) concerns late-19th-century soldiers who fought the Apaches. His short stories were collected in *The Return of the Weed* (1936), *Figures in a Landscape* (1940), and *The Peach Stone* (1967).

In addition to novels, Horgan wrote historical sketches and books that sympathetically depicted the successive Native American, Spanish, Mexican, and Anglo-American frontier cultures of the Southwest. Both his two-volume *Great River: The Rio Grande in North American History* (1954) and the biography *Lamy of Santa Fe* (1975) won Pulitzer Prizes. He also produced poetry, drama, and children's books.

Horton, George Moses (b. 1797?, Northampton County, N.C.—d. 1883?) Poet, one of the first professional black writers in America.

A slave from birth, Horton was relocated in 1800 to a plantation near the University of North Carolina. From the 1820s, university students regularly commissioned him to create love poems, including clever acrostic compositions based on the names of their lovers. He received literary training from Caroline Lee Hentz, a student who also published his verse in newspapers and tried unsuccessfully to engineer his release from slavery.

Horton's first book of poetry, *The Hope of Liberty* (1829; retitled *Poems by a Slave*), includes love lyrics as well as hopeful poems about freedom from enslavement. Probably because of fears of punishment, *The Poetical Works of George M. Horton, The Colored Bard of North Carolina* (1845) addressed the issue of slavery only obliquely. His last and largest volume of verse was *Naked Genius* (1865).

Hough \\'həf\\, **Emerson** (b. June 28, 1857, Newton, Iowa—d. April 30, 1923, Evanston, Ill.) Novelist and lawyer.

After graduating from Iowa State University in 1880, he studied law and moved to New Mexico to practice. There his growing interest in frontier life led him to write essays and sketches about cowboys and miners. In 1889 he moved to

Chicago and worked for *Forest and Stream* magazine. He later wrote a regular column, "Out of Doors," for the *Saturday Evening Post.*

Hough's first book, *The Singing Mouse Stories* (1895), was followed by *The Story of the Cowboy* (1897), the best-seller *The Mississippi Bubble* (1902), *The Way to the West* (1903), *The Story of the Outlaw* (1907), *The Sowing* (1909), *John Rawn* (1912), and *The Passing of the Frontier* (1918), among others. His highly successful *Covered Wagon* (1922) was made into the first important western film (1923). For juveniles he wrote the popular "Young Alaskans" series.

Hough was a leading advocate for conservation and the national parks; his report on Yellowstone National Park influenced Congress to pass a law protecting the park's few remaining buffalo.

Hovey \\'həv-ē\\, **Richard** (b. May 4, 1864, Normal, Ill.—d. Feb. 24, 1900, New York City) Poet, translator, and dramatist whose works consistently reflected his optimism and his faith in a vital United States.

After graduating in 1885 from Dartmouth, Hovey studied art and theology. He lectured on aesthetics at Columbia University, where he became professor of English at Barnard College. His first major work was *Launcelot and Guenevere* (1891), the first part of a planned three-trilogy scheme—each trilogy to consist of a masque, a tragedy, and a drama. He managed to complete the first trilogy and only the masque, *Taliesin* (1896), of the second. With the poet Bliss Carman he collaborated on *Songs from Vagabondia* (1894), *More Songs from Vagabondia* (1896), and *Last Songs from Vagabondia* (1901). Hovey's other works include *Seaward* (1893), an elegy on Thomas William Parsons, and *Along the Trail* (1898), a book of verse on the Spanish-American War.

Howard, Bronson (Crocker) (b. Oct. 7, 1842, Detroit, Mich.—d. Aug. 4, 1908, Avon, N.J.) Journalist, dramatist, and founder-president of the first American society for playwrights.

Howard had his first success with *Saratoga*, produced in 1870 at a time when dramas of American life written by Americans were practically nonexistent; its success encouraged other native playwrights. *The Henrietta* (1887), a satire on business, was followed by the hugely successful *Shenandoah* (1889), which established Charles Frohman as a great producer. Howard's other plays include *The Banker's Daughter* (1878), first produced in 1873 as *Lillian's Last Love*; *Wives* (1879); *Young Mrs. Winthrop* (1882); and *One of Our Girls* (1885). He described his craft in *Autobiography of a Play* (1914).

Howard, Richard (b. Oct. 13, 1929, Cleveland, Ohio) Poet, critic, and translator influential in introducing modern French poetry and fiction to American readers.

Educated at Columbia University and the Sorbonne, Howard worked as a lexicographer before becoming a freelance critic and translator. He taught at the University of Cincinnati, Yale, and the University of Houston (1987–97), and has served as poetry editor of *The Paris Review*.

Beginning with his first volume, *Quantities* (1962), much of Howard's poetry has been in the form of dramatic monologues in which historic and literary personages address the reader directly. His other volumes of poetry include *Untitled Subjects* (1969, Pulitzer Prize), *Two-Part Inventions* (1974), *Misgivings* (1979), *Lining Up* (1984), *No Traveller* (1989), *Like Most Revelations* (1994), and *Trappings* (1999). In *Alone with America* (1969), he analyzes the work of 41 contemporary American poets. He has translated a vast body of work from the French, including works by Charles Baudelaire, Simone de Beauvoir, Roland Barthes, Alain Robbe-Grillet, Claude Simon, Jean Genet, Marcel Proust, Stendhal, and Jean Cocteau.

Howard, Sidney Coe (b. June 26, 1891, Oakland, Calif.—d. Aug. 23, 1939, Tyringham, Mass.) Playwright whose works helped to bring psychological as well as theatrical realism to the American stage.

Howard graduated from UC–Berkeley in 1915 and studied under George Pierce Baker at his Harvard 47 Workshop. He served on the editorial staff of *Life* magazine in 1919–22 and in 1923 became a feature writer for W. R. Hearst's *International Magazine*.

Howard's best-known play was *They Knew What They Wanted* (1924, Pulitzer Prize), the story of an aging Italian immigrant in California and his mail-order bride, which became the basis of Frank Loesser's musical *The Most Happy Fella* (1957). Other well-known plays are *The Silver Cord* (1926) and *Yellow Jack* (1934; with Paul de Kruif), a dramatized documentary of the conquest of yellow fever. His other plays include *Lute Song* (1930; with Will Irwin) and *Dodsworth* (1934; adapted from Sinclair Lewis's novel). His numerous translations and adaptations of European dramas include *The Late Christopher Bean* (1932; from a play by René Fauchois) and *Salvation* (1928; with Charles MacArthur). His screenplays include *Arrowsmith* (1932), *Dodsworth* (1936), and *Gone with the Wind* (1939, Academy Award). He died in an accident on his farm.

Howe, E(dgar) W(atson) (b. May 3, 1853, Treaty, Ind.—d. Oct. 3, 1937, Atchison, Kan.) Editor, novelist, and essayist known for his iconoclasm and pessimism.

An apprentice printer at age 12, Howe worked at the trade in Missouri, Iowa, Nebraska, and Utah (1867–72). At 19 he became publisher of the *Golden* (Colo.) *Globe,* and in 1877 he cofounded the *Atchison* (Kan.) *Daily Globe*, which became famous through the frequent reprinting throughout the United States of his articles and comments, whose homespun wisdom earned Howe the sobriquet "the Sage of Potato Hill." His first and most successful novel, *The Story of a Country Town* (1883), was the first realistic novel of Midwestern small-town life. He retired from the *Globe* in 1911 to publish and edit *Howe's Monthly* (1911–33), consisting largely of his own caustic observations, and wrote essays, travel books, and an autobiography, *Plain People* (1929). His journalistic writing was collected in *The Indignations of E. W. Howe* (1933) and other books.

Howe, Irving (b. June 11, 1920, New York City—d. May 5, 1993, New York City) Literary and social critic and educator.

Howe was educated at CCNY, where he became part of a brilliant young group of young Jewish radicals, and he later taught at Brandeis and Stanford universities and the City University of New York. He wrote critical works on Sherwood Anderson (1951), William Faulkner (1952), and Thomas Hardy (1967), and he synthesized his political and literary interests in *Politics and the Novel* (1957), *Decline of the New* (1970), and *A World More Attractive* (1963). He edited the works of George Gissing, Edith Wharton, Leon Trotsky, and George Orwell, and from 1953 was editor of the left-wing periodical *Dissent,* which he cofounded. He also coedited *Favorite Yiddish Stories* (1974), *The Best of Sholom Aleichem* (1979), and *The Penguin Book of Modern Yiddish Verse* (1987).

His *World of Our Fathers* (1976) is a major sociocultural study of the Eastern European Jews who immigrated to New York between 1880 and 1924. *Celebrations and Attacks* (1978) is a collection of his critical articles, and *A Margin of Hope* (1982) deals with his own involvement with culture and politics.

Howe, Julia Ward *originally* Julia Ward (b. May 27, 1819, New York City—d. Oct. 17, 1910, Newport, R.I.) Author, abolitionist, and social reformer best known for her "Battle Hymn of the Republic."

Howe worked in the abolitionist movement from her early years. The stirring "Battle Hymn," composed to the rhythm of the folk song "John Brown's Body," was first published in the *Atlantic Monthly* in February 1862. Moved by the economic plight of Civil War widows, Howe worked for equal educational, professional, and business opportunities for women. She founded the New England Woman Suffrage Association in 1868 and served many years as its president (1868–77, 1893–1910). She edited *Woman's Journal* from 1870 to 1890, and also wrote such nonfiction works as *Sex and Education* (1874), travel books, drama, verse, a biography of Margaret Fuller (1883), an autobiography (1899), and songs for children. In 1908 she became the first woman elected to the American Academy of Arts and Letters.

Howells, William Dean (b. March 1, 1837, Martins Ferry, Ohio—d. May 11, 1920, New York City) Novelist and critic preeminent in late 19th-century American letters.

Howells grew up in various Ohio towns and began work early as a typesetter and reporter. Meanwhile he taught himself languages, becoming well read in German, Spanish, and English classics, and began contributing poems to the *Atlantic Monthly*. His campaign biography of Abraham Lincoln (1860) financed a trip to New England, where he met the great men of the literary establishment, including Hawthorne and Emerson. Following Lincoln's victory, Howells received a consulship at Venice (1861–65), which enabled him to marry. On his return to the U.S. he became assistant editor (1866–71) and then editor (1871–81) of the *Atlantic*, in which he began publishing reviews and articles interpreting American writers. He immediately recognized the worth of Henry James, and he was the first to take Mark Twain seriously as an artist.

Their Wedding Journey (1872) and *A Chance Acquaintance* (1873) were his first realistic novels of uneventful middle-class life. There followed several international novels, contrasting American and European manners. *A Modern Instance* (1882) is a powerful novel about the disintegration of a marriage. Howells's best work depicts the American scene as it changed from a simple, egalitarian society where luck and pluck were rewarded to one in which social and economic gulfs were becoming unbridgeable. His best-known work, THE RISE OF SILAS LAPHAM (1885), deals with a self-made businessman's efforts to fit into Boston society.

In 1887 he made a plea for clemency for the condemned Haymarket anarchists, labor leaders convicted of murder after a violent riot in Chicago; believing they had been convicted for their political beliefs, he risked both livelihood and reputation in the cause. In 1888 he left Boston for New York. His deeply shaken social faith was reflected in his later novels, such as the strongly pro-labor *Annie Kilburn* (1888) and *A Hazard of New Fortunes* (1890), one of his finest works, which dramatizes the competitive life of New York, where a representative group of characters try to establish a magazine.

––––––––––

Hubbard, Elbert (Green) (b. June 19, 1856, Bloomington, Ill.—d. May 7, 1915, at sea off Ireland) Editor, publisher, and author.

After a number of years as a freelance newspaperman and businessman, Hubbard retired in 1892 and founded the Roycroft Press in 1895 at East Aurora, N.Y., basing it on the model of William Morris's communal Kelmscott Press in England, where old handicrafts were revived. From 1895 he issued his famous monthly "Little Journey" booklets, pleasant biographical essays on famous persons in which fact was interwoven with comment and satire. From 1895 he also published the avant-garde magazine *The Philistine*, which he ultimately wrote single-handedly. The didactic essay "A Message to Garcia," in which the importance of perseverance was drawn as a moral from a Spanish-American War incident, appeared in an 1899 number of *The Philistine* and became widely famous. In 1908 Hubbard began to edit and publish a second monthly, *The Fra*.

Little Journeys (14 vols., 1915), and *Selected Writings* (14 vols., 1923) are valuable collections of Hubbard's writings. His *Scrap Book* (1923) and *Note Book* (1927) were published after his death in the sinking of the liner *Lusitania*.

––––––––––

Hubbard, L(afayette) Ron(ald) (b. 1911, Tilden, Neb.—d. Jan. 25, 1986, San Luis Obispo, Calif.) Science-fiction novelist and founder of the Church of Scientology.

After studying engineering at George Washington University, Hubbard became a successful science-fiction novelist in the 1930s; in his stories, the righteous hero typically uses mental powers to defeat his enemies. His colorful accounts of his life included claims to have taken part in exploratory expeditions around the world. After serving in the wartime navy, he published *Dianetics* (1950), which detailed his theories of the human mind; it would become a perennial best-seller. Building on Dianetics' self-fulfillment ambitions, in 1954 he founded the Church of Scientology to teach methods of developing the mind and will. He increasingly nurtured beliefs in a global plot to destroy him, and his organization's increasing wealth indeed led to charges of fraud; in 1978 an FBI raid revealed evidence of wiretapping, burglaries, and theft of government documents, and in 1980 the tax-exempt status of his "church" was challenged. Hubbard remained in seclusion on his yacht for his last six years. Many of his novels, including *Fear* (1951) and *Battlefield Earth* (1982; film, 2000), became bestsellers, and works under his name, including the series *Mission Earth* (1985–87), have continued to appear regularly since his death.

Hughes, (James Mercer) Langston (b. Feb. 1, 1902, Joplin, Mo.—d. May 22, 1967, New York City) Poet and writer who became one of the foremost interpreters to the world of the American black experience.

Hughes first came to notice when his poem THE NEGRO SPEAKS OF RIVERS, written the summer after his graduation from high school in Cleveland, was published in the NAACP journal *Crisis* (1921). After briefly attending Columbia University (1921–22), he worked as a steward on a freighter bound for Africa, later sojourning in Paris and Rome. Upon his return he took a variety of menial jobs while continuing to write. While working as a busboy in a hotel in Washington, D.C., Hughes put three of his poems beside the plate of Vachel Lindsay in the dining room. The next day, newspapers around the country reported that Lindsay had discovered a Negro busboy poet. A scholarship to Lincoln University followed, and before Hughes received his degree in 1929 his first two books had been published.

Langston Hughes

The Weary Blues (1926), which includes "Dream Variation," was warmly received. *Fine Clothes to the Jew* (1927) was criticized harshly for its title and its frankness, but Hughes himself felt it represented a step forward. A few months after graduation, *Not Without Laughter* (1930), his first novel, had a cordial reception. In 1931 he collaborated with Zora Neale Hurston on the play MULE BONE. In the 1930s he traveled widely in the Soviet Union, Haiti, and Japan and served as a newspaper correspondent (1937) in the Spanish Civil War; his poetry of the era became highly political. His *Montage of a Dream Deferred*, containing the famous poem HARLEM, was published in 1951. A posthumous book of poems, *The Panther and the Lash* (1967), reflected the anger and militancy of blacks in the 1960s.

Hughes's nonpoetical literary output was highly diverse. In 1934 he published a collection of short stories, *The Ways of White Folks*. He wrote *A Pictorial History of the Negro in America* (1956) and edited the anthologies *The Poetry of the Negro* (1949) and *The Book of Negro Folklore* (1958; with Arna Bontemps). He produced two volumes of autobiography, *The Big Sea* (1940) and *I Wonder as I Wander* (1956). His numerous works for the stage included the lyrics for Kurt Weill's "American opera" *Street Scene*. He translated the poetry of Federico García Lorca and Gabriela Mistral. He was widely known for his comic character Jesse B. Semple, nicknamed Simple, who appeared in Hughes's columns in the *Chicago Defender* and the *New York Post,* later collected in several volumes.

Humphreys, Josephine (b. Feb. 2, 1945, Charleston, S.C.) Novelist noted for her sensitive evocations of family life in the American South.

Humphreys studied creative writing at Duke University and later at Yale and the University of Texas, and has taught at Baptist College in Charleston (1970–77). Her first novel, *Dreams of Sleep* (1983), examines a faltering marriage that is saved by a third party. Her later novels, similarly set in the South, include *Rich in Love* (1987; film, 1992), *The Fireman's Fair* (1991), and the Civil War story *Nowhere Else on Earth* (2000).

Huneker \\ˈhə-ni-kər\\, **James G(ibbons)** (b. Jan. 31, 1860, Philadelphia— d. Feb. 9, 1921, Brooklyn, N.Y.) Critic and writer.

Huneker studied piano in Philadelphia, Paris, and New York, taught piano at the National Conservatory of Music (1886–98), and was both music and drama critic for the *New York Recorder* and (from 1900 to 1912) for the *New York Sun*. The brilliance of his style made his criticism—which ranged widely over many fields—some of the most influential in the country. His published works included *Mezzotints in Modern Music* (1899), *Chopin* (1900), *Overtones: A Book of Temperaments* (1904), *Iconoclasts: A Book of Dramatists* (1905), *Franz Liszt* (1911), *Egoists: A Book of Supermen* (1909), and *Ivory Apes and Peacocks* (1915). He also wrote the novel *Painted Veils* (1920), the short-story collections *Melomaniacs* (1902) and *Visionaries* (1905), and the autobiographical *Old Fogy* (1913) and *Steeplejack* (1920).

Hunter, Evan *originally* Salvatore Albert Lombino (b. Oct. 15, 1926, New York City) Prolific writer of best-selling fiction, of which more than 50 books have been crime stories published under the pseudonym Ed McBain.

Hunter graduated from Hunter College in 1950. His best-known novel was among his earliest: *The Blackboard Jungle* (1954), a story of violence in a New York high school that became the basis of a popular film. After his *Strangers When We Meet* (1958) and *A Matter of Conviction* (1959; U.S. title, *The Young Savages*) became best-sellers, he wrote the screenplays for both (1960–61), as well as for Alfred Hitchcock's *The Birds* (1962) and several later films. He has written several novels on the theme of family tensions, including *Mothers and Daughters* (1961), *Last Summer* (1968), *Sons* (1969), and *Streets of Gold* (1974).

Hunter has been most prolific as a crime novelist. Nearly all his Ed McBain books are "police procedurals"—a genre he virtually invented—set in the 87th Precinct of a city much like New York. The first, *Cop Hater* (1956), was followed by such titles as *Fuzz* (1968), *Widows* (1991), and *Mischief* (1993); many have been made into films. Hunter has also written children's stories and stage plays.

Hunter, Kristin *or* **Kristin Hunter-Lattany** *originally* Kristin Elaine Eggleston (b. Sept. 12, 1931, Philadelphia) Novelist who has examined American racial relations in stories for both young people and adults.

Hunter began writing for the *Pittsburgh Courier,* a black newspaper, at 14 and continued while attending the University of Pennsylvania. She won a 1955 television contest with her script *Minority of One*, about school integration. In her first and best-known novel, *God Bless the Child* (1964), three generations of women confront choices forced on them by their skin tones. Despite harshly realistic settings, her subsequent fiction tended to optimism. *The Landlord* (1966; film, 1970) tells of a misanthropic white landlord transformed by his new black tenants. In *The Survivors* (1975) a lonely dressmaker befriends a neglected 13-year-old boy despite his involvement with dishonest, sometimes brutal acquaintances. Her books for young readers include *The Soul Brothers and Sister Lou* (1968), its sequel *Lou in the Limelight* (1981), *Boss Cat* (1971), *Guests in the Promised Land* (1973), *The Lakestown Rebellion* (1978), and *Do Unto Others* (2000).

Hurst, Fannie (b. Oct. 18, 1889, Hamilton, Ohio—d. Feb. 23, 1968, New York City) Novelist, dramatist, and screenwriter.

Born into a Jewish family, Hurst graduated from Washington University and did graduate work at Columbia. From early on she was preoccupied with such social issues as equal pay for equal work and relief of the oppressed Jews of Eastern Europe. After she succeeded in getting a story published in 1912, the *Saturday Evening Post* asked for all her future stories. The first of her nine story collections, *Just Around the Corner,* appeared in 1914. Her popular novels, which would eventually number 17, began to appear in 1921; the most widely read were *Back Street* (1931; films, 1932, 1941, 1961) and *Imitation of Life* (1933; films, 1939, 1954). Though her work was labeled sentimental by critics, she was for a time the country's second-highest-paid writer. A friend of Eleanor Roosevelt, she chaired the Women's National Housing Commission (1936–37) and a committee on workers' compensation (1940) and served on the advisory committee to the Works Progress Administration (1940–41). She worked energetically to raise funds for wartime German refugees. In the 1950s she hosted a television talk show.

Fannie Hurst

Zora Neale Hurston

Hurston, Zora Neale (b. Jan. 7, 1901?, Eatonville, Fla.—d. Jan. 28, 1960, Fort Pierce, Fla.) Folklorist and writer who celebrated black culture in the voice of the rural black South.

Hurston attended Howard University and won a scholarship to Barnard College, where she studied anthropology with Franz Boas. Though she initially practiced scientific ethnology along the lines taught by Boas, she ultimately rejected the conventional academic anthropology in favor of personal involvement with her heritage.

In 1931 she collaborated with Langston Hughes on the play MULE BONE. Her first novel, *Jonah's Gourd Vine* (1934), was well received, though some critics considered it uneven. Her second novel, THEIR EYES WERE WATCHING GOD (1937), was widely acclaimed but controversial among blacks because of her refusal to portray blacks as victims of the myth of inferiority. Her later novels were *Moses, Man of the Mountain* (1939) and *Seraph on the Suwanee* (1948). Hurston's fiction, which influenced such writers as Ralph Ellison and Toni Morrison, is celebratory in tone and rooted in a rural black South reminiscent of her hometown, and her characters act freely within their rich heritage and narrow social position. *Mules and Men* (1935), about Florida blacks, and *Tell My Horse* (1938), about Haiti and voodoo, were both ethnographic works. DUST TRACKS ON A ROAD (1942) is her autobiography. Hurston's increasing conservatism in her later years, which led her to oppose school integration, alienated her from many of her black contemporaries.

Hutchinson, Thomas (b. Sept. 9, 1711, Boston—d. June 3, 1780, London) Colonial administrator.

Hutchinson served in local and provincial legislatures (1758–49) of the Massachusetts Bay province before becoming lieutenant governor (1758–71) and chief justice of the superior court (1760–69). Though he attended the Albany Congress of 1754, which projected a plan of union among the colonies, as a Loyalist he resisted the gradual movement toward independence. After he was accused of instigating the repugnant Stamp Act of 1765, a mob sacked his home. The embittered Hutchinson thereafter increasingly distrusted the rebels and secretly advised Parliament to pass repressive measures. As acting governor at the time of the Boston Massacre in 1770, he strictly administered British law and became more unpopular. Letters to English friends expressing his views became public in 1773 and aroused additional protest. Later that year, against the legislature's advice, he insisted that a shipment of imported tea land before being given clearance papers, providing the occasion for the Boston Tea Party. In 1774, replaced by Gen. Thomas Gage as military governor, he went to England to act as an adviser to George III, hoping in vain to return to Boston after the unrest was quelled.

He completed his valuable *History of the Colony and Province of Massachusetts Bay* (3 vols., 1764–1828) before his death.

Ignatow \ig-'nä-tō\, **David** *originally* David Ignatowsky (b. Feb. 7, 1914, Brooklyn, N.Y.—d. Nov. 17, 1997, East Hampton, N.Y.) Poet whose works addressed social and personal issues in meditative, vernacular free verse.

The son of an immigrant bookbinder, Ignatow worked for a time as a journalist with the WPA Federal Writers' Project. His first book of poetry, *Poems* (1948), was followed by *The Gentle Weight Lifter* (1955), many of whose pieces, as well as many in *Say Pardon* (1961) and *Figures of the Human* (1964), are written in the form of parables.

Ignatow's thematic range, as well as his reputation, expanded significantly with *Rescue the Dead* (1968), which explored family, marriage, nature, and society. In *Facing the Tree* (1975), *The Animal in the Bush* (1977), and *Tread the Dark* (1978), he further examined death and the art of poetry. Later collections include *Whisper to the Earth* (1981), *Leaving the Door Open* (1984), and *Shadowing the Ground* (1991). *The Notebooks of David Ignatow* was published in 1973, and his memoir *The One in the Many* in 1988. From the 1960s, he taught poetry at several American colleges and universities. In 1977 he was awarded the Bollingen Prize.

Inge \'iŋ\, **William (Motter)** (b. May 3, 1913, Independence, Kan.—d. June 10, 1973, Hollywood Hills, Calif.) Playwright.

Inge was one of the first dramatists to deal with life in the small towns of the Midwest. His first play, *Farther Off from Heaven* (1947), was produced with the help of Tennessee Williams; 10 years later it was revised for Broadway as *The Dark at the Top of the Stairs* (film, 1960) to critical acclaim.

He enjoyed notable success throughout the 1950s, when he wrote his best-known plays: *Come Back, Little Sheba* (1950; film, 1952); PICNIC (1953; film, 1956), for which he won a Pulitzer Prize; and BUS STOP (1955; film, 1956). His later plays—*A Loss of Roses* (1960; film, *The Stripper*, 1963), *Natural Affection* (1963), *Where's Daddy?* (1966), and *The Last Pad* (1970)—were less successful, but his original screenplay for *Splendor in the Grass* (1961) received an Academy Award. His shorter works include *Glory in the Flower* (1958), *To Bobolink, for Her Spirit* (1962), *The Boy in the Basement* (1962), and *Bus Riley's Back in Town* (1962; film, 1965). Depressed by his waning capacity to write, he committed suicide.

Ingraham \'iŋ-grə-həm, 'iŋ-grə-,ham; 'iŋ-grəm\, **Joseph Holt** (b. Jan. 25, 1809, Portland, Me.—d. Dec. 18, 1860, Holly Springs, Miss.) Novelist and clergyman.

Ingraham taught at Jefferson College in Mississippi, then turned to writing. His first book was *The South-West, by a Yankee* (1835). *The Pirate of the Gulf* (2 vols., 1836), a fictionalized tale of Jean Laffite, was the first of his many sensational and gory adventure books. Often styling himself "Professor Ingraham," he apparently wrote over 80 novels, many of them serialized in periodicals and most of them great successes. They included *Burton, or the Sieges* (2 vols., 1838), *The Quadroone, or St. Michael's Day* (2 vols., 1841), *Rafael, or the Twice Condemned* (1845), and *Ringold Griffitt, or the Raftsman of the Susquehannah* (1847).

In 1852 he became an Episcopal priest, and he served as rector of churches in Mississippi, Alabama, and Tennessee. Three late religious romances—*The Prince of the House of David* (1855), *The Pillar of Fire* (1859), and *The Throne of David* (1860)—proved at least as popular as his earlier novels.

Ingraham, Prentiss (b. Dec. 22, 1843, Adams County, Miss.—d. Aug. 16, 1904, Beauvoir, Miss.) Novelist.

The son of J. H. Ingraham, he left college to enlist in the Confederate army in 1861. He became a commander of scouts in Texas, and after the war went to Mexico to fight under Benito Juárez. He thereafter continued his life as a soldier of fortune in Austria, Crete, Africa, and Cuba.

In 1870 he settled in London and began to write, using his experiences and imagination to produce hundreds of sensational novels for the Dime Library and Half-Dime Library. He later lived in New York and Chicago and became a close friend of Buffalo Bill Cody, about whom he wrote over 200 books. His 700-odd novels included *The Beautiful Rivals* (1884), *Buck Taylor, King of the Cowboys* (1887), *Darkie Dan* (1888), *Cadet Carey of West Point* (1890), *Trailing with Buffalo Bill* (1899), and *The Girl Rough Riders* (1903). He also wrote successful plays and many short stories and poems.

Irving, John (Winslow) (b. March 2, 1942, Exeter, N.H.) Novelist.

After graduating from Phillips Exeter Academy, Irving attended the universities of Pittsburgh, Vienna, New Hampshire, and Iowa. He taught until the late 1970s, when he began to write full-time. His early novels—*Setting Free the Bears* (1968), *The Water-Method Man* (1972), and *The 158-Pound Marriage* (1974)—received favorable notices, but he first achieved a breakthrough to fame with the hugely popular *The World According to Garp* (1978; film, 1982). Infused with comedy and violence, it chronicles the tragic life and death of the novelist T. S. Garp. Like his other works, it was noted for its engaging story line, colorful characterizations, macabre humor, and examination of contemporary issues. His later novels, all major best-sellers, include *The Hotel New Hampshire* (1981; film, 1984), *The Cider House Rules* (1985; film, 1999, Academy Award), *A Prayer for Owen Meany* (1989), *A Son of the Circus* (1994), *A Widow for One Year* (1998), and *The Fourth Hand* (2001). His short-story collection *Nowhere Man* was published in 1992.

Irving, Washington (b. April 3, 1783, New York City—d. Nov. 28, 1859, Tarrytown, N.Y.) Writer called the "first American man of letters."

The last and favorite of 11 children, Irving avoided a college education but intermittently read law. A series of his whimsically satirical essays appeared over the signature of "Jonathan Oldstyle, Gent." in the *Morning Chronicle* (1802–3). In 1806 he passed the bar examination, and he soon set up as a lawyer. In 1807–8 his chief occupation was the writing (with his brother William and James K. Paulding) of a series of 20 periodical essays titled SALMAGUNDI.

Washington Irving

He next wrote A HISTORY OF NEW YORK . . . BY DIEDRICH KNICKERBOCKER (1809), a comic history of the Dutch regime in New York, prefaced by a mock-pedantic account of the world from creation onward. In 1815 he sailed on business to England, and he would remain there and in Europe for the next 17 years. In London he published THE SKETCH BOOK (1819–20), a collection of stories and essays that mixes satire and whimsicality with fact and fiction, and its tremendous success in both England and the United States assured him that he could live by his pen. In 1822 he produced the sequel *Bracebridge Hall*.

Early in 1826 he joined the diplomatic corps in Spain, where he wrote the nonfiction *Columbus* (1828) and *The Companions of Columbus* (1831). His absorption in the legends of the Moorish past resulted in *A Chronicle of the Conquest of Granada* (1829) and *The Alhambra* (1832), a Spanish counterpart of *The Sketch Book*.

In 1832 he finally returned to New York, where he was warmly received. After a journey west, he produced in rapid succession *A Tour of the Prairies* (1835), *Astoria* (1836), and *The Adventures of Captain Bonneville U.S.A.* (1837). Except for four years as minister to Spain (1842–46), he spent the rest of his life at his home on the Hudson River, "Sunnyside" in Tarrytown, where he wrote biographies of Oliver Goldsmith (1849), Muhammad (1849–50), and George Washington (5 vols., 1855–59).

Isherwood \ˈish-ər-ˌwu̇d\, **Christopher (William Bradshaw-)** (b. Aug. 26, 1904, High Lane, Cheshire, England—d. Jan. 4, 1986, Santa Monica, Calif.) Anglo-American novelist and playwright.

Educated at Cambridge University, Isherwood briefly attended medical school but left to teach school in Germany (1929–33). He gained recognition with his first two novels, *All the Conspirators* (1928) and *The Memorial* (1932), and collaborated with his school friend W. H. Auden on the verse dramas *The Dog Beneath the Skin* (1935), *The Ascent of F6* (1936), and *On the Frontier* (1938). In Berlin he observed the decay of the Weimar Republic and the rise of Nazism; his novels about this period—*Mr. Norris Changes Trains* (1935) and *Goodbye to Berlin* (1939), later published together as THE BERLIN STORIES—established his reputation. They formed the basis for the play *I Am a Camera* (1951), which was adapted to become the hit musical *Cabaret* (1966; film, 1972). In 1938 he published *Lions and Shadows*, an account of his university years.

The coming of World War II prompted Isherwood and Auden to immigrate to the United States. In 1939 Isherwood settled in southern California, where he taught and collaborated on screenplays. Having turned to pacifism and the self-abnegation of Indian Vedanta and become a follower of Swami Prabhavananda, he produced several works on Vedanta and translations with Prabhavananda in the following decades, including one of the *Bhagavadgita* (*The Song of God*, 1951). The short novel *A Single Man* (1964) presents a single day in the life of a lonely, middle-aged homosexual. Isherwood's avowedly autobiographical works include a self-revealing memoir of his parents, *Kathleen and Frank* (1971); a retrospective biography of himself in the 1930s, *Christopher and His Kind* (1977); and a study of his relationship with Prabhavananda, *My Guru and His Disciple* (1980).

Jackson, Helen Hunt *originally* Helen Maria Fiske (b. Oct. 15, 1830, Amherst, Mass.—d. Aug. 12, 1885, San Francisco) Poet and novelist best known for her novel *Ramona*.

    The daughter of an Amherst College professor, she was a close friend of Emily Dickinson. She turned to writing (usually under the pseudonyms Saxe Holm and H.H.) after the deaths of her first husband and two sons. In 1875 she married William Jackson and moved to Colorado. A prolific writer of minor works, Jackson is remembered primarily for her later efforts on behalf of American Indians. *A Century of Dishonor* (1881) arraigned government Indian policy. Her subsequent appointment to a federal commission investigating the plight of Indians on missions provided material for *Ramona* (1884), which aroused public sentiment on behalf of the Indians but has been admired chiefly for its picturesque and romantic setting in old California.

Jackson, Shirley (Hardie) (b. Dec. 14, 1916, San Francisco—d. Aug. 8, 1965, North Bennington, Vt.) Novelist and short-story writer best known for her story THE LOTTERY.

    Jackson graduated from Syracuse University in 1940 and married the critic Stanley Edgar Hyman. *Life Among the Savages* (1953) and *Raising Demons* (1957) are fictionalized memoirs about life with their four children; their light, comic tone contrasts sharply with the dark pessimism of Jackson's other works. "The Lottery," a chilling tale whose meaning has been much debated, provoked widespread outrage when it was first published in the *New Yorker* in 1948. Jackson's six finished novels, especially the classics *The Haunting of Hill House* (1959; films, 1963, 1999) and *We Have Always Lived in the Castle* (1962), confirmed her reputation as a master of gothic horror and psychological suspense. Her later years saw a sharp physical and psychological decline. Three short-story collections and an unfinished novel were published after her death from heart failure at 48.

Jacobs, Harriet (Ann) (b. 1813, Edenton, N.C.—d. 1897, Washington, D.C.) Slave and writer.

    Born to slaves, Jacobs was taught to read by her mistress; on the latter's death in 1825, she was bequeathed to a relative. She fought off sexual advances by her new master but became the lover of a white neighbor, bearing two children. In 1835 she escaped, reasoning that her master would sell the children to their father. She lived in hiding in an attic in her grandmother's house until 1842, when she was able to escape north and was reunited with her children. After passage of the fugitive-slave law in 1850, her former master tried to seize her in New York, and she fled to Massachusetts. In 1852 an abolitionist friend purchased her freedom.

    After friends encouraged her to inform northern women about the abuse of women slaves, she spent five years writing her autobiography, *Incidents in the Life of a Slave Girl, Written by Herself*; it was published in 1861 under the pseudonym

Linda Brent. During and after the Civil War, she and her daughter worked to provide health care and education for black refugees around Washington, D.C. Her book, originally thought to be a novel by a white woman, was largely forgotten until the 1980s, when its authenticity was confirmed.

Henry James

James, Henry (b. April 15, 1843, New York City—d. Feb. 28, 1916, London, England) Novelist and, as a naturalized English citizen from 1915, a great figure in transatlantic culture.

The son of the theologian Henry James and the brother of William James, he grew up in Manhattan but spent much of his childhood abroad. After graduating from Harvard College and briefly attending its law school, he devoted himself to literature, publishing his first story at 21. While writing regular criticism for the *Nation* (1865–69), he was encouraged to pursue fiction by W. D. Howells, editor of the new *Atlantic Monthly*, in whom James found a friend and mentor, and between them James and Howells inaugurated the era of American realism.

James made the first of many trips to Europe as an adult in 1869, and within five years he had decided to live abroad permanently. Thus began his long expatriation, whose initial products (in 1876) were the novel RODERICK HUDSON, his first collection of travel writings, and a collection of tales. During 1875–76 he lived in Paris, writing literary and topical letters for the *New York Tribune* and working on his novel THE AMERICAN (1877). Late in 1876 he crossed to London, where he would write the major fiction of his middle years. In 1878 he achieved international renown with DAISY MILLER (1879), and he further enhanced his prestige with *The Europeans* that same year. He ended this first phase of his career by producing his masterpiece, THE PORTRAIT OF A LADY (1881). His reputation was thus founded on a series of witty tales of the "self-made" young "American girl," the bold and brash American innocent who insists upon American standards in European society.

In the middle phase of his career, James wrote two novels dealing with social reformers and revolutionaries, THE BOSTONIANS (1886) and THE PRINCESS CASAMASSIMA (1886). These were followed by THE TRAGIC MUSE (1890), in which he projected a study of the London and Paris art studios and the stage. After failing to win success as a playwright, he spent several years seeking to adapt the techniques of drama to his fiction, as evidenced by WASHINGTON SQUARE (1880), and the result was a complete change in his storytelling methods. In the novelette THE ASPERN PAPERS (1888), THE SPOILS OF POYNTON (1897), WHAT MAISIE KNEW (1897), THE TURN OF THE SCREW (1898), and THE AWKWARD AGE (1899), he began to use the methods of alternating "picture" and dramatic scene, close adherence to a given angle of vision, and a withholding of information from the reader, presenting only what the characters see.

The experiments of this "transition" phase led to three great novels that represent James's final phase: THE WINGS OF THE DOVE (1902), THE AMBASSADORS (1903), and THE GOLDEN BOWL (1904), along with such short stories as THE BEAST IN THE JUNGLE (1903). His intense concern with the novel as an art form is reflected in THE ART OF FICTION (1884), the prefaces to the volumes of his collected works, and his many literary essays.

James, William   (b. Jan. 11, 1842, New York City—d. Aug. 26, 1910, Chocorua, N.H.) Psychologist and philosopher.

William James

Son of the philosopher Henry James and brother of the novelist Henry James, he received a broad early education in Europe and the United States and studied art and science before earning his medical degree in 1869 from Harvard, where he returned to teach in 1872—first physiology, then psychology (he established the country's first laboratory for psychological research), and finally philosophy. His first major work, the monumental *Principles of Psychology* (1890), treated thinking and knowledge as instruments in the struggle to live. The book won wide acclaim from both scientists and the general public, and made James a leader of the psychological movement of functionalism. However, he would go beyond his radically empiricist psychology, using it as a tool to explore larger philosophical, ethical, and religious questions.

His most famous work, THE VARIETIES OF RELIGIOUS EXPERIENCE (1902), written to reconcile religion and science, remains a greatly admired classic in the field. In 1907, the year he retired from teaching, James expanded on the ideas of Charles S. Peirce in *Pragmatism*; in it he asserted that the meaning of any idea must be analyzed in terms of the succession of experiential consequences it leads to, and that truth and error depend solely on these consequences. The book established him as a leader of the Pragmatist movement.

His other works, most of which address the controversy raised by *Pragmatism*, included *A Pluralistic Universe* (1909), *The Meaning of Truth* (1909), *Some Problems of Philosophy* (1911), and *Essays in Radical Empiricism* (1912).

Jameson \\'jām-sən\\, **J(ohn) Franklin** (b. Sept. 19, 1859, near Boston— d. Sept. 28, 1937, Washington, D.C.) Historian.

Jameson obtained a Ph.D. from Johns Hopkins in 1882, where he stayed to teach (1882–88). After teaching at Brown University (1888–1901) and the University of Chicago (1901–5), he became director of historical research at the Carnegie Institution of Washington (1905–28) and chief of the manuscript division of the Library of Congress (1928–37). His work in overseeing the systematic publication of historical documents held in governmental and private collections made available vast new scholarly resources.

In 1884 he helped found the American Historical Association, and he was subsequently managing editor of *American Historical Review* (1895–1901, 1905–28). His many scholarly books include *Dictionary of United States History* (1894) and *The American Revolution Considered as a Social Movement* (1926), and he edited *Original Narratives of Early American History* (19 vols., 1906–17).

Randall Jarrell

Jarrell \ja-'rel\, **Randall** (b. May 6, 1914, Nashville, Tenn.—d. Oct. 14, 1965, Chapel Hill, N.C.) Poet, novelist, and critic noted for revitalizing the reputations of Robert Frost and Walt Whitman in the 1950s.

Childhood was a major theme of Jarrell's verse. In 1942 he joined the air force, and his first book of verse, *Blood for a Stranger*, was published. Many of his best poems appeared in *Little Friend, Little Friend* (1945) and *Losses* (1948), both of which dwell on his wartime experiences.

He taught briefly at Sarah Lawrence College (1946–47), and his only novel, the sharply satirical *Pictures from an Institution* (1954), is about a similar progressive girls' college. His criticism was collected in *Poetry and the Age* (1953), *A Sad Heart at the Supermarket* (1962), and the posthumous *Third Book of Criticism* (1969). His other poetry collections include *The Seven-League Crutches* (1951), *The Woman at the Washington Zoo* (1960), and *The Lost World* (1965). From 1947 until his death, he taught at the University of North Carolina at Greensboro. He was killed when he stepped in front of a moving car.

Jay, John (b. Dec. 12, 1745, New York City—d. May 17, 1829, Bedford, N.Y.) First chief justice of the Supreme Court (1789–95).

A successful lawyer, Jay initially favored reconciliation with Britain but soon became a staunch supporter of American independence. A delegate to the first Continental Congress (1774), he drafted *The Address to the People of Great Britain,* stating the claims of colonists. He helped draft New York's first constitution, was elected the state's first chief justice, and in 1778 was chosen president of the Continental Congress. In 1782 he helped negotiate favorable terms from Britain in the 1783 treaty that ended the American Revolution. From 1784 to 1789 he served as U.S. secretary for foreign affairs. A supporter of the new U.S. Constitution, he collaborated with Alexander Hamilton and James Madison by writing five essays for *The Federalist.* In 1789 he was appointed the country's first chief justice, in which capacity he was instrumental in shaping early Supreme Court procedures. In *Chisholm v. Georgia,* he affirmed the subordination of the states to the federal government. In 1794 Washington sent him to Britain to help avert war over accumulated grievances. The commercial agreement he negotiated, called the Jay Treaty, was criticized as too pro-British. Jay resigned from the Court in 1795 and was elected governor of New York (1795–1801).

Jeffers \'jef-ərz\, **(John) Robinson** (b. Jan. 10, 1887, Pittsburgh, Pa.—d. Jan. 20, 1962, Carmel, Calif.) One of the most controversial American poets of the 20th century, who viewed human life as a frantic, often contemptible struggle within a net of passions.

Educated in literature, medicine, and forestry, Jeffers enjoyed inherited wealth, which allowed him to devote his life to writing poetry. His shorter lyrics as well as his sprawling narrative poems celebrate the coastal scenery near Carmel, Calif., where he and his wife moved in 1916. His third book, *Tamar and*

Other Poems (1924), brought him fame and revealed the unique style, eccentric contempt for humanity, and love of the harsh, eternal beauties of nature that he would develop in such later volumes as *Cawdor* (1928), *Thurso's Landing* (1932), *Give Your Heart to the Hawks* (1933), and *Be Angry at the Sun* (1941). His brilliant adaptation of Euripides' *Medea,* produced in 1946, was followed by other Greek adaptations, which paralleled his own work's frequent reliance on Greek myth.

Jefferson, Thomas (b. April 2, 1743, Shadwell, Va.—d. July 4, 1826, Monticello, Va.) Drafter of the Declaration of Independence and third president of the United States (1801–9).

Thomas Jefferson

After studies at William and Mary College, Jefferson read law and became a planter and lawyer; from 1769 he was a member of the Virginia House of Burgesses. In 1774 his "Summary View of the Rights of British America" made him famous as an early advocate of American independence. A delegate to the Continental Congress, he was appointed to the committee to draft the Declaration of Independence, and became its principal author.

After serving as governor of Virginia (1779–81), he was a delegate to the Congress (1783–85), where he drafted territorial provisions that were included in the Northwest Ordinances. In 1785 he was appointed U.S. minister to France. In 1790 George Washington appointed him the first U.S. secretary of state; he resigned in 1793 over conflict with Alexander Hamilton. His wide-ranging *Notes on the State of Virginia* (1784) enhanced his already high intellectual reputation and extended it into the fields of science and general scholarship.

Jefferson became vice president in 1797 under Pres. John Adams, whom he succeeded in 1801. As president, he oversaw the Louisiana Purchase and authorized the Lewis and Clark Expedition. He avoided entanglement in the Napoleonic Wars by signing the Embargo Act. In 1809 he retired to his home, Monticello, to pursue his many interests in science, philosophy, and architecture. Possibly the most broadly learned citizen of the entire country, he amassed an impressive library, which would become the core of the Library of Congress when the latter was burnt in the War of 1812. In 1819 he founded and designed the University of Virginia.

In 1813, after a long estrangement, Jefferson and Adams became reconciled and began a voluminous correspondence, exchanging views on national issues that illuminated much of the founders' philosophies. Their letters were later published in many editions as *The Adams–Jefferson Letters.*

Jewett \\'jü-ət\\, **Sarah Orne** (b. Sept. 3, 1849, South Berwick, Maine—d. June 24, 1909, South Berwick) Writer of regional fiction.

The daughter of a country doctor, on whose rounds she experienced a great variety of rural life, Jewett determined early in her teens to write about the rapidly disappearing traditions of provincial life about her, and by age 28 she was an established writer. Outstanding among her 20 volumes are the novels *Deephaven*

(1877), *A Country Doctor* (1884), and THE COUNTRY OF THE POINTED FIRS (1896), regarded as her finest achievement, and the story collection *A White Heron* (1886). The books contain realistic sketches of aging Maine natives, whose manners, idioms, and pithiness she recorded with pungency and humor, sympathetically but without sentimentality. She virtually never left the state of Maine. A disabling accident all but ended her writing career in 1902.

Jhabvala \'jäb-vä-lə\, **Ruth Prawer** *originally* Ruth Prawer (b. May 7, 1927, Cologne, Germany) Novelist and screenwriter.

Born to German parents, Prawer fled the Nazi regime with her family in 1939, settling in England. She received an M.A. from London University in 1951, married Cyrus Jhabvala the same year, and moved to India with him. In 1961 she began a long association with the filmmakers James Ivory and Ismail Merchant, for whom she has written over a dozen screenplays, including *Shakespeare Wallah* (1965), *The Bostonians* (1984), *A Room with a View* (1986, Academy Award), *Howard's End* (1992, Academy Award), and *The Remains of the Day* (1993). Her early fiction is set in India; the novel *Heat and Dust* (1975) won the Booker Prize. In 1975 she moved to New York and in 1986 she became an American citizen; her later novels, including *Three Continents* (1987) and *Poet and Dancer* (1993), are set in America. The stories in *East into Upper East* (1998) are set in New Delhi and New York.

Johnson, Charles S(purgeon) (b. July 24, 1893, Bristol, Va.—d. Oct. 27, 1956, Louisville, Ky.) Sociologist, educator, and writer.

After graduating from Virginia Union University, Johnson studied sociology at the University of Chicago and later worked for the Chicago Commission on Race Relations (1919–21). His first important book, *The Negro in Chicago* (1922), was a sociological study of the 1919 race riot in that city. He soon moved to New York City, where he directed research for the National Urban League and also founded and edited (1923–28) the intellectual journal *Opportunity*, a major voice of the Harlem Renaissance. In 1928 he became chairman of the social-sciences department at Fisk University, and in 1946 he was chosen the university's first black president. His books included *The Negro in American Civilization* (1930), *The Negro College Graduate* (1936), *Growing Up in the Black Belt* (1941), and *Patterns of Negro Segregation* (1943).

Johnson, Denis (b. 1949, Munich, Germany) Novelist and poet.

Born to a U.S. government worker, he lived in the United States, Japan, and Germany, before returning to Washington as a teenager. After college, he taught for several years, but in the 1970s he became a drug addict and alcoholic.

His first collection of poetry, *The Man Among the Seals* (1969), was followed by *Inner Weather* (1976) and *The Incognito Lounge* (1982). His first novel, *Angels* (1983), won favorable notice for its harsh depiction of the addict's life, and several of his subsequent novels—which include *Fiskadoro* (1985), *The Stars at Noon* (1986), *Resuscitation of a Hanged Man* (1991), *Already Dead* (1997), and *The Name of the World* (2000)—have similarly relied on those experiences. Johnson's work has been much praised for its imagination and unpredictability. His stories have been collected in *Jesus' Son* (1992).

Johnson, Diane *originally* Diane Lain Johnson Murray (b. April 28, 1934, Moline, Ill.) Writer known for worldly and satiric novels about women in crisis.

Educated at Stephens College, the University of Utah, and the University of California, since 1968 she has taught at UC–Davis while spending much of each year in Paris. The heroine of her first novel, *Fair Game* (1965), exploited by a series of lovers, eventually finds a man who will foster her desire to grow into a more complete person. In *Loving Hands at Home* (1968) a woman leaves her Mormon husband but fails to succeed on her own in the wider world. *Burning* (1971) satirizes Southern California life. *The Shadow Knows* (1974) concerns a divorced mother whose secure life is shattered when she becomes convinced she is marked for violence. Later novels include *Lying Low* (1978), *Persian Nights* (1987), *Health and Happiness* (1990), *Le Divorce* (1997), and *Le Mariage* (2000). Johnson has also written a well-received novelistic biography of George Meredith's first wife (1972), the biography *Dashiell Hammett* (1983), and the screenplay *The Shining* (1980; with Stanley Kubrick).

Johnson, James Weldon (b. June 17, 1871, Jacksonville, Fla.—d. June 26, 1938, Wiscasset, Maine) Poet, diplomat, and anthologist of African-American culture.

After graduating from Atlanta University, Johnson read law, was admitted to the bar in Florida, and began practicing there. During this period he and his brother, the composer J. Rosamond Johnson (1873–1954), began writing songs, and in 1901 the two moved to New York, where they wrote some 200 songs for the Broadway stage.

From 1906 to 1914 he held various diplomatic posts. His novel AUTOBIOGRAPHY OF AN EX-COLORED MAN (published anonymously, 1912) attracted little attention until it was reissued under his own name in 1927, while Johnson was serving as executive secretary of the NAACP (1920–30). From 1930 he taught at Fisk University.

Fifty Years and Other Poems (1917) was followed by the pioneering anthologies *Book of American Negro Poetry* (1922) and *American Negro Spirituals* (1925, 1926), collaborations with his brother, with whom he also collaborated on the anthem "Lift Every Voice and Sing." Johnson's best-known original poetry collection is GOD'S TROMBONES (1927), a group of black dialect sermons in verse. *Along This Way* (1933) is an autobiography.

Jolas \zhō-ˈlä\, **Eugene** (b. Oct. 26, 1894, Union City, N.J.—d. May 26, 1952, Paris, France) Founder, with his wife and Elliot Paul, of the revolutionary literary quarterly *transition*.

Raised in Lorraine, France, Jolas worked as a journalist both in the United States and France. His wife, Maria, born Maria McDonald (1893–1987), moved to Europe to study voice in 1913. Soon after their marriage in 1926, the couple moved to Paris, where Eugene sought to provide a forum for international writers by establishing the periodical *transition*. English-language writers whose works would appear in its pages during its short life (1927–30, 1932–39) included Ernest Hemingway, Samuel Beckett, and most significantly James Joyce. Jolas's own poetry reflecting his beliefs that language should be recreated and should rely on dreams and the subconscious for inspiration; his best volume was *The Language of Night* (1932).

Maria served essentially as managing and production editor of *transition*, as well as a translator of the foreign pieces it published. She also established the Bilingual School of Neuilly (1932–40) and translated 12 novels by Nathalie Sarraute.

Jones, James (Ramon) (b. Nov. 6, 1921, Robinson, Ill.—d. May 9, 1977, Southampton, Long Island, N.Y.) Writer best known for his novels of World War II.

The strongest influence on Jones's writing was his service in the army from 1939 to 1945. He used his experience of the Pearl Harbor attack and day-to-day military life in his first novel, *From Here to Eternity* (1951, National Book Award; film, 1953), about a charismatic serviceman who dies shortly after the outbreak of war in Hawaii. In his second novel, *Some Came Running* (1957; film, 1958), Jones drew on his life in Illinois after the war. His next two novels, *The Pistol* (1958) and the acclaimed *The Thin Red Line* (1962; films, 1964, 1998), return to his wartime experiences. Jones lived as an expatriate in Paris from 1958 until 1974. Later novels included *Go to the Widow-Maker* (1967) and *The Merry Month of May* (1971). *Whistle*, published posthumously in 1978, completes the trilogy that includes *From Here to Eternity* and *The Thin Red Line*.

Jones, LeRoi See **Amiri Baraka**

Jong \ˈjȯŋ, ˈzhȯŋ\, **Erica** *originally* Erica Mann (b. March 26, 1942, New York City) Novelist and poet.

After attending Barnard College and Columbia University (M.A., 1965), she taught poetry in several New York colleges. Her first collection of poems, *Fruits and Vegetables* (1971), was followed by *Half Lives* (1973). Jong became a sensation with the publication of her first novel, *Fear of Flying* (1973), with its frank description of a woman's sexual desires and her search for liberation; more than 12 million copies would eventually be sold. She continued her semiautobiographical story in *How to Save Your Own Life* (1977) and *Parachutes and Kisses* (1984). Her other novels include *Fanny* (1980), *Witches* (1981), *Serenissima* (1987), *Any Woman's Blues* (1990), and *Inventing Memory* (1997). Her poems have been collected in *Loveroot* (1975) and *Becoming Light* (1991); *The Devil at Large* (1992) discusses her friend Henry Miller; *Fear of Fifty* (1994) is a memoir.

Jordan, June (b. July 9, 1936, New York City—d. June 14, 2002, Berkeley, Calif.) Versatile author of poetry, essays, and drama.

The daughter of Jamaican immigrants, Jordan grew up in Brooklyn and attended Barnard College and the University of Chicago. Her marriage to a white graduate student (1965–75) ended in divorce. From 1967 to 2002, she taught English, literature, and African studies, principally at SUNY–Stony Brook and UC–Berkeley, where she fought for the inclusion of black studies and third-world studies in university curricula and advocated acceptance of Black English.

Her first poetry collection, *Who Look at Me*, appeared in 1969; her subsequent collections included *Some Changes* (1971), *Things That I Do in the Dark* (1977), *Living Room* (1985), *Naming Our Destiny* (1989), *Poetic Justice* (1991), and *Kissing God Goodbye* (1997). In the 1970s she wrote books for children and adolescents. Her first novel was *His Own Where* (1971). As both journalist and poet, Jordan wrote about feminism, racism, abortion rights, and opportunity for minorities; her essays are collected in *Civil Wars* (1981), *On Call* (1985), *Technical Difficulties* (1992), and *Affirmative Acts* (1998).

Josephson, Matthew (b. Feb. 15, 1899, Brooklyn, N.Y.—d. March 13, 1978, Santa Cruz, Calif.) Biographer and historian.

As a radical expatriate in Paris in the 1920s, Josephson was an associate editor of *Broom* (1922–24), which featured both American and European writers, and later an editor of *transition* (1928–29). His first book was the authoritative biography *Zola and His Time* (1928). Other highly praised biographies followed, including *Victor Hugo* (1942) and *Stendhal* (1946), which helped regenerate American interest in Stendhal's work. He addressed American economics in perhaps his best-known work, *The Robber Barons* (1934), which chronicles the lives of such figures as John D. Rockefeller and Andrew Carnegie, and much later in *The Money Lords* (1972).

Judson, E(dward) Z(ane) C(arroll) *pseudonym* **Ned Buntline** (b. March 20, 1823, Stamford, N.Y.—d. July 16, 1886, Stamford) Adventurer and writer, an originator of the "dime novels" popular during the late 19th century.

Judson's early stories were based on the exploits of his own astonishingly picaresque career, which began as a cabin boy in the navy. He left the navy in 1844, reputedly to fight Indians and travel in the West. He contributed stories to the *Knickerbocker Magazine* and in 1844 established the short-lived *Ned Buntline's*

Magazine in Cincinnati. He later moved to Nashville and founded the sensational-ist and jingoist newspaper *Ned Buntline's Own*, which he took to New York when he was forced to leave town after killing the husband of his mistress. He joined the Union Army during the Civil War but was discharged in 1864 for drunkenness. In 1869 he met William F. Cody, whom he dubbed "Buffalo Bill" and would portray as the hero of a series of his dime novels. He also wrote a play for Cody, *The Scouts of the Plains* (1872), patterned on his life; not only did Cody himself act in the play, but so also did "Wild Bill" Hickok, whose nickname was likewise Judson's invention.

Judson's 400 dime novels and serials were sensational stories of swash-buckling heroes and violence, but none matched the outrageously eventful life of their author.

Justice, Donald (Rodney) (b. Aug. 12, 1925, Miami, Fla.) Poet and editor best known for finely crafted verse that frequently illuminates the pain of loss and the desolation of an unlived life.

Educated at the Universities of Miami, North Carolina, and Iowa and at Stanford University, Justice later taught English and writing at several colleges. His poetry collections include *The Summer Anniversaries* (1960), *Night Light* (1967), *Departures* (1973), and *Selected Poems* (1979, Pulitzer Prize). He also published the essay collection *Platonic Scripts* (1984) and *The Sunset Maker: Poems, Stories, A Memoir* (1987). Having considered becoming a composer as a young man, he has retained a lifelong interest in music, writing the librettos for three operas, including *The Death of Lincoln* (1988; with music by Edwin Lon-don). Among books he has edited or coedited are *The Collected Poems of Weldon Kees* (1960), *Contemporary French Poetry* (1965), and *Syracuse Poems* (1968). He was awarded the Bollingen Prize in 1991.

Kantor \\'kan-tər\\, **(Benjamin) MacKinlay** (b. Feb. 4, 1904, Webster City, Iowa—d. Oct. 11, 1977, Sarasota, Fla.) Author of popular novels and short stories.

After finishing high school, Kantor became a reporter on the local newspaper. He lived some years in Chicago, but returned to Iowa as a columnist for the *Des Moines Tribune*. After publishing many short stories, he won recognition with a novel about Gettysburg, *Long Remember* (1934). After service in World War II he became a screenwriter in Hollywood, where he helped Robert E. Sherwood adapt *Glory for Me* (1945), Kantor's verse novel about three American servicemen returning to civilian life, for the film *The Best Years of Our Lives* (1946, Academy Award). His highly acclaimed *Andersonville* (1955, Pulitzer Prize) concerned the notorious Civil War prisoner-of-war camp. In his long career Kantor published more than 30 novels, including the historical novels *Spirit Lake* (1961) and *Valley Forge* (1975), and several popular collections of short stories on subjects ranging from Chicago gangsters to life in the Ozarks.

Kaplan, Justin (b. Sept. 5, 1925, New York City) Writer, biographer, and book editor known for his acclaimed literary biographies.

A graduate of Harvard, Kaplan left graduate school in 1946 to become an editor at a publishing house, where he worked with Bertrand Russell, Will Durant, Níkos Kazantzákis, and C. Wright Mills. He has since taught at Harvard, Emerson College, and Griffith University in Australia.

His first book, the biography *Mr. Clemens and Mark Twain* (1966), won a Pulitzer Prize and a National Book Award. *Lincoln Steffens* (1974), about the prominent journalist and muckraker, and *Walt Whitman* (1980, American Book Award) were also highly praised. Kaplan edited the 16th edition of *Bartlett's Familiar Quotations* (1992).

Kaufman, Bob (*originally* Robert Garnell) (b. April 18, 1925, New Orleans—d. Jan. 12, 1986, San Francisco) Innovative poet who became an important figure of the Beat movement.

With a black Roman Catholic mother, a German-Jewish father, and a grandmother who believed in voodoo, Kaufman was exposed to a variety of religious influences, and eventually adopted Buddhism. After settling in San Francisco in 1958 he became involved in the city's bohemian artistic community and wrote witty, surreal poetry inspired by the rhythms of bebop jazz. Three broadside poems he published in 1959 were later included in his collection *Solitudes Crowded with Loneliness* (1965). In 1965 he cofounded the poetry magazine *Beatitude*. He worked as a street performer in both San Francisco and New York, becoming known for his striking eccentricity.

In the early 1960s Kaufman was one of the most popular American poets among European readers. His second collection, *Golden Sardine*, appeared in 1967. After seeing the televised assassination of John F. Kennedy in 1963, he took a vow of silence, and he did not speak or write again until 1973. After that

K

he wrote prolifically, producing poems with literary themes that were published with earlier works in *The Ancient Rain: Poems, 1956–1978* (1981). In 1978 he retreated into solitude for the rest of his life.

Kaufman, George S(imon) (b. Nov. 16, 1889, Pittsburgh, Pa.—d. June 2, 1961, New York City) Playwright noted for his collaboration with other authors on some of the most successful plays and musicals of the 1920s and '30s.

After attending public school in Pittsburgh and Paterson, N.J., Kaufman worked briefly as a salesman. He began contributing to the satirical column of Franklin P. Adams ("F.P.A.") in the *New York Evening Mail*, and in 1912 was given his own column in the *Washington Times*. He was a drama critic for the *New York Times* from 1917 to 1930, during which time he became a member of the Algonquin Round Table.

His first successful play, written with Marc Connelly, was *Dulcy* (1921). His other collaborations with Connelly included *Merton of the Movies* (1922), one of the first satires on Hollywood, and *Beggar on Horseback* (1924). *The Butter and Egg Man* (1925), a satire on theatrical production, was the only play he wrote alone. Among his other collaborations were the musical *Of Thee I Sing* (1931, Pulitzer Prize), with Morrie Ryskind and the Gershwin brothers; *Dinner at Eight* (1932), *Stage Door* (1936), and *The Land Is Bright* (1941), with Edna Ferber; *The Solid Gold Cadillac* (1953), with Howard Teichmann; *Silk Stockings* (1955), with Abe Burroughs; and a number of memorable successes with Moss Hart that included *Once in a Lifetime* (1930), *Merrily We Roll Along* (1934), *You Can't Take It with You* (1936, Pulitzer Prize), and *The Man Who Came to Dinner* (1939). He cowrote the screenplays for the Marx Brothers films *The Cocoanuts* (1929), *Animal Crackers* (1930), and *A Night at the Opera* (1935). Kaufman's range was wide, varying in tone with his collaborators, but brilliant satire and caustic wit were his forte.

Kazin \ˈkāz-ən\, **Alfred** (b. June 5, 1915, Brooklyn, N.Y.—d. June 5, 1998, New York City) Teacher, editor, and literary critic.

Kazin attended CCNY and Columbia University, then worked as a freelance book reviewer for various periodicals. At 27 he published a sweeping historical study of modern American literature, *On Native Grounds* (1942), tracing the social and political movements that inspired successive stages of literary development in America, whose brilliance won him instant recognition.

Many of Kazin's later works dealt with the forces that drive an individual to write. His sketches of literary personalities revealed much about both the writers and their eras. Kazin felt that with increasing technological domination of society, literature had diminished in importance as a vehicle of personal growth and political definition, and in such critical works as *Bright Book of Life* (1973), *An American Procession* (1984), *A Writer's America* (1988), and *God and the Amer-*

ican Writer (1997), his critical and political sensibilities were inextricably inter-
twined. Among the books he edited were *The Portable Blake* (1946), *The Stature
of Theodore Dreiser* (1955), and *The Works of Anne Frank* (1959). His celebrated
autobiographical works include *A Walker in the City* (1951), *Starting Out in the
Thirties* (1965), and *New York Jew* (1978).

Keillor \ˈkē-lər\, **Garrison (Edward)** (b. Aug. 7, 1942, Anoka, Minn.)
Radio entertainer and writer.

    Keillor began writing for the *New Yorker* while a student at the University of
Minnesota, and thereafter continued as a staff writer for the magazine until 1992.
He also began working for Minnesota Public Radio in 1969, and in 1974 he created the public-radio humor and variety show *A Prairie Home Companion,* about
the fictional Minnesota town Lake Wobegon. Hosted by the genial Keillor, and
broadcast nationally from 1980, it became a great success with public-radio audiences. He ended the show in 1987, started a new show, *The American Radio Company,* in 1989, and replaced it with a revived *Prairie Home Companion* in 1993.

    Keillor's books, most of them semiautobiographical, with the deadpan
humor of his radio persona, include *Happy to Be Here* (1981), the huge best-
seller *Lake Wobegon Days* (1985), *Leaving Home* (1987), *We Are Still Married*
(1989), *WLT: A Radio Romance (1991), The Book of Guys* (1993), *The Sandy
Bottom Orchestra* (1996), *Wobegon Boy* (1997), *Me* (1999), and *Love Me* (2003).

Keller, Helen (Adams) (b. June 27, 1880, Tuscumbia, Ala.—d. June 1, 1968,
Westport, Conn.) Writer and educator.

    Deprived by illness of sight and hearing at the age of 19 months, Keller
soon became mute as well. At age 7 she began to be instructed by Anne Sullivan,
who taught her the names of objects by pressing the manual alphabet into her
palm; Sullivan remained with Keller until her own death in 1936. Having learned
to read and write in Braille, she attended schools for the deaf, and in 1904 she
graduated from Radcliffe College. In 1913 she began lecturing (with the aid of an
interpreter), primarily on behalf of the American Foundation for the Blind, for
which she later established a $2 million endowment fund, and her lecture tours
took her several times around the world. By 1937 she prompted the organization
of commissions for the blind in 30 states. She also worked for women's suffrage
and involved herself in socialist and humanitarian causes.

Helen Keller

    Her articles about her condition appeared in *Ladies' Home Journal* and
other magazines, and she wrote of her life in several books, including *The Story
of My Life* (1902), *Optimism* (1903), *The World I Live In* (1908), *My Religion*
(1927), *Helen Keller's Journal* (1938), and *The Open Door* (1957). Keller's
childhood training with Anne Sullivan was depicted in William Gibson's play
The Miracle Worker (1959; film, 1962).

Kelly, George (Edward) (b. Jan. 16, 1887, Philadelphia—d. June 18, 1974, Bryn Mawr, Pa.) Playwright, actor, and director whose dramas of the 1920s depict the foibles of the American middle class.

Kelly followed his elder brother into vaudeville as an actor, writing his first sketches for his own performance. His first success on Broadway was *The Torch-bearers* (1922), a satire on the social and aesthetic pretensions of the little-theater movement then flourishing. His next play, *The Show-Off* (1924), became a comedy classic, and was filmed three times (1926, 1934, 1946). In the savage drama *Craig's Wife* (1925; films, 1936, 1950) he shifted his vision to the upper middle class. Kelly's film scripts include those for the screen versions of his plays.

Kennan, George F(rost) (b. Feb. 16, 1904, Milwaukee) Diplomat and historian.

After graduating from Princeton University, Kennan entered the foreign service, studied Russian language and culture at the University of Berlin (1929–31), and was assigned to the U.S. embassy in Moscow (1933–35). He served in other posts in Europe, returning to Moscow during and after World War II. His concept of "containment," published in a highly influential anonymous article in 1947, was adopted as the basis of U.S. foreign policy toward the Soviet Union.

From 1956 to 1974 Kennan was professor of historical studies at Princeton's Institute for Advanced Study, a tenure broken only by a stint as ambassador to Yugoslavia (1961–63). In the late 1950s he revised his containment views, advocating instead a program of U.S. "disengagement" from areas of conflict with the Soviet Union.

A prolific and admired author, Kennan wrote such important books as *American Diplomacy* (1951), *Realities of American Foreign Policy* (1954), and *Soviet-American Relations* (1956–58), whose first volume, *Russia Leaves the War* (1956), won both the Pulitzer Prize and the National Book Award, as did the first volume of his *Memoirs* (1967).

Kennedy, John Pendleton (b. Oct. 25, 1795, Baltimore—d. Aug. 18, 1870, Newport, R.I.) Statesman and writer best remembered for his historical fiction.

Kennedy was admitted to the Maryland bar in 1816. He served three terms in the U.S. Congress (1838–39, 1841–45), and as secretary of the navy under Millard Fillmore he organized Matthew Perry's expedition to Japan. Meanwhile, using the pen name of Mark Littleton, he wrote historical novels, including *Swallow Barn* (1832), sketches of the post-revolutionary life of gentlemen on Virginia plantations, and *Rob of the Bowl* (1838), a tale of colonial Maryland. His major work of nonfiction is *Memoirs of the Life of William Wirt* (1849), about a prosecuting attorney in the trial of Aaron Burr.

Kennedy, William (b. Jan. 16, 1928, Albany, N.Y.) Novelist and journalist.

Kennedy graduated from Siena College in 1949 and worked as a journalist in New York and Puerto Rico, where he began writing fiction. In 1963 he returned to Albany, which became the source of his literary inspiration. His first novel, *The Ink Truck* (1969), concerns a colorful columnist who leads a strike at his newspaper in a city resembling Albany. Kennedy combined history, fiction, and black humor in the first novel of his "Albany cycle," *Legs* (1975), about Jack "Legs" Diamond, a gangster who was killed in Albany in 1931. *Billy Phelan's Greatest Game* (1978) chronicles the life of a small-time streetwise hustler who sidesteps the powerful Albany political machine. *Ironweed* (1983, Pulitzer Prize; film, 1987), which made Kennedy's name widely known, tells the story of the hustler's father. *O Albany!* (1983) is a spirited nonfictional account of the city's politics and history. The Albany cycle continued with *Quinn's Book* (1988), *Very Old Bones* (1992), and *The Flaming Corsage* (1996). Kennedy also wrote the screenplays for *The Cotton Club* (1984; with Francis Ford Coppola) and *Ironweed* (1987).

Kennedy, X. J. *originally* Joseph Charles Kennedy (b. Aug. 21, 1929, Dover, N.J.) Author of witty verse for children as well as for adults.

Kennedy studied at Seton Hall and Columbia universities, served in the navy, and returned to studies at the Sorbonne and the University of Michigan. He served as poetry editor of the *Paris Review*, and subsequently taught at Tufts University (1963–79).

Beginning with his first collection, *Nude Descending a Staircase* (1961), and with rare subsequent exceptions, Kennedy's poems are in rhyming stanzas and traditional meters and forms. They exhibit vivid language and frequent humor, including parody and satire. His *Cross Ties* was published in 1985. Composing poems and stories for his own children led him to write the nonsense verse collection *One Winter Night in August* (1975). Children misbehave hilariously and are punished outrageously in the nonsense poems published in *Brats* (1986), *Fresh Brats* (1990), *Drat These Brats!* (1993), and *Uncle Switch* (1997); *The Kite That Braved Old Orchard Beach* (1991) includes serious, even poignant verses. His widely used textbooks include *An Introduction to Poetry, Literature,* and *The Bedford Reader*. With his wife, Dorothy M. Kennedy, he wrote and edited the children's anthologies *Knock at a Star* (1982) and *Talking Like the Rain* (1992).

Kenner, (William) Hugh (b. Jan. 7, 1923, Peterborough, Ontario, Canada) Canadian-American critic known for his witty and readable books on modernist writers.

Kenner studied at the University of Toronto and Yale University, and taught at UC–Santa Barbara (1950–73), Johns Hopkins University (1973–90), and the University of Georgia (1990–99). In his influential books *The Poetry of Ezra*

Pound (1951) and *The Pound Era* (1971), he described Pound as the central figure in modernist literature and helped reestablish the poet's battered reputation. Of comparable importance were his studies of James Joyce in *Dublin's Joyce* (1955), *Flaubert, Joyce and Beckett* (1962), *Joyce's Voices* (1978), and *Ulysses* (1980). He has focused on T. S. Eliot, G. K. Chesterton, Wyndham Lewis, and others in such other works as *Gnomon* (1958), *The Counterfeiters: An Historical Comedy* (1968), *A Homemade World: The American Modernist Writers* (1975), *A Colder Eye: The Modern Irish Writers* (1983), and *A Sinking Island: The Modern English Writers* (1988).

Jack Kerouac

Kerouac \'ker-ə-ˌwak\, **Jack** (*originally* Jean-Louis) (b. March 12, 1922, Lowell, Mass.—d. Oct. 21, 1969, St. Petersburg, Fla.) Poet, novelist, and leader and spokesman of the Beat movement.

Of French-Canadian descent, Kerouac learned English as a schoolboy. He studied briefly at Columbia University (1940–41), then saw wartime service in the merchant marine and the navy (1942–43), from which he was discharged for psychological reasons. Back in New York, he met William S. Burroughs and Allen Ginsberg while living near Columbia, and began a restless, marginal, adventurous, drug-taking, bohemian life that would continue for many years.

A trip across the country in 1947 resulted in a first draft of the novel *On the Road* in 1948. His novel *The Town and the City* (1950) dealt with his hometown and New York. Inspired by jazz and a notion of "spontaneous bop prose," he rewrote *On the Road*, typing on a continuous roll of paper, in three weeks in 1951. The book's long-delayed publication in 1957 proved one of the most stunning literary events of the decade. The wild, unedited spontaneity of its prose shocked more polished writers, drew public attention to a widespread subterranean culture of poets, folksingers, hipsters, mystics, and eccentrics, and made Kerouac a well-known and charismatic figure. He gave prose and poetry readings (often backed up by jazz musicians) and made other public appearances, and his life was followed by legions of young people.

His study of Buddhism in 1954 lent a strongly Buddhistic bent to many of his later writings, all essentially autobiographical, which include *The Dharma Bums* (1958), *The Subterraneans* (1958), *Doctor Sax* (1959), *Lonesome Traveler* (1960), and *Desolation Angels* (1965). In his later years he became embittered and more deeply drug- and alcohol-dependent, and his death at 47 resulted from alcoholic-related causes. *Visions of Cody* was published posthumously in 1972.

Kesey \'kē-zē\, **Ken (Elton)** (b. Sept. 17, 1935, La Junta, Colo.—d. Nov. 10, 2001, Eugene, Ore.) Writer who became a hero of the 1960s counterculture.

Kesey was educated at the University of Oregon and Stanford University. He later served as an experimental subject at a Veterans Administration hospital, taking mind-altering drugs and reporting on their effects. This experience and his work as a hospital aide provided the background for his best-known novel, *One*

Flew Over the Cuckoo's Nest (1962; film, 1975), which was read enthusiastically by young people in the late 1960s. He further examined values in conflict in *Sometimes a Great Notion* (1964; film, 1971), about loggers in Oregon.

In the nonfiction *Kesey's Garage Sale* (1973), *Demon Box* (1986), and *The Further Inquiry* (1990), Kesey wrote of his travels and psychedelic experiences with his Merry Pranksters, a group that traveled together in a bus beginning in the 1960s, whose adventures were also recounted by Tom Wolfe in *The Electric Kool-Aid Acid Test* (1968). With 13 graduate students he wrote the mystery novel *Caverns* (1990) under the joint pseudonym of O. U. Levon. A later novel is *Sailor Song* (1992). He also published children's books.

Ken Kesey

Keyes \'kīz\, **Frances Parkinson** *originally* Frances Parkinson Wheeler (b. July 21, 1885, Charlottesville, Va.—d. July 3, 1970, New Orleans) Novelist.

After attending private schools in Boston, Geneva, and Berlin, Wheeler in 1904 married Henry W. Keyes, who would later be elected governor of New Hampshire (1917). When he was elected U.S. Senator in 1919, the couple moved to Washington, D.C., where they led an active social life. In 1920 Frances Keyes began writing a monthly column, "Letters from a Senator's Wife," for *Good Housekeeping* magazine, for which she was a contributing editor from 1923 to 1935.

She wrote over 50 popular novels, many of which featured successful heroines; they included *The Old Gray Homestead* (1919), *Senator Marlowe's Daughter* (1933), *Written in Heaven* (1937), *All That Glitters* (1941), *Came a Cavalier* (1947), *Dinner at Antoine's* (1948), *Joy Street* (1950), *The Royal Box* (1954), and *The Chess Players* (1960). She also wrote several books with religious themes, collections of poetry, and four autobiographical works.

Kilmer, (Alfred) Joyce (b. Dec. 6, 1886, New Brunswick, N.J.—d. July 30, 1918, near Seringes, France) Poet known chiefly for his 12-line verse "Trees."

Kilmer's first volume of verse, *Summer of Love* (1911), showed the influence of W. B. Yeats and the Irish poets. After his conversion to Roman Catholicism, he attempted to model his poetry on that of Coventry Patmore and the 17th-century Metaphysical poets. "Trees" first appeared in *Poetry* magazine in 1913; it would subsequently be memorized by millions of schoolchildren, though it was not admired by critics. His books include *Trees and Other Poems* (1914), *The Circus and Other Essays* (1916), *Main Street and Other Poems* (1917), and *Literature in the Making* (1917). He joined the staff of the *New York Times* in 1913. In 1917 he edited *Dreams and Images*, an anthology of modern Catholic poetry. He was killed in action during World War I and posthumously awarded the Croix de Guerre.

Joyce Kilmer

Kincaid, Jamaica *originally* Elaine Potter Richardson (b. May 25, 1949, St. John's, Antigua and Barbuda) Novelist and essayist.

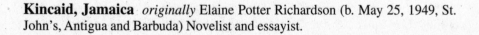

Kincaid came to the United States in 1966. From 1976 to 1995 she was a staff writer for the *New Yorker* magazine. Her works, many of them set in the Caribbean of her youth, include the story collection *At the Bottom of the River* (1983), the novels *Annie John* (1985) and *Lucy* (1990), the essay collection *A Small Place* (1988), and the nonfiction works *The Autobiography of My Mother* (1996), *My Brother* (1997), and *My Garden Book* (1999).

Martin Luther King

King, Martin Luther, Jr. *originally* Michael Luther King, Jr. (b. Jan. 15, 1929, Atlanta, Ga.—d. April 4, 1968, Memphis, Tenn.) Civil-rights leader.

Son of a prominent minister, King was educated at Morehouse College, Crozer Theological Seminary, and Boston University (Ph.D., 1955). While a student, he became an adherent of nonviolence philosophies. Having been ordained a Baptist minister in 1954, he was appointed pastor of a church in Montgomery, Ala. As head of the Montgomery Improvement Association, he directed the boycott that brought about desegregation of the city's public-transport system.

In 1957 he formed the Southern Christian Leadership Conference and began lecturing nationwide, urging active nonviolence to achieve civil rights for blacks. In 1960 he returned to Atlanta to join his father as copastor of Ebenezer Baptist Church. He was arrested for protesting segregation at a lunch counter and jailed; the case drew national attention, and presidential candidate John F. Kennedy interceded to obtain his release. He led antidiscrimination demonstrations and voter registration drives in Selma and Birmingham, Ala. In 1963 King helped organize the huge March on Washington, where he delivered his famous "I Have a Dream" sermon-speech. The march helped bring about passage of the Civil Rights Act of 1964, and King was awarded the 1964 Nobel Peace Prize. He broadened his advocacy to address the plight of the poor of all races and to oppose the Vietnam War. While in Memphis, Tenn., supporting a strike by sanitation workers, he was assassinated by a sniper, James Earl Ray.

Though King's eloquence gained most attention in his speeches, he was also the author of several books, including *Stride Toward Freedom* (1958), *Why We Can't Wait* (1964), and *Where Do We Go From Here?* (1967).

King, Stephen (Edwin) (b. Sept. 21, 1947, Portland, Maine) Novelist whose books revived the genre of horror fiction in the late 20th century.

King graduated from the University of Maine in 1970 and later supported himself by teaching and working at menial jobs while writing short stories. His first published novel, *Carrie* (1974), about a tormented teenage girl gifted with telekinetic powers, was an immediate popular success, and was the first of many novels in which King blended horror, the macabre, fantasy, and science fiction, including *Salem's Lot* (1975), *The Shining* (1977), *The Stand* (1978), *The Dead Zone* (1979), *Firestarter* (1980), *Cujo* (1981), *Christine* (1983), *Pet Sematary* (1983), *It* (1986), *Misery* (1987), *The Tommyknockers* (1987), *The Dark Half* (1989), *The Stand* (1990), *Dolores Claiborne* (1992), *Insomnia* (1994), *Rose*

Madder (1995), *Bag of Bones* (1998), *Dreamcatcher* (2001), and *From a Buick 8* (2002). The serial novel *The Green Mile* was published as six separate novellas (1996). King's short-story collections include *Night Shift* (1978), *Skeleton Crew* (1985), and *Nightmares and Dreamscapes* (1993). Several books, including *Thinner* (1984), have been published under the pseudonym Richard Bachman. King has explored a remarkable range of terror-producing themes, from vampires, rabid dogs, deranged killers, and a pyromaniac to ghosts, extrasensory perception and telekinesis, and biological warfare. His themes often resonate disturbingly with contemporary anxieties. Though his work has sometimes been disparaged as undisciplined and inelegant, its immense success has been firmly founded on realistic detail, forceful plotting, and a remarkable capacity to involve and terrify the reader. His name has become synonymous with the genre of horror fiction, and most of his novels have been successfully adapted for the screen.

Kingsolver, Barbara (b. April 8, 1955, Annapolis, Md.) Writer and political activist whose novels concern the strength and endurance of the poor and disenfranchised people of the Southwest.

Kingsolver grew up in eastern Kentucky, the daughter of a physician who treated the rural poor. After graduating from DePauw University, she did graduate work in biology and ecology at the University of Arizona.

Her novel *The Bean Trees* (1988) concerns a woman and the young Cherokee girl with whom she moves from rural Kentucky to the Southwest. In *Animal Dreams* (1990) a disconnected woman returns to live in her small Arizona hometown. *Pigs in Heaven* (1993) is a sequel to her first novel. Kingsolver has also written the nonfiction works *Holding the Line: Women in the Great Arizona Mine Strike of 1983* (1989) and *High Tide in Tucson* (1995) and a short-story collection, *Homeland and Other Stories* (1989). Her poetry collection, *Another America/Otra America* (1991), in English with Spanish translation, concerns the struggles of impoverished women against sexual and political abuse, war, and death. *The Poisonwood Bible* (1998) is set in postcolonial Africa; *Prodigal Summer* (2000) deals with ecological issues in Appalachia.

Kingston, Maxine Hong *originally* Maxine Hong (b. Oct. 27, 1940, Stockton, Calif.) Writer whose novels and nonfiction works explore the myths, realities, and cultural identities of Chinese and American families.

The daughter of Chinese immigrants, Kingston learned English as a second language and studied at UC–Berkeley. She taught 10 years in Hawaiian public school before publishing her first book. *The Woman Warrior* (1976, National Book Critics Circle Award) recalls her own girlhood, blending fact and fantasy in recreating the history of her female relatives in China. In the equally admired *China Men* (1980, American Book Award), she used biographical, mythological, and fantasy elements to tell the story of her father's life in China and his accommodations to life in America. The protagonist of *Tripmaster Monkey: His Fake*

Book (1988) is a young man in 1960s San Francisco who lives without regard to consequences. *The Fifth Book of Peace* (2003) blends memoir and fiction.

Kinnell \kə-'nel\, **Galway** (b. Feb. 1, 1927, Providence, R.I.) Poet known for his examinations of the primitive bases of existence obscured by the overlay of civilization.

Educated at Princeton University and the University of Rochester, Kinnell worked for the University of Chicago in the early 1950s, and has since taught at a number of colleges while living principally in Vermont.

His poems, often spiritually inflected and visionary, search for significance in such circumstances as the individual's relationship with violence and inevitable death, the plight of the urban dispossessed, attempts to hold death at bay, and the regenerative power of nature. His collections include *What a Kingdom It Was* (1960), *Flower Herding on Mount Monadnock* (1964), *Body Rags* (1967), the extraordinary *Book of Nightmares* (1971), *The Avenue Bearing the Initial of Christ into the New World* (1974), *Mortal Acts, Mortal Words* (1980), *Selected Poems* (1982, National Book Award and Pulitzer Prize), and *When One Has Lived a Long Time Alone* (1990). His translations include *The Poems of François Villon* (1965) and *The Essential Rilke* (1999). *Black Light* (1966) is a novel.

Kirk, Russell (Amos) (b. Oct. 19, 1918, Plymouth, Mich.—d. April 29, 1994, Mecosta, Mich.) Writer and lecturer.

After attending Michigan State College and Duke University (M.A., 1941), Kirk taught at Michigan State (1946–53) before pursuing a career as a lecturer and writer. In 1955 he helped found the conservative journal *National Review,* and he became its educational columnist (1956–83). He wrote a syndicated newspaper column (1962–75) and contributed over 500 articles to periodicals in the U.S. and abroad, while also giving numerous lectures on college campuses.

His many books, which earned him a reputation as one of the preeminent American conservative intellectuals of the second half of the century, include *The Conservative Mind: From Burke to Santayana* (1953; 7th ed., 1986), considered a major work in modern conservative thought; *A Program for Conservatives* (1954); *Eliot and His Age* (1971); and *The Roots of American Order* (1974). He edited *The Portable Conservative Reader* (1982), and also wrote several fantasy novels and story collections.

Kirkland, Joseph (b. Jan. 7, 1830, Geneva, N.Y.—d. April 29, 1894, Chicago) Novelist whose trilogy of Midwestern pioneer life contributed to the development of realistic fiction.

Kirkland was influenced by the English realist Thomas Hardy and by his own mother, Caroline Kirkland, whose realistic accounts of the family's life in backwoods Michigan were published in the 1840s. *Zury: The Meanest Man in Spring County* (1887), the first book of his trilogy, was followed by *The McVeys*

(1888), depicting the grimness of village life, and *The Captain of Company K* (1891), about the Civil War.

Kirkwood, James (b. Aug. 22, 1924, Los Angeles—d. April 21, 1989, New York City) Librettist, novelist, and playwright.

Son of the silent-film stars Lila Lee and James Kirkwood, the young Kirkwood appeared on Broadway in *Junior Miss*, *Small Wonder*, and *Welcome Darling*. With Nicholas Dante he wrote the text for the Broadway musical *A Chorus Line* (1975), about dancers auditioning for a musical, for which he won both a Tony award and a Pulitzer Prize; the show closed in 1990 as the longest-running musical in Broadway history. The most popular of his novels were the coming-of-age story *Good Times, Bad Times* (1968) and *P.S. Your Cat Is Dead!* (1972); his other novels were *There Must Be a Pony!* (1960), *Some Kind of Hero* (1975), and *Hit Me with A Rainbow* (1979). He also wrote such plays as *U.T.B.U.: Unhealthy To Be Unpleasant* (1966) and the comedy *Legends* (1987).

Kirstein \\'kər-ˌstēn\\, **Lincoln** (b. May 4, 1907, Rochester, N.Y.—d. Jan. 5, 1996, New York City) Writer, editor, dance authority, and cofounder and director of the New York City Ballet.

Born into a wealthy family, as a student at Harvard University Kirstein founded and edited (1927–34) the literary journal *Hound and Horn*, whose contributors would include T. S. Eliot, Ezra Pound, and E. E. Cummings.

Lincoln Kirstein

He became involved in ballet when he helped Romola Nijinsky write the biography of her famous husband. In 1933 he persuaded the young dancer George Balanchine to come to the United States to found a ballet school and company. Several ballet companies founded by the two men culminated in the great New York City Ballet (1948), which Kirstein served as general director until 1989. His books include the classic history *Dance* (1935), *The Classic Ballet* (1952; with Muriel Stuart), *Movement and Metaphor* (1970), and *Nijinsky Dancing* (1975), as well as a novel, two poetry collections, several studies of modern artists, and three volumes of memoirs.

Kizer \\'kī-zər\\, **Carolyn (Ashley)** (b. Dec. 10, 1925, Spokane, Wash.) Poet whose work reflects her advocacy of feminism and concern for human rights.

After attending Sarah Lawrence College, Kizer did graduate work at Columbia University and the University of Washington. In 1959 she cofounded *Poetry Northwest*, which she edited until 1965. After serving in Pakistan as literary specialist for the State Department (1964–65, 1966–70), she became the first director of literary programs for the National Endowment for the Arts, and later taught at several universities.

Her collections include *Poems* (1959), *The Ungrateful Garden* (1961), *Knock upon Silence* (1965), *Midnight Was My Cry* (1971), *Mermaids in the Basement: Poems for Women* (1984), *Yin* (1984, Pulitzer Prize), *The Nearness of*

You (1986), and *Harping On* (1996). "Pro Femina" is a well-known satiric poem about women writers. She has also published essay collections, translations, and anthologies.

Kleinzahler \\'klīn-ˌzä-lər\\, **August** (b. 1949, Jersey City, N.J.) Poet.

Kleinzahler attended the University of Wisconsin and graduated from the University of Victoria in British Columbia. He worked at various jobs before moving to San Francisco in 1981. He has since given poetry workshops at colleges and universities and to the homeless. His poems tend to reflect an urban landscape. His poetry collections include *A Calendar of Airs* (1978), *Storm over Hackensack* (1985), *Earthquake Weather* (1989), *Like Cities, Like Storms* (1992), *Red Sauce, Whiskey, and Snow* (1995), *Green Sees Things in Waves* (1998), and *Live from the Hong Kong Nile Club* (1999).

Knight, Etheridge (b. April 19, 1931, Corinth, Miss.—d. March 10, 1991, Indianapolis, Ind.) Poet who emerged as a robust voice of the black aesthetic movement with his *Poems from Prison*.

Born into poverty, Knight dropped out of school in the eighth grade and later served 10 years in the army. Arrested for robbery in 1960, he was imprisoned for eight years. The poet Gwendolyn Brooks visited the prison and encouraged his writing, and he would recount his prison experience in verse in *Poems from Prison* (1968) and in both poetry and prose in the anthology *Black Voices from Prison* (1970). On his release in 1968 he married the poet SONIA SANCHEZ, and he thereafter taught at various universities. His poetry combined the energy and bravado of African-American "toasts" (long narrative poems recited in a mixture of street slang, specialized argot, and obscenities) with a sensitive concern for freedom from oppression. He experimented with rhythmic forms of punctuation in *Belly Song* (1973), which addressed the themes of ancestry, racism, and love. In *Born of a Woman* (1980) he introduced the concept of the poet as a "meddler" who forms a trinity with the poem and the reader. Much of his verse was collected in *The Essential Etheridge Knight* (1986).

Knight, Sarah Kemble *originally* Sarah Kemble *known as* **Madame Knight** (b. April 19, 1666, Boston—d. Sept. 25, 1727, New London, Conn.) Colonial teacher, businesswoman, and diarist.

Her vivid and often humorous diary of an unchaperoned journey on horseback from Boston to New York in 1704, published more than a century later as *The Journal of Mme Knight* (1825), is considered one of the most authentic chronicles of 18th-century colonial life in America. One of very few works of its era to be published that was not written by a clergyman, it was a precursor of a type of literature based on regional caricature.

Knowles \\'nōlz\\, John (b. Sept. 16, 1926, Fairmont, W.Va.—d. Nov. 29, 2001, Ft. Lauderdale, Fla.) Author best known for his first published novel, A SEPARATE PEACE.

Knowles attended Phillips Exeter Academy and Yale University, and contributed articles to various publications in the early 1950s before becoming a full-time novelist. *A Separate Peace* (1959; film, 1972) chronicles the competitive friendship of two students at a New England preparatory school during World War II. Acclaimed when it appeared, it has enjoyed an extraordinarily durable life on high-school reading lists. Its sequel, *Peace Breaks Out* (1981), tells of a troubled young teacher recently returned from World War II. Knowles's other novels, most of them psychological examinations of characters caught in conflict between the wild and the pragmatic sides of their personalities, include *Morning in Antibes* (1962), *Indian Summer* (1966), *The Paragon* (1971), *Spreading Fires* (1974), *A Vein of Riches* (1978), *A Stolen Past* (1983), and *The Private Life of Axie Reed* (1986). *Phineas* (1968) is a collection of six short stories.

Koch \\'kōk\\, Kenneth (b. Feb. 27, 1925, Cincinnati, Ohio—d. July 6, 2002, New York City) Teacher, playwright, and poet noted especially for his witty, often surreal, and sometimes epic poetry.

Koch attended Harvard University and received his doctorate from Columbia, where he would subsequently teach for decades. With the publication of *Poems* (1953), he became one of the leading poets of the so-called New York school, a loose-knit group that included Frank O'Hara, John Ashbery, and James Schuyler.

Koch's work is noted for its whimsical humor and unusual juxtapositions. He wrote two Byronic epics in ottava rima: *Ko; or, A Season on Earth* (1959) and *The Duplications* (1977), as well as the long prose poem *The Burning Mystery of Anna in 1951* (1979). Many of his shorter verses were collected in *Selected Poems* (1991). For two 1994 collections, *On the Great Atlantic Rainway* and *One Train*, he received the Bollingen Prize. Two dozen short plays and 10 screenplays were collected in *A Change of Hearts* (1973); a later collection of plays, *The Gold Standard,* appeared in 1996. He is best known for teaching poetry writing and appreciation to children and the elderly, as described in the widely used *Wishes, Lies, and Dreams* (1970), *Rose, Where Did You Get That Red?* (1973), and *I Never Told Anybody* (1977). He also wrote the novel *The Red Robins* (1975) and the short stories of *Hotel Lambosa* (1993).

Komunyakaa \\ˌkō-mən-'yä-kə, ˌkä-\\, Yusef *originally* **James Willie Brown, Jr.** (b. April 29, 1947, Bogalusa, La.) Poet.

Komunyakaa attended the University of Colorado and Colorado State University (M.A., 1978) and taught in New Orleans public schools before joining the faculty of Afro-American studies at Indiana University in 1987. Since 1997 he has taught creative writing at Princeton University. His collections of poetry include *Lost in the Bonewheel Factory* (1979), *Dien Cai Dau* (1988), and *Magic*

City (1992). *Neon Vernacular* (1993) received the Pulitzer Prize. His later collections include *Ploughshares Spring* (1997), *Thieves of Paradise* (1998), and *Talking Dirty to the Gods* (2000). His prose is collected in *Blue Notes* (2000).

Koontz \\'künts\\, **Dean R(ay)** (b. July 9, 1945, Everett, Pa.) Novelist.

After college Koontz taught high-school English in Pennsylvania before moving to California in 1969 to write full-time. He has written over 60 science-fiction and horror novels, many of them best-sellers, including *Star Quest* (1968), *Hell's Gate* (1970), *The Crimson Witch* (1971), *Warlock* (1972), *The Key to Midnight* (1976), *Whispers* (1980), *Phantoms* (1983), *Strangers* (1986), *Watchers* (1987; films, 1994, 1998), *Hideaway* (1992), *Intensity* (1995), *Fear Nothing* (1998), *False Memory* (1999), and *From the Corner of His Eye* (2000). He has also written crime, suspense, and gothic novels under such pseudonyms as David Axton, Brian Coffey, Deanna Dwyer, K. R. Dwyer, John Hill, Leigh Nichols, and Owen West.

Kopit \\'kō-pit\\, **Arthur (Lee)** (b. May 10, 1937, New York City) Playwright.

Kopit attended Harvard University, where seven of his plays were produced while he was still a student. He has since taught at Wesleyan and Yale universities and CCNY.

Praised for his ease with language, his impressive theatricality, and his skewering of American popular culture, Kopit has written plays on a range of subjects. His best-known work is *Oh Dad, Poor Dad, Mama's Hung You in the Closet and I'm Feelin' So Sad* (1960; film, 1967); subtitled "a pseudoclassical tragifarce in a bastard French tradition," it parodies the Theater of the Absurd and the conventions of avant-garde drama. *The Day the Whores Came Out to Play Tennis and Other Plays* (1965) includes *Chamber Music* and *Sing to Me Through Open Windows*. Kopit's other plays include *Indians* (1969; film, *Buffalo Bill and the Indians,* 1976), *Wings* (1978), the parodic *The End of the World with Symposium to Follow* (1984), and *The Road to Nirvana* (1991), a racy satire of Hollywood. He has written the books for several musicals, including *Nine* (1983) and *Phantom* (1999).

Kornbluth \\'kȯrn-,blu̇th\\, **C(yril) M.** (b. 1923, New York City—d. March 21, 1958, Waverly, N.Y.) Writer whose science fiction reflects a dark, acerbic view of the future.

Kornbluth began publishing science-fiction stories as a teenager, when he and a group of young writers called the Futurians, including Isaac Asimov and Frederik Pohl (who would be his frequent coauthor), composed and edited most of the tales in such magazines as *Astonishing Stories* and *Super Science Stories*. After army service in World War II, he attended the University of Chicago. His well-plotted fiction (much of it serialized in *Galaxy Science Fiction* under almost

20 pseudonyms) was noted for its vision, social concern, and biting, pessimistic tone. Critical of stories presenting science as humanity's ultimate savior, he examined the dangers of sophisticated technologies allowed to run amok. With Judith Merril he wrote *Outpost Mars* (1952; revised as *Sin in Space*, 1961) and *Gunner Cade* (1952). Among his collaborations with Pohl were *The Space Merchants* (1953), *Search the Sky* (1954), *Gladiator-at-Law* (1955), and *Wolfbane* (1959). On his own he wrote *Takeoff* (1952), a detective novel about the first space flight, and *The Syndic* (1953), about organized crime in a future United States. His essay "The Failure of the Science Fiction Novel as Social Criticism" appeared in 1959 after his untimely death of heart failure.

Kosinski \kō-ˈsin-skē\, **Jerzy (Nikodem)** *originally* Jerzy Lewinkopf (b. June 14, 1933, Lodz, Poland—d. May 3, 1991, New York City) Polish-American writer whose novels were studies of individuals in controlling and bureaucratic societies.

Born to Jewish parents, Kosinski claimed to have been separated from them at the age of 6 at the outbreak of World War II and to have wandered through Poland and Russia, living by his wits and under continual suspicion, experiences which he said rendered him mute until 1947. He studied at the University of Lodz, receiving degrees in history and political science, and then taught sociology at the Polish Academy of Sciences (1955–57). In 1959 he immigrated to the United States and taught himself English, then published two nonfiction anticommunist works, *The Future Is Ours, Comrade* (1960) and *No Third Path* (1962), under the pen name Joseph Novak.

His celebrated novel THE PAINTED BIRD (1965) was followed by *Steps* (1968, National Book Award) and *Being There* (1970; film, 1979), and he became a well-known public figure. Later novels include *The Devil Tree* (1973), *Cockpit* (1975), *Blind Date* (1977), *Passion Play* (1979), *Pinball* (1981), and *The Hermit of 69th Street* (1988). He died a suicide. Questions about the extraordinary events of his early life had arisen during his lifetime, and later research confirmed that most of them had been fabricated.

Kostelanetz \ˌkȯs-tə-ˈlä-nets\, **Richard (Cory)** (b. May 14, 1940, New York City) Avant-garde writer, artist, critic, and editor.

Kostelanetz attended Brown and Columbia universities and King's College, London, and has since been a visiting professor or guest artist at a variety of institutions and has lectured widely.

He became associated in the 1960s with the avant-garde group of artists known as Fluxus. His output, which has included performance pieces, recordings, art, and films, has been bewildering in its size and variety. In 1971, employing a radically formalist approach, he produced the novel *In the Beginning*, which consists of the alphabet, in single- and double-letter combinations, unfolding over 30 pages. Among his other challenging writings are *Recyclings: A Literary Autobiography*

(1974, 1984), *Politics in the African-American Novel* (1991), *Published Encomia, 1967–91* (1991), *On Innovative Art(ist)s* (1992), *Wordworks* (1993), *Minimal Fictions* (1994), and *Ecce Kosti* (1996).

Krieger \\'krē-gər\\, **Murray** (b. Nov. 27, 1923, Newark, N.J.—d. Aug. 5, 2000, Laguna Beach, Calif.) Literary critic known for his studies of the special nature of the language of imaginative literature.

Krieger held the first American chaired professorship in literary criticism, at the University of Iowa, and later taught in the University of California system, where in 1967 he founded the influential School of Criticism and Theory at its Irvine campus. Believing that poetic language has a unique capacity to reveal vision and meaning beyond the scope of everyday language, he set forth his ideas in *The New Apologists for Poetry* (1956), *The Tragic Vision* (1960), and *The Classic Vision* (1971). Among the earliest literary critics to insist on the importance of literary theory, he also stated, in *The Play and Place of Criticism* (1967), that language provides order and meaning to human experience. Among his later works are *Theory of Criticism* (1976), *Poetic Presence and Illusion* (1979), *Arts on the Level* (1981), *Words About Words About Words* (1988), *A Reopening of Closure* (1989), and *Ekphrasis* (1992).

Krutch \\'krüch\\, **Joseph Wood** (b. Nov. 25, 1893, Knoxville, Tenn.—d. May 22, 1970, Tucson, Ariz.) Writer, critic, naturalist, and conservationist.

Krutch graduated from the University of Tennessee and received his doctorate from Columbia University. From 1924 to 1952 he was the influential drama critic for the *Nation*, and he taught at Columbia from 1937 to 1953. He wrote three critical biographies, *Edgar Allan Poe* (1926), *Samuel Johnson* (1944), and *Henry David Thoreau* (1948), the latter two reflecting his growing interest in commonsense philosophy and natural history. *The Modern Temper* (1929) was an early critical work. He turned his attention to the natural world after moving to Arizona, where he produced such books as *The Measure of Man* (1954), *The Voice of the Desert* (1955), *The Great Chain of Life* (1956), and his autobiography, *More Lives Than One* (1962).

Kumin \\'kyü-min\\, **Maxine** *originally* Maxine Winokur (b. June 6, 1925, Philadelphia) Poet, novelist, and children's author.

After graduating from Radcliffe College, Kumin taught English at several colleges. In the 1950s she met the poet ANNE SEXTON, who influenced her stylistic development and with whom she would collaborate on several children's books. Kumin's first book of poetry, *Halfway*, was published in 1961. *The Privilege* (1965) and *The Nightmare Factory* (1970) address issues of Jewish identity and family. Her New Hampshire farm was the inspiration for *Up Country* (1972, Pulitzer Prize). Critics have compared Kumin to Robert Frost and H. D. Thoreau for her precise, unsentimental evocations of rural New England and the rhythms of daily life. Her later works include the acclaimed *The Retrieval System* (1978), *Our Ground Time Here Will Be Brief* (1982), and *Looking for Luck* (1992).

Her many children's books also reflected her love of nature and interest in family. She has also published four novels, the story collection *Why Can't We Live Together Like Civilized Human Beings?* (1982), and a memoir, *Inside the Halo and Beyond* (2000). She served as poetry consultant to the Library of Congress 1981–82.

Kunitz \\'kyü-nits\\, **Stanley (Jasspon)** (b. July 29, 1905, Worcester, Mass.) Poet noted for his subtle craftsmanship and complexity.

Kunitz attended Harvard University and subsequently worked as an editor. He was 24 when his first poetry collection, *Intellectual Things* (1930), was published. His collection *Passport to the War* (1944), like his first book, contained meticulously crafted, intellectual verse. Most of the poems from these works were reprinted in *Selected Poems 1928–1958* (1958), which won the Pulitzer Prize.

With *The Testing-Tree* (1971), which included "The Illumination" and "King of the River," Kunitz departed from the formal structure and rational approach of his earlier verse to write shorter, looser, more emotional poetry. His later collections include *The Terrible Threshold* (1974), *The Coat Without a Seam* (1974), *The Lincoln Relics* (1978), *The Wellfleet Whale and Companion Poems* (1983), and *Next-to-Last Things* (1985). For *Passing Through* (1995) he received a National Book Award. He has also edited numerous literary anthologies, including *Twentieth Century Authors* (1942), and has translated Russian literature. He taught at Columbia University for many years. In 1987 he received the Bollingen Prize. In 2000, at the age of 95, he was named U.S. Poet Laureate.

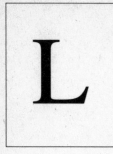

L

La Farge \lə-'färzh, lə-'färj\, **Oliver (Hazard Perry)** (b. Dec. 19, 1901, New York City—d. Aug. 2, 1963, Albuquerque, N.M.) Anthropologist, short-story writer, and novelist who acted as a spokesman for Native Americans through his political actions and his fiction.

After studies at Harvard, La Farge made archaeological and ethnological expeditions to Arizona, Guatemala, and Mexico. His first novel, *Laughing Boy* (1929; film, 1934), a poetic but realistic story of the clash of white and Navajo cultures, which rejected the popular sentimental image of the Indian in contemporary literature, was awarded the Pulitzer Prize. Later novels include *The Sparks Fly Upward* (1931) and *The Enemy Gods* (1937). *All the Young Men* (1935) is a short-story collection, and *Raw Material* (1945) is an autobiography.

L'Amour \lä-'mȯr, lä-'mu̇r\, **Louis (Dearborn)** (b. March 22, 1908, Jamestown, N.D.—d. June 10, 1988, Los Angeles) Prolific and best-selling author of more than 100 books, mostly formula westerns with authentic portrayals of frontier life.

L'Amour left school at 15 and traveled the world before beginning his writing career in the 1940s, when he began publishing stories in magazines. He stopped using pseudonyms (including Tex Burns and Jim Mayo) after *Hondo*, his first novel (1953), became a successful film. His books, which consistently reflect a "manifest destiny" attitude toward the winning of the West, have sold over 200 million copies in 20 languages. More than 30 of his books—including *Kilkenny* (1954), *The Burning Hills* (1956), *Guns of the Timberland* (1955), and *How the West Was Won* (1963)—have formed the basis of films.

Langer \'laŋ-ər\, **William L(eonard)** (b. March 16, 1896, Boston—d. Dec. 26, 1977, Boston) Historian.

After graduating from Harvard University, Langer taught school and served in World War I. He obtained his Ph.D. from Harvard in 1923 and returned there to teach from 1927 until his retirement in 1964. During World War II he was chief of research in the Office of Strategic Services, and he served as a consultant to several government departments in the postwar years.

His many books on military and diplomatic history include *The Franco-Russian Alliance* (1929), *European Alliances and Alignments* (1931), and *Diplomacy of Imperialism* (1935); he cowrote *The Challenge to Isolation* (1952) and *The Undeclared War* (1953). He was also editor of *An Encyclopedia of World History* (1940; 5th ed., 1972) and of the series of books with the general title *The Rise of Modern Europe* (from 1932). From 1921 to 1942 he was married to the philosopher Suzanne K. Langer.

Lanier \lə-'nir\, **Sidney** (b. Feb. 3, 1842, Macon, Ga.—d. Sept. 7, 1881, Lynn, N.C.) Poet and musician whose verse often suggests the rhythms and thematic development of music.

In 1867 Lanier published his first book, the novel *Tiger-Lilies*, a mixture of German philosophy, Southern traditional romance, and his own experiences as a soldier in the Civil War. He practiced law before accepting a position as first flutist in Baltimore's Peabody Orchestra in 1873.

"Corn" (1875), a poem treating agricultural conditions in the South, and "The Symphony" (1875), treating industrial conditions in the North, brought him national recognition. Adverse criticism of his "Centennial Meditation" in 1876 launched him on an intensive and inventive investigation of verse technique that he continued until his death and that produced the remarkable *Science of English Verse* (1880). The small collection *The Song of the Chattahoochee,* with its famous title poem, was published in 1877. Appointed a lecturer at Johns Hopkins University in 1879, he collected his lectures in *The English Novel* (1883) and *Shakspere and His Forerunners* (1902).

Lardner, Ring(gold Wilmer) (b. March 6, 1885, Niles, Mich.—d. Sept. 25, 1933, East Hampton, N.Y.) One of the most gifted American satirists and story-tellers.

Ring Lardner

Lardner began his writing career in 1905 as a reporter for the *South Bend* (Ind.) *Times*. He went on to work at newspapers in Chicago, where he established a reputation as a sportswriter specializing in baseball stories. From 1913 to 1919 he wrote a daily column for the *Chicago Tribune* and from 1919 to 1927 a humorous weekly column for the Bell syndicate. Meanwhile, in 1914, he had begun publishing fiction and had won popular success with his comic stories about the baseball player Jack Keefe, some of which were collected in *You Know Me, Al* (1916).

Lardner moved to New York in 1919, and he first attracted serious critical interest with his collection *How to Write Short Stories (with Samples)* (1924), in which appeared some of his best stories—"My Roomy," "Champion," "The Golden Honeymoon," and "Some Like Them Cold." Equally good was his next collection, *The Love Nest* (1926), which was similarly admired for its narrative skill, convincing vernacular language, and hilarious satire. He collaborated on two plays that had Broadway runs: *Elmer the Great* (1928; with George M. Cohan) and *June Moon* (1929; with George S. Kaufman). His spoof autobiography, *The Story of a Wonder Man*, appeared in 1927.

His son, the screenwriter Ring Lardner, Jr. (1915–2000), wrote the scripts for such films as *Woman of the Year* (1942, Academy Award) and *M*A*S*H* (1970, Academy Award); one of the Hollywood Ten, he was blacklisted during the McCarthy era.

Larsen, Nella (b. April 13, 1891, Chicago—d. March 30, 1964, New York City) Novelist and short-story writer of the Harlem Renaissance.

Larsen was born to a Danish mother and a West Indian father who died when she was 2. She worked as a nurse in New York, married a physicist, and was introduced to the Harlem Renaissance circle. Her first story was published in

1926. Her first novel, *Quicksand* (1928), concerns a young, headstrong, biracial woman who becomes mired in an emotional morass of her own creation. Her second novel, *Passing* (1929), centers on two light-skinned women, one of whom marries a black man and settles in Harlem, while the other marries a white man but cannot reject her black cultural ties. In 1930 Larsen became the first black woman awarded a Guggenheim fellowship. Though she completed at least one more novel, she never published again.

Lattimore, Richmond (Alexander) (b. May 6, 1906, Baoding prefecture, China—d. Feb. 26, 1984, Rosemont, Pa.) Poet and translator renowned for his translations of Greek classics.

While in college, Lattimore wrote poetry that touched on Greek, Anglo-Saxon, and Norse traditions. He later focused on composing lyric poetry; his *Poems from Three Decades* was published in 1972. His translations include Homer's *Iliad* (1951) and *Odyssey* (1967) and *The Four Gospels and the Revelation* (1979); with David Grene he edited *The Complete Greek Tragedies* (1959). His disciplined but poetic translations of Aeschylus, Euripides, Aristophanes, Pindar, and the *Iliad* were particularly highly praised. He also wrote books of criticism, including *Story Patterns in Greek Tragedy* (1964). He taught Greek at Bryn Mawr College from 1935 to 1971.

Laughlin \ˈläk-lin\, **James** (b. Oct. 30, 1914, Pittsburgh, Pa.—d. Nov. 12, 1997, Norfolk, Conn.) Publisher and poet, founder of New Directions press.

After graduating from Harvard, Laughlin lived in Italy with Ezra Pound, who would become a major influence on his life and work. Returning to America, he founded New Directions in 1936, relying on his inherited wealth to tide over the marginally profitable venture. Initially he intended to concentrate on ignored yet influential avant-garde writers of the period—Pound's *Cantos* and William Carlos Williams's *Paterson* were among the works he eventually issued—but he was soon also publishing novels by such authors as Henry James and F. Scott Fitzgerald. Editions of Dylan Thomas, Lawrence Ferlinghetti, Tennessee Williams, and Vladimir Nabokov proved very popular, and the press also produced a large body of translations of foreign authors, including Hermann Hesse, Pablo Neruda, Jorge Luis Borges, and Boris Pasternak. Despite its small size, the house became perhaps the most distinguished literary publisher in the United States. Laughlin himself wrote poetry noted for its warmth, imagination, and biographical frankness; his *Collected Poems* were published in 1992. His prose writings include memoirs of Pound, *Random Essays* (1989), and *Random Stories* (1990).

Lawson, John Howard (b. Sept. 25, 1894, New York City—d. Aug. 11, 1977, San Francisco) Playwright, screenwriter, and member of the "Hollywood Ten."

Lawson's early plays, such as *Roger Bloomer* (1923) and especially *Processional* (1925), are notable examples of Expressionism. His later plays became strongly ideological and proletarian: *The International* (1928) depicted a world revolution of the proletariat; *Gentlewoman* (1934) denounced American decadence; *Marching Song* (1937) concerned a sit-down strike. In 1928 he began writing screenplays, and in 1933 he became the founding president of the Screen Writers Guild. His film scripts include *Action in the North Atlantic* (1943) and *Sahara* (1943). In 1936 he published *Theory and Technique of Playwriting* (1936), which was revised as *Theory and Technique of Playwriting and Screenwriting* (1949). Having joined the Communist Party in 1934, he was jailed (1948–49) and blacklisted for refusing to testify about his political allegiances. He later explored American culture and film in *The Hidden Heritage* (1950), *Film in the Battle of Ideas* (1953), and *Film: The Creative Process* (1964).

Lazarus **ˈ**laz-ə-rəs**, Emma** (b. July 22, 1849, New York City—d. Nov. 19, 1887, New York City) Writer best known for her sonnet "The New Colossus," written to the Statue of Liberty.

Lazarus was born into a wealthy Jewish family and educated privately. Her first book, *Poems and Translations* (1866), published in her teens, caught the attention of Ralph Waldo Emerson. At 21 she published *Admetus and Other Poems* (1871). She also wrote the prose romance *Alide*, based on Goethe's autobiography, the tragedy *The Spagnoletto*, and the translations *Poems and Ballads of Heinrich Heine* (1881). Around 1881, outraged by the Russian pogroms, she began working for the relief of new immigrants. Her *Songs of a Semite* (1882) contains much of her best work. The sonnet "The New Colossus" (1883), written to express her faith in America as a refuge for the oppressed, closes with the lines:

> "Give me your tired, your poor,
> Your huddled masses, yearning to breathe free,
> The wretched refuse of your teeming shore.
> Send these, the homeless, tempest-tost to me,
> I lift my lamp beside the golden door!"

It was chosen to be inscribed on a bronze plaque inside the base of the Statue of Liberty, which was dedicated in 1886.

Leavitt **ˈ**le-vət**, David (Adam)** (b. June 23, 1961, Pittsburgh) Novelist.

Since graduating from Yale University, Leavitt has worked as a writer full-time; he lives in Italy and California. His novels include *The Lost Language of Cranes* (1986), *Equal Affections* (1989), *The Page Turner* (1998), and *Martin Bauman* (2000). His short stories have been collected in *Family Dancing* (1984) and *A Place I've Never Been* (1990); *Arkansas* (1997) is a set of novellas. Leavitt has coedited *The Penguin Book of Gay Short Fiction* (1994) and *Pages Passed from Hand to Hand* (1998), a survey of gay literature. After the publication of the historical tour de force *While England Sleeps* (1993), he was attacked for his unacknowledged borrowing from the Spanish Civil War memoirs of British poet Stephen Spender and for his candid portrayal of homoerotic love.

Lee, (Nelle) Harper (b. April 28, 1926, Monroeville, Ala.) Novelist.

After graduating from Huntington College and studying law at the University of Alabama, Lee worked as an airline reservation clerk in New York in the 1950s before devoting herself to writing. She expanded one of her short stories into the novel *To Kill a Mockingbird* (1960). The book, which dealt with racist prejudice and violence in a small Southern town as seen through the eyes of a white child, was a great popular success, won the Pulitzer Prize, and was adapted as a highly successful film. Lee has since published only a few short essays; granting few interviews, she has continued to live in her hometown with her sister, an attorney.

Ursula K. Le Guin

Le Guin \lə-'gwin\, **Ursula K(roeber)** (b. Oct. 21, 1929, Berkeley, Calif.) Writer of tales of science fiction and fantasy.

Daughter of the distinguished anthropologist Alfred Kroeber, Le Guin attended Radcliffe College and Columbia University. The methods of anthropology have influenced her science-fiction stories, which have often featured highly detailed descriptions of alien societies. Her first three novels, *Rocannon's World* (1966), *Planet of Exile* (1966), and *City of Illusions* (1967), introduced beings from the planet Hain, who established human life on habitable planets, including the earth. Her Earthsea series—*A Wizard of Earthsea* (1968), *The Tombs of Atuan* (1971), *The Farthest Shore* (1972, National Book Award), and *Tehanu* (1990)— was written for children but attracted a large adult readership.

Among Le Guin's most important novels are THE LEFT HAND OF DARKNESS (1969), *The Dispossessed* (1974), *The Word for World Is Forest* (1972), *Always Coming Home* (1985), and *The Telling* (2000). She has also written non-science fiction and a number of other children's books, including the "Catwings" series. Her essays have been collected in *The Language of the Night* (1979) and *Dancing at the Edge of the World* (1989).

Leiber \'lī-bər\, **Fritz** *in full* Fritz Reuter Leiber, Jr. (b. Dec. 24, 1910, Chicago—d. Sept. 5, 1992, San Francisco) Writer noted for his innovative sword-and-sorcery, contemporary horror, and satiric science fiction.

The son of actors, Leiber studied at the University of Chicago and worked as an actor before becoming a book and magazine editor. His first published story, "Two Sought Adventure" (1939), introduced the characters Grey Mouser and Fafhrd, whom he would feature in a series of swashbuckling adventure fantasies collected in *The Three of Swords* (1989) and *Swords' Masters* (1990). He began publishing his pioneering horror stories with modern urban settings with "Smoke Ghost" (1941) and continued in such early novels as *Gather, Darkness!* (1950) and *Conjure Wife* (1953; films, 1944, 1962). In the early 1950s, the leftist Leiber published savagely satiric works about a chaotic, crumbling America, including the short story "Coming Attraction" (1950) and the novel *The Green Millennium* (1953). The satire is less harsh in his later fiction, which includes *The Big Time* (1957, Hugo Award), *The Silver Eggheads* (1961), *The Wanderer* (1964, Hugo Award), *A Specter is Haunting Texas* (1969), and *Ship of Shadows* (1979, Hugo Award). His later short stories, which include "Gonna Roll the Bones" (1967), "Ill Met in Lankhmar" (1970), and "Belsen Express" (1975), are among his most admired works.

Leland \'lē-lənd\, **Charles Godfrey** (b. Aug. 15, 1824, Philadelphia— d. March 20, 1903, Florence, Italy) Poet and writer best known for the "Hans Breitmann Ballads."

Leland studied for two years in Germany, where he became fascinated with German culture. In 1853 he turned to journalism and worked for a number of years on P. T. Barnum's *Illustrated News*, the *Philadelphia Evening Bulletin*, and *Vanity Fair,* while publishing translations of Heinrich Heine's poetry. He also edited *Graham's Magazine*, where he published the first of his humorous German-English poems, "Hans Breitmann's Barty" (1857). Written in a mixture of German and broken English imitative of the German immigrants who had recently flooded into America, the immensely popular poems were later collected in *The Breitmann Ballads* (complete edition, 1895).

L'Engle \'leŋ-gəl\, **Madeleine** *originally* Madeleine Camp (b. Nov. 29, 1918, New York City) Author of imaginative juvenile literature concerned with the conflict of good and evil, the nature of God, and individual responsibility.

L'Engle pursued a career in the theater before publishing her first novel, *The Small Rain* (1945), about an aspiring pianist who chooses her art over her personal relationships. After writing her first children's book, *And Both Were Young* (1949), she began a series of juvenile fictional works about the Austin family—*Meet the Austins* (1960), *The Moon by Night* (1963), *The Twenty-four Days Before Christmas* (1964), *The Young Unicorns* (1968), and *A Ring of Endless Light* (1980).

In A WRINKLE IN TIME (1962), she introduced a group of young children who engage in a cosmic battle against a great evil that abhors individuality. Their story continued in *A Wind in the Door* (1973), *A Swiftly Tilting Planet* (1978), and *Many Waters* (1986). L'Engle has also continued to write fiction and poetry for adults. She discussed her own life in *A Circle of Quiet* (1972), *The Summer of the Great-Grandmother* (1974), *The Irrational Season* (1977), *Walking on Water* (1980), *Two Part Invention* (1988), *Bright Evening Star* (1997), and *The Other Dog* (2001).

Madeleine L'Engle

Leonard, Elmore *in full* Elmore John Leonard, Jr. (b. Oct. 11, 1925, New Orleans) Author of popular crime novels known for their black humor, colorful cast of characters, and uncannily realistic dialogue.

Leonard served in the navy (1943–46) before graduating from the University of Detroit. While composing scripts for advertising and educational films, he began writing western novels and short stories. The 1957 films *3:10 to Yuma* and *The Tall T* were based on his novelettes, and his Western novel *Hombre* (1961) was also adapted for film in 1967. His first crime novel, *The Big Bounce*, was published in 1969.

There followed a series of novels set primarily in Detroit and Florida, including *Fifty-two Pickup* (1974), *Swag* (1976), *Unknown Man No. 89* (1977), *The Switch* (1978), *Stick* (1983), and *LaBrava* (1983). *Glitz* (1985) brought him to major national attention. Its best-selling successors have included *Bandits* (1987), *Touch* (1987), *Freaky Deaky* (1988), *Rum Punch* (1992; film, *Jackie Brown,* 1997), *Get Shorty* (1990; film, 1995), *Maximum Bob* (1991), *Pronto* (1993), *Riding the Rap* (1995), *Out of Sight* (1996; film, 1998), *Cuba Libre* (1998), and *Be Cool* (1999), all characterized by hypervivid characterization and dialogue, deft plotting, and cynical humor.

Leopold, (Rand) Aldo (b. Jan. 11, 1886, Burlington, Iowa—d. April 21, 1948, near Baraboo, Wis.) Environmentalist and writer.

After graduating from Yale University and earning a master's degree from its new school of forestry, Leopold worked for the U.S. Forest Service, mainly in the Southwest (1909–28). At his insistence, the Forest Service set aside 500,000 acres of the Gila National Forest as the system's first officially designated wilderness area. From 1933, when he published the text *Game Management,* he taught at the University of Wisconsin. He became a director of the Audubon Society in 1935, the same year he helped found the Wilderness Society. *A Sand County Almanac* (1949), published after Leopold's death while fighting a wildfire, called for the preservation of ecosystems and for cultivation of a reverence for land that he called the "land ethic"; read by millions over the decades since its publication, it has had an important influence on the environmental movement.

Lerner, Max(well Allen) *originally* Mikhail Lerner (b. Dec. 20, 1902, Minsk, Russia—d. June 5, 1992, New York City) Editor and columnist.

Lerner came to America with his parents in 1907, graduated from Yale University, and received a Ph.D. from the Brookings Graduate School of Economics and Government. He later served as editor of the Encyclopaedia of the Social Sciences (1927–32) and of the *Nation* magazine (1936–38), and from 1949 he was a widely read columnist for the *New York Post,* where his liberal views gradually put him at odds with the paper as it became more conservative. He taught at many institutions, most notably Brandeis (1949–73). In his best-known book,

America as a Civilization (1957), he discussed the nation's "tenacious cult of property"; his other books include *It Is Later Than You Think* (1938) and *The Age of Overkill* (1962).

Le Sueur \lə-'sür\, **Meridel** (b. Feb. 22, 1900, Murray, Iowa—d. Nov. 14, 1996, Hudson, Wis.) Author who espoused feminism and social reform in her fiction, journalism, and poetry.

Le Sueur grew up on the Midwestern plains, where she was influenced by her family's socialist heritage and by the stories and poetry she heard from Indian women. She quit high school, traveled to Hollywood with her cousin Lucille Le Sueur (renamed Joan Crawford) to act in silent films, and moved to New York in the late 1920s to begin writing fiction and journalism.

The lives of women in the Great Depression was the subject of her first novel, *The Girl*; though written in 1939, it was not published until 1978. Her short stories, including those collected in *Salute to Spring* (1940), were widely admired. *North Star Country* (1945) is a history of the settling of the Midwest; *Crusaders* (1955) is a biography of her parents. In the postwar years, while under FBI surveillance for her political views, she wrote a series of highly praised children's books on American history and folklore. Her other works include the nonfiction *Conquistadores* (1973) and *The Mound Builders* (1974); the poetry collection *Rites of Ancient Ripening* (1975); *Harvest: Collected Stories* (1977); *Ripening: Selected Work, 1927–80* (1982); and the novel *The Dread Road* (1991).

Levertov \'lev-ər-ˌtȯf\, **Denise** (b. Oct. 24, 1923, Ilford, Essex, England—d. Dec. 27, 1997, Seattle, Wash.) Anglo-American poet.

Daughter of a Russian Jew who became an Anglican priest, Levertov was encouraged at age 12 by T. S. Eliot to pursue a career as a poet. As a civilian nurse during World War II, she served in London throughout the bombings. She settled in New York in 1947 with her husband. Her first volume of verse, *The Double Image* (1946), was followed by *Here and Now* (1957) and the acclaimed *With Eyes at the Back of Our Heads* (1959). Five more volumes appeared in the 1960s, including *The Jacob's Ladder* (1962), *O Taste and See* (1964), and *The Sorrow Dance* (1967). She cotranslated the Buddhist work *In Praise of Krishna: Songs from the Bengali* (1967). Opposed to the war in Vietnam, she was active in the War Resisters League and edited for it the collection *Out of the War Shadow* (1967). *Relearning the Alphabet* (1970) discloses her growing concern with social issues. In *Footprints* (1972) she reverted to the mystical tone of her earlier works. Her later efforts include essays and prose, as in *The Poet in the World* (1973), and several more poetry collections, including *Freeing the Dust* (1975), *Candles in Babylon* (1982), *Breathing the Water* (1987), *A Door in the Hive* (1989), and *Evening Train* (1992).

Levin \\'lev-in\\, **Meyer** (b. Oct. 8, 1905, Chicago—d. July 9, 1981, Jerusalem, Israel) American-Israeli author of novels and nonfiction about the Jewish people and Israel.

Levin first became known with the novel *Yehuda* (1931). *The Old Bunch* (1937), traces the lives of several young Chicago Jews from 1921 to 1934. Later notable works are *Citizens* (1940) and *Compulsion* (1956; film, 1959), the latter about the notorious Leopold-Loeb murder case.

Beginning in 1933 Levin worked for *Esquire* magazine. He was a reporter for the Loyalists in the Spanish Civil War and a war correspondent during World War II. After the war he produced a documentary film, *The Illegals* (1948), about the journey of Jewish immigrants from Poland to Israel.

Levin was partly responsible for bringing Anne Frank's diary to light, and his obsessive interest in its dramatization involved him in decades of litigation with her family. He settled in Israel in 1958. His only comic novel, *Gore and Igor*, was published in 1968. Two works on the early settlement of Israel—*The Settlers* (1972) and *The Harvest* (1978)—were not well received. *The Architect* (1981) was based on the career of Frank Lloyd Wright.

Levine \\lə-'vēn\\, **Philip** (b. Jan. 10, 1928, Detroit, Mich.) Poet of American urban working-class life.

After studies at Wayne State University and the University of Iowa, Levine worked at various industrial jobs before he began teaching at colleges and universities. In his poetry he has attempted to speak for those whose intelligence, emotions, and imagination are constrained by tedious and harsh working conditions. Despite his concern with modern life's brutalities, he has also written poems of love and joy. His numerous collections include *On the Edge* (1963), *They Feed The Lion* (1972), *Ashes* (1979), and *A Walk with Tom Jefferson* (1988). After a visit to Barcelona, he wrote *The Names of the Lost* (1976) in honor of the Loyalists who fought in the Spanish Civil War. *What Work Is* (1991) won the National Book Award, and *Simple Truth* (1994) received a Pulitzer Prize.

Lewis, Meriwether (b. Aug. 18, 1774, near Charlottesville, Va.—d. Oct. 11, 1809, near Nashville, Tenn.) Explorer.

After serving in the army, Lewis in 1801 became private secretary to Pres. Thomas Jefferson, who selected him to lead the first overland expedition to the Pacific Northwest. Lewis asked that William Clark, a former army colleague, share the command. In 1804 the Lewis and Clark Expedition set out from St. Louis to explore the new lands added to the United States after the Louisiana Purchase. The two men led a party of about 40 men up the Missouri River to winter in present-day North Dakota. The next spring they hired Toussaint Charbonneau and his Shoshone wife, Sacagawea, as guides and interpreters. The expedition traveled over the Continental Divide and canoed down several rivers to the mouth of the Columbia River on the Pacific coast. After wintering in present-day Oregon, the group returned to St. Louis to great acclaim in September 1806, having traveled over 4,000 miles.

Named governor of the Louisiana Territory, Lewis died at 35 under mysterious circumstances in an inn en route to Washington, D.C. Clark was named superintendent of Indian affairs, and also served as governor of the Missouri Territory (1813–22).

The journals kept by Lewis and others, edited by Nicholas Biddle and published in 1814, helped reinforce U.S. claims to the Oregon country. In blunt, forthright, minimal prose, they document the Indian tribes, wildlife, and geography of the vast region traversed, providing a matchless account of the discovery of a new world.

Lewis, (Harry) Sinclair (b. Feb. 7, 1885, Sauk Center, Minn.—d. Jan. 10, 1951, near Rome, Italy) Novelist and social critic who punctured American complacency with his broadly drawn, widely popular satirical novels.

Sinclair Lewis

The son of a Midwestern doctor, Lewis attended Yale University, where he edited its literary magazine, and later traveled the country and worked in New York publishing houses. His first novel, *Our Mr. Wrenn* (1914), written while he was also writing with ever-increasing success for such popular magazines as the *Saturday Evening Post* and *Cosmopolitan,* attracted favorable notice but few readers. The publication of his sixth novel, MAIN STREET, in 1920 made his reputation. It was followed by a string of successful and admired novels, many of which offended conservative sensibilities, including BABBITT (1922), ARROWSMITH (1925, Pulitzer Prize—refused), ELMER GANTRY (1927), *The Man Who Knew Coolidge* (1928), and DODSWORTH (1929). In 1930 he received the Nobel Prize for Literature, the first ever given to an American. Lewis's later books fell short of the standards of his work in the 1920s. IT CAN'T HAPPEN HERE (1935), which dramatized the possibilities of a fascist takeover of the United States, was produced as a play by the Federal Theater with 21 companies in 1936. *Cass Timberlane* (1945) shocked some readers with its sexual frankness; *Kingsblood Royal* (1947) is a novel of race relations; *World So Wide* (1951) was his 22nd and final novel. Lewis was married to the journalist Dorothy Thompson from 1928 to 1942.

Liebling \lē-bliŋ\, A(bbott) J(oseph) (b. Oct. 15, 1904, New York City—d. Dec. 28, 1963, New York City) Journalist.

After graduating from Columbia University, Liebling worked for several New York newspapers, including the *World Telegram* (1931–35). In 1935 he was hired by Harold Ross onto the staff of the *New Yorker* magazine, where he would remain the rest of his life. He wrote on a wide variety of subjects, including boxing, food, language, France, horse racing, and politicians. During World War II he covered such major initiatives as the African campaign, D-Day, and the liberation of Paris. His vivid, energetic, often humorous prose became an influential model for the magazine's other nonfiction writers. Most of his 15 books are compilations of his articles; they include *Back Where I Came From* (1938), *The Road Back to Paris* (1944), *The Wayward Pressman* (1947), *Chicago* (1952), *Normandy Revisited* (1958), and *The Earl of Louisiana* (1961). From 1959 he was married to the writer Jean Stafford.

Abraham Lincoln

Lincoln, Abraham (b. Feb. 12, 1809, near Hodgenville, Ky.—d. April 14, 1865, Washington, D.C.) 16th president of the United States (1861–65).

Born in poverty, he moved with his family to Indiana and Illinois. Largely self-taught, he became a lawyer. He served in the state legislature (1834–41), moving to Springfield, Ill., during his tenure, and in the U.S. House of Representatives (1847–49). A supporter of the new Republican Party in its antislavery stand, in 1858 he ran for U.S. Senate against the incumbent, Stephen A. Douglas; though he was unsuccessful, their eloquent debates brought Lincoln to national attention. In 1860 he won the Republican presidential nomination and was elected president. Though Lincoln had expressed a moderate view on slavery during the campaign, opposing only its extension into new states, the South seceded and the Civil War began in 1861.

The war dominated Lincoln's administration. To unite the North and influence foreign opinion, he issued the landmark Emancipation Proclamation in 1863. His extraordinary Gettysburg Address later that year further ennobled the war's purpose; it contains the most celebrated language ever spoken by an American politician. He was reelected in 1864, and in his eloquent Second Inaugural Address he called for moderation in reconstructing the South and in building a harmonious Union. Five days after the war's end, he was shot by the fanatic John Wilkes Booth. His reputation among U.S. presidents remains unsurpassed.

Lincoln's other celebrated writings include his "House Divided" speech of 1858, a prelude to the Lincoln–Douglas debates; his Cooper Union Speech of February, 1860, leading up to his nomination; his Message to Congress of December 1, 1862; and his moving "Letter to Mrs. Bixby," a woman who had lost five sons in combat. More widely known during his lifetime than his serious oratory were his pithy and often humorous aphorisms.

Lindbergh, Anne Morrow *originally* Anne Spencer Morrow (b. June 22, 1906, Englewood, N.J.—d. Feb. 7, 2001, Passumpic, Vt.) Writer and poet.

A graduate of Smith College, Morrow married Charles Lindbergh in 1929. She accompanied her husband on many of his flights around the world and became a pilot herself in 1931. In 1932 their child was kidnapped and murdered; the incessant publicity surrounding the case caused them to move to England in 1935.

Her first book, *North To the Orient*, was published that year, and it was followed by *Listen! the Wind* (1938); both books recounted their pioneering flights in 1931 and 1933. The Lindberghs returned to the United States in 1940. Her novel

The Steep Ascent appeared in 1944. Subsequent books included the best-selling collection of poetic essays *Gift from the Sea* (1955), *The Unicorn and Other Poems* (1956), the novel *Dearly Beloved* (1962), *Earth Shine* (1969), and excerpts from her diaries and letters in such acclaimed books as *Bring Me a Unicorn* (1972), *Locked Rooms and Open Doors* (1974), and *War Within and Without* (1980).

Lindsay, Howard and Russel Crouse, (respectively b. March 29, 1889, Waterford, N.Y.—d. Feb. 11, 1968, New York City; b. Feb. 20, 1893, Findlay, Ohio—d. April 3, 1966, New York City) Team of playwrights and producers who coauthored successful humorous plays.

Lindsay and Crouse first collaborated on a revision of Cole Porter's musical *Anything Goes* (1934; film, 1936), and they teamed again with Porter for *Red, Hot and Blue!* (1936). Their longest-playing drama was a 1939 production based on Clarence Day's book *Life with Father* (film, 1947), which ran for 3,213 performances and in which Lindsay played Father opposite his real-life wife, Dorothy Stickney. *Arsenic and Old Lace* (1940; film, 1944) was another huge success and joined *Life with Father* as one of the longest-running plays in Broadway history. The pair won the Pulitzer Prize for *State of the Union* (1945; film, 1948), a satire of American politics. They later wrote the books for Irving Berlin's *Call Me Madam* (1950; film, 1953) and Rodgers and Hammerstein's *The Sound of Music* (1959; film, 1965), among other musicals.

Lindsay, (Nicholas) Vachel (b. Nov. 10, 1879, Springfield, Ill.—d. Dec. 5, 1931, Springfield) Poet known for his powerfully rhythmic works written for recital.

The son of an energetically idealistic minister's daughter, Lindsay attended the Art Institute of Chicago and was soon wandering throughout the country from 1906 to 1912 reciting his poems and preaching a gospel of beauty in return for food and shelter in an attempt to revive poetry as an oral art form of the common people. He first received widespread recognition in 1913 when *Poetry* magazine published "General William Booth Enters into Heaven," about the founder of the Salvation Army. Studded with vivid imagery and bold rhymes, his poems express his wide-eyed visions of love and nature (as in "The Tree of Laughing Bells") and his idealistic passion for progressive democracy (as in "Bryan, Bryan, Bryan, Bryan" and "The Eagle That Is Forgotten"). Lindsay's dramatic recitals of his most rhythmically exciting works came to draw large audiences and brought him fame.

His best volumes of verse, many of them self-illustrated, include *Rhymes to Be Traded for Bread* (1912), *General William Booth Enters into Heaven and Other Poems* (1913), *The Congo and Other Poems* (1914), with its immensely popular title poem, and *The Chinese Nightingale and Other Poems* (1917). Depressed and unstable in his later years, he committed suicide by drinking poison.

Lippmann \\'lip-mən\\, **Walter** (b. Sept. 23, 1889, New York City—d. Dec. 14, 1974, New York City) Newspaper commentator and author.

After graduating from Harvard University, Lippmann published *A Preface to Politics* (1913), a penetrating critique of popular prejudices. In 1914 he helped found the liberal *New Republic* magazine. His writings there influenced Pres. Woodrow Wilson, who, after selecting Lippmann to help formulate his famous Fourteen Points and develop the concept of the League of Nations, sent him to the post–World War I peace negotiations for the Treaty of Versailles.

Lippmann began writing columns in 1921 for the reformist *New York World,* which he served two years (1929–31) as editor. Moving to the *New York Herald-Tribune*, he began his long-running column, "Today and Tomorrow." Eventually syndicated worldwide, the column won two Pulitzer Prizes and made Lippmann one of the most respected political columnists in the world.

Over the decades he contributed articles to over 50 magazines. His numerous books included the influential *Public Opinion* (1922), *The Phantom Public* (1925), and *A Preface to Morals* (1929), all of which endorse "liberal democracy." In *The Good Society* (1937) he criticized the collectivist tendencies of the New Deal, which he had initially supported. Later works include *The Cold War* (1947) and *Essays in the Public Philosophy* (1955). Lippmann's analyses over many years earned him a special Pulitzer Prize citation in 1958.

Locke, Alain (LeRoy) (b. Sept. 13, 1886, Philadelphia—d. June 9, 1954, New York City) Educator, writer, and philosopher, a leader and one of the chief interpreters of the HARLEM RENAISSANCE.

Graduated in philosophy from Harvard University, Locke became the first black Rhodes scholar, studying at Oxford (1907–10) and the University of Berlin (1910–11). He subsequently taught almost 40 years at Howard University, where he headed the philosophy department.

Believing that the artist was the key to improving American race relations, Locke encouraged black authors to seek subjects in black life and adopt high artistic standards. He familiarized American readers with the Harlem Renaissance by editing a special Harlem issue for *Survey Graphic,* which he expanded into the important anthology *The New Negro* (1925). He edited the *Bronze Booklet* studies of cultural achievements by blacks, and he annually reviewed black literature in *Opportunity* and *Phylon*. His many books include *Four Negro Poets* (1927), *The Negro in America* (1933), *Frederick Douglass* (1935), *Negro Art—Past and Present* (1936), *The Negro and His Music* (1936), and *The Negro in Art* (1941).

Lofting, Hugh (b. Jan. 14, 1886, Maidenhead, Berkshire, England—d. Sept. 26, 1947, Santa Monica, Calif.) Anglo-American author and illustrator of a series of children's classics about Doctor Dolittle.

Lofting moved to the United States in 1912, but the ambience of all his books is English. The character Dr. Dolittle, a chubby, gentle, eccentric physician to animals, was originally created to entertain Lofting's children in letters he sent from the front during World War I. *The Story of Dr. Dolittle*, the first of his series, appeared in 1920 and won instant success. From 1922 to 1928 he wrote one Dr. Dolittle book a year, and these seven are generally considered the best of the series—certainly the sunniest. Wearying of his hero, Lofting tried to get rid of him by sending him to the moon (*Dr. Dolittle in the Moon*, 1928), but popular demand compelled him to relent in 1933. The last book of the series was published posthumously. Lofting's other books include *The Story of Mrs. Tubbs* (1923) and its sequel, *Tommy, Tilly, and Mrs. Tubbs* (1934).

London, Jack *originally* John Griffith Chaney (b. Jan. 12, 1876, San Francisco—d. Nov. 22, 1916, Glen Ellen, Calif.) Novelist and short-story writer known for his vivid tales of the wilderness.

Jack London

Deserted by his father, a roving astrologer, London was raised in Oakland, Calif., by his spiritualist mother and stepfather. He worked as a sailor and saw much of the United States as a hobo riding freight trains and as a member of one of the many protest armies of the unemployed born of the panic of 1893. He was jailed for vagrancy and in 1894 became a militant socialist. He educated himself at public libraries, and at age 19 he crammed a four-year high-school course into one year and entered UC–Berkeley. After a year he left to seek a fortune in the Klondike gold rush of 1897.

London studied magazines and then set himself an energetic daily schedule of writing. Within two years, stories of his Alaskan adventures, though often crude, began to win acceptance for their fresh subject matter and virile force. His first book, *The Son of the Wolf* (1900), gained a wide audience. His reputation was further enhanced by the grim short story TO BUILD A FIRE (1908). For the rest of his life he produced steadily, and he completed 50 books of fiction and nonfiction, including many romantic depictions of elemental struggles for survival as well as socialist tracts, in 17 years. In 1910 he settled in California, where he built his grandiose Wolf House.

London's hastily written output is of uneven quality. His Alaskan stories—THE CALL OF THE WILD (1903), WHITE FANG (1906), and *Burning Daylight* (1910)—in which he dramatized, in turn, atavism, adaptability, and the appeal of the wilderness, are outstanding. His autobiographical novels include *The Road* (1907); *Martin Eden* (1909), perhaps his most enduring work; and *John Barleycorn* (1913). Other important works are THE SEA-WOLF (1904), with its Nietzschean superman hero, and THE IRON HEEL (1907), a fantasy of the future that is a terrifying anticipation of fascism.

Alcoholic and financially improvident, he committed suicide at the age of 40.

Henry Wadsworth
Longfellow

Longfellow, Henry Wadsworth (b. Feb. 27, 1807, Portland, Mass. [now in Maine]—d. March 24, 1882, Cambridge, Mass.) The most popular American poet of the 19th century.

After graduating from Bowdoin College in 1825, Longfellow traveled in Europe, returning in 1829 to become a professor and librarian at Bowdoin. When offered a professorship at Harvard, with another opportunity to go abroad, he accepted and spent a year in Heidelberg, where he fell under the influence of German Romanticism.

He returned to Harvard in 1836. In 1839 he published *Hyperion*, a romantic novel, and *Voices of the Night,* containing "The Psalm of Life" and "The Light of the Stars," which became immediately popular. "The Wreck of the Hesperus," included in *Ballads and Other Poems* (1841), swept the nation, as did EVANGE-LINE (1847), an idyll of the former French colony of Acadia. Many of the poems in these collections evinced the gentleness, simplicity, and idealized vision of the world that were to be his hallmarks.

After presiding over Harvard's modern-language program for 18 years, Longfellow left teaching in 1854. In 1855 he published HIAWATHA, whose public success was immediate. He translated Dante's *Divine Comedy* (1865–67), producing one of the most notable translations to that time, and wrote six sonnets on Dante that are among his finest poems.

Tales of a Wayside Inn (1863), modeled roughly on Chaucer's *Canterbury Tales*, reveals his narrative gift; the first poem, PAUL REVERE'S RIDE, became a national favorite. In 1872 he published what was intended to be his masterpiece, *Christus: A Mystery*, a trilogy dealing with Christianity from its beginnings, and he followed it with two fragmentary dramatic poems, "Judas Maccabaeus" and "Michael Angelo," neglected works that were later seen to contain some of his most effective writing. In the last decades of his life he was the best-known and best-loved poet in America.

Longstreet, Augustus Baldwin (b. July 9, 1790, Augusta, Ga.—d. July 9, 1870, Oxford, Miss.) Jurist, writer, and educator.

After graduating from Yale University in 1813, Longstreet studied law and established a law practice in Greensboro, Ga. He served briefly on the state's superior court (1822–25) before returning to Augusta in 1827.

For the Milledgeville (Ga.) *Southern Recorder,* he began writing a series of humorous sketches of Georgia life. Compiled in his very popular book *Georgia Scenes* (1835), they represent an early example of local-color writing and frontier humor.

In 1838 Longstreet became a Methodist minister, and he subsequently served as president, successively, of Emory College (1839–48), the University of Mississippi (1849–56), and the University of South Carolina (1857–65). An ardent advocate of secession and a believer in the compatibility of slavery and Christianity, he continued to write vindications of the South after the Civil War.

Lopez \\'lō-₁pez\\, **Barry (Holstun)** (b. Jan. 6, 1945, Port Chester, N.Y.)
Writer best known for his books on natural history and the environment.

Lopez's collection of Native American trickster stories, *Giving Birth to Thunder, Sleeping with His Daughter: Coyote Builds North America*, appeared in 1977. The critically acclaimed *Of Wolves and Men* (1978) combines scientific information, folklore, and essays on the wolf's role in human culture. *Arctic Dreams* (1986, National Book Award), his best-known work, employs natural history as a metaphor for wider moral issues. Lopez's other works include the linked fictional narratives *Desert Notes* (1976), *River Notes* (1979), and *Field Notes* (1994); a volume of short fiction, *Winter Count* (1981); and the essay collections *Crossing Open Ground* (1988) and *About This Life* (1998).

Lorde \\'lȯrd\\, **Audre (Geraldine)** (b. Feb. 18, 1934, New York City—d. Nov. 17, 1992, St. Croix, Virgin Islands) Poet, essayist, and autobiographer known for her passionate writings on lesbian feminism and racial issues.

Born to Grenadan immigrants, Lorde studied at Hunter College and Columbia University and later worked as a librarian. Her first volume of poetry, *The First Cities* (1968), focused on personal relationships. *Cables to Rage* (1970) contained the first poetic expression of her lesbianism. *From a Land Where Other People Live* (1973), *New York Head Shop and Museum* (1974), and *Coal* (1976) were more rhetorical and political. In *The Black Unicorn* (1978), often called her finest poetic work, she turned from the urban themes of her early work, looking instead to Africa, and wrote on her role as mother and daughter, using rich imagery and mythology.

The poet's 14-year battle with cancer is examined in *The Cancer Journals* (1980), which includes a feminist critique of the medical profession. *A Burst of Light* (1988), its sequel, won a National Book Award. She also wrote the novel *Zami* (1982), and the essay collection *Sister Outsider* (1984). Her last poetry collection, *Undersong*, was published in 1992.

Lovecraft, H(oward) P(hillips) (b. Aug. 20, 1890, Providence, R.I.—d. March 15, 1937, Providence) Author of fantastic and macabre short novels and stories.

A precocious but sickly child, Lovecraft declined to enter college and became an autodidact, reading deeply in languages and science. While maintaining a voluminous correspondence and writing newspaper columns, he published some 50 stories in his lifetime, most in the magazine *Weird Tales,* but remained obscure. After his death at 46 from lymphoma, his friends began to publish collections of his works, and he gradually gained renown as a master of horror. His Cthulhu Mythos series of tales describe ordinary New Englanders' encounters with horrific beings of extraterrestrial origin. His other stories deal with similar phenomena in which horror and morbid fantasy acquire an unexpected verisimilitude. *The Case of Charles Dexter Ward* (1928), *At the Mountains of Madness*

(1931), and *The Shadow Over Innsmouth* (1936) are considered his best short novels. Lovecraft's poetic language set an unusually high literary standard for the genre. Some 30 films have been made from his works.

Lowell, Amy (b. Feb. 9, 1874, Brookline, Mass.—d. May 12, 1925, Brookline) Critic, lecturer, and a leading Imagist poet.

Born into a distinguished Brahmin family, Lowell began to devote herself seriously to poetry at 28 but published nothing until 1910. Her first volume, *A Dome of Many-Coloured Glass* (1912), was succeeded by *Sword Blades and Poppy Seed* (1914), which included her first poems in free verse and what she called "polyphonic prose." That year she became, with Ezra Pound, the leading exponent of Imagism, a successor to French Symbolism. The early collections were followed by *Men, Women, and Ghosts* (1916), *Pictures of the Floating World* (1919), *Can Grande's Castle* (1918), *What's O'Clock* (1925), and the posthumously published *East Wind* (1926) and *Ballads for Sale* (1927), among other volumes. *A Critical Fable* (1922), an imitation of her kinsman J. R. Lowell's *A Fable for Critics*, was published anonymously and stirred widespread speculation until she revealed her authorship. Her critical works include *Six French Poets* (1915), *Tendencies in Modern American Poetry* (1917), and *John Keats* (2 vols., 1925).

Lowell's vivid and powerful personality and her independence and zest made her conspicuous, as did her scorn of convention. Though a bold experimenter in form and technique, she remained conservative at the core, retaining conventional verse forms and in her last years severing connections with all radical schools of poetry.

James Russell Lowell

Lowell, James Russell (b. Feb. 22, 1819, Cambridge, Mass.—d. Aug. 12, 1891, Cambridge) Poet, critic, essayist, editor, and diplomat whose major significance probably lies in the interest in literature he helped develop in America.

Lowell graduated from Harvard and in 1840 took his degree in law, which he never practiced. In 1844 he married the poet Maria White, who had inspired his poems in *A Year's Life* (1841). Another early work, *Conversations on Some of the Old Poets* (1845), contained critical essays that included pleas for the abolition of slavery. From 1845 to 1850 he wrote some 50 antislavery articles for periodicals and began serial publication of his BIGLOW PAPERS on the same subject. The year 1848 saw the publication of Lowell's two other most important works: THE VISION OF SIR LAUNFAL, an enormously popular long poem extolling the brotherhood of man; and *A Fable for Critics*, a witty verse evaluation of contemporary American authors.

The death of three of his children was followed by the death of his wife in 1853. Henceforth his literary production would comprise mainly prose essays on topics in literature, history, and politics. In 1855 he was appointed Smith professor of modern languages at Harvard, succeeding H. W. Longfellow. In 1857 he helped found the *Atlantic Monthly*; during its four years under his editorship, it became the focus of the New England literary renaissance.

With Charles Eliot Norton, he edited the *North American Review* from 1864 to 1872. A series of his critical essays on literary figures were collected with other essays in *Among My Books* (1870, 1876). After serving as minister to Spain (1877–80) and ambassador to Britain (1880–85), he retired from public life.

Lowell, Robert *in full* Robert Traill Spence Lowell, Jr. (b. March 1, 1917, Boston—d. Sept. 12, 1977, New York City) Poet noted for his complex, confessional poetry.

Born into an illustrious Brahmin family, Lowell attended Harvard but graduated from Kenyon College in 1940, the year he married the novelist Jean Stafford. His first major work, *Lord Weary's Castle* (1946), won the Pulitzer Prize; it contains two of his most praised poems: THE QUAKER GRAVEYARD IN NANTUCKET and "Colloquy in Black Rock," celebrating the feast of Corpus Christi.

After being divorced in 1948, he married the writer Elizabeth Hardwick the next year (divorced 1972). After a few years abroad, they settled in Boston in 1954. His LIFE STUDIES (1959, National Book Award) contains an autobiographical essay, "91 Revere Street," and a series of 15 confessional poems, including "Waking in Blue," which tells of his confinement in a mental hospital, and SKUNK HOUR, which dramatically conveys his mental turmoil.

Lowell's activities in the civil-rights and antiwar campaigns of the 1960s lent a more public note to his next three books of poetry: FOR THE UNION DEAD (1964), *Near the Ocean* (1967), and *Notebook 1967–68* (1969). His trilogy of plays, *The Old Glory*, which views American culture over the span of history, appeared in 1965. His later poetry volumes include *The Dolphin* (1973, Pulitzer Prize) and *Day by Day* (1977). His translations include *Phaedra* (1963) and *Prometheus Bound* (1969); *Imitations* (1961), free renderings of various European poets; and *The Voyage and Other Versions of Poems by Baudelaire* (1968).

Luce \\'lüs\\, **Clare Boothe** *originally* Ann Clare Boothe (b. March 10, 1903, New York City—d. Oct. 9, 1987, Washington, D.C.) Playwright, politician, and celebrity, noted for her satiric wit.

She held editorial positions at *Vogue* and *Vanity Fair* in the early 1930s, and some of her satiric articles for *Vanity Fair* were collected in *Stuffed Shirts* (1931). In 1935 she married the magazine publisher Henry R. Luce. After an earlier play failed, she wrote *The Women* (1936), a comedy that ran for 657 performances on Broadway; *Kiss the Boys Goodbye* (1938), a satire on American life; and *Margin for Error* (1939), an anti-Nazi play. All three were adapted into films. After succeeding her stepfather in the U.S. House of Representatives (1943–47) as a Republican from Connecticut, she remained influential in the Republican Party nationally, served as ambassador to Italy (1953–56), and in 1983 received the Presidential Medal of Freedom.

Ludlum, Robert (b. May 25, 1927, New York City—d. March 12, 2001, Naples, Fla.) Popular suspense novelist.

After graduating from Wesleyan University, Ludlum became an actor on Broadway and in television (1952–60). He began producing his own plays in New York and New Jersey before turning to writing full-time in 1969.

His first book, *The Scarlatti Inheritance* (1971), was followed by numerous other mysteries and suspense novels, some written under the pen names Jonathan Ryder and Michael Shepherd. His later books, most of them major best-sellers, include *The Matlock Paper* (1973), *The Gemini Contenders* (1976), *The Bourne Identity* (1980; film, 1988), *The Holcroft Covenant* (1985; film, 1985), *The Matarese Circle* (1979), *The Bourne Supremacy* (1986), *The Parsifal Mosaic* (1982), *The Aquitaine Progression* (1984), *The Road to Omaha* (1992), *The Apocalypse Watch* (1995), and *The Prometheus Deception* (2000).

Luhan \\'lü-ˌhän\\, **Mabel Dodge** *originally* Mabel Ganson (b. Feb. 26, 1879, Buffalo, N.Y.—d. Aug. 13, 1962, Taos, N.M.) Salon hostess whose autobiographical volumes contain candid depictions of well-known Americans of her era.

Born into a wealthy family, she lived near Florence, Italy, from 1903 to 1912, where her remarkable salon drew such figures as Eleonora Duse and Isadora Duncan. Back in New York, she made her home a meeting place for such intellectuals and radicals as Amy Lowell, John Reed, and Walter Lippmann, and helped organize the epochal Armory Show of new art in 1913. In 1918 she moved to Taos to become the center of an artist's colony; there, in 1923, she married her fourth husband, Tony Luhan, a Pueblo Indian. Luhan's multivolume autobiography, *Intimate Memories*—consisting of *Background* (1933), *European Experiences* (1935), *Movers and Shakers* (1936), and *Edge of Taos Desert* (1937)—is largely devoted to recording her relationships with her illustrious friends with little regard for propriety or privacy. *Lorenzo in Taos* (1932) is a sometimes painfully intimate account of her friendship with D. H. Lawrence and his wife.

Lumpkin, Grace (b. 1892?, Milledgeville, Ga.—d. March 23, 1980, Columbia, S.C.) Writer and political activist.

Lumpkin grew up in South Carolina, and taught school after finishing college. She later worked for the YWCA before moving in 1925 to New York City, where she worked for a religious newspaper. Distressed by the poverty and social injustices she reported on, she joined the Communist Party. Her first novel, *To Make My Bread* (1932), concerns an Appalachian farmer's struggle to find work in Southern textile mills. Considered an example of proletarian literature, it won approval from the Communist Party, which began supporting her writing efforts. Her next novel was *A Sign for Cain* (1935). In the late 1930s she became disillusioned with communism and left the party; moving to the radical right, she joined the religious Moral Re-Armament movement. Her novel *The Wedding* appeared in 1939. In the 1950s she testified at U.S. Senate hearings against the Communist Party. Her last book, *Full Circle*, appeared in 1962.

Lurie \'lu̇r-ē\, **Alison** (b. Sept. 3, 1926, Chicago) Writer whose urbane and witty novels usually feature upper-middle-class academics in a university setting.

Lurie graduated from Radcliffe College in 1947 and later taught English and then children's literature for decades at Cornell University. Her widely read novel *The War Between the Tates* (1974) concerns the way the wife of a professor at Corinth University deals with her husband's infidelity. *Foreign Affairs* (1984, Pulitzer Prize) describes the separate, unexpected affairs of two Corinth academics during a sabbatical in England. Lurie's other works, almost all set in academia, include *Love and Friendship* (1962), *The Nowhere City* (1965), *Imaginary Friends* (1967), *Real People* (1969), *Only Children* (1979), *The Truth About Lorin Jones* (1988), and *The Last Resort* (1998). She has written books for children, including *The Heavenly Zoo* (1979) and *Fabulous Beasts* (1981), as well as works about children's literature. Her short stories were collected in *Women and Ghosts* (1994). *The Language of Clothes* (1981) discusses the psychology of fashion.

M

MacArthur, Charles (Gordon) (b. Nov. 5, 1895, Scranton, Pa.—d. April 21, 1956, New York City) Journalist, dramatist, and screenwriter remembered for his comedies written with Ben Hecht.

At 17 MacArthur moved to Chicago to begin a career in journalism. After working at the *Chicago Tribune* and the *Chicago Herald-Examiner*, he moved to New York to work for the *New York American* and began writing plays.

MacArthur and Hecht began their long partnership with *The Front Page* (1928; film, 1931), a highly successful stage comedy about a star reporter who is drawn into his own story. They again achieved success with *Twentieth Century* (1932; film, 1934), a lively satire of the entertainment industry. Later stage collaborations included *Jumbo* (1934), *Ladies and Gentlemen* (1939), and *Swan Song* (1946). The pair also wrote many successful screenplays in the 1930s, among them *Crime Without Passion* (1934) *The Scoundrel* (1935, Academy Award), *Soak the Rich* (1936), and *Wuthering Heights* (1939), and codirected several of the films made from them. MacArthur's solo screenplays included *The Sin of Madelon Claudet* (1931), with an acclaimed performance by his second wife, Helen Hayes; *Rasputin and the Empress* (1932); and *The Senator Was Indiscreet* (1947).

Macdonald, Cynthia (b. Feb. 2, 1928, New York City) Poet known for the sardonic tone and grotesque imagery with which she has commented on the mundane.

After teaching English at Sarah Lawrence College (1970–75) and Johns Hopkins University (1975–78), Macdonald founded the creative writing program at the University of Houston in 1979. *Amputations* (1972), her first volume of poetry, attracted attention with its startling imagery; almost all its poems concern freakish people who have undergone amputation either physical or symbolic. *Transplants* (1976) continues the theme of separateness and alienation, placing its subjects in threatening environments. *(W)holes* (1980) similarly focuses on grotesques and incongruous surroundings. MacDonald's later works include *Alternate Means of Transport* (1985), *Living Wills* (1991), and *I Can't Remember* (1997). She wrote the libretto for Thomas Benjamin's opera *The Rehearsal* (1978).

Macdonald, Dwight (b. Mar. 24, 1906, New York City—d. Dec. 19, 1982, New York City) Literary and social critic.

After graduating from Yale University, Macdonald became a staff writer for *Fortune* magazine (1929–36). During World War II he founded the antiwar magazine *Politics*, which featured the works of such writers as André Gide, Albert Camus, and Marianne Moore. Politically active, he sequentially supported such ideologies as Stalinism, Trotskyism, and anarchism. Later, as a pacifist, he strongly opposed the Vietnam War. One of the first serious film critics, he was a staff writer for the *New Yorker* from 1951 to 1971, also writing film reviews for *Esquire* magazine (1960–66). He wrote numerous essays on political and social issues, and his books include *Henry Wallace* (1948), *The Root Is Man* (1953),

The Memoirs of a Revolutionist (1957), the well-known *Against the American Grain* (1962), and *Politics Past* (1970).

MacDonald, John D(ann) (b. July 24, 1916, Sharon, Pa.—d. Dec. 28, 1986, Milwaukee, Wis.) Author of mysteries and science fiction, best remembered for his 21 crime novels featuring Travis McGee.

Having graduated from Syracuse University and received an M.B.A. from Harvard, MacDonald began contributing science-fiction and suspense stories to pulp magazines in the mid-1940s. His first full-length novel was *The Brass Cupcake* (1950). In his 44th novel, *The Deep Blue Good-By* (1964), he introduced the private investigator Travis McGee, a tough, eccentric "salvage consultant" who lives on a houseboat in Fort Lauderdale. Transcending the usual formula of sex and violence, MacDonald investigated contemporary social and moral concerns through McGee and his erudite sidekick Meyer. Books in the series (whose titles all include color names) include *One Fearful Yellow Eye* (1966), *A Tan and Sandy Silence* (1971), and *Cinnamon Skin* (1982). Among his science-fiction novels are *Wine of the Dreamers* (1951), *Ballroom of the Skies* (1952), and *The Girl, the Gold Watch, and Everything* (1962). Notable among his other books are *The Neon Jungle* (1953), *Condominium* (1977), and *One More Sunday* (1984).

Macdonald, Ross *originally* Kenneth Millar (b. Dec. 13, 1915, Los Gatos, Calif.—d. July 11, 1983, Santa Barbara, Calif.) Mystery writer credited with elevating the detective novel to the level of literature with his compactly written tales of murder and despair.

Millar's family moved to Canada in 1919, and he only returned to the United States in 1941 to attend the University of Michigan, where he would obtain his Ph.D. in 1952. By then he had written several novels, including *The Dark Tunnel* (1944), *Trouble Follows Me* (1946), and *The Three Roads* (1948), under his real name. As John Macdonald he wrote *The Moving Target* (1949; reissued as *Harper,* 1966; film, 1966), in which he introduced the shrewd private investigator Lew Archer. He assumed the pen name John Ross Macdonald for such Lew Archer mysteries as *The Way Some People Die* (1951), *The Ivory Grin* (1952), *Find a Victim* (1954), and *The Name Is Archer* (1955). To avoid confusion with John D. MacDonald, he adopted the name Ross Macdonald for *The Barbarous Coast* (1956), *The Doomsters* (1958), and *The Galton Case* (1959). Such later novels as *The Underground Man* (1971) and *Sleeping Beauty* (1973) reflected his abiding interest in conservation. Among crime novelists he came to enjoy a reputation as a literary figure that rivaled or surpassed that of Dashiell Hammett and Raymond Chandler.

MacKaye \mə-ˈkī**, Percy (Wallace)** (b. March 16, 1875, New York City—d. Aug. 31, 1956, Cornish, N.H.) Poet, playwright, and writer of pageants.

MacKaye was introduced to the theater by his father, Steele MacKaye, with whom he initially collaborated. Infected by his father's enthusiasm for bringing poetry and drama to large participant groups and uniting the stage arts, music, and poetry through masques and communal chanting, he wrote such pageants as *The Canterbury Pilgrims* (1903) and, as coauthor, *St. Louis: A Civic Masque*, which was performed in 1914 with 7,500 participants. His most noteworthy works are the historical play *The Scarecrow* (1908), the pageant-masque *Caliban* (1916), and the regional play *This Fine Pretty World* (1923); *The Mystery of Hamlet* (1945) consists of a series of four verse plays. In *The Civic Theatre* (1912) he advocated amateur community theatricals. In 1929 he became advisory editor to *Folk-Say*, a journal of American folklore.

MacKaye \mə-ˈkī\, **(James Morrison) Steele** (b. June 6, 1842, Buffalo, N.Y.—d. Feb. 25, 1894, Timpas, Colo.) Playwright, actor, theater manager, and inventor.

In 1873 MacKaye became the first American to act Hamlet in London. At Harvard, Cornell, and elsewhere, he lectured on the philosophy of aesthetics. In New York City he founded the St. James, Madison Square, and Lyceum theaters. He wrote almost 30 plays, including the popular *Hazel Kirke* (1880), *Paul Kauvar* (1887), and *Money Mad* (1889), acting in them in 17 different roles. He organized the first school of acting in the U.S., which later became the American Academy of Dramatic Art, and patented more than 100 theatrical inventions, including folding theater seats. Percy MacKaye was his son.

MacLeish \mə-ˈklēsh\, **Archibald** (b. May 7, 1892, Glencoe, Ill.—d. April 20, 1982, Boston) Poet, playwright, and public official whose concern for liberal democracy figured in much of his work.

After graduating from Yale and obtaining a law degree from Harvard, MacLeish moved to France in 1923 to perfect his poetic craft. The verse he published during his expatriate years—*The Happy Marriage* (1924), *The Pot of Earth* (1925), *Streets in the Moon* (1926), and *The Hamlet of A. MacLeish* (1928)—shows the fashionable influence of Ezra Pound and T. S. Eliot and includes the frequently anthologized "Ars Poetica" (1926). He returned to become editor of *Fortune* magazine (1928–38). *New Found Land* (1930) reveals his simple lyric eloquence and includes the well-known "You, Andrew Marvell."

Archibald MacLeish

In the 1930s his concern about the menace of fascism began to manifest itself in his works. *Conquistador* (1932, Pulitzer Prize), an epic about the conquest and exploitation of Mexico, was the first of his "public" poems. Others were collected in *Frescoes for Mr. Rockefeller's City* (1933), *Public Speech* (1936), and *America Was Promises* (1939). His radio verse plays include *The Fall of the City* (1937), *Air Raid* (1938), and *The Great American Fourth of July Parade* (1975). MacLeish served as Librarian of Congress (1939–44) and assistant secretary of state (1944–45), and was Boylston Professor at Harvard from

1949 to 1962. His *Collected Poems: 1917–1952* (1952) won the Pulitzer Prize, as did *J.B.* (1958), a verse drama based on the story of Job that had a successful Broadway run.

Madhubuti \ˌmäd-hü-ˈbü-tē\, **Haki R.** *originally* Don Luther Lee (b. Feb. 23, 1942, Little Rock, Ark.) Author, publisher, and teacher.

Lee attended graduate school at the University of Iowa and joined the faculty of Chicago State University in 1984. His poetry has been characterized by anger at social and economic injustice and celebration of African-American culture; written in black slang and dialect, it has been seen as influential on the developing language of rap music. The collection *Don't Cry, Scream* (1969) was introduced by Gwendolyn Brooks. Collections published under the Swahili name Haki R. Madhubuti have included *Book of Life* (1973) and *Killing Memory, Seeking Ancestors* (1987). His numerous prose books on topical issues and self-empowerment include *Black Men: Obsolete, Single, Dangerous?* (1990) and *Tough Notes* (2002). Lee founded the Third World Press in 1967, and in 1969 he established the Institute of Positive Education, a school for black children.

Madison, James (b. March 16, 1751, Port Conway, Va.—d. June 28, 1836, Montpelier, Va.) Fourth president of the United States (1809–17).

After graduating from the College of New Jersey, Madison returned to Virginia to begin his political career. He was elected to the state constitutional convention in 1776 and gained prominence as an advocate for religious freedom. At the 1787 Constitutional Convention he influenced the planning and ratification of the U.S. Constitution; his active participation and his careful notes on the debates earned him the title "father of the Constitution." He collaborated with Alexander Hamilton and John Jay on the influential essays in the *Federalist* in support of the document, 29 of which appeared over his pseudonym, "Publius."

James Madison

As a member of the new House of Representatives (1789–97), he sponsored the Bill of Rights and became a leader of the Jeffersonian Republicans. As U.S. secretary of state (1801–9) under Thomas Jefferson, he helped develop U.S. foreign policy that led to the Louisiana Purchase. Elected president in 1808, he was occupied by the trade and shipping embargo problems caused by France and Britain that led to the War of 1812. His second term as president was marked principally by the war, during which he reinvigorated the army, and by his approval of the nation's first protective tariff. In 1817 he retired to his Virginia estate with his wife, Dolley, whose political acumen he had long prized. He continued to write articles and letters, and he served 10 years as rector of the University of Virginia. His writings were edited in nine volumes in 1900–10.

Mailer, Norman (b. Jan. 31, 1923, Long Branch, N.J.) Novelist and journalist, one of the major figures in American letters of the later 20th century.

Norman Mailer

Mailer studied aeronautical engineering at Harvard University and was drafted into the wartime army. After the war he enrolled at the Sorbonne, where he wrote the novel THE NAKED AND THE DEAD (1948; film, 1958), which many critics embraced as the finest American novel of World War II. His second and third novels, *Barbary Shore* (1951) and *The Deer Park* (1955), were greeted with critical hostility and mixed reviews, respectively. His next important work, the long essay *The White Negro* (1957), was a sympathetic study of a marginal social type, the "hipster." In 1959 he made a bid for attention with *Advertisements for Myself*, a miscellany whose naked self-revelation won the admiration of a younger generation. *An American Dream* (1965; film, 1966) is about a man who murders his wife; the admired novel *Why Are We in Vietnam?* (1967) is about a young man on an Alaska hunting trip.

A controversial figure whose egotism and bluff belligerence often antagonized critics and readers, Mailer won increasingly respectful attention as he shifted from fiction to journalism. *The Armies of the Night* (1968, Pulitzer Prize, National Book Award) is a personally engaged account of the Washington peace demonstrations of October 1967, in which he was jailed and fined. *Miami and the Siege of Chicago* (1969), an account of the two presidential conventions from a similarly engaged perspective, was also admired. He reported on the first manned space flight to the moon in *Of a Fire on the Moon* (1970). *The Prisoner of Sex* (1971) dealt controversially with the women's movement.

The Executioner's Song (1979), a "nonfiction novel" about the life of the murderer Gary Gilmore, won great critical admiration and a second Pulitzer Prize. *Ancient Evenings* (1983), a novel of ancient Egypt, baffled many readers. It was followed by the mystery thriller *Tough Guys Don't Dance* (1984) and the 1,200-page *Harlot's Ghost* (1991), about the CIA.

From 1952 to 1963 Mailer was an editor of the leftist journal *Dissent*, and in 1955 he cofounded the *Village Voice*.

Bernard Malamud

Malamud \\'mal-ə-ˌməd\\, **Bernard** (b. April 26, 1914, Brooklyn, N.Y.— d. March 18, 1986, New York City) Novelist and short-story writer who made parables out of Jewish immigrant life.

A son of Russian Jews, Malamud was educated at CCNY and Columbia University. His first novel, THE NATURAL (1952), is a fable about a baseball hero gifted with miraculous powers. THE ASSISTANT (1957) concerns a young Gentile hoodlum and an old Jewish grocer. THE FIXER (1966), set in czarist Russia, won a Pulitzer Prize and a National Book Award. His other novels are *A New Life* (1961), *The Tenants* (1971), *Dubin's Lives* (1979), and *God's Grace* (1982).

Malamud's genius is most apparent in his short stories, collected in THE MAGIC BARREL (1958, National Book Award), *Idiots First* (1963), *Pictures of Fidelman* (1969), and *Rembrandt's Hat* (1973), in which grim city neighborhoods are visited by magical events and their hardworking residents have glimpses of love and self-sacrifice. Though told in spare, compressed prose, they include bursts of emotional, metaphorical language.

Malcolm X *originally* Malcolm Little *later* El-Hajj Malik El-Shabazz (b. May 19, 1925, Omaha, Neb.—d. Feb. 21, 1965, New York City) Black militant leader.

Growing up in Lansing, Mich., Malcolm Little saw his house burned down by the Ku Klux Klan; his father was later murdered, and his mother placed in a mental institution. He moved to Boston to live with his sister and drifted into petty crime. In 1946, while in prison for burglary, he was converted to the Black Muslim (Nation of Islam) faith, principally by his sister. Released in 1952, he met the sect's leader, Elijah Muhammad and changed his last name to "X" as a rejection of his "slave name." Sent on speaking tours around the country, he soon became the sect's most effective speaker and organizer. He derided the civil-rights movement and rejected both integration and racial equality, calling instead for black separatism, black pride, and the use of violence for self-protection.

After sharp disagreements with Elijah, he left the sect in 1964 to form his own organization. After a pilgrimage to Mecca, he converted to orthodox Islam and modified his views of black separatism. Rival Black Muslims made threats against his life, and in 1965 he was shot to death at 39 at a rally in a Harlem ballroom. The posthumously published *Autobiography of Malcolm X* (1965), written by Alex Haley from interviews, became a classic of black American autobiography.

Malone, Dumas (b. Jan. 10, 1892, Coldwater, Miss.—d. Dec. 27, 1986, Charlottesville, Va.) Editor, historian, and biographer of Thomas Jefferson.

After receiving his doctorate from Yale University, Malone taught at Yale, Columbia, and the University of Virginia, where he was Thomas Jefferson Foundation Professor of History. He edited the *Dictionary of American Biography* (1929–36) and the *Political Science Quarterly* (1953–58) and served as director of the Harvard University Press (1936–43). His masterwork is the six-volume *Jefferson and His Time* (1948–81). His other writings include *The Public Life of Thomas Cooper* (1926), *Saints in Action* (1939), and *Empire for Liberty* (2 vols., 1960; with Basil Rauch).

Mamet \\'mam-it\\, **David (Alan)** (b. Nov. 30, 1947, Chicago) Playwright, director, and screenwriter noted for his often desperate working-class characters and for his distinctive dialogue.

Mamet began writing plays while attending Goddard College. Returning to Chicago, he worked at various factory jobs, at a real estate agency, and as a taxi driver, experiences that would later provide background for his plays. In 1973 he cofounded the St. Nicholas Theater Co.

Most of Mamet's plays have focused on male characters and power relationships, and many deal with corporate and personal corruption. His rapid-fire dialogue, studded with obscenities, repeatedly edges from the intensely realistic into the surreal. The plays include *The Duck Variations* (1972), *Sexual Perversity in Chicago* (1974; film, 1986), which brought his name to wide attention, AMERICAN BUFFALO (1976, New York Drama Critics Circle Award; film, 1995), *A Life in the Theater* (1977), and *Speed-the-Plow* (1987). GLENGARRY GLEN ROSS (1983;

film, 1992) won the Pulitzer Prize. *Oleanna* (1992; film, 1995) examines sexual harassment in academia. *The Cryptogram* (1994) depicts a child's nightmarish glimpses of dark aspects of his family life. Later plays include *The Old Neighborhood* (1997) and *Boston Marriage* (1999).

Mamet has enjoyed great success writing screenplays for such films as *The Postman Always Rings Twice* (1981), *The Verdict* (1982), *Tin Men* (1987), *The Untouchables* (1987), and *Hoffa* (1992). He both wrote and directed *House of Games* (1987), *Things Change* (1988), *Homicide* (1991), and *The Spanish Prisoner* (1998), among other films. His nonfiction books and essay collections include *Writing in Restaurants* (1986), *On Directing Film* (1991), *The Cabin* (1992), and *On Acting* (1999), and he has also written children's stories and plays.

Manchester, William (b. April 1, 1922, Attleboro, Mass.) Historian, educator, and novelist.

Manchester began his journalistic career at the *Daily Oklahoman* (1945–46) and moved to the *Baltimore Sun* (1947–55), where he eventually became an associate editor. He has since been associated with Wesleyan University in various capacities, from 1990 as professor emeritus of history. His best-known book is *Death of a President* (1967), on the assassination of John F. Kennedy. His gifts as a biographer are displayed in *A Rockefeller Family Portrait* (1959), *American Caesar: Douglas MacArthur* (1978), and *The Last Lion,* a biography of Winston Churchill (2 vols., 1983–88; vol. 3 projected). His best-selling *The Glory and the Dream* (1974) traces several decades of 20th-century American history.

Edwin Markham

Markham \\'mär-kəm\\, **Edwin** *originally* Charles Edward Anson Markham (b. April 23, 1852, Oregon City, Ore.—d. March 7, 1940, New York City) Poet and lecturer best known for his poem of social protest "The Man with the Hoe."

Markham grew up unhappily on an isolated ranch in California and eventually became a public-school administrator. In 1899 he gained national fame with the publication in the *San Francisco Examiner* of "The Man with the Hoe." Inspired by Millet's famous painting, Markham made the French peasant the symbol of the exploited classes throughout the world. The great success of his first book of verse, *The Man with the Hoe and Other Poems* (1899), enabled him to devote himself to writing and lecturing. *Lincoln and Other Poems* (1901), with the poem "Lincoln, the Man of the People," also enjoyed success. Later volumes—*Shoes of Happiness* (1915), *Gates of Paradise* (1920), *New Poems* (1932), and *The Star of Araby* (1937)—have the commanding rhetoric but lack the passion of the early works.

Marquand \\'mär-ˌkwänd, 'mär-kwənd; mär-'kwänd\\, **J(ohn) P(hillips)** (b. Nov. 10, 1893, Wilmington, Del.—d. July 16, 1960, Newburyport, Mass.) Novelist who recorded the shifting patterns of middle- and upper-class American society.

Marquand grew up in comfortable circumstances until his father's business failure, when he was sent to live with relatives in Newburyport. This experience of reduced status and security made him acutely conscious of social gradations and their psychological corollaries. After graduating from Harvard, he was soon having his stories published in the *Saturday Evening Post*. Beginning in 1935 with "Mr. Moto Takes a Hand," many were chapters in serial novels that had as their hero the resourceful Japanese intelligence agent Mr. Moto. The six Mr. Moto novels would lead to a series of eight films starring Peter Lorre (1937–39).

Marquand's three most characteristic novels were satirical but sympathetic studies of a crumbling New England gentility: *The Late George Apley* (1937, Pulitzer Prize; film, 1947), *Wickford Point* (1939), and *H. M. Pulham, Esquire* (1941; film, 1942). Three later novels—*So Little Time* (1943), *Repent in Haste* (1945), and *B. F.'s Daughter* (1946)—deal with the dislocations of wartime America. He regained his former level in *Point of No Return* (1949), a painstakingly accurate social study of a New England town. *Melville Goodwin, U.S.A.* (1951) concerns a professional soldier, and *Sincerely, Willis Wayde* (1955) is a sharply satiric portrait of a big-business promoter. *Women and Thomas Harrow* (1958) is partly autobiographical.

Marqués \mär-'kās\, **René** (b. Oct. 4, 1919, Arecibo, Puerto Rico—d. March 22, 1979, San Juan, Puerto Rico) Playwright, short-story writer, critic and Puerto Rican nationalist.

After college in Puerto Rico, Marqués studied at the University of Madrid and Columbia University. His best-known play, *La carreta* (1956; "The Oxcart"), concerns a rural Puerto Rican family that immigrates to New York in search of its fortune but fails. In 1959 he published three plays in the collection *Teatro*: *La muerte no entrará en palacio* ("Death Will Not Enter the Palace"), a political allegorical play in which a governor betrays his youthful ideals; *Un niño azul para esa sombra* ("A Blue Child for That Shadow"); and the successful *Los soles truncos* ("Maimed Suns"). He also published three short-story collections—*Otro d'a nuestro* (1955; "Another of Our Days"), *En una ciudad llamada San Juan* (1960; "In a City Called San Juan"), and *Inmersos en el silencio* (1976; "Immersed in Silence")—and the novels *La v'spera del hombre* (1959; "The Eve of Man") and *La mirada* (1975; "The Glance"). A collection of his essays, *Ensayos* (1966), echoes his imaginative writing in examining the problem of national identity in Puerto Rico.

Marquis \'mar-kwis\, **Don(ald Robert Perry)** (b. July 29, 1878, Walnut, Ill.—d. Dec. 29, 1937, New York City) Newspaperman, poet, and playwright, creator of the characters Archy the cockroach and Mehitabel the cat—wry, down-and-out philosophers of the 1920s.

Marquis began his career as a reporter on the *Atlanta Journal*. When in 1907 Joel Chandler Harris established *Uncle Remus's Magazine*, Marquis became his associate editor. In 1912 he left Atlanta for New York, where, writing the column "The Sun Dial" for the *Evening Sun* and "The Lantern" for the *Herald Tribune*, he became one of the best known of literary journalists. His stories about Archy and Mehitabel, originally published in "The Sun Dial," were first collected in ARCHY AND MEHITABEL (1927).

His collections of humorous poetry, satirical prose, and plays include *Danny's Own Story* (1912), *Dreams and Dust* (1915), *Hermione* (1916), *The Old Soak* (1916; dramatized 1926), *Sonnets to a Red Haired Lady* (1922), *The Dark Hours* (1924), and *Out of the Sea* (1927). After his death, *archy and mehitabel* was combined with several sequels into *the lives and times of archy and mehitabel* (1940).

Marshall, Paule *originally* Paule Burke (b. April 9, 1929, Brooklyn, N.Y.) Novelist whose works have emphasized the need for black Americans to reclaim their African heritage.

The Barbadian background of Marshall's parents was to inform all her work. She graduated from Brooklyn College and worked at *Our World* magazine from 1953 to 1956. Her autobiographical first novel, BROWN GIRL, BROWNSTONES (1959), about the American daughter of Barbadian parents who travels to their homeland as an adult, was acclaimed for its dialogue.

Soul Clap Hands and Sing (1961), a collection of four novellas, presents four aging men who come to terms with their earlier refusal to affirm lasting values. Her short story "Reena" (1962) was one of the first pieces of fiction to feature a college-educated, politically active black woman as its protagonist; frequently anthologized, it was included in *Reena and Other Stories* (1983). *The Chosen Place, the Timeless People* (1969), set on a Caribbean island, concerns a philanthropic attempt to modernize an impoverished and oppressed society. Marshall's most eloquent statement of her belief in African-Americans' need to rediscover their heritage was PRAISESONG FOR THE WIDOW (1983), which established her reputation as a major writer. *Daughters* (1991) concerned a West Indian woman in New York who returns home to assist her father's reelection campaign and an epiphany after confronting her personal and cultural past.

Mason, Bobbie Ann (b. May 1, 1940, Mayfield, Ky.) Short-story writer and novelist known for her evocation of rural Kentucky life.

Reared on a dairy farm, Mason graduated from the University of Kentucky and moved to New York City. She attended SUNY–Binghamton and the University of Connecticut; her doctoral dissertation was published as *Nabokov's Garden: A Guide to Ada* (1974). After 1979, she began publishing stories in the *New Yorker*, the *Atlantic*, and elsewhere.

Mason received critical acclaim for *Shiloh and Other Stories* (1982), her first collection of stories, which described the lives of working-class people in a shifting rural society now dominated by chain stores, television, and superhighways. *In Country* (1985), her first novel, was also steeped in mass culture, leading one critic to speak of Mason's "shopping-mall realism." Many critics praised her realistic regional dialogue, though some compared the novel unfavorably to her shorter works. Her later works include the novels *Spence + Lila* (1988) and *Feather Crowns* (1993), the story collections *Love Life* (1989) and *Midnight Magic* (1998), and the memoir *Clear Springs* (1999).

Masters, Edgar Lee (b. Aug. 23, 1869, Garnett, Kan.—d. March 5, 1950, Philadelphia) Poet and novelist, best known as author of SPOON RIVER ANTHOLOGY.

Masters grew up on his grandfather's farm near New Salem, Ill., and moved to Chicago to practice law. His first volume of verse (1898) was followed by the blank-verse drama *Maximilian* (1902), *The New Star Chamber and Other Essays* (1904), *Blood of the Prophets* (1905), and a series of plays issued between 1907 (*Althea*) and 1911 (*The Bread of Idleness*).

In 1909 Masters was introduced to *Epigrams from the Greek Anthology* and was seized by the idea of composing a similar series of free-verse epitaphs in the form of monologues. The result was *Spoon River Anthology*, in which the former inhabitants of the community of Spoon River speak from the grave of their unfulfilled lives.

Though Masters continued to publish volumes of verse almost yearly, including *Domesday Book* (1920) and *The New Spoon River* (1924), the quality of his work never again rose to the same level. Among his novels are *Mitch Miller* (1920) and *The Nuptial Flight* (1923). His controversial revisionist biography of Abraham Lincoln (1931) was followed by biographies of Walt Whitman (1937), Mark Twain (1938), and his friend and fellow poet Vachel Lindsay, the subject of his best biography (1935). His autobiography is *Across Spoon River* (1936).

Mather \\'ma-<u>th</u>ər, -thər\\, **Cotton** (b. Feb. 12, 1663, Boston—d. Feb. 13, 1728, Boston) Puritan leader and writer.

Son of Increase Mather and grandson of John Cotton, Mather earned a master's degree at 18 from Harvard University. Ordained a Congregational minister in 1685, he joined his father as pastor of Boston's North Church, where he would remain the rest of his life.

His early writings provoked a revolt that led to the ouster of Edmund Andros, the unpopular British governor of Massachusetts, and he later influentially supported the new colonial charter of 1691. His *Memorable Providences Relating to Witchcrafts and Possessions* (1689) contributed to the hysteria that resulted in the 1692 Salem witchcraft trials, though Mather disapproved of their excesses; *Wonders of the Invisible World* (1693) was a narrative of some of the trials. Of his 450 works on a wide variety of subjects, the best-known was *Magnalia Christi Americana* (1702), which remained the most complete history of New England for many years. The moral essays in *Bonifacius, or Essays to Do Good* (1710) offered instruction in humanitarian acts, some of its ideas being far ahead of his time. As Harvard College became increasingly secular, Mather promoted

Cotton Mather

the founding of Yale as a new bastion of the faith. His learning in the natural history of the New World, evident in his *Curiosa Americana* (1712–24), won him membership in the Royal Society of London. The most famous of the Puritan divines, he was perhaps the best-known American at his death.

Mather, Increase (b. June 21, 1639, Dorchester, Massachusetts Bay Colony—d. Aug. 23, 1723, Boston) Puritan leader.

Son of the Puritan cleric Richard Mather, Mather was educated at Harvard College and Trinity College, Dublin. He returned to Boston in 1661 and became minister of North Church in 1661, where he remained until his death; he was joined there by his son Cotton in 1685. He won concessions from William III in the new colonial charter granted in 1691. From 1685 he also served as president of Harvard; controversies over the new charter and the colonial governor, both supported by Mather, led to his dismissal in 1701.

Mather wrote over 150 books, most of them on theology. *An Essay for the Recording of Illustrious Providences* (1684) is a compilation of stories showing the hand of divine providence in rescuing people from natural and supernatural disasters. His *Case of Conscience Concerning Evil Spirits Personating Men* (1693) helped end the Salem witchcraft trials.

Matthews, (James) Brander (b. Feb. 21, 1852, New Orleans—d. March 31, 1929, New York City) Essayist, drama critic, novelist, and academic.

Educated at Columbia University, Matthews subsequently taught literature there from 1892 until 1900, when he became the first professor of dramatic literature in America. A prominent figure in New York theatrical and literary groups, he founded both the Authors' Club and the Players' Club. He wrote many short stories and critical essays, spent many years as a regular critic for the *New York Times*, and wrote or edited more than 40 books, including *The Development of the Drama* (1903). *A Confident Tomorrow* (1899) is considered his best novel. His sound scholarship was revealed in such works as *French Dramatists of the 19th Century* (1881), *Molière* (1910), and *Shakspere as a Playwright* (1913).

Matthiessen \\'math-əs-ᵊn\\, **F(rancis) O(tto)** (b.Feb. 19, 1902, Pasadena, Calif.—d. April 1, 1950, Boston) Educator and critic.

Educated at Yale, Oxford (as a Rhodes scholar), and Harvard (Ph.D., 1927), Matthiessen taught English at Harvard from 1929 until his death.

His early critical works include *Translation: An Elizabethan Art* (1931) and *The Achievement of T. S. Eliot* (1935). His best-known work, the highly influential *American Renaissance* (1941), helped establish American literature as an academic subject. *Henry James* (1944) and *The James Family* (1947) led to a revival of interest in the writer. A political leftist and homosexual, Matthiessen died a suicide at 48 following severe depression. His *Theodore Dreiser* (1951) and *The Responsibilities of the Critic* (1952) were published posthumously.

Matthiessen, Peter (b. May 22, 1927, New York City) Novelist and naturalist whose work has dealt with the destructive effects of encroaching technology on preindustrial cultures and the natural environment.

Peter Matthiessen

After serving in the navy, Matthiessen attended the Sorbonne and Yale University, then returned to Paris, where he and George Plimpton founded the *Paris Review* in 1953.

A dedicated naturalist, he has written some 20 books of nonfiction, including *Wildlife in America* (1959), an important and prescient history of the destruction of North American wildlife; *The Cloud Forest* (1961), about the South American wilderness; *Under the Mountain Wall* (1962), about a scientific expedition to New Guinea; *Blue Meridian* (1971), about the great white shark; *The Tree Where Man Was Born* (1972), an illustrated book on Africa; *The Snow Leopard* (1978, National Book Award), a mystical account of tracking the rare snow leopard in remote Nepal; and *In Sand Rivers* (1981) and *African Silences* (1991), about declining African wildlife. *In the Spirit of Crazy Horse* (1983), about the 1973 conflict between federal agents and the American Indian Movement at Wounded Knee, S.D., was the subject of a prolonged libel suit that blocked all but an initial printing and was not settled until 1990. *Dragon River* (1986) tells of his Zen apprenticeship and ordination as a Zen priest.

His novels include *Race Rock* (1954); the acclaimed *At Play in the Fields of the Lord* (1965; film, 1991), a surrealistic work about missionaries and Indians in the Amazon rain forest; *Far Tortuga* (1975), about a doomed Caribbean turtle-fishing expedition; and a trilogy about a murder in the Everglades consisting of *Killing Mister Watson* (1990), *Lost Man's River* (1997), and *Bone by Bone* (1999). *On the River Styx* (1989) is a short-story collection.

Maupin \\'mȯ-pin\\, **Armistead** (b. May 13, 1944, Washington, D.C.) Novelist known for his *Tales of the City* series.

Maupin's career as a fiction writer was launched when his *Tales of the City* was published as a serial in the *San Francisco Chronicle* in 1976–77, then as a book in 1978. The story, set in San Francisco, focuses on three characters—Mary Ann Singleton, a naive young woman from Cleveland; Michael "Mouse" Tolliver, her homosexual friend; and their motherly landlady, Anna Madrigal, a transsexual. The author's compassion and lively humor made *Tales of the City* a cult favorite, and five popular sequels followed: *More Tales of the City* (1980), *Further Tales of the City* (1982), *Baby Cakes* (1984), *Significant Others* (1987), and *Sure of You* (1989). Though their tone is generally lighthearted, the characters confront serious personal and political issues including loneliness, parenthood, and AIDS. Several television miniseries have been made from the stories.

Maupin broke from the series to write *Maybe the Moon* (1992), the story of a dwarf actress. *The Night Listener* (2000) is autobiographical.

Maxwell, William *originally* William Maxwell Keepers, Jr. (b. Aug. 16, 1908, Lincoln, Ill.—d. July 31, 2000, New York City) Author known for his spare, evocative stories and novels about small-town Midwestern life.

Maxwell taught at the University of Illinois before joining the staff of the *New Yorker*, where he would remain from 1936 to 1976, earning a formidable reputation as an editor for his work with John Cheever, J. D. Salinger, John Updike, and many other writers. His first novel, *Bright Center of Heaven* (1934), was followed by *They Came Like Swallows* (1937), about the effect of an influenza epidemic on a close family (the death of Maxwell's own mother from influenza would mark much of his writing). *The Folded Leaf* (1945), perhaps his best-known work, describes the love between two small-town boys. In *Time Will Darken It* (1948) a long visit from relatives disrupts a family; in *The Château* (1961) American travelers encounter postwar French culture. *So Long, See You Tomorrow* (1980) returns to the subject of two boys' friendship, this one disrupted by a parent's murder of his spouse and suicide; it won Maxwell the William Dean Howells Medal for the best American fiction published in the preceding five years. He wrote three short-story collections: *The Old Man at the Railroad Crossing* (1966), *Over by the River* (1977), and *Billie Dyer* (1992).

Mayhew \\'mā-hyü\\, **Jonathan** (b. Oct. 8, 1720, Chilmark, Mass.—d. July 9, 1766, Boston) Religious leader and writer.

After graduating from Harvard College, Mayhew became pastor of West Church, Boston, in 1747. He soon began to move away from older Puritan beliefs with sermons questioning the divine right of kings and ecclesiastical absolutism. He was probably the first American clergyman to abandon traditional Trinitarian doctrine, a step which initiated the movement toward Unitarian congregationalism.

His sermons supporting the rights of the individual, which led John Adams to pronounce him a "transcendent genius," had a great effect on Boston colonists. They were supplemented by letters to newspapers and by pamphlets, which made him an early influence in the movement toward independence. In *The Snare Broken* (1766), provoked by the Stamp Act, he justified civil disobedience and even rebellion.

McAlmon \\mə-'kȯl-mən\\, **Robert (Menzies)** (b. March 9, 1896, Clifton, Kan.—d. Feb. 2, 1956, Desert Hot Springs, Calif.) Author and publisher, an exemplar of the literary expatriate in Paris during the 1920s.

In 1920 McAlmon moved to Chicago and then to New York, where he and William Carlos Williams founded the little magazine *Contact*. In 1921 he married the English writer Bryher (Annie Winifred Ellerman) and moved to Paris.

After publishing a book of his short stories, *A Hasty Bunch* (1922), at his own expense, he founded his own publishing company; Contact Editions, which published his short-story collection *A Companion Volume* (1923), his autobiographical novel *Post-Adolescence* (1923), and works by Williams, Bryher, Gertrude Stein, and Ernest Hemingway.

His best-received work was the novel *Village: As It Happened Through a Fifteen Year Period* (1924), a bleak portrait of an American town. Later books include *Distinguished Air (Grim Fairy Tales)* (1925), the poetry collection *The Portrait of a Generation* (1926), the epic poem *North America, Continent of Conjecture* (1929), and the Paris memoir *Being Geniuses Together* (1938).

McBain, Ed See **Hunter, Evan**

McCarthy, Cormac *originally* Charles McCarthy, Jr. (b. July 20, 1933, Providence, R.I.) Writer in the Southern gothic tradition whose novels about wayward characters in the rural South and Southwest are noted for their dark violence and dense prose.

Readers were introduced to McCarthy's difficult narrative style in the novel *The Orchard Keeper* (1965). Later novels include *Outer Dark* (1968), about two incestuous siblings; *Child of God* (1974), which tells of a lonely man's descent into depravity; and *Suttree* (1979), about a man who overcomes his fixation on death. After *Blood Meridian* (1985), a violent frontier tale, McCarthy achieved popular fame with *All the Pretty Horses* (1992, National Book Award, National Book Critics Circle Award), the coming-of-age story of two Texans who travel to Mexico and the first volume of his "Border Trilogy," which would be completed by *The Crossing* (1994) and *Cities of the Plain* (1999). *The Stonemason* (1994) is a five-act play about four generations of a black family in Louisville.

McCarthy, Mary (Therese) (b. June 21, 1912, Seattle, Wash.—d. Oct. 25, 1989, New York City) Novelist and critic noted for bitingly satiric commentaries on marriage, the impotence of intellectuals, and the role of women in urban America.

Orphaned at 6, McCarthy suffered a bitterly unhappy childhood. After graduating from Vassar College, she began her career writing book reviews. She served on the editorial staff of *Partisan Review* from 1937 to 1948. She married four times, the second time (1938–45) to EDMUND WILSON, who encouraged her to begin writing fiction.

Her first novel, THE COMPANY SHE KEEPS (1942), concerns a fashionable woman who experiences divorce and psychoanalysis. *The Oasis* (1949) is about the failure of a utopian community of intellectuals. *The Groves of Academe* (1952) is a satiric examination of higher education during the era of the anti-communist "witch hunts." THE GROUP (1963), her most popular novel, follows the

Mary McCarthy

lives of eight Vassar graduates. In *Birds of America* (1971) American innocence is confronted with European sophistication. *Cannibals and Missionaries* (1979) is about the hijacking of a committee flying to Iran to investigate the shah's atrocities. She also wrote two memoirs, MEMORIES OF A CATHOLIC GIRLHOOD (1957) and *How I Grew* (1987).

McClure, Michael (Thomas) (b. Oct. 20, 1932, Marysville, Kan.) Poet.

McClure grew up in Seattle and moved in 1954 to San Francisco, where he became an original member of the Beat movement. His first book, *Passage*, appeared in 1956. From 1962 he taught at the California College of Arts and Crafts. McClure's poems and plays, which incorporate obscure and hallucinatory images, often concern nature and biology and show the influence of the poet's Buddhism. His poetry collections include *The New Book* (1961), *Star* (1970), *September Blackberries* (1974), and *Fragments of Perseus* (1983). Early productions of *The Beard* (1965), which features Billy the Kid and Jean Harlow, were repeatedly closed for obscenity. His later play *Josephine, the Mouse Singer* (1980) has seen numerous productions. McClure's other plays include *Gargoyle Cartoons* (1971) and *Gorf* (1976). In recent years he has declaimed his poetry to piano accompaniment by the rock musician Ray Manzarek.

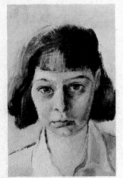
Carson McCullers

McCullers, Carson *originally* Lula Carson Smith (b. Feb. 19, 1917, Columbus, Ga.—d. Sept. 29, 1967, Nyack, N.Y.) Writer of novels and stories that depict the inner lives of lonely people.

A series of strokes suffered as a child left McCullers partly paralyzed; she would suffer further strokes as an adult. She studied at Columbia University and NYU and eventually settled in New York's Greenwich Village. Her stories, usually set in small Southern communities, depict the inner lives of lonely, wounded people. Her first novel, THE HEART IS A LONELY HUNTER, appeared in 1940 (film, 1968); many have regarded it as her finest work. In THE MEMBER OF THE WEDDING (1946; film, 1952), a motherless 12-year-old girl yearns to go on her brother's honeymoon; McCullers adapted it into a successful stage play in 1950. REFLECTIONS IN A GOLDEN EYE (1941; film, 1967) is a highly colored psychological horror story set in a peacetime Southern army camp. The widely read BALLAD OF THE SAD CAFÉ, a novelette published with short stories in 1951, was dramatized by Edward Albee in 1963 (film, 1991).

McCutcheon \mə-'kəch-ən**, George Barr** (b. July 26, 1866, near Lafayette, Ind.—d. Oct. 23, 1928, New York City) Author of popular novels.

McCutcheon attended Purdue University briefly but left to become a newspaper reporter. He was city editor of the *Lafayette Daily Courier* from 1893, resigning after his novel GRAUSTARK (1901), set in a mythical middle European kingdom, achieved popular success. *Brewster's Millions* (1902), a comic fantasy about an ordinary man who must spend a huge amount of money in a short time, was also highly successful and was eventually filmed seven times. Altogether, McCutcheon published some 40 works of fiction, including more swashbuckling tales of Graustark.

McElroy \\'mak-əl-ˌrȯi\\, **Joseph (Prince)** (b. Aug. 21, 1930, New York City) Novelist and short-story writer known for his intricate, lengthy, complex fiction.

McElroy received his doctorate from Columbia University in 1961. His first novel, *A Smuggler's Bible* (1966), is made up of eight disconnected chapters separated by authorial commentary. *Lookout Cartridge* (1974), perhaps his best and most accessible work, is a political thriller about a filmmaker who searches London and New York for movie footage that may have recorded a crime. *Plus* (1976) is about a rebellious, disembodied brain that operates a computer in outer space. The admired *Women and Men* (1986) is a 1,191-page novel about a journalist and a feminist who live in the same New York apartment building but never meet. *The Letter Left to Me* (1988) centers on a letter of advice written by the late father of a 15-year-old boy. *Actress in the House* was published in 2003.

McGinley, Phyllis (b. March 21, 1905, Ontario, Ore.—d. Feb. 22, 1978, New York City) Poet and author of books for young people, best known for her light verse celebrating suburban home life.

McGinley's poetry began to appear in such magazines as the *New Yorker* and the *Atlantic* in the 1920s. Her witty, technically expert verse, though often dismissed as light, is often fundamentally serious. Her best-known collections are *A Pocketful of Wry* (1940) and *Times Three* (1960, Pulitzer Prize). *Sixpence in Her Shoe* (1964) collected a popular series of essays about being a wife in the suburbs. *Saint-Watching* (1969) is an engaging treatment of saints' lives. Her numerous works for juveniles include *The Horse Who Lived Upstairs* (1944) and *The Make-Believe Twins* (1953).

McGuane, Thomas *in full* Thomas Francis McGuane III (b. Dec. 11, 1939, Wyandotte, Mich.) Author noted for his novels of violent action.

McGuane's durably popular first novels, *The Sporting Club* (1969; film, 1971), *The Bushwhacked Piano* (1971), and *Ninety-two in the Shade* (1973; film, 1975), presented the central plot and theme of his fiction: a man, usually from a secure family, who exiles himself from society to an isolated locale, then finds a reason (such as alienation, attraction to a woman, or rights to territory) to oppose another man in a succession of acts of escalating violence and revenge.

His novels' locales—Key West, northern Michigan, Montana—and his scenes of fishing and personal combat suggest the influence of Hemingway. While his early novels were noted for their stylistic extravagance, a growing plainness of style developed in his later novels, which include *Panama* (1978), *Nobody's Angel* (1981), *Something To Be Desired* (1984), *Keep the Change* (1989), and *Nothing but Blue Skies* (1992). *An Outside Chance* (1980) is a collection of his sports essays, *Some Horses* (1999) contains essays about horses, which he keeps on his Montana ranch, and *The Longest Silence* (1999) tells of his love of fishing. His stories have been collected in *To Skin a Cat* (1986) and *Barrel Fever* (1999). His screenplays include *Rancho Deluxe* (1975), *The Missouri Breaks* (1976), and *Tom Horn* (1980).

Claude McKay

McKay \mə-ˈkā\, **Claude** (*originally* Festus Claudius) (b. Sept. 15, 1890, Jamaica, British West Indies—d. May 22, 1948, Chicago) Jamaican-American poet and novelist.

Before moving to the United States in 1912, McKay wrote two volumes of Jamaican dialect verse, *Songs of Jamaica* (1911) and *Constab Ballads* (1912). After attending Tuskegee Institute and Kansas State Teachers College, he moved to New York in 1914, where he began contributing to the *Liberator*, a leading avant-garde journal. With the publication of two volumes of poetry, *Spring in New Hampshire* (1920) and *Harlem Shadows* (1922), he emerged as the first and most militant voice of the Harlem Renaissance. After 1922 he lived abroad successively in the Soviet Union, France, Spain, and Morocco. His *Home to Harlem* (1928) became the most popular novel written by an American black to that time; in it and his next novel, *Banjo* (1929), he tried to capture the vitality of the black vagabonds of urban America and Europe. There followed a collection of short stories, *Gingertown* (1932), and another novel, *Banana Bottom* (1933). In all these works McKay searched among the common folk for a distinctive black identity.

After returning to America in 1934, he wrote for such journals and newspapers as the *New Leader* and New York's *Amsterdam News*. He also wrote an autobiography, *A Long Way from Home* (1937), and the study *Harlem: Negro Metropolis* (1940).

McKuen \mə-ˈkyü-ən\, **Rod (Marvin)** (b. April 29, 1933, Oakland, Calif.) Singer, composer, and poet.

McKuen began working as a disc jockey for an Oakland radio station at 16. His first book, *Elephants in the Rice Paddies* (1954), highly critical of the U.S. Army, was inspired by his army experiences in Korea (1953–55). He returned to San Francisco in 1955 and began singing in nightclubs and composing songs. In 1959 he moved to New York, where he composed music for television and continued to perform. He honed his singing style in France in the early 1960s, working with Jacques Brel and other performers. Back in America later in the decade, he began to enjoy great success as a poet and singer. Such collections as *Stanyan Street and Other Sorrows* (1966), *Listen to the Warm* (1967), *Lonesome Cities* (1968), and *In Someone's Shadow* (1969) enjoyed popular sales far greater than those of any other poet, though they were derided by critics for their vague and undemanding sweetness. His later collections include *Come to Me in Silence* (1973), *Looking for a Friend* (1980), and *The Sound of Solitude* (1984). He also recorded over 50 records and wrote music for such films as *Joanna* (1968) and *The Prime of Miss Jean Brodie* (1969).

McMaster, John Bach (b. June 29, 1852, Brooklyn, N.Y.—d. May 24, 1932, Darien, Conn.) Historian.

While working as an engineer (1874–77), McMaster published works on bridge and dam construction. As an instructor at the College of New Jersey (1877–83), he began to write a history of the United States. Publication of the first volume of his *History of the People of the United States from the Revolution to the Civil War* in 1883 brought him recognition as an innovator in historical writing and an offer to teach history at the University of Pennsylvania, where he would remain until his retirement in 1920. The ninth and final volume of his great work did not appear until 1913. McMaster's emphasis on the social and economic forces that influenced history originated a major genre of historical writing that is still practiced. His talent for narrative and ingenuity in interpretation made his primary- and secondary-school textbooks popular throughout the country. His other works included *Benjamin Franklin as a Man of Letters* (1887) and *The United States in the World War* (2 vols., 1918–20).

McMillan, Terry (b. Oct. 18, 1951, Port Huron, Mich.) Novelist whose work often portrays spirited black women and their discouragements in relationships with black men.

Born into a lower-middle-class family headed by an abusive father, McMillan graduated from UC–Berkeley and did graduate work in film at Columbia University. In her first novel, *Mama* (1987), a black woman manages to raise five children after forcing her drunken husband to leave. *Disappearing Acts* (1989) concerns two dissimilar people who begin an intimate relationship. *Waiting to Exhale* (1992; film, 1995) follows four black middle-class women, each looking for the love of a worthy man; it achieved sales virtually unprecedented among black American authors, and was followed by another huge success, *How Stella Got Her Groove Back* (1996; film, 1998). *A Day Late and a Dollar Short* (2001) concerns family relationships. In 1990 MacMillan edited the anthology of black fiction *Breaking Ice*. Her work, often disparaged by critics, has aroused enthusiasm among black women and hostility among black men.

McMurtry, Larry (Jeff) (b. June 3, 1936, Wichita Falls, Texas) Novelist noted for works set on the frontier, in contemporary small towns, and in increasingly urbanized and industrial areas of Texas.

McMurtry did graduate work at Rice and Stanford universities and started a used-book store in Washington, D.C., before beginning to publish. His first novel, *Horseman, Pass By* (1961; filmed as *Hud*, 1963), is set in the Texas ranching country. The isolation and claustrophobia of small-town life are examined in *The Last Picture Show* (1966; film, 1971). The frontier epic *Lonesome Dove* (1985, Pulitzer Prize) was the first novel of an epic frontier series that also includes *Streets of Laredo* (1993), *Dead Man's Walk* (1995), and *Comanche Moon* (1997). Urban Houstonites appear in *Moving On* (1970), *All My Friends Are Going to Be Strangers* (1972), and *Terms of Endearment* (1975; film, 1983). Other novels include *Leaving Cheyenne* (1963; filmed as *Lovin' Molly*, 1974), *Cadillac Jack* (1982), *The Desert Rose* (1983), *Buffalo Girls* (1990), and *The Evening Star* (1992). McMurtry's great popular success has been consistently paralleled by the critical admiration his works have evoked.

McPhee, John (Angus) (b. March 8, 1931, Princeton, N.J.) Author of accessible, informative books on a wide variety of topics, particularly profiles of figures in sports, science, and the environment.

Educated at Princeton and Cambridge universities, he became an associate editor at *Time* (1957–64) and since 1965 has been a staff writer at the *New Yorker*. His first book, *A Sense of Where You Are* (1965), was based on his *New Yorker* article on Bill Bradley, and he profiled tennis players in *Levels of the Game* (1969) and *Arthur Ashe Remembered* (1993), a conservationist in *Encounters with the Archdruid* (1971), and a boat craftsman in *The Survival of the Bark Canoe* (1975).

He focused on New Jersey in *The Pine Barrens* (1968), the Scottish Highlands in *The Crofter and the Laird* (1970), Alaska in *Coming into the Country* (1977), and Switzerland in *La Place de la Concorde Suisse* (1984). A series of books on the geology of the West included *Basin and Range* (1981), *Rising From the Plains* (1986), and *Assembling California* (1993). He examined the citrus industry in *Oranges* (1967), aeronautical engineering in *The Deltoid Pumpkin Seed* (1973), nuclear terrorism in *The Curve of Binding Energy* (1974), and geology in *Annals of the Former World* (1998, Pulitzer Prize). Among his essay collections are *A Roomful of Hovings* (1968), *The John McPhee Reader* (1976), *Giving Good Weight* (1979), and *Table of Contents* (1985).

McPherson \mək-'fir-sən\, **James Alan** (b. Sept. 16, 1943, Savannah, Ga.) Short-story writer whose realistic, character-driven fiction examines racial tension, the mysteries of love, and the pain of isolation.

McPherson studied law at Harvard and Yale universities. His short story "Gold Coast" won a contest in the *Atlantic* in 1968, and he became a contributing editor of the magazine in 1969. He received his M.F.A. from the University of Iowa in 1971. In 1968 he published his first volume of short fiction, *Hue and Cry*. The stories in his next collection, *Elbow Room* (1977), including "Elbow Room,"

"A Loaf of Bread," and "Widows and Orphans," balance bitterness with hope; it became the first work of fiction by an African-American to win a Pulitzer Prize. His nonfiction has included *Railroad* (1977), *A World Unsuspected* (1987), *The Prevailing South* (1988), *Confronting Racial Differences* (1990), the memoir *Crabcakes* (1997), and *A Region Not Home* (2000). Since 1981 he has taught at the Iowa Writers' Workshop.

Mead, Margaret (b. Dec. 16, 1901, Philadelphia—d. Nov. 15, 1978, New York City) Anthropologist and writer.

    After graduating from Barnard College, Mead studied at Columbia University under Franz Boas and Ruth Benedict, earning her Ph.D. in 1929. She did fieldwork in Samoa, where she gathered material for the first and most famous of her 23 books, *Coming of Age in Samoa* (1928), which presented evidence in support of cultural determinism with respect to the formation of personality and temperament. A characteristic example of her reliance on observation rather than statistics for data, it was criticized after Mead's death for its methodological approach and findings.

    Her later books, many of which sold in large numbers, included *Sex and Temperament in Three Primitive Societies* (1935), *Male and Female* (1949), *Continuities in Cultural Evolution* (1964), and *Culture and Commitment* (1970). With Gregory Bateson, her husband from 1936 to 1951, she collaborated on *Balinese Character* (1942).

    From 1926 to 1978 Mead served in curatorial positions at the American Museum of Natural History. In her later years she became a prominent voice on such wide-ranging issues as women's rights and nuclear proliferation, and her fame owed as much to the force of her personality and her outspokenness as it did to the quality of her scientific work.

Melville, Herman *originally* Herman Melvill (b. Aug. 1, 1819, New York City—d. Sept. 28, 1891, New York City) Author best known for his novels of the sea, including his masterpiece, MOBY-DICK.

Herman Melville

    A bout of scarlet fever in 1826 left Melville with permanently weakened eyesight. He enrolled at Albany (N.Y.) Classical School in 1835, and in 1839 he shipped out as cabin boy on the *St. Lawrence*, a merchant ship bound for Liverpool. In 1841, after a grinding search for work and a brief teaching job, he sailed on the whaler *Acushnet* to the South Seas. In June 1842 it anchored in the Marquesas Islands, in present-day French Polynesia; Melville's adventures there, somewhat romanticized, became the subject of his first novel, TYPEE (1846). The voyage was unproductive, and Melville joined an uprising that landed the mutineers in a Tahitian jail, from which he escaped without difficulty. His carefree roving through the islands after his escape confirmed his bitterness against colonial and especially missionary debasement of the Polynesian peoples. He based his second book, OMOO (1847), on these events.

In 1847 Melville began MARDI (1849) and became a regular contributor to a literary journal. *Typee* and *Omoo* had provoked immediate enthusiasm and outrage, but when *Mardi* appeared the public and critics alike found its wild, allegorical fantasy and medley of styles incomprehensible. Concealing his disappointment, he quickly wrote REDBURN (1849) and WHITE-JACKET (1850) in the manner expected of him. In 1850 he bought a farm, "Arrowhead," near Nathaniel Hawthorne's home at Pittsfield, Mass. Their initially close relationship reanimated Melville's creative energies. On his side, it was dependent, almost mystically intense, but to the cooler, withdrawn Hawthorne, such depth of feeling so openly declared was uncongenial, and the two men gradually drew apart.

Moby-Dick, published in 1851, brought its author neither acclaim nor reward. Increasingly a recluse, he embarked almost at once on PIERRE (1852), which proved another critical and financial disaster. ISRAEL POTTER (1855) enjoyed modest success. Meanwhile, Melville had published important stories in *Putnam's Monthly Magazine*—BARTLEBY THE SCRIVENER (1853), THE ENCANTADAS (1854), and BENITO CERENO (1855)—reflecting the despair and the contempt for human hypocrisy and materialism that increasingly possessed him. Similar in theme was THE CONFIDENCE-MAN (1857), the last of his novels to be published in his lifetime.

The Civil War furnished the subject of his first volume of verse, *Battle-Pieces and Aspects of the War* (1866), published privately. Four months later, an appointment as a customs inspector on the New York docks finally brought him a secure income. His second collection of verse, *John Marr, and Other Sailors*, appeared in 1888, again privately published. By then he had been in retirement for three years, assisted by legacies from friends and relatives. *Timoleon* (1891) was his final verse collection. More significant was the return to prose that culminated in his last work, BILLY BUDD, FORETOPMAN, which remained unpublished until 1924. Although by the end of the 1840s he had been among the most celebrated of American writers, his death evoked but a single obituary notice. Only after years of neglect did modern criticism finally secure his reputation as one of the greatest American writers.

Mencken, H(enry) L(ouis) (b. Sept. 12, 1880, Baltimore—d. Jan. 29, 1956, Baltimore) Controversialist, humorous journalist, and pungent critic of American life.

Mencken became a reporter for the *Baltimore Morning Herald* and later joined the staff of the *Baltimore Sun*, for which he would work most of his life. From 1914 to 1923 he and George Jean Nathan edited the *Smart Set*, then the magazine most influential in the growth of American literature. In 1924 the two founded the AMERICAN MERCURY, and Mencken edited it until 1933.

Mencken was the most influential American literary critic in the 1920s, and often used literary criticism as a point of departure to jab at American weaknesses. His reviews and miscellaneous essays filled six volumes, aptly titled *Prejudices* (1919–27). He fulminated against writers he regarded as fraudulently successful and proselytized for such outstanding newcomers as Theodore

Dreiser and Sinclair Lewis. He jeered at American sham, pretension, provincialism, and prudery, and ridiculed organized religion, business, and the middle class (the "booboisie"). In the 1930s his opinions became increasingly conservative and sometimes reactionary.

In *The American Language* (1919), he attempted to bring together examples of American expressions and idioms. The book grew with each reissue through the years, and in 1945 and 1948 he published substantial supplements. By the time of his death, Mencken was perhaps the leading authority on the language of his country.

H.L. Mencken

His autobiographical trilogy, *Happy Days* (1940), *Newspaper Days* (1941), and *Heathen Days* (1943), is devoted to his experiences in journalism. The manuscript for *My Life as Author and Editor* (1993) had been sealed, at Mencken's request, until 35 years after his death.

Merrill, James (Ingram) (b. March 3, 1926, New York City—d. Feb. 6, 1995, Tucson, Ariz.) Poet known for the fine craftsmanship and wit of his lyric and epic poems.

Son of a founder of the Merrill Lynch brokerage house, Merrill attended Amherst College and was thereafter free to pursue writing without financial concern. *Jim's Book* (1942) and the volumes that followed revealed his mastery of poetic form and technique but were also deemed stiff and artificial. With *Water Street* (1962), critics noted a growing ease and the development of a personal vision. The interactions between art and life and between memory and experience became the major motifs of this transitional stage, during which his *Nights and Days* (1966) won a National Book Award.

Not until the publication of the epic poetry in *Divine Comedies* (1976, Pulitzer Prize, Bollingen Prize), *Mirabell: Books of Number* (1978, National Book Award), and *Scripts for the Pageant* (1980, National Book Critics Circle Award)—a trilogy later published in *The Changing Light at Sandover* (1982)—did Merrill achieve wider public appreciation. He used a Ouija board in composing some of the poetry in the trilogy, which is a serious yet witty summation of his lifelong concerns. Selections of his poetry appeared in *From the First Nine* (1982) and *Selected Poems, 1946–1985* (1992). Merrill also wrote two novels, two plays, and a memoir, *A Different Person* (1993). His last volume of poetry, *A Scattering of Salts* (1995), was posthumously published.

Merton, Thomas (b. Jan. 31, 1915, Prades, France—d. Dec. 10, 1968, Bangkok, Thailand) Roman Catholic monk known for his prolific writings on spiritual and social themes.

Merton was educated at Cambridge and Columbia universities. After teaching English at Columbia and at St. Bonaventure University, he joined a contemplative Trappist order in the Cistercian Abbey of Gethsemani, near Louisville, Ky. He was ordained a priest in 1949.

Merton's first published works were collections of poems: *Thirty Poems* (1944), *A Man in the Divided Sea* (1946), and *Figures for an Apocalypse* (1948). With publication of the autobiographical *Seven Storey Mountain* (1948), he gained an international reputation. His early works were strictly spiritual, but in the early 1960s his writings tended toward social criticism, while many of his later works reveal an insight into Oriental philosophy and mysticism unusual in a Westerner. His only novel, *My Argument with the Gestapo*, written in 1941, was published posthumously in 1969. His other writings include *The Waters of Siloe* (1949), a history of the Trappists; *Seeds of Contemplation* (1949); *The Living Bread* (1956), a meditation on the Eucharist; *Contemplation in a World of Action* (1971), an insightful book of essays; and *The Asian Journal of Thomas Merton* (1973).

Merwin, W(illiam) S(tanley) (b. Sept. 30, 1927, New York City) Poet and translator known for the spare style of his poetry in which he expressed his concerns about the alienation of humans from their environment.

After graduating from Princeton University, Merwin worked as a tutor in Europe and freelance translator. He received critical acclaim for his first collection of poetry, *A Mask for Janus* (1952). His early poems include both lyrical works and philosophical narratives based on myth and folk tales. Subsequent collections include *Green with Beasts* (1956), *The Drunk in the Furnace* (1960), and *The Moving Target* (1963). The poems of *The Lice* (1967) reflect his despair over human mistreatment of the rest of creation and his strongly held environmentalist and pacifist views. He won a Pulitzer Prize for *The Carrier of Ladders* (1970). Among his later collections are *The Compass Flower* (1977), *Finding the Islands* (1982), *The Rain in the Trees* (1988), *Travels* (1993), *The Vixen* (1995), and *The River Sound* (1999). His acclaimed translations, often collaborations with others, range from plays of Euripides and Lorca to Dante's *Purgatorio* to the epic *Poem of the Cid* and *Song of Roland* to ancient and modern works from Chinese, Sanskrit, and Japanese. In 1979 he received the Bollingen Prize.

Metalious \mə-ˈta-lē-əs**, Grace** *originally* Grace de Repentigny (b. Sept. 8, 1924, Manchester, N.H.—d. Feb. 25, 1964, Boston) Popular novelist.

After graduating from high school, she married George Metalious, a schoolteacher. The couple and their three children later moved to Gilmanton, N.H., a small town where they lived in near-poverty.

Metalious began writing in 1954 and *Peyton Place,* whose characters were based on the town's residents and their secret scandals, was published in 1956. Helped by reviews that emphasized its sex scenes, it was a best-seller within a month and would go on to sell over 8 million copies. Shocked by the notoriety, most residents shunned Metalious after its publication. The book became a film in 1957 and a television series in the 1960s.

Her later novels include *Return to Peyton Place* (1959; film, 1961), *The Tight White Collar* (1960), and *No Adam in Eden* (1963). Though her books sold over 15 million copies, she earned little money from them. Increasingly alcoholic, she died of liver disease at 39.

Michener \\'mich-nər\\, **James A(lbert)** (b. 1907—d. Oct. 16, 1997, Austin, Texas) Novelist and short-story writer best known for his epic and detailed novels.

A foundling discovered in Doylestown, Pa., Michener was raised as a Quaker. After attending Swarthmore College and studying in Europe, he taught college-level social sciences and worked as a book editor. He saw wartime service as a naval historian in the South Pacific (1944–46), where his early fiction is based. He won a Pulitzer Prize for *Tales of the South Pacific* (1947), which became the basis of Rodgers and Hammerstein's musical *South Pacific* (1949). The Pacific was also the setting for *The Bridges at Toko-Ri* (1953; film, 1954), *Sayonara* (1954; film, 1957), and *Hawaii* (1959; film, 1966).

Michener's novels were typically detailed and massive in scope, and he researched them extensively (with the help of assistants). In his later years, he turned his interest to American landscapes in such books as *Centennial* (1974), *Chesapeake* (1978), and *Alaska* (1988). *Space* (1982) was a fictional chronicle of the U.S. space program. His later works include *Poland* (1983), *Mexico* (1992), and the memoir *The World Is My Home* (1992). In 1977 he received the Presidential Medal of Freedom.

Millay \\mi-'lā\\, **Edna St. Vincent** (b. Feb. 22, 1892, Rockland, Maine—d. Oct. 19, 1950, Austerlitz, N.Y.) Poet and dramatist who came to personify romantic rebellion and bravado in the 1920s.

Millay grew up in Camden, Maine, and her poetic work is filled with the imagery of coast and countryside. Her first poems were published in the children's magazine *St. Nicholas*. Acclaim greeted RENASCENCE when it was included in *The Lyric Year* in 1912; it brought Millay to the attention of a benefactor who made it possible for her to attend Vassar. For a time she supported herself in New York by writing short stories under a pseudonym and as an actress and playwright. In 1923 she married, and she lived thereafter on a farm in the Berkshires.

Her first book, *Renascence and Other Poems* (1917), was full of the romantic and independent temper of youth. The line "My candle burns at both ends," from a poem in *A Few Figs from Thistles* (1920), was taken up as the watchword of the "flaming youth" of the era and brought her a renown she came to despise. In 1921 she published *Second April* as well as three verse plays: *Two Slatterns and a King*, *The Lamp and the Bell*, and *Aria da Capo*. The title poem of *The Harp Weaver* (1923, Pulitzer Prize) is thought to have been inspired by her mother. She wrote the libretto for Deems Taylor's opera *The King's Henchman*,

Edna St. Vincent Millay

mounted at the Metropolitan Opera in 1927. Her major later works include *The Buck in the Snow* (1928), the sonnet sequence *Fatal Interview* (1931), and *Wine from These Grapes* (1934).

Arthur Miller

Miller, Arthur (b. Oct. 17, 1915, New York City) Playwright who has combined social awareness with a searching concern for his characters' inner lives.

Raised in modest circumstances, Miller worked his way through the University of Michigan. His first public success was with *Focus* (1945), a novel about anti-Semitism. ALL MY SONS (1947; film, 1948), about a manufacturer of faulty war materials, was his first important play. DEATH OF A SALESMAN (1948, Pulitzer Prize; film, 1951) is the tragedy of a small man destroyed by false values that are largely those of his society; hugely acclaimed, it was soon regarded as one of the greatest American dramas of its century.

THE CRUCIBLE (1953; films, 1957, 1996) was based on the Salem witchcraft trials of 1692, which Miller analogized to the widespread investigation of subversive activities of the 1950s. The short plays *A Memory of Two Mondays* and *A View from the Bridge* (film, 1962) were staged on the same bill in 1955. AFTER THE FALL (1964) was inspired by Miller's failed marriage to Marilyn Monroe (1956–60), for whom he wrote a part in the screenplay *The Misfits* (1961). *Incident at Vichy* (1964) concerns collaboration with the Nazis. *The Price* (1968) continued his exploration of guilt and responsibility in the strained relationship between two brothers. *The Archbishop's Ceiling* (1977) dealt with the Soviet treatment of dissidents. *The American Clock* (1980) was set in the Great Depression. Miller produced several one-act plays in the 1980s; *I Can't Remember Anything* and *Clara* were published together as *Danger, Memory!* (1986). His other full-length plays include *Playing for Time* (1981), *The Ride Down Mount Morgan* (1991), *The Last Yankee* (1991), and *Resurrection Blues* (2002).

Henry Miller

Miller, Henry (Valentine) (b. Dec. 26, 1891, New York City—d. June 7, 1980, Pacific Palisades, Calif.) Writer and perennial bohemian whose autobiographical novels had a liberating influence on mid-20th-century literature.

Miller was brought up in Brooklyn, and he wrote about his childhood experiences there in *Black Spring* (1936). In 1930 he moved to France. TROPIC OF CANCER (1934) is based on his hand-to-mouth existence in depression-era Paris. *Tropic of Capricorn* (1939) draws on his earlier New York phase.

Because of their sexual frankness, his major works were banned as obscene in Britain and the United States until 1961, though they were widely known earlier from copies smuggled in from France. In 1964 the U.S. Supreme Court rejected earlier state court findings that the "Tropics" books were obscene.

A visit to Greece in 1939 inspired *The Colossus of Maroussi* (1941). *The Air-Conditioned Nightmare* (1945) is a sharply critical account of a tour of the United States. After settling in California's Big Sur, he produced his Rosy Crucifixion trilogy—*Sexus*, *Plexus*, and *Nexus* (U.S. edition, 1965)—which traces the stages by which the hero-narrator becomes a writer, again with considerable sexual candor. Other important books include the essay collections *The Cosmological Eye* (1939) and *The Wisdom of the Heart* (1941). Various volumes of his correspondence have been published: with Lawrence Durrell (1963), to Anaïs Nin (1965), and with Wallace Fowlie (1975).

Miller, J(oseph) Hillis (b. March 5, 1928, Newport News, Va.) Literary critic initially associated with the Geneva group of critics and later with deconstruction.

Miller graduated from Oberlin College and received his Ph.D. from Harvard in 1952. He thereafter held positions at Johns Hopkins (1953–72), Yale (1972–86), and UC–Irvine (from 1986).

With the Geneva group of critics, Miller argued in his earlier works that literature is a tool for understanding the mind of the writer. His criticism emphasized theological concerns, as in *Poets of Reality: Six Twentieth-Century Writers* (1965), *The Form of Victorian Fiction* (1968), and *The Disappearance of God: Five Nineteenth-Century Writers* (1963). By 1970, however, he had joined the deconstructionist critics at Yale, and his subsequent scholarship has been steeped in arcane language and has expressed the belief that language itself is a work's sole reality. His criticism in this vein includes *Fiction and Repetition* (1982) and *The Linguistic Moment* (1985).

Miller, Joaquin (*originally* Cincinnatus Hiner) (b. Sept. 8, 1837, near Liberty, Ind.—d. Feb. 17, 1913, Oakland, Calif.) Poet and journalist whose best work conveys a sense of the majesty and excitement of the Old West.

Miller led a picaresque early life in California among miners and gamblers. In Oregon he owned a newspaper (the *Eugene Democratic Register*) and served as a county judge. His first books of poems, *Specimens* (1868) and *Joaquin et al.* (1869), attracted little attention. In 1870 he traveled to England, where *Pacific Poems* (1871) was privately printed. *Songs of the Sierras* (1871), on which his reputation mainly rests, was loudly acclaimed in England, while generally derided in the United States for its excessive romanticism. His other books of poetry include *Songs of the Sunlands* (1873), *The Ship in the Desert* (1875), *The Baroness of New York* (1877), and *Memorie and Rime* (1884). His best-known poem is "Columbus"; its refrain, "On, sail on!" was once familiar to millions of American schoolchildren.

Miller, May (b. Jan. 26, 1899, Washington, D.C.—d. Feb. 8, 1995, Washington, D.C.) Playwright and poet associated with the Harlem Renaissance.

Miller graduated from Howard University in 1920, earning an award for her one-act play *Within the Shadows,* and afterwards taught secondary school while continuing to write. A prizewinning play, *The Bog Guide* (1925), helped establish her in the black cultural scene, and she became the most widely published woman playwright of the Harlem Renaissance. She openly addressed racial issues in plays such as *Scratches* (1929), *Stragglers in the Dust* (1930), and *Nails and Thorns* (1933). She also wrote many historical plays, four of which (including *Harriet Tubman* and *Sojourner Truth*) were anthologized in *Negro History in Thirteen Plays* (1935). She retired from teaching in 1943 and became a prolific poet, publishing seven volumes that included *Into the Clearing* (1959) and *Dust of Uncertain Journey* (1975).

Miller, Perry (Gilbert Eddy) (b. Feb. 25, 1905, Chicago—d. Dec. 9, 1963, Cambridge, Mass.) Literary historian.

Miller earned his doctorate from the University of Chicago in 1931, then joined the faculty of Harvard University, where he taught American literature until his death. His first book, *Orthodoxy in Massachusetts* (1933), established him in the field of 17th-century American studies, where he would remain pre-eminent among scholars. *The New England Mind* (1939) toppled conventional notions about the Puritans and became the standard work on early New England intellectual history. His other works on the 17th century included studies of Jonathan Edwards (1948, 1949) and *Roger Williams* (1953). He turned to the 19th century in such later works as *The Raven and the Whale* (1956), *Consciousness in Concord* (1958), and *The Golden Age of American Literature* (1959).

Milosz \\'mē-lȯsh\\, Czeslaw (b. June 30, 1911, Szetejnie, Lithuania) Polish-American poet, translator, and critic.

Milosz was a socialist by the time he published his first book of verse at 21, and during the Nazi occupation of Poland he was active in the resistance. He served briefly as a diplomat for communist Poland before emigrating to America, where he taught Slavic literature at UC–Berkeley until his retirement in 1978. His well-known essay collection *The Captive Mind* (1953) condemned the continuing accommodation of many Polish intellectuals to communism. His poetry, including the well-known *Bells in Winter* (1978), *Facing the River* (1995), *Roadside Dog* (1998), and *The Second Space* (2002), displays a classical style and frequent preoccupation with philosophical and political issues. Milosz has also published novels, including *The Seizure of Power* (1955) and *The Issa Valley* (1981), a *History of Polish Literature* (1969), further essay collections admired for their quietly expressed depth of thought, translations, and an autobiography (1988). All his works have continued to be written in Polish; Milosz has assisted other poets in translating them into English and other languages. He was awarded the Nobel Prize in 1980.

Mitchell, Donald Grant (b. April 12, 1822, Norwich, Conn.—d. Dec. 15, 1908) Farmer and writer known for nostalgic, sentimental books on American life.

After graduating from Yale, Mitchell returned home to farm his ancestral land. He served briefly at the U.S. consulate in Liverpool before ill health forced him to resign. From 1846 he wrote articles for the *Morning Courier* and *New York Enquirer* under the pseudonym Ik Marvel. From 1850 he also edited the satirical magazine *Lorgnette* (1850). His earliest books, *Fresh Gleanings* (1847) and *The Battle Summer* (1850), record incidents of his travels in Europe and the French revolution of 1848. With *Reveries of a Bachelor* (1850) he gained immediate fame, and in 1851 he published *Dream Life*. His quiet, simple, archaic style has been compared to that of the English author Jerome K. Jerome.

In 1855 he bought Edgewood, an estate near New Haven, intending to farm full-time. Having always considered his agricultural projects more important than his writing, he tried to build a model farm. Of his several further volumes of essays, most deal with farming life.

Mitchell, Joseph (Quincy) (b. July 27, 1908, Fairmont, N.C.—d. May 24, 1996, New York City) Journalist.

After studying at the University of North Carolina, Mitchell moved to New York in 1929 and worked for several newspapers, including the *World Telegram* (from 1931). In 1938 he joined the staff of the *New Yorker* magazine, for which he wrote articles, profiles, and vignettes of New York life into the early 1960s. He found his frequently odd subjects in the unexplored corners of the city, and brought them to life with his sharp intelligence, eye for detail, and deft style. Mitchell's books, most of them collections of his *New Yorker* pieces, included *My Ears Are Bent* (1938), *McSorley's Wonderful Saloon* (1943), *Old Mr. Flood* (1948), *The Bottom of the Harbor* (1960), and *Joe Gould's Secret* (1965), whose title story was filmed in 2000. In 1992 *Up in the Old Hotel*, a collection of most of his previously published pieces, became an unexpected best-seller.

Mitchell, Margaret (b. Nov. 8, 1900, Atlanta, Ga.—d. Aug. 16, 1949, Atlanta) Author of the enormously popular novel GONE WITH THE WIND.

Educated at Smith College, Mitchell subsequently wrote for the *Atlanta Journal*. After leaving the newspaper she spent 10 years writing her one book, *Gone with the Wind*, a novel about the Civil War and Reconstruction as seen from the Southern point of view. In the first six months after its publication in 1936, a million copies were sold, 50,000 of them in one day, and it quickly became almost certainly the largest-selling novel in the history of U.S. publishing to its time. Before the author's death after being struck by a car, sales had totaled 8 million in 40 countries.

Mitchell, S(ilas) Weir (b. Feb. 15, 1829, Philadelphia—d. Jan. 4, 1914, Philadelphia) Physician and author who excelled in novels of psychology and historical romance.

Mitchell served as an army surgeon during the Civil War, and his experiences were the basis for "The Case of George Dedlow" (1866), a story about an amputee notable for its psychological insight and realistic war scenes. *Wear and Tear* (1871) and *Fat and Blood* (1877), both medical popularizations, were best-sellers. Mitchell also published short stories, poems, and children's stories anonymously. Of his later novels, the most notable are *Roland Blake* (1886), *Hugh Wynne* (1898), *Circumstance* (1901), *Constance Trescott* (1905), and *The Red City* (1908). His poetry, which lacks his novels' psychological insight and contemporaneity, appears in such collections as *The Hill of Stones* (1882) and *The Wager* (1900).

Momaday \\'mäm-ə-ˌdā\\, **N(avarre) Scott** (b. Feb. 27, 1934, Lawton, Okla.) Author of works centered on his Kiowa Indian heritage.

Momaday grew up on an Oklahoma farm and on Southwestern reservations, graduated from the University of New Mexico, and earned his doctorate at Stanford University in 1963. His first novel and best-known work, the Pulitzer Prize–winning *House Made of Dawn* (1968), narrates from several points of view the dilemma of a young man returning home to his Kiowa pueblo after a stint in the army.

Momaday's second novel, *The Ancient Child*, appeared in 1989. His limited-edition collection of Kiowa Indian folktales, *The Journey of Tai-me* (1967), was enlarged as *The Way to Rainy Mountain* (1969), illustrated by his father, Alfred Momaday. His poetry is collected in *Angle of Geese* (1974), *The Gourd Dancer* (1976), and *In the Bear's House* (1997). *The Names* (1976) tells of his early life and his respect for his ancestors. *In the Presence of the Sun* (1992) contains selected stories and poems, and *The Man Made of Words* (1997) contains both essays and stories.

Monroe, Harriet (b. Dec. 23, 1860, Chicago—d. Sept. 26, 1936, Arequipa, Peru) Founder and longtime editor of POETRY magazine.

Monroe worked on various Chicago newspapers as an art and drama critic while privately writing verse and verse plays. Her poem "Cantata" celebrates Chicago history, and her heroic "Columbian Ode" (1892) was recited at the dedication of Chicago's World's Columbian Exposition. In founding *Poetry,* she secured the backing of wealthy Chicago patrons and invited contributions from a wide range of poets. Her open-minded, inclusive editorial policy and awareness of the importance of the contemporary poetic revolution made *Poetry* the principal organ for modern English-language poetry and made Monroe a major influence in its development. Her autobiography, *A Poet's Life,* was published posthumously in 1938.

Moody, William Vaughn (b. July 8, 1869, Spencer, Ind.—d. Oct. 17, 1910, Colorado Springs, Colo.) Poet, playwright, and educator.

After studies at Harvard University (A.M., 1894), Moody taught English and rhetoric at the University of Chicago from 1895 to 1907. His works included *Poems* (1901) and a trilogy of dramas in verse: *The Masque of Judgment* (1900), *The Fire-Bringer* (1904), and *The Death of Eve,* which he left incomplete at his death. He also wrote two prose dramas: *The Great Divide* (1907), about the competing strains of Puritanism and wide-ranging adventurism in the American character, enjoyed great success and is regarded as the finest American drama of its decade; *The Faith Healer* (1909) was admired by the critics but not successful. He also cowrote a successful textbook, *A First View of English Literature* (1905).

Moore, Clement Clarke (b. July 15, 1779, New York City—d. July 10, 1863, Newport, R.I.) Scholar now chiefly remembered for the ballad that begins "'Twas the night before Christmas."

A wealthy New York City landowner, Moore attended Columbia College. His chief scholarly work is *A Compendious Lexicon of the Hebrew Language* (1809). From 1821 to 1850 he taught Oriental and Greek literature at General Theological Seminary. It is said that he composed "A Visit from St. Nicholas" to amuse his children on Christmas 1822, and that, unknown to him, a houseguest copied it and gave it to the *Troy* (N.Y.) *Sentinel*, where it was published anonymously on Dec. 23, 1823. In 2000 it was determined that the poem (not claimed by Moore as his own until 1844) was in all likelihood the work of the gentleman poet Henry Livingston, Jr.

Moore, Marianne (Craig) (b. Nov. 15, 1887, St. Louis, Mo.—d. Feb. 5, 1972, New York City) Poet whose work distilled moral and intellectual insights from the close and accurate observation of objective detail.

Moore graduated in 1909 from Bryn Mawr College, and from 1919, living with her mother in Brooklyn, N.Y., she devoted herself to writing, contributing poetry and criticism to many journals in the United States and England.

In 1921 her first book, *Poems*, was published in London by the poet H.D. without Moore's knowledge. Her first American volume was *Observations* (1924). These initial collections, containing such well-known poems as "To a Steam Roller," "The Fish," "When I Buy Pictures," "Peter," "The Labors of Hercules," and POETRY (the source of her often-quoted admonition that poets should present imaginary gardens with real toads in them) exhibit Moore's love of animals and natural history, her exquisite concision, and her creation of a mosaic of oddly juxtaposed images and texts leading unerringly to a conclusion that, at its best, is both surprising and inevitable.

In 1925, already regarded as one of America's leading younger poets, she became acting editor of *The Dial*, an influential journal of literature and the arts, and served until it was discontinued in 1929. Her *Collected Poems* (1951) won the Pulitzer and Bollingen Prizes and the National Book Award. She also published a translation of *The Fables of La Fontaine* (1954); a volume of critical papers, *Predilections* (1955); and *Idiosyncrasy and Technique: Two Lectures* (1958). Her disciplined and elegant verse won her the admiration of fellow poets throughout her long career, and in her late years the winningly eccentric Moore, with her cape and tricornered hat, became a beloved icon of sprightly gentility.

More, Paul Elmer (b. Dec. 12, 1864, St. Louis, Mo.—d. March 9, 1937, Princeton, N.J.) Scholar and conservative critic and philosopher, one of the leading exponents of the New Humanism in literary criticism.

More was educated at Washington University and later at Harvard, where he met Irving Babbitt. He thereafter taught at Bryn Mawr College and Princeton University, while also working as a literary editor. Like Babbitt, with whom he led the neo-Christian New Humanists, More became an uncompromising advocate of traditional critical standards and classical restraint.

His best-known work is his *Shelburne Essays* (11 vols., 1904–21), a collection of articles and reviews named for his retreat in Shelburne, N.H. Also notable are *Platonism* (1917), *The Religion of Plato* (1921), *Hellenistic Philosophies* (1923), *New Shelburne Essays* (3 vols., 1928–36), and the autobiography *Pages from an Oxford Diary* (1937). His monumental *The Greek Tradition* (5 vols., 1924–31) is generally thought to be his finest work.

Morison, Samuel Eliot (b. July 9, 1887, Boston, Mass.—d. May 15, 1976, Boston) Biographer and historian who recreated in vivid prose notable maritime stories of modern history.

Morison received his doctorate from Harvard University and, after further study and teaching abroad, returned to teach at Harvard for 40 years. To give authenticity to his writing, he undertook numerous voyages himself, sailed the ocean routes followed by Columbus, and during wartime served on 12 ships as a commissioned officer in the naval reserve.

His principal writings are *The Growth of the American Republic* (1930; with H. S. Commager); *Admiral of the Ocean Sea* (1942, Pulitzer Prize), a biography of Columbus; *John Paul Jones* (1959, Pulitzer Prize); the 15-volume *History of U.S. Naval Operations in World War II* (1947–62); *The Oxford History of the American People* (1965); and *The European Discovery of America* (2 vols., 1971, 1974).

Morley, Christopher (Darlington) (b. May 5, 1890, Haverford, Pa.—d. March 28, 1957, Roslyn Heights, Long Island, N.Y.) Writer whose versatile works are lighthearted, vigorous displays of language.

Morley gained popularity with his literary columns in the *New York Evening Post* and the *Saturday Review of Literature* and from collections of essays and columns such as *Shandygaff* (1918). His novels include *The Haunted Bookshop* (1919), the innovative *The Trojan Horse* (1937), a combination of prose, verse, and dramatic dialogue that satirizes the devotion to luxury, and the sentimental best-seller *Kitty Foyle* (1939; film, 1940). *The Old Mandarin* (1947) is a collection of witty free verse. He also edited two editions of Bartlett's *Familiar Quotations* (1937, 1948).

Morris, Wright (Marion) (b. Jan. 6, 1910, Central City, Neb.—d. April 29, 1998, Mill Valley, Calif.) Novelist known for his works set on the Nebraska plains.

Morris's journeys with his father around America in the 1920s and '30s led to his first novel, *My Uncle Dudley* (1942), in which a group of people travel across country by car. *The Field of Vision* (1956) won the National Book Award; it and such later novels as the admired *Ceremony in Lone Tree* (1960) describe the failed and frustrated lives of residents of small Midwestern towns. Later works include the paired novels *Fire Sermon* (1971) and *A Life* (1973); *The Fork River Space Project* (1977); and *Plains Song, for Female Voices* (1980, American Book Award). Morris also wrote such books of nonfiction as the essay collections *About Fiction* (1975) and *Earthly Delights, Unearthly Adornments* (1978) and the memoirs *Will's Boy* (1981), *Solo* (1983), and *A Cloak of Light* (1985), and published five books combining his own photographs and text.

Morrison, Toni *originally* Chloe Anthony Wofford (b. Feb. 18, 1931, Lorain, Ohio) Writer and editor noted for her examination of the black experience, and particularly the experience of black women.

Toni Morrison

Morrison grew up in a working-class Midwestern neighborhood. She attended Howard University, where she toured as an actress with its repertory company, and received her master's degree from Cornell. In 1965, after teaching at Texas Southern University and Howard, she became an editor at Random House, where she would remain until 1983. Since the late 1980s she has taught at Princeton University.

Her first book, THE BLUEST EYE (1970), is a novel of initiation. Her second novel, SULA (1973), examines (among other issues) the dynamics of friendship and the expectations for conformity within the black community. She used a male narrator in the brilliant SONG OF SOLOMON (1977), whose publication brought her to national attention. In 1981 she published *Tar Baby*. The celebrated BELOVED (1987) won the Pulitzer Prize. *Jazz* (1992) concerns a couple that moves from the deep South to Harlem early in the 20th century. *Paradise* (1998) tells of a women's shelter in an all-black Oklahoma town. *Love* (2003) ranges from the 1940s to the 1990s. Morrison's "magic realist" use of fantasy and myth, mastery of ambiguity, and sinuous poetic style have given her works great strength and texture. She edited *The Black Book* (1974), a pictorial history of African-American life; *Playing in the Dark: Whiteness and the Literary Imagination* (1992) is a work of criticism. In 1993 she became the second American woman, and the first African-American, to receive the Nobel Prize for Literature.

Morton, Sarah Wentworth *originally* Sarah Wentworth Apthorp (b. August 1759, Boston—d. May 14, 1846, Quincy, Mass.) Poet.

The daughter of a merchant, she grew up in Braintree (now Quincy), and in 1781 she married Perez Morton, a lawyer. She had written verse since her childhood, and in 1789 she began sending poems to the newly established *Massachusetts Magazine*. Under the pen name Philenia, she published the long verse narrative *Ouâbi* (1790), an Indian tale of the "noble savage" type. As her poems continued to appear in literary magazines, Philenia became the foremost American female poet of her period. The long poem *Beacon Hill* (1797) and its sequel, *The Virtues of Society* (1799), were uniquely American works of the early national period. Her last work was *My Mind and Its Thoughts* (1823).

Morton was long considered the anonymous author of the first American novel, *The Power of Sympathy* (1789), based on a scandal involving Morton's husband and sister, ending in the latter's suicide, but in 1894 its author was identified as William Hill Brown.

Morton, Thomas (b. 1590?, England—d. 1647?) Colonist and writer.

Little is known of Morton's early life, but he was in Massachusetts in 1624 as the leader of a settlement within the town of modern Quincy. At his settlement, called Merry Mount, he encouraged wild festivities and attacked the solemn Puritan way of life. By providing firearms and supplies to the Indians, he gained a virtual monopoly of the local fur trade. The Puritans despised him and in 1627 cut down a maypole he had erected. Twice arrested and sent to England (1628, 1630), he twice returned. After his second return he attempted to have the Puritans' charter revoked.

His *New England Canaan* (1637), a partly satirical description of New England, caused consternation among the colonists. In 1643 he was forced out of Massachusetts; arrested and imprisoned in Boston (1644–45) when he tried to return, he was again banished.

Morton was later the subject of a story by Nathaniel Hawthorne, two novels by John L. Motley (1839, 1849), and Howard Hanson's opera *Merry Mount* (1934).

Mosley \ˈmōz-lē\, **Walter** (b. Jan. 12, 1952, Los Angeles) Author of mystery stories noted for their realistic portrayals of segregated inner-city life.

Mosley attended Goddard College and Johnson State College, and worked as a potter and computer programmer before publishing his first novel, *Devil in a Blue Dress* (1990; film, 1995). Set in 1948, it introduces Ezekiel "Easy" Rawlins, an unwilling amateur detective from the Watts section of Los Angeles. Other novels featuring Rawlins include *A Red Death* (1991), *White Butterfly* (1992), *Black Betty* (1994), *A Little Yellow Dog* (1996), and *Gone Fishin'*(1997). The popular and admired series uses period detail and slang to create authentic settings and characters, especially the earnest, complex Rawlins. *RL's Dream*

(1995) concerns an old blues musician. *Blue Light* (1998) ventures into science fiction. The story collections *Always Outnumbered, Always Outgunned* (1997) and *Walkin' the Dog* (1999) introduce the ex-convict Socrates Fortlow. His recent work includes *Fear Itself* (2003) and *The Man in My Basement* (2004).

Moss, Howard (b. Jan. 22, 1922, New York City—d. Sept. 16, 1987, New York City) Poet and poetry editor of the *New Yorker* magazine for almost 40 years.

Moss graduated from the University of Wisconsin in 1943 and published the first of 12 volumes of his poetry, *The Wound and the Weather*, in 1946. He joined the *New Yorker* staff in 1948, and throughout his long tenure there he showcased the works and helped establish the careers of such poets as Sylvia Plath, Richard Wilbur, and Elizabeth Bishop. His own *Selected Poems* (1971) won the National Book Award. Moss also published volumes of criticism and was an accomplished playwright, whose plays include *The Folding Green* (1958), *The Oedipus Mah-Jongg Scandal* (1968), and *The Palace at 4 A.M.* (1972).

Motley, John Lothrop (b. April 15, 1814, Boston—d. May 29, 1877, Dorsetshire, England) Historian and diplomat.

After graduating from Harvard College in 1831, Motley traveled in Europe and studied in Germany before returning to Boston in 1835 to live on his father's estate. Devoting himself to literature, he wrote two novels (1839, 1849) about the anti-Puritan colonist Thomas Morton, but gained only slight success.

He spent five years researching and writing *The Rise of the Dutch Republic* (1856); noted for its brilliant style, drama, and strong feeling for liberty and democracy, the book became greatly popular, though it was attacked from the outset for its dubious interpretations. *The History of the United Netherlands* (4 vols., 1860–67) and *The Life and Death of John of Barneveld* (2 vols., 1874) were less successful. Motley also served as U.S. minister to Austria (1861–67) and to Britain (1869–70).

Muir \\'myu̇r\\, **John** (b. April 21, 1838, Dunbar, Scotland—d. Dec. 24, 1914, Los Angeles) Naturalist.

Muir immigrated with his family to Wisconsin in 1849. Though he attended the University of Wisconsin (1859–63), he refused to abide by its curriculum and took no degree. He subsequently made extensive journeys on foot through the Midwest and Canada. After an accident damaged his eye in 1867, he abandoned a promising career as an inventor and turned to nature.

His journals from a walking trip from Indianapolis to the Gulf of Mexico were later published as *A Thousand-Mile Walk to the Gulf* (1916). In 1868 he moved to California, where he spent several years studying its natural history, ranging as far afield as the Northwest and Alaska (where he discovered Glacier

Bay). Later trips would take him to South America, Africa, and Australia. From 1876 he insistently urged Congress to adopt a forest conservation policy. In the 1890s he wrote numerous articles for *Scribner's Monthly* and *Century* magazines that resulted in the establishment of Yosemite National Park and passage of a bill allowing the president to create forest preserves from the public domain. In 1892 he became the chief founder of the Sierra Club, which he served as president until 1914. He persuaded Pres. Theodore Roosevelt to greatly increase the amount of protected public land.

Muir's books, which were influential in mobilizing public support for his preservationist cause, include *The Mountains of California* (1894), *Our National Parks* (1901), *My First Summer in the Sierras* (1911), *The Yosemite* (1912), *Travels in Alaska* (1915), and *Steep Trails* (1918).

Mukherjee \\'mü-kər-jē\\, **Bharati** (b. July 27, 1940, Calcutta, India) Indian-American novelist and short-story writer.

Mukherjee attended the Universities of Calcutta and Baroda before immigrating to the United States in 1961, where she earned a doctorate at the University of Iowa Writers' Workshop. She moved to Canada with her Canadian husband, Clark Blaise, and taught at McGill University before returning to the United States in 1980.

Mukherjee's work is characterized by cultural clashes and undercurrents of violence. Her first novel, *The Tiger's Daughter* (1972), tells of a sheltered Indian woman jolted by immersion in American culture, then again shocked by her return to a violent Calcutta. *Wife* (1975) details the descent into madness of an Indian woman trapped in New York City by the fears and passivity engendered by her upbringing. The story collection *Darkness* (1985) includes the acclaimed "The World According to Hsü." *The Middleman and Other Stories* (1988) features third-world immigrants to America, who are also the subject of the later novels *Jasmine* (1989), *The Holder of the World* (1993), and *Leave It to Me* (1997). Mukherjee has also written nonfiction works, including two with her husband, *Days and Nights in Calcutta* (1977) and *The Sorrow and the Terror* (1987).

Mumford, Lewis (b. Oct. 19, 1895, Flushing, N.Y.—d. Jan. 26, 1990, Amenia, N.Y.) Architectural critic, urban planner, and historian.

After studies at several colleges in New York City, from which he never obtained a degree, Mumford became an associate editor of the *Dial* in 1919. From 1931 to 1963 he wrote influential architectural criticism and urban commentary for the *New Yorker*.

His early writings established him as an authority on American architecture, art, and urban life. His many books include *Sticks and Stones* (1924), *The Golden Day* (1926) and *The Brown Decades* (1931). In his "Renewal of Life" series—*Technics and Civilization* (1934), *The Culture of Cities* (1938), *The Con-*

dition of Man (1944), and *The Conduct of Life* (1951)—Mumford criticized the dehumanizing tendencies of modern technological society and urged that it be brought into harmony with humanistic goals and aspirations. *The City in History* (1961, National Book Award), a key work, provided a sweeping historical study of the city's role in human civilization. Mumford's late works include *The Myth of the Machine* (2 vols., 1967–70), a critical reassessment of technology's role in human development.

Murray, Albert L(ee) (b. May 12, 1916, Nokomis, Ala.) Essayist and critic whose writings assert the vitality and influence of black people in forming American traditions.

Murray attended Tuskegee Institute, where he began his long friendship with Ralph Ellison, and later New York University. He joined the air force in 1943 and retired as a major in 1962. His essay collection *The Omni-Americans* (1970) used historical fact, literature, and music to attack false perceptions of black American life. *South to a Very Old Place* (1971) recorded his visit to scenes of his segregated boyhood in the 1920s. In *Stomping the Blues* (1976), he maintained that blues and jazz musical styles developed as affirmative responses to misery. His novels include *Train Whistle Guitar* (1974), *The Spyglass Tree* (1991), and *Seven League Boots* (1995). He cowrote Count Basie's autobiography, *Good Morning Blues* (1985). The essay collection *Blue Devils of Nada* appeared in 1995. *Trading Twelves* (2000) contains his correspondence with Ellison.

Vladimir Nabokov

Nabokov \nə-'bȯ-kəf, 'nab-ə-kȯf\, **Vladimir (Vladimirovich)** (b. April 22, 1899, St. Petersburg, Russia—d. July 2, 1977, Montreux, Switzerland) Russian-American-Swiss novelist and critic.

Born into the Russian aristocracy, Nabokov had an English-speaking governess as a child. He began his career as a poet, publishing two collections of verse before the family fled Russia in 1919. He studied at Trinity College, Cambridge, and lived in Germany and France from 1922 until 1940. By 1925 he had settled on prose as his principal medium. His avowedly autobiographical first novel, *Mary* (1926), contains descriptions of his first serious romance as well as of the Nabokov family estate, both later described in his celebrated autobiography, SPEAK, MEMORY (1951). He did not again draw so heavily on personal experience until PNIN (1957), an episodic novel about an émigré professor partly based on his experiences teaching at Cornell (1948–59).

His second novel, KING, QUEEN, KNAVE (1928), marked a turn to the highly stylized form that would thereafter characterize his art. His novels' subject matter is principally the problem of art itself presented in various figurative disguises. Thus, *The Defense* (1930) is seemingly about chess, *Despair* (1936) about murder, and INVITATION TO A BEHEADING (1938) about politics, but each makes statements about art that are central to understanding the book as a whole. Beginning with THE GIFT (published serially, 1937–38), parody became another common feature of his novels.

He immigrated to the United States in 1940 and initially worked at Harvard University as an lepidopterist, a field in which he also achieved a considerable reputation. His first novels in English, *The Real Life of Sebastian Knight* (1941) and *Bend Sinister* (1947), do not rank with his best Russian work. The extraordinary LOLITA (1955) is another subtle allegory. Its subject matter caused it to be widely banned, but the controversy and the critical excitement the novel aroused made it an international best-seller, and as a result, Nabokov, now wealthy, was able to leave Cornell and move to Switzerland in 1959. The brilliant PALE FIRE (1962) extends and completes the mastery of unorthodox structure first displayed in *The Gift*. ADA (1969) parodies the family chronicle.

Nabokov's major critical works are an irreverent book about Gogol (1944) and a monumental translation of Pushkin's *Eugene Onegin* with commentary (4 vols., 1964). He also produced numerous short stories and novellas, mostly originally written in Russian.

Nasby \'naz-bē\, **Petroleum V(esuvius)** *pseudonym of* David Ross Locke (b. Sept. 20, 1833, Binghamton, N.Y.—d. Feb. 15, 1888, Toledo, Ohio) Humorist who influenced public issues during and after the Civil War.

From an early age Locke worked for newspapers in New York and Ohio. In 1861, as editor of the *Findlay* (Ohio) *Jeffersonian*, he published the first of many satirical letters under the name Petroleum V. Nasby. For more than 20 years he contributed "Nasby Letters" to the *Toledo Blade*, which under his editorship gained national circulation. Many of the letters appeared also in book form, including *The Nasby Papers* (1864) and *The Diary of an Office Seeker* (1881). An ardent Unionist and foe of slavery, Locke vigorously supported the Northern cause. His chief weapon was a heavy irony, with his character Nasby, a coarse and vicious Copperhead, illiterately arguing the Southern position.

Nash, (Frederic) Ogden (b. Aug. 19, 1902, Rye, N.Y.—d. May 19, 1971, Baltimore) Writer of humorous poetry who won a large following for his audacious verse.

　　After briefly attending Harvard University, Nash sold his first verse (1930) to the *New Yorker*, whose editorial staff he joined in 1932. With publication of his first collection, *Hard Lines* (1931), he began a 40-year career during which he produced 20 volumes of verse with such titles as *The Bad Parents' Garden of Verse* (1936), *I'm a Stranger Here Myself* (1938), and *Everyone but Thee and Me* (1962). He wrote the lyrics for Kurt Weill's musical *One Touch of Venus* (1943) and Vernon Duke's *Two's Company* (1952), as well as several children's books. His audacious, quotable rhymes are jarringly off or disconcertingly exact, and his ragged stanzas vary from lines of one word to others that meander the length of a paragraph, often interrupted by inapposite digressions. Nash claimed to have learned his prosody from the blunders of the poet Julia Moore, the "Sweet Singer of Michigan."

Nathan, George Jean (b. Feb. 14, 1882, Fort Wayne, Ind.—d. April 8, 1958, New York City) Author, editor, and drama critic.

　　Beginning in 1906, Nathan was at various times drama critic for numerous magazines and newspapers, but his name is particularly associated with the *Smart Set*, of which he was coeditor (1914–23) with H. L. Mencken, and with the influential *American Mercury*, which he and Mencken founded in 1924. With Eugene O'Neill and others, he cofounded the *American Spectator* in 1932. As a critic he championed the plays of Ibsen, Strindberg, Shaw, O'Neill, O'Casey, and Saroyan. He published more than 30 volumes of lively essays, and edited the annual *Theatre Book of the Year* (1943–51)

Naylor, Gloria (b. Jan. 25, 1950, New York City) Novelist known for her strong depictions of black women.

　　Naylor was the child of former sharecroppers. After working with the Jehovah's Witnesses, she attended Brooklyn College and Yale University. Her first novel, THE WOMEN OF BREWSTER PLACE (1982), won the National Book Award for its powerful dramatization of the struggles of seven women living in a blighted urban neighborhood. *Linden Hills* (1985) deals with the destructive materialism of upwardly mobile suburban blacks. *Mama Day* (1988) blends stories from Shakespeare's *The Tempest* with black folklore, and *Bailey's Cafe* (1992) centers on a Brooklyn diner that offers an oasis for the suffering. *The Men of Brewster Place* (1998) is a sequel to her first novel.

Gloria Naylor

Neal, John (b. Aug. 25, 1793, Portland, Me.—d. June 20, 1876, Portland, Me.) Journalist and writer.

Orphaned as an infant, Neal grew up in Portland but soon moved to Baltimore. After a business failure, he began writing articles for local newspapers. He also composed two narrative poems, a tragedy in verse, and a series of popular novels—*Keep Cool* (1817), *Logan* (1822), *Errata* (2 vols., 1823), *Seventy-Six* (1823), and *Randolph* (1823)—that made him, after J. F. Cooper, perhaps the best-known fiction writer in America and among the first to adopt a distinctly American style. In 1824 he moved to England, where he became the first American to write regularly for major British journals. In a long anonymous survey of American writers for *Blackwood's* magazine, he exalted himself and slighted Cooper. In 1827 he returned and settled in Portland, Me., where he continued writing stories and articles and several more popular novels, including *Rachel Dyer* (1828) and *The Down-Easters* (1833). His autobiography, *Wandering Recollections of a Somewhat Busy Life* (1869), displays his characteristically American style.

Neihardt \\'nī-ˌhärt\\, **John G(neisenau)** (b. Jan. 8, 1881, near Sharpsburg, Ill.—d. Nov. 3, 1973, Columbia, Mo.) Poet, novelist, and short-story writer whose works focus on the American Indians, especially the Sioux.

Neihardt wrote literary criticism for various newspapers, worked for the Bureau of Indian Affairs, and later taught at the University of Missouri (1948–66). His early contact with both whites and Indians in Kansas and Nebraska led him to write such works as *The Lonesome Trail* (1907), a collection of short stories about pioneering heroes and the Omahas. The lyric sequence *A Bundle of Myrrh* (1908) established his reputation as a lyric poet. He was instrumental in transcribing the oral autobiography of Black Elk in BLACK ELK SPEAKS (1932). He spent almost 30 years on his major work, *A Cycle of the West* (1949), a series of five book-length narrative poems that paint a vital picture of the frontier and those who battled to control it. The novel *When the Tree Flowered* (1951) was one of his last works.

Nemerov \\'nem-ər-ˌȯf\\, **Howard** (b. March 1, 1920, New York City—d. July 5, 1991, University City, Mo.) Poet, novelist, and critic whose poetry, marked by irony and self-deprecatory wit, is often about nature.

Brother of the photographer Diane Arbus, Nemerov graduated from Harvard and served as a pilot in World War II. After the war he taught at various colleges, including Bennington College and Washington University. His first book of verse, *The Image and the Law* (1947), was followed by many others, including *The Salt Garden* (1955), *Mirrors and Windows* (1958), *Blue Swallows* (1967), *Gnomes and Occasions* (1973), *Sentences* (1980), and *War Stories* (1987). His fiction includes *The Melodramatists* (1949); *The Homecoming Game* (1957), a tale of a professor who flunks his small college's football hero; and *A Commodity of Dreams and Other Stories* (1960). Among his considerable body of critical writing are *Journal of the Fictive Life* (1965), *Reflections on Poetry and Poetics* (1972), and *Figures of Thought* (1978). His *Collected Poems* (1977) received the Pulitzer Prize and the National Book Award. He served as consultant in poetry to the Library of Congress (1963–64) and later as poet laureate of the United States (1988–90).

Nevins \\'nev-inz\\, **Allan** (b. May 20, 1890, Camp Point, Ill.—d. March 5, 1971, Menlo Park, Calif.) Historian known for his huge history of the Civil War and biographies of American political and industrial figures.

Nevins was educated at the University of Illinois. His first book, *The Life of Robert Rogers* (1914), concerns a Colonial American soldier who fought on the Loyalist side. He joined the *New York Evening Post* as an editorial writer and for many years worked as a journalist, during which time he also compiled *American Social History as Recorded by British Travellers* (1923) and wrote two works on U.S. history.

In 1928 he accepted a post at Columbia University, where he would remain for 30 years. There he produced an immense and impressive body of work, including the Pulitzer Prize–winning biographies *Grover Cleveland* (1932) and *Hamilton Fish* (1936), as well as a biography of John Charles Frémont (2 vols., 1939). His most ambitious work was a vast history of the Civil War that comprised *Ordeal of the Union* (2 vols., 1947), *The Emergence of Lincoln* (2 vols., 1950), and *The War for Union* (4 vols., 1959–71). He also wrote notable works on John D. Rockefeller (1940) and Henry Ford (3 vols., 1954–63; with F. E. Hill) and the politician Herbert Lehman (1963). In 1948, seeking to preserve interviews with notable figures whose views of current affairs would interest future historians, he inaugurated at Columbia the country's first oral history program.

Niebuhr \\'nē-ˌbùr, 'nē-bər\\, **Reinhold** (b. June 21, 1892, Wright City, Mo.—d. June 1, 1971, Stockbridge, Mass.) Theologian.

Son of a clergyman, Niebuhr graduated from Yale Divinity School (M.A., 1915) and was ordained to the ministry of the Evangelical Synod of North America. From 1915 to 1928 he was pastor of Bethel Evangelical Church in Detroit. His years in that industrial city made him a critic of capitalism and an advocate of socialism. In 1928 he joined the faculty of New York's Union Theological Seminary, where he taught until his retirement in 1960.

His *Moral Man and Immoral Society* (1932), attacking the form of Christianity whose focus on a "gospel of love" rendered it inadequate to deal with such serious problems as political coercion, marked the beginning of the neo-orthodox movement in America. In the postwar years Niebuhr turned against doctrinaire leftism without abandoning his deep social concern. His later influential writings—including *The Nature and Destiny of Man* (2 vols., 1941–43), *Faith and History* (1949), *The Self and Dramas of History* (1955), *Beyond Tragedy* (1961), and *Man's Nature and His Communities* (1965)—criticize liberal Protestant thought and emphasized the persistence of evil in human nature and social institutions, emphasizing historicity as an element in human moral development.

Nin \\'nēn, 'nin\\, **Anaïs** *in full* Angela Anais Juana Antolina Rosa Edelmira Nin y Culmell (b. Feb. 21, 1903, Neuilly, France—d. Jan. 14, 1977, Los Angeles) French-American writer whose literary reputation rests on her published personal diaries.

The daughter of the Cuban composer Joaquín Nin, Nin launched her literary career with the study *D. H. Lawrence* (1932). In the early 1940s she moved to New York, where she printed and published her fiction at her own expense. Not until 1966, with publication of the first volume of her voluminous diaries, did she win recognition as a writer. The diaries' success provoked interest in her earlier *Cities of the Interior*, a five-volume roman-fleuve consisting of *Ladders to Fire* (1946), *Children of the Albatross* (1947), *The Four-Chambered Heart* (1950), *A Spy in the House of Love* (1954), and *Solar Barque* (1958). Her other fiction includes the story collection *Under a Glass Bell* (1944), the novels *House of Incest* (1936), *Seduction of the Minotaur* (1961), and *Collages* (1964), three novelettes collected in *Winter of Artifice* (1939), and the erotic works *Delta of Venus* (1977) and *Little Birds* (1979). The posthumously published *Incest* (1992) recounts a long incestuous relationship with her father.

Nin's literary contribution, which shows the influence of the Surrealist movement and her study of psychoanalysis, was a subject of controversy in her lifetime and afterward. Some critics have admired her lyrical style, psychological insight, and unique expression of femininity, while others have dismissed her work as self-indulgent and narcissistic.

Norris, (Benjamin) Frank(lin) (b. March 5, 1870, Chicago—d. Oct. 25, 1902, San Francisco) Novelist and short-story writer, the first important American author to embrace naturalism.

Norris's family moved to San Francisco when he was 14. After doing adventurous work as an overseas and domestic correspondent, he published the novel *Moran of the Lady Letty* (1898). His first important novel, MCTEAGUE (1899), tells of a dentist who murders his miserly wife and meets his own end fleeing through Death Valley. *A Man's Woman* appeared in 1900. Influenced by the works of Émile Zola, he produced his masterpiece, THE OCTOPUS (1901), the first novel of the projected trilogy *The Epic of the Wheat*, which depicts the struggle of California wheat growers against a monopolistic railway corporation. Its second novel, *The Pit* (1903), deals with wheat speculation on the Chicago Board of Trade. Its intended final volume, *The Wolf*, was unwritten when Norris died at 32 of a botched appendix operation. The novel *Vandover and the Brute*, published posthumously in 1914, is a study of moral degeneration. Despite their romanticizing tendencies, Norris's novels present a vividly authentic and highly readable picture of life in California at the turn of the century. His collected writings were published in 10 volumes in 1928.

Norton, Andre (*originally* Alice Mary) (b. Feb. 17, 1912, Cleveland, Ohio) Prolific best-selling author of science-fiction and fantasy adventure novels for juveniles and adults.

Norton's 18 years as a children's librarian in the Cleveland Public Library enabled her to become familiar with children's literature. She legally changed her name to Andre Norton in 1934, when her historical fantasy *The Prince Commands* was published. While working for the science-fiction publisher Gnome Press in the 1950s, she wrote her first novel in the genre, *Star Man's Son, 2250 A.D.* (1952). Norton's fast-moving science fiction and fantasy tales usually feature adolescents undergoing rites of passage—tests of physical, emotional, and moral strength. Her detailed and colorful depictions of future earth, distant planets, and fantasy lands draw on her wide readings in history, biology, travel, archaeology, anthropology, mythology, folklore, and magic. Among her more than 100 books, the most noted include a series of some 35 works, beginning with *Witch World* (1963), set on a matriarchal planet. In 1983 she became the first woman named a Grand Master by the Science Fiction and Fantasy Writers of America.

Norton, Charles Eliot (b. Nov. 16, 1827, Cambridge, Mass.—d. Oct. 21, 1908, Cambridge) Scholar, man of letters, idealist, and reformer.

After graduating from Harvard, Norton ran his own importing firm, opened a night school in Cambridge, directed a housing experiment in Boston, and worked zealously as an editor for the Union cause. He coedited the *North American Review* with J. R. Lowell (1864–68) and was one of the founders of the *Nation* (1865). His course in the history of art at Harvard (1873–97) was the first in the United States, and he wrote major works on art and architecture. A friend of many literary figures, including Thomas Carlyle, R. W. Emerson, John Ruskin, and H. W. Longfellow, he produced valuable editions of their letters and other biographical material. He also edited collections of poetry, notably that of John Donne (1805, 1905) and Anne Bradstreet (1897). His best literary work was probably his prose translation of Dante's *Divine Comedy* (1891–92). His letters were published in 1913.

Nugent, Richard Bruce (b. July 2, 1906, Washington, D.C.—d. May 27, 1987, Hoboken, N.J.) Writer, artist, and actor associated with the Harlem Renaissance.

Nugent's introduction to Langston Hughes in 1925 signaled the beginning of his lifelong fascination with the arts and his literary and political contribution to the Harlem Renaissance. He explored issues of sexuality and black identity in his poems, short stories, and erotic drawings. "Shadows," his first published poem, was included in Countee Cullen's anthology *Caroling Dusk* (1927). His one-act musical *Sadhji*, published in *Plays of Negro Life* (1927), is an African morality tale about a chieftain's beautiful wife beloved by her stepson, who in turn is loved by a male friend. In 1926 Nugent (writing as Richard Bruce) contributed the story "Smoke, Lilies, and Jade," about a 19-year-old artist's sexual encounter with another man, to the only issue of *Fire!!*

Nye, Bill *pseudonym of* Edgar Wilson Nye (b. Aug. 25, 1850, Shirley, Maine—d. Feb. 22, 1896, Arden, N.C.) Journalist and one of the major American humorists in the later 19th century.

Settling in Laramie, Wyo., in 1876, Nye contributed to the *Denver Tribune* and *Cheyenne Sun*. His humorous squibs and tales in the *Laramie Boomerang*, which he helped found in 1881, were widely read and reprinted. Collected, they form the substance of numerous published volumes, from *Bill Nye and Boomerang* (1881) to *Bill Nye's History of the U.S.* (1894). He later returned to Wisconsin, where he had grown up, and for several years wrote for the *New York World*. In 1886 he lectured with the poet James Whitcomb Riley, the combination of Nye's wit and Riley's sentiment proving extremely popular.

Oates, Joyce Carol (b. June 16, 1938, Lockport, N.Y.) Prolific prose writer noted for her depictions of violence and evil.

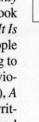

Oates graduated from Syracuse University and received her doctorate from the University of Wisconsin. Her first collection of short stories, *By the North Gate* (1963), was soon followed by her first novel, *With Shuddering Fall* (1964). She wrote prolifically thereafter, averaging about two books (chiefly short stories and novels) per year. Her best-known novels include *A Garden of Earthly Delights* (1967), *Expensive People* (1968), and THEM (1969, National Book Award), which form a trilogy; *Do with Me What You Will* (1973); and *Because It Is Bitter and Because It Is My Heart* (1990). Oates has typically portrayed people whose intensely experienced lives end in bloodshed and self-destruction owing to larger forces beyond their control, and who often are the victims of random violence. Also significant is a parodic gothic series that includes *Bellefleur* (1980), *A Bloodsmoor Romance* (1982), and *Mysteries of Winterthurn* (1984). She has written under the pseudonym Rosamond Smith. In addition to over 40 novels and novellas and over 25 story collections, she has published plays, poems, essays, and literary criticism. She has taught at the University of Detroit (1961–67), the University of Windsor (1967–78), and Princeton University (from 1978).

O'Brien, Fitz-James (b. c.1828, County Limerick, Ireland—d. April 6, 1862, Cumberland, Md.) Irish-American journalist, playwright, and author whose psychologically penetrating tales of pseudoscience and the uncanny made him a forerunner of modern science fiction.

O'Brien initially worked as a journalist in London. In 1852 he moved to New York City and soon became an important figure in that city's bohemia. But his work, though published in the leading periodicals of the day, won him neither the reputation he thought he merited nor the financial security he desired. He died from wounds received as a Union soldier in the Civil War.

His best-known stories include "The Diamond Lens" (1858), about a man who falls in love with a being he sees through a microscope in a drop of water, which appeared in the first issue of the *Atlantic Monthly*; "What Was It?" (1859), in which a man is attacked by a thing he apprehends with every sense but sight; and "The Wondersmith" (1859), in which robots are fashioned only to turn upon their creators.

O'Brien, (William) Tim(othy) (b. Oct. 1, 1946, Austin, Minn.) Novelist noted for his writings about American soldiers in the Vietnam War.

O'Brien fought in Vietnam, rising to the rank of sergeant. He subsequently did graduate work at Harvard and briefly worked as a reporter for the *Washington Post*. He collected his newspaper and magazine articles about his war experiences in *If I Die in a Combat Zone, Box Me Up and Ship Me Home* (1973). By turns meditative and brutally realistic, it was praised for its honest portrayal of a soldier's emotions.

The Vietnam War is present in all of O'Brien's novels. One of the two protagonists in *Northern Lights* (1975) is a wounded war hero. A soldier abandons his platoon in Vietnam to try to walk to Paris in the harsh, surreal, and lyrical *Going after Cacciato* (1978, National Book Award). A man's lifelong fear of dying from a nuclear bombing is the subject of *The Nuclear Age* (1981), while *The Things They Carried* (1990) returns to the theme of Vietnam. *In the Lake of the Woods* (1994) concerns the long-lingering psychological aftereffects of the war. In *Tomcat in Love* (1998) O'Brien's tone finally shifts to comedy.

Occom \'ä-kəm\, **Samson** (b. 1723, New London, Conn.—d. July 14, 1792, Oneida community, N.Y.) Mohegan Indian preacher and writer.

Occom was converted to Christianity in 1741 and studied theology under Rev. Eleazar Wheelock (1743–47). He subsequently become a teacher to the Montauk tribe. Ordained in 1759, he became a Presbyterian missionary to the Montauks.

As a recruiter of Indian students for Wheelock's charity school, he was sent to England in 1765–67 and made numerous successful fund-raising appearances. On his return he became estranged from Wheelock, who decided to expand his school into a college for white missionaries; it was chartered in 1769 as Dartmouth College. In his later years Occom worked as minister and teacher to the Stockbridge Oneida community.

In 1772 he published *A Sermon, Preached at the Execution of Moses Paul, an Indian*, the first text written by an Indian in English. In 1774 he published *A Choice Collection of Hymns and Spiritual Songs*; for writing several of the hymns, he is regarded as the earliest Presbyterian hymn-writer in America.

O'Connor, Edwin (Greene) (b. July 29, 1918, Providence, R.I.—d. March 23, 1968, Boston) Novelist.

After graduating from the University of Notre Dame, O'Connor worked as a radio announcer, then served in the coast guard (1942–45). He settled in Boston and began to write full time. He wrote several short stories for the *Atlantic Monthly*, and his first novel, *The Oracle*, appeared in 1951. While working on his second novel, he helped the comedian Fred Allen edit his radio scripts into a book.

In 1956 he published *The Last Hurrah*, a novel about big-city politics based on the career of Boston's James Michael Curley; a best-seller, it was made into a successful movie by John Ford (1958). *The Edge of Sadness* (1961, Pulitzer Prize) again mines Boston Irish culture with its story of a demoralized middle-aged priest and an elderly patriarch. O'Connor's last novels are *I Was Dancing* (1964) and *All in the Family* (1966).

O'Connor, (Mary) Flannery (b. March 25, 1925, Savannah, Ga.—d. Aug. 3, 1964, Milledgeville, Ga.) Novelist and short-story writer whose symbol-laden works, usually set in the rural South, are centrally concerned with the individual's relationship to God.

O'Connor graduated from Georgia State College for Women and did graduate work at the University of Iowa. Her first published short story appeared in *Accent* in 1946. Her first novel, WISE BLOOD (1952), combines the keen ear for common speech, caustic religious imagination, and flair for the grotesque that were to characterize her subsequent work. With the publication of further short stories, first collected in A GOOD MAN IS HARD TO FIND (1955), she came to be regarded as a master of the form. Her other works of fiction are a novel, *The Violent Bear It Away* (1960), and the story collection EVERYTHING THAT RISES MUST CONVERGE (1965). Long crippled by lupus erythematosus, which would cause her death at 39, O'Connor lived modestly, writing and raising peafowl on her mother's ancestral farm. A collection of occasional prose pieces, *Mystery and Manners*, appeared posthumously in 1969. Her *Complete Stories* (1971) won the National Book Award. Her letters, which provide valuable insight into the role of Roman Catholicism in her life and art, were published as *The Habit of Being* (1979).

Odets \ō-'dets**, Clifford** (b. July 18, 1906, Philadelphia—d. Aug. 14, 1963, Hollywood, Calif.) Leading dramatist of the theater of social protest in the United States during the 1930s.

Clifford Odets

Odets acted for repertory companies from 1923 to 1928, and joined the Group Theatre in 1931. His first play, WAITING FOR LEFTY (1935), used both the auditorium and the stage for action and was an effective plea for labor unionism, and helped establish his and the company's reputation. *Awake and Sing!* (1935) was a naturalistic family drama, and GOLDEN BOY (1937; film, 1939) was about an Italian-American prizefighter. *Paradise Lost* (1935) deals with the tragic life of a middle-class family.

In 1936 Odets moved to Hollywood to write screenplays, including *Sweet Smell of Success* (1961), and he directed several successful films, including *None but the Lonely Heart* (1944). His many later plays include *Clash by Night* (1941; film, 1952), *The Big Knife* (1949; film, 1955), *The Country Girl* (1950; film, 1954), and *The Flowering Peach* (1954), but many thought he failed to fulfill the enormous promise of his early years.

O'Hara, Frank (*originally* Francis Russell) (b. June 27, 1926, Baltimore—d. July 25, 1966, Fire Island, N.Y.) Poet who gathered images from an urban environment to represent personal experience.

O'Hara studied piano at the New England Conservatory, served in World War II, and later attended Harvard and the University of Michigan. During the 1960s, as an assistant curator at the Museum of Modern Art, O'Hara wrote catalogs for the exhibits he curated and sent his perceptive criticism of new art to such periodicals as *Art News*. Meanwhile, local theaters were producing many of his experimental one-act plays, including *Try! Try!* (1960), about a soldier's return to his wife and her new lover.

He nevertheless considered himself primarily a poet. His music- and art-influenced poems, which mark him as a member of the New York school of poets (with his friends John Ashbery, Kenneth Koch, and James Schuyler), are often random-seeming but lyrical mixtures of quotations, gossip, phone numbers, commercials—any mote of experience he found appealing. Beginning with *A City Winter* (1952), he published seven collections in his lifetime. His *Collected Poems* (1971) appeared after he was run over by a vehicle on the beach.

John O'Hara

O'Hara, John (Henry) (b. Jan. 31, 1905, Pottsville, Pa.—d. April 11, 1970, Princeton, N.J.) Novelist and short-story writer whose sparingly styled fiction stands as a social history of upwardly mobile Americans from the 1920s through the 1940s.

Born into a well-to-do family, O'Hara attended several boarding schools. In 1928 his stories—many of them set in the typical small town of Gibbsville, the fictional equivalent of O'Hara's hometown of Pottsville—began to appear in the *New Yorker*, with which he would enjoy a long association. His highly acclaimed first novel, *Appointment in Samarra* (1934), explored the disintegration and death of an upper-class inhabitant of a small city. The popular *Butterfield 8* (1935; film, 1960), about a call girl, cemented his reputation. *Ten North Frederick* (1955; film, 1958) received a National Book Award. Some of O'Hara's other best-selling novels were likewise adapted for stage and screen, including *A Rage to Live* (1949; film, 1965) and *From the Terrace* (1958; film, 1960). *Pal Joey* (1940) became a hit Rodgers and Hart musical. His short stories were collected in such volumes as *Waiting for Winter* (1966) and *And Other Stories* (1968). O'Hara was fascinated by the effects of class, money, and sexuality on Americans, and his fictional representations of Hollywood and Broadway are thick with the snobbery of social structure, while the influence of his experience as a critic and reporter in New York is seen in his objective and nonexperimental style.

Olds, Sharon (b. Nov. 19, 1942, San Francisco) Poet best known for her powerful, often erotic, imagery of the body and the family.

Olds studied at Stanford and Columbia universities, and has since taught poetry at numerous colleges, principally NYU. Her first collection, *Satan Says* (1980), described her early sexual life in frank language, making clear her disdain for poetic politesse. *The Dead and the Living* (1984, National Book Critics Circle Award) refined her poetic voice. Her poems honoring the dead encompassed family members and victims of political violence; those addressed to the living continued her exploration of the life of the body, a theme she further developed in *The Gold Cell* (1987) and *The Matter of This World* (1987). *The Father* (1992) concerned her father's death from cancer; *The Wellspring* (1996) and *Blood, Tin, Straw* (1999), continued her intimate exposition—free of bitterness and self-pity—of her own life.

Oliver, Mary (b. Sept. 10, 1935, Cleveland, Ohio) Poet whose work has reflected a deep communion with the natural world.

Oliver worked for a time as secretary to Edna St. Vincent Millay's sister, and Millay's influence is apparent in her first book of poetry, *No Voyage* (1963). Some of these lyrical nature poems are set in the Ohio of Oliver's youth. Her childhood plays a more central role in *The River Styx, Ohio* (1972), in which she attempted to recreate the past through memory and myth. *The Night Traveler* (1978) explores the themes of birth, decay, and death through the conceit of a classical journey into the underworld. *American Primitive* (1983, Pulitzer Prize) glorifies the natural world, reflecting the American fascination with the ideal of the pastoral life. In *House of Light* (1990) Oliver explores the rewards of solitude in nature. *New and Selected Poems* (1992) won the National Book Award. *A Poetry Handbook* (1994) and *Rules for the Dance* (1998) discuss the craft of poetry; *Blue Pastures* (1995) is a collection of prose pieces.

Olmsted \'ōm-ˌsted, 'äm-, -stəd\, **Frederick Law** (b. April 26, 1822, Hartford, Conn.—d. Aug. 28, 1903, Brookline, Mass.) Landscape architect and writer.

Olmsted's restricted eyesight limited his education, but he worked briefly as an apprentice to a topographic engineer. After his eyesight improved, he attended lectures in science and engineering at Yale University. From 1844 he studied scientific farming, and in 1847 he began his own farm and nursery business. During an extensive holiday in Europe, he became greatly impressed with English landscaping, and he wrote about his observations in the popular *Walks and Talks of an American Farmer in England* (1852). In the 1850s he traveled through the South and provided unbiased reports of the slaveholding states in three books, later compiled in the well-received *Journey and Explorations in the Cotton Kingdom* (1861). In 1865 he and E. L. Godkin founded the *Nation*, a reformist journal of politics and the arts that would eventually become the country's longest-lived weekly.

In 1857 Olmsted was appointed superintendent of New York's newly planned Central Park; with the architect Calvert Vaux, he won a competition to design the park. He went on to design such other parks as Prospect Park in Brooklyn, South Park in Chicago, the Boston park system, and such grounds as Stanford University, the Capitol at Washington, D.C., Niagara Falls, the 1893 World's Columbian Exposition in Chicago, and Biltmore, the Vanderbilt estate at Asheville, N.C. He was considered the outstanding landscape architect of his time, and his works remain unequaled.

Olsen, Tillie *originally* Tillie Lerner (b. Jan. 14, 1913, Omaha, Neb.) Author known for her powerful fiction about the inner lives of the working poor, women, and minorities.

Olsen's early adulthood was devoted to political activism and to rearing a family. Her first novel, begun at 19, was set aside for 35 years. Though she found it too painful to finish, she eventually published the reconstructed manuscript as *Yonnondio: From the Thirties* (1974). It tells of the Holbrook family, who struggle during the Depression era to survive as coal miners, tenant farmers, and meat packers. She is principally known for *Tell Me A Riddle* (1961), a collection of three short stories and a novella, each a small masterpiece, in which she uses rhythmic, metaphoric language to give a voice to otherwise inarticulate characters. In her later works she addressed feminist themes and concerns, especially as related to women writers. The essay collection *Silences* (1978) contains a long piece on Rebecca Harding Davis, whose writing career failed after she married.

Olson, Charles (John) (b. Dec. 27, 1910, Worcester, Mass.—d. Jan. 10, 1970, New York City) Avant-garde poet and literary theorist, notable for his influence on American poetry in the late 1950s.

After obtaining degrees from Wesleyan and Harvard universities, Olson taught at Clark University, Harvard, and Radcliffe College, but his real influence began in the late 1940s as an instructor and then as rector (1951–56) at the experimental Black Mountain College in North Carolina. He first gained recognition for *Call Me Ishmael* (1947), a study of the literary influences on Melville's *Moby-Dick*. His concepts of poetry, contained in his 1950 essay *Projective Verse*, influenced such poets as Robert Creeley, Robert Duncan, and Denise Levertov. His *Maximus Poems* (1953, 1956) contains a long poetic sequence that was continued in subsequent volumes, while *In Cold Hell, in Thicket* (1953) and *The Distances* (1960) contain some of his best-known shorter poems.

Olson, Elder (James) (b. March 9, 1909, Chicago—d. July 25, 1992, Albuquerque, N.M.) Poet, playwright, and Neo-Aristotelian critic.

After graduating from the University of Chicago, Olson taught there from 1942 until 1977. With his teachers and colleagues, he became known for his responses to the New Criticism. In *Critics and Criticism,* the Neo-Aristotelian manifesto edited by his colleague R. S. Crane (1952), and in such later works as *Tragedy and the Theory of Drama* (1961) and *The Theory of Comedy* (1968), he argued for a systematic, comprehensive, and pluralistic approach to criticism based on Aristotle's *Poetics*, attacking the New Critics for focusing on poetic diction and arguing that criticism should concentrate on poetic wholes. His own poetry embodies rich imagery, a serious and elegiac tone, sharp wit, and metaphysical themes in such collections as *Thing of Sorrow* (1934), *The Scarecrow Christ* (1954), *Olson's Penny Arcade* (1975), and *Last Poems* (1984).

O'Neill, Eugene (Gladstone) (b. Oct. 16, 1888, New York City—d. Nov. 27, 1953, Boston) One of the greatest American playwrights.

The son of a popular actor, O'Neill attended Princeton University for a year, after which he shipped to sea, lived a derelict's existence on the waterfronts of Buenos Aires, Liverpool, and New York, submerged himself in alcohol, and attempted suicide. He began to write plays in 1912 while recovering from tuberculosis at a sanitarium in Connecticut.

His one-act sea drama *Bound East for Cardiff* (1916) was produced by the experimental Provincetown Players, which would also stage his other early plays. His first full-length play, *Beyond the Horizon*, was produced on Broadway in 1920 and won the Pulitzer Prize. O'Neill's capacity for work would thenceforth prove staggering: between 1920 and 1943 he would complete 20 long plays and a number of shorter ones. His most distinguished short plays include the early sea dramas *In the Zone*, *The Long Voyage Home*, and *The Moon of the Caribbees*, written between 1913 and 1917 but not produced until 1924 (with *Bound East for Cardiff*) under the overall title *S.S. Glencairn*; THE EMPEROR JONES (1921; film, 1933); and THE HAIRY APE (1923; film, 1944).

Eugene O'Neill

Among his most celebrated long plays are ANNA CHRISTIE (1922, Pulitzer Prize; film, 1930); DESIRE UNDER THE ELMS (1925; film, 1958) and MOURNING BECOMES ELECTRA (1931), both of which evoked the starkness and inevitability of Greek tragedy that he felt in his own life; and THE GREAT GOD BROWN (1926) and STRANGE INTERLUDE (1928, Pulitzer Prize), in which he used such experimental stage techniques as expressionistic dialogue and spoken asides, which have since become common. Following a long succession of tragic visions, including *Mourning Becomes Electra* (1931; film, 1947), his only comedy, the lighthearted and nostalgic AH, WILDERNESS! appeared on Broadway (1933; film, 1935). THE ICEMAN COMETH (1946), the most complex and perhaps the finest of his tragedies, appeared in 1946.

O'Neill's plays were written from an intensely personal point of view, deriving directly from the scarring effects of his tragic relationships with his family—his mother and father, who loved and tormented each other; his older brother, who both loved and corrupted him and died of alcoholism in middle age; and O'Neill himself, caught and torn between love for and rage at all three. Even in his last writings, his youth continued to absorb his attention. The posthumous production of LONG DAY'S JOURNEY INTO NIGHT (1956, Pulitzer Prize; film, 1962) brought to light an agonizingly autobiographical play, one of his greatest. Its sequel, the admired A MOON FOR THE MISBEGOTTEN (1952), was produced the following year.

In 1936 O'Neill became the second American to be awarded the Nobel Prize for Literature.

Oppen \\'äp-ən, 'ȯp-ən\\, **George** (b. April 24, 1908, New Rochelle, N.Y.—d. July 7, 1984, Sunnyvale, Calif.) Poet and political activist, one of the chief proponents of objectivism.

Oppen grew up in San Francisco and briefly attended Oregon State University. From 1930 to 1933 he and his wife ran the To Publishers press, which published *An "Objectivist" Anthology* (1932); edited by Louis Zukofsky and containing work by Ezra Pound, T. S. Eliot, and William Carlos Williams, it proved a seminal work in the history of American poetry.

Oppen's own first book of poems, *Discrete Series*, was published in 1934. His spare, precise style earned him a reputation as one of the foremost objectivist poets, who celebrated simplicity over formal structure and rhyme and emphasized the poem as an object in itself, not as a vehicle of meaning or association. He became active in the Communist Party in the mid-1930s; in 1950 he fled to Mexico City to avoid persecution, but he returned in 1958 and began writing poetry again. *The Materials* (1962) was his first book of poetry in 28 years. Most critics agree that his best work is *Of Being Numerous* (1968, Pulitzer Prize). His *Collected Poems* was published in 1975, and *Primitive*, his last collection, in 1978.

Owen, Robert Dale (b. Nov. 9, 1801, Glasgow, Scotland—d. June 24, 1877, Lake George, N.Y.) Social reformer.

In 1825 Owen emigrated with his father, the reformer Robert Owen, to establish a self-sufficient socialist community at New Harmony, Ind. He edited the *New Harmony Gazette* until 1827, when he met the radical reformer Frances Wright. The two moved to New York City, where Owen edited the *Free Enquirer*, a newspaper at the center of radical free thought. In 1832 he returned to New Harmony. While serving in the Indiana legislature (1836–38) he secured funds for public education, and in the U.S. House of Representatives (1843–47) he introduced the bill establishing the Smithsonian Institution.

He was appointed U.S. chargé d'affaires at Naples in 1853 and minister to Italy in 1855. On his return in 1858, he became an outspoken proponent of emancipation; a letter he wrote on the subject to Abraham Lincoln in 1862 is said to have greatly influenced the president. In 1863 Owen headed a committee to investigate the condition of the freedmen and wrote a book on his findings, *The Wrong of Slavery* (1864). He spent his final years writing a novel, *Beyond the Breakers* (1870), and his autobiography, *Threading My Way* (1874).

Ozick \\'ō-zik\\, **Cynthia** (b. April 17, 1928, New York City) Novelist, short-story writer, and essayist whose works seek to define the challenge of remaining Jewish in contemporary American life.

The child of Russian-Jewish immigrants who ran a pharmacy in the Bronx, Ozick was educated at NYU and Ohio State University. Her first novel, *Trust* (1966), is the story of a woman's rejection of her wealthy Jewish family and search for her renegade father in Europe. In subsequent books such as *Bloodshed and Three Novellas* (1976), she struggled with the idea that the creation of art (a pagan activity) is in direct opposition to principles of Judaism, which forbids the creation of idols. The psychological aftermath of the Holocaust became a major theme of her work, especially in *Levitation: Five Fictions* (1982) and the novel *The Cannibal Galaxy* (1983). Ozick has often drawn on traditional Jewish mysticism, yet her later works have turned away from the theme of the sacred and the profane. Her novel *The Messiah of Stockholm* (1987) is in part a meditation on the nature of writing. The two moving Holocaust-related stories that make up *The Shawl* (1989) won O. Henry first prizes. *The Puttermesser Papers* (1997) contains outlandish tales from the life of a middle-aged civil-service lawyer in New York City. Ozick's essay collections include *Art and Ardor* (1987), *Metaphor and Memory* (1989), and *Fame and Folly* (1996).

Page, Thomas Nelson (b. April 23, 1853, near Beaver Dam, Va.—d. Nov. 1, 1922, Oakland, Calif.) Author whose work fostered romantic legends of Southern plantation life.

Page attended Washington College and the University of Virginia and practiced law until 1893, when he devoted himself exclusively to writing and lecturing, except for a period as ambassador to Italy (1913–19). He first won notice with the story "Marse Chan," about a loyal old black servant, in the *Century* magazine. This and similar stories, most of which hark back nostalgically to the antebellum era, were collected in *In Ole Virginia, Marse Chan, and Other Stories* (1887). Among his essays and social studies are *Social Life in Old Virginia* (1897) and *The Old Dominion—Her Making and Her Manners* (1908). His other works include the children's tale *Two Little Confederates* (1888), *The Burial of the Guns* (1894), *The Old Gentlemen of the Black Stock* (1897), and *Red Rock* (1898).

Paine, Thomas (b. Jan. 29, 1737, Thetford, England—d. June 8, 1809, New York City) Writer and political pamphleteer.

After an early life of failed prospects in England, Paine arrived in Philadelphia in 1774, where he helped edit the *Pennsylvania Magazine*. He also published numerous articles anonymously.

Thomas Paine

In January 1776 he wrote his famous *Common Sense,* a 50-page pamphlet eloquently advocating independence. Over 500,000 copies were quickly sold, and Paine's fiery eloquence greatly strengthened the colonists' resolve.

During the American Revolution, while serving as an aide to Gen. Nathanael Greene, he began writing his 16 *Crisis* papers (1776–83), signed "Common Sense." The first paper, beginning "These are the times that try men's souls," was ordered by Gen. George Washington to be read to the dispirited troops at Valley Forge and reignited their will to fight.

In 1787 Paine returned to England, where he became involved in the debate over the French Revolution. *The Rights of Man* (1791–92), written in defense of republicanism, was seen as an attack on the monarchy and he was indicted for treason. He escaped to France, where he was made an honorary French citizen, but his criticism of the Reign of Terror sent him to prison. Released in 1794, he wrote *The Age of Reason* (1794, 1796), which attacked organized religion and supported deism.

In 1802 Paine returned to the United States. Criticized for his deist writings and little remembered for his service to the Revolution, he died in poverty.

Palés Matos \pä-ˈlāz-ˈmä-tōs\, **Luis** (b. March 20, 1898, Guayama, Puerto Rico—d. Feb. 23, 1959, San Juan, Puerto Rico) Writer often considered Puerto Rico's most distinguished lyric poet.

Palés Matos wrote his first poetry, which was collected in *Azaleas* (1915), in imitation of modernist trends, but he soon found his own direction in his personal interpretation (as a white man) of black culture. His poems on black themes gave impetus to the developing concern of Latin Americans with their African heritage, and enriched the vocabulary of Spanish verse with words, themes, symbols, images, and rhythms from African folklore and dance. Though he was best known and most influential for his "Negro" poetry, Palés Matos's reflective and introspective personality found expression in poetry of many other moods and themes. *Poesía, 1915–56* (1957), a collection of much of his poetry, reveals his more personal side as a lyric poet.

Paley, Grace *originally* Grace Goodside (b. Dec. 11, 1922, New York City) Poet and short-story writer known for her seriocomic portrayals of working-class New Yorkers and her political activism.

Born in the Jewish Bronx, whose accents would be vividly reproduced in her fiction, Paley attended Hunter College and the New School for Social Research and joined the faculty of Sarah Lawrence College in 1966. During the 1960s she was actively involved in the opposition to the Vietnam War, and she continued her political activism after the war ended.

Her first volume of short stories, *The Little Disturbances of Man* (1959), was praised for its realistic dialogue. It was followed by the equally admired *Enormous Changes at the Last Minute* (1974) and *Later the Same Day* (1985), both of which continued her compassionate, often comic, exploration of ordinary individuals struggling against loneliness. Many of the stories feature the character of Faith, Paley's alter ego. She has also published several volumes of poems, including *Leaning Forward* (1985) and *Begin Again* (1992).

Paretsky \pǝ-'ret-skē\, **Sara** (b. June 8, 1947, Ames, Iowa) Mystery writer who helped break the gender barrier in detective fiction with her popular novels featuring V. I. Warshawski.

After earning a doctorate at the University of Chicago, Paretsky worked for an insurance company until she began to write full-time in 1985. Her wisecracking, independent, passionate, compassionate, Polish-Italian-Jewish Chicago female private detective was created in *Indemnity Only* (1982), in which V. I. uncovers an insurance scam involving shady insurance agents, a union leader, and a gangster. In other V. I. Warshawski novels, V. I. becomes the target of violence and learns of conspiracies involving big business, organized crime, and even the Roman Catholic church. Paretsky has dealt with social issues including abortion rights, the treatment of the homeless and the elderly, and corporate polluters in such novels as *Deadlock* (1984), *Killing Orders* (1985), *Bitter Medicine* (1987), *Burn Marks* (1990), *Guardian Angel* (1992), *Tunnel Vision* (1994), and *Hard Time* (1999). Many consider *Blood Shot* (1988) her best novel. In the 1980s she helped found Sisters in Crime to promote the work of women mystery writers and to challenge the publication of crime stories marked by gratuitous violence against women.

Parker, Dorothy *originally* Dorothy Rothschild (b. Aug. 22, 1893, West End, N.J.—d. June 7, 1967, New York City) Short-story writer and poet remembered for her witty remarks.

Born to a wealthy family and partly educated in a convent, Parker was drama critic for *Vanity Fair* from 1917 to 1920. In 1919, she and two other writers for the magazine—Robert Benchley and Robert Sherwood—formed the nucleus of the informal luncheon club known as the Algonquin Round Table, where her rapier wit became celebrated. From 1927 until 1933 she contributed a personal kind of book review to the *New Yorker* as "Constant Reader"; some were collected in *A Month of Saturdays* (1971). In 1929 her story "Big Blonde" won the O. Henry award for short fiction. Three books of her light, witty, and sometimes cynical verse, including the best-selling *Enough Rope* (1926), were collected in *Collected Poems: Not So Deep as a Well* (1936). *Laments for the Living* (1930) and *After Such Pleasures* (1933) were collections of her deft and bittersweet short stories, combined and augmented in 1939 as *Here Lies*. She also reported on the Spanish Civil War and collaborated on several plays and on such screenplays as *A Star Is Born* (1937, Academy Award) and *Saboteur* (1942) until her leftish sympathies made her a liability in postwar Hollywood.

Parkman, Francis (b. Sept. 16, 1823, Boston—d. Nov. 8, 1893, Jamaica Plain, Mass.) Historian.

Parkman graduated from Harvard University, and after earning a law degree in 1846 he set out on a journey into the Great Plains and along the Oregon Trail, where he recorded the sights and sounds of the largely unexplored territory. He published his observations in a series of magazine articles, which were compiled in his best-selling book *The California and Oregon Trail* (1849; later called *The Oregon Trail*).

He then began his massive work of history, the seven-part *France and England in North America*, which covered the colonial period from its beginnings to 1763. The first volume appeared in 1851. Poor health interrupted his research until 1865; in the interim period he developed his interest in horticulture and published his *Book of Roses* (1866).

Once able to resume work on his magnum opus, he published six more volumes—including *Pioneers of France in the New World* (1865), *Montcalm and Wolfe* (1884), and *A Half-Century of Conflict* (1892)—between 1865 and 1892. The work is noted for its character portrayal and literary artistry, and Parkman's extensive and critical use of documentation represent a major contribution to historiography.

Parks, Gordon (b. Nov. 30, 1912, Fort Scott, Kan.) Author, photographer, and film director who documented black American life.

A high-school dropout, Parks worked odd jobs before becoming a photojournalist in the late 1930s. His first books were *Flash Photography* (1947) and *Camera Portraits* (1948). As a staff photographer for *Life* magazine (1948–72), he became known for his portrayals of ghetto life, black nationalists, and the civil-rights movement. A photo essay about a child from a Brazilian slum was expanded into a television documentary (1962) and a book with poetry (1978), both titled *Flavio*. His first work of fiction was *The Learning Tree* (1963). His forthright autobiographies, *A Choice of Weapons* (1966), *To Smile in Autumn* (1979), and *Voices in the Mirror* (1990), won critical admiration. He combined poetry and photography in *A Poet and His Camera* (1968), *Whispers of Intimate Things* (1971), *In Love* (1971), and *Moments Without Proper Names* (1975). His other books include the essay collection *Born Black* (1971), the novel *Shannon* (1981), and *Arias in Silence* (1994). He also directed such films as *The Learning Tree* (1969) and *Shaft* (1971).

Parrington \\'par-iŋ-tən\\, **Vernon Louis** (b. Aug. 3, 1871, Aurora, Ill.—d. June 16, 1929, Winchcombe, Gloucestershire, England) Writer and teacher noted for his far-reaching appraisal of American literary history.

Parrington was educated at the College of Emporia and Harvard University, and later taught principally at the University of Washington (1908–29). His major work on American literary history was published in *Main Currents in American Thought* (2 vols., 1927), which won a Pulitzer Prize. The incomplete third volume was published posthumously in 1930. The work, now regarded as a classic, represents an interpretation of the development of American thought through its literature, in terms of the concept of democratic idealism. He also wrote *The Connecticut Wits* (1926) and *Sinclair Lewis, Our Own Diogenes* (1927).

Parton, James (b. Feb. 9, 1822, Canterbury, England—d. Oct. 17, 1891, Newburyport, Mass.) Biographer.

Parton immigrated to the United States with his widowed mother in 1827. He taught school in the 1840s, then worked as an editor on Nathaniel P. Willis's *New York Home Journal* until 1854. He would marry Willis's sister Sara in 1856.

In 1854 he convinced the publishers Mason Brothers to advance him money for a book project. His *Life of Horace Greeley* (1855), unique among biographies of its time for its realism and writerly skill, became a best-seller. Parton's success continued with biographies of Aaron Burr (1857), Andrew Jackson (3 vols., 1859–60), Benjamin Franklin (2 vols., 1864), John Jacob Astor (1865), George Washington (1872), his wife, using her pseudonym, Fanny Fern (1873), Thomas Jefferson (1874), and Voltaire (2 vols., 1881), virtually all of which were great successes with both readers and critics and many of which remain readable and valuable today. Between these important works he continued to turn out numerous volumes of shorter biographical sketches.

Parton, Sara Payson Willis *originally* Grata Payson Willis, *pseudonym* **Fanny Fern** (b. July 9, 1811, Portland, Maine—d. Oct. 10, 1872, New York City) One of the most popular American women writers in the 19th century.

Parton's sketches, often dealing with domestic life, were originally published in periodicals in Boston and New York. They were first collected in *Fern Leaves from Fanny's Port-Folio* (1853), which sold a remarkable 100,000 copies its first year. The success of this and other books led to an offer by the *New York Ledger* that made Parton one of America's first women newspaper columnists. From 1855 until her death, she reached an audience estimated at 500,000 readers weekly. Her writings are considered valuable mostly as a source for social history and as a mirror of popular taste in the mid-19th century. In addition to her articles, she wrote a number of best-selling books, including *Ruth Hall* (1855) and *A New Story Book for Children* (1864).

Patchen \\'pach-ən\\, **Kenneth** (b. Dec. 13, 1911, Niles, Ohio—d. Jan. 8, 1972, Palo Alto, Calif.) Experimental poet, novelist, painter, and graphic designer.

Patchen published many collections of verse from 1936 on, notably *Collected Poems* (1968), and several notable novels, including the surreal, hallucinatory *Journal of Albion Moonlight* (1941), *Memoirs of a Shy Pornographer* (1945), and *See You in the Morning* (1948). He also wrote plays and other works, all of which exhibit a combination of high idealism, abhorrence of violence, isolation from the mainstream of American thought, and shock at materialistic secularism. Loosely associated with the Beats, from 1957 Patchen was an important practitioner of poetry-and-jazz performance.

Patten, Gilbert (b. Oct. 25, 1866, Corinna, Me.—d. Jan. 16, 1945, Vista, Calif.) Novelist.

Patten sold his first story to a pulp magazine at 17, and he continued to write popular fiction from then on. After spending a month in Omaha, Neb., in 1889, he considered himself an expert on the West and began writing stories under the pseudonyms William West and Wyoming Will.

In 1896 he began writing under the pen name Burt L. Standish and created his famous fictional character Frank Merriwell, of Fardale Academy and later Yale. Patten's 200-odd books about his brilliant, athletic, and—above all—morally upright hero eventually sold over 125 million copies and were greatly popular with American boys for over 25 years. Merriwell even appeared in a comic strip from 1931 and in a radio program from 1934.

Working for Street & Smith pulp-fiction publishers, Patten earned only a small salary and no royalties. He wrote over 40 other books but never made a fortune. An ardent socialist, he died in poverty.

Paulding, James Kirke (b. Aug. 22, 1778, Dutchess County, N.Y.—d. April 6, 1860, Hyde Park, N.Y.) Dramatist, novelist, and public official chiefly remembered for his early advocacy and use of native American material in literature.

James Kirke Paulding

Together with the brothers William and Washington Irving, Paulding founded *Salmagundi* (1807–8), a New York periodical consisting mainly of light satires on local subjects. A member of the "Knickerbocker school," he satirized England's conduct toward America during the War of 1812 in *The Diverting History of John Bull and Brother Jonathan* (1812) and *The Lay of the Scottish Fiddle* (1813), a burlesque of Sir Walter Scott. Further broadsides in the "literary war" with England included two later satires, *A Sketch of Old England* (1822) and *John Bull in America* (1825).

The advantages and hardships of western migration are the theme of "The Backwoodsman" (1818), a poem written to encourage American writers to find literary themes in their own country rather than Europe. Novels such as *Koningsmarke* (1823), *Westward Ho!* (1832), and *The Old Continental* (1846) represent Paulding's attempts to employ the American scene in fiction. In the play *The Lion of the West* (performed 1831), he introduced frontier humor to the stage and contributed to the growing legend of Davy Crockett. He served as secretary of the navy 1837–41 under his friend President Martin Van Buren.

John Howard Payne

Payne, John Howard (b. June 9, 1791, New York City—d. April 9, 1852, Tunis, Tunisia) Playwright and actor.

A precocious actor and writer, Payne wrote his first play, *Julia*, when he was 15. He enjoyed instant but fleeting success on his acting debut in 1809, and in 1813 he left for England and Europe, where he would spend the next 20 years, in hopes of reviving his success. In Paris the actor François-Joseph Talma introduced him to French drama, from which he would adapt many of his more than 60 plays, following the techniques and themes of the European Romantic blank-verse dramatists. There he also met Washington Irving, with whom he would collaborate on some 10 plays. Payne's finest original play, *Brutus* (produced 1818), remained popular for 70 years. His other important dramas include *Clari*, which included Payne's famous song "Home, Sweet Home"; *Charles the Second* (1824), written with Irving; and *Thérèse* (1821), a French adaptation.

Peabody \\'pē-ˌbäd-ē, 'pē-bə-dē\\, **Elizabeth (Palmer)** (b. May 16, 1804, Billerica, Mass.—d. Jan. 3, 1894, Jamaica Plain, Mass.) Educator and participant in the Transcendental movement.

After being educated at a small private school by her mother, Peabody started her own school in Boston in 1820. From 1825 to 1834 she was secretary to William Ellery Channing, the early leader of American Unitarianism. She then joined Bronson Alcott at his Temple School, which she wrote about in *Record of a School* (1835). Two years later she became involved in adult education in Boston. In 1839 she opened her West Street bookstore, which became a kind of club for Boston's intellectual community. On her own printing press she published translations from German by Margaret Fuller and three of Nathaniel Hawthorne's earliest books. For two years she published and wrote articles for the *Dial*, the literary monthly of the Transcendental movement. Inspired by German models, Peabody opened a kindergarten in 1860, the first in the United States, and she devoted herself thereafter to organizing public and private kindergartens and to lecturing and writing in the field. Her letters were published in 1984. Her sisters married Hawthorne and Horace Mann.

Percy, Walker (b. May 28, 1916, Birmingham, Ala.—d. May 10, 1990, Covington, La.) Novelist who wrote of the search for faith and love in the New South, a place transformed by industry and technology.

Walker Percy

Percy graduated from the University of North Carolina and studied medicine at Columbia University. He contracted tuberculosis while working as a pathologist at New York's Bellevue Hospital; during his recuperation he read widely (especially in European existentialism), decided on a career in writing, and converted to Roman Catholicism. Catholicism and existentialism would both be powerful influences on his works.

During the 1950s Percy wrote articles for philosophical, literary, and psychiatric journals. His first and best-known novel, THE MOVIEGOER (1961, National Book Award), introduced his concept of "malaise," a disease of despair born of the rootless modern world. His other novels include *The Last Gentleman* (1966), *Love in the Ruins* (1971), *Lancelot* (1977), *The Second Coming* (1980), and *The Thanatos Syndrome* (1987). He also wrote such nonfiction as *The Message in the Bottle* (1975), a sophisticated philosophical treatment of semantics.

Perelman \ˈper-əl-mən, *commonly* ˈpərl-mən\, **S(idney) J(oseph)** (b. Feb. 1, 1904, Brooklyn, N.Y.—d. Oct. 17, 1979, New York City) Humorist, a master of wordplay in books, movies, plays, and essays.

After graduating from Brown University, Perelman married the sister of his classmate Nathanael West and was soon writing such early, frenetic Marx Brothers film classics as *Monkey Business* (1931) and *Horse Feathers* (1932). From 1931 he regularly contributed essays to the *New Yorker* magazine under such absurd titles as *Beat Me, Post-Impressionist Daddy* and *No Starch in the Dhoti*. He collaborated with Kurt Weill on the musical *One Touch of Venus* (1943), and later collaborated on the screenplay for *Around the World in 80 Days* (1956, Academy Award). His magazine pieces were collected in a long series of books, including *Strictly from Hunger* (1937), *Westward Ha!; or, Around the World in Eighty Clichés* (1948), and *The Road to Miltown; or, Under the Spreading Atrophy* (1957). In all his works Perelman's densely packed humor, characterized by an exquisite sense of cliché and mimicry, combines with a varied vocabulary to create effects of comic nihilism and literary parody.

Perry, Bliss (b. Nov. 25, 1860, Williamstown, Mass.—d. Feb. 13, 1954, Exeter, N.H.) Scholar and editor especially noted for his work in American literature.

Educated at Williams College and the Universities of Berlin and Strassburg, Perry subsequently taught at Williams (1886–93), Princeton (1893–1900), and Harvard (1907–30). From 1899 to 1909 he edited the *Atlantic Monthly*. He edited the works of Edmund Burke, Sir Walter Scott, and Ralph Waldo Emerson, and was general editor (1905–9) of the Cambridge edition of the major American poets. He wrote books on Walt Whitman, John Greenleaf Whittier, Thomas Carlyle, and Emerson, as well as novels, short fiction, essays, an autobiography, studies of poetry, and collections of fiction and essays.

Petrakis \pə-'trä-kis\, **Harry Mark** (b. June 5, 1923, St. Louis, Mo.) Novelist and short-story writer.

The son of an Eastern Orthodox priest, Petrakis briefly attended the University of Illinois and then held a variety of jobs to support himself while writing. His novels and stories are mostly exuberant and sensitive stories of the lives of Greek immigrants in urban America, usually Chicago. They include *Lion at My Heart* (1959), *The Odyssey of Kostas Volakis* (1963), the best-selling *A Dream of Kings* (1966; film, 1969), *The Hour of the Bell* (1976), *Nick the Greek* (1979), *Days of Vengeance* (1983), *Ghost of the Sun* (1990), a sequel to *A Dream of Kings,* and *Twilight of the Ice* (2003). He also published collections of short stories, a biography, and the autobiography *Stelmark* (1970).

Petry \'pē-trē\, **Ann** *originally* Ann Lane (b. Oct. 12, 1908, Old Saybrook, Conn.—d. April 28, 1997, Old Saybrook) Novelist whose works offered a unique perspective on black life in small-town New England.

Petry earned a pharmaceutical degree and practiced pharmacy until her marriage brought her to New York City, where she wrote for the *Amsterdam News* and the *Peoples' Voice* of Harlem and later studied creative writing at Columbia University.

Her first novel, THE STREET (1946), sold more than a million copies and was acclaimed for its portrayal of a working-class black woman who dreams of escaping Harlem but is inevitably thwarted by poverty and racism. *Country Place* (1947) depicts the disillusionment and corruption among a group of white people in a small Connecticut town. *The Narrows* (1953) is the story of a Dartmouth-educated black man who tends bar in the black section of Monmouth, Conn., and his tragic love affair with a rich white woman. Petry's short stories were collected in *Miss Muriel and Other Stories* (1971). Her biographies for children include *Harriet Tubman* (1955) and *Tituba of Salem Village* (1964).

Phelps, William Lyon (b. Jan. 2, 1865, New Haven, Conn.—d. Aug. 21, 1943, New Haven) Scholar and critic who did much to popularize the teaching of contemporary literature.

Phelps attended Yale and Harvard universities and taught at Yale from 1892 to 1933. In 1895 he began teaching the first American college course in the modern novel. There and in his *Essays on Russian Novelists* (1911), he was influential in introducing Russian novelists to American readers.

He was a popular lecturer and critic, and his literary essays that appeared in *Scribner's Magazine* and other periodicals, his syndicated newspaper column, "A Daily Thought," and such books as *What I Like in Poetry* (1934) brought him a wide audience. His *Autobiography with Letters* was published in 1939.

Piercy, Marge (b. March 31, 1936, Detroit) Feminist poet and novelist.

After studies at the University of Michigan and Northwestern University (M.A., 1958), Piercy worked some years in the civil-rights movement. From 1969 she devoted her attention to the women's movement, and she remains an outspokenly feminist poet and novelist.

Her first novel, *Going Down Fast* (1969), like her subsequent novels, features a female protagonist and focuses on women's roles in American society. It was followed by *Small Changes* (1973), *Vida* (1980), *Braided Lives* (1982), *He, She, and It* (1991), *The Longings of Women* (1994), *Storm Tide* (1998), and *Three Women* (2000). Her many books of poetry, which have likewise reflected her feminism, include *Breaking Camp* (1968), *Hard Loving* (1969), *Living in the Open* (1976), *Available Light* (1988), *Mars and Her Children* (1992), and *Early Grrrl* (1999).

Pinsky, Robert (b. Oct. 20, 1940, Long Branch, N.J.) Poet and critic.

A graduate of Rutgers and Stanford universities, Pinsky has taught at Wellesley College, UC–Berkeley, and Boston University. The title poem of his first collection, *Sadness and Happiness* (1975), comments on his own life. His long poem *An Explanation of America* (1979) probes personal and national myths. Vivid imagery characterizes his other collections, which include *History of My Heart* (1984), *The Want Bone* (1990), *The Figured Wheel* (1996), and *Jersey Rain* (2000). *Landor's Poetry* (1968), *The Situation of Poetry* (1976), and *Poetry and the World* (1988) are among his critical writings. He has served as poetry editor of the *New Republic* and *Slate*. He has cotranslated poems by Czeslaw Milosz, in *The Separate Notebooks* (1984), and published an acclaimed translation of Dante's *Inferno* (1995). He devised and published an interactive quest romance, *Mindwheel* (1985), to be played on computers. As U.S. Poet Laureate (1997–2000) he energetically and inventively promoted the reading and teaching of poetry nationwide; *America's Favorite Poems* (1999), coedited by Pinsky, was one product of his multifaceted Favorite Poem Project.

Plath, Sylvia (b. Oct. 27, 1932, Boston, Mass.—d. Feb. 11, 1963, London, England) Poet best known for her carefully crafted pieces noted for their personal imagery and intense focus, often on themes of alienation, death, and self-destruction.

The daughter of an entomologist who died when she was 8, Plath was driven to excel as a writer from an early age and published her first poem that same year. At Smith College she experienced a mental breakdown, made an early suicide attempt, and submitted to electroshock treatment, experiences she would later recount in her only novel, THE BELL JAR (1963), published under a pseudonym. While attending Cambridge University on a Fulbright grant, she married the poet Ted Hughes, and the couple had two children. She published the poetry collection *The Colossus* in 1960. After separating from Hughes, she committed suicide at 30. Works published after her death include the collections ARIEL (1965)—which won her posthumous fame—and *Crossing the Water* (1971) as well as *Johnny Panic and the Bible of Dreams* (1977), a book of short stories and other prose. Her *Collected Poems* (1981) won the Pulitzer Prize. Though little known at the time of her death, by the mid-1970s Plath was considered a major contemporary poet, admired for the febrile intensity of her verse. Her life eventually became more famous than her poetry, as she was seized on as a martyr by some who saw her suicide as a consequence of harsh treatment by Hughes, a notion that was largely dispelled by biographers and such publications as her unabridged journals (2000).

Edgar Allan Poe

Poe, Edgar Allan *originally* Edgar Poe (b. Jan. 19, 1809, Boston—d. Oct. 7, 1849, Baltimore) Poet, critic, and short-story writer famous for his cultivation of mystery and the macabre in fiction.

After his father abandoned the family and his mother died in 1811, Poe was taken into the home of John Allan, a Richmond merchant. He briefly attended the University of Virginia before his gambling debts caused a break with his foster father and he moved to Boston, where in 1827 he published a pamphlet containing TAMERLANE and other youthful Byronic poems. Out of money, he joined the army (1827–29). After a few months at West Point Military Academy, he was expelled, moved to New York City, and began to write journalism and stories. In 1833 his MS. FOUND IN A BOTTLE won $50 from a Baltimore weekly. By 1835 he was in Richmond as editor of the *Southern Literary Messenger*, the first of several periodicals he was to edit or write for. There he married his 13-year-old cousin. In 1839 he became coeditor of *Burton's Gentleman's Magazine* in Philadelphia, for which he wrote some of his best-known stories of supernatural horror. His *Tales of the Grotesque and Arabesque* appeared later that year.

In addition to his stories Poe continued to write his musical, sensuous poetry, which, though less highly regarded today than formerly, has always remained popular. THE BELLS in particular is a showcase of sound effects. In 1845 his most famous poem, THE RAVEN, brought him national fame.

Poe's life was irregular and eccentric, and alcohol was his constant bane. He attempted suicide in 1848 after his wife's early death, and although he was soon engaged again, he died delirious and impoverished in a Baltimore hotel at 40.

His writing is characterized by a strange duality. On the one hand, he was an idealist and a visionary, and his sensitivity to women inspired his most touching lyrics, including ANNABEL LEE. But more generally, in such verses as ULALUME and in his prose tales, his familiar mode of escape from the world was through eerie thoughts, impulses, or fears. From these materials he drew the startling effects of his tales of death (THE FALL OF THE HOUSE OF USHER, THE MASQUE OF THE RED DEATH, THE PREMATURE BURIAL), wickedness and crime (THE BLACK CAT, THE CASK OF AMONTILLADO, THE TELL-TALE HEART), and survival after dissolution (LIGEIA). When his characters are not in the clutch of mysterious forces or onto the untrodden paths of the beyond, a story may center on the anguish of imminent death (THE PIT AND THE PENDULUM).

His close observation of minute details is evident in the long narratives (*The Narrative of Arthur Gordon Pym*) and in many of the descriptions that introduce the tales. His powers of ratiocination are manifested in his analytical tales (THE GOLD BUG) and science-fiction tales, and importantly in such detective narratives as THE MURDERS IN THE RUE MORGUE and "The Purloined Letter," which initiated the modern detective story.

Poe's genius was early recognized abroad. No one did more to persuade the world of his greatness than the French poets Charles Baudelaire and Stéphane Mallarmé. His role in French literature was that of a poetic master model and guide to criticism, and French Symbolism relied on his "Philosophy of Composition," borrowed from his imagery, and used his examples to generate the modern theory of "pure poetry."

Pohl \\'pōl\\, **Frederik** (b. Nov. 26, 1919, New York City) Science-fiction writer whose best work embodies social criticism and explores the long-range consequences of technology in an ailing society.

As one of the Futurians, an important group of young socially conscious science-fiction writers and enthusiasts, Pohl was working as an editor of science-fiction magazines by 21. After service in the wartime air corps, he worked briefly in an advertising agency before returning to writing and editing. In his most famous work, *The Space Merchants* (1953; a collaboration with C. M. Kornbluth), the "copysmith star class" for a powerful advertising agency leads a project to colonize Venus in order to create consumers in space; a chilling portrait of a world dominated by the economic perspective of advertising executives, it made Pohl's reputation. He wrote several other books with Kornbluth, including *Gladiator-at-Law* (1955); samples can be found in *Our Best* (1987). His nearly 30 other novels (some also written with Jack Williamson) include *The Age of the Pussyfoot* (1969), *Man Plus* (1976), and *Chernobyl* (1987). He also produced almost 200 short stories, many under pseudonyms; his numerous collections include *Pohlstars* (1984). His works repeatedly won the Hugo and Nebula awards. In 1978 he published the memoir *The Way the Future Was*. Recent novels include *O Pioneers!* (1998) and *The Far Shore of Time* (1999).

Porter, Gene Stratton *originally* Geneva Stratton (b. Aug. 17, 1863, Wabash County, Ind.—d. Dec. 6, 1924, Los Angeles) Novelist.

Growing up in rural Indiana, Stratton developed the deep appreciation for nature that would stay with her throughout her life. In 1886 she married Charles D. Porter, and around 1895 she began contributing a column on nature photography to the magazines *Recreation* and *Outing*. With the success of a short story in *Metropolitan* magazine in 1901, she decided on a career in fiction.

Her first successful novel was *Freckles* (1904), a sentimental tale of a poor and apparently orphaned boy who is the self-appointed guardian of the Limberlost Swamp; the book eventually sold nearly 2 million copies. Her later bestsellers, mostly sentimental romances, include *A Girl of the Limberlost* (1909), *The Harvester* (1911), *Laddie* (1913), *A Daughter of the Land* (1918), and *The Keeper of the Bees* (1925). In 1920 she and her family moved to California, where in 1922 she organized a film company to produce movie versions of her stories. She died in an automobile accident.

Katherine Anne Porter

Porter, Katherine Anne (Maria Veronica Callista Russell) (b. May 15, 1890, Indian Creek, Texas—d. Sept. 18, 1980, Silver Spring, Md.) Writer whose long short stories have a richness of texture and complexity of character delineation usually achieved only in the novel.

Porter worked as a journalist in Chicago and Denver before leaving in 1920 for Mexico, the scene of several of her stories. "Maria Concepción," her first published story (1922), was later included in her first collection, FLOWERING JUDAS (1930).

The title story of her next collection, PALE HORSE, PALE RIDER (1939), is a poignant tale of youthful romance cruelly thwarted by the man's death in an influenza epidemic. In it and the two other stories in the volume, "Noon Wine" and "Old Mortality," there appears Porter's spirited semiautobiographical heroine, Miranda. *The Leaning Tower* (1944) depicts in its title story a young Texas artist in Berlin during the rise of Nazism. The ascendancy of Nazism also haunts SHIP OF FOOLS (1962; film, 1965), Porter's only novel.

Porter's *Collected Short Stories* (1965) won the National Book Award and the Pulitzer Prize. Her essays, articles, and book reviews were collected in *The Days Before* (1952). Her last work, *The Never-Ending Wrong* (1977), deals with the Sacco-Vanzetti murder trial.

Porter, William Sydney See **O. Henry**

Post, Emily *originally* Emily Price (b. Oct. 27, 1872 or Oct. 3, 1873, Baltimore—d. Sept. 25, 1960, New York City) Authority on social behavior.

Educated privately in New York, Price was a popular debutante. In 1892 she married Edwin M. Post, a banker. After their divorce in 1906, financial circumstances forced her to begin writing, and she produced newspaper articles on interior decoration and several light novels. At her publisher's suggestion, she undertook her major work, *Etiquette in Society, in Business, in Politics, and at Home* (1922). Written in a charming and lively style, the book differed from other etiquette guides in being directed to a broad popular audience, and it proved immediately popular. Later retitled *Etiquette: The Blue Book of Social Usage*, the guide went through 10 editions and 90 printings before Post's death.

Beginning in 1931, Post spoke on good taste on radio programs and wrote a newspaper column that was eventually syndicated to over 200 newspapers. Her later books included *The Personality of a House* (1930), *Children Are People* (1940), and *Motor Manners* (1950).

Potok \\'pō-täk\\, **Chaim** (*originally* Herman Harold) (b. Feb. 17, 1929, New York City—d. July 23, 2002, Merion, Pa.) Rabbi whose novels introduced the world of Orthodox Jews into American fiction.

The son of Polish immigrants, Potok was reared in an Orthodox home. Drawn to the less restrictive Conservative doctrine, he was ordained a Conservative rabbi after attending Yeshiva University and Jewish Theological Seminary. He was named managing editor of *Conservative Judaism* in 1964 and received his doctorate in philosophy from the University of Pennsylvania in 1965, the year he became editor in chief of the Jewish Publication Society. Throughout his career Potok has written scholarly and popular articles and reviews. His first novel, the best-selling *The Chosen* (1967; film, 1981), was the first novel from a major publisher to portray Orthodox Judaism in America. The story of the son of a Hasidic rabbi and his friend, whose Orthodox father encourages him to study secular subjects, it established Potok's reputation. *The Promise* (1969) followed the same characters to young adulthood. *My Name Is Asher Lev* (1972) tells of a young artist in conflict with his Hasidic family. Potok's next four novels—the autobiographical *In the Beginning* (1975), *The Book of Lights* (1981), *Davita's Harp* (1985), and *The Gift of Asher Lev* (1990)—further explored religious-secular conflicts. His last book was *Old Men at Midnight* (2001). Potok's nonfiction writings include *Wanderings* (1978), a history of the Jews.

Pottle, Frederick A(lbert) (b. Aug. 3, 1897, Lovell, Maine—d. May 16, 1987, New Haven, Conn.) Scholar who became the foremost authority on James Boswell.

Pottle graduated from Colby College and earned a Ph.D. from Yale University, where he would teach until his retirement in 1966. Almost all of his scholarly career was devoted to the editing of Boswell's journals and letters, 13,000 pages of which were purchased by Yale in 1949. Their publication began in 1950 with *Boswell's London Journal, 1762–1763;* 12 more volumes were published during Pottle's lifetime. Among his other works are *James Boswell: The Earlier Years, 1740–1769* (1966).

Ezra Pound

Pound, Ezra (Loomis) (b. Oct. 30, 1885, Hailey, Idaho—d. Nov. 1, 1972, Venice, Italy) American-Italian poet and critic who exercised a broad and profound influence on 20th-century literature.

Pound graduated from Hamilton College and in 1906 received his M.A. from the University of Pennsylvania. After briefly teaching college in Indiana, he sailed for Europe in 1908, avid to escape American provinciality and immerse himself in European culture. In Venice he published, at his own expense, his first book of poems, *A lume spento* (1908). He moved on to England, where he published several books of poems, including *Personae* (1909). In 1912 he became European correspondent for *Poetry* magazine, and his extraordinary energy, brilliance, and confidence soon made him a dominant figure in Anglo-American literature. As the central figure in IMAGISM, he edited its first anthology (*Des Imagistes*, 1914), and he helped promote such writers as W. B. Yeats, James Joyce, Ernest Hemingway, Robert Frost, D. H. Lawrence, and T. S. Eliot, whose *Waste Land* he brilliantly edited.

After World War I Pound published two important long poems, "Homage to Sextus Propertius," in the book *Quia Pauper Amavi* (1919), and HUGH SELWYN MAUBERLEY (1920) before moving to the continent. He lived four years in Paris before moving to Rapallo, Italy, which would be his home for the next 20 years. Around this time he began publishing volumes of THE CANTOS, the epic series of poems he was to continue to work on throughout his life. (All 117 completed cantos would be posthumously published in 1970.) He also began to develop interests outside of literature, and his investigations in the areas of culture and history would lead to the eccentrically brilliant but fragmentary prose work *Guide to Kulchur* (1938). Following the worldwide depression of the 1930s, he turned more and more to history, especially economic history. He became obsessed with monetary reform, involved himself in politics, and declared his admiration for Benito Mussolini.

Between 1941 and 1943, when Italy and the United States were at war, he made several hundred broadcasts over Rome Radio, often openly condemning the U.S. war effort. He was arrested for treason by U.S. forces in 1945 and spent six months in a prison camp near Pisa. There, under harsh physical conditions, he wrote *The Pisan Cantos*, the most moving section of his long poem-in-progress; published in 1948, these would earn him the first Bollingen Prize ever awarded.

Returned to the United States to face trial for treason, he was pronounced "insane and mentally unfit for trial" by a panel of doctors and spent 12 years (1946–58) in Saint Elizabeth's Hospital for the criminally insane in Washington, D.C. Through many of his years there, in protest at his treatment, he did not utter a word. After his release, effected partly through the efforts of fellow poets, he returned to Italy, where, in semi-seclusion and no longer writing, he would spend the rest of his life.

Powell, Dawn (b. 1897, Mt. Gilead, Ohio—d. Nov. 14, 1965, New York City) Novelist.

After graduating from Lake Erie College, she married Joseph R. Gousha in 1920, and they settled in New York's Greenwich Village, which would be the setting of many of her stories. Her first novel, *She Walks in Beauty* (1928), was followed by *The Bride's House* (1929), *Dance Night* (1931), *Turn, Magic Wheel* (1936), *My Home Is Far Away* (1944), *The Locusts Have No King* (1948), *A Time to Be Born* (1952), *The Wicked Pavilion* (1954), and *The Golden Spur* (1962). Though noted for her satiric wit and admired in literary circles, Powell was not widely read. Many of her novels were reissued in the 1990s, and an edition of her diaries appeared in 1998.

Powers, J(ames) F(arl) (b. July 8, 1917, Jacksonville, Ill.—d. June 12, 1999, Collegeville, Minn.) Novelist and short-story writer.

After studying at Northwestern University, he refused (as a pacifist) to be inducted into the army during World War II and was jailed for over a year. After his release, he worked as a hospital orderly while writing short stories, several of which appeared in the *New Yorker* and other magazines; they were collected in *Prince of Darkness* (1947) and *The Presence of Grace* (1956). In his first novel, the acclaimed *Morte d'Urban* (1962, National Book Award), he wrote about his favorite subject, Roman Catholic priests in the Midwest, in a satiric yet compassionate style. His later works include the short-story collection *Look How the Fish Live* (1975) and a second novel, *Wheat That Springeth Green* (1988).

Powers, Richard (b. 1957) Author known for his intellectually ambitious novels of technology and the capacities and limitations of the mind and body.

He received bachelor's and master's degrees in English from the University of Illinois, worked as a technical writer and computer programmer before publishing his first books, and has taught at Illinois since 1992. His novels, mazelike in their intricacy and widely regarded as brilliant, weave parallel stories which tend to reflect on the relationships between biology, technology, and the human mind, often probing the nature of thought itself. They include *Three Farmers on Their Way to a Dance* (1985), about the eve of World War I and what it portended for the century; *Prisoner's Dilemma* (1988), about a family within the context of history; the greatly admired *Gold Bug Variations* (1991), a mystery that hinges on genetics and information science; *Operation Wandering Soul* (1993), about an inner-city pediatrics ward; *Galatea 2.2* (1996), about the development of a computer that can pass an English-literature exam; *Gain* (1998), about cancer and corporate greed; and *Plowing the Dark* (2000), about the development of virtual-reality technology in the 1980s.

Prescott, William H(ickling) (b. May 4, 1796, Salem, Mass.—d. Jan. 28, 1859, Boston) Historian.

Born to a prosperous family, Prescott graduated from Harvard College in 1814. He was forced by poor health and the accidental blinding of one eye to forgo a career in law. He undertook serious historical studies and wrote several articles for the *North American Review* in 1821. His literary friends encouraged him to pursue Spanish themes, and his first major work was *History of the Reign of Ferdinand and Isabella the Catholic* (1838).

He continued to focus on 16th-century Spain and its colonies in his famous *History of the Conquest of Mexico* (3 vols., 1843) and *History of the Conquest of Peru* (2 vols., 1847). His rigorous use of original sources in these great works earned him a reputation as America's first scientific historian. Vividly imagined and dramatized, both won wide popularity. His last large work, unfinished at his death, was *A History of the Reign of Philip the Second, King of Spain* (3 vols., 1855–58).

Price, (Edward) Reynolds (b. Feb. 1, 1933, Macon, N.C.) Writer whose stories are set in his home state of North Carolina.

Price attended Duke University and Merton College, Oxford (as a Rhodes Scholar), before beginning his long teaching career at Duke. His first novel, *A Long and Happy Life* (1957), introduced his memorable young heroine, the naive, spirited Rosacoke Mustian. Rosacoke also appears in Price's short-story collection *The Names and Faces of Heroes* (1963), and in the novel *A Generous Man* (1966) her brother Milo experiences his sexual awakening. *Good Hearts* (1988) resumes the story of Rosacoke in her middle age, while searching the backwoods for a retarded brother, a dog, and an escaped python. Price went on to write such novels as *Love and Work* (1968), the admired *The Surface of the Earth* (1975), *The Source of Light* (1981), and *Kate Vaiden* (1986, National Book Critics Circle Award). Having largely lost the use of his legs around 1986 as the result of a brain tumor, he has since been confined to a wheelchair. Later novels have included *The Tongues of Angels* (1990), *Blue Calhoun* (1992), and *Roxanna Slade* (1998). He has also written poetry, plays, essays, memoirs, and biblical translations. His *Collected Stories* appeared in 1993.

Prokosch \ˈprō-ˌkȯsh\, **Frederic** (b. May 17, 1908, Madison, Wis.—d. June 6, 1989, Plan-de-Grasse, France) Writer who became famous with his early novels and whose literary stature rose as his fame declined.

Having received a master's degree from Haverford College at 18, Prokosch went on to obtain a Ph.D. from Yale and a second M.A. from the University of Cambridge. His first novel, *The Asiatics* (1935), is the picaresque story of a young American who travels from Beirut across vivid Asian landscapes to China. His other novels of the 1930s, especially the travel adventure *The Seven Who Fled* (1937) and *Night of the Poor* (1939), were also well received. Meanwhile, with his own press he published many of his own poems. His fourth novel, *The Skies of Europe* (1941), includes a portrait of Adolf Hitler as a failed artist.

During World War II Prokosch was American cultural attaché in Sweden, and he remained in Europe after the war. There he wrote several more novels, including the travel adventures *Storm and Echo* (1948) and *Nine Days to Mukalla* (1953) and a fictional biography of Byron, *The Missolonghi Manuscript* (1968). He published four volumes of original poems and translated works of Euripides, Louise Labé, and Friedrich Hölderlin. *Voices* (1983) is a memoir of his encounters with leading literary figures.

Proulx \'prü\, (Edna) Annie (b. Aug. 22, 1935, Norwich, Conn.) Novelist and short-story writer.

Proulx studied toward a doctorate in economic history but left school to practice journalism. While raising a family in rural Vermont, she wrote how-to books while also submitting stories to men's outdoor magazines.

After publication of her first story collection, *Heart Songs* (1988), she turned to writing novels, which better accommodated her dense plots and complex characterizations. *Postcards* (1992), her first novel, used the device of picture postcards mailed from the road over 40 years' time to illustrate changes in American life; with it, Proulx became the first woman to win the PEN/Faulkner Award. In *The Shipping News* (1993, Pulitzer Prize, National Book Award), the protagonist and his dysfunctional family of two young daughters and a sensible old aunt depart for Newfoundland after the accidental death of his unfaithful wife. *Accordion Crimes* (1996) follows an accordion from Sicily in 1896 to Florida in 1990, recounting the violence that attends the lives of its owners. The highly praised collection *Close Range: Wyoming Stories* (1999), including "The Half-Skinned Steer" and "Brokeback Mountain," further enhanced her already high reputation. Writing mostly about men, Proulx's prose alternates between vividly lyrical evocations of landscape and sensitive but brutally direct depictions of the mental states of inarticulate people and the violence that often surrounds them.

Purdy, James (b. July 17, 1923, Fremont, Ohio) Novelist and short-story writer whose works present a vision of human alienation, indifference, and cruelty.

After studies at the University of Chicago and in Mexico, Purdy worked as an interpreter in Latin America, France, and Spain. His first two works—*Don't Call Me by My Right Name and Other Stories* (1956) and the novella *63: Dream Palace* (1956)—were initially rejected for publication and were privately printed, but later met with critical favor.

Purdy's fiction, which has generally remained obscure despite the admiration it has evoked from leading writers, combines grotesquerie, violence, and sexual deviation and trauma in a gothic mixture. *Malcolm* (1959), about a 15-year-old boy in a fruitless search for his identity, was adapted for the stage by Edward Albee. *The Nephew* (1960) and *Cabot Wright Begins* (1964) further develop the bleak worldview propounded in *Malcolm*. *Eustace Chisholm and the*

Works (1967) is vividly brutal and homoerotic. In the trilogy *Sleepers in Moon-Crowned Valleys*—consisting of *Jeremy's Vision* (1970), *The House of the Solitary Maggot* (1974), and *Mourners Below* (1981)—Purdy explores small-town American life and destructive family relationships. His later novels include the ambitious *Narrow Rooms* (1978), *I Am Elijah Thrush* (1972), *In a Shallow Grave* (1976), *Candles of Your Eyes* (1986), and *Gertrude of Stony Island Avenue* (1998). He has also written several collections of stories, plays, and poems.

Putnam, Samuel (Whitehall) (b. Oct. 10, 1892, Rossville, Ill.—d. Jan. 15, 1950, Lambertville, N.J.) Editor, publisher, and author best known for his translations.

After incomplete studies at the University of Chicago, Putnam worked for various Chicago newspapers before becoming a literary and art critic for the *Chicago Evening Post* (1920–26). In 1927 he moved to Europe, where he financed his ventures as an editor and publisher by translating works by French and Italian writers. Returning to the United States in 1933, he contributed regularly to such left-wing magazines as *Partisan Review*, the *New Masses*, and the *Daily Worker* until the mid-1940s, when his interests shifted to Latin-American and Spanish literature. He produced an authoritative translation of Euclides da Cunha's Brazilian prose epic *Os sertões* (1944; *Rebellion in the Backlands*), and spent 17 years on a translation of *Don Quixote*, which appeared to high praise in 1949. *Marvelous Journey* (1948) surveys the history of Brazilian literature. The memoir *Paris Was Our Mistress* (1947) depicts the American expatriate community in Paris in the 1920s and '30s.

Puzo \\'pü-zō\\, **Mario** (b. Oct. 15, 1920, New York City—d, July 2, 1999, Bay Shore, N.Y.) Novelist and screenwriter.

Puzo dropped out of school to work to support his family, then served in World War II. After the war he studied at the New School for Social Research and Columbia University. While working as a civil servant, he began writing pulp stories for men's magazines. His first two novels, *The Dark Arena* (1955) and *The Fortunate Pilgrim* (1964), attracted good reviews but few buyers.

Though he lacked personal knowledge of organized crime, thorough research provided the necessary details, and *The Godfather* (1969), the story of a Mafia family and its strong bonds, became a phenomenal success, selling over 20 million copies worldwide. Puzo collaborated on the scripts for the three movies based on its characters (1972, 1974, 1990), winning Academy Awards for the first two. His later novels included *Fools Die* (1978), *The Sicilian* (1984; film, 1987), *The Last Don* (1996), and *Omerta* (2000).

Pyle, Ernie (*originally* Ernest Taylor) (b. Aug. 3, 1900, near Dana, Ind.—d. April 18, 1945, Ie Shima, Ryukyu Islands) Journalist.

Pyle studied journalism at Indiana University and left school to become a reporter for a small-town newspaper. In 1935, after various editorial jobs, he acquired a roving assignment for the Scripps-Howard newspaper chain; his daily experiences furnished him material for a column that eventually appeared in as many as 200 newspapers.

His coverage of the World War II military campaigns in North Africa, Sicily, Italy, and France brought him a Pulitzer Prize in 1944 and several other awards. His columns were greatly popular, mainly because of his understanding of the ordinary soldier in war. He was with the U.S. forces in the Pacific on Iwo Jima; during the Okinawa campaign he visited the nearby island of Ie Shima, where he was killed at 44 by Japanese machine-gun fire.

Compilations of Pyle's columns appeared in *Ernie Pyle in England* (1941), *Here Is Your War* (1943), *Brave Men* (1944), and *Last Chapter* (1946). The movie *G.I. Joe* (1945) was about his coverage of the Italian campaign.

Pyle, Howard (b. March 5, 1853, Wilmington, Del.—d. Nov. 9, 1911, Florence, Italy) Illustrator, painter, and author best known for his children's books.

Pyle's magazine and book illustrations are among the finest of the turn-of-the-century period in the Art Nouveau style. Many of his children's stories, both told and illustrated with vividness and historical accuracy, have become classics—most notably *The Merry Adventures of Robin Hood* (1883), *Otto of the Silver Hand* (1888), *Men of Iron* (1892), *Jack Ballister's Fortunes* (1895), several books on Arthurian legend, and his own folktales in *Pepper & Salt* (1886), *The Wonder Clock* (1888), and *The Garden Behind the Moon* (1895). He established the Brandywine School in 1900, where he taught such artists as N. C. Wyeth and Maxfield Parrish.

Pynchon \\'pin-chən\\, **Thomas** (b. May 8, 1937, Glen Cove, Long Island, N.Y.) Novelist and short-story writer whose works combine black humor and fantasy to depict human alienation in the chaos of modern society.

Pynchon studied physics at Cornell and worked briefly as a technical writer before devoting himself to fiction. His first novel, *V.* (1963), is a cynically absurd tale of a middle-aged Englishman's search for "V.," an elusive, supernatural adventuress. Like his later novels, it combines black humor and fantasy to depict human alienation in the chaos of modern society. In his next book, *The Crying of Lot 49* (1966), Pynchon described a woman's strange quest to discover the mysterious, conspiratorial Tristero System in a futuristic world of closed societies. His masterpiece, the extraordinary GRAVITY'S RAINBOW (1973, National Book Award), similarly based on the idea of conspiracy, is filled with descriptions of paranoid fantasies, grotesque imagery, and esoteric mathematical language. Heated disagreement over *Gravity's Rainbow* resulted in failure to award the Pulitzer Prize for fiction in 1974, but it would receive the William Dean Howells Medal as the best American fiction of its half-decade.

Pynchon's next novel, *Vineland*, was not published until 1990. The huge *Mason & Dixon* (1997) combines historical fact (the drawing of the Mason-Dixon Line) with outrageous fantasy. Of his few short stories, most notable are "Entropy" (1960), a neatly structured tale in which he first used extensive technical language and scientific metaphors, and "The Secret Integration" (1964), collected in *Slow Learner* (1984), which explores small-town bigotry and racism. Pynchon has lived in hiding or incognito for decades, refusing to grant interviews or be photographed.

Queen, Ellery *pseudonym of* Frederic Dannay (*originally* Daniel Nathan) and Manfred Bennington Lee (*originally* Manford Lepofsky) (respectively b. Oct. 20, 1905, Brooklyn, N.Y.—d. Sept. 3, 1982, White Plains, N.Y.; b. Jan. 11, 1905, Brooklyn, N.Y.—d. April 3, 1971, near Waterbury, Conn.) Cousins who co-authored a series of more than 35 detective novels featuring the character Ellery Queen.

Dannay (an advertising art director) and Lee (a film publicity agent) first collaborated, on impulse, on an entry for a detective-story contest; the success of the result, *The Roman Hat Mystery* (1929), started Ellery Queen on his career. The two took turns creating plots and writing stories about the sleuth Queen, whose adventures were adapted for radio, television, and film. For their stories about a later detective creation, Drury Lane, they used the pseudonym Barnaby Ross.

The two men also published a dozen short-story collections, cofounded *Ellery Queen's Mystery Magazine* in 1941, and edited some 35 anthologies.

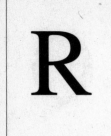

R

Rabe \\'rāb\\, **David (William)** (b. March 10, 1940, Dubuque, Iowa) Playwright known for his grotesque humor, satire, and surreal fantasy.

After studies at Loras College and Villanova University, Rabe was drafted into the army, and his experiences in a Vietnam hospital-support unit became the basis for several acclaimed dramas. *The Basic Training of Pavlo Hummel* (1969) depicts Vietcong ruthlessness and the brutalization of American troops, and shows the effects of the war on combatants and noncombatants alike. In *Sticks and Bones* (1972, Tony Award), a blinded, distraught veteran returns to his middle-American family; *Streamers* (1975; film, 1983) concerns violent racial and sexual tensions in a Virginia army camp. Other plays include *The Orphan* (1975), a reworking of the *Oresteia*; *In the Boom Boom Room* (1975), about the rape of a go-go dancer; *Hurlyburly* (1985; film, 1998) and *Those the River Keeps* (1991), a drama and its "prequel" about disillusionment and cynicism in Hollywood; *The Crossing Guard* (1995; film, 1995), about revenge; *Recital of the Dog* (1993), about a man's descent into madness; *A Question of Mercy* (1998), about terminal illness and suicide; and *Corners* (2000), about Mafia "honor." Rabe wrote an original screenplay for the Vietnam film *Casualties of War* (1989).

Rahv \\'räv\\, **Philip** *originally* Ivan Greenberg (b. March 10, 1908, Kupin, Ukraine, Russian Empire—d. Dec. 22, 1973, Cambridge, Mass.) Ukrainian-American critic, cofounder of the *Partisan Review*.

Rahv immigrated to the United States by himself at 14. He never finished high school, but eked out a living by teaching Hebrew (one of his six languages), joined the Communist Party, and began contributing to the *New Masses,* the *Nation,* the *New Republic*, and the *New Leader*. In 1933 he and William Phillips founded the PARTISAN REVIEW as a radical intellectual journal; he would continue to edit it until 1969, though his politics altered with the years. An important arbiter of literary taste, his books included *Fourteen Essays on Literary Themes* (1949), *Image and Idea* (1957), *Myth and the Powerhouse* (1965), and *Literature and the Sixth Sense* (1969), and he edited such volumes as *The Partisan Reader* (1946, with Phillips), *The Discovery of Europe* (1947), *Literature in America* (1958), and *Modern Occasions* (1966).

Rand \\'rand\\, **Ayn** *originally* Alisa Zinovievna Rosenbaum (b. Feb. 2, 1905, St. Petersburg, Russia—d. March 6, 1982, New York City) Russian-American writer who embodied her philosophy of Objectivism in her perennially best-selling novels.

After graduating from the University of Petrograd, Rand immigrated to the United States in 1926 and found work as a screenwriter in Hollywood. In 1935 her first play, *The Night of January 16th,* began a successful New York run. Her first novel, *We, the Living,* appeared in 1936, and her second, *Anthem,* in 1938. In 1940 her play *The Unconquered* had a short Broadway run. THE FOUNTAINHEAD (1943; film, 1949), which became a durable best-seller, depicts its architect-hero as a superman whose egoism and genius prevail over timid traditionalism and social conformism. The Objectivist philosophy embodied in the book, inspired by Nietzsche, held that all real achievement is the product of individual ability and effort, that laissez-faire capitalism is most congenial to the exercise of talent, and that selfishness is a virtue, altruism a vice. Rand's reversal of the traditional Judeo-Christian ethic made her a beacon for an avid and self-renewing cult of libertarian-conservative followers. The allegorical ATLAS SHRUGGED (1957), another perennial best-seller, combines science fiction and a political message. Rand also wrote a number of nonfiction works expounding her beliefs, including *For the New Intellectual* (1961) and *The Virtue of Selfishness* (1964), and edited two journals propounding her ideas, *The Objectivist* (1962–71) and *The Ayn Rand Letter* (1971–76).

Ransom, John Crowe (b. April 30, 1888, Pulaski, Tenn.—d. July 4, 1974, Gambier, Ohio) Poet and critic, leading theorist of the Southern literary renaissance that began after World War I.

Ransom was educated at Vanderbilt University, and later taught English there (1914–37). At Vanderbilt he became the leader of the Fugitives, a group of poets who published the influential literary magazine *The Fugitive* (1922–25) and shared a belief in the South and its regional traditions. His own poetry collections included *Chills and Fever* (1924) and *Two Gentlemen in Bonds* (1927). He was among those Fugitives—including Allen Tate and Robert Penn Warren—who became known as the Agrarians; their collective manifesto *I'll Take My Stand* (1930) criticized the idea that industrialization was the answer to the needs of the South.

From 1937 until his retirement in 1958 he taught at Kenyon College, where he founded and edited (1939–59) the KENYON REVIEW. His literary studies include *God Without Thunder* (1930) and *The World's Body* (1938), in which he contends that poetry and science furnish different but equally valid knowledge about the world. His *The New Criticism* (1941) provided the name for the influential mid-20th-century critical school known as NEW CRITICISM. Later volumes include *Poems and Essays* (1955) and *Beating the Bushes* (1972).

Rawlings, Marjorie Kinnan *originally* Marjorie Kinnan (b. Aug. 8, 1896, Washington, D.C.—d. Dec. 14, 1953, St. Augustine, Fla.) Novelist who founded a regional literature of backwoods Florida.

After graduating from the University of Wisconsin, Rawlings worked as a journalist for 10 years while trying to write stories she could sell. Visiting Florida in 1926, she became enchanted by the landscape, and in 1928 she acquired an orange grove in Cross Creek, Hawthorn, where she devoted herself to writing fiction. She finally succeeded with her award-winning short story "Gal Young 'Un" (1933; film, 1979). Her first novel, *South Moon Under* (1933), was followed by *Golden Apples* (1935) and the book for which she is best known, THE YEARLING (1938, Pulitzer Prize; film, 1946).

Rawlings took her material from the people and land around her, and her books are less fiction than vivid factual reporting. Her books—which also include the story collection *When the Whippoorwill* (1940), *Cross Creek* (1942; film, 1983), a mystical autobiographical description of her discovery of her Florida home, and *The Sojourner* (1953)—have been acclaimed for their magical description of landscape.

Opie Read

Read, Opie (Percival) (b. Dec. 22, 1852, Nashville, Tenn.—d. Nov. 2, 1939, Chicago) Journalist, humorist, novelist, and lecturer.

Inspired by Benjamin Franklin's autobiography, Read became a printer and reporter. He later edited the *Little Rock Gazette* (1878–81) and cofounded and edited (1882–91) the *Arkansas Traveler*, a weekly humor and literary journal. His dozens of books specialize in the homespun humor of life in Kentucky, Tennessee, and Arkansas; they include *Len Gansett* (1888), *A Kentucky Colonel* (1890), *The Jucklins* (1895), *My Young Master* (1896), and the autobiography *I Remember* (1930).

Rechy, John (Francisco) (b. March 10, 1934, El Paso, Texas) Novelist whose semiautobiographical works explore the worlds of sexual and social outsiders.

Of half-Mexican extraction, Rechy graduated from Texas Western College and later studied at New York's New School for Social Research. He has since taught creative writing, principally at USC.

In *City of Night* (1963), his first and best-received novel, a young homosexual hustler makes his way to New Orleans for Mardi Gras; a best-seller, it is regarded as a pioneering work of gay literature. The widely read *Numbers* (1967) and *This Day's Death* (1969) deal with obsession and identity. *The Vampires* (1971) concerns the nature of evil, and *The Fourth Angel* (1972) records the adventures of four thrill-seeking adolescents. The nonfictional *The Sexual Outlaw* (1977) is Rechy's "prose documentary" of three days and nights in the Los Angeles sexual underground. His other novels include *Rushes* (1979), *Bodies and Souls* (1983), *Marilyn's Daughter* (1988), *The Miraculous Day of Amalia Gómez* (1991), and *The Coming of the Night* (1999).

Reed, Ishmael (Scott) (b. Feb. 22, 1938, Chattanooga, Tenn.) Author of poetry, essays, and satiric novels.

Reed grew up in Buffalo, N.Y., studied at the University of Buffalo, and moved to New York City, where he cofounded the *East Village Other* (1965), an underground newspaper that achieved a national reputation. Since the 1960s he has taught at UC–Berkeley.

His first novel, *The Free-Lance Pallbearers*, appeared in 1967. It was followed by *Yellow Back Radio Broke-Down* (1969), *Mumbo Jumbo* (1972), regarded as his finest work, *The Last Days of Louisiana Red* (1974), *Flight to*

Canada (1976), *The Terrible Twos* (1982) and its sequel *The Terrible Threes* (1989), and *Japanese By Spring* (1993). The novels, which have sparked controversy among his fellow African-Americans, are marked by surrealism, satire, and sharp political and racial commentary. They have often depicted human history as a cycle of battles between oppressed people and their oppressors; their characters and actions are an antic mixture of inverted stereotypes, revisionist history, and prophecy. Reed has also written several admired poetry volumes, as well as essay collections.

Reed, John (b. Oct. 22, 1887, Portland, Ore.—d. Oct. 19, 1920, Moscow, U.S.S.R.) Poet-adventurer whose short life as a revolutionary writer and activist made him the hero of a generation of radical intellectuals.

John Reed

Born into a wealthy Portland family, Reed graduated from Harvard and in 1913 began writing for a socialist newspaper, the *Masses*, while also writing poetry, several collections of which he would privately publish. In 1914 he covered the revolutionary fighting in Mexico and recorded his impressions in *Insurgent Mexico*. Frequently arrested for organizing and defending strikes, he rapidly became established as a radical leader and helped form the U.S. Communist Party.

He covered World War I for *Metropolitan* magazine; out of this experience came *The War in Eastern Europe* (1916). That year he married the writer Louise Bryant. They reached Russia in time to witness the 1917 Bolshevik revolution, which he enthusiastically supported; he became a friend of Vladimir Lenin, and he reported his intimate view of the revolution in his best-known book, *Ten Days That Shook the World* (1919).

When the U.S. Communist Party and the Communist Labor Party split in 1919, Reed became the leader of the latter. Indicted for sedition, he escaped to the Soviet Union, where he died of typhus at 32; he was buried with other Bolshevik heroes beside the Kremlin wall.

Reese, Lizette W(oodworth) (b. Jan. 9, 1856, Baltimore County, Md.—d. Dec. 17, 1935, Baltimore) Poet whose work draws on the images of her rural childhood.

Reese taught for most of her life in the Baltimore public schools. Her lyric talent was strikingly evident in her first book, *A Branch of May* (1887), which was followed by *A Handful of Lavender* (1891). Her fresh images, condensed form, and sincerity of emotion broke with conventional sentimentality and foreshadowed 20th-century lyricism. Her best-known poem is the widely anthologized sonnet "Tears" (1899). Her *Selected Poems* (1926) was followed by several other volumes of verse, two books of reminiscences, *A Victorian Village* (1929) and *The York Road* (1931), and a posthumous novel, *Worleys* (1936).

Remarque \rə-'märk\, **Erich Maria** (b. June 22, 1898, Osnabrück, Germany—d. Sept. 25, 1970, Locarno, Switzerland) Novelist.

Drafted into the German army at 18, Remarque served in World War I and was wounded several times. After the war he worked as a racing-car driver and sportswriter while writing his novel. He is chiefly remembered for *Im Westen nichts Neues* (1929; *All Quiet on the Western Front*), which became perhaps the best-known and most representative novel of World War I. It describes the daily routine of ordinary soldiers who seem to have no past or future apart from their life in the trenches. Its title, the language of routine communiqués, is typical of its cool, terse style, which records the daily horrors of war in laconic understatement. It had an immediate international success, as did the American film made from it in 1930.

Remarque left Germany for Switzerland in 1932, and his books were banned by the Nazis in 1933. In 1939 he moved to the United States, where he was naturalized in 1947. He later settled in Switzerland with his second wife, the actress Paulette Goddard. His later works included *The Road Back* (1931), *Arc de Triomphe* (1946; film, 1948), and *The Black Obelisk* (1956).

Rexroth \'reks-ˌroth\, **Kenneth** (b. Dec. 22, 1905, South Bend, Ind.—d. June 6, 1982, Santa Barbara, Calif.) Painter, essayist, poet, and translator, an early champion of the Beat movement.

Largely self-educated, Rexroth spent his youth as a wanderer, casual laborer, and labor organizer, becoming associated with various leftist and avant-garde movements, while also studying art at the Chicago Art Institute and New York's Art Students League. He later wrote for the *Nation* (1953–68) and was a columnist for the *San Francisco Examiner* (1960–68). In the 1950s he became an important exponent of the loosely defined group of West Coast writers that became known as the Beats. His own early poetry was experimental, influenced by Surrealism; his later work was praised for its tight form and its wit and humanistic passion. His *Complete Collected Shorter Poems* appeared in 1967, *Complete Collected Longer Poems* in 1968, and *New Poems* in 1974. His other works include the essay collections *Bird in the Bush* (1959), *Assays* (1962), *The Alternative Society* (1970), and *With Eye and Ear* (1970). *An Autobiographical Novel* was published in 1966, and the history *American Poetry in the Twentieth Century* and the volume of verse plays *Beyond the Mountains* in 1971. Rexroth also published numerous translations of Japanese, Chinese, Greek, Latin, and Spanish poetry.

Rhodes, James Ford (b. May 1, 1848, Cleveland, Ohio—d. Jan. 22, 1927, Brookline, Mass.) Businessman and historian.

Rhodes left college after two years to travel in Europe. On his return to Cleveland, he entered the iron and coal business with his father, brother, and brother-in-law (Mark Hanna). The company prospered, and by 1885 he had acquired a fortune that permitted him to retire.

Long interested in history, he wrote many articles and reviews for the *Magazine of Western History* and began the monumental project that established his reputation as a historian: the *History of the United States from the Compromise of*

1850 (7 vols., 1893–1906). The work earned the high esteem of professional historians for its scientific (i.e., objective and detached) historical scholarship.

Rhodes moved to Cambridge, Mass., in 1891 and to Boston in 1895, and in 1898 he was elected president of the American Historical Association. The most esteemed of his later works, his *History of the Civil War, 1861-1865* (1917), won the Pulitzer Prize.

Rice, Alice Hegan *originally* Alice Caldwell Hegan (b. Jan. 11, 1870, Shelbyville, Ky.—d. Feb. 10, 1942, Louisville) Writer best known for *Mrs. Wiggs of the Cabbage Patch*.

At the age of 16 she worked at a mission Sunday school in a Louisville slum known as the Cabbage Patch. Her experiences there, particularly her acquaintance with a warm, humorous old woman who lived there, resulted in *Mrs. Wiggs of the Cabbage Patch* (1901), published under her maiden name. A sentimental story of courage in the face of poverty, it became a perennial best-seller. In 1902 she married the poet Cale Young Rice. Long devoted to social causes, she cofounded the Cabbage Patch Settlement House in 1910. In addition to *Mrs. Wiggs*, she wrote many other novels noted for their pathos and humor, including *Mr. Opp* (1909), and an autobiography, *The Inky Way* (1940).

Rice, Anne *originally* Anne O'Brien (b. Oct. 14, 1941, New Orleans) Novelist.

Married at 20, Rice earned degrees from San Francisco State College (M.A., 1971) and later held a variety of jobs while becoming a writer. Her first book, *Interview with the Vampire* (1976; film, 1994), marked the beginning of her greatly successful "Vampire Chronicles," set in New Orleans, which also includes *The Vampire Lestat* (1985), *The Queen of the Damned* (1988), *The Tale of the Body Thief* (1992), *Memnoch the Devil* (1995), *The Vampire Armond* (1998), and *Merrick* (2000).

Rice's other novels include *The Feast of All Saints* (1980), *The Mummy* (1989), *Violin* (1997), *Pandora* (1998), and the books of the "Lives of the Mayfair Witches" series: *The Witching Hour* (1990), *Lasher* (1993), and *Taltos* (1994). Under the pseudonym A. N. Roquelaure, she wrote the collection of erotic novels compiled in *The Sleeping Beauty Novels* (1991). Her other pseudonym, Anne Rampling, appears on the traditional novels *Exit to Eden* (1985) and *Belinda* (1986).

Rice, Elmer *originally* Elmer Leopold Reizenstein (b. Sept. 28, 1892, New York City—d. May 8, 1967, Southampton, Hampshire, England) Playwright, director, and novelist noted for his innovative and polemical plays.

Rice's first work, the melodramatic *On Trial* (1914), was the first stage play to employ the motion-picture technique of flashbacks, in this case to present the recollections of witnesses at a trial. In *The Adding Machine* (1923), Rice adapted techniques from German Expressionist theater. He collaborated with Dorothy Parker on *Close Harmony* (1924). His most important play, STREET SCENE (1929), won a Pulitzer Prize; Kurt Weill used it as the basis of his first, and highly popular, "American opera." *Counsellor-at-Law* (1931) was a critical look at the legal profession. In *We, the People* (1933), *Between Two Worlds* (1934), *Judgment Day* (1934), and other polemical plays of the 1930s, Rice treated the evils of Nazism, the poverty of the Great Depression, and racism. *Dream Girl* (1945) was the last of his plays to enjoy great success. In 1938 he cofounded the Playwrights Company. He also wrote several novels and an autobiography, *Minority Report* (1963).

Adrienne Rich

Rich, Adrienne (Cecile) (b. May 16, 1929, Baltimore) Poet, scholar, teacher, and critic.

Rich attended Radcliffe College, and before her graduation her poetry was chosen by W. H. Auden for publication in the Yale Younger Poets series. The resulting volume, *A Change of World* (1951), reflected her formal mastery. *The Diamond Cutters* (1955) was followed by *Snapshots of a Daughter-in-Law* (1963), in which she moved toward looser, more personal forms. Her fourth collection, *Necessities of Life* (1966), was written almost entirely in free verse. Throughout the 1960s and '70s her increasing commitment to the women's movement and to a lesbian-feminist aesthetic politicized and lent power to much of the poetry in such volumes as *Leaflets* (1969), the acclaimed *Diving into the Wreck* (1973, National Book Award), *The Dream of a Common Language* (1978), *A Wild Patience Has Taken Me This Far* (1981), *An Atlas of the Difficult World* (1991), and *Dark Fields of the Republic* (1995). Rich's critical works include the admired study of motherhood *Of Woman Born* (1976, National Book Award), *On Lies, Secrets, and Silence* (1979), *Blood, Bread, and Poetry* (1986), *What Is Found There* (1993), and *Arts of the Possible* (2001).

Richter \ˈrik-tər\, **Conrad (Michael)** (b. Oct. 13, 1890, Pine Grove, Pa.—d. Oct. 30, 1968, Pottsville, Pa.) Novelist and short-story writer known for his lyrical fiction about early America.

Richter became the editor of the *Patton* (Pa.) *Courier* at 19. He later founded a juvenile magazine, which he liquidated before moving to New Mexico in 1928. In an era when many American writers steeped themselves in European culture, Richter was fascinated with American history, and he spent years researching frontier life. He is best known for THE SEA OF GRASS (1936; film, 1947) and his AWAKENING LAND trilogy of pioneer life: *The Trees* (1940), *The Fields* (1946), and *The Town* (1950, Pulitzer Prize). Richter's stories are usually told through a contemporary narrator, allowing the reader to see the present and past as a continuum. His later novels include *The Light in the Forest* (1953; film, 1958) and the autobiographical *The Waters of Kronos* (1960, National Book Award).

Riding, Laura *or* **Laura Riding Jackson** *originally* Laura Reichenthal (b. Jan. 16, 1901, New York City—d. Sept. 2, 1991, Sebastian, Fla.) Poet, critic, and prose writer influential among the avant-garde in the 1920s and '30s.

After attending Cornell University, Riding came to be associated with the Fugitives, a prominent group of Southern writers. From 1926 to 1939 she lived abroad, mostly with the poet and critic Robert Graves. Together they established the Seizin Press (1927–38) and published the journal *Epilogue* (1935–38). Their *Survey of Modernist Poetry* (1927) developed ideas of close textual analysis that influenced New Criticism.

In 1941 Riding married the critic Schuyler B. Jackson, and until his death in 1968 they worked together on lexicographical studies. She completed their unique *Rational Meaning: A New Foundation for the Definition of Words* in 1974, though it remained unpublished until 1997. She had ceased to write poetry, which she renounced as "inadequate." Her prose writings, including her late philosophical work *The Telling* (1972), were highly esteemed among a small readership. Her *Collected Poems* (1938) was revised in 1980, and *First Awakenings: The Early Poems* was published in 1992. In 1991 she received the Bollingen Prize for *The Word "Woman."*

Riis \\'rēs\\, **Jacob A(ugust)** (b. May 3, 1849, Ribe, Denmark—d. May 26, 1914, Barre, Mass.) Journalist and social reformer.

Riis immigrated to the United States at 21 and eventually found work as a police reporter for the *New York Tribune* (1877–88) and the *New York Evening Sun* (1888–99). In covering New York's Lower East Side, he reported on the deplorable living conditions in the tenements. His photographs of the slum dwellings, for which he used the newly invented flashbulb to illuminate their squalid rooms and hallways, remain classics to this day. He compiled his findings in *How the Other Half Lives* (1890), which shocked the nation's social conscience and led to the first significant New York legislation to curb the slum landlords' abuses.

He carried on his crusade in such later books as *The Children of the Poor* (1892) and *Children of the Tenements* (1903), while publishing numerous articles and lecturing widely to arouse public sentiment. His autobiography, *The Making of an American*, appeared in 1901.

Riley, James Whitcomb (b. Oct. 7, 1849, Greenfield, Ind.—d. July 22, 1916, Indianapolis) Poet remembered for nostalgic dialect verse, often called "the Hoosier poet."

Riley gained his reputation with a series of poems in Hoosier dialect ostensibly written by a farmer (Benj. F. Johnson, of Boone) and contributed to the *Indianapolis Daily Journal*. They were later published as *The Old Swimmin' Hole and 'Leven More Poems* (1883). The later volumes of verse by "the poet of the common people," characterized by their kindly humor, pathos, sincerity, and naturalness, are *Pipes o' Pan at Zekesbury* (1888), *Old-Fashioned Roses* (1888), *The Flying Islands of the Night* (1891), *A Child-World* (1896), and *Home Folks*

James Whitcomb Riley

(1900). His best-known poems include "When the Frost Is on the Punkin," LITTLE ORPHANT ANNIE, "The Raggedy Man," and "An Old Sweetheart of Mine." His works enjoyed great popular success, as did his regular public readings of them. His poems were collected in his *Complete Works* (10 vols., 1916).

Rinehart, Mary Roberts *originally* Mary Roberts (b. Aug. 12, 1876, Pittsburgh, Pa.—d. Sept. 22, 1958, New York City) Novelist and playwright best known for her mystery stories.

Trained as a nurse, she married a physician and only took up writing as a result of financial difficulties in 1903. Her *The Man in Lower Ten*, serialized in 1907, was followed by her first book, *The Circular Staircase* (1908). Often writing a novel a year, she produced such works as *The Amazing Interlude* (1917), *The Breaking Point* (1922), and *Haunted Lady* (1942). In addition to mysteries, she wrote a long series of comic tales in the *Saturday Evening Post* about a dauntless spinster named Tish and her adventures with two friends. Of her plays, mostly written with Avery Hopwood, the most successful was *The Bat*, based on *The Circular Staircase* (1920; film, 1959). She also wrote romances and travel books, some of which reflected her experiences as a World War I correspondent.

George Ripley

Ripley, George (b. Oct. 3, 1802, Greenfield, Mass.—d. July 4, 1880, New York City) Journalist and reformer, the leading promoter and director of Brook Farm.

Ripley entered the Unitarian ministry after graduating from Harvard Divinity School in 1826. As pastor of Boston's Purchase Street Church, he became a member of the Transcendental Club and an editor of the *Dial*, the Transcendentalists' principal organ. A spokesman for the utopian socialist ideas of the French social reformer Charles Fourier, he left the pulpit in 1841 to found and direct the utopian agricultural and educational commune BROOK FARM in nearby West Roxbury. Brook Farm closed in 1847, and to pay off its debts Ripley took a job with Horace Greeley's *New York Tribune*, where, as its book reviewer, he became an arbiter of taste and culture for much of the reading public. His financial position nevertheless remained precarious until the publication of *The Cyclopedia* (1862), a widely acclaimed reference book that he coedited.

Robbins, Harold *originally* Francis Kane (b. May 21, 1916, New York City—d. Oct. 14, 1997, Palm Springs, Calif.) Novelist.

Orphaned at birth and raised in foster homes, Kane assumed the name Rubins from a foster family but later changed it to Robbins. He began speculating on crop futures at 19, was a millionaire by 20, then lost his fortune speculating unsuccessfully in sugar. After filing for bankruptcy, he took a job with Universal Pictures. Dissatisfied with its films, he bet the head of production $100 that he himself could write better stories. His *Never Love a Stranger* (1948; film, 1958) made him a best-selling author. *The Dream Merchants* (1949; film, 1980) and *A Stone for Danny Fisher* (1952) followed. He realized international fame with *The Carpetbaggers* (1961; film, 1964), based on the life of Howard Hughes. Virtually all of Robbins's gossipy-style formulaic works featured the triple themes of sex, money, and power. His 23 books—including *The Stiletto* (1960; film, 1969), *The Adventurers* (1966; film, 1970), *The Betsy* (1971; film, 1977), *The Pirate* (1974), *The Lonely Lady* (1976), *Dreams Die First* (1977), *The Story-teller* (1982), *The Predators* (1998), and *The Secret* (2000)—were distributed in over 40 countries and have sold some 750 million copies.

Robbins, Tom (*originally* Thomas Eugene) (b. July 22, 1936, Blowing Rock, N.C.) Countercultural novelist noted for his eccentric characters, playful optimism, and self-conscious wordplay.

Robbins dropped out of college to hitchhike across the United States, served in the air force in Korea, earned a master's degree in Far Eastern studies, and worked as a journalist and art critic before beginning to write his novels. *Another Roadside Attraction* (1971) is about a native of rural Washington who steals the mummy of Jesus Christ. *Even Cowgirls Get the Blues* (1976; film, 1993) is the story of a female hitchhiker with an enormous thumb. Robbins's later novels include *Still Life with Woodpecker* (1980), *Jitterbug Perfume* (1984), *Skinny Legs and All* (1990), *Half Asleep in Frog Pajamas* (1994), and *Fierce Invalids Home from Hot Climates* (2000). Highly imaginative and anarchically humorous though not profound, his novels have earned him a steady following among the generation that came of age in the 1960s and '70s.

Roberts, Elizabeth Madox (b. Oct. 30, 1886, Perryville, Ky.—d. March 13, 1941, Orlando, Fla.) Novelist, poet, and short-story writer noted for her accurate portrayal of Kentucky life.

Roberts suffered from ill health all her life, and only completed her studies at the University of Chicago in 1921. Her first novel, *The Time of Man* (1926), concerns a poor white woman living in Kentucky. Its rich texture, contrasting inner growth with outward hardship, and its account of life in Kentucky brought her international acclaim. *The Great Meadow* (1930), her best-known novel, describes a woman's spiritual return to the wilderness. Roberts's subsequent books generally dealt with similar themes and settings, and several later novels were similarly successful, but her fame declined in the 1930s. She also wrote two books of short stories, *The Haunted Mirror* (1932) and *Not By Strange Gods* (1941), and three books of poetry, *In the Great Steep's Garden* (1915), *Under the Tree* (1922), and *Song in the Meadow* (1940).

Roberts, Kenneth (Lewis) (b. Dec. 8, 1885, Kennebunk, Maine—d. July 21, 1957, Kennebunkport, Maine) Journalist and novelist who wrote fictional reconstructions of the American Revolution.

Roberts was a staff correspondent of the *Saturday Evening Post* from 1919 until 1928, when he devoted himself to writing fiction. Believing that the past is only poorly understood through historical accounts, he wrote *Arundel* (1930), a fictional treatment of the Revolutionary War. He is best known for *Northwest Passage* (1937; film, 1940), about the frontier soldier Major Robert Rogers, and *Rabble in Arms* (1933), a celebration of Revolutionary heroes who fought the British under conditions of great hardship. *Oliver Wiswell* (1940) was written from the Loyalist point of view. His other works, most of them very successful, include *The Lively Lady* (1931), *Lydia Bailey* (1947; film, 1952), and *Boon Island* (1956). Roberts researched his books minutely, and set several of them in his home state, which he considered a last outpost of rugged individualism.

Robinson, Edwin Arlington (b. Dec. 22, 1869, Head Tide, Maine—d. April 6, 1935, New York City) Poet best known for his short dramatic poems about the people in a small New England village.

After his family suffered financial reverses, Robinson cut short his attendance at Harvard and moved to New York, where he worked as a timekeeper on subway construction, enduring years of poverty and obscurity before his poetry began to attract attention. From *The Children of the Night* (1897) to *The Man Against the Sky* (1916), his best poetic form was the dramatic lyric, as exemplified in the latter's title poem. Among his best poems of this period are RICHARD CORY, MINIVER CHEEVY, "For a Dead Lady," "Flammonde," and "Eros Turannos." Many tell the stories of tragic and despairing lives in Tilbury Town, a fictional location modeled on Gardiner, Maine, where he grew up.

In 1905 Robinson's work attracted the attention of Theodore Roosevelt, who gave him a sinecure at the U.S. Customs House in New York (1905–9). *Merlin* (1917), the first of his long blank-verse narrative poems based on the King Arthur legends, was followed by *Lancelot* (1920) and *Tristram* (1927, Pulitzer Prize). His *Collected Poems* (1921, Pulitzer Prize) was followed by *The Man Who Died Twice* (1924, Pulitzer Prize) and *Amaranth* (1934), the most acclaimed of his later narrative poems; later short poems include MR. FLOOD'S PARTY, "Many Are Called," and "The Sheaves." He was perhaps the most honored American poet of his time, though his work has been somewhat less read in the decades since his death.

Robinson, James Harvey (b. June 29, 1863, Bloomington, Ill.—d. Feb. 16, 1936, New York City) Historian.

After earning degrees at Harvard University (M.A., 1888) and the University of Freiburg (Ph.D., 1890), Robinson taught European history at the University of Pennsylvania (1891–95) and Columbia University (1895–1919). His notion of "new history" was explicated in *The New History* (1911); there he called for historians to use the social sciences in historical scholarship, and to pay attention to social, cultural, scientific, and intellectual history in addition to politics and economics, while contending controversially that the study of the past should serve primarily to improve the present.

Robinson resigned from Columbia in 1919 to help found the New School for Social Research, but soon left the school to devote himself to writing. In 1921 he published his popular success *The Mind in the Making* (1921), an optimistic survey of intellectual history. The waning of his optimism became evident in *The Ordeal of Civilization* (1926). He also wrote several influential and widely used college textbooks, among them *An Introduction to the History of Western Europe* (1902) and *The Development of Modern Europe* (2 vols., 1907–8; with Charles A. Beard).

Roethke \\ˈret-kē, ˈreth-kē\\, **Theodore** (b. May 25, 1908, Saginaw, Mich.— d. Aug. 1, 1963, Bainbridge Island, Wash.) Poet.

Roethke was educated at the University of Michigan and Harvard University. He later taught at several institutions, notably the University of Washington (1947–63). From 1935 on, his career was interrupted by hospitalizations for breakdowns and manic depression.

His first book of poetry, *Open House*, called "completely successful" by W. H. Auden, was published in 1941; like his later works, it contains short, highly controlled poems that exhibit his introspection and intense lyricism. It was followed by *The Lost Son* (1948) and *Praise to the End!* (1951). By now his work was receiving extremely favorable attention; *The Waking* (1953) won a Pulitzer Prize; *Words for the Wind* (1957) won a National Book Award and the Bollingen Prize, and *The Far Field* (1964) won a second National Book Award. His *Collected Poems* were published in 1966. *I Am! Says the Lamb* (1961) is a collection of children's poems. His essays and lectures are collected in *On the Poet and His Craft* (1965).

Rogers, Will(iam Penn Adair) (b. Nov. 4, 1879, near Oologah, Indian Territory [now in Oklahoma]—d. Aug. 15, 1935, near Point Barrow, Alaska) Humorist and entertainer.

Of part-Cherokee parentage, Rogers attended a series of boarding schools and subsequently worked as a cowboy on his father's ranch. While traveling abroad, he joined a Wild West show as a rope twirler, and on his return he transferred his act to vaudeville, gradually adding an offhand humorous patter in a Southwestern drawl, which audiences loved. He made his first New York appearance in 1905, and in 1915 he joined Ziegfeld's Follies, where his talk began to include political humor.

In 1922 he began writing a weekly column for the *New York Times* that was soon syndicated nationally. Noted for its good-natured but sharp criticism of contemporary public figures and affairs, it eventually reached an audience estimated at 40 million, and his radio talks made his comfortable drawl a beloved presence in tens of millions of households nationwide. He also wrote a series of books in a similar vein, including *Rogerisms, the Cowboy Philosopher on Prohibition* (1919), *The Illiterate Digest* (1924), and *There's Not a Bathing Suit in Russia* (1927).

He began appearing in films in 1918, and enjoyed great success as an actor during the Depression in such films as *A Connecticut Yankee* (1931), *State Fair* (1933), *David Harum* (1934), and *Steamboat Round the Bend* (1935). His death in a plane crash with the pilot Wiley Post was widely mourned.

Rolvaag \\'rœl-ˌvȯg, *Engl* 'rōl-ˌväg\\, **O(le) E(dvart)** (b. April 22, 1876, Dönna Island, Helgeland, Norway—d. Nov. 5, 1931, Northfield, Minn.) Norwegian-American novelist and educator noted for his realistic portrayals of Norwegian settlers on the Dakota prairies and of the clash between transplanted and native cultures in the United States.

After working as a fisherman, Rolvaag immigrated to the United States in 1896. He was educated at St. Olaf College, and would spend most of his life there as a teacher of Norwegian and the history of Norwegian immigration. He wrote and originally published his works in Norwegian, and worked closely with the translators of the English versions.

Two novels from 1925 were translated as GIANTS IN THE EARTH (1927). His finest work, it tells of Norwegian immigrant life on the South Dakota prairies in the 1870s, representing its positive aspects in Per Hansa, the negative aspects in his wife Beret. *Peder Victorious* (1929) and *Their Fathers' God* (1931) continued the story to the second generation. Rolvaag's other novels include *Pure Gold* (1920, translated 1930), *The Boat of Longing* (1921, translated 1933), and *The Third Life of Per Smevik* (1912, translated 1971).

Eleanor Roosevelt

Roosevelt, (Anna) Eleanor (b. Oct. 11, 1884, New York City—d. Nov. 7, 1962, New York City) Humanitarian, diplomat, and writer.

The niece of Pres. Theodore Roosevelt, she was schooled in England, and in 1905 she married her distant cousin Franklin D. Roosevelt. She raised their five children and became active in politics after her husband was crippled by polio in 1921.

As First Lady from 1933 to 1945, Roosevelt traveled around the United States to report on living and working conditions and public opinion for her husband, on whose policies she exerted considerable influence. She supported such causes as child welfare and civil rights. She wrote a syndicated newspaper column, "My Day," and numerous articles and books, including *This Is My Story* (1937), *The Moral Basis of Democracy* (1940), *This I Remember* (1949), *On My Own* (1958), and an *Autobiography* (1961).

During World War II she traveled to military bases worldwide to raise morale. After her husband's death in 1945, she was appointed a delegate to the United Nations. As chair of its Commission on Human Rights (1946–51), she helped draft the Universal Declaration of Human Rights. In the 1950s she traveled widely for the U.N., and her humanitarian work made her the most admired woman in the world.

Roosevelt, Theodore (b. Oct. 27, 1858, New York City—d. Jan. 6, 1919, Oyster Bay, N.Y.) President of the United States, writer, naturalist, and soldier.

Theodore Roosevelt

Born into a prominent New York family, Roosevelt was sickly from birth but set about determinedly to overcome his weakness, acquiring a passion for the vigorous life. He graduated with honors from Harvard, and soon entered the New York legislature, where he became a notably independent Republican leader. After the death of his wife in 1884, he left politics to ranch in the Dakota Territory. He also began writing historical works, including *The Naval War of 1812* (1882). In 1886 he returned to run unsuccessfully for governor, then again retired to write such books as *Hunting Trips of a Ranch Man* (1885), biographies of Thomas Hart Benton and Gouverneur Morris, and *The Winning of the West* (4 vols., 1889–96). As a civil-service commissioner (1889–95) and head of the city's police commissioners (1895–97), he gained national prominence for his battles against corruption. At the start of the Spanish-American War in 1898 he joined Col. Leonard Wood in organizing a cavalry unit, later called the Rough Riders; his book *The Rough Riders* appeared in 1899. He returned to New York a hero and was elected governor.

Elected vice president in 1900, he became president after William McKinley's assassination in 1901, and his first term saw the passage of the Sherman Antitrust Act. Elected in his own right in 1904, he passed consumer-protection laws, set aside vast tracts of land as national forests and parks, and began construction of the Panama Canal. For mediating an end to the Russo–Japanese War, he was awarded the Nobel Peace Prize in 1906.

After declining to run for reelection in 1908, Roosevelt traveled in Africa and Europe. In 1912, failing to win the Republican nomination for president, he organized the Bull Moose (Progressive) Party and ran as its nominee. He continued to write numerous books, including *Progressive Principles* (1913), *History as Literature* (1913), and *America and the World War* (1915). His lifetime output also includes some 2,000 articles on history, politics, travel, and nature, and more than 150,000 personal letters.

Rosten \\'rȯs-tən\\, **Leo (Calvin)** (b. April 11, 1908, Lodz, Poland—d. Feb. 19, 1997, New York City) Author and social scientist known for his popular books on Yiddish and for his comic novels about the immigrant night-school student Hyman Kaplan.

At age 3 Rosten immigrated with his parents to Chicago. He earned a doctorate from the University of Chicago in 1937, worked as a screenwriter, and held a series of wartime government-information jobs before joining the staff of *Look* magazine in 1949, where he would remain until 1971, while also lecturing at Columbia University.

In 1937 Rosten (as Leonard Q. Ross) published *The Education of H*Y*M*A*N K*A*P*L*A*N*. Based on his experiences teaching English to immigrants, it is full of puns and malapropisms based on the fractured English of the cherubic, naive Kaplan, for whom the plural of "sandwich" is "delicatessen," and was acclaimed for its high spirits and its comic mastery of Yiddish-inflected English. Two sequels followed, *The Return of H*Y*M*A*N K*A*P*L*A*N* (1959) and *O K*A*P*L*A*N! My K*A*P*L*A*N!* (1976).

At *Look* Rosten edited a series of articles that formed the basis of *A Guide to the Religions of America* (1955), noted for its readability and scholarly accuracy. *The Story Behind the Painting* (1962), a respected popular art-history book, also grew from a magazine assignment. He enjoyed instant success with *The Joys of Yiddish* (1968), a comic but solidly researched dictionary of Yiddish words and their many nuances, which he expanded in *The Joys of Yinglish* (1989).

Roth, Henry (b. Feb. 8, 1906, Tysmenica, Galicia, Austria-Hungary [now Tismenitsya, Ukraine]—d. Oct. 13, 1995, Albuquerque, N.M.) Author known for his novel CALL IT SLEEP.

Roth's family arrived in the United States when he was an infant, and he graduated from the City College of New York. *Call It Sleep,* his autobiographical novel about a young Jewish immigrant, appeared in 1934 to laudatory reviews but only sold 4,000 copies before going out of print. In the late 1950s, Alfred Kazin, Irving Howe, and others revived public interest in the book, which came to be recognized as a Jewish-American classic and a masterpiece of 1930s proletarian literature. Roth attempted to write a second novel shortly after finishing the first, and brought out short stories in the *New Yorker*, but he published no more novels for decades, during which he held a variety of jobs and lived in Maine and New Mexico. He began writing again in the late 1960s, and the story and essay collection *Shifting Landscape* appeared in 1987. He began a projected six-volume series, *Mercy of a Rude Stream,* that returned to the themes of *Call It Sleep*, but only completed its first three volumes—*A Star Shines Over Mt. Morris Park* (1994), *A Diving Rock on the Hudson* (1995), and *From Bondage* (1996)—before his death.

Roth, Philip (Milton) (b. March 19, 1933, Newark, N.J.) Novelist who first gained notice for works about Jewish middle-class life and the painful entanglements of sexual and familial love.

After attending Bucknell University and doing graduate work at the University of Chicago, Roth achieved fame with *Goodbye, Columbus* (1959, National Book Award; film, 1969), whose title novella candidly depicts the boorish materialism of a Jewish middle-class suburban family. His admired first novel, *Letting Go* (1962), was followed by *When She Was Good* (1967), but he did not recapture the success of his first book until the appearance of the outrageous PORTNOY'S COMPLAINT (1969).

Several minor works, including *The Breast* (1972) and *The Professor of Desire* (1977), were followed by the important *The Ghost Writer* (1979), centering on the aspiring young writer Nathan Zuckerman. *Zuckerman Unbound* (1981) and *The Anatomy Lesson* (1983) trace Zuckerman's subsequent life and career. All three were republished with the novella *The Prague Orgy* as *Zucker-man Bound* (1985). *The Counterlife* (1986, National Book Critics Circle Award) was the fourth novel in the series. The memoir *Patrimony* (1991, National Book Critics Circle Award) concerns the loss of Roth's father. In *Operation Shylock* (1993) a narrator named Philip Roth meets his double, who also calls himself Philip Roth, in Jerusalem. *Sabbath's Theater* (1995), the hilariously scabrous story of an aging, sex-obsessed puppeteer, won the National Book Award, and *American Pastoral* (1997), about an "all-American" Jew whose daughter becomes a terrorist, received the Pulitzer Prize. *The Human Stain* (2000) is an ironic story about a professor who falls victim to political correctness.

Rowlandson \\'rō-lənd-sən\\, **Mary** *originally* Mary White (b. c.1637, England—d. Jan. 5, 1710/11, Wethersfield, Conn.) Colonial writer.

White emigrated to America as a child and in 1653 moved to the frontier village of Lancaster, Mass. In 1656 she married Joseph Rowlandson, Lancaster's first regular minister. In 1676, during King Philip's War, Indians attacked Lancaster and took 24 captives, including Rowlandson and her children. She was kept a prisoner for three months before being ransomed back to her husband; her children were returned later.

Her husband died in 1678, and around that time she wrote an vivid account of her captivity for her children. *The Soveraignty & Goodness of God, Together with the Faithfulness of His Promises Displayed; Being a Narrative of the Captivity and Restauration of Mrs. Mary Rowlandson*, published in 1682, soon became a classic, and it remains one of the best firsthand accounts of 17th-century Indian life and of Puritan–Indian conflicts in early New England.

Rowson \\'rau̇-sən\\, **Susanna** *originally* Susanna Haswell (b. c.1762, Portsmouth, Hampshire, England—d. March 2, 1824, Boston) Anglo-American actress, educator, and author.

Daughter of a naval lieutenant, she had several books published in London before *Charlotte Temple* (1791), a conventional, sentimental story of seduction and remorse, which became immensely popular. After being republished in Philadelphia in 1794, it became the first best-seller in America.

In 1792, with her husband, William Rowson, she went on the stage; the two performed in Scotland before moving to the United States in 1793. She became a strong partisan of America (as against Britain), founded a boarding school in Massachusetts, and edited the *Boston Weekly Magazine* (1802–5). Among her many other works are such novels as *Rebecca* (1792), *Sarah, the Exemplary Wife* (1813), and *Charlotte's Daughter* (1828); such plays as *Slaves in Algiers* (1794) and the musical *The Volunteers* (1795); and such textbooks as *A Spelling Dictionary* (1807) and *Biblical Dialogues Between a Father and His Family* (1822).

Rukeyser \'rük-ī-zər, 'rùk-ī-zər\, **Muriel** (b. Dec. 15, 1913, New York City—d. Feb. 12, 1980, New York City) Poet and activist best known for her poems concerning social and political issues.

While studying at Vassar College and Columbia University, Rukeyser contributed poems of a personal nature to *Poetry* magazine. Her *Theory of Flight* (1935) won the Yale Series of Younger Poets award. She broadened her experience by passionate involvement in the issues of the day. She attended the Scottsboro trials (a major civil-rights case) and witnessed the opening events of the Spanish Civil War, and the scope of her poetry widened accordingly. *U.S. 1* (1938) describes the oppressed poor along the industrial Atlantic seaboard; the sequence "The Book of the Dead," about West Virginia miners dying of silicosis, is considered one of her best works. Her use of fragmented, emotional imagery is sometimes thought lavish, but her poetry has been praised for its power and acuity. Her *Collected Poems* was published in 1978.

In addition to her 14 volumes of poetry, she translated the poetry of such writers as Octavio Paz and Gunnar Ekelöf, and wrote criticism, books for juveniles, and well-received biographies of Wendell Willkie and Willard Gibbs.

Rule, Jane (b. March 28, 1931, Plainfield, N.J.) American-Canadian writer known for her exploration of lesbian themes.

After graduating from Mills College, Rule studied briefly at University College, London, and Stanford University, then taught in Massachusetts before moving to Vancouver in 1956, where she taught intermittently at the University of British Columbia until 1972.

Rule's characters are usually rewarded for following their hearts and punished for emotional cowardice. *Desert of the Heart* (1964; film, *Desert Hearts*, 1984), her first and best-known novel, is considered a lesbian classic. *This Is Not for You* (1970) is written as an (unmailed) letter to the narrator's best friend, whose love she denies at the cost of her own happiness. *Against the Season* (1971) explores the interwoven lives of several people in a small town. Later novels include *The Young in One Another's Arms* (1977), *Contract with the World* (1980), *Memory Board* (1987), and *After the Fire* (1989). Her story collections include *Theme for Diverse Instruments* (1975), *Outlander* (1981), and *Inland Passage* (1985). In *Lesbian Images* (1975) she discusses her own sexuality and the history of lesbianism and addresses the work of 12 lesbian writers. Other essays are collected in *A Hot-Eyed Moderate* (1985).

Rumaker \'rü-₁mā-kər\, **Michael** (b. March 5, 1932, Philadelphia) Author whose early fiction reflected the disaffection of the Beat generation.

Rumaker graduated with honors from Black Mountain College. In the memoir *Robert Duncan in San Francisco* (1996) he describes the new vitality the Beat movement brought to all the arts. From the late 1950s Rumaker's short stories, such as "The Desert" (1957), were frequently anthologized. He was hospitalized for an emotional breakdown from 1958 to 1960; his novel *The Butterfly* (1962) tells of a young man struggling back from an emotional breakdown. *Exit 3* (1966; U.S. title, *Gringos*) contains short fictions rife with marginal characters and random violence. *A Day and a Night at the Baths* (1979) and *My First Satyrnalia* (1981) are accounts of initiation into New York's homosexual community. His later works include *To Kill a Cardinal* (1992) and *Pagan Days* (2001).

Runyon \ˈrən-yən\, **(Alfred) Damon** (b. Oct. 4, 1884, Manhattan, Kan.—d. Dec. 10, 1946, New York City) Journalist and short-story writer, best known for his collection *Guys and Dolls*.

Runyon enlisted in the army at 18 and fought in the Philippines in the Spanish-American War. He later wrote for newspapers in the West for 10 years. Though he gained a reputation as a political and feature reporter, his passion was for sports. In 1911 he moved to New York, where he joined the *New York American*. He covered the New York baseball clubs for many years, as well as boxing and other sports, focusing on human interest rather than strictly reporting facts. Over the years he wrote three syndicated columns, "Both Barrels," "As I See It," and "The Brighter Side." His stories about a racy section of Broadway, published in the *Saturday Evening Post* and elsewhere, were first collected in *Guys and Dolls* (1931). The book is representative of Runyon's style in its use of an exaggerated version of local idiom (dubbed "Runyonese") to portray the gamblers, promoters, fight managers, and racetrack bookies he encountered on the street. The stories were adapted by Frank Loesser for a celebrated stage musical (1950) through which Runyon posthumously earned his greatest fame. His later collections include *Blue Plate Special* (1934) and *Money from Home* (1935). His successful screenplays include *Lady for a Day* (1933), *Little Miss Marker* (1934), and *A Slight Case of Murder* (1938; based on a play written with Howard Lindsay).

S

Sagan \\'sā-gən\\, **Carl (Edward)** (b. Nov. 9, 1934, Brooklyn, N.Y.—d. Dec. 20, 1996, Seattle, Wash.) Astronomer and science writer.

After obtaining his Ph.D. from the University of Chicago in 1960, Sagan worked on planetary astronomy and the Search for Extraterrestrial Intelligence (SETI) project at the Smithsonian Astrophysical Observatory (1962–68). In 1968 he became director of the Laboratory of Planetary Studies at Cornell University.

With the publication of *The Cosmic Connection* (1973), he gained prominence as a popular science writer and commentator noted for his clear writing and enthusiasm. *The Dragons of Eden* (1977) won a Pulitzer Prize. In 1980 he coproduced and narrated the television series *Cosmos*, whose companion book became the best-selling English-language science book of all time. In the 1980s he studied the environmental effects of nuclear war and helped popularize the term "nuclear winter."

His other writings include *Atmospheres of Mars and Venus* (1961), *Planetary Exploration* (1970), *Broca's Brain* (1979), the novel *Contact* (1985), *Nuclear Winter* (1985), and *The Demon-Haunted World* (1996).

Said \\sä-'ēd\\, **Edward W(illiam)** (b. Nov. 1, 1935, Jerusalem—d. Sept. 24, 2003, New York City) Palestinian-American critic who studied literature in light of sociocultural politics.

Born to a well-to-do Christian family, Said grew up in Cairo. He attended a New England boarding school and Princeton University and earned his doctorate from Harvard before joining the Columbia University faculty in 1963. His first book, *Joseph Conrad and the Fiction of Autobiography* (1966), expanded on his doctoral thesis. In his best-known and most influential work, *Orientalism* (1978), he examined Western stereotypes about the Orient, specifically the Islamic world, and argued that Orientalist scholarship is based on Western imperialism. His books about Middle Eastern politics include *The Question of Palestine* (1979), *After the Last Sky* (1986), and *The Politics of Dispossession* (1994). Among his other books are *Beginnings: Intention and Method* (1975), *The World, the Text, and the Critic* (1983), and *Culture and Imperialism* (1993).

Salinger \\'sal-in-jər\\, **J(erome) D(avid)** (b. Jan. 1, 1919, New York City) Writer whose novel THE CATCHER IN THE RYE won him legions of admirers.

Salinger's stories began to appear in periodicals in 1940. He served in the wartime army, and was hospitalized for stress. His name and writing style became increasingly associated with the *New Yorker*, which published almost all his later stories. Some of the best made use of his wartime experiences: "For Esmé—With Love and Squalor" (1950) describes a soldier's poignant encounter with two British children, and "A Perfect Day for Bananafish" (1948) concerns the suicide of the sensitive, despairing veteran Seymour Glass.

Major critical and popular recognition came with the publication of *The Catcher in the Rye* in 1951. Its humor and colorful language place it in the tradition of *Huckleberry Finn* and the stories of Ring Lardner, but its hero, like most of Salinger's younger characters, views his life with an added dimension of precocious self-consciousness. The book has sold millions of copies in the decades since its publication. *Nine Stories* (1953) added to his reputation.

Eastern mysticism began to color Salinger's writings in the 1950s. FRANNY AND ZOOEY (1961) brought together two earlier *New Yorker* stories; both deal with the Glass family, as do the two stories in *Raise High the Roof Beam, Carpenters and Seymour: An Introduction* (1963). He moved to Cornish, N.H., in 1953, and his reclusive habits in his later years made his personal life a matter of intense speculation among devotees. Successive candid memoirs by his young lover (1998) and his daughter (2000) evoked intense controversy.

Saltus \\'sȯl-təs\\, **Edgar Evertson** (b. Oct. 8, 1855, New York City—d. July 31, 1921, New York City) Novelist and popular historian.

Educated at Yale and abroad, Saltus received a law degree from Columbia in 1880 but never practiced. He wrote a popularized history of the Roman emperors, *Imperial Purple* (1893), and another of the Russian czars, *Imperial Orgy* (1920), as well as books on Balzac and Schopenhauer. *Anatomy of Negation* (1886) is a study of antitheistic philosophies from earliest times. His novels, popular in their time for their wit and their shockingly erotic incidents, include *Mr. Incoul's Misadventure* (1887), *Vanity Square* (1906), and *Daughters of the Rich* (1912), and reveal Saltus as one of the few Americans to adopt the sophisticated cynicism, art-for-art's-sake credo, and mannerisms of the European school of Decadents.

Sanchez \\'san-chez\\, **Sonia (Benita)** *originally* Wilsonia Driver (b. Sept. 9, 1934, Birmingham, Ala.) Poet, playwright, and educator.

Sanchez graduated from Hunter College and briefly studied at NYU. From 1966 she has taught in a succession of institutions, chiefly Temple University. In the 1960s she published poetry in numerous journals. She married the writer and ex-convict ETHERIDGE KNIGHT in 1968, and her first book, *Homecoming* (1969), contained invective against "white America" and "white violence." Thereafter she continued to write on what she called "neoslavery," the social and psychological enslavement of blacks. Much of her verse is written in black speech patterns, eschewing traditional English grammar and pronunciations. Her later collections include *I've Been a Woman* (1978), the well-known *homegirls & handgrenades* (1984), and *Under a Soprano Sky* (1986).

Sandburg, Carl (August) (b. Jan. 6, 1878, Galesburg, Ill.—d. July 22, 1967, Flat Rock, N.C.) Poet, historian, novelist, and folklorist.

When the Spanish-American War broke out in 1898, Sandburg enlisted in the infantry. These early years he would later describe in his autobiography, *Always the Young Strangers* (1953). From 1910 to 1912 he was an organizer for the Social Democratic Party and secretary to the mayor of Milwaukee. Moving to

Carl Sandburg

Chicago in 1913, he became an editor of *System*, a business magazine, and later joined the staff of the *Chicago Daily News*.

In 1914 a group of his poems, including the well-known CHICAGO, appeared in *Poetry* magazine (they would be issued as *Chicago Poems* in 1916) and made an instant and favorable impression. In Whitmanesque free verse, Sandburg eulogized American workers: "Pittsburgh, Youngstown, Gary, they make their steel with men" (*Smoke and Steel*, 1920). In *Good Morning, America* (1928) he seemed to have lost some of his faith in democracy, but from the depths of the Great Depression he wrote *The People, Yes* (1936), a poetic testament to the common man. His popular biography *Abraham Lincoln: The Prairie Years* (2 vols., 1926) was followed by the huge *Abraham Lincoln: The War Years* (4 vols., 1939), which won the Pulitzer Prize. Between the two sets he published a biography of his brother-in-law, *Steichen, the Photographer* (1929).

By the postwar years he had become a venerable national figure. In 1948 he produced a long novel, REMEMBRANCE ROCK, that recapitulates the American experience from Plymouth Rock to World War II. His *Complete Poems* (1950) won him another Pulitzer Prize. The folk songs he sang before delighted audiences were issued in two popular collections, *The American Songbag* (1927) and *New American Songbag* (1950). He also wrote four books for children— ROOTABAGA STORIES (1922), *Rootabaga Pigeons* (1923), *Rootabaga Country* (1929), and *Potato Face* (1930).

Sandoz \'san-dōz\, **Mari** (*originally* Marie Susette) (b. 1901, Sheridan County, Neb.—d. March 10, 1966, New York City) Biographer and novelist known for her scrupulously researched books of the early American West.

Sandoz's early days as a student and teacher in rural Nebraska—a rigorous life that left her blind in one eye at 13—prepared her to depict pioneer and Indian life realistically. She wrote almost 80 stories while in college, but her first success came in her mid-30s, with *Old Jules* (1935), a story of her father's hard farm life. Her many other books include the biography *Crazy Horse* (1942); *Cheyenne Autumn* (1953; film, 1964), about Indians leaving a reservation to return home; *The Buffalo Hunters* (1954), about the white settlers' slaughter of bison and its social impact on the West; and *The Battle of the Little Bighorn* (1966).

Santayana \ˌsän-tä-ˈyä-nä, *commonly* ˌsan-tə-ˈyan-ə\, **George** *originally* Jorge Augustín Nicolás Ruiz de Santillana (b. Dec. 16, 1863, Madrid, Spain—d. Sept. 26, 1952, Rome, Italy) Spanish-American philosopher, poet, and humanist.

Born of Spanish parents, he never relinquished his Spanish citizenship, and, though he was to write in English with subtlety and poise, he did not begin to learn the language until taken at 8 to join his mother in Boston. He graduated from Harvard College and studied in Berlin before returning to Harvard to complete his doctorate. In 1889 he joined its philosophy faculty, where he formed a brilliant triumvirate with the older William James and Josiah Royce.

The Sense of Beauty (1896), an important work on aesthetics, discusses the nature and elements of aesthetic feelings. The vital affinity between aesthetic and moral faculties is illustrated in *Interpretations of Poetry and Religion* (1900), particularly in its discussion of Browning. His five-volume *Life of Reason* (1905–6) is a major theoretical work. Much later, in *Realms of Being* (4 vols., 1927–40), he would recast his whole system of thought. His essays were gathered into *Three Philosophical Poets: Lucretius, Dante, and Goethe* (1910) and *Winds of Doctrine* (1913), which discusses Shelley's poetry and Henri Bergson's and Bertrand Russell's philosophies.

Living in Europe when his mother died in 1912, he retired from teaching and never returned to America. In 1924 he settled permanently in Rome, where he produced works that consolidated his reputation as a critic and man of letters. Most of his energies in his later years went into speculative philosophy. His only novel, *The Last Puritan* (1935), became a best-seller. His autobiography, *Persons and Places* (3 vols., 1944–53), though admired, revealed him as an opponent of democracy and liberalism.

Saroyan \sə-'rȯi-ən\, **William** (b. Aug. 31, 1908, Fresno, Calif.—d. May 18, 1981, Fresno) Writer who made his initial impact in the Great Depression with brash, irreverent stories celebrating the joy of living in spite of poverty, hunger, and insecurity.

The son of an Armenian immigrant, Saroyan left school at 15 and continued his education by reading and writing on his own. His first collection of stories, *The Daring Young Man on the Flying Trapeze* (1934), was soon followed by another collection, *Inhale and Exhale* (1936). His first play, *My Heart's in the Highlands*, was produced by the Group Theatre in 1939. In 1940 Saroyan refused the Pulitzer Prize for his play *The Time of Your Life* (1939; film, 1948), claiming it was no better than anything else he had written.

William Saroyan

Saroyan's conviction of the basic goodness of all people, especially the obscure and naive, and of the value of life is evident throughout his work, and his mastery of the vernacular makes his characters vibrantly alive. Most of his stories are based on his childhood and family, notably the collection *My Name is Aram* (1940) and the novel THE HUMAN COMEDY (1943; film, 1943, Academy Award). Novels such as *Rock Wagram* (1951) and *The Laughing Matter* (1953) were inspired by his marriage, fatherhood, and divorce. He also wrote several enjoyable memoirs, including *Here Comes, There Goes You Know Who* (1961), *Not Dying* (1963), *Days of Life and Death and Escape to the Moon* (1971), and *Places Where I've Done Time* (1975).

Sarton, May (*originally* Eleanore Marie) (b. May 3, 1912, Wondelgem, Belgium—d. July 16, 1995, York, Maine) Poet, novelist, and essayist on the themes of mind-body conflict, creativity, lesbianism, and the trials of age and illness.

Daughter of the historian of science George Sarton, she worked as an actress while writing poetry from an early age. Her novels, which often earned greater acclaim from the public than from critics, increasingly reflected the concerns of her own life. Her early fiction, such as *The Single Hound* (1938) and *A Shower of Summer Days* (1952), was set in Europe and showed only glimpses of autobiography. *Mrs. Stevens Hears the Mermaids Singing* (1965), considered her most important novel, addresses issues of artistic expression. Her later novels include *As We Are Now* (1973), *A Reckoning* (1978), *The Magnificent Spinster* (1985), and *The Education of Harriet Hatfield* (1989).

Sarton preferred writing poetry to prose. Of her many volumes of poetry, *The Land of Silence* (1953), *In Time Like Air* (1958), and *A Private Mythology* (1966) are cited as among her best, the last for its varied forms and invocation of Japanese, Indian, and Greek cultures. Her *Collected Poems* (1993) demonstrated her range of subjects and styles. Her late autobiographical writings, including *After the Stroke* (1989), *Endgame* (1992), and *Encore* (1993), offer meditations on illness and aging.

Schlesinger \'shlā-ziŋ-ər, 'shle-sin-jər\, **Arthur M(eier)** (b. Feb. 27, 1888, Xenia, Ohio—d. Oct. 30, 1965, Boston) Historian and educator.

After earning a doctorate from Columbia University, Schlesinger taught at Midwestern universities until 1924, when he joined the Harvard University faculty. There he became one of the century's most influential teachers of American history, training a significant number of the nation's finest historians. Through a long series of works beginning with *The Colonial Merchants and the American Revolution* (1917), he helped broaden the study of U.S. history by emphasizing social and urban developments. His greatest production was *A History of American Life* (13 vols., 1928–43), which he coedited with Dixon Ryan Fox; a comprehensive survey of the country's cultural, social, and economic development, it includes the distinguished volume *The Rise of the City, 1878-1898* (1933) by Schlesinger himself.

Schlesinger, Arthur M(eier), Jr. (b. Oct. 15, 1917, Columbus, Ohio) Historian.

After studies at Harvard and Cambridge universities, Schlesinger made his reputation with his first book, the much-admired *The Age of Jackson* (1945, Pulitzer Prize). He joined the Harvard faculty in 1946. His greatest work was the three-volume *The Age of Roosevelt* (1957–60), beginning with *The Crisis of the Old Order*. Active in Democratic politics, Schlesinger helped found the liberal Americans for Democratic Action and was a speechwriter for Adlai Stevenson's presidential campaigns. He served as a special assistant for Latin-American affairs in John F. Kennedy's administration, whose history he later recounted in *A Thousand Days* (1965; Pulitzer Prize, National Book Award). His other books include *The Vital Center* (1949), *The Bitter Heritage* (1967), *The Imperial Presi-*

dency (1973), and *The Cycles of American History* (1986). From 1967 until 1995 he taught at the City University of New York.

Schulberg \\'shül-bərg\\, **Budd (Wilson)** (b. March 27, 1914, New York City) Novelist, screenwriter, and journalist.

The son of a film producer, Schulberg grew up in Hollywood, attended Dartmouth College, and became a script reader and then a screenwriter. His first novel, *What Makes Sammy Run* (1941), about an unprincipled studio mogul, was a great success. During and after World War II, he served in the military and was commended for collecting visual evidence of Nazi war crimes for the Nuremberg trials. *The Harder They Fall* (1947) is a fictional exposé of corruption in professional boxing. The main character of *The Disenchanted* (1950) is based on F. Scott Fitzgerald. Called before Congress for his political activities in 1947, Schulberg cooperated with the committee, naming 15 colleagues as Communist Party members. His screenplays include the original *On the Waterfront* (1954, Academy Award); those for *The Harder They Fall* (1956) and *A Face in the Crowd* (1957) were based on his own novels. In the 1960s he helped establish the Douglass House Watts Writers Workshop in the Watts district of Los Angeles after riots there, and in 1971 he founded the Frederick Douglass Creative Arts Center in New York. In *Moving Pictures* (1981), he described his Hollywood childhood; *Love, Action, Laughter, and Other Sad Tales* was published in 1989.

Schuyler \\'skī-lər\\, **James (Marcus)** (b. Nov. 9, 1923, Chicago—d. April 12, 1991, New York City) Poet, playwright, and novelist associated with the New York school of poets.

Schuyler attended college in West Virginia, served in the navy (1943–47), and lived in Italy before settling in New York. There he met the other principal poets of what would become known as the New York school—Frank O'Hara, John Ashbery, and Kenneth Koch—and began to write for *Art News*. An acute observer of natural landscapes, he would become known for describing common experiences with familiar images in compact lines of varied rhythm. His best-known volumes of poetry are *Freely Espousing* (1969), *The Crystal Lithium* (1972), whose title poem examines the variability of experience while describing a beach in winter, and *Hymn to Life* (1974). Among his other verse collections are *Salute* (1960), *May 24th or So* (1966), *A Sun Cab* (1972), *Song* (1976), *The Fireproof Floors of Witley Court* (1976), *The Home Book* (1977), *The Morning of the Poem* (1980, Pulitzer Prize), and *A Few Days* (1985). He also wrote plays and novels, including *A Nest of Ninnies* (1969; with Ashbery).

Schwartz, Delmore (b. Dec. 8, 1913, Brooklyn, N.Y.—d. July 11, 1966, New York City) Poet, short-story writer, and critic noted for his lyrical descriptions of cultural alienation and the search for identity.

Delmore Schwartz

Educated at the University of Wisconsin, NYU, and Harvard, Schwartz later taught at Harvard and other schools. His first book, *In Dreams Begin Responsibilities* (1939), which brought him immediate fame, included the title story and a group of lyrical and imaginative poems. Subsequent publications included *Shenandoah* (1941), a verse play; *Genesis, Book I* (1943), a long introspective poem; and *The World Is a Wedding* (1948) and *Successful Love* (1961), short-story collections dealing primarily with middle-class Jewish family life.

Schwartz's lucid literary criticism was published in various periodicals, and he served as an editor for *Partisan Review* (1943–55). His *New and Selected Poems* (1959) received the Bollingen Prize. Brilliant but increasingly alcoholic and mentally unstable, he died alone in a New York hotel at 52. He was the model for the title character in Saul Bellow's *Humboldt's Gift* (1975).

Seaman, Elizabeth Cochrane See **Nellie Bly**

Selby, Hubert, Jr. (b. July 23, 1928, New York City) Novelist and screenwriter.

Selby left school at 15, served in the merchant marine during World War II, and held a variety of odd jobs. He gained instant notoriety for the brutal and graphic narrative realism of his first book, *Last Exit to Brooklyn* (1964; film, 1989). His later work, several of them in a similar vein, include *The Room* (1971), *The Demon* (1976), *Requiem for a Dream* (1978; film, 2000), *Song of the Silent Snow* (1986), and *The Willow Tree* (1998). He has also written several screenplays, including *Day and Night* (1986) and *Soldier of Fortune* (1990).

Maurice Sendak

Sendak \'sen-dak\, **Maurice (Bernard)** (b. June 10, 1928, New York City) Illustrator and author of children's books.

The son of Polish-Jewish immigrants, Sendak attended Dartmouth College and received formal art training at New York's Art Students League. The first children's books he illustrated were Marcel Aymé's *The Wonderful Farm* (1951) and Ruth Krauss's *A Hole Is to Dig* (1952). Both were successful, and Sendak went on to illustrate more than 80 children's books by such writers as Meindert De Jong, Else Holmelund Minarik, and Randall Jarrell. With *Kenny's Window* (1956), he began both writing and illustrating stories. These include the miniature four-volume *Nutshell Library* (1962) and the important trilogy composed of *Where the Wild Things Are* (1963, Caldecott Medal), *In the Night Kitchen* (1970), and *Outside Over There* (1981). In these and other books, his children confront their sometimes terrifying imaginings and emerge unharmed. In 1975 he wrote and directed the animated television special *Really Rosie*; with Carole King, he adapted it as a musical in 1978. In addition to creating opera versions of some of his own stories, including *Where the Wild Things Are,* Sendak has designed several other works for the stage, notably a production of Mozart's *Magic Flute* (1980). He is the only American illustrator to have received the international Hans Christian Andersen Medal (1970).

Seton, Anya (*originally* Ann) (b. c.1904, New York City—d. Nov. 8, 1990, Old Greenwich, Conn.) Author of best-selling, exhaustively researched, romantic historical and biographical novels.

The daughter of Ernest Thompson Seton, she traveled extensively with her parents and used these and later travels as inspirations for her books. In 1941 she published her first book, *My Theodosia*, a novel about the daughter of Aaron Burr. She is best known for her gothic romance *Dragonwyck* (1944; film, 1946) and her novel *Foxfire* (1950; film, 1955), about a white woman who marries a Southwest Indian. Among her many other novels are *The Turquoise* (1946), *The Hearth and Eagle* (1948), the historical romance *Katherine* (1954), *The Winthrop Woman* (1958), and a number of dark romances with English settings, including *Devil Water* (1962), *Avalon* (1965), and *Green Darkness* (1972).

Seton, Ernest Thompson or **Ernest Seton-Thompson** *originally* Ernest Evan Thompson (b. Aug. 14, 1860, South Shields, Durham, England—d. Oct. 23, 1946, Seton Village, Santa Fe, N.M.) Naturalist and writer known for his animal stories.

Seton's family immigrated to Canada in 1866. He gained experience as a naturalist by trailing and hunting in the prairie country of Manitoba, which he would use as the basis for his animal stories. His most popular book, *Wild Animals I Have Known* (1898), is a collection of those empathetic but harshly unsentimental stories, illustrated by himself. Other popular volumes included *The Biography of a Grizzly* (1900), *Lives of the Hunted* (1901), and *Two Little Savages* (1903), as well as books of woodcraft and other skills.

Ernest Thompson Seton

Having moved to the United States, he gained a wide reputation as a lecturer and advocate for nature and contributed thousands of articles to magazines. Deeply concerned with the future of the prairie, he fought to establish Indian reservations and parks for animals threatened by extinction. To provide children with opportunities for nature study, he founded the Woodcraft Indians organization in 1902, and he chaired the committee that established the Boy Scouts of America in 1910.

Seuss, Dr. See **Theodor Seuss Geisel**

Sewall \\'sü-əl\\, **Samuel** (b. March 28, 1652, Bishopstoke, England—d. Jan. 1, 1730, Boston) Colonial merchant and judge.

Sewall immigrated to America as a boy and graduated from Harvard College in 1671. In 1681 he became manager of the printing press for the New England colonies. He was appointed to the governor's council in 1684 and, though not trained in the law, to the superior court, where, as chief justice, he became known for his clear and compassionate decisions. In 1692 he was named to a special commission to try the Salem witchcraft cases, in which 19 people were condemned to death. Sewall was the only judge to later admit the error of these decisions, standing silently in Boston's Old South Church in 1697 while his confession of error and guilt was read aloud.

As a writer, he is best remembered for his *Diary* (3 vols., published 1878–82), which describe the life of the late New England Puritans. His other writings included an early antislavery appeal, *The Selling of Joseph* (1700), and *A Memorial Relating to the Kennebeck Indians* (1721), an argument for humane treatment of Indians.

Sexton, Anne *originally* Anne Gray Harvey (b. Nov. 9, 1928, Newton, Mass.—d. Oct. 4, 1974, Weston, Mass.) Poet whose work is noted for its confessional intensity.

A lifelong resident of New England, Sexton worked briefly as a model and a librarian before suffering the first of her severe depressions after the births of her children. Urged to write poetry by her psychiatrist, she studied under Robert Lowell at Boston University, where she met Sylvia Plath and other poets. She later taught briefly at a high school and later at Harvard and other universities.

Her first book of poetry, *To Bedlam and Part Way Back* (1960), is an intense examination of her mental breakdowns and subsequent recoveries. In *All My Pretty Ones* (1962) and *Live or Die* (1966, Pulitzer Prize) she continues her probing treatment of her personal life and continuing emotional illness. Her later volumes include *Love Poems* (1969), *Transformations* (1971), and *The Book of Folly* (1972). Her last poems were published after her suicide at 45, in *The Awful Rowing Toward God* (1975), *45 Mercy Street* (1976), and *Uncollected Poems with Three Stories* (1978), as was *No Evil Star: Selected Essays, Interviews, and Prose* (1985).

Shange \ˈshäŋ-gä\, **Ntozake** *originally* Paulette Williams (b. Oct. 18, 1948, Trenton, N.J.) Author of plays, poetry, and fiction noted for their feminist themes and racial and sexual anger.

The daughter of a surgeon, Williams met many luminaries of the jazz world as a child in her parents' home. She graduated from Barnard College and earned her master's degree from USC. She adopted an African name in 1971, and began to appear as a dancer and reciter. Her 1975 theater piece (or "choreopoem") *For Colored Girls Who Have Considered Suicide/When the Rainbow Is Enuf* quickly brought her fame. A set of 20 poems on the power of black women to survive despair and pain, for performance by seven actors, it ran for seven months off-Broadway before moving to Broadway, and was later produced throughout the country and on television.

Shange has since created a number of other theater works that employed poetry, dance, and music while abandoning conventions of plot and character development, the most popular being her 1980 adaptation of Brecht's *Mother Courage*, featuring a black family during the Civil War. Her poetry collections include *Nappy Edges* (1978) and *Ridin' the Moon in Texas* (1987), and her novels include *Sassafrass, Cypress & Indigo* (1982), *Betsey Brown* (1985), and *Liliane: Resurrection of the Daughter* (1994).

Shapiro, Karl (Jay) (b. Nov. 10, 1913, Baltimore—d. May 18, 2000, New York City) Poet and critic whose verse ranges from passionately physical love lyrics to sharp social satire.

Shapiro came to critical attention in 1942 with the collection *Person, Place and Thing*. He served in the army during World War II, and his *V-Letter and Other Poems* (1944), with "Elegy for a Dead Soldier," won the Pulitzer Prize. His later works include *Poems of a Jew* (1958), *White-Haired Lover* (1968), and *Adult Bookstore* (1976), as well as such works of criticism as *Beyond Criticism* (1953), *In Defense of Ignorance* (1960), and *The Poetry Wreck* (1975). Shapiro was consultant in poetry to the Library of Congress 1946–47, and editor of *Poetry* magazine 1950–56. From 1956 he taught at the Universities of Nebraska, Illinois, and California. His *Collected Poems* was published in 1978, and *New & Selected Poems* in 1987. *Poet: An Autobiography in Three Parts* appeared in 1988. In 1968 he received the Bollingen Prize.

Shaw, Irwin *originally* Irwin Gilbert Shamforoff (b. Feb. 27, 1913, New York City—d. May 16, 1984, Davos, Switzerland) Prolific playwright, screenwriter, and author of acclaimed short stories and best-selling novels.

Shaw began his career at 21 by writing scripts for radio shows. He wrote his antiwar one-act play *Bury the Dead* for a 1935 contest; though it lost, it was produced the next year. He wrote his first screenplay, *The Big Game*, in 1936. His stories, which appeared in such magazines as the *New Yorker* and *Esquire* beginning in the late 1930s, were praised for their plotting, naturalness of narration, and characterization.

Shaw's experiences in the army in Europe during World War II led to his writing *The Young Lions* (1948; film, 1958), a novel about three young soldiers; it became a best-seller, and thereafter he devoted most of his career to writing novels. Among the best-known of his 12 novels are *Two Weeks in Another Town* (1960; film, 1962), *Evening in Byzantium* (1973; film, 1978), and *Beggarman, Thief* (1977). Probably his most popular novel, though it was derided by critics, was *Rich Man, Poor Man* (1970).

Sheed \\'shēd\\, **Wilfrid (John Joseph)** (b. Dec. 27, 1930, London, England) Author of satirical fiction as well as essays, biographies, and other nonfiction works.

Sheed's parents, authors themselves, founded Sheed & Ward, a leading Roman Catholic publishing firm. The family immigrated to the United States in 1940, though Sheed returned to England to study at Oxford. In 1959 he began writing film, drama, and book criticism for magazines and newspapers in New York.

The lives of individuals working in the mass media are the subjects of most of his comic novels. Journalists battle over the editorial pecking order in *Office Politics* (1966), while compulsive analysis and perfectionism destroy the life of a critic in *Max Jamison* (1970). A reporter views the moral hypocrisy of a candidate in *People Will Always Be Kind* (1973). His other novels include *The Hack* (1963), *Transatlantic Blues* (1978), and *The Boys of Winter* (1987). Among his nonfiction books are *Frank and Maisie: A Memoir with Parents* (1985), the biographies *Muhammad Ali* (1975) and *Clare Boothe Luce* (1982), the essay collections *The Good Word & Other Words* (1978) and *Essays in Disguise* (1990), and *Baseball and Lesser Sports* (1991).

Sheehan, Neil (b. Oct. 27, 1936, Holyoke, Mass.) Journalist.

After graduating from Harvard University, Sheehan served in the army (1959–62). He went to Vietnam as bureau chief for United Press International, and as a correspondent for the *New York Times* from 1964 he reported on the Vietnam War from Saigon and later Washington, D.C. In 1971 he obtained the classified Pentagon Papers from Daniel Ellsberg; his story in the *Times* about the secret history of the war related in the documents resulted in strenuous government attempts to halt publication and became perhaps the most celebrated news story of the decade.

Sheehan's first book, *The Arnheiter Affair* (1972), deals with the flawed captain of a naval vessel. He spent some 15 years on his best-known work, *A Bright Shining Lie* (1988); a biography of Col. John Paul Vann that illuminates much of the war's history, it won universal acclaim and received the Pulitzer Prize. It was followed by *After the War Was Over* (1992).

His wife, Susan Sheehan, is the author of several admired studies of the lives of members of the American underclass, including *Is There No Place on Earth for Me?* (1983, Pulitzer Prize).

Sheldon, Sidney (b. Feb. 11, 1917, Chicago) Novelist and producer.

Sheldon worked as a script reader before beginning to write film scripts for several studios. His screenplay for *The Bachelor and the Bobby-Soxer* (1947) won an Academy Award; he also collaborated on the screenplays for such movies as *Easter Parade* (1948) and *Annie Get Your Gun* (1950). He both wrote and directed *Dream Wife* (1953) and *The Buster Keaton Story* (1957). In the 1960s he created and produced the television shows *I Dream of Jeannie* and *The Patty Duke Show*. In the 1970s he began to publish a series of best-selling (if not critically admired) novels, including *The Naked Face* (1970; film, 1985), *The Other Side of Midnight* (1974; film, 1977), *Bloodline* (1977; film, 1979), *Rage of Angels* (1980; film, 1983), *If Tomorrow Comes* (1985; film, 1986), *Memories of*

Midnight (1990; film, 1991), *Nothing Lasts Forever* (1994), *The Best Laid Plans* (1997), and *The Sky Is Falling* (2000).

Shepard, Sam *originally* Samuel Shepard Rogers (b. Nov. 5, 1943, Fort Sheridan, Ill.) Playwright and actor whose plays have adroitly blended images of the American West, science fiction, and elements of popular and youth culture.

After a year of college, Shepard joined a touring company of actors and in 1963 moved to New York to pursue his theatrical interests as well as songwriting and rock-band drumming. His earliest attempts at playwriting, a rapid succession of one-act dramas, found a receptive audience off-off-Broadway, and in the 1965–66 season he won Obie awards for *Chicago*, *Icarus's Mother*, and *Red Cross*.

He lived in England from 1971 to 1974, and two notable plays, *The Tooth of Crime* (1972)—a brutal fantasy on American celebrity—and *Geography of a Horse Dreamer* (1974), premiered in London. In late 1974 he became playwright-in-residence at San Francisco's Magic Theater, where most of his subsequent plays have had their first productions.

Shepard's works of the mid-1970s showed a heightening of earlier techniques and themes. In *Killer's Head* (1975), the rambling monologue—part of his stock-in-trade—blends horror and banality in a murderer's last thoughts before electrocution. *Angel City* (1976) depicts the destructive machinery of the Hollywood entertainment industry, and *Suicide in B-Flat* (1976) exploits the potentials of music as an expression of character.

Curse of the Starving Class (1976), the Pulitzer Prize–winning BURIED CHILD (1979), TRUE WEST (1981), and FOOL FOR LOVE (1983; film, 1985), like several other works, examine tempestuous blood relationships in a fragmented society. His other plays include *La Turista* (1966), *Operation Sidewinder* (1970), *The Unseen Hand* (1970), *Seduced* (1979), *A Lie of the Mind* (1985), *Simpatico* (1995), *The Late Henry Moss* (2000), and several plays cowritten with the director Joseph Chaikin. The husband of the actress Jessica Lange, Shepard has also written a number of screenplays, including *Paris, Texas* (1984), has become well known as a screen actor, and has directed feature films.

Sherwood, Robert E(mmet) (b. April 4, 1896, New Rochelle, N.Y.—d. Nov. 14, 1955, New York City) Playwright whose works reflect his involvement in social and political problems.

A graduate of Harvard, Sherwood enlisted in the Canadian army and suffered exposure to mustard gas in World War I. Working as drama editor of *Vanity Fair* (1919–20) and as an editor of the humor magazine *Life* (1920–28), he was an original member of the Algonquin Round Table, the center of a New York literary coterie. His first play, *The Road to Rome* (1927), criticizes the pointlessness of war, a recurring theme in his work. The heroes of THE PETRIFIED FOREST (1935; film, 1936) and *Idiot's Delight* (1936, Pulitzer Prize; film, 1939) begin as detached cynics but recognize

their own moral bankruptcy and sacrifice themselves for their fellowmen. In ABE LIN-
COLN IN ILLINOIS (1939, Pulitzer Prize; film, 1940) and *There Shall Be No Night*
(1941, Pulitzer Prize), in which his pacifist heroes decide to fight, Sherwood suggests
that a person can make his own life significant only by losing it for others. In 1938 he
helped establish the Playwrights' Company, which became a major producing company. He also wrote the screenplays for such films as *The Scarlet Pimpernel* (1935),
Rebecca (1940), and *The Best Years of Our Lives* (1946, Academy Award).

The Lincoln play led to his introduction to Eleanor Roosevelt and ulti-
mately to his working for Franklin D. Roosevelt as speechwriter and adviser.
From his association with Roosevelt came much of the material for the book
Roosevelt and Hopkins (1948, Pulitzer Prize).

Shields, Carol *originally* Carol Warner (b. June 2, 1935, Oak Park, Ill.—d. July
16, 2003, Victoria, B.C.) Novelist.

After graduating from Hanover College, she married a Canadian, and the
couple moved to Canada in 1957, where they reared five children. After earning a
master's degree in 1975, she taught many years at the University of Manitoba,
and in 1996 was named chancellor of the University of Winnipeg. Her first books
were the poetry collections *Others* (1972) and *Intersect* (1974). Her first novel,
Small Ceremonies (1976), was followed by *The Box Garden* (1977), *Happen-
stance* (1980), *A Fairly Conventional Woman* (1982), the mystery *For Swann*
(1987), and *The Republic of Love* (1992). Her acclaimed semiautobiographical
novel *The Stone Diaries* (1993) won a Pulitzer Prize. Her later novels include
Larry's Party (1997), *Dressing Up for the Carnival* (2000), and *Unless* (2002).
Many of her works examine friendships between women.

Shillaber \'shil-ˌā-bər\, **Benjamin P(enhallow)** (b. July 12, 1814,
Portsmouth, N.H.—d. Nov. 25, 1890, Chelsea, Mass.) Poet and humorist.

After working as a newspaper printer's apprentice, Shillaber joined the
Boston Post as a printer in 1838. In 1847 he created his fictional alter ego, Mrs.
Partington, whose humorous commentary soon made him a national figure. From
1851 to 1853 he published the humor weekly *The Carpet-Bag,* in which
appeared the work of such humorists as the young Mark Twain and Artemus
Ward. After it failed, he returned to the *Boston Post* as a reporter. From 1856 to
1866 he wrote for the *Saturday Evening Gazette,* while also giving humorous
lectures around the country. The best-known of his books, *Life and Sayings of
Mrs. Partington* (1854), sold 50,000 copies within weeks of its publication. His
later books include *Knitting-Work* (1859) and *Lines in Pleasant Places* (1874).
He also wrote a series of children's books featuring Ike Partington.

Shirer \'shīr-ər\, **William L(awrence)** (b. Feb. 23, 1904, Chicago—d. Dec.
28, 1993, Boston) Journalist, historian, and novelist best known for his massive
Rise and Fall of the Third Reich.

In the 1920s, '30s, and '40s, Shirer was stationed in Europe and India as a correspondent for the *Chicago Tribune* and the Universal News Service. From 1937 to 1941 he also served as radio broadcaster for CBS, relaying to America news of the European crises leading to World War II. His impassioned alarms about the Nazi danger earned him several journalistic awards.

Shirer collected his impressions of European political events in *Berlin Diary* (1941), which gained an international audience for its simple documentation of survival amidst horror. In the 1950s he began his research for the comprehensive but readable *Rise and Fall of the Third Reich* (1960, National Book Award). His other major historical work, *The Collapse of the Third Republic* (1960), is considered by some the best one-volume study of France during the interwar period. In *Gandhi: A Memoir* (1980) he recalled his interviews with Gandhi in the early 1930s. His three-volume set of memoirs is collectively entitled *Twentieth-Century Journey* (1976–90). *Love and Hatred: The Troubled Marriage of Leo and Sonya Tolstoy* was published posthumously in 1994.

Showalter \\'shō-ˌwȯl-tər\\, **Elaine** (b. Jan. 21, 1941, Boston) Literary critic and founder of "gynocritics," a school of criticism concerned with the history, themes, genres, and structures of literature by women.

Showalter studied English at Bryn Mawr College, Brandeis University, and UC–Davis (Ph.D., 1970), then joined the faculty of Douglass College, where she developed women's studies courses. She published her doctoral thesis as her first book, *A Literature of Their Own* (1977), a study of British women novelists in which she created a critical framework for analyzing literature by women. As a result of the book, gynocritics became the leaders of American feminist criticism. *The Female Malady* (1985) was a historical examination of women and the practice of psychiatry. Her other books include *Sexual Anarchy: Gender and Culture at the Fin de Siècle* (1990) and *Sister's Choice: Tradition and Change in American Women's Writing* (1991). She has also edited several volumes, including *The New Feminist Criticism* (1985) and *Daughters of Decadence: Women Writers of the Fin de Siècle* (1993).

Sigourney \\'sig-ər-nē\\, **L(ydia) H(oward)** *originally* Lydia Howard Huntley (b. Sept. 1, 1791, Norwich, Conn.—d. June 10, 1865, Hartford, Conn.) Popular writer, educator, and one of the few American women of her time to succeed at a literary career.

Her first work, *Moral Pieces in Prose and Verse* (1815), was intended for the use of her pupils at the school she had opened in Hartford. Her best-known prose work (which included *Biography of Pious Persons,* 1832, and *How to Be Happy,* 1833) was *Letters to Young Ladies* (1833). In all she wrote almost 70 books and more than a thousand articles, relying on sentimental conventions of moral and religious themes, death and piety being her most popular subjects. She was perhaps the most widely read American poet during her lifetime, earning the sobriquet "the sweet singer of Hartford," but was not respected by her literary contemporaries.

Silko \\'sil-kō\\, **Leslie Marmon** (b. 1948, Albuquerque, N.M.) Poet and novelist.

While growing up on the Laguna Pueblo reservation in New Mexico, Silko (whose ancestry is mixed) learned Laguna traditions and myths from senior family members. After attending the University of New Mexico, she published the poetry collection *Laguna Woman* (1974). *Ceremony* (1977) was the first novel ever published by a Native American woman. Noted for its close observation of human nature and its nonchronological narrative, it follows its half-Laguna, half-white protagonist Tayo home to his reservation after World War II; his future bleak, he learns Laguna folklore and ceremonies that restore him. *Storyteller* (1981) is a collection of poetry, tribal stories, fiction, and photographs, and *The Delicacy and Strength of Lace* (1986) is a collection of letters exchanged by Silko and James A. Wright. In her second novel, *Almanac of the Dead* (1991), Indians whose lives and values are in tune with nature retake America from the environmentally destructive, personally perverse, and brutal whites. *Gardens in the Dunes* (1999) is a historical novel of the Ghost Dance.

Silverberg, Robert (b. Jan. 15, 1935, New York City) Science-fiction writer.

After studying comparative literature at Columbia University, Silverberg worked as a writer for science-fiction magazines, producing hundreds of stories under many pseudonyms. His early novels include *Revolt on Alpha C* (1955), *Collision Course* (1961), and *The Silent Invaders* (1963). His novel *Thorns* (1967) marked a transition to more complex works, which later included *Nightwings* (1969, Hugo Award), *A Time of Changes* (1971, Nebula Award), the best-selling *Lord Valentine's Castle* (1980), *Valentine Pontifex* (1983), *Gilgamesh in the Outback* (1987, Hugo Award), *At Winter's End* (1988), *Enter a Soldier. Later: Enter Another* (1990, Hugo Award), *Kingdoms of the Wall* (1993), *Mountains of Majipoor* (1995), and *Lord Prestimion* (1999). Silverberg has also written dozens of nonfiction and juvenile books and has edited several science-fiction and fantasy anthologies, including *Legends* (2000).

Simic \\'sim-ik, *originally* 'sē-mēch\\, **Charles** (b. May 9, 1938, Belgrade, Yugoslavia) Poet who evoked his eastern European heritage and his childhood experiences to comment on the dearth of spirituality in contemporary life.

Simic and his mother immigrated to the United States when he was 16 to be reunited with his father. After graduating from New York University, he began translating the works of Yugoslavian poets into English. Since 1974 he has taught at the University of New Hampshire.

Simic's first volume of poetry, *What the Grass Says* (1967), was well received by critics, who cited its rural European imagery. Among his many subsequent collections, most of them exhibiting a whimsical, humorous surrealism haunted by a sense of loss, are *Somewhere Among Us a Stone Is Taking Notes* (1969), *Dismantling the Silence* (1971), *School for Dark Thoughts* (1978), *Unending Blues* (1986), and *The World Doesn't End: Prose Poems* (1989), which received the Pulitzer Prize. Later collections include *The Book of Gods and Devils* (1990), *Dime-Store Alchemy* (1992), a collection of prose pieces written as a tribute to the artist Joseph Cornell, *Hotel Insomnia* (1993), *Walking the Black Cat* (1996), and *Jackstraws* (1999).

Simms, William Gilmore (b. April 17, 1806, Charleston, S.C.—d. June 11, 1870, Charleston) Outstanding Southern man of letters known especially for his historical novels.

A child prodigy, Simms had mastered four languages by 10, was publishing poetry in newspapers by 16, and had edited a magazine and published a volume of poetry by 19. As a state legislator and magazine and newspaper editor, he would become embroiled in political and literary quarrels as an upholder of slavery, but his novels remained admired in the North as well as the South.

Simms's strength was his racy and masculine English prose style and his humorous treatment of his rowdy frontier characters. His gift as a teller of tales in the oral tradition and his careful preparation of historical materials earned him comparison with James Fenimore Cooper. *The Yemassee* (1835), set in colonial times, was his most popular novel. Notable among the others are *Pelayo* (1838), with its 8th-century setting, and *Vasconselos* (1853), set in the 16th century. A series set during the Revolution includes *The Partisan* (1835), *The Kinsmen* (1841), *Katherine Walton* (1851), *Woodcraft* (1854), and *Eutaw* (1856). He also wrote two noteworthy romances about frontier life in the South, *Richard Hurdis* (1838) and *Border Beagles* (1840); the story collection *The Wigwam and the Cabin* (1845); and a *History of South Carolina* (1840). He published 19 volumes of poetry. Most popular of his biographies were those of Francis Marion (1844) and Chevalier Bayard (1847). His criticism is represented in *Views and Reviews of American Literature* (1845).

Simon, Kate *originally* Kaila Grobsmith (b. Dec. 5, 1912, Warsaw, Poland—d. Feb. 4, 1990, New York City) Memoirist and travel writer whose work was noted for its readability and wit.

Simon's family immigrated to the United States in 1917 and settled in New York, where she later took editorial positions at *Publisher's Weekly* and the *New Republic*. Her first guidebook, *New York Places and Pleasures* (1959), was well received, and she later won praise for similar guides to Italy, London, Mexico, and Paris, written with elegance and verve. Her three memoirs, BRONX PRIMITIVE (1982), *A Wider World* (1986), and *Etchings in an Hourglass* (1990), won acclaim for their unsentimental evocation of her working-class immigrant Jewish family life.

Simon, (Marvin) Neil (b. July 4, 1927, New York City) Playwright, screenwriter, television writer, and librettist, one of the most popular playwrights in the history of the American theater.

Simon briefly attended college and served in the army before working as a writer for Phil Silvers, Sid Caesar, and other television comics throughout the 1950s, an experience he would later portray in the play *Laughter on the 23rd Floor* (1994). His autobiographical *Come Blow Your Horn* (1961; film, 1963) ran for two years on Broadway. It was the first of a string of theatrical successes unparalleled in American theater history, including *Barefoot in the Park* (1963; film, 1967), *The Odd Couple* (1965, Tony Award; film, 1968), *The Star-Spangled Girl* (1966; film, 1971), *Plaza Suite* (1968; film, 1971), *Last of the Red Hot Lovers* (1969; film, 1972), *The Prisoner of Second Avenue* (1971; film, 1975), *The Sunshine Boys* (1972; film, 1975), *California Suite* (1976; film, 1978), *Chapter Two* (1977; film, 1979), *I Ought to Be in Pictures* (1980; film, 1982), an admired trilogy of autobiographical plays consisting of *Brighton Beach Memoirs* (1983; film, 1986), *Biloxi Blues* (1985, Tony Award; film, 1988), and *Broadway Bound* (1986); and the acclaimed *Lost in Yonkers* (1991, Pulitzer Prize, Tony Award; film, 1993). He has written screenplays for the film adaptations of most of his plays, more of which more have been turned into films than those of any other playwright in history. His original screenplays include *The Out-of-Towners* (1970), *The Heartbreak Kid* (1972), and *The Goodbye Girl* (1977). He wrote the books for the musicals *Little Me* (1962), *Sweet Charity* (1966), *Promises, Promises* (1968), and *They're Playing Our Song* (1979).

Simpson, Louis (Aston Marantz) (b. March 27, 1923, Jamaica) Jamaican-American poet and critic.

Of Scottish-Russian ancestry, Simpson moved to New York at 17, graduated from Columbia University, and worked as a book editor before earning his doctorate from Columbia and taking teaching positions there and later at UC–Berkeley and (from 1967) SUNY–Stony Brook.

His conventional early poetry—that of *The Arrivistes* (1949) and *Good News of Death* (1955)—gave way to experimental free verse in *A Dream of Governors* (1959). Having come to believe that poetic expression should be original and natural, he abandoned poetic conventions with the publication of *At the End of the Open Road* (1963), which won him the Pulitzer Prize. His later collections include *Adventures of the Letter I* (1971), *Searching for the Ox* (1976), *Caviare at the Funeral* (1980), *The Best Hour of the Night* (1983), and *In the Room We Share* (1990). Simpson has also produced several critical studies of other poets, including *Three on the Tower* (1975) and *A Revolution of Taste* (1978); the anthology *Modern Poets of France* (1996); and the autobiographical *North of Jamaica* (1972) and *The King My Father's Wreck* (1994).

Sinclair, Upton (Beall) (b. Sept. 20, 1878, Baltimore—d. Nov. 25, 1968, Bound Brook, N.J.) Novelist and socialist polemicist, whose THE JUNGLE is a landmark among naturalistic proletarian novels.

Born to an eminent but financially straitened family, Sinclair began earning money by writing at 15, and supported himself with literary hackwork while doing graduate work at Columbia University. An assignment from a socialist weekly led him to write *The Jungle* (1906), his sixth novel and first popular success. Published at his own expense after several publishers rejected it, it became an immensely influential best-seller. He used the proceeds to open a socialist colony in Englewood, N.J., which was abandoned when the building was destroyed by fire in 1907.

A long series of other muckraking novels—among them *King Coal* (1917), *Oil!* (1927), based on the Teapot Dome Scandal, and *Boston* (1928), based on the Sacco-Vanzetti trial—followed, but none achieved the popularity of *The Jungle*. Sinclair again reached a wide audience with his Lanny Budd series, 11 contemporary historical novels constructed around an implausible antifascist hero, beginning with *World's End* (1940) and including *Dragon's Teeth* (1942, Pulitzer Prize).

During the economic crisis of the 1930s, he organized the EPIC (End Poverty in California) socialist reform movement. He ran repeatedly but unsuccessfully for public office as a Socialist; running as a Democrat for governor of California in 1934, he was only narrowly defeated. His autobiographical *American Outpost* (1932) was reworked and extended in *The Autobiography of Upton Sinclair* (1962).

Singer, Isaac Bashevis *Yiddish* Yitskhok Bashevis Zinger (b. July 14?, 1904, Radzymin, Poland, Russian Empire—d. July 24, 1991, Miami, Fla.) Polish-American writer of novels, short stories, and essays in Yiddish.

Born into a family of Hasidic rabbis, Singer received a traditional Jewish education at the Warsaw Rabbinical Seminary. His first novel, *Satan in Goray*, was published in installments in Poland shortly before he immigrated to the United States in 1935. Settling in New York, he initially worked for the Yiddish-language daily *Forverts (Forward),* using the pseudonym Varshavski.

Though Singer's works became most widely known in their English versions, he continued to write almost exclusively in Yiddish, personally supervising the translations. In his most important novels he depicts Jewish life in Poland and the United States in a rich blend of irony, wit, and wisdom flavored with the occult and the grotesque. They include THE FAMILY MOSKAT (1950), THE MAGICIAN OF LUBLIN (1960), *The Slave* (1962), *The Manor* (1967), *The Estate* (1969),

Isaac Bashevis Singer

Enemies, a Love Story (1972), *Shosha* (1978), and *The Penitent* (1983). His superb short stories, published in such collections as *Gimpel the Fool* (1957), *The Spinoza of Market Street* (1961), *Short Friday* (1964), *The Seance* (1968), *A Crown of Feathers* (1973, National Book Award), *Old Love* (1979), and *The Image* (1985), include the well-known GIMPEL THE FOOL and THE SPINOZA OF MARKET STREET.

Singer's most ambitious narratives, *The Family Moskat* and the continuous story spun out in *The Manor* and *The Estate*, chronicle the changes in and eventual breakup of large Jewish families during the late 19th and early 20th centuries as their members are differently affected by the secularism and assimilationist opportunities of the modern era. His shorter novels examine characters tempted by evil in various forms. His short stories, like his novels, are saturated with Jewish folklore, legends, and mysticism and display an incisive understanding of human weakness.

In 1978 Singer was awarded the Nobel Prize for Literature.

Singer, I(srael) J(oshua) (b. Nov. 30, 1893, Bigoraj, Poland, Russian Empire—d. Feb. 10, 1944, New York City) Polish-American writer in Yiddish, noted for his realistic historical novels.

The son of a Hasidic rabbi, Singer was the older brother of Isaac Bashevis Singer. He began writing tales of Hasidic life in 1915, then worked as a journalist in Warsaw in the 1920s and early 1930s. Several collections of his short stories were published during this time; the short story "The Pearl" was his first international success. His novel *Yoshe Kalb*, a description of Hasidic life in Galicia, appeared in 1932, the year before he immigrated to the United States. His subsequent writings appeared in serialized form in New York's Yiddish daily *Forverts (Forward)*.

Like his brother, Singer wrote multigenerational family novels, but he firmly placed his vivid characters in a larger historical and socioeconomic setting. *The Brothers Ashkenazi* (1936), his masterpiece, examines the rivalry of two very different brothers whose fortunes parallel that of their birthplace, the city of Lodz. *The Family Carnovsky* (1943) traces an assimilated German-Jewish family for several decades until its members must immigrate to the United States after the Nazi takeover. Singer also wrote short stories and plays.

Cornelia Otis Skinner

Skinner, Cornelia Otis (b. May 30, 1901, Chicago—d. July 9, 1979, New York City) Actress and author.

Skinner made her professional stage debut with her father, the eminent tragedian Otis Skinner, in *Blood and Sand* (1921), and she collaborated with him in writing her first play, *Captain Fury of the Holy Innocents* (1925). During the 1930s she wrote and staged a series of "monodramas," including *The Wives of Henry VIII* (1931) and *Edna, His Wife* (1937). In 1939 she won high praise performing in *Candida;* she confirmed her acting reputation in productions of such plays as *Theatre* (1941), *Lady Windermere's Fan* (1946), *Paris '90* (1952), and *The Pleasure of His Company* (1958), which she wrote with Samuel Taylor. Her diverse writing abilities were evident in her best-selling memoir *Our Hearts Were Young and Gay* (1942, with Emily Kimbrough) and in a moving biography of Sarah Bernhardt, *Madame Sarah* (1966).

Smiley, Jane (Graves) (b. Sept. 26, 1949, Los Angeles) Novelist.

Smiley studied at Vassar College and the University of Iowa (Ph.D., 1978), and has taught at Iowa State University since 1981. Her first novel, *Barn Blind* (1980), was followed by *At Paradise Gate* (1981), *Duplicate Keys* (1984), the short-story collection *The Age of Grief* (1987), *The Greenlanders* (1988), and the novellas *Ordinary Love & Good Will* (1989). *A Thousand Acres* (1991), a contemporary story inspired by *King Lear*, received a Pulitzer Prize and became a major best-seller. Her later books include *Moo* (1995), an academic satire set at a midwestern agricultural college; *The All-True Travels and Adventures of Lidie Newton* (1998), a historical novel set in "bleeding Kansas" before the Civil War; and *Horse Heaven* (2000), a satire about horse racing.

Smith, Charles Henry See **Bill Arp**

Smith, Dave (*originally* David Jeddie) (b. Dec. 19, 1942, Portsmouth, Va.) Poet and educator.

Educated at the University of Virginia and Ohio University (Ph.D., 1976), Smith has since taught at such institutions as the University of Utah (1976–80), Virginia Commonwealth University (1982–89), and Louisiana State University (from 1990), and is an editor of the *Southern Review*. Collections of his poetry, much of which first appeared in the *New Yorker*, include *Cumberland Station* (1976), *Goshawk, Antelope* (1979), *The Roadhouse Voices* (1985), *Cuba Night* (1990), *Fate's Kite* (1995), *Floating on Solitude* (1996), and *The Wick of Memory* (2000). He has also written the novel *Onliness* (1981) and the poem-and-story collection *Southern Delights* (1984), and he has coedited *The Morrow Anthology of Younger American Poets* (1985) and edited *The Essential Poe* (1991).

Smith, John (baptized Jan. 6, 1580, Willoughby, England—d. June 1631, London, England) English explorer and colonist.

After a period as a military adventurer, Smith joined an English group preparing to establish a colony in North America. He and about 100 others arrived in Chesapeake Bay in 1607 and established the first permanent English settlement at Jamestown, Va.; Smith became the colony's leader. From there he undertook a series of river voyages that enabled him to draw a remarkably accurate map of Virginia. On one voyage he was captured by Indians and saved from

John Smith

death by the chief's daughter, Pocahontas. In 1609 he was forced by an injury to return to England. Eager for further exploration, he contacted the Virginia Company of Plymouth and sailed in 1614 to the area he named New England, whose coast he carefully mapped.

Smith wrote and talked about the New World for the rest of his life. His writings include his *Map of Virginia with a Description of the Country, . . .* (1612), a similar *Description of New England* (1625), and his well-known *Generall Historie of Virginia, New England, and the Summer Isles* (1624). His vivid descriptions of the New World whetted the colonizing appetite of prospective English settlers.

Smith, Lee (b. Nov. 1, 1944, Grundy, Va.) Author of fiction about her native South.

Smith's first novel, *The Last Day the Dog Bushes Bloomed* (1968), was written while she was in college. Her generally comic stories are set in the contemporary South; eschewing the gothic and grotesque, they are filled with the details of everyday life. *Fancy Strut* (1973) was widely admired, as was her fourth novel, *Black Mountain Breakdown* (1980), and the short-story collection *Cakewalk* (1981). Critics noted her powerful characterizations of rural Southerners in the novel *Oral History* (1983), a history of a family over the course of 100 years. Her later books include the novels *Family Linens* (1985), *Fair and Tender Ladies* (1988), *The Devil's Dream* (1992), *Saving Grace* (1995), and *The Christmas Letters* (1996), and the story collections *Me and My Baby View the Eclipse* (1990) and *News of the Spirit* (1997).

Smith, Seba *pseudonym* **Major Jack Downing** (b. Sept. 14, 1792, Buckfield, Maine—d. July 28, 1868, Patchogue, N.Y.) Editor and humorist.

Smith graduated from Bowdoin College and worked as a newspaper editor before founding Maine's first daily newspaper, the *Portland Courier*, in 1829. The next year there began appearing the fictional letters of Major Jack Downing, a common man magnified as oracle, a Yankee full of horse sense and wise saws, and a threadbare office seeker exposing follies in the "mobocracy" of the Andrew Jackson presidency. Shameless pirating of Smith's invention led to his collecting the letters in book form in 1833. Another series of letters appeared in the *Daily National Intelligencer* from 1847 to 1853; these were collected in *My Thirty Years Out of the Senate* (1859). Smith's *Way Down East* (1854) was a popular collection of stories depicting the New England Yankee character.

Smith, Thorne *originally* James Thorne Smith, Jr. (b. 1892, Annapolis, Md.—d. June 21, 1934, Florida) Humorist.

After attending Dartmouth College, Smith worked in advertising. He served in the navy in World War I; his comic stories for the service newspaper *Broadside* were published as *Biltmore Oswald* (1918) and *Out o' Luck* (1919) and became widely popular. His best-known work, the whimsical comedy *Topper* (1926), inspired two films (1937, 1979) and a television series (1953–55); *Topper Takes a Trip* (1932; film, 1939) is a sequel. His other books, mainly farce and fantasy, include *The Stray Lamb* (1929), *The Night Life of the Gods* (1931), *Rain in the Doorway* (1933), and *Skin and Bones* (1933). He also wrote a prankish mystery, *Did She Fall?* (1930). His unfinished novel *The Passionate Witch* (published 1941; with Norman Matson) was adapted as the movie *I Married a Witch* (1942) and later inspired the television series *Bewitched* (1964–72). He died of a heart attack at 42.

Smith, William Jay (b. April 22, 1918, Winnfield, La.) Lyric poet who has written for both adults and children.

Smith spent much of his childhood on an army post, a period he recalled in *Army Brat* (1980). Educated at Washington University (M.A., 1941), he served in the navy (1941–45), did further graduate work at Columbia University and the universities of Oxford and Florence, and later taught at several colleges. His first collections of poems, *Poems* (1947) and *Celebration at Dark* (1950), revealed the breadth of his narrative range. Though he began to experiment with free verse with *The Tin Can* (1966), he is known for his strict adherence to traditional metrical forms. He began collecting his whimsical poems for children in *Laughing Time* (1955) and *Boy Blue's Book of Beasts* (1957); his later children's poetry included *Typewriter Town* (1960), *Ho for a Hat!* (1964), and *Laughing Time* (1990). He also edited several volumes of children's poetry, including *The Golden Journey* (1965; with Louise Bogan). His *Collected Poems* was published in 1990; *The World Below the Window* (1998) contains only serious adult poetry. He has also edited and translated poetry from several languages; his notable translations include Jules Laforgue's *Selected Writings* (1956). *The Spectra House* (1961) is a study of literary hoaxes and lampoons. In 1968–70 Smith was consultant in poetry to the Library of Congress.

Snodgrass, W(illiam) D(e Witt) (b. Jan. 5, 1926, Wilkinsburg, Pa.) Poet.

Snodgrass received his M.A. and M.F.A. degrees from the University of Iowa, and since 1980 he has taught at the University of Delaware. His first collection, *Heart's Needle* (1959), marked by careful formal control and a sensitive and solemn delineation of his experience of losing his daughter through divorce, won the Pulitzer Prize. *After Experience* (1968) exemplifies similar formal and thematic concerns. His later work—including *Remains* (1970), *If Birds Build with Your Hair* (1979), *D. D. Byrde Calling Jennie Wrenn* (1984), *The Death of Cock Robin* (1989), and *The Fuehrer Bunker* (1995)—employs free verse. His other writing includes several volumes of translations of European ballads, including *Selected Translations* (1998), and *In Radical Pursuit* (1975), a volume of criticism.

Snyder, Gary (Sherman) (b. May 8, 1930, San Francisco) Poet early identified with the Beat movement and later an important spokesman for communal living and ecological activism.

Snyder attended Reed College and studied Asian languages at UC–Berkeley. In the early 1950s he became associated with the Beats, whom he introduced to Buddhism, and he studied Zen in Japan from 1958 to 1966.

He published his first poetry collection in 1959. His poetry is rooted in ancient, natural, and mythic experience, and his style exhibits influences ranging from Whitman to Pound to haiku. Prominent in his first two books of poems, *Riprap* (1959) and *Myths and Texts* (1960), are images and experiences drawn from his work as a logger and forest ranger in the Northwest. In *The Back Country* (1967) and *Regarding Wave* (1969), the fusion of religion into everyday life reflects his interest in Eastern philosophies. Later collections include *Turtle Island* (1974, Pulitzer Prize), *Axe Handles* (1983), and *No Nature* (1992). Snyder's prose works include *Earth House Hold* (1969); *The Old Ways* (1977), on tribal life; *He Who Hunted Birds in His Father's Village* (1979), on Haida Indian myth; *The Real Work* (1980); *Passage Through India* (1984), about an Asian pilgrimage; and *The Practice of the Wild* (1990). In 1997 Snyder received the Bollingen Prize for his ongoing poetic cycle *Mountains and Rivers Without End*.

Sontag \\'sän-ˌtag\\, **Susan** *originally* Susan Rosenblatt (b. Jan. 16, 1933, New York City) Intellectual and novelist known for her essays on modern culture.

Sontag entered UC–Berkeley at 15, graduated from the University of Chicago, studied literature and philosophy at Harvard and the Sorbonne, and taught philosophy at several institutions before publishing her first novel, *The Benefactor* (1963). Already a contributor to such periodicals as *Partisan Review* and *Commentary*, she came to national attention in 1964 with the essay "Notes on 'Camp,'" and her brilliance, daring, and radical politics, combined with her striking good looks, soon brought her fame of a kind rarely achieved by American intellectuals. A second novel, *Death Kit* (1967), was followed by the influential *Against Interpretation* (1968), whose title essay argued against the ferreting out of symbols in literary texts. Her later collections of French-influenced essays would display her serious philosophical approach to aspects of modern culture rarely taken seriously at the time, including films and popular music. Another essay collection, *Styles of Radical Will* (1969), was followed by *On Photography* (1977), *Illness as Metaphor* (1977), *Under the Sign of Saturn* (1980), and *AIDS and Its Metaphors* (1988). She later successfully took up the challenge of the historical novel, producing the best-selling *The Volcano Lover* (1992), about Admiral Nelson and Emma Hamilton, and *In America* (2000, National Book Award), about the actress Helena Modrzejewska. She has also written screenplays and edited writings by Roland Barthes and Antonin Artaud.

Sorrentino \\ˌsȯr-en-ˈtē-nō\\, **Gilbert** (b. April 27, 1929, Brooklyn, N.Y.) Poet and experimental novelist.

Educated at Brooklyn College, Sorrentino cofounded (with LeRoi Jones and others) the journal *Neon* (1956), which would feature works by Beat writers; he was later book editor for *Kulchur* (1961–65). His poetry collections include *The Darkness Surrounds Us* (1960), *Black and White* (1964), *The Perfect Fiction* (1968), and *The Orangery* (1978). Among his avant-garde novels, in which he has followed the dictum that "form not only determines content but form *invents* content," are *The Sky Changes* (1966), each chapter of which is named for a town the protagonists visit; *Imaginative Qualities of Actual Things* (1971), a plotless, digressive satire of the 1960s art scene; *Splendide-Hôtel* (1973), a novelistic defense of poetry arranged in 26 alphabetical sections; *Mulligan Stew* (1979), a multilevel mélange of Joycean proportions that satirizes creativity, considered by some an apotheosis of avant-garde fiction; the admired *Aberration of Starlight* (1980), set in 1939; *Odd Number* (1985), which deals with unanswered questions; *Rose Theatre* (1987), each chapter of which is written in a different narrative style; *Misterioso* (1989), an exhaustive alphabetical catalog of everything discussed in *Odd Number* and *Rose Theatre*; and *Under the Shadow* (1991), 59 vignettes with recurring characters and images.

Southern, Terry (b. May 1, 1924, Alvarado, Texas—d. Oct. 29, 1995, New York City) Writer of satirical novels and screenplays.

After service in the wartime army, Southern studied at the University of Chicago, Northwestern University, and the Sorbonne. His first novel, *Flash and Filigree* (1958), satirizes medical and legal institutions. *Candy* (1958; written with Mason Hoffenberg), a hilarious parody of pornography about a libidinous young woman, gained him wide notoriety when it finally appeared in America in 1964. His other novels include *The Magic Christian* (1959; film, 1971), *Blue Movie* (1970), and *Texas Summer* (1991). *Red-Dirt Marijuana* (1967) is an admired collection of short stories and essays. One of the major American screenwriters of the 1960s, he wrote the scripts for such films as *Dr. Strangelove* (1964), *The Loved One* (1965), *The Cincinnati Kid* (1966), *Casino Royale* (1967), *Barbarella* (1967), *Easy Rider* (1969), and *The End of the Road* (1970). With his books and movies Southern probably contributed as much as any writer to setting the anarchic, absurdist tone of the 1960s counterculture.

Southworth, Emma *originally* Emma Dorothy Eliza Nevitte (b. Dec. 26, 1819, Washington, D.C.—d. June 30, 1899, Georgetown, Washington, D.C.) One of the most popular of America's 19th-century sentimental novelists.

After teaching school for five years, Nevitte married Frederick Southworth, an itinerant inventor. When the couple separated in 1844, she turned to writing to support her family. Her first novel, *Retribution* (1849), sold 200,000 copies. Writing as Mrs. E. D. E. N. Southworth, she went on to produce 66 more novels over the next 50 years, many of them first published serially in such magazines as the *Saturday Evening Post* and *New York Ledger*. Such novels as *The Curse of Clifton* (1852), *The Hidden Hand* (1859), and *The Fatal Marriage* (1863) reached wide audiences in the United States and Europe, and *Ishmael* and *Self-Raised* (both 1876) were huge successes. Her domestic stories, which relied on sentimental plots of the gothic genre that reflected prevailing values of piety and domesticity, are said to have contributed two new character types to American fiction: the self-made man and the independent woman.

Sparks, Jared (b. May 10, 1789, Willington, Conn.—d. March 14, 1866, Cambridge, Mass.) Editor and biographer.

Born into poverty, Sparks was educated at Harvard College and Harvard Divinity School, and became a Unitarian minister in 1819. In 1823 he purchased the *North American Review,* which under his editorship (until 1830) became the arbiter of literature in New England. In 1839, at Harvard, he became the first professor of secular history in the United States, and he served as president of the college from 1849 to 1853.

After writing a life of Gouverneur Morris (3 vols., 1932), he edited the *Writings of George Washington* (12 vols., 1834–37), *The Works of Benjamin Franklin* (10 vols., 1836–40), *The Diplomatic Correspondence of the American Revolution* (12 vols., 1829–30), and *The Library of American Biography* (25 vols., 1834–48). Though he published much valuable historical material, the value of his efforts was impaired by his editing methods, since he omitted passages likely to cause international ill will and sometimes embellished his subjects' writings. The exacting scholarly standards of a later age rendered much of his work obsolete.

Spillane \spi-'lān\, **Mickey** (*originally* Frank Morrison) (b. March 9, 1918, Brooklyn, N.Y.) Writer of pulp detective fiction.

A college dropout, Spillane began his career by writing for comic books and pulp magazines. His first novel—*I, The Jury* (1947; films, 1953, 1982)—introduced the detective Mike Hammer, who would appear in 12 other highly popular novels saturated with brutal violence and sex, including *My Gun Is Quick* (1950; film, 1957), *Vengeance Is Mine* (1950), *The Big Kill* (1951), and *Kiss Me Deadly* (1952; film, 1955). Having converted to the Jehovah's Witnesses, Spillane wrote no novels from 1953 to 1961; he resumed with *The Deep* (1961). He played the role of Hammer in the 1963 film version of *The Girl Hunters* (1962). *Day of the Guns* (1964) initiated a series featuring the international agent Tiger Mann. Among Spillane's later books were *The Erection Set* (1972), *The Last Cop Out* (1973), *The Killing Man* (1989), and *Black Alley* (1996), his thirteenth Mike Hammer novel. At his height in the 1950s, Spillane was perhaps the best-selling writer in the world.

Spingarn \'spin-ˌgärn\, **J(oel) E(lias)** (b. May 17, 1875, New York City—d. July 26, 1939, New York City) Critic and social reformer.

Born into a wealthy family, Spingarn studied at Columbia University (Ph.D. 1899), and thereafter taught comparative literature at Columbia until 1911. His several works of criticism and poetry include a *History of Literary Criticism in the Renaissance* (1899), *The New Criticism* (1911), *The New Hesperides and Other Poems* (1911), *Creative Criticism* (1917), and *Poetry and Religion* (1924). In 1919 he helped found the publishing firm of Harcourt, Brace, for which he served as literary adviser until 1932. In his later years he became a well-known horticulturist.

In 1909 Spingarn founded the National Association for the Advancement of Colored People (NAACP), of which he was successively chairman of the board (1913–19), treasurer (1919–30), and president (1930–39). In 1914 he established the prestigious Spingarn Medal, given annually to an African-American in recognition of merit and achievement. His brother, Arthur B. Spingarn (1878–1971), succeeded him as president of the NAACP.

Stafford, Jean (b. July 1, 1915, Covina, Calif.—d. March 26, 1979, White Plains, N.Y.) Short-story writer and novelist.

Stafford's admired first novel, *Boston Adventure* (1944), sold 400,000 copies and guaranteed her a position of prominence in literary circles. She followed it with two more novels, *The Mountain Lion* (1947) and *The Catherine Wheel* (1952), as well as children's books. She is principally remembered for her short stories, which appeared in such journals as the *New Yorker*, the *Kenyon Review*, and *Partisan Review*. Her *Collected Stories* (1969) won a Pulitzer Prize.

Stafford's personal life was marked by alcoholism, breakdowns, and illness and by troubled marriages to the writers Robert Lowell (1940–48), Oliver Jensen, and A. J. Liebling.

Standish, Burt L. See **Gilbert Patten**

Stanton, Elizabeth Cady *originally* Elizabeth Cady (b. Nov. 12, 1815, Johnstown, N.Y.—d. Oct. 26, 1902, New York City) Social reformer and women's-suffrage leader.

While studying law in her father's office, Cady learned of the discriminatory laws under which women lived. In 1840 she married the abolitionist Henry B. Stanton. By now a tireless agitator for women's rights, she helped secure passage in 1848 of a New York state law giving property rights to married women.

In 1848 she and Lucretia Mott organized the first women's-rights convention at Seneca Falls, N.Y. Stanton's "Declaration of Sentiments," modeled on the Declaration of Independence, detailed the inferior status of women and called for extensive reforms.

Elizabeth Cady Stanton

From 1851 she joined forces with Susan B. Anthony and traveled widely to speak at conventions and before legislatures. In addition to writing countless letters and pamphlets, as well as articles and essays for numerous periodicals, she coedited the women's-rights newspaper *The Revolution* (1868–70). In 1869 she became the founding president of the National Woman Suffrage Association, a post she would hold until 1892.

Stanton helped compile the first three volumes (1881–86) of the six-volume *History of Woman Suffrage* (1881–1922). In 1898 she published an autobiography, *Eighty Years and More*.

Stedman, Edmund Clarence (b. Oct. 8, 1833, Hartford, Conn.—d. Jan. 18, 1908, New York City) Poet, critic, and editor.

Educated at Yale University, Stedman ran his own brokerage house from 1864 to 1908. Despite a time-consuming business career, his great energy and deep learning combined to make him a highly productive and influential figure in American letters. His critical writings appeared in such books as *Victorian Poets* (1875), *Poets of America* (1885), and *The Nature and Elements of Poetry* (1892), and he assembled such important anthologies as the *Library of American Literature* (11 vols., 1888–90), *Victorian Anthology* (1896), and *American Anthology* (1900), while also producing editions of such writers as Edgar Allan Poe and Walter Savage Landor. His own sentimental poetry appeared in *Poetical Works* (1875), *Hawthorne and Other Poems* (1877), *Lyrics and Idylls* (1879), and *Mater Coronata* (1900).

Steel, Danielle *originally* Danielle Fernande Schuelein (b. Aug. 14, 1947, New York City) Novelist.

Reared in Paris and New York, Steel graduated from New York's Lycée Français at 15 and attended New York University. She married a wealthy French banker and became vice president of an advertising agency from 1968 to 1971, when she turned to writing novels and poetry. Her first paperback novel, *Going Home* (1973), sold only moderately well, but she continued to write after divorcing and remarrying and while rearing her children. Her fourth novel, *The Promise* (1978), was an instant best-seller. Her first hardcover novel was *The Ring* (1980), a multigenerational, international saga. It was followed by a long string of best-selling books, most of which feature strong yet glamorous women who overcome obstacles to secure love, a career, and a family. Often published at a rate of more than one a year, they include *Changes* (1984), *Full Circle* (1984), *Secrets* (1985), *Wanderlust* (1986), *Kaleidoscope* (1984), *Fine Things* (1987), *Zoya* (1988), *Daddy* (1989), *Star* (1989), *Message from Nam* (1990), *No Greater Love* (1991), *Heartbeat* (1991), *Crossings* (1982), *Accident* (1994), *The Ghost* (1998), and her 50th novel, *Journey* (2000). Though never noticed by critics, Steel's novels have sold more than 400 million copies, making her one of the world's most successful writers.

Steffens, (Joseph) Lincoln (b. April 6, 1866, San Francisco—d. Aug. 9, 1936, Carmel, Calif.) Journalist, lecturer, political philosopher, and social reformer.

Steffens graduated from the University of California and later studied in France and Germany. During nine years of New York newspaper work, he discovered abundant evidence of corruption of politicians by businessmen and among the police. He served as managing editor of *McClure's Magazine* (1901–6), where he published the influential articles later collected as *The Shame of the Cities* (1904) and became a leader among the writers dubbed "muckrakers" by his friend Theodore Roosevelt. *The Struggle for Self-Government* (1906) addressed issues of corruption at the state level. Both books relied on careful research rather than sensationalism to make their points. He won a wide audience with his many lecture tours, in which, using comic irony, he jolted his listeners into awareness of the ethical paradox of private interest in public affairs, and revealed the shortcomings of the popular dogmas that connected economic success with moral worth and national progress with individual self-interest. In 1906, he and such colleagues as Ida Tarbell and Finley Peter Dunne bought *American Magazine*, which they made into the nation's leading reform journal.

Political events in Mexico and Russia turned his attention from reform to revolution, and he lived in Europe from 1919 to 1927. After a trip to St. Petersburg in 1919 he wrote "I have seen the future; and it works." His unorthodox radicalism lost him his American audience in the 1920s, but he became a legendary figure for the younger expatriates. His somewhat unillusioned *Autobiography* (2 vols., 1931) was a great success.

Stegner, Wallace (Earle) (b. Feb. 18, 1909, Lake Mills, Iowa—d. April 13, 1993, Santa Fe, N.M.) Author of fiction and history set mainly in the West.

Stegner graduated from the Universities of Utah and Iowa and later taught principally at Stanford University, where from 1945 to 1971 he developed its highly respected creative-writing program. His fifth novel, *The Big Rock Candy Mountain* (1943), the story of an American family moving from place to place in the West, seeking their fortune, was his first critical and popular success. Among his later novels are *The Preacher and the Slave* (1950; later titled *Joe Hill*), the best-selling *A Shooting Star* (1961), *Angle of Repose* (1971, Pulitzer Prize), and *The Spectator Bird* (1976, National Book Award).

Stegner's nonfiction includes two histories of the Mormon settlement of Utah, *Mormon Country* (1942) and *The Gathering of Zion* (1964), a biography of John Wesley Powell, *Beyond the Hundredth Meridian* (1954), and a book of essays, *Where the Bluebird Sings to the Lemonade Spring* (1992). All his writings are informed by a deep sense of the American experience and the "geography of promise" that the West symbolizes.

Stein, Gertrude (b. Feb. 3, 1874, Allegheny, Pa.—d. July 27, 1946, Neuilly-sur-Seine, France) Avant-garde writer, eccentric, salon hostess, and self-styled genius.

Born to a wealthy Jewish family, Stein spent her girlhood in Oakland, Calif. After studying philosophy at Radcliffe College and medicine at Johns Hopkins, she moved to Paris, where from 1903 she lived with her brother Leo,

Gertrude Stein

who became an important art critic. In 1909 her lover Alice B. Toklas (1877–1967) joined the household, and Leo moved out in 1914.

The Steins were among the first collectors of works by the Cubists and other experimental painters, including Picasso (who painted Gertrude's portrait), Matisse, and Braque, several of whom became her friends. At her salon they mingled with expatriate American writers, such as Sherwood Anderson and Ernest Hemingway, and other visitors drawn by her literary reputation (and Toklas's cooking), and her literary and artistic judgments became highly influential. In such works as TENDER BUTTONS (1914) she tried to achieve Cubistic effects through fragmentation, extreme simplification, and endless, slightly varied repetitions.

Her first published book, *Three Lives* (1909), about three working-class women, is regarded as a minor masterpiece. THE MAKING OF AMERICANS (written 1906–11, published 1925), was too convoluted for general readers, for whom she remained essentially the author of such orphic lines as "Rose is a rose is a rose is a rose." She expounded her theories of writing in *Composition as Explanation* (1926), based on lectures she gave at Oxford and Cambridge. Her only book to reach a wide public was THE AUTOBIOGRAPHY OF ALICE B. TOKLAS (1933), actually Stein's own autobiography. The U.S. performance of FOUR SAINTS IN THREE ACTS (1934), which Virgil Thomson had set as an opera, led to a triumphal American lecture tour in 1934–35. Thomson later scored *The Mother of Us All* (1947), about Susan B. Anthony. Stein became a near-legendary figure in her later years, during which she and Toklas survived the German occupation of France.

John Steinbeck

Steinbeck, John (Ernst) (b. Feb. 27, 1902, Salinas, Calif.—d. Dec. 20, 1968, New York City) Novelist.

Steinbeck attended Stanford University intermittently between 1920 and 1926 but did not earn a degree. He worked as a manual laborer while writing, and his experiences lent authenticity to his depictions of the lives of the workers in his stories. He spent much of his life in California's Monterey County.

His first three novels—*Cup of Gold* (1929), *The Pastures of Heaven* (1932), and *To a God Unknown* (1933)—were unsuccessful, but he achieved popularity with TORTILLA FLAT (1935; film, 1942), an affectionately told story of Mexican-Americans. *In Dubious Battle* (1936) is a classic account of a strike by farm workers. The novella OF MICE AND MEN (1937; films, 1939, 1999) is a tragic story about the strange, complex bond between two migrant laborers. Another notable achievement of this period was THE RED PONY (1937; film, 1949). THE GRAPES OF WRATH (1939, Pulitzer Prize; film, 1940), the story of the migration of a dispossessed family from the Oklahoma Dust Bowl to California and their subsequent exploitation by a ruthless system of agricultural economics, earned him international fame. It was the last of his naturalistic novels of the 1930s with proletarian themes, works which, with their rich symbolic structures, effectively convey the mythopoetic and symbolic qualities of his characters.

During World War II Steinbeck wrote several effective pieces of propagandistic fiction, among them *The Moon Is Down* (1942; film, 1943), a novel of Norwegians under the Nazis, and also served as a war correspondent. His immediate postwar work—CANNERY ROW (1945; film, 1982), THE PEARL (1947; film, 1948), *The Wayward Bus* (1947; film, 1957)—contained the familiar elements of his social criticism but were more relaxed and sentimental in tone. His later writings were slighter works of entertainment and journalism, including the highly popular *Travels with Charley* (1962), interspersed with three attempts to reassert his stature as a major novelist: *Burning Bright* (1950), EAST OF EDEN (1952; film, 1955), and *The Winter of Our Discontent* (1961). In critical opinion, none equaled his earlier achievement. Outstanding among his original screenplays were *Forgotten Village* (1941) and *Viva Zapata!* (1952). He received the Nobel Prize for Literature in 1962.

Steiner, (Francis) George (b. April 23, 1929, Paris, France) Influential French-American literary critic who has studied the relationship between literature and society, particularly in light of modern history.

Steiner was born in Paris of émigré Austrian parents and educated at the Sorbonne, the University of Chicago, and Harvard and Oxford universities. Though he became an American citizen in 1944, he has since spent most of his time in Europe. He was an editor at the *Economist* (1952–56) and worked at Princeton's Institute for Advanced Study (1956–58) before teaching at Cambridge University and the University of Geneva.

His first book, *Tolstoy or Dostoevsky* (1959), compares the two authors on the basis of historical, biographical, and philosophical data. *Language and Silence* (1967) examines the dehumanizing effect of World War II and the Holocaust on literature. It and subsequent writings on language and the Holocaust have reached a wide, nonacademic audience. The intersection of culture and linguistics that underlies translation and multilingualism are explored in *Extraterritorial* (1971) and *After Babel* (1975). Among Steiner's other critical works are *The Death of Tragedy* (1961), *In Bluebeard's Castle* (1971), *On Difficulty* (1978), *Martin Heidegger* (1979), *Antigones* (1984), and *Real Presences* (1989). His fiction includes *Anno Domini* (1964), *The Portage to San Cristóbal of A. H.* (1981), and *Proofs and Three Parables* (1992).

Sterling, Bruce (b. April 14, 1954, Brownsville, Texas) Science-fiction writer, a leading exponent of the cyberpunk subgenre.

In 1976 Sterling graduated from the University of Texas and published his first story, "Man-Made Self." His first novel, *Involution Ocean* (1977), describes a dystopian planet where inhabitants escape their confusing lives through drug abuse. The characters in *The Artificial Kid* (1980) struggle to gain stability in a world of fast-paced change. The novel *Schismatrix* (1985) and the story collection *Crystal Express* (1989) examine the contrasting philosophies of the Shapers (who alter themselves genetically) and the Mechanists (who alter themselves with prosthetic devices). In *Islands in the Net* (1988) the heroine is drawn into the geopolitics of a vast information network. *The Difference Engine* (1990; written with William Gibson) is a novel about Charles Babbage and his 19th-century proto-computer. *Heavy Weather* (1994) and *Holy Fire* (1996) are later novels, *Globalhead* (1992) is a story collection, and *The Hacker Crackdown* discusses computer crime and civil liberties. Sterling also edited the important cyberpunk anthology *Mirrorshades* (1986).

Stern, Richard G(ustave) (b. Feb. 25, 1928, New York City) Novelist and short-story writer.

Educated at the University of North Carolina, Harvard University, and the University of Iowa, Stern taught at the University of Chicago from 1955. His novels include *Golk* (1960), a humorous examination of the television industry; *Europe: or, Up and Down with Schreiber and Baggish* (1961), about two middle-aged American men in postwar Germany; *Stitch* (1965), about an expatriate American sculptor, modeled on Ezra Pound; *Other Men's Daughters* (1973), an autobiographical account of a professor in love with a student; *Natural Shocks* (1978), in which a journalist must deal with the deaths of those close to him; and *A Father's Words* (1986), about a divorced father's relationship with his grown children. *Teeth, Dying, and Other Matters* (1964) is a collection of short fiction, a play, and an essay. *The Books in Fred Hampton's Apartment* (1973) contains miscellaneous pieces. Stern's other compilations include the story collections *Noble Rot* (1989) and *Shares* (1992), and *One Person and Another: On Writers and Writing* (1993).

Wallace Stevens

Stevens, Wallace (b. Oct. 2, 1879, Reading, Pa.—d. Aug. 2, 1955, Hartford, Conn.) Poet whose work explores the interaction of reality and the human interpretation of reality.

Stevens attended Harvard University, worked briefly for the *New York Herald Tribune*, earned a degree at the New York Law School (1904), and began practicing law in New York City. His first published poems, aside from college verse, appeared in *Poetry* in 1914, and thereafter he was a frequent contributor to literary magazines. In 1916 he joined an insurance firm in Hartford; in 1934 he was named vice president, and he held that position until his death. His life was notably uneventful.

At 44 he published his extraordinary first collection, *Harmonium* (1923); it sold fewer than 100 copies. In such poems as "Le Monocle de Mon Oncle," "Sunday Morning," and "Peter Quince at the Clavier"; Stevens's own favorites, "Domination of Black" and "The Emperor of Ice-Cream"; "Sea Surface Full of Clouds," in which waves are described in terms of umbrellas, French phrases, and varieties of chocolate; and "The Comedian as the Letter C," in which he examines the artist's relation to society, *Harmonium* introduces the imagination-reality theme that would occupy Stevens's creative lifetime, making his work so unified that three decades later he considered calling his collected poems "The Whole of Harmonium." It displayed his most dazzling verbal brilliance; his later work tended to relinquish surface luster for philosophical rigor.

In the 1930s and early 1940s, the imagination-reality theme was to reappear, though not to the exclusion of others, in *Ideas of Order* (1935), *The Man with the Blue Guitar* (1937), and *Parts of a World* (1942). *Transport to Summer* (1947) incorporated two long sequences that had appeared earlier: "Notes Towards a Supreme Fiction" and "Esthétique du Mal," in which he argued that beauty is inextricably linked with evil. *The Auroras of Autumn* (1950, National Book Award) contains some of his finest work.

Not until late in life was Stevens widely read at all or recognized as a major poet by more than a few. In 1950 he became the second recipient of the Bollingen Prize. Not until the appearance of the *Collected Poems* (1954) did he receive a Pulitzer Prize (along with a National Book Award). He has since been acclaimed by some as the greatest American poet of the 20th century. A volume of his critical essays, *The Necessary Angel*, appeared in 1951.

Stewart, Donald Ogden (b. Nov. 30, 1894, Columbus, Ohio—d. Aug. 2, 1980, London, England) Humorist, actor, playwright, and screenwriter.

A graduate of Yale, Stewart served in World War I before taking up humorous writing in 1921. His *Parody Outline of History* (1921) was an instant success, and he was received into the Algonquin Round Table literary circle. He enjoyed success with satirical novels before making his New York acting debut in *Holiday* in 1928; he subsequently appeared in his own first play, *Rebound* (1930), and coauthored the musical *Fine and Dandy* (1930). He achieved his most enduring success as a screenwriter, usually of adaptations of plays or novels. His scripts included *Laughter* (1930), *Smilin' Through* (1932), *Dinner at Eight* (1933), *Holiday* (1938), *Marie Antoinette* (1938), *The Philadelphia Story* (1940, Academy Award), and *An Affair to Remember* (1957), most of them marked by witty dialogue. Falling victim to the postwar anticommunist frenzy, he was one of many Hollywood figures to be blacklisted, and in 1951 he left Hollywood for England. His autobiography, *By a Stroke of Luck*, appeared in 1975.

Stockton, Frank R. (*originally* Francis Richard) (b. April 5, 1834, Philadelphia—d. April 20, 1902, Washington, D.C.) Popular novelist and short-story writer of mainly humorous fiction.

Stockton worked as a wood engraver before beginning to contribute children's stories to periodicals. From 1873 to 1881 he was assistant editor of *St. Nicholas Magazine* for young people. Among his most popular children's stories were those collected in *Ting-a-Ling Tales* (1870), *The Floating Prince* (1881), and *The Bee-Man of Orn* (1887). He is best known as the author of the intriguingly unresolved title story of *The Lady, or the Tiger?* (1884). His adult novel *Rudder Grange* (1879) recounts the whimsically fantastic and amusing adventures of a family living on a canal boat. Its success encouraged two sequels, *Rudder Grangers Abroad* (1891) and *Pomona's Travels* (1894). *The Casting Away of Mrs. Lecks and Mrs. Aleshine* (1886), his best and most successful work, tells of two middle-aged women on a sea voyage to Japan who become castaways on a deserted island. A sequel, *The Dusantes,* appeared in 1888.

Stoddard, Richard Henry (b. July 2, 1825, Hingham, Mass.—d. May 12, 1903, New York City) Poet, critic, and editor.

The son of a seaman, Stoddard was raised in poverty. He worked as a reviewer and editor for the *New York World* (1860–70) and the *New York Mail and Express* (1880–1903), later taking diplomatic posts as well. He wrote successful book on travel early on, as well as three novels on social themes. His poetry includes *Abraham Lincoln, An Horatian Ode* (1865), *Songs of Summer* (1857), and *The Book of the East* (1867). For the last 30 years of the century, his house was a leading gathering place for writers and artists. His autobiography, *Recollections Personal and Literary,* was published in 1903. His wife, Elizabeth Drew (1823–1902), was a well-regarded novelist and poet.

Stone, Irving *originally* Irving Tennenbaum (b. July 14, 1903, San Francisco— d. Aug. 26, 1989, Los Angeles) Writer of popular historical biographies.

Stone first came to prominence with *Lust for Life* (1934; film, 1956), a fictionalized biography of Vincent van Gogh. In this and the later works he would term "bio-history," through meticulous and exhaustive research, he verified and expanded his preconception of a selected historical character, then acquired the basis for reconstructed dialogue by immersing himself in the subject's native environment and reading all available original documents. His other novels, all of them best-sellers, include *President's Lady* (1951; film, 1953), about Rachel and Andrew Jackson; *Love Is Eternal* (1954), about Abraham and Mary Todd Lincoln; the highly popular *The Agony and the Ecstasy* (1961; film, 1965), about Michelangelo; *The Passions of the Mind* (1971), about Sigmund Freud; and *The Origin* (1980), about Charles Darwin. Stone's nonfiction works include *Clarence Darrow for the Defense* (1941) and *They Also Ran* (1943), biographies of 19 defeated presidential candidates.

Stone, Robert (Anthony) (b. Aug. 21, 1937, New York City) Author of novels about individuals in conflict with decaying, late-20th-century Western societies.

Stone served in the navy before attending New York and Stanford universities. *A Hall of Mirrors* (1967), his first novel, revolves around a right-wing New Orleans radio station and its chaotic "Patriotic Revival"; Stone adapted it for a screen version, *WUSA* (1970). Like most of his later novels, its power resides in its stark handling of a violent political confrontation. *Dog Soldiers* (1974, National Book Award) brought the corruption of the Vietnam War home; its film version, *Who'll Stop the Rain?* (1978), used Stone's screenplay. *A Flag for Sunrise* (1981) concerns four individuals in a corrupt, poverty-stricken Central American country ripe for revolution. *Children of Light* (1986) features a debauched screenwriter and a schizophrenic actress, both in decline. *Outerbridge Reach* (1992) tells of a foundering marriage and an around-the-world sailboat race. *Damascus Gate* (1998) concerns Israel and the Arab world. *Bear and His Daughter* (1997) is a short-story collection.

Stout, Rex (Todhunter) (b. Dec. 1, 1886, Noblesville, Ind.—d. Oct. 27, 1975, Danbury, Conn.) Author of genteel mystery stories, many of which feature the elegantly eccentric and reclusive detective Nero Wolfe.

Born to Quaker parents, Stout worked successfully in finance for a number of years, which enabled him to retire in 1927 and devote himself to writing. After producing several moderately successful novels, he turned to the form of the detective story, and by 1927 he was earning his living exclusively from his detective novels and novellas. In *Fer-de-Lance* (1934) he introduced Nero Wolfe, an obese, brilliant aesthete who solves crimes without leaving his New York apartment, and whose epicurean passions for fine food and orchids were paralleled in those of his author. The mysteries, which include *League of Frightened Men* (1935; film, 1937), *Black Orchids* (1942), and *A Family Affair* (1975), are narrated by Archie Goodwin, Wolfe's wisecracking link to the outside world. All of Stout's 46 Wolfe mysteries achieved great success.

Stowe \\'stō\\, Harriet Beecher *originally* Harriet Elizabeth Beecher (b. June 14, 1811, Litchfield, Conn.—d. July 1, 1896, Hartford, Conn.) Writer and philanthropist known for her antislavery novel UNCLE TOM'S CABIN.

Harriet Beecher Stowe

Stowe was the daughter of the famous Congregationalist minister Lyman Beecher and the sister of the preacher Henry Ward Beecher and the educator Catherine Beecher. After 1832 she taught in Cincinnati, where she contributed stories and sketches to local journals and compiled a school geography. She continued to write after her school closed in 1836 and after her marriage that year to a professor of theology and their move to Maine.

In Cincinnati, separated only by the Ohio River from a slaveholding community, she came in contact with fugitive slaves and learned about southern life from friends and from her own visits. These experiences prompted her to write *Uncle Tom's Cabin* (1852), published serially in the antislavery paper *National Era*. She reinforced her story with *The Key to Uncle Tom's Cabin* (1853), in which she accumulated a large number of documents and testimonies against slavery.

In 1853, on a journey to Europe, she was lionized in England. Much later, British public opinion would turn against her with publication of the article "The True Story of Lord Byron's Life" (1869), alleging an incestuous love affair between the poet and his half sister. In the novel *Dred: A Tale of the Great Dismal Swamp* (1856), she depicted the deterioration of a society resting on a slave basis. When the *Atlantic Monthly* was established the next year, she found a ready vehicle for her writings, which she also published in two of her brother's papers, the *Independent* of New York and the *Christian Union*. She thereafter led the life of a woman of letters, writing novels, of which *The Minister's Wooing* (1859) is best known, and many studies of social life in both fiction and essay.

Strand, Mark (b. April 11, 1934, Summerside, Prince Edward Island, Canada) Poet and translator whose often surreal poetry explores the boundaries of the self and the external world.

Raised in the United States and South America and educated at Antioch College, Yale University (where he studied painting with Joseph Albers), and the University of Iowa, Strand has since taught at several universities, including the University of Utah (1981–93).

Influenced by Latin-American surrealism and such European writers as Franz Kafka, Strand's poetry, especially his earliest works, is known for its symbolic imagery and minimalist sensibility. His collections include *Sleeping with One Eye Open* (1964), *Reasons for Moving* (1968), *Darker* (1970), *The Story of Our Lives* (1973), *The Late Hour* (1978), *The Continuous Life* (1990), *Dark Harbor* (1993), a book-length poem for which he received the Bollingen Prize, and *Blizzard of One* (1998, Pulitzer Prize). Among his translations of poetry by South American writers are *18 Poems from the Quechua* (1971) and Rafael Alberti's *The Owl's Insomnia* (1973). He has edited *The Contemporary American Poets* (1969), *New Poetry of Mexico* (1970), and, with Charles Simic, *Another Republic: 17 European and South American Writers* (1976). *The Monument* (1978) is an irreverent prose miscellany. A short-story collection, *Mr. and Mrs. Baby*, was published in 1985. He has also written several children's books and works of art criticism. He served as U.S. poet laureate (1990–91).

Stratemeyer \'strat-ə-ˌmī-ər\, **Edward** (b. Oct. 4, 1862, Elizabeth, N.J.—d. May 10, 1930, Newark, N.J.) Writer of popular juvenile fiction, whose Stratemeyer Literary Syndicate produced the Rover Boys, Hardy Boys, Tom Swift, Bobbsey Twins, and Nancy Drew series.

Stratemeyer began working as a clerk after high school, while also writing stories in imitation of Horatio Alger, who chose Stratemeyer to finish his uncompleted works. He sold his first magazine story in 1888. In 1893 he became editor of the boys' magazine *Good News*, to which he contributed stories, and in 1896 he added the editorship of *Bright Days*. His first book, *Richard Dare's Venture* (1894), spawned its own series, and Stratemeyer was soon writing several series concurrently (each under a separate pseudonym), including the *Bound to Win, Old Glory, Pan-American, Colonial, Mexican War, Frontier, Civil War,* and *Flag of Freedom* series. His highly successful *Rover Boys' Series for Young Americans* began in 1899, and his *Boy Hunters* series in 1906. Later series included the *Motor Boys* and *Boy Scouts* series and the immensely successful *Tom Swift, Hardy Boys, Nancy Drew,* and *Bobbsey Twins* series.

In 1906 he founded the Stratemeyer Literary Syndicate, and began supplying characters and plot outlines to a stable of hack writers, several of whom might contribute to a given series under a single pseudonym. After his death, his company was largely directed by his daughter, Harriet Stratemeyer Adams (1893?–1982), who under pseudonyms wrote some 200 of the *Nancy Drew, Dana Girls, Hardy Boys, Bobbsey Twins,* and *Tom Swift, Jr.* stories. In 1984 the Syndicate was acquired by Simon & Schuster.

Sturgeon, Theodore *originally* Edward Hamilton Waldo (b. Feb. 26, 1918, Staten Island, N.Y.—d. May 8, 1985, Eugene, Ore.) Science-fiction writer.

After selling his first short story in 1937, Sturgeon was soon publishing regularly in science-fiction magazines under several pseudonyms. He was especially prolific in the years 1946–58. His most noted work is *More Than Human* (1953), about six outcast children with extrasensory powers. In *Venus Plus X* (1960) he envisioned a utopia achieved by eliminating all sexual differences. His other science-fiction and fantasy novels include *The Dreaming Jewels* (or *The Synthetic Man;* 1950), *The Cosmic Rape* (1958), and *Some of Your Blood* (1961). Sturgeon was unusual among his peers in writing about loneliness, romantic love, and sex. His stories were considered daring for dealing with the problems of hermaphrodites, exiled lovers, and homosexuals. He also wrote western, historical, and mystery novels.

Styron, William (Clark) (b. June 11, 1925, Newport News, Va.) Novelist noted for his tragic, violent themes and rich, Faulknerian prose style.

After graduating from Duke University, Styron joined the expatriate community in Paris in the 1950s. His first novel, *Lie Down in Darkness* (1951), set in his native tidewater Virginia, tells of a disturbed young woman from a loveless middle-class family who fights for her sanity before committing suicide. His next work, the novella *The Long March* (1956), chronicles a brutal forced march undertaken by Marine recruits. *Set This House on Fire,* about American expatriates in France, appeared in 1960. His fourth novel, THE CONFESSIONS OF NAT TURNER (1967), a complexly psychological and controversial tour de force and a vivid evocation of slavery, won the Pulitzer Prize and later the William Dean Howells Medal as the best American fiction of its half-decade.

Styron's subsequent works include a play, *In the Clap Shack* (1972); the novel SOPHIE'S CHOICE (1979, American Book Award; film, 1982); *This Quiet Dust* (1982), a collection of essays on his fiction's dominant themes; *Darkness Visible* (1990), a best-selling account of his depression; and *A Tidewater Morning* (1993), a story collection.

Susann \sü-ˈzan\, **Jacqueline** (b. Aug. 20, 1921, Philadelphia—d. Sept. 21, 1974, New York City) Novelist.

Susann studied ballet and drama in New York, where she worked as a model and an actress, appearing in over 20 Broadway plays and road-company productions. She began writing in the 1960s; her first book was the nonfiction *Every Night, Josephine!* (1963), about her poodle. Avid for fame and wealth, she achieved instant success with *Valley of the Dolls* (1966; film, 1967), a sex- and fantasy-filled novel for women, scorned by critics as crudely written soft pornography, that became one of the best-selling American novels of all time and made Susann a highly visible public figure. Her next novel, *The Love Machine* (1969; film, 1971), was another phenomenal success. Her later books included *Once Is Not Enough* (1973; film, 1975) and the posthumously published *Dolores* (1976) and *Yargo* (1978).

Swenson, May (b. May 28, 1919, Logan, Utah—d. Dec. 4, 1989, Ocean View, Del.) Poet whose work is noted for its engaging nature imagery, intricate wordplay, and eccentric typography.

Educated at Utah State University, Swenson later moved to New York and worked for New Directions press (1959–66), and subsequently taught at several colleges. Her first volume of poetry was *Another Animal* (1954); later collections include *A Cage of Spines* (1958), *To Mix with Time* (1963), *Poems to Solve* (1966), *Iconographs* (1970), *More Poems to Solve* (1971), *New & Selected Things Taking Place* (1978), and *In Other Words* (1987). *Half Sun, Half Sleep* (1967) included translations of poetry by six Swedish authors. She cotranslated from the Swedish *Windows and Stones, Selected Poems of Tomas Tranströmer* (1972). Her collection *Nature* (1994) was published posthumously. She received the Bollingen Prize in 1981.

Taggard \\ˈtag-ərd\\, **Genevieve** (b. Nov. 28, 1894, Waitsburg, Wash.—d. Nov. 8, 1948, New York City) Poet.

Born to missionary parents, Taggard grew up from 1896 in Hawaii. After graduating from UC–Berkeley, she moved to New York City, found a job with a publishing firm, joined a radical literary circle, and became a frequent contributor to radical magazines. In 1921 she helped found the *Measure,* a poetry journal, and served on its editorial board until its demise in 1926. She taught English at several colleges, including Sarah Lawrence College (1935–46). Her first volume of verse, *For Eager Lovers* (1922), was followed by *Hawaiian Hilltop* (1923), *Words for the Chisel* (1926), and *Travelling Standing Still* (1928), *Not Mine to Finish* (1934), *Calling Western Union* (1936), and *Slow Music* (1946). Her lyric verse mingled intellectual, personal, social, and aesthetic concerns. Her *Life and Mind of Emily Dickinson* (1930) was long regarded as one of the best interpretations of Dickinson.

Tan, Amy (Ruth) (b. Feb. 19, 1952, Oakland, Calif.) Author of novels about Chinese-American women.

The daughter of Chinese immigrants, Tan did graduate work in linguistics at UC–Santa Cruz and UC–Berkeley and subsequently worked as a technical writer. Her semiautobiographical novel *The Joy Luck Club* (1989; film, 1993), which contrasts the hardships that immigrant women experienced in China with the very different lives of their American daughters, achieved enormous success and was widely adopted in high-school and college classes. *The Kitchen God's Wife* (1991), another major success, took up similar themes, as did her next novels, *The Hundred Secret Senses* (1995) and *The Bonesetter's Daughter* (2001). Tan has also written the children's stories *The Moon Lady* (1992) and *The Chinese Siamese Cat* (1994).

Tarbell \\ˈtär-bəl\\, **Ida M(inerva)** (b. Nov. 5, 1857, Erie County, Pa.—d. Jan. 6, 1944, Bridgeport, Conn.) Investigative journalist, lecturer, and chronicler of American industry.

After graduating from Allegheny College, Tarbell worked as a teacher and editor before resuming her studies at the Sorbonne and the Collège de France in Paris (1891–94). From 1894 to 1906 she was on the staff of *McClure's* magazine. A set of articles on Napoleon resulted in a book-length biography (1895), which sold in large numbers, and she followed it with other biographies. *The History of the Standard Oil Company* (2 vols., 1904), originally serialized by *McClure's,* a notably thorough and well-researched account of the rise of a business monopoly and its use of unfair practices, resulted in a federal investigation and the eventual dissolution of Standard Oil of New Jersey in 1911, and earned her membership in the group of journalists characterized as "muckrakers" by Theodore Roosevelt. She left *McClure's* in 1906 to purchase (with such other reformers as Lincoln Steffens and Finley Peter Dunne) *American Magazine,* which she coedited from

Ida M. Tarbell

391

1906 to 1915. She subsequently became a popular lecturer. Her diverse other writings include several more on business practices and eight books on Abraham Lincoln. Her autobiography, *All in the Day's Work*, was published in 1939.

Booth Tarkington

Tarkington, (Newton) Booth (b. July 29, 1869, Indianapolis, Ind.—d. May 19, 1946, Indianapolis) Novelist and dramatist, best known for his satirical and sometimes romanticized pictures of Midwesterners.

Tarkington studied at Purdue and Princeton universities but took no degree. He won early recognition with the melodramatic novel *The Gentleman from Indiana* (1899), about corruption in the lawmaking process. His humorous portrayals of boyhood and adolescence, PENROD (1914), *Penrod and Sam* (1916; film, 1937), SEVENTEEN (1916; film, 1940), and *Gentle Julia* (1922), became young-people's classics. He was equally successful with his portrayals of Midwestern life and character, particularly in the trilogy *Growth*—consisting of *The Turmoil* (1915), THE MAGNIFICENT AMBERSONS (1918, Pulitzer Prize; film, 1942), *The Midlander* (1923)—and *The Plutocrat* (1927). ALICE ADAMS (1921, Pulitzer Prize; film, 1935), a searching character study, is perhaps his most finished novel. He continued his delineations of female character in *Claire Ambler* (1928), *Mirthful Haven* (1930), and *Presenting Lily Mars* (1933; film, 1943). He also wrote many plays, including an adaptation of his immensely popular romance *Monsieur Beaucaire* (1901; film, 1946). *The World Does Move* (1928) is a memoir.

Allen Tate

Tate, (John Orley) Allen (b. Nov. 19, 1899, Winchester, Ky.—d. Feb. 9, 1979, Nashville, Tenn.) Poet, teacher, novelist, and leading exponent of the New Criticism.

At Vanderbilt University Tate helped found the *Fugitive* (1922–25), a poetry magazine that concentrated largely on the South. With other Fugitive poets he contributed to the important symposium *I'll Take My Stand* (1930), a conservative manifesto defending the traditional agrarian society of the South. From 1934 he taught at several schools, including Princeton and the University of Minnesota (1951–68). Under his editorship in the mid-1940s, the literary journal *Sewanee Review* acquired wide importance.

In Tate's best-known poem, "Ode to the Confederate Dead" (1926), the dead symbolize the emotions he is no longer able to feel. His poems of the 1930s broaden the theme of disjointedness by showing its effect on society, as in "The Mediterranean" (1932). In his later poems he suggested that only through the subjective wholeness of the individual can society itself be whole; this view emerged tentatively in "Seasons of the Soul" (1943) and confidently in "The Buried Lake" (1953). His only novel, *The Fathers* (1938), refashions the Jason-Medea myth to promulgate agrarian beliefs. *Essays of Four Decades* appeared in 1969. In both his criticism and his poetry, Tate emphasized the writer's need for a tradition to adhere to; he found his own tradition in the culture of the conservative, agrarian South, and later in Roman Catholicism, to which he was converted in 1950.

Taylor, (James) Bayard (b. Jan. 11, 1825, Kennett Square, Pa.—d. Dec. 19, 1878, Berlin, Germany) Author known for his lively travel narratives and his translation of Goethe's *Faust*.

In 1844 Taylor's first volume of verse, *Ximena*, was published. A long trip to Europe financed by the *Saturday Evening Post* and the *United States Gazette* resulted in the extremely popular compilation of travel letters *Views Afoot* (1846). In 1847 he began a career in journalism in New York. *Eldorado* (1850) is his account of the California Gold Rush. He continued his trips—to the Orient, Africa, and Russia—and such books as *A Journey to Central Africa* (1854), *The Land of the Saracen* (1855), and *Poems of the Orient* (1855) marked him as a modern Marco Polo. In 1862 he became secretary of the U.S. legation at St. Petersburg, and in 1878 minister to Germany. Of his works in this later period, the translation of *Faust* (1870–71) remains his best known.

Bayard Taylor

Taylor, Edward (b. 1645?, in or near Coventry, Warwickshire, England— d. June 24, 1729, Westfield, Mass.) Poet of colonial British North America.

Unwilling to subscribe to a required oath of conformity because of his staunch adherence to Congregational principles, Taylor gave up schoolteaching in England, immigrated to New England, and entered Harvard College. After his graduation in 1671, he served as minister and physician in the frontier village of Westfield, Mass., where he remained until his death.

Taylor's manuscript *Poetical Works* came into the possession of Yale in 1883, but not until 1939 was any of his poetry published, whereupon he was immediately recognized as the finest poet of 18th-century America, even though his poetic models, principally such Metaphysical poets as John Donne, had long been out of favor, especially in England, at the time he was writing. The important poems fall into two broad divisions. "God's Determinations Touching His Elect" is an extended verse sequence setting forth the grace and majesty of God as a drama of sin and redemption; the "Sacramental Meditations," about 200 in number, were described by Taylor as "Preparatory Meditations Before My Approach to the Lord's Supper."

Taylor, John (b. Dec. 19?, 1753, Caroline County, Va.—d. Aug. 21, 1824, Caroline County, Va.) Political philosopher.

After serving in the American Revolution, Taylor was elected several times to the Virginia legislature (1779–81, 1783–85, 1796–1800) and the U.S. Senate (1792–94, 1803, 1822–24), where he was known as a strong supporter of states' rights and of Thomas Jefferson. He became widely known through his political writings. *An Inquiry into the Principles and Policy of the Government of the United States* (1814) and *Construction Construed and Constitutions Vindicated* (1820) were wordy but important defenses of agrarian democracy against the assaults of a too-powerful central government and the monied mercantile classes. His other writings, including the essay collection *The Arator* (1813), dealt with his experiments in scientific agriculture. Having always regarded himself as a farmer, he spent most of his life on his plantation, "Hazelwood."

Taylor, Peter (Hillsman) (b. Jan. 8, 1917, Trenton, Tenn.—d. Nov. 2, 1994, Charlottesville, Va.) Writer known for his portraits of Tennessee gentry caught in a changing society.

Taylor attended Vanderbilt University, then the center of a Southern literary renaissance led by Allen Tate, R. P. Warren, and J. C. Ransom, before transferring to Southwestern College to study with Tate and completing his degree under Ransom at Kenyon College. He thereafter taught at a number of schools, principally the University of Virginia (from 1967).

He is best known for his short stories, usually set in contemporary Tennessee, which reveal conflicts between old rural society and the rough, industrialized "New South." His first collection, *A Long Fourth* (1948), was praised for its subtle depictions of family disintegration. In the novella *A Woman of Means* (1950), regarded by many as his finest work, a young narrator recalls his wealthy stepmother's nervous collapse and reveals the tension between her city ways and his father's rural values. *The Widows of Thornton* (1954), *Happy Families Are All Alike* (1959), and *Miss Leonora When Last Seen* (1963) secured his reputation as a master of short fiction. Later works include the story collections *In the Miro District* (1977) and *The Old Forest* (1985), containing THE OLD FOREST; the much-admired novel *A Summons to Memphis* (1986, Pulitzer Prize); and *The Oracle at Stoneleigh Court* (1993), a collection of short stories and plays.

Sara Teasdale

Teasdale, Sara (b. Aug. 8, 1884, St. Louis, Mo.—d. Jan. 29, 1933, New York City) Poet whose short, personal lyrics were noted for their classical simplicity and quiet intensity.

Privately educated, Teasdale traveled in Europe and the Mideast from 1905 to 1907. She made frequent trips to Chicago, where she eventually became part of Harriet Monroe's *Poetry* magazine circle. After rejecting Vachel Lindsay, whose good friend she would remain the rest of her life, she married a businessman in 1914 and moved to New York City. She divorced him in 1929 and lived in virtual retirement and reclusion as a semi-invalid until her suicide.

Her first book, *Sonnets to Duse*, was printed privately in 1907. From the beginning, her work was well received. Her technically polished poems adhered to simple forms but gained in subtlety and depth over time. With *Rivers to the Sea* (1915) she was established as a popular poet; for *Love Songs* (1917) she became the first person to win Columbia University's Poetry Society Prize, soon to be renamed the Pulitzer Prize. Her familiar "Let It Be Forgotten" is included in *Flame and Shadow* (1920). As her technical competence increased, her work became simpler and more austere, as in the haunting "An End" (from *Dark of the Moon*, 1926). Many of the poems in her last book, *Strange Victory* (1933), foreshadow her own death.

Terhune \tər-ˈhyün\, **Albert Payson** (b. Dec. 21, 1872, Newark, N.J.—d. Feb. 18, 1942, near Pompton Lakes, N.J.) Writer known for his popular stories about dogs.

Terhune graduated from Columbia University, traveled in Egypt and Syria, and in 1894 joined the staff of the *New York Evening World*. His first book was *Syria from the Saddle* (1896); his first novel, *Dr. Dale* (1900), was written with his mother, herself a novelist. He published more than 12 books before leaving the *World* in 1916. The first of his popular dog stories, *Lad, a Dog*, appeared in 1919 (film, 1962). He went on to write more than 25 more books, nearly all of them novels in which dogs played conspicuous parts, including *Bruce* (1920), *The Heart of a Dog* (1924), *Lad of Sunnybank* (1928), and *A Book of Famous Dogs* (1937).

Albert Payson Terhune

Terkel \\'tər-kəl\\, **Studs** (*originally* Louis) (b. May 16, 1912, New York City) Interviewer and writer.

Terkel grew up in Chicago and graduated from the University of Chicago and its law school (J.D., 1934). He gave up a legal career to become a radio disk jockey and interviewer, exposure that led to his own television show in 1950. In 1953, blacklisted for his leftist leanings, he returned to radio and conducted his interview program at the same station, WFMT, for 45 years.

His first book was *Giants of Jazz* (1956). In the 1960s, at the suggestion of his future editor, he began the first of a series of books based on interviews of the kind he had long conducted. *Division Street: America* (1967), about race and class divisions in Chicago, was followed by *Hard Times* (1970), about the Depression; the hugely successful *Working* (1974), on Americans and their jobs; *The Good War* (1984; Pulitzer Prize), about World War II; *The Great Divide* (1988), about America during the Reagan administration; *Race* (1992), on American feelings about race; and *Coming of Age* (1995), about his aging contemporaries.

Terry, Lucy (b. 1730, West Africa—d. 1821, Vermont) Poet, storyteller, and activist of the colonial and postcolonial period.

Taken by slave traders from Africa to Rhode Island as a child, she worked as a household slave in Deerfield, Mass., until 1756, when she married Abijah Prince, a free black, and in 1764 they settled in Guilford, Vt., where their six children were born. Her only surviving work, the doggerel poem "Bars Fight" (1746), commemorates white settlers killed in an encounter with Indians in 1746. The earliest existing poem by an African-American, it was transmitted orally for over 100 years before appearing in print in 1855. A persuasive orator, Terry successfully negotiated a land case before the U.S. Supreme Court, and delivered a three-hour address to the Williams College board of trustees in a vain attempt to gain admittance for her son.

Theroux \\thə-'rü\\, **Paul (Edward)** (b. April 10, 1941, Medford, Mass.) American-English novelist, travel writer, and essayist.

After graduating from the University of Massachusetts, Theroux taught English in Malawi, Uganda—where he established an important friendship with V. S. Naipaul—and Singapore before moving to England to devote all his time to writing. Several early novels, including *Girls at Play* (1969) and *Saint Jack* (1973; film, 1979), focus on the social and cultural dislocation of Westerners in postcolonial Africa and Southeast Asia. He first achieved commercial success with the travel book *The Great Railway Bazaar* (1975), describing a four-month train journey through Asia. His later novels include *The Family Arsenal* (1976), the highly successful *The Mosquito Coast* (1981; film, 1986), *Half Moon Street* (1984; film, 1986), *Millroy the Magician* (1993), *My Other Life* (1996), and *Kowloon Tong* (1997). His later travel books include *The Old Patagonian Express* (1979), *The Kingdom by the Sea* (1983), and *The Happy Isles of Oceania* (1992). He has also published collections of essays. He is known for his sharp-edged prose and humor and his sometimes cynical harshness toward its subjects, irrespective of their origins.

Thomas, Audrey *originally* Audrey Grace Callahan (b. Nov. 17, 1935, Binghamton, N.Y.) American-Canadian writer.

Thomas settled in Canada after graduating from Smith College, did graduate work at the University of British Columbia, and lived in Ghana (1964–66) before returning to British Columbia. She has written about domestic life and women's search for independence, often throwing her characters' inner conflicts into relief by transplanting them to foreign lands. Use of wordplay and fragments of popular culture have characterized her experimental style. The stories of *Ten Green Bottles* (1967) are told by an unhappy female narrator of varying circumstances but consistent character. Thomas's alter ego, Isobel Cleary, narrates the novels *Mrs. Blood* (1970), *Songs My Mother Taught Me* (1973), and *Blown Figures* (1974), which uses Africa as a metaphor for the unconscious. Later works include the story collections *Real Mothers* (1981), *Goodbye Harold, Good Luck* (1986), and *The Wild Blue Yonder* (1990), and the novels *Latakia* (1979), *Graven Images* (1993), and *Isobel Gunn* (1999).

Thomas, Augustus (b. Jan. 8, 1857, St. Louis—d. Aug. 12, 1934, Nyack, N.Y.) Playwright.

As a youth Thomas worked as a page at the state capitol and at the U.S. House of Representatives, where he began a lifelong interest in public speaking. He worked in the St. Louis railroad yards (1871–78) while studying acting and playwriting. In 1888 he moved to New York, where his drama *Alabama* was produced in 1891; the story of a family conflict after the Civil War, it earned wide acclaim for its use of American material. Among his numerous other plays, which total some 65 original or adapted works, all written in a distinctly American mode, are *In Mizzoura* (1893), *Colonel George of Mount Vernon* (1895), and the successful *Arizona* (1899). His later works, mostly farces, include the very popular *The Witching Hour* (1907), *The Harvest Moon* (1909), the acclaimed *As a Man Thinks* (1911), and *The Copperhead* (1918).

Noted for his wit, Thomas was popular as a public speaker. He served as president of the American Dramatists' Association (1906–11) and of the National Institute of Arts and Letters (1914–16).

Thomas, Lewis (b. Nov. 25, 1913, Flushing, N.Y.—d. Dec. 3, 1993, New York City) Physician, essayist, and administrator known for his collections of reflections on the larger truths evoked by the study of biology.

Son of a doctor, Thomas attended Princeton University and Harvard Medical School (M.D., 1937), served in the Navy Medical Corps, and taught at Johns Hopkins and Tulane universities and the University of Minnesota. In 1954 he moved to the NYU School of Medicine, which he left as dean to teach at Yale. From 1973 to 1984 he was president of New York's Memorial Sloan-Kettering Cancer Center.

His first book, the widely admired *The Lives of a Cell* (1974, National Book Award), collected 29 essays originally written for the *New England Journal of Medicine*. Like his later books, most of which are similarly essay collections that exhibit a benignly philosophical consideration of biology in lucid prose, include *The Medusa and the Snail* (1979), *Late Night Thoughts on Listening to Mahler's Ninth Symphony* (1983), and *The Fragile Species* (1992).

Thomas, Lowell (Jackson) (b. April 6, 1892, Woodington, Ohio—d. Aug. 29, 1981, Pawling, N.Y.) Explorer, lecturer, author, journalist, and preeminent radio commentator.

After earning masters' degrees from the University of Denver and Princeton University, Thomas was commissioned by Woodrow Wilson to do film journalism in wartime Europe and the Mideast, where he eventually followed T. E. Lawrence into the Arabian Desert and filed the exclusive story and pictures that helped make Lawrence legendary. He gained renown as a globetrotter, circling the globe by airplane in 1926–27, and his films and written records of his expeditions established his reputation for adventure. Joining CBS in 1930, he soon became known for his nightly news broadcasts, which continued for nearly two generations. He appeared on television from its earliest days. His more than 50 books include *With Lawrence in Arabia* (1924), *Kabluk of the Eskimo* (1932), *Back to Mandalay* (1951), and *The Seven Wonders of the World* (1956). The first volume of his autobiography bore his sign-on phrase, *Good Evening, Everybody* (1976); his sign-off—"So long, until tomorrow!"—became the title of the second (1977).

Thomas, Norman (Mattoon) (b. Nov. 20, 1884, Marion, Ohio—d. Dec. 19, 1968, Huntington, N.Y.) Social reformer and politician.

Thomas graduated from Princeton University at the head of his class, was ordained a Presbyterian minister in 1911, and became pastor of New York's East Harlem Church. In 1918 he left his parish post to become secretary of the pacifist

Fellowship of Reconciliation. In 1920 he helped found the American Civil Liberties Union, and from 1922 to 1937 he was codirector of the League for Industrial Democracy. A member of the Socialist Party from 1918, Thomas was its candidate for governor (1924) and mayor (1925, 1929), and served as its leader from 1926. From 1928 to 1948 he was its candidate for U.S. president in every election. He staunchly opposed both communism and fascism, and many of his most important proposals (including low-cost housing, a five-day work week, minimum-wage laws, and abolition of child labor) were eventually passed into law.

A tireless and brilliant speaker, he also wrote many books, including *Is Conscience a Crime?* (1927), *Socialism on the Defensive* (1938), *We Have a Future* (1941), *A Socialist's Faith* (1951), *The Test of Freedom* (1954), *Mr. Chairman, Ladies and Gentlemen* (1955), *The Prerequisites for Peace* (1959), and *Socialism Reexamined* (1963).

Dorothy Thompson

Thompson, Dorothy (b. July 9, 1894, Lancaster, N.Y.—d. Jan. 30, 1961, Lisbon, Portugal) Newspaperwoman and writer, one of the 20th century's most famous journalists.

The daughter of a Methodist minister, Thompson attended the Lewis Institute in Chicago and Syracuse University. After World War I she went to Europe as a freelance correspondent and became famous for an exclusive interview with Empress Zita of Austria after Emperor Charles's unsuccessful attempt in 1921 to regain the throne of Hungary. She married Sinclair Lewis in 1928 (divorced 1942) and briefly led a domestic life, but soon returned to Europe. Her reporting on the Nazi movement so infuriated Adolf Hitler that she became the first American correspondent to be expelled from Germany, and she subsequently lectured widely against the Hitler regime. From 1936 her newspaper column "On the Record" was published in the *New York Herald Tribune*; syndicated from 1941 to 1958, it eventually appeared in 170 daily papers. Her many books include *New Russia* (1928), *I Saw Hitler!* (1932), *Refugees: Anarchy or Organization* (1938), *Let the Record Speak* (1939), and *The Courage to Be Happy* (1957).

Thompson, Hunter S(tockton) (b. July 18, 1937, Louisville, Ky.) Journalist and novelist.

After serving time in a juvenile detention center as a teenager, Thompson was obliged to enter the air force, where he wrote a sports column for a service periodical. He thereafter worked as a journalist in Puerto Rico and South America before moving to San Francisco in 1964, where he joined the Beat and budding counterculture movements. He began writing for such newspapers and magazines as the *National Observer* (1961–63), the *Nation* (1964–66), *High Times* (1977–82), the *San Francisco Chronicle* (1985–90), and most importantly *Rolling Stone* (1970–84), and has also been a political analyst for several European magazines.

He gained notoriety with his first book, the arresting nonfiction account *Hell's Angels* (1966), based on a year spent as a member of the motorcycle group. His novel *Fear and Loathing in Las Vegas* (1972; film, 1988), a hilarious story of an LSD-fueled trip to Las Vegas, became an underground classic. *Fear and Loathing on the Campaign Trail '72* (1973) is an insightful nonfiction account of the presidential race in a similar mode. These works earned Thompson a larger-than-life reputation and made him the model for the character Duke in the popular *Doonesbury* comic strip. His shorter pieces have been collected in *The Great Shark Hunt* (1977), *Generation of Swine* (1988), *Songs of the Doomed* (1990), and *Better Than Sex* (1994). His 1959 novel *The Rum Diary* was first published in 1998. *The Proud Highway* (1997) and *Fear and Loathing in America* (2000) are collections of his correspondence.

Thompson, Jim (*originally* James Myers) (b. Sept. 27, 1906, Anadarko, Okla.—d. April 7, 1977, Los Angeles) Writer of pulp novels of the hard-boiled genre.

The son of a sheriff with a checkered career, Thompson worked in odd jobs and briefly attended the University of Nebraska before becoming affiliated with the Federal Writers' Project in the 1930s. He later wrote for the *New York Daily News* and the *Los Angeles Times Mirror*. He published his first (non-crime) novel in 1942. Though blacklisted during the anticommunist scare of the early 1950s for his earlier membership in the Communist Party, he was summoned to Hollywood by Stanley Kubrick to cowrite screenplays for *The Killing* (1956) and *Paths of Glory* (1957).

Thompson's reputation rests on his novels, which consistently display his ability to enter the minds of the criminally insane. *The Killer Inside Me* (1952; film, 1976) is a chilling depiction of a criminally warped mind; its narrator, like most of Thompson's narrators, speaks directly and colloquially to the reader. *After Dark, My Sweet* (1955; film, 1990) presents a mentally imbalanced narrator who becomes embroiled in a kidnapping scheme with his lover but kills himself rather than harm her. Of his approximately 25 other novels, the best-known are *A Hell of a Woman* (1954; film, *Série noire,* 1979), *The Grifters* (1963; film, 1990), and *Pop. 1280* (1964; film, *Coup de tourchon,* 1981). The posthumous publication of two Thompson omnibuses—*Hardcore* (1986) and *More Hardcore* (1987)—and the short-story collection *Fireworks* (1988) revived interest in his largely dismissed and forgotten novels, which are now regarded as classic hard-boiled crime fiction.

Thompson, William T(appan) (b. Aug. 31, 1812, Ravenna, Ohio—d. March 24, 1882, Savannah, Ga.) Humorist remembered for his character sketches of Southern backwoodsmen.

Thompson worked briefly on a Philadelphia newspaper before moving to Georgia in the early 1830s. In 1838 he founded the *Augusta Mirror*, a literary journal, and he would go on to found several more such journals. Discovering that the South would not support literary periodicals, in 1850 he founded the *Savannah Morning News* and continued as its editor until his death. Influenced by A. B. Longstreet, he wrote amusing dialect letters from a Georgia Cracker known as Major Jones for the *Morning News*; collected in 1843 as *Major Jones's Courtship*, they achieved nationwide popularity, and two other volumes followed.

Henry David Thoreau

Thoreau \'thȯ-rō, 'thər-ō, *commonly* thə-'rō, thȯ-'rō\, **Henry David** (b. July 12, 1817, Concord, Mass.—d. May 6, 1862, Concord) Essayist, poet, and practical philosopher best known for having lived the doctrines of Transcendentalism, recording his experience in his masterwork, WALDEN.

Thoreau graduated from Harvard and taught several years in a school he started with his brother John. A canoe trip in 1839, later recounted in A WEEK ON THE CONCORD AND MERRIMACK RIVERS (1849), convinced him that he should instead be a poet of nature. He soon met Ralph Waldo Emerson, who had recently settled in Concord and begun to attract kindred spirits there, out of whose heady speculations and affirmatives would come New England Transcendentalism. In 1837, at Emerson's suggestion, Thoreau began keeping a journal that would eventually cover thousands of pages, and he began publishing writings on the outdoors in the *Dial,* the Transcendentalist magazine.

In 1842, having grown restless, he moved to New York to cultivate its literary market, but he returned to Concord the next year, confirmed in his distaste for city life and disappointed by his failure. In spring of 1845, at 27, he began to build a hut on the shores of Walden Pond, a lake two miles from Concord, on land Emerson owned. From the outset the move gave him profound satisfaction. When not busy weeding his bean rows and trying to protect them from hungry woodchucks or occupied with fishing, swimming, or rowing, he spent long hours observing and recording the local flora and fauna and making journal entries which he would later polish and include in *Walden*.

Midway in his two-year Walden sojourn, Thoreau had spent a night in jail protesting the Mexican-American War, an event he reflected on in the famous and influential essay CIVIL DISOBEDIENCE (1849). When he left Walden, his life lost much of its illumination. Slowly his Transcendentalism drained away as he turned to a variety of tasks to support himself. The observant and humorous accounts of various journeys he made in this period were published posthumously in *Excursions* (1863), THE MAINE WOODS (1864), *Cape Cod* (1865), and *A Yankee in Canada* (1866). He became a dedicated abolitionist and actively helped speed fleeing slaves north on the Underground Railroad while lecturing and writing against slavery. He died at 44. His vivid and fruitful journals were published in 14 volumes in 1906.

Thorpe, Thomas Bangs (b. March 1, 1815, Westfield, Mass.—d. Sept. 20, 1878, New York City) Humorist, one of the most effective portrayers of frontier life before Mark Twain.

Thorpe studied painting in New York and at 18 exhibited his "Ichabod Crane" at the American Academy of Fine Arts. In 1836 he moved to Louisiana, where he published a succession of newspapers. His "The Big Bear of Arkansas" (1841), republished in *Mysteries of the Backwoods* (1846), was so outstanding a tall tale that historians would give the name "Big Bear school" to a group of Thorpe's contemporaries.

He wrote three books about his experiences with Zachary Taylor's army in the Mexican-American War. Following a political defeat, he returned to New York and published his finest sketches as *The Hive of the Bee Hunter* (1854). He saw service in New Orleans as a Union colonel during the Civil War, then returned to New York to spend his remaining years painting, working at the customhouse, and writing for magazines.

Thurber, James (Grover) (b. Dec. 8, 1894, Columbus, Ohio—d. Nov. 2, 1961, New York City) Humorist and cartoonist.

Thurber held several newspaper jobs before moving in 1926 to New York, where he became a reporter for the *Evening Post*. In 1927 he became managing editor and staff writer at Harold Ross's recently established *New Yorker* magazine, where over the decades he would make a major contribution to its style and substance. He would later write a colorful account of his associates there in *The Years with Ross* (1959).

Thurber, who considered himself primarily a writer, first published a cartoon in the *New Yorker* in 1931, though his drawings had been used earlier to illustrate *Is Sex Necessary?* (1929), a collaboration with his colleague E. B. White. The stock characters of Thurber's cartoons—the snarling wife, her timid, hapless husband, and a roster of serene, silently observing animals—have become classics of urban mythology.

Though he left the *New Yorker* staff in 1933, he remained a leading contributor of humor and cartoons. In 1940 failing eyesight forced him to curtail his drawing, and by 1952 he had to abandon it as his blindness became nearly total.

His collections of stories include *My Life and Hard Times* (1933), a whimsical group of autobiographical pieces; *Fables for Our Time* (1940), a stylistically simple and charming yet clear-sighted appraisal of human foibles; and *The Thurber Album* (1952), a second collection of family sketches. "The Secret Life of Walter Mitty" (1939; films, 1946, 2001), about a henpecked husband who retreats into a series of heroic fantasies, is his most famous story. With Elliott Nugent he wrote the play *The Male Animal* (1941), a humorously written plea for academic freedom. His fantasies for children, *The 13 Clocks* (1950) and *The Wonderful O* (1957), are classic modern fairy tales.

Thurman, Wallace Henry (b. Aug. 16, 1902, Salt Lake City, Utah—d. Dec. 22, 1934, New York City) Editor, critic, novelist, and playwright associated with the Harlem Renaissance.

Thurman moved to Harlem in 1925, and by the time he became managing editor of the black periodical *Messenger* in 1926 he had immersed himself in the Harlem literary scene and was encouraging such writers as Langston Hughes and Zora Neale Hurston to contribute to his publication. That summer Hughes asked Thurman to serve as founding editor of the literary and art magazine *Fire!!*. Despite outstanding contributors, it folded after one issue. Two years later he published *Harlem*, again with work by the younger Harlem Renaissance writers, but it too survived only one issue.

In 1929 Thurman's play *Harlem*, written with William Rapp, opened to mixed reviews, though its bawdy treatment of Harlem life made it a popular success. His first novel, *The Blacker the Berry* (1929), like his unfinished play *Black Cinderella*, dealt with color prejudice within the black community. He is best known for his novel *Infants of the Spring* (1932), a satire of what he believed were the overrated creative figures of the Harlem scene; some reviewers welcomed his bold insights, while others vilified him as a race traitor. Thurman's death at 32 resulted from tuberculosis aggravated by alcoholism.

Timrod, Henry (b. Dec. 8, 1828, Charleston, S.C.—d. Oct. 6, 1867, Columbia, S.C.) Poet known as "the laureate of the Confederacy."

The son of a bookbinder, Timrod attended Franklin College (later the University of Georgia) and briefly read law in Charleston. In 1860 a collection of his poems was published. In his best-known essay, "Literature in the South" (1859), he decried the lack of respect accorded Southern writers in both the North and the South. He enlisted in the Confederate army, but was discharged for health reasons. He was later part-owner and an editor of the *South Carolinian* in Columbia. After the city was burned by Union forces, he suffered from poverty and chronic ill health, and he died of tuberculosis at 38.

In 1873 his lifelong friend the poet Paul Hamilton Hayne edited *The Poems of Henry Timrod*. Among Timrod's poems celebrating the South are "Ode Sung at the Occasion of Decorating the Graves of the Confederate Dead," "The Cotton Boll," and "Ethnogenesis." His *Complete Poems* appeared in 1899.

Tolson, Melvin B(eaunorus) (b. Feb 6, 1898, Moberly, Mo.—d. Aug. 29, 1966, Dallas, Texas?) Poet who explored African-American issues in a modernist style.

After graduate work at Columbia University, Tolson taught at Wiley College (1924–47) and Langston University (from 1947). Writing after the Harlem Renaissance but adhering to its ideals, he remained hopeful of a better political and economic future for blacks; his abiding optimism, as well as his concern with poetic form, set him apart from many contemporaries. His first collection, *Rendezvous with America* (1944), includes his popular "Dark Symphony," a poem in six "movements" that contrasts European-American and African-American history. Its success led to his appointment as poet laureate of Liberia in 1947. *Harlem Gallery: Book I, The Curator* (1965), which he intended as the first volume of a five-volume history of black Americans, is written in a sophisticated modernist idiom. He is best known for the epic *Gallery of Harlem Portraits* (published in 1979 but written much earlier); modeled on Edgar Lee Masters's *Spoon River Anthology*, it uses blues lyrics, dramatic monologues, and free (often very prose-like) verse to portray a culturally and racially diverse community.

Toomer, Jean (*originally* Nathan Eugene) (b. Dec. 26, 1894, Washington, D.C.—d. March 30, 1967) Poet and novelist associated with the Harlem Renaissance.

After attending several colleges and universities and working at a variety of jobs, including schoolteaching, Toomer turned to lecturing and writing. Though he published extensively in the *Dial* and other little magazines and wrote several experimental plays, his reputation is based on a single work, the experimental novel CANE (1923), made up of poems, short stories, and a play. In 1926 he attended the Gurdjieff Institute in France, dedicated to the expansion of consciousness and meditation, and on his return he led Gurdjieff groups in Harlem and Chicago, founding a similar institution in Portage, Wis., in 1931. Though he influenced other black writers, only after his death was he recognized as a writer of note.

Trilling, Lionel (b. July 4, 1905, New York City—d. Nov. 5, 1975, New York City) Literary critic and teacher whose criticism was informed by psychological, sociological, and philosophical methods and insights.

Trilling began teaching at Columbia University in 1932 before earning his doctorate from Columbia six years later, and he would remain there until his retirement in 1975. His critical writings include studies of Matthew Arnold (1939) and E. M. Forster (1943), as well as collections of literary essays, including *The Liberal Imagination* (1950), *Beyond Culture* (1965), *Sincerity and Authenticity* (1972), and *Mind in the Modern World* (1972). He also wrote *Freud and the Crisis of Our Culture* (1955) and edited Ernest Jones's massive *Life and Work of Sigmund Freud* (1962). His single novel, *The Middle of the Journey* (1947), based on the life of Whittaker Chambers, concerns the moral and political development of the liberal mind in the 1930s and '40s. Trilling's criticism typically examines literature in the context of its moral and cultural context. In his later years he was perhaps the most famous and influential critic in America. His wife was the critic Diana Trilling (1905–1996).

Trumbull, John (b. April 24, 1750, Westbury, Conn.—d. May 11, 1831, Detroit, Michigan Territory) Poet and jurist known for his political satire, a leader of the HARTFORD WITS.

A member of a distinguished family, Trumbull entered Yale College at 13 (having passed the entrance exams at 7). After studies under John Adams, he practiced law for 50 years in New Haven and Hartford.

As a Yale student he wrote correct but undistinguished Neoclassical elegies as well as brilliant comic verse that he circulated among friends. His burlesque "Epithalamium" (1769) combined wit and scholarship. His many essays in the style of Joseph Addison were published in the *Boston Chronicle* (1770) and the *Connecticut Journal* (1773). As a tutor at Yale he wrote *The Progress of Dulness* (1772–73), an attack on the college's educational methods. In the Revolutionary era he turned to patriotic themes; his major work was the highly popular 3,000-line comic epic *M'Fingal* (1776–82), which acquired an exaggerated reputation as anti-Tory propaganda. His literary production declined after 1782, as he became increasingly involved in law and politics, eventually serving 11 years on the Connecticut Supreme Court.

Sojourner Truth

Truth, Sojourner *originally* Isabella (b. 1797?, Ulster Country, N.Y.—d. Nov. 26, 1883, Battle Creek, Mich.) Evangelist and social reformer.

Born into slavery, she was freed after passage of New York's Emancipation Act of 1827 and moved to New York City, where she worked as a domestic, taking the surname Van Wagener from the owners who freed her. She became active as an evangelist, initially as a follower of the zealot Elijah Pierson, and in 1843 left New York to travel and preach, adopting the name Sojourner Truth at the command of the disembodied voices she had long heard. She soon added abolitionism and women's suffrage to her religious messages, and she became widely known as an advocate of both causes in her adopted state of Massachusetts. In 1850 she set out on a lecture tour of the Midwest, where her magnetic speaking style—which, despite her illiteracy, evoked comparisons with her frequent speaking partner Frederick Douglass—drew large crowds. She supported herself by selling copies of her autobiography, *The Narrative of Sojourner Truth*, written with Olive Gilbert.

In the 1850s she settled in Battle Creek, Mich. During the Civil War she gathered supplies for black volunteer regiments. In 1864 she was received at the White House by Abraham Lincoln, who appointed her to the National Freedmen's Relief Association, and she counseled former slaves, particularly in matters of resettlement, and encouraged the migration of freedmen to Kansas and Missouri. She continued to appear before suffrage gatherings the rest of her life.

Barbara Tuchman

Tuchman \'tək-mən\, **Barbara** *originally* Barbara Wertheim (b. Jan. 30, 1912, New York City—d. Feb. 6, 1989, Greenwich, Conn.) Writer of popular histories marked by trenchant intelligence and a masterly style.

Educated at Radcliffe College, Tuchman worked as a research assistant for the Institute of Pacific Relations, then as a correspondent for the *Nation* and other periodicals. She first gained notice with her third book, *The Zimmermann Telegram* (1958), a study of the World War I document in which Germany promised Mexico parts of the American Southwest in return for wartime support. The next of a string of critically and popularly acclaimed historical works, *The Guns of August* (1962, Pulitzer Prize), describes the military errors and miscalculations of the month when World War I began, and was released to universal acclaim. *The Proud Tower* (1966) surveys European and American society, culture, and politics in the 1890s. *Stilwell and the American Experience in China, 1911–45* (1970, Pulitzer Prize) is a study of the United States' relationship with 20th-century China as epitomized in the wartime experiences of Gen. Joseph Stilwell. *A Distant Mirror* (1978) presents a vivid picture of the events, personalities, and texture of life in 14th-century France. Tuchman's later works were *The March of Folly* (1984), about the disastrous errors throughout history that have resulted in war, and *The First Salute* (1988), about the naval and diplomatic aspects of the American Revolution.

Tuckerman, Frederick Goddard (b. Feb. 4, 1821, Boston—d. May 9, 1873, Greenfield, Mass.) Poet.

Born into a wealthy family, Tuckerman graduated from Harvard Law School in 1842 and practiced briefly, but retired to Greenfield, Mass., in 1847 to pursue his interests in literature, botany, and astronomy. He published several poems in literary magazines, which were collected and privately printed in *Poems* (1860). Though some of them won favorable notice from Emerson and Longfellow, Tuckerman was virtually forgotten until 1931, when Witter Bynner published an edition of his sonnets which sparked a revival of interest in his work and a new appreciation for his attempt to develop a distinctively American style.

Turner, Frederick Jackson (b. Nov. 14, 1861, Portage, Wis.—d. March 14, 1932, San Marino, Calif.) Historian.

After graduating from the University of Wisconsin and Johns Hopkins University (Ph.D., 1890), Turner taught at Wisconsin (1889–1910) and Harvard (1910–24). Deeply influenced by his Wisconsin childhood, he rejected the doctrine that American institutions could be traced mainly to European origins, and demonstrated his theories in a series of groundbreaking essays. In the famous essay "The Significance of the Frontier in American History," he asserted that the American character had been shaped by frontier life and the end of the frontier era. Turner's "frontier thesis" rose to become the dominant interpretation of American history for the next half-century and longer. Later he focused on sectionalism as a force in U.S. development. His essays were collected in *The Frontier in American History* (1920) and *The Significance of Sections in American History* (1932), which was awarded the Pulitzer Prize.

Turow \tù-'rō**, Scott** (b. April 12, 1949, Chicago) Best-selling novelist, creator of a genre of legal crime and suspense novels written by lawyers.

Turow was educated at Harvard Law School, and his first book, *One L* (1977), was an influentially critical account of his first year there that became a classic for law students. His first novel, the hugely popular *Presumed Innocent* (1987; film, 1990), was written while he was an assistant U.S. attorney in Chicago; it tells the story of Rusty Sabich, a deputy prosecutor assigned to investigate the murder of a female colleague with whom he has had an affair. *The*

Scott Turow

Burden of Proof (1990) begins with the suicide of an attorney's wife. In *Pleading Guilty* (1993) a firm's top litigator vanishes with $5 million. *The Laws of Our Fathers* (1996) evokes the radical legacy of the 1960s. *Personal Injuries* (1999) deals with judicial corruption. All Turow's novels are marked by notably complex and ingenious plots and deftly controlled tension.

Mark Twain

Twain, Mark *pseudonym of* **Samuel Langhorne Clemens** (b. Nov. 30, 1835, Florida, Mo.—d. April 21, 1910, Redding, Conn.) Humorist, writer, and lecturer who won a worldwide audience for his stories of youthful adventures, especially TOM SAWYER, LIFE ON THE MISSISSIPPI, and HUCKLEBERRY FINN.

Clemens grew up in Hannibal, Mo., on the west bank of the Mississippi. At 13 he was apprenticed to a local printer. When his older brother Orion established the *Hannibal Journal*, Samuel became a compositor for the paper. After working for a time as an itinerant printer, he rejoined Orion in Keokuk, Iowa, until the fall of 1856, when he began another period of wandering with a commission to write comic travel letters for the *Keokuk Daily Post*. Only five letters appeared, for on the way down the Mississippi he signed on as an apprentice to a steamboat pilot, and for almost four years he plied the Mississippi, after 1859 as a licensed pilot in his own right, until the Civil War put an end to steamboat traffic.

In 1861 he joined Orion in a trip to the Nevada Territory and became a writer for Virginia City's *Territorial Enterprise*. There, on Feb. 3, 1863, "Mark Twain" was born when he signed a humorous travel account with that pseudonym, a riverman's term for water "two fathoms deep" and thus just barely safe for navigation. In 1864 he left Nevada for California. At a mining camp he heard the story which, retold as THE CELEBRATED JUMPING FROG OF CALAVERAS COUNTY (1865), would make him famous.

In 1866 he visited Hawaii as a correspondent for the *Sacramento Union*, publishing letters on his trip and later giving popular lectures. He then set out on a world tour for California's largest paper, the *Alta California*. The letters he wrote over the next five months for it and for Horace Greeley's *New York Tribune* caught the public fancy and, when revised for publication in 1869 as THE INNOCENTS ABROAD, established Twain as a popular favorite.

He married in 1870 and moved with his wife to Hartford in 1871. In 1872 he published ROUGHING IT, a chronicle of an overland stagecoach journey and of his adventures in the Pacific islands. He collaborated with his neighbor Charles Dudley Warner on *The Gilded Age* (1873), a satire on financial and political malfeasance that gave a name to the expansive post–Civil War era.

He continued to lecture with great success both at home and (in 1872–73) in England. In 1876 he published *Tom Sawyer*, a narrative of youthful escapades. It was followed in 1880 by *A Tramp Abroad*, in 1881 by THE PRINCE AND THE PAUPER, and in 1883 by the autobiographical *Life on the Mississippi*. His next novel, *Huckleberry Finn* (1884), is generally considered his finest and one of the masterpieces of American fiction. In 1889 he published A CONNECTICUT YANKEE IN KING ARTHUR'S COURT, in which a commonsensical Yankee is transported back in time to medieval Britain.

Various unsuccessful financial speculations, including his own publishing firm, left him bankrupt in the early 1890s, but the returns from PUDD'NHEAD WILSON (1894), *Personal Recollections of Joan of Arc* (1895), a lecture tour around the world, and *Following the Equator* (1897), his account of the tour, made him solvent again. THE MAN THAT CORRUPTED HADLEYBURG was published with other stories and sketches in 1900.

In 1903 he and his family settled near Florence, Italy. His wife died six months later, and he expressed his grief, loneliness, and pessimism about humanity in several late works, including LETTERS FROM THE EARTH (published 1962) and *The Mysterious Stranger* (published 1916).

Tyler, Anne (b. Oct. 25, 1941, Minneapolis, Minn.) Novelist and short-story writer.

Tyler spent much of her youth in North Carolina, studied Russian at Duke University, and did graduate work at Columbia before settling in Baltimore in 1967, rearing a family, and turning to writing full-time. Her first published novel, *If Morning Ever Comes* (1964), is typical of her work in its polished prose and its understated examination of personal isolation and the difficulties of communication. Her subsequent novels, most of them comedies of manners marked by compassionate wit and precise details of domestic life, have often focused on eccentric middle-class people living in chaotic, disunited families. They include *The Tin Can Tree* (1965), *A Slipping-Down Life* (1970), *The Clock Winder* (1972), *Celestial Navigation* (1974), *Searching for Caleb* (1975), *Earthly Possessions* (1977), and *Morgan's Passing* (1980). She won fame with *Dinner at the Homesick Restaurant* (1982), which was followed by the equally acclaimed *The Accidental Tourist* (1985; film, 1988) and *Breathing Lessons* (1988, Pulitzer Prize). Her later novels have included *Saint Maybe* (1991), *Ladder of Years* (1995), and *Patchwork Planet* (1998).

Tyler, Royall (*originally* William Clark) (b. July 18, 1757, Boston—d. Aug. 26, 1826, Brattleboro, Vt.) Lawyer, teacher, and dramatist.

Tyler attended Harvard, fought as a major in the American Revolution, then settled into a law practice, eventually serving six years as chief justice of the Vermont Supreme Court. A meeting with Thomas Wignell, star comedian of New York's American Company, led him to write *The Contrast,* which premiered in 1787. A light comedy echoing Oliver Goldsmith and Richard Brinsley Sheridan, it contains a Yankee character notable as a distinctly American type, the prototype of many such in years to follow. It was the first comedy by a native American to be professionally produced; very successful, it was produced often in later years. Tyler wrote several more plays as well as the satirical novel *The Algerine Captive* (1797). He and Joseph Dennie, using the pseudonyms Colon and Spondee, wrote a series of pro-Federalist satires in prose and verse, which were collected in 1801 as *The Spirit of the Farmers' Museum.*

U

Underwood, Francis Henry (b. Jan. 12, 1825, Enfield, Mass.—d. Aug. 7, 1894, Edinburgh, Scotland) Author and lawyer, a founder of the *Atlantic Monthly*.

After attending Amherst College and the University of Kentucky, Underwood practiced law in Kentucky and Massachusetts before joining the publishing house Phillips, Sampson in 1854. The antislavery atmosphere of the Northeast and Underwood's close observation of slavery in Kentucky led him to the idea of publishing a literary magazine to oppose slavery, and by 1857 he had gained the support of such liberal writers as Emerson, Thoreau, Longfellow, H. B. Stowe, O. W. Holmes, and J. R. Lowell and persuaded his firm to publish the magazine. With Lowell as editor and himself as assistant editor, the *Atlantic Monthly* began publication in November 1857. Underwood left the magazine in 1859 after it was purchased by another firm. He later wrote biographies of Lowell, Longfellow, and John Greenleaf Whittier, as well as several short stories and novels. His best-known book is *Quabbin: The Story of a Small Town* (1893), an account of his Enfield boyhood.

Updike, John (Hoyer) (b. March 18, 1932, Shillington, Pa.) Writer of novels, short stories, and poetry, known for his careful craftsmanship and subtle depiction of "American, Protestant, small-town, middle-class" life.

After studying English at Harvard and art at Oxford, Updike began an association in 1955 with the *New Yorker* magazine, to which he would contribute editorials, poetry, stories, and criticism throughout his prolific career. His poetry—intellectual, witty pieces on the absurdities of modern life—was first gathered in *The Carpentered Hen* (1958), which was followed by his first novel, *The Poorhouse Fair* (1958). RABBIT, RUN (1960; film, 1970) concerns a star high-school athlete, Harry "Rabbit" Angstrom, who is inarticulately baffled by his early decline when bound by marriage and small-town life. Three subsequent novels, *Rabbit Redux* (1971), *Rabbit Is Rich* (1981, Pulitzer Prize, American Book Award), and *Rabbit at Rest* (1990, Pulitzer Prize, William Dean Howells Medal), follow Rabbit, with humor and pathos, through his unheroic life, which reflects the changing decades of late-20th-century America. *The Centaur* (1963, National Book Award) and *Of the Farm* (1965) are notable among his other novels set in his native Pennsylvania. Most of his later fiction is set in New England, where he has lived since the 1960s.

His other novels include the controversial *Couples* (1968), *Marry Me* (1976), *The Coup* (1976), *The Witches of Eastwick* (1984; film, 1987), *S.* (1988), *Brazil* (1994), and *In the Beauty of the Lilies* (1996). The Jewish novelist Bech is the subject of *Bech: A Book* (1970), *Bech Is Back* (1982), and *Bech at Bay* (1998). Updike's acclaimed short-story collections include PIGEON FEATHERS (1962), *Museums and Women* (1972), and *Trust Me* (1987). His criticism and other nonfiction have been collected in such volumes as *Picked-Up Pieces* (1975), *Hugging the Shore* (1983), *Just Looking* (1989), and *Odd Jobs* (1991). Updike's mastery of virtually every genre of literature had led many to regard him, by the end of the century, as America's foremost man of letters.

Uris \\ˈyu̇r-is\\, **Leon (Marcus)** (b. Aug. 3, 1924, Baltimore—d. June 21, 2003, Shelter Island, N.Y.) Writer known for his panoramic, action-filled novels.

Son of a Polish-Jewish immigrant, Uris dropped out of high school and served in the Marines in World War II. His first novel, *Battle Cry* (1953; film, 1955), is the story of a battalion of Marines in the war. A success, it was soon followed by *The Angry Hills* (1955; film, 1959), an account of the Jewish brigade from Palestine that fought with the British army in Greece. *Exodus* (1958; film, 1960) deals with the struggle to establish and defend the state of Israel; it became the greatest best-seller of any American work of fiction in two decades. *Mila 18* (1961) concerns the Jewish uprising against the Nazis in the Warsaw Ghetto; *Topaz* (1967; film, 1969) deals with Russian involvement in Cuba; *QB VII* (1970) concerns Nazi war crimes; *Trinity* (1976) is a chronicle of a Northern Irish farm family from the 1840s to 1916; *The Haj* (1984) depicts the lives of Palestinian Arabs from World War I to the Suez war of 1956; *Mitla Pass* (1988) is an account of the Sinai campaign of 1956; *Redemption* (1995) is a sequel to *Trinity*; *A God in Ruins* (1999) concerns the presidential candidates in 2008.

V

Van Dine, S. S. *pseudonym of* Willard Huntington Wright (b. Oct. 15, 1888, Charlottesville, Va.—d. April 11, 1939, New York City) Critic, editor, and author of a series of best-selling detective novels.

Brother of the avant-garde painter Stanton MacDonald-Wright, Wright became literary editor of the *Los Angeles Times* in 1907 and in 1912 moved to New York, where he was briefly editor of *Town Topics* and the *Smart Set* and produced the poetry collection *Songs of Youth* (1913), the novel *The Man of Promise* (1916), such critical works as *Modern Painting* (1915) and *What Nietzsche Taught* (1915), and, with H. L. Mencken and George Jean Nathan, the travel book *Europe After 8:15* (1914). While convalescing from an illness, he studied thousands of detective stories and determined to improve on the genre. As S. S. Van Dine, he published *The Benson Murder Case* (1926), the first of a dozen novels featuring the brilliant but arrogant art connoisseur and amateur sleuth Philo Vance, which would include *The "Canary" Murder Case* (1927), *The Greene Murder Case* (1928), and *The Bishop Murder Case* (1929). The successful series, written in ornate prose, inspired numerous films and radio programs. Wright also edited the seminal anthology *The Great Detective Stories* (1927).

Van Doren, Carl (Clinton) (b. Sept. 10, 1885, Hope, Ill.—d. July 18, 1950, Torrington, Conn.) Author and teacher whose writings range from novels to surveys of literature and biographies.

Educated at Columbia University (Ph.D., 1911), Van Doren taught there until 1930, during which period he was one of a group of academicians who helped establish American literature and history as an integral part of university programs. He served as managing editor of the *Cambridge History of American Literature* (1917–21) and literary editor of the *Nation* (1919–22) and *Century Magazine* (1922–25). His best-selling biography *Benjamin Franklin* (1938) won a Pulitzer Prize. Other important works include *The American Novel* (1921), *Contemporary American Novelists* (1922), *American and British Literature Since 1890* (1925; with his brother, Mark Van Doren), and *What Is American Literature?* (1935). He also wrote studies of Thomas Love Peacock (1911), James Branch Cabell (1925), Jonathan Swift (1930), and Sinclair Lewis (1933). His autobiography, *Three Worlds,* appeared in 1936. *The Great Rehearsal* (1948) was a plea for world government.

Van Doren, Mark (b. June 13, 1894, Hope, Ill.—d. Dec. 10, 1972, Torrington, Conn.) Poet, writer, and eminent teacher.

Like his older brother Carl, Van Doren obtained his doctorate from Columbia University (1920). As a teacher at Columbia for four decades (1920–59), he exercised a profound influence on generations of students. His literary criticism includes *The Poetry of John Dryden* (1920); *Shakespeare* (1939); *Nathaniel Hawthorne* (1949); and *The Happy Critic* (1961). In *The Noble Voice* (1946) he considers 10 long poems by authors ranging from Homer through Byron. His *Introduction to Poetry* (1951) examines shorter classic poems.

Throughout a lengthy period of experiment in poetry, he upheld the writing of verse in traditional forms. He published the first of more than 20 volumes of verse, *Spring Thunder,* in 1924. His *Collected Poems* (1939) won the Pulitzer Prize. He wrote three book-length narrative poems—*Jonathan Gentry* (1931), *Winter Diary* (1935), and *The Mayfield Deer* (1941)—and the verse play *The Last Days of Lincoln* (1959). He also served as literary editor (1924–28) and film critic (1935–38) of the *Nation,* wrote three novels—*The Transients* (1935), *Windless Cabins* (1940), and *Tilda* (1943)—as well as plays and several volumes of short stories, and edited various anthologies. In 1922 he married Dorothy Graffe, author of five novels and the memoir *The Professor and I.*

Van Duyn \van-'dīn\, **Mona (Jane)** (b. May 9, 1921, Waterloo, Iowa) Poet noted for her examination of daily life, mixing the prosaic with the unusual.

After attending Iowa State Teachers College and the University of Iowa, Van Duyn and her husband, Jarvis Thurston, cofounded (1947) and coedited (until 1960) the literary quarterly *Perspective.* Her first volume of poetry, *Valentines to the Wide World*, appeared in 1959. She won wide recognition with *To See, To Take* (1970), which received both the National Book Award and Bollingen Prize. Her other works include *A Time of Bees* (1964), *Merciful Disguises* (1973), and *Near Changes* (1990, Pulitzer Prize). *Firefall* and *If It Be Not I: Collected Poems 1959–1982* were published in 1993. She was the first woman U.S. Poet Laureate (1992–93). Frequently described as a "domestic poet" who celebrates married love, Van Duyn has found in love and art the possibility of redemption— "but against that rage slowly may learn to pit / love and art, which are compassionate"—and has used wry humor, insight, irony, and technical skill to find meaning and possibility in a merciless world.

Van Dyke, Henry (b. Nov. 10, 1852, Germantown, Pa.—d. April 10, 1933, Princeton, N.J.) Short-story writer, poet, and essayist.

Educated at Princeton, Van Dyke graduated from its theological seminary in 1877 and became a minister at New York's Brick Presbyterian Church (1883–99), later returning to teach at Princeton (1899–1913, 1919–23). His early works "The Story of the Other Wise Man" (1896) and "The First Christmas Tree" (1897) were first read aloud as sermons and quickly brought him recognition. His other stories and anecdotal tales were gathered into such volumes as *The Ruling Passion* (1901), *The Blue Flower* (1902), *The Unknown Quantity* (1912), *The Valley of Vision* (1919), and *The Golden Key* (1926). Van Dyke's popularity extended to his verse, collected in *Poems* (1920).

Van Loon \van-'lōn\, **Hendrik Willem** (b. Jan. 14, 1882, Rotterdam, the Netherlands—d. March 11, 1944, Old Greenwich, Conn.) Popular historian.

Van Loon emigrated to the United States in 1902, graduated from Cornell University, and earned his doctorate from the University of Munich in 1911. As an Associated Press journalist, he witnessed the 1905 Russian Revolution and the outbreak of World War I. Though he had hoped to teach history, he found more lucrative work as a lecturer on modern European history. His first book, *The Fall of the Dutch Republic* (1913), was followed by *The Golden Book of the Dutch Navigators* (1916). In 1921 his *Story of Mankind*, a history for young people, became a best-seller and won the American Library Association's first John Newbery Medal. His later popular histories include *The Story of the Bible* (1923), *Tolerance* (1925), *America* (1927), and *Man the Miracle Maker* (1928). Characterized by the engaging anecdotal style with which historical figures are described, these popular works are also distinctively illustrated by Van Loon himself. His later books included the best-selling *Van Loon's Geography* (1932), *The Arts* (1937), and *Van Loon's Lives* (1942).

Carl Van Vechten

Van Vechten \van-ˈvek-tən\, **Carl** (b. June 17, 1880, Cedar Rapids, Iowa— d. Dec. 21, 1964, New York City) Novelist and music and drama critic, an influential figure in New York literary circles in the 1920s and an early enthusiast of black culture.

After studying at the University of Chicago, Van Vechten moved to New York in 1906 and worked as a music critic at the *New York Times* and later as its correspondent in Paris, where he became part of Gertrude Stein's circle. Back in New York, he became an important early critic of modern dance. His elegant, sophisticated novels, including *Peter Whiffle* (1922) and *The Tattooed Countess* (1924), became very popular. The controversial novel *Nigger Heaven* (1926) sparked wide interest in the Harlem Renaissance among whites. He also wrote extensively on music and published an autobiography, *Sacred and Profane Memories* (1932), after which he vowed to write no more and to devote his time to photography; his photographic portraits of celebrated figures, especially in the arts, are some of the finest of their kind. His extensive collection of books on black Americana, the James Weldon Johnson Memorial Collection, is now at Yale University. He also established the Carl Van Vechten Collection at the New York Public Library and the George Gershwin Memorial Collection at Fisk University.

Veblen \ˈve-blən\, **Thorstein (Bunde)** (b. July 30, 1857, Manitowoc County, Wis.—d. Aug. 3, 1929, near Menlo Park, Calif.) Economist and social scientist.

Veblen earned his Ph.D. in philosophy from Yale University in 1884. After vain attempts to secure a teaching post, he returned home to work on the farm for seven years. His first published essay led to an invitation to join the economics faculty at the University of Chicago in 1892. That year he helped found the *Journal of Political Economy*, which he edited until 1905 and in which many of his early essays appeared.

In 1899 his first book, *The Theory of the Leisure Class*, brought him immediate fame as a social critic. With dry wit and idiosyncratic diction, he applied Darwin's evolutionary theories to the study of modern economic life, highlighting the competitive and predatory nature of the business world, coining the term "conspicuous consumption" to describe the upper classes' invidious display of wealth. His *Theory of Business Enterprise* (1904) further clarified his harsh view of the American economy.

Veblen's indifferent teaching style and marital infidelity led to his forced resignation from Chicago in 1906 and from Stanford University in 1909. His later books, in which he applied his iconoclastic progressivism to a wide variety of topics, include *The Instinct of Workmanship* (1914), *An Inquiry into the Nature of Peace* (1917), *The Higher Learning in America* (1918), *The Vested Interests and the State of the Industrial Arts* (1919), and *The Engineers and the Price System* (1921). In 1919 he helped found New York's New School for Social Research, and he taught there until 1926, when he retired to a mountain cabin in California. His reputation was highest in the 1930s, when the economic depression appeared to vindicate his criticism of the business system.

Very \ˈvir-ē, ˈver-ē\, **Jones** (b. Aug. 28, 1813, Salem, Mass.—d. May 8, 1880, Salem) Transcendentalist poet and Christian mystic.

Descended from a seafaring family, Very was educated at Harvard College and Harvard Divinity School. At Harvard he became a Greek tutor, but he had begun writing religious sonnets as early as 1837, insisting that they were all "communicated" to him. After he began to relate his mystic beliefs and visions, his colleagues forced his resignation, questioning his sanity. He first came to notice for his critical essays, and such contemporaries as R. W. Emerson and W. C. Bryant praised his poetry for its beauty and simplicity. His *Essays and Poems* was published in 1839 under Emerson's supervision. In 1843 Very was licensed to preach as a Unitarian minister, but he retired around 1858 and went into virtual seclusion for the rest of his life.

Vidal \ˈvē-ˌdäl, vē-ˈdäl\, **Gore** (*originally* Eugene Luther) (b. Oct. 3, 1925, West Point, N.Y.) Prolific novelist, playwright, and essayist, noted for his irreverence and intellectual adroitness.

Son of a pioneer aviator and New Deal administrator, Vidal graduated from Phillips Exeter Academy and served in the army in World War II. Thereafter he resided in many parts of the world, including Europe, North Africa, and Central America; for many years he has lived in Italy. His first novel, *Williwaw* (1946), published when he was 21, was based on his wartime experiences and won wide praise. His third novel, *The City and the Pillar* (1948), shocked the public and critics with its direct and unadorned examination of a homosexual main character, and the five novels that followed, including *Messiah* (1954), were ignored or received coolly by critics. Abandoning novels, he turned to writing for the stage, television, and films and was successful in all three media. His best-known dramatic works from the next decade were the hits *Visit to a Small Planet* (produced for television, 1955; on Broadway, 1957; film, 1960) and *The Best Man* (play, 1960; film, 1964).

He returned to writing novels with *Julian* (1964), a sympathetic portrait of Julian the Apostate. *Washington, D.C.* (1967), an ironic examination of political morality in the U.S. capital, was followed by a series of popular novels that vividly recreated prominent figures and events across the entire span of American history—*Burr* (1973), *1876* (1976), *Lincoln* (1984), *Empire* (1987), *Hollywood* (1990), and *The Golden Age* (2000). Another success was the remarkable comedy *Myra Breckenridge* (1968; film, 1970), which lampooned both transsexuality and contemporary American culture; many regard it as his finest novel. In bitingly ironic essays in such collections as *Reflections upon a Sinking Ship* (1969), *The Second American Revolution* (1982), and *A View from the Diners Club* (1991), he has incisively analyzed American politics and government from an iconoclastically leftist perspective. His many screenplays include *Suddenly Last Summer* (1960) and *Bob Roberts* (1993). *Palimpsest* (1996) is a memoir.

Vollmann \ˈvōl-mən\, William T. (b. 1959) Novelist.

After studying comparative literature at Cornell University, Vollmann worked for a period as a computer programmer. His novels, noted for their length as well as their sensationalist, sexual, and surrealistic subject matter, include *You Bright and Risen Angels* (1987), *Whores for Gloria* (1991), *Butterfly Stories* (1993), *Open All Night* (1995), and *The Royal Family* (2000). *The Ice-Shirt* (1990), *Fathers and Crows* (1992), and *The Rifles* (1995) are volumes from his ongoing *Seven Dreams* series, a fictional history of the Indians and Europeans in the New World. His short stories have been collected in *The Rainbow Stories* (1989), *13 Stories and 13 Epitaphs* (1991), and *The Atlas* (1996). *An Afghanistan Picture Show* (1992) is a nonfiction account. His fiction, admired by many critics, has attracted a devoted following especially among younger readers. Known for his frequent personal immersion in the milieus about which he writes, he has befriended prostitutes in Thailand, lived in the war zones of Afghanistan and Somalia, and traveled to the North Pole.

Vonnegut \ˈvän-ə-ˌgət\, Kurt, Jr. (b. Nov. 11, 1922, Indianapolis, Ind.)
Writer noted for pessimistic satirical novels that use fantasy and science fiction to highlight the horrors and ironies of the 20th century.

After studying biochemistry at Cornell University and anthropology at the University of Chicago, Vonnegut served in World War II, was captured by the Germans, and survived the Allied firebombing of Dresden. His first novel, *Player Piano* (1952), visualizes a completely mechanized and automated society whose dehumanizing effects are unsuccessfully resisted by the scientists and workers in a factory town. *The Sirens of Titan* (1959) is a quasi-science-fiction novel in which the history of the human race is considered an accident attendant on an alien planet's search for a spare part for a spaceship. This he followed with *Mother Night* (1961), CAT'S CRADLE (1963), *God Bless You, Mr. Rosewater* (1965), and SLAUGHTERHOUSE-FIVE (1969; film, 1972), novels whose blunt, mordant, absurdist humor won him a huge readership especially among young people in the 1960s and '70s.

His later novels include *Breakfast of Champions* (1973), *Slapstick* (1976), *Jailbird* (1979), *Deadeye Dick* (1983), *Galápagos* (1985), *Bluebeard* (1987), *Hocus Pocus* (1990), and *Timequake* (1997). He has also written several plays, including *Happy Birthday, Wanda June* (1970); several works of nonfiction; and several collections of short stories, chief among them *Welcome to the Monkey House* (1968).

W

Wakoski \wə-ˈkäs-kē\, **Diane** (b. Aug. 3, 1937, Whittier, Calif.) Poet known for her examinations of loss, pain, and desire in verse that often reproduces incidents from her own turbulent life.

Wakoski studied at UC–Berkeley, where she first published her poems, and moved to New York after graduating. *Coins & Coffins* (1962), the first of more than 60 published collections, contains "Justice Is Reason Enough," about the suicide of an imaginary twin brother. In *The George Washington Poems* (1967) she addresses Washington as an archetypal figure. *Waiting for the King of Spain* (1976) concerns an imaginary monarch. *The Collected Greed: Parts 1–13* (1984), in which "greed" is defined as "failing to choose," is a major work bringing together years of previously published poetry. Later collections, which often focus on the natural world and on the cultural and popular ideas by which personal lives are structured, include *Emerald Ice: Selected Poems 1962–1987* (1988) and the four-volume *Archaeology of Movies and Books* (1991–98). Wakoski has taught at Michigan State University since 1976, and is particularly known for her performances of her own poetry.

Alice Walker

Walker, Alice (Malsenior) (b. Feb. 9, 1944, Eatonton, Ga.) Novelist, poet, essayist, and short-story writer.

Born into a large sharecropping family, Walker was accidentally blinded in one eye as a child. After attending Spelman and Sarah Lawrence colleges, she moved to Mississippi and became involved with the civil rights movement. She also began teaching and publishing short stories and essays and her first book of poetry, *Once* (1968). Her first novel, *The Third Life of Grange Copeland* (1970), traces a family's attempt to conquer a kind of emotional slavery that exists across three generations. She published the story collection *In Love & Trouble* in 1973, before moving to New York to complete *Meridian* (1976), a novel about a young woman in the civil rights movement.

She later moved to California, where she published a second story collection, *You Can't Keep a Good Woman Down* (1981), which was followed by her most famous work, THE COLOR PURPLE (1982, Pulitzer Prize; film, 1985), an epistolary novel written in black English vernacular telling the story of a poor black woman's struggle for racial and sexual equality. After releasing the essay collection *In Search of Our Mothers' Gardens* (1983) and the poetry collection *Horses Make a Landscape Look More Beautiful* (1984), she cofounded Wild Trees Press (1984–88). Her later novels include *The Temple of My Familiar* (1989), *Possessing the Secret of Joy* (1992), about genital mutilation in Africa, and *By the Light of My Father's Smile* (1998). Walker has also written juvenile literature and critical essays on such writers as Zora Neale Hurston and Flannery O'Connor.

Walker, Margaret (Abigail) *or* **Margaret Walker Alexander** (b. July 7, 1915, Birmingham, Ala.—d. Nov. 30, 1998, Chicago) Novelist and poet, one of the leading black woman writers of the mid-20th century.

Born into a cultivated and intellectual family, Walker graduated from Northwestern University and joined the Federal Writers' Project in Chicago, where she began a brief literary relationship with the novelist Richard Wright. While attending the University of Iowa she wrote the acclaimed volume of poetry *For My People* (1942), which celebrates black American culture and history and calls for a racial awakening.

Walker joined the faculty at Jackson State College in 1949. After decades of work, she completed her novel *Jubilee* in 1966, as her doctoral dissertation for the University of Iowa; it is based on the life of her great-grandmother, and chronicles the progress of a slave family in the mid to late 19th century. *How I Wrote Jubilee* (1972) traces the writing of the novel. Her second volume of poetry, *Prophets for a New Day* (1970), compares the black leaders of the civil rights movement to the biblical prophets. *October Journey* (1973) consists mostly of poems commemorating her personal heroes. After retiring from teaching in 1979, she published *Richard Wright: Daemonic Genius* (1988), the poetry collection *This Is My Century* (1989), and the essay collection *On Being Female, Black, and Free* (1997).

Wallace, David Foster (b. Feb. 21, 1962, Ithaca, N.Y.) Novelist.

A graduate of Amherst College, Wallace was a graduate student at the University of Arizona when his first novel, *The Broom of the System* (1987), was published to excellent reviews. It was followed by his first collection of short stories, *Girl with Curious Hair* (1989). The nonfiction *Signifying Rappers* appeared in 1990. Wallace's frequently hallucinatory and transgressive writing has been compared to the adventurous works of William S. Burroughs, Don DeLillo, and Thomas Pynchon. He spent four years researching and writing the 1,079-page novel *Infinite Jest* (1996), a bizarre tour de force that involves the owners of a tennis academy and the patients at a halfway house. It was followed by the nonfiction collections *A Supposedly Fun Thing I'll Never Do Again* (1997) and *Brief Interviews with Hideous Men* (1999). Wallace has taught at Illinois State University.

Wallace, Irving (b. March 19, 1916, Chicago—d. June 29, 1990, Los Angeles) Popular novelist.

Wallace began work as a freelance writer and interviewer for magazines in 1931. During World War II he was a screenwriter with an army movie unit. After the war he moved to Hollywood to work as a screenwriter. He became a full-time novelist after the publication of his first best-seller, *The Chapman Report* (1960; film, 1962), based on the Kinsey research on sexual behavior. He popularized many subjects in such other best-sellers as *The Prize* (1962; film, 1963), about the Nobel Prize; *The Man* (1964; film, 1972), about integration; and *The Word* (1972), about religion. His other popular novels included *The Fan Club* (1974), *The Pigeon Project* (1979), *The Almighty* (1982), *The Miracle* (1984), *The Celestial Bed* (1987), and *The Guest of Honor* (1988). From 1975 to 1983, he and his family edited several editions of *The People's Almanac*.

Lew Wallace

Wallace, Lew(is) (b. April 10, 1827, Brookville, Ind.—d. Feb. 15, 1905, Crawfordsville, Ind.) Soldier, lawyer, diplomat, and author remembered for the historical novel BEN-HUR.

Son of a governor of Indiana, Wallace left school at 16 and became a copyist in the county clerk's office, reading in his leisure time. He began his study of law in his father's office but left to recruit volunteers for the Mexican War. In the Civil War he served with the Union forces and attained the rank of major general of volunteers. In 1865 he returned to his law practice, which was interrupted by service in two diplomatic positions and as governor of New Mexico Territory (1878–81).

Though he also wrote poetry and a play, his literary reputation rests on three historical novels: *The Fair God* (1873), a story of the Spanish conquest of Mexico; the enormously popular *Ben-Hur* (1880; films, 1925, 1959); and *The Prince of India* (1893), about the Byzantine Empire. His autobiography appeared in 1906.

Walrond \'wȯl-rənd\, **Eric (Derwent)** (b. 1898, Georgetown, British Guiana [now Guyana]—d. 1966, London, England) Caribbean-born writer associated with New York's Harlem Renaissance.

Walrond grew up in Guiana, Barbados, and Panama, where he worked as a government clerk and a reporter. In 1918 he immigrated to New York, where he attended CCNY and Columbia University. He thereafter worked as an editor and writer for black papers, including *Negro World* (1923–25) and *Opportunity* (1925–27). His articles (including "The New Negro Faces America," 1923) and short fiction (including "On Being Black," 1922, "Cynthia Goes to the Prom," 1923, and "The Voodoo's Revenge," 1925) were realistic examinations of racism in America. The stories in his only book, the collection *Tropic Death* (1926), including "The Yellow One," "The Palm Porch," and "Subjection," are set against a lush Caribbean backdrop and juxtapose impressionistic images of natural beauty with terse descriptions of misery and death. Walrond left the United States in 1927 to travel throughout Europe.

Ward, Artemus *pseudonym of* Charles Farrar Browne (b. April 26, 1834, Waterford, Maine—d. March 6, 1867, Southampton, Hampshire, England) One of the most popular 19th-century American humorists, whose lecture techniques influenced Mark Twain and others.

Starting as a printer's apprentice, Browne went to Boston to work as a compositor for *The Carpet-Bag*, a humor magazine. After several years as an editor for the *Toledo Commercial* and the *Cleveland Plain Dealer*, he became staff writer for *Vanity Fair* in New York in 1859. While working on the *Plain Dealer*, Browne created the character Artemus Ward, the manager of an itinerant sideshow who "commented" on a variety of subjects in letters to the *Plain Dealer*, *Punch*, and *Vanity Fair*. The most obvious features of his humor are puns and gross misspellings. In 1861 Browne turned to lecturing under the name Artemus Ward. Though his books—including *Artemus Ward: His Book* (1862), *Artemus Ward: His Travels* (1865), and *Artemus Ward in London* (1867)—were popular, it was his deadpan lecturing that brought him fame.

Ward, Elizabeth Stuart Phelps *or* **Elizabeth Stuart Phelps** *originally* Mary Gray Phelps (b. Aug. 31, 1844, Boston—d. Jan. 28, 1911, Newton, Mass.) Popular 19th-century author and feminist.

Daughter of a clergyman, Mary Phelps assumed the name of her mother, a popular writer, after the latter's death in 1852. She published her first piece, in *Youth's Companion,* at 13. In 1868 she published *The Gates Ajar*, her greatest success; a sentimental religious novel about a girl's struggle to renew her faith despite the death of a beloved brother, it was immediately popular, selling 80,000 copies in the United States and 100,000 in England.

Phelps subsequently wrote 56 more books, in addition to poetry, pamphlets, and short articles. Her later work, much of it similarly religious, was often concerned with the domestic status of women. *The Story of Avis* (1877) and *Doctor Zay* (1882), for example, focus on the problems of women facing the demands of both career and marriage. Phelps also advocated the causes of labor, temperance, and antivivisection in her novels. Her autobiography, *Chapters from a Life*, was published in 1896.

Ward, Nathaniel (b. 1578?, Haverhill, England—d. October 1652, Shenfield, England) Puritan minister and writer.

After studying at Cambridge University, Ward practiced law until 1618, when he was inspired to join the Anglican ministry. He served in a London parish from 1624 until he was dismissed for nonconformity in 1633. He left England in 1634, a time of Puritan persecution, and settled in the colony of Massachusetts, where he became minister of Agawam (now Ipswich). After resigning his pastorate in 1638, he was engaged by the colony's General Court to compile its first code of law; the Body of Liberties, enacted in 1641, was the first true bill of rights in America. On his return to England, Ward issued *The Simple Cobler of Aggawam* (1647), a vigorously written satirical pamphlet defending the status quo and attacking religious tolerance.

Warren, Mercy Otis *originally* Mercy Otis (b. Sept. 25, 1728, Barnstable, Mass.—d. Oct. 19, 1814, Plymouth, Mass.) Poet and historian.

The sister of the political activist James Otis, she managed to absorb an education from her brothers' tutors. In 1754 she married James Warren, a political leader, and came to know most of the leaders of the Revolution personally. From her vantage point at the center of events from 1765 to 1789, Warren was ideally situated to recount the events of the Revolutionary era. Her several plays include the satires *The Adulateur* (1772), which foretold the Revolution, *The Defeat* (1773), and *The Group* (1775), which conjectures what would happen if the British king abrogated the Massachusetts charter of rights. Her *Observations on the New Constitution* (1788) opposed its ratification. In 1790 she published *Poems, Dramatic and Miscellaneous*. In 1805 she completed her three-volume *History of the Rise, Progress, and Termination of the American Revolution,* which remains especially useful for its knowledgeable comments on the important personages of the day. Her feminist concerns are reflected in her correspondence with Abigail Adams.

Warren, Robert Penn (b. April 24, 1905, Guthrie, Ky.—d. Sept. 15, 1989, Stratton, Vt.) Novelist, poet, critic, and teacher, known for his treatment of moral dilemmas in a South beset by erosion of its traditional rural values.

At Vanderbilt University Warren joined the group of poets who called themselves the Fugitives. He was later among several Fugitives who joined with other Southerners to publish the important essay anthology *I'll Take My Stand* (1930), a plea for the agrarian way of life in the South. After graduation, he studied at UC–Berkeley, Yale, and Oxford (as a Rhodes scholar), and he later taught at several colleges, including Vanderbilt, the University of Minnesota, and Yale (1961–73). With Cleanth Brooks and Charles W. Pipkin he founded and edited the *Southern Review* (1935–42), one of the most influential American literary magazines of its time.

His first novel, *Night Rider* (1939), based on the tobacco war (1905–8) between the independent growers in Kentucky and the large tobacco companies, anticipates much of his later fiction in the way it treats a historical event with tragic irony, emphasizes violence, and portrays individuals caught in moral quandaries. His best-known novel is ALL THE KING'S MEN (1946, Pulitzer Prize; film, 1949), based on the career of Huey Long. His other novels include *At Heaven's Gate* (1943), *World Enough and Time* (1950), *Band of Angels* (1956), and *The Cave* (1959). His long narrative poem *Brother to Dragons* (1953), about the murder of a slave by two nephews of Thomas Jefferson, is essentially a versified novel, and his poetry generally exhibits many of the concerns of his fiction. His other volumes of poetry include *Promises* (1957, Pulitzer Prize), *You, Emperors, and Others* (1960), *Audubon: A Vision* (1969), *Now and Then* (1978, Pulitzer Prize), *Rumor Verified* (1981), and *Chief Joseph* (1983). The story collection *The Circus in the Attic* (1948) includes "Blackberry Winter," considered one of his finest achievements; *Selected Essays* (1958) is a collection of critical writings. In 1986 Warren was named the first poet laureate of the United States.

Washington, Booker T(aliaferro) (b. April 5, 1856, Franklin County, Va.—d. Nov. 14, 1915, Tuskegee, Ala.) Educator and reformer.

Born a slave, he moved with his mother to West Virginia after emancipation. He began working in a salt furnace at 9. He worked his way through the Hampton Normal and Agricultural Institute as a janitor, graduating in 1875, and returned to teach there in 1879. When the Tuskegee Normal and Industrial Institute was founded in 1881 as a teacher-training school for blacks, Washington was chosen as its first principal. Under his guidance it thrived and grew impressively, eventually changing its name to Tuskegee University.

By the 1890s Washington had become the most prominent black leader in America. In a speech in Atlanta in 1895, he stated his conviction that blacks could best gain equality in America by improving their economic situation through education—particularly industrial training—rather than by demanding equal rights. His "Atlanta Compromise" was sharply criticized by other black leaders—including W. E. B. du Bois, who would become Washington's great intellectual opponent—though many blacks and most whites supported his views.

Washington's many books included the autobiographical UP FROM SLAVERY (1901), *Tuskegee and Its People* (1905), *The Life of Frederick Douglass* (1907), *The Story of the Negro* (1909), and *My Larger Education* (1911).

Wasserstein \'wäs-ər-ˌstīn\, **Wendy** (b. Oct. 18, 1950, Brooklyn, N.Y.) Playwright whose work probes, with humor and sensibility, the responses of college-educated women to their own aspirations and to modern feminism.

Wasserstein was educated at Mount Holyoke College, CCNY, and the Yale School of Drama. Her first play, *Any Woman Can't* (1973), is a cutting farce on one of her major themes, a woman's attempts to succeed in an environment dominated by men. Two other early works were *Uncommon Women and Others* (1978) and *Isn't It Romantic* (1984), which explore women's attitudes toward marriage and society's expectations of women. In *The Heidi Chronicles* (1989, Pulitzer Prize, Tony Award), a successful art historian discovers that her independent life choices have alienated her from men as well as women. *The Sisters Rosenzweig* (1993) continues the theme into middle age. *An American Daughter* (1997) concerns a woman nominated to the post of surgeon general. Other works include the play *When Dinah Shore Ruled the Earth* (1975; with Christopher Durang), the musical *Miami* (1986), and the screenplay for *The Object of My Affection* (1998).

Webster, Daniel (b. Jan. 18, 1782, Salisbury, N.H.—d. Oct. 24, 1852, Marshfield, Mass.) Orator, lawyer, and politician.

Though born to a humble family, Webster managed to graduate from Dartmouth College. After reading law, he was admitted to the Boston bar in 1805. He served in Congress as a Federalist from New Hampshire (1813–17); after returning to Boston in 1816 he built a prosperous law practice and represented Massachusetts in Congress (1823–27). He argued several precedent-setting cases before the U.S. Supreme Court in which he upheld federal authority over states' rights. As a U.S. senator (1827–41, 1845–52) he became famous as one of the greatest American orators of all time, employing his skills in support of the

Union. A celebrated debate with Robert Hayne of South Carolina (1830) ended with the invocation "Liberty *and* Union, now and forever, one and inseparable." Appointed secretary of state by W. H. Harrison in 1841, he negotiated the Webster-Ashburton Treaty (1842), which settled the Canada–Maine boundary. His belief that preservation of the Union was more important than the abolition of slavery led him to support the Compromise of 1850, permitting slavery in lands ceded by Mexico and incorporating the Fugitive Slave Act, a position that led many antislavery advocates to denounce him. He was bitterly disappointed at being passed over for his party's presidential nomination in 1848. In 1850 he served again as secretary of state.

An 18-volume edition of Webster's eloquent writings was published in 1903.

Webster, Noah (b. Oct. 16, 1758, West Hartford, Conn.—d. May 28, 1843, New Haven, Conn.) Lexicographer who gave American English a dignity and vitality of its own.

Webster interrupted his studies at Yale to serve briefly in the Revolutionary War; he received his degree in 1778. While teaching in Goshen, N.Y., he became dissatisfied with the disregard for American culture that he found in children's textbooks. Seeking to promote a distinctively American education, he published *The American Spelling Book* (1783), the famed "Blue-Backed Speller" that would go on to sell some 100 million copies through many decades, making it perhaps the best-selling book in American history. Largely through his *Speller*, Webster is principally responsible for the differences that exist today between British and American spelling. Encountering difficulties in state-by-state copyrighting, he influentially lobbied for a national copyright law, which was passed in 1790.

In 1793 Webster founded two pro-Federalist newspapers, for which he wrote articles on politics and many other subjects until he sold both in 1803. In 1806 he produced his first dictionary; its innovations included perhaps the first separation of *i* and *j* and of *u* and *v*. In 1807 he began work on the landmark *American Dictionary of the English Language* (1828), which reflected his belief that spelling, grammar, and usage should be based on the living, spoken language. It included about 70,000 entries, including many that had not appeared in any earlier dictionary. The dictionary's success ensured that by the late 19th century Webster's name had become synonymous with American dictionaries. In 1821 he and Samuel Dickinson founded Amherst College. Also a scientist, Webster published such important works as *A Brief History of Epidemic and Pestilential Diseases* (1799), which became a standard medical work, and *Experiments Respecting Dew* (1809), a pioneer work that foreshadowed work of later census and weather bureaus.

Weems, Mason Locke *known as* **Parson Weems** (b. Oct. 11, 1759, Anne Arundel County, Md.—d. May 23, 1825, Beaufort, S.C.) Author and bookseller.

Weems studied for the ministry in England and was ordained an Anglican priest in 1784. He preached regularly until 1792, after which he engaged primarily in writing, publishing, and bookselling. In 1794 he became an agent for the publisher Mathew Carey, and for the rest of his life he traveled the Atlantic seaboard selling Carey's books along with his own self-improvement pamphlets, his almanacs, and eventually his own full-length books. His best-selling *Life and Memorable Actions of George Washington* (1800) contained in its fifth edition the famous account of young Washington's felling of the cherry tree—apocryphal, like most of the anecdotes in the biography. Weems also wrote biographies of Gen. Francis Marion, Benjamin Franklin, and William Penn.

Wells-Barnett, Ida *originally* **Ida B(ell) Wells** (b. July 16, 1862, Holly Springs, Miss.—d. March 25, 1931, Chicago) Advocate for the rights of blacks and women.

The daughter of slaves, Wells lost her parents early and became financially responsible for her five siblings, whom she supported through teaching from age 14. After moving to Memphis, she attended summer sessions at Fisk University. Removed from a train for refusing to sit in the segregated car in 1884, she took her case to court and won, though a higher court overturned her victory and she lost her teaching job. Turning to journalism, she began writing for black-owned newspapers, and bought an interest in the *Memphis Free Speech and Headlight*. When three black businessmen were lynched in 1892, she wrote a scathing editorial, the start of her campaign against lynching. After the *Free Speech* offices were destroyed and her life was threatened, she moved to New York and continued her work, eventually touring Britain in hopes of bringing international anti-lynching pressure to bear on the United States. In 1895 she married Ferdinand Barnett and began writing for his newspaper, the *Chicago Conservator.* Her book *A Red Record* (1895) provides a detailed look at lynching. In 1910 she founded the Chicago Negro Fellowship League and in 1913 the Alpha Suffrage Club, perhaps the first black female-suffrage club.

Welty, Eudora (b. April 13, 1909, Jackson, Miss.—d. July 23, 2001, Jackson) Short-story writer and novelist whose work focused on regional manners in the South.

Welty was educated at the Mississippi State College for Women, the University of Wisconsin, and Columbia University's School of Advertising. During the Depression she worked as a photographer on the Works Progress Administration's guide to Mississippi, and photography remained a lifelong interest. She also worked as a writer for a Jackson radio station and newspaper before her fiction began to win critical acclaim. Her readership grew steadily after publication of *A Curtain of Green* (1941), a volume of short stories containing the much-anthologized "Petrified Man" and WHY I LIVE AT THE P.O. Her novels include *The Robber Bridegroom* (1942), DELTA WEDDING (1946), THE PONDER HEART (1954), *Losing Battles* (1970), and *The*

Optimist's Daughter (1972, Pulitzer Prize). *The Wide Net* (1943), *The Golden Apples* (1949), and *The Bride of the Innisfallen* (1955) are collections of short stories; her *Collected Stories* appeared in 1980. *The Eye of the Story* (1978) is a volume of essays. The autobiographical *One Writer's Beginnings* (1984), which originated in a series of lectures given at Harvard, beautifully evokes her sheltered life in Jackson and how her early fiction grew out of it.

Welty's works combine humor and psychological acuity with a sharp ear for regional speech patterns. Her main subject is the intricacies of human relationships, particularly as revealed in intimate social encounters. Her themes include the subjectivity and ambiguity of people's perception of character and the presence of virtue hidden beneath an obscuring surface of convention, insensitivity, and social prejudice. Welty's outlook is hopeful, and love appears as a redeeming presence amid isolation and indifference.

Wescott, Glenway (b. April 11, 1901, Kewaskum, Wis.—d. Feb. 22, 1987, Rosemont, N.J.) Novelist and essayist.

Independently wealthy, Wescott entered the University of Chicago but dropped out to live abroad, especially in France (1925–33), where he wrote two collections of poems and several short stories and novels, including *The Grandmothers* (1927), the best-selling novel of a pioneer family that made him famous. *Goodbye, Wisconsin* (1928) is a collection of stories about the people and region of his birth. He returned to America in 1934. *The Pilgrim Hawk* (1940), a love story that takes place in a single afternoon, is regarded by some as his best work. *Apartment in Athens* (1945) also enjoyed popular success. His friends and acquaintances included many literary figures; he remembered Katherine Anne Porter, Somerset Maugham, Isak Dinesen, Colette, and others in *Images of Truth* (1962).

West, Dorothy (b. June 2, 1907, Boston—d. Aug. 16, 1998, Boston) Novelist, short-story writer, and journalist.

West began writing short stories at 7; she published several in the *Boston Post,* winning several prizes. Having moved to New York to study journalism at Columbia University, she participated in Harlem Renaissance circles. She traveled to the Soviet Union with other blacks to make a film exposing American racial inequality, but it was never completed. In 1934 she founded the literary magazine *Challenge,* and in 1937 she founded *New Challenge;* though only one issue of the latter ever appeared, it reflected her increasing class- and race-consciousness. She later worked for the WPA's Federal Writers' Project while continuing to publish short stories in various magazines. In 1945 she moved to Martha's Vineyard, where she wrote weekly for the *Martha's Vineyard Gazette.* Her novel *The Living Is Easy* (1948) satirized the concerns of affluent black Bostonians. She did not publish another novel until 1995, when *The Wedding,* about wealthy blacks on Martha's Vineyard, became a great success.

West, (Mary) Jessamyn (b. July 18, 1902, Jennings County, Ind.—d. Feb. 23, 1984, Napa, Calif.) Novelist and short-story writer.

West's mother was a Quaker, and West graduated from Whittier College, a Quaker institution, in 1923. While working on her Ph.D. at UC–Berkeley, she was diagnosed with terminal tuberculosis, but was nursed back to health by her mother. While convalescing, she listened to stories of her mother's Indiana childhood and of earlier pioneer forebears that inspired her to write her first stories, tales of the Quakers Jess and Eliza Birdwell. They appeared in the *Atlantic Monthly, Harper's,* and *Ladies' Home Journal,* and a collection was published as *The Friendly Persuasion* (1945; film, 1956). West's first novel, *The Witch Diggers,* appeared in 1951. It was followed by other novels and story collections, including a continuation of the Birdwells' story, *Except for Me and Thee* (1969), as well as an autobiography and a collection of poems.

West, Nathanael *originally* Nathan Weinstein (b. Oct. 17, 1903, New York City—d. Dec. 22, 1940, near El Centro, Calif.) Writer best known for satiric novels of the 1930s.

Nathanael West

Of middle-class Jewish immigrant parentage, West graduated from Brown University. During a 15-month stay in Paris he completed his first novel, *The Dream Life of Balso Snell*, about an odd assortment of grotesque characters inside the Trojan horse; it was published in 1931 in an edition of only 500 copies. After his return to New York, he supported himself by working as a hotel manager, giving free or low-rent rooms to such struggling fellow writers as Dashiell Hammett, James T. Farrell, and Erskine Caldwell. His second novel, MISS LONELYHEARTS (1933; film, 1958), deals with an advice columnist whose manipulative attempts to solace his correspondents end in ironic defeat and his own murder. In *A Cool Million* (1934), West mocks the American success dream popularized by Horatio Alger by portraying a hero who slides from bad to worse while doing what he supposes to be the right thing. In his last years he worked as a screenwriter in Hollywood. THE DAY OF THE LOCUST (1939; film, 1975), which dramatizes the false world and people on the fringes of the movie industry, has been called by some the best novel ever written about Hollywood.

West was killed with his wife (Eileen McKenney, the subject of Ruth McKenney's popular book *My Sister Eileen,* 1938) in an automobile accident at 37. Never widely read during his lifetime, his work attracted wide attention only after World War II, at first in France. Publication in 1957 of his *Complete Works* sparked new interest in West's work in the United States.

Westcott, Edward Noyes (b. Sept. 27, 1846, Syracuse, N.Y.—d. March 31, 1898, Syracuse) Novelist and banker.

Westcott attended schools in Syracuse until age 16, when he became a junior clerk in a local bank; he would devote his next 30 years to the banking business. In 1895, while recuperating in the Adirondacks from tuberculosis, he began to write *David Harum*, the story of a shrewd, crusty small-town banker in upstate New York with an abundant fund of humor, an obvious talent for horse-trading, and a strong streak of Yankee decency. He died six months before its publication. A best-seller, it was dramatized and twice made into a film; more than a million copies were sold over the next four decades.

Whalen, Philip (Glenn) (b. Oct. 20, 1923, Portland, Ore.—d. June 26, 2002, San Francisco) Poet who emerged from the Beat movement.

Whalen served in the wartime army air corps (1943–46) and later attended Reed College, rooming with Gary Snyder, before joining the West Coast's nascent Beat movement. Like other Beats, he was contemptuous of structured, academic writing and interested in Asian religions, personal freedom, and literary experimentation, but his poetry differed from his Beat colleagues in being generally apolitical, whimsical, and steeped in the quotidian. In 1960 he published *Like I Say* and *Memoirs of an Interglacial Age*, both candid reflections of his beatnik life. His poetry of the 1960s culminated in *Every Day* (1965) and *On Bear's Head* (1969). He was ordained a Zen Buddhist priest in 1973. His later collections include *Decompressions* (1978), *Enough Said* (1980), and *Heavy Breathing* (1983). He was the author of two novels, *You Didn't Even Try* (1967) and *Imaginary Speeches for a Brazen Head* (1972).

Edith Wharton

Wharton, Edith *originally* Edith Newbold Jones (b. Jan. 24, 1862, New York City—d. Aug. 11, 1937, St.-Brice-sous-Forêt, France) Author known for her stories and novels about the upper-class society into which she was born.

Born into a distinguished family, Wharton was educated privately at home and in Europe. In 1885 she married Edward Wharton, a wealthy Boston banker, and a few years later resumed the literary career she had begun tentatively as a young girl. Her major literary model was the older Henry James, who became a close friend; her work reveals James's concern for form and ethical issues, and James himself did much to promote her work.

The best of her early tales were collected in *The Greater Inclination* (1899). Her novel *The Valley of Decision* (1902) was followed in 1905 by the critically and popularly successful THE HOUSE OF MIRTH, which established her as a leading writer. After 1907 she lived in France, visiting the United States only at rare intervals. In 1913 she was divorced from her husband, who had been committed to a mental hospital.

In the two decades following *The House of Mirth*—before the quality of her work began to decline under the demands of writing for women's magazines—she wrote numerous novels, including *The Reef* (1912), THE CUSTOM OF THE COUNTRY (1913), *Summer* (1917), and THE AGE OF INNOCENCE (1920, Pulitzer Prize). Her best-known work is perhaps the long tale ETHAN FROME (1911), which exploits the grimmer possibilities of the New England farm life she had observed from her home in Lenox, Mass. She also wrote many short stories and poems, several books of travel reflecting her interest in architecture and landscape gardening, and the manual *The Writing of Fiction* (1925).

Her novel *Twilight Sleep* was a best-seller in 1927, but the most ambitious project of her later years was the novel *Hudson River Bracketed* (1929) and its sequel, *The Gods Arrive* (1932), books comparing the cultures of Europe and the region of the United States she knew. Her best writing of that period was in the posthumous *The Buccaneers* (1938). Her autobiography, *A Backward Glance*, appeared in 1934.

Wharton, William *originally* Albert W. DuAime (b. 1925, Philadelphia) Novelist best known for his innovative first novel, *Birdy.*

Trained as a painter at UCLA, DuAime worked as an artist for almost 25 years—during which time he and his family settled in France, where they have long lived on a houseboat on the Seine—before the publication of *Birdy* (1979; film, 1984), a critical and popular success. Hospitalized as a result of his service in World War II, Birdy seems to want only to become a bird; a childhood friend, likewise a scarred veteran, tries to help him. Wharton's second novel, *Dad* (1981), tells of a middle-aged painter living in France who returns to the United States to care for his ailing parents. Further novels include the World War II story *A Midnight Clear* (1982; film, 1992); *Scumbler* (1984), about an American artist in Paris; *Pride* (1985), a story of the Depression; *Tidings* (1987); and *Last Lovers* (1991). Wharton himself illustrated his seventh novel, *Franky Furbo* (1989).

Wheatley, Phillis (b. c.1753, Senegal?—d. Dec. 5, 1784, Boston) First black woman poet and, after Anne Bradstreet, the second American woman poet of note.

Apparently of Fulani origin, she was transported to America on the slaver *Phillis* and sold in 1761, at around age 7, to John Wheatley, a Boston merchant. The Wheatleys soon recognized her talents and taught her to read and write English and Latin. Around age 14 she began writing poetry, taking Pope and other Neoclassical writers as models. Her elegy (1770) on the death of the evangelist George Whitefield attracted much attention, and to a surprising degree she gained acceptance in Boston society. She was taken to London in 1773, where her poise and learning won her social success. Her *Poems on Various Subjects, Religious and Moral*, consisting of 39 poems, was published under the sponsorship of the Countess of Huntingdon, and Wheatley's reputation spread in Europe and subsequently in America, where the volume was issued more than a decade later. Her poetry, largely of the occasional type, reflects Christian concerns with morality and piety. Critics long contended that her significance stemmed from the attention she drew to her education, but later reevaluations have called attention to her technical mastery and suggested evidence of African influences.

She was manumitted on her return to America in 1773. Mrs. Wheatley, whose illness had prompted her return, died in 1774, and Phillis remained with the family until John's death in 1778, when she married a free black man who later failed in business and was sent to debtors' prison. At the end of her life Wheatley was working as a servant, and she died in poverty. A memoir was published in 1834, and her letters in 1864.

White, Edmund (Valentine) (b. Jan. 13, 1940, Cincinnati, Ohio) Writer of novels, short fiction, and nonfiction whose work focuses on male homosexual society in America.

After studying Chinese at the University of Michigan, White worked in book and magazine publishing in New York; he has since lived several years in France and has taught at various institutions, including Columbia, Yale, Brown, and Princeton universities. He is a frequent contributor of articles, reviews, and commentary to such periodicals as the *New York Times Book Review*, the *New York Review of Books, Mother Jones*, and *Architectural Digest*.

White's nonfiction includes *The Joy of Gay Sex* (1977; with Charles Silverstein), *States of Desire: Travels in Gay America* (1980), and a biography of Jean Genet (1993, National Book Critics Circle Award). Among his novels are *Forgetting Elena* (1973), *Nocturnes for the King of Naples* (1978), *A Boy's Own Story* (1982), *Caracole* (1985), *The Beautiful Room Is Empty* (1988), *The Farewell Symphony* (1997), and *The Married Man* (2000). His play *Blue Boy in Black* was produced Off-Broadway in 1963.

White, E(lwyn) B(rooks) (b. July 11, 1899, Mount Vernon, N.Y.—d. Oct. 1, 1985, North Brooklin, Maine) Leading essayist and literary stylist.

White graduated from Cornell University and worked as a reporter and freelance writer until 1927, when he joined the *New Yorker* magazine, with which he would be associated the rest of his career. In 1929 he married Katherine Sergeant Angell, its first fiction editor, and that same year he and James Thurber published *Is Sex Necessary?*, a spoof of sex manuals. From 1938 to 1943 he contributed a monthly column to *Harper's* magazine, collected in *One Man's Meat* (1942). In 1959 he revised and published *The Elements of Style*, a typewritten manual for students used in class by his Cornell professor William Strunk, Jr.; it became a standard writer's guide, and millions of copies have since been used in high-school and college courses. In 1941 he edited with his wife *A Subtreasury of American Humor*. His three books for children—STUART LITTLE (1945), CHARLOTTE'S WEB (1952), and *The Trumpet of the Swan* (1970)—are considered classics. His other works include *The Second Tree from the Corner* (1954) and *Points of My Compass* (1962). Collections of his letters (1976), essays (1977), and poems and sketches (1981) appeared in his later years, and he received a special Pulitzer Prize citation in 1978.

White, Theodore H(arold) (b. May 6, 1915, Boston—d. May 15, 1986, New York City) Journalist, historian, and novelist, known for his astute, suspenseful accounts of presidential elections.

After graduating from Harvard in 1938, White served as one of *Time* magazine's first foreign correspondents; stationed in East Asia from 1939 to 1945, he drew on his experience for the book *Thunder Out of China* (1946;with Annalee Jacoby). He later became European correspondent for the Overseas News Agency (1948–50) and for the *Reporter* (1950–53), and wrote *Fire in the Ashes* (1953) about postwar Europe. Having analyzed other cultures, he was well equipped to tackle the American scene in *The Making of the President, 1960* (1961) and *The Making of the President, 1964* (1965). Instantly accepted as the standard histories of the campaigns (the earlier book became the first winner of the Pulitzer Prize for general nonfiction), they present their subjects by intelligently juxtaposing events and treating politicians as personalities rather than symbols, conveying a genuine excitement about American institutions and politics. White's approach was felt to have elevated this type of history to an art form, and he went on to analyze the elections of 1968 and 1972 in similar books. His other books include *The Mountain Road* (1958), *Breach of Faith: The Fall of Richard Nixon* (1975), and the autobiographical *In Search of History* (1978).

White, William Allen (b. Feb. 10, 1868, Emporia, Kan.—d. Jan 29, 1944, Emporia) Journalist who became known as "The Sage of Emporia."

White held positions on the *El Dorado* (Kansas) *Republican* and the *Kansas City Star* before purchasing the *Emporia Daily and Weekly Gazette* (1895). In his *Gazette* editorials he espoused liberal Republicanism; his 1896 editorial "What's the Matter With Kansas?" attacked the platform of the Populist Party and helped the Republican candidate, William McKinley, win the presidency. In 1912 White broke ranks to support Theodore Roosevelt's Bull Moose Progressive Party. In 1923 he won a Pulitzer Prize for editorial writing; collections of his editorials later appeared as *The Editor and His People* (1924) and *Forty Years on Main Street* (1937). He ran unsuccessfully for governor of Kansas in 1924. His numerous other books included several novels and biographies of Woodrow Wilson and Calvin Coolidge. His posthumously published *Autobiography* (1946) received a Pulitzer Prize.

Whitehead, Alfred North (b. Feb. 15, 1861, Ramsgate, England—d. Dec. 30, 1947, Cambridge, Mass.) Anglo-American mathematician and philosopher.

Whitehead entered Cambridge University in 1880, and remained there as a fellow and lecturer until 1910. His focus on mathematics and logic produced such major works as *A Treatise on Universal Algebra* (1898) and the epochal *Principia Mathematica* (3 vols., 1910–13), a collaboration with the young Bertrand Russell, which sought to establish the whole of mathematics on a rigorously logical basis. The treatise is regarded as one of the greatest intellectual achievements of the 20th century. Whitehead's other books include *An Introduction to Mathematics* (1910), *The Principles of Natural Knowledge* (1919), and *The Concept of Nature* (1920).

He taught at the University of London from 1911 until 1924, then accepted a position in Harvard University's philosophy department in 1924. He held the post until his retirement in 1936, and remained a major intellectual influence internationally until his death. Several of his later works—which often stress individuality, creative interaction, and a pantheistic approach to religion, in an attempt to modify what Whitehead saw as a contemporary overemphasis on science and determinism—became widely popular, including *Science and the Modern World* (1925), *Religion in the Making* (1926), *The Aims of Education* (1928), *Process and Reality* (1929), and *Adventures of Ideas* (1933).

Walt Whitman

Whitman, Walt(er) (b. May 31, 1819, West Hills, Long Island, N.Y.— d. March 26, 1892, Camden, N.J.) Journalist, essayist, and poet whose LEAVES OF GRASS revolutionized American literature.

Whitman grew up in Brooklyn, left school at 12, and started work as a journeyman printer in 1835. A year later he began teaching and thereafter he held a great variety of jobs while writing and editing for several periodicals. He spent much of his time walking and observing in New York City and Long Island, visited the theater frequently, developed a strong love of music, especially opera, and read widely.

No publisher's or author's name appeared on the first edition of *Leaves of Grass* in 1855, but the cover had a portrait of Whitman, "broad shouldered, rouge fleshed, Bacchus-browed, bearded like a satyr." Its poems, which included I SING THE BODY ELECTRIC, addressed the nation's citizens, urging them to be large and generous in spirit, a new race of races nurtured in political liberty, and celebrated an idealized American life. It was hailed by such figures as Emerson, but scandalized many with its frank sensuousness. In 1856, after much rewriting, the second edition of *Leaves of Grass* appeared. It contained revisions of the poems of the first edition and several new ones, including the "Sun-down Poem" (later renamed CROSSING BROOKLYN FERRY). All his later poems would be incorporated into successive editions of *Leaves of Grass*

From 1857 to 1859 he edited the *Brooklyn Times*, and his way of life became bohemian. This period up to 1860, when the third edition of *Leaves of Grass* was published, was that of the "I" who was "turbulent, fleshy, sensual, eating, drinking and breeding." Notable in the 1860 volume the "Calamus" poems, which record a personal crisis of some intensity in his life, apparently a homosexual love affair; "Premonition" (later titled "Starting from Paumanok"), which records the violent emotions that often drained the poet's strength; SONG OF MYSELF, asserting the beauty of the human body, physical health, and sexuality; and OUT OF THE CRADLE ENDLESSLY ROCKING.

When his brother was wounded at Fredericksburg, Whitman went there in 1862 to care for him, and for the rest of the Civil War he spent much time cheering and caring for wounded Union and Confederate soldiers in hospitals. DRUM-TAPS (1965) showed his readers a new kind of poetry, ranging from his early oratorical excitement to his later awareness of the horrors of war. *Sequel to*

Drum-Taps (1865) contained a great elegy on Lincoln, whose assassination had devastated Whitman: WHEN LILACS LAST IN THE DOORYARD BLOOM'D. The war also had its effect on his larger views, some of which emerged in the prose of DEMOCRATIC VISTAS (1871). His last works, aside from the ninth (authorized) edition of *Leaves of Grass* (1891–92), were the prose *Specimen Days & Collect* (1882–83) and *November Boughs* (1888), a collection of 62 new poems. Long celebrated as the most seminal of all American poets, Whitman's powerful and enduring influence can be seen in poets as diverse as Wallace Stevens, Fernando Pessoa, Pablo Neruda, and Allen Ginsberg.

Whittemore, Reed *in full* Edward Reed Whittemore II (b. Sept. 11, 1919, New Haven, Conn.) Teacher and poet.

Whittemore cofounded the literary magazine *Furioso* while a student at Yale University. He served in the army air forces during World War II and afterwards revived and edited *Furioso* and its successor, *The Carleton Miscellany*, while teaching at Carleton College. From 1968 to 1984 he taught at the University of Maryland, and in 1988 he revived the journal *Delos*.

Characters and quotations from literature inspired many of the whimsical poems in his first collection, *Heroes & Heroines* (1946). Daily life, the seasons, nature, and modern culture are his subjects in *An American Takes a Walk* (1956) and *The Self-Made Man* (1959). In the 1960s, while his humorous tone remained, a note of sadness began to make itself felt in such collections as *The Boy from Iowa* (1962); in *Fifty Poems Fifty* (1970) and *The Mother's Breast and the Father's House* (1974) his bitterness emerges as well. His later collections include *The Past, the Future, the Present* (1990). Among his prose works are the biography *William Carlos Williams* (1975) and the group portrait *Six Literary Lives* (1993). Whittemore twice served as Consultant in Poetry to the Library of Congress (1964–65, 1984–85).

Whittier \ˈhwit-ē-ər, ˈwit-ē-ər\, **John Greenleaf** (b. Dec. 17, 1807, near Haverhill, Mass.—d. Sept. 7, 1892, Hampton Falls, Mass.) Author and abolitionist noted for his vivid and deeply truthful portrayals of rural New England life.

Born on a farm, of Puritan and Quaker ancestry, Whittier had limited formal education but was acquainted with poetry from an early age. Wordsworth, Coleridge, and Charles Lamb were lasting favorites, but his deepest admiration was for Milton, whose role as apostle of freedom and goad to righteous living he sought to imitate.

John Greenleaf Whittier

Encouraged by the abolitionist William Lloyd Garrison, he wrote copiously and enthusiastically. When his father convinced him of the impracticality of poetry as a vocation, he turned to journalism. He edited newspapers in Boston and Haverhill and by 1830 had become editor of the *New England Weekly Review*, New England's most important Whig journal. During this period he was also writing verse, sketches, and tales of New England, and in 1831 he published his first volume of poems, *Legends of New England*.

By 1843 he had broken with Garrison, but he continued actively to support humanitarian causes as an expression of his strong Quaker faith. He also became more active in literature. In the next two decades he published eight more volumes, which included the poems "Songs of Labor" (1850), "Maud Muller" (1854), "The Barefoot Boy" (1855), and "Barbara Frietchie" (1863). Most of his literary prose, including his one novel, *Leaves from Margaret Smith's Journal* (1849), was also published during this period.

The Civil War years encompassed the deaths of several friends and his beloved sister Elizabeth, who with their mother had influenced him greatly. But national and personal grief furthered his literary maturity. The publication in 1866 of his best-known poem, SNOW-BOUND, in a collection of the same name, was followed by other triumphs in *The Tent on the Beach* (1867), *Among the Hills* (1868), and *The Pennsylvania Pilgrim* (1872).

Wideman, John Edgar (b. June 14, 1941, Washington, D.C.) Writer admired for his intricate literary style in novels about black men in urban America.

Until age 10 Wideman lived in Homewood, a black working-class section of Pittsburgh, which would later become the setting of many of his novels. An outstanding scholar and athlete at the University of Pennsylvania, he became the second African-American to receive a Rhodes scholarship to Oxford. He joined the Penn faculty in 1966, and the next year he published his first novel, *A Glance Away*, about a reformed drug addict and a gay English professor. *Hurry Home* (1970), is the story of an alienated black intellectual. *The Lynchers* (1973) was his first novel to focus on interracial issues. He left Pennsylvania to teach at the University of Wyoming (1975–85). His historical *Homewood Trilogy* comprised the novels *Hiding Place* (1981) and *Sent for You Yesterday* (1983) and the story collection *Damballah* (1981). In the nonfiction *Brothers and Keepers* (1984) he contemplated the role of the black intellectual by studying his relationship with his brother, convicted of murder. After joining the University of Massachusetts faculty in 1985, he published the story collection *Fever* (1989); the nonfiction *Fatheralong* (1994), part of which deals with his relationship with his son, who killed a classmate in 1986; and the novels *Philadelphia Fire* (1990) and *The Cattle Killing* (1996), based on incidents of white-on-black violence in 20th- and 18th-century Philadelphia.

Wiesel \vē-ˈzel\, **Elie** (*originally* Elizer) (b. Sept. 30, 1928, Sighet, Romania) Romanian-American novelist whose works provide a sober yet passionate testament of the destruction of European Jewry during World War II.

Wiesel's early life, spent in a small Hasidic community, was a rather hermetic existence of prayer and contemplation and was barely touched by the war until 1944, when all the Jews of the town (annexed by Hungary in 1940) were deported to Auschwitz, where his mother and younger sister were killed. He was then sent as a slave laborer to Buchenwald, where his father was killed. After the war he settled in France, studied at the Sorbonne, and wrote for French and Israeli newspapers. He moved to the United States in 1956, and has since taught at such institutions as CCNY and Boston University.

While living in France, he was urged by François Mauriac to bear witness to what he had experienced in the concentration camps. The outcome was his first book (and only work in Yiddish), *And the World Remained Silent,* abridged as *Night* (1958), a semiautobiographical novel of a young boy's spiritual reaction to Auschwitz that is one of the most powerful literary expressions of the Holocaust. All his subsequent works have been written in French, and all concern in some manner his wartime experiences and his reflections on their broader significance. They include *Dawn* (1960) and *The Accident* (1961), which round out the *Night* trilogy; *The Town Beyond the Wall* (1962), a novel examining human apathy; *A Beggar in Jerusalem* (1968), which ponders why people kill; *Souls on Fire* (1972), an admired collection of Hasidic tales; *The Testament* (1980); *The Fifth Son* (1983); *Twilight* (1987); *The Forgotten* (1989), in which a Holocaust survivor develops Alzheimer's disease; and the memoir *All Rivers Run to the Sea* (1995). Wiesel was awarded the Nobel Peace Prize in 1986.

Wiggin, Kate Douglas *originally* Kate Douglas Smith (b. Sept. 28, 1856, Philadelphia—d. Aug. 24, 1923, Harrow, Middlesex, England) Novelist and leader in kindergarten education.

Smith moved to California with her family when she was about 17; there she trained to be a kindergarten teacher and established the Silver Street Kindergarten (1878) in San Francisco, the first free kindergarten in the West. In 1881 she married Samuel Bradley Wiggin; after his death in 1889 she traveled to Europe, and the experience led her to write three popular novels for adults: *A Cathedral Courtship* (1893), *Penelope's Progress* (1898), and *Penelope's Irish Experiences* (1901). By far her most popular book was *Rebecca of Sunnybrook Farm* (1903; films, 1917, 1938); the tale of a spirited girl sent to live with her two disagreeable aunts, it became a children's classic and one of the century's bestselling books. Wiggin remarried in 1895 and divided her time between America and England.

Wigglesworth, Michael (b. Oct. 18, 1631, Yorkshire?, England—d. June 10, 1705, Malden, Mass.) Clergyman, physician, and author of rhymed treatises expounding Puritan doctrines.

Wigglesworth immigrated to America in 1638 with his family and settled in New Haven, Conn. In 1651 he graduated from Harvard College, where he was a tutor and a fellow. He was pastor at Malden, Mass., from 1656 until his death. In addition to his clerical duties, he practiced medicine and wrote numerous poems, including "A Short Discourse on Eternity," "Vanity of Vanities," and *God's Controversy with New England* (published 1871). The first two were appended to *The Day of Doom: or a Poetical Description of the Great and Last Judgment* (1662), a long poem in ballad measure using horrific imagery. The most widely read poet of early New England, Wigglesworth declined in popularity together with Puritanism and has since been considered a writer of doggerel verse.

Wilbur, Richard (Purdy) (b. March 1, 1921, New York City) Poet, critic, editor, and translator noted for his urbane and well-crafted verse.

Wilbur was educated at Amherst College and Harvard University. With *The Beautiful Changes* (1947) and *Ceremony* (1950), he established himself as an important young writer of technically and formally exquisite poems. He produced a superb translation of Molière's *The Misanthrope* in 1955, and followed it with equally admired versions of such other Molière plays as *Tartuffe* (1963), *The School for Wives* (1971), *The Learned Ladies* (1977), and *Sganarelle* (1994), and of Racine's *Andromache* (1982). His own collection *Things of This World* (1956) won great acclaim, including the Pulitzer Prize and National Book Award. His later collections include *Advice to a Prophet* (1961), *Walking to Sleep* (1969, Bollingen Prize), *The Mind Reader* (1976), *New and Collected Poems* (1988, Pulitzer Prize), and *Mayflies* (2000). He also wrote the lyrics for Leonard Bernstein's musical version of Voltaire's *Candide* (1957), such children's books as *Loudmouse* (1963) and *Opposites* (1973), and criticism that has been collected in *Responses* (1976). In 1987 he was named the second poet laureate of the United States.

Wilcox, Ella Wheeler *originally* Ella Wheeler (b. Nov. 5, 1850, Johnstown Center, Rock County, Wis.—d. Oct. 30, 1919, Short Beach, Conn.) Poet, novelist, and journalist.

Wheeler's first published work appeared when she was 14, and by 18 she was contributing substantially to the family income. Her first collection of poems, *Drops of Water* (1872), consisted of temperance verses; it was followed by *Shells* (1873), religious and moral poems, and *Maurine* (1876), a sentimental narrative poem. The initial rejection of her next collection, *Poems of Passion,* on grounds of immorality ensured financial success when it was put out by another publisher in 1883. In 1884 Wheeler married Robert M. Wilcox; the couple traveled widely and entertained many artists and writers. Wilcox's literary output continued unabated; she published some 20 volumes, including a number of novels and the autobiography *The World and I* (1912), and wrote a daily poem for a newspaper syndicate for several years. Influenced in her later years by theosophy and spiritualism, she attempted (successfully, by her account) to contact her husband's spirit after his death in 1916. The sentimentality of her writing displeased critics but endeared her to millions of readers.

Wilder, Laura Ingalls *originally* Laura Ingalls (b. Feb. 7, 1867, Lake Pepin, Wis.—d. Feb. 10, 1957, Mansfield, Mo.) Author of children's fiction based on her own youth as a pioneer in the Midwest.

Wilder spent 12 years editing the *Missouri Ruralist,* but only began to write fiction in her sixties at her daughter's suggestion. Her enduringly popular autobiographical novels—*Little House in the Big Woods* (1932), *Farmer Boy* (1933), *Little House on the Prairie* (1935), *On the Banks of Plum Creek* (1937), *By the Shores of Silver Lake* (1939), *The Long Winter* (1940), *Little Town on the Prairie* (1941), and *These Happy Golden Years* (1943)—center on the unrest of the men and the patience of the women who were pioneers in the mid-19th century, celebrating their peculiarly American spirit and independence.

Wilder, Thornton (Niven) (b. April 17, 1897, Madison, Wis.—d. Dec. 7, 1975, Hamden, Conn.) Writer known for his innovative novels and plays.

The son of a diplomat, Wilder grew up in China, graduated from Yale University, and later studied archaeology in Rome. His first novel, *The Cabala* (1926), though set in 20th-century Rome, is essentially a fantasy about the death of the pagan gods. His most popular novel, THE BRIDGE OF SAN LUIS REY (1927, Pulitzer Prize), examines the lives of five people who died in the collapse of a bridge in Peru in the 18th century. *The Woman of Andros* (1930) is an interpretation of Terence's *Andria. Heaven's My Destination* (1934) concerns a quixotically good hero in a contemporary setting. His later novels are *The Ides of March* (1948), *The Eighth Day* (1967), and *Theophilus North* (1973).

Wilder's plays, much better known than his novels, engage the audience in make-believe by having the actors address the spectators directly, by discarding props and scenery, and by treating time in an unrealistic manner through such devices as having the same characters appear in different historical periods and using deliberate anachronisms. His depiction of small-town New England life in OUR TOWN (1938, Pulitzer Prize) was embraced nationwide as the ideal of American community and decency; taken up by high-school and community groups throughout the country, it became perhaps the most frequently performed play ever written by an American. Notable among his other plays are *The Long Christmas Dinner* (1931), THE SKIN OF OUR TEETH (1942, Pulitzer Prize), and THE MATCHMAKER (1954), which was adapted as the musical *Hello, Dolly!* (1964).

Williams, C(harles) K(enneth) (b. Nov. 4, 1936, Newark, N.J.) Poet.

Educated at Bucknell University and the University of Pennsylvania, Williams was a contributing editor for *American Poetry Review* from 1972 and has taught at Princeton University while living part of each year in Paris. His first collection of verse, *Lies* (1969), contains lyrical yet vituperative short-lined poems railing against human callousness and dishonesty. *I Am the Bitter Name* (1972) inveighs against the military-industrial complex and the complacency of governments. A stylistic and thematic departure is evident in *With Ignorance* (1977); an exploration of the American psyche rather than a diatribe, its long-lined, conversational poems have a dramatic and investigative quality. His later works include *Tar* (1983), *Flesh and Blood* (1987, National Book Critics Circle Award), *A Dream of Mind* (1992), and *Repair* (2000, Pulitzer Prize).

Williams, Roger (b. 1603?, London, England—d. Jan. 27/March 15, 1683, Providence, R.I.) Religious leader and founder of Rhode Island.

Educated at Cambridge, Williams arrived in Boston in 1631, seeking freedom to pursue his Nonconformist religious ideals. He settled in the separatist Plymouth colony, but moved to Salem in 1633 after his insistence that only direct purchase of land from the Indians gave just title to it alienated him from the colony. Banished by the civil authorities in Salem for his dangerous views on land rights and separation of church and state, he founded the town of Providence and the colony of Rhode Island on land purchased from the Narragansett Indians in 1636. Providence became a haven for Quakers, Jews, and others whose religion was not tolerated in the Massachusetts Bay colony.

While in England to receive a charter for Rhode Island (1643–44), Williams published *A Key into the Language of America* (1643) and *The Bloudy Tenent of Persecution* (1644), a defense of religious liberty in the face of Puritan attempts to establish a single colonial church. Among his other writings were *Christenings Make Not Christians* (1645) and *The Hireling Ministry None of Christ's* (1652). During a return trip to England to have the charter confirmed (1651–54), he befriended the poet John Milton. Williams served as Rhode Island's first president and was of constant service as a peacemaker with the Narragansetts (whose language he knew), though he helped defend the colony from them in King Philip's War (1675–76).

Tennessee Williams

Williams, Tennessee (*originally* Thomas Lanier) (b. March 26, 1911, Columbus, Miss.—d. Feb. 25, 1983, New York City) Dramatist whose plays reveal a world of human frustration in which sex and violence often underlie a pervasive atmosphere of romantic gentility.

Son of a shoe salesman and an Episcopal priest's daughter, Williams became interested in playwriting while at the University of Missouri and Washington University. Little theater groups produced some of his work, encouraging him to study dramatic writing at the University of Iowa. His first recognition came when *American Blues* (1939), a group of one-act plays, won a Group Theatre award.

Success came with THE GLASS MENAGERIE (1945; films, 1950, 1987), which portrays a declassed Southern family living in a tenement. Williams's next major play, A STREETCAR NAMED DESIRE (1947; film, 1951), the story of the ruin of one member of a once-genteel Southern family, won a Pulitzer Prize. It was followed by the successful *Summer and Smoke* (1948; film, 1961) and *The Rose Tattoo* (1951; film, 1955). In 1953 *Camino Real*, a complex and bizarre work set in a mythical, microcosmic town whose inhabitants include Lord Byron and Don Quixote, was a commercial failure, but CAT ON A HOT TIN ROOF (1955; film, 1958) received a Pulitzer Prize, and THE NIGHT OF THE IGUANA (1961; film, 1964) and *Orpheus Descending* (1958; films, 1959, 1990) were also successful. In SUD-DENLY, LAST SUMMER (1958; film, 1959) Williams deals with lobotomy, pederasty, and cannibalism, and in SWEET BIRD OF YOUTH (1959; film, 1962) the gigolo hero is castrated for having infected a politician's daughter with venereal disease.

Williams's frequent ill health during the 1960s culminated in a severe mental and physical breakdown in 1969, and his plays of the 1960s and 1970s were less successful. They include *Period of Adjustment* (1960; film, 1962), *The Milk Train Doesn't Stop Here Anymore* (1962), *Small Craft Warnings* (1972), *Vieux Carré* (1977), *A Lovely Sunday for Crève Coeur* (1978–79), and *Clothes for a Summer Hotel* (1980). He also wrote numerous short stories, in such collections as *One Arm* (1948) and *Hard Candy* (1954), as well as two novels, *The Roman Spring of Mrs. Stone* (1950; film, 1961) and *Moise and the World of Reason* (1975), essays, poetry, film scripts (including *Baby Doll*, 1956, based on two short plays), and a memoir (1975). His works have been translated and performed around the world.

Williams, William Appleman (b. June 12, 1921, Atlantic, Iowa—d. March 5, 1990, Newport, Ore.) Historian, founder of the New Left school of American history.

Williams graduated from the U.S. Naval Academy in 1944 and served in the navy during World War II, earning a Purple Heart. He earned his Ph.D. at the University of Wisconsin (1950) and taught at a number of colleges before taking a position in 1968 at Oregon State University, where he remained until his retirement in 1986. Especially critical of America's role in the Cold War and Vietnam, he wrote Marxist-oriented revisionist histories of the United States that condemned American imperialism around the globe. His works include *American-Russian Relations, 1781–1947* (1952), *The Roots of the Modern American Empire* (1969), and *America Confronts a Revolutionary World: 1776–1976* (1976).

Williams, William Carlos (b. Sept. 17, 1883, Rutherford, N.J.—d. March 4, 1963, Rutherford) Poet known for the clarity and discreteness of his imagery.

Trained as a pediatrician at the University of Pennsylvania, Williams thereafter divided his life between poetry writing and medical practice in his hometown. By his third volume, *Al Que Quiere!* (1917) his style—which he termed "objectivism" and regarded as an outgrowth of imagism—had become distinctly his own, and he was embraced by the avant-garde. His fresh, direct impressions of the sensuous world are embodied in such well-known works as "Lighthearted William," "By the Road to the Contagious Hospital," and "The Red Wheelbarrow," the latter two published in SPRING AND ALL (1923).

During the Depression of the 1930s, his images became less a celebration of the world and more a catalog of its wrongs. Such poems as "Proletarian Portrait" and "The Yachts" reveal his skill in conveying attitudes by presentation rather than explanation. His most celebrated work, the five-volume PATERSON (1946–58), evokes a complex vision of America and modern life through images of the industrial New Jersey city.

A prolific writer of prose, Williams analyzed the American character and culture through essays on historical figures in *In the American Grain* (1925). He also wrote a trilogy of novels—*White Mule* (1937), *In the Money* (1940), and *The Build-Up* (1952). Among his notable short stories are "Jean Beicke," "A Face of Stone," "The Use of Force," and "The Farmers' Daughters." He also published the play *A Dream of Love* (1948) and an autobiography (1951). He received the Bollingen Prize in 1953, and PICTURES FROM BRUEGHEL (1962) earned him a posthumous Pulitzer Prize.

Willis, Nathaniel P(arker) (b. Jan. 20, 1806, Portland, Maine—d. Jan. 20, 1867, near Tarrytown, N.Y.) Journalist, editor, and author.

Willis grew up in Portland and Boston and graduated from Yale in 1827. He edited and published the *American Monthly* (1829–31), then became a freelance foreign correspondent for the *New York Mirror* (1832–36), reporting from Europe and the Middle East. Collections of his letters to the *Mirror* were published as *Pencillings by the Way* (1835) and *Loiterings of Travel* (1840). During the same period he also published *Melanie and Other Poems* (1835) and a series of sketches. Traveling in the United States, 1836–39, he wrote two successful plays. He became coeditor of the *New Mirror* (later the *Evening Mirror*). Continuing to divide his time between Europe and the United States, he published two more collections of travel letters, a collection of short stories, and a novel, *Paul Fane* (1857). From 1846 until the end of the Civil War he was copublisher and editor of the *New York Home Journal*. During his lifetime he was one of America's most widely read authors, though even at the time his writing was criticized as sentimental and affected. His sister, Sara Parton, became famous under the pseudonym Fanny Fern.

Wills, Garry (b. May 22, 1934, Atlanta) Journalist and historian.

Raised a Catholic, Wills entered a seminary after high school, but decided against becoming a priest. He earned a Ph.D. at Yale (1961) and subsequently taught history at Johns Hopkins University (1962–80) before joining the faculty of Northwestern University. An article he sent to William F. Buckley led to a staff position on the conservative *National Review,* where he remained until his criticism of government Vietnam policy led to a split with Buckley. He has written on figures as diverse as G. K. Chesterton (*Chesterton*, 1961), Richard Nixon (*Nixon Agonistes*, 1990), John Wayne (*John Wayne's America*, 1997), and St. Augustine (*St. Augustine*, 1999), and has contributed to many periodicals, notably the *New York Review of Books*. Almost all his books have concerned either the Catholic church or American history; they include *Bare Ruined Choirs* (1972), about contemporary Catholicism; *Inventing America* (1978), about Jefferson and the Declaration of Independence; *Explaining America* (1981), about the *Federalist*; *Reagan's America* (1986), a political biography; *Lincoln at Gettysburg* (1992, Pulitzer Prize) about the Gettysburg Address; *A Necessary Evil* (1999), on American distrust of government, and *Papal Sin* (2000), on the history of papal dishonesty.

Wilson, August *originally* Frederick August Kittel (b. April 27, 1945, Pittsburgh, Pa.) Playwright known for his cycle of plays, each set in a different decade of the 20th century, about black American life.

The son of a German-born baker who largely abandoned his family, Wilson grew up in poverty, quit school at 15 after a teacher questioned his authorship of a paper, and adopted his black mother's surname. He joined the black aesthetic movement in the late 1960s, cofounded (1968) and directed Pittsburgh's Black Horizons Theater, and published poetry in such journals as *Black World* and *Black Lines*.

Wilson's first published play was *Black Bart and the Sacred Hills* (1981). *Jitney* (1982), set in a cab-service office in the 1970s, was the first in Wilson's series of plays exploring aspects of black life decade by decade. MA RAINEY'S BLACK BOTTOM opened on Broadway in 1984; set in Chicago in 1927, it centers on a verbally abusive blues singer, her fellow black musicians, and their white manager. The celebrated *Fences* (1985, Pulitzer Prize, Tony Award), set in the 1950s, concerns the generational conflict that results from a former baseball player's rage at having been denied the success he felt he deserved. It confirmed Wilson's status as the leading black playwright of his time, and, in the opinion of some, the equal of any dramatist in America. His chronicle continued with JOE TURNER'S COME AND GONE (1986), about neighbors in a Pittsburgh boardinghouse in 1911; *The Piano Lesson*, (1987, Pulitzer Prize, Tony Award), set in the 1930s and concerning a family's ambivalence about selling an heirloom; *Two Trains Running* (1990), set in a Pittsburgh coffeehouse in the 1960s; and *Seven Guitars* (1995), set in the 1940s.

Wilson, Edmund (b. May 8, 1895, Red Bank, N.J.—d. June 12, 1972, Talcottville, N.Y.) Preeminent critic and essayist of his time.

Educated at Princeton, Wilson worked as a newspaper reporter in New York before becoming managing editor of *Vanity Fair* (1920–21) and associate editor of the *New Republic* (1926–31). His first critical work, AXEL'S CASTLE (1931), was an influential international survey of the Symbolist poets. His next major book, TO THE FINLAND STATION (1940), was a sweeping historical study of the thinkers who laid the groundwork for the Russian Revolution. Until 1940 he was a contributor to the *New Republic*, and much of his work for it was collected in *Travels in Two Democracies* (1936), *The Triple Thinkers* (1938), and THE WOUND AND THE BOW (1941). In later years he was closely associated with the *New Yorker* magazine.

Edmund Wilson

After World War II Wilson learned to read Hebrew and produced the best-selling study *The Scrolls from the Dead Sea* (1955). *Red, Black, Blond and Olive* (1956) compares the Zuni, Haitian, Soviet Russian, and Israeli cultures (1956); *Apologies to the Iroquois* (1960) is a sympathetic study of New York State's Indian tribes; PATRIOTIC GORE (1962) is an important analysis of Civil War literature; *O Canada* (1965) examines Canadian culture.

In other works, including *The Fruits of the MLA* (1968), which attacked the Modern Language Association's editions of American authors for their pedantry, Wilson gave evidence of his crotchety character. Many of his plays were collected in *Five Plays* (1954) and *The Duke of Palermo and Other Plays* (1969). His poetry appears in *Poets, Farewell* (1929), *Notebooks of Night* (1942) and *Night Thoughts* (1961). The short-story collection MEMOIRS OF HECATE COUNTY (1946) encountered censorship problems. Wilson's only novel was the early *I Thought of Daisy* (1929). He edited his friend F. Scott Fitzgerald's posthumous papers and notebooks, from which he published *The Crack-Up* (1945) as well as the uncompleted novel *The Last Tycoon* (1941). Wilson's own journals were published posthumously in five volumes. He received the Presidential Medal of Freedom in 1963. He was married five times, from 1938 to 1946 to Mary MCCARTHY.

Wilson, Harriet E. *originally* Harriet Adams (b. 1828?, Milford, N.H.?—d. 1863?, Boston?) Author of *Our Nig,* probably the first African-American novel written in English in the United States.

Almost nothing is known of Wilson's life until 1850. She may have been an indentured servant in Milford before leaving to work as a domestic in Massachusetts. In 1851 she married Thomas Wilson, a fugitive slave; he ran off to sea before the birth of their son, and the abandoned wife eventually left the baby in a white foster home in New Hampshire in order to find work. In the preface to *Our Nig, or, Sketches from the Life of a Free Black, in a Two-Story White House, North. Showing that Slavery's Shadows Fall Even There. By "Our Nig."* (1859), Wilson states that she wrote the novel to make money to reclaim her son, who died of a fever in 1860. The book is largely autobiographical. Its mixed-race protagonist, Frado, is abandoned by her white mother and mistreated by the bigoted white family that employs her as an indentured servant; she eventually marries but is deserted by her husband. After 1863 Wilson disappears from official public records.

Wilson, Harry Leon (b. May 1, 1867, Oregon, Ill.—d. June 28, 1939, Carmel, Calif.) Author.

Wilson left school at 16 to find work, and traveled from Illinois to California, trying his hand at a number of jobs before starting to write for a living. In 1892 he moved to New York and became assistant editor of *Puck*; he was editor from 1896 to 1902. Many of his novels from this period, such as *The Spenders*

(1902) and *The Seeker* (1904), have western or rural settings. While living in Europe (1905–12), he collaborated with Booth Tarkington on plays, of which their best-known was *The Man from Home* (1907). After 1912 he lived in Carmel, Calif., where he wrote sentimental and comic stories for the *Saturday Evening Post*. His most famous novel is *Ruggles of Red Gap* (1915; films, 1918, 1923, 1935). The novel *Merton of the Movies* (1922; films, 1924, 1932, 1947), about a hapless young man's Hollywood adventures, was adapted for the stage by Marc Connelly and George S. Kaufman.

Wilson, Lanford (Eugene) (b. April 13, 1937, Lebanon, Mo.) Playwright, a pioneer of the off-off Broadway and regional theater movements.

Wilson moved to New York after graduating from the University of Chicago and became associated with the Café Cino, an important avant-garde performance venue. The one-act plays *Home Free!* and *The Madness of Lady Bright* (published together in 1968) were first performed in 1964; the former involves a pair of incestuous siblings, the latter an aging transvestite. *Balm in Gilead* (1965), his first full-length play, is set in an all-night restaurant crowded with hustlers and junkies. *The Rimers of Eldritch* (1967) examines small-town life. Like his later plays they incorporate experimental staging, simultaneous dialogue, and deferred character exposition.

Lanford Wilson

In 1969, with his long-time associate Marshall Mason and others, Wilson founded the Circle Theater (later Circle Repertory Company), which he would direct until 1995, building it into one of the most significant theaters in New York. He achieved commercial success with *The Hot L Baltimore* (1973) and *The Mound Builders* (1975). A cycle of plays about the effects of war on a family from Missouri included *The 5th of July* (1978), *Talley's Folly* (1981, Pulitzer Prize), and *Talley and Son* (1985). His other plays include *The Gingham Dog* (1969), *Lemon Sky* (1970), *Burn This* (1987), *Redwood Curtain* (1993), *By the Sea* (1996), *Book of Days* (1998), and *Rain Dance* (2002).

Wilson, Woodrow (b. December 28, 1856, Staunton, Va.—d. Feb. 3, 1924, Washington, D.C.) Political scientist, university president, and president of the United States.

Son of a minister, Wilson attended the College of New Jersey (now Princeton), and received his Ph.D. from Johns Hopkins in 1886. From 1890 to 1902 he taught at Princeton, and he served as its president from 1902 to 1910, pushing through major reforms. In 1910, having acquired a national reputation, he was elected governor of New Jersey; once in office, he kept his ambitiously reformist campaign promises. In 1912 he was elected president of the United States, defeating W. H. Taft and Theodore Roosevelt. His early reforms included lowering tariff rates, initiating an income tax, creating the Federal Reserve (1913), and recognizing the legality of labor unions and strikes. Foreign policy proved more difficult; entanglements with Mexico led to Gen. John Pershing's being dispatched to chase down the

Woodrow Wilson

guerrilla leader Pancho Villa. Despite the 1915 sinking of the *Lusitania*, Wilson maintained U.S. neutrality during World War I through his reelection (1916), but entered the war in April 1917 following renewed German attacks on American ships. His high-minded "Fourteen Points" speech, which called for arms reductions, open diplomacy, trade liberalization, and a league of nations, became the basis for peace negotiations in 1918. The resultant Treaty of Versailles was opposed by Henry Cabot Lodge. On a cross-country speaking tour to raise support for it and the League of Nations, Wilson collapsed from a stroke; crippled, he urged his supporters to oppose the treaty rather than accept Lodge's amendments, and it was twice voted down by the Senate. In 1919 Wilson was awarded the Nobel Peace Prize.

His writings include the brilliant *Congressional Government* (1885), *The State* (1889), *Division and Reunion, 1829–1889* (1893), *George Washington* (1897), *A History of the American People* (1902), and *Constitutional Government in the United States* (1908).

Winsor, Justin (b. Jan. 2, 1831, Boston—d. Oct. 22, 1897, Cambridge, Mass.) Historian and librarian.

Winsor left Harvard University without graduating in order to study in Europe for two years. On his return he spent the next dozen years writing articles, poems, and stories. In 1868 he became head librarian of the Boston Public Library; in 1877 he became head librarian for Harvard University. He was a founder and first president (1876–88) of the American Library Association, and he helped found *Library Journal*. As a historian, he edited the *Memorial History of Boston* (4 vols., 1880–81) and the *Narrative and Critical History of America* (8 vols., 1884–94), and wrote several other works of American history.

Winters, (Arthur) Yvor (b. Oct. 17, 1900, Chicago—d. Jan. 25, 1968, Palo Alto, Calif.) Poet, critic, and teacher who held that literature should be evaluated for its moral and intellectual content as well as its aesthetic appeal.

Educated at the Universities of Chicago and Colorado and Stanford University, Winters taught at Stanford from 1928 to 1966. He wrote one book of short stories and several books of poetry; his *Collected Poems* (1960) won the Bollingen Prize. He is best known for his literary criticism. His attacks on Expressionism and on such literary idols as T. S. Eliot and Henry James aroused much controversy, and he increasingly advocated an adherence to formalism. His major critical works, including *Primitivism and Decadence: A Study of American Experimental Poetry* (1937), *Maule's Curse* (1938), and *The Anatomy of Nonsense* (1943), were collected as *In Defense of Reason* (1947). *Forms of Discovery* appeared in 1967.

Winthrop, John (b. Jan. 22, 1588 [Jan 12, Old Style], Edwardstone, Suffolk, England—d. March 26, 1649, Boston) First governor of Massachusetts Bay Colony.

Winthrop established a law practice in London but, as a Puritan of deep religious convictions, became troubled by the future of religion in England. In 1629 he joined other Puritans in the Cambridge Agreement, a promise to settle in New England in return for the right to self-government, and in 1628 he helped organize the Massachusetts Bay Company. He landed in New England in 1630 and founded the settlement that was to become Boston.

As governor for 12 one-year terms, Winthrop opposed democratic tendencies and the clergy's efforts to share control of the colony. Initially lenient toward dissenters, he forcefully opposed Anne Hutchinson and her followers (1636–38). He led the United Colonies of New England in their defense against the Indians (1643) and defended the colony from parliamentary interference (1645–46). Three volumes of his richly informative journal were published together as *The History of New England from 1630 to 1649* (1825–26).

Wise, John (b. Aug. 1652, Roxbury, Mass.—d. April 8, 1725, Ipswich, Mass.) Religious leader.

Wise was the first son of an indentured servant to graduate from Harvard College (1673). He preached in various Congregational parishes before accepting a post in Ipswich, Mass., where he served the rest of his life. He spoke up for democracy and individual rights long before that position was popular, and was temporarily deprived of his parish for his opposition to a land tax (1687). He opposed the move led by Increase and Cotton Mather that would have given clergy control of churches; his pamphlet *The Churches' Quarrel Espoused* (1710) crushed their movement. His best-known tract, *A Vindication of the Government of New England Churches* (1717) was a plea for democracy in both church and civil affairs; its language was echoed in the Declaration of Independence.

Wister, Owen (b. July 14, 1860, Philadelphia—d. July 21, 1938, North Kingstown, R.I.) Novelist whose THE VIRGINIAN helped establish the cowboy as a folk hero and stock fictional character.

Owen Wister

Grandson of the English actress Fanny Kemble, Wister grew up in an intellectual household, graduated from Harvard Law School, and practiced two years in Philadelphia. He spent his summers in the West, and from 1891, after the enthusiastic acceptance by *Harper's* of two of his Western sketches, he devoted himself to a literary career. *The Virginian* (1902; films, 1929, 1946), a humorous account of a "tenderfoot" in Wyoming, was a great popular success. *Roosevelt: The Story of a Friendship, 1880–1919* (1930) details his long acquaintance with his Harvard classmate. His other novels, none of which approached *The Virginian* in popularity, include *Red Men and White* (1896), *Lin McLean* (1898), *Philosophy 4* (1904), and *Lady Baltimore* (1906). He also wrote books for children. His collected writings were published in 11 volumes in 1928, and his journals and letters (1885–95) were published in *Owen Wister Out West* (1958).

Woiwode \'wī-wůd-ē\, **Larry (Alfred)** (b. Oct. 30, 1941, Carrington, N. D.) Writer whose fiction reflects his early childhood in a tiny town on the North Dakota plains where five generations of his family had lived.

Woiwode first published his fiction while at the University of Illinois, and his short stories and poetry soon began to appear in such magazines as the *New Yorker, Harper's*, the *Paris Review*, and the *Atlantic*. He has taught at Dartmouth College, SUNY–Binghamton, and other institutions.

His acclaimed first novel, *What I'm Going to Do, I Think* (1969), is a study of a newly married couple. *Beyond the Bedroom Wall* (1975) is a multigenerational saga of a North Dakota family; *Born Brothers* (1988) continues the story of Charles and Jerome Neumiller, who also appear in the collection *The Neumiller Stories* (1989). *Poppa John* (1981) concerns an out-of-work television actor. *Indian Affairs* (1992) is a sequel to his first novel. Woiwode has also published the collected-poems volume *Even Tide* (1977), the story collection *Silent Passengers* (1993), and the memoir *What I Think I Did* (1996).

Thomas Wolfe

Wolfe, Thomas (Clayton) (b. Oct. 3, 1900, Asheville, N.C.—d. Sept. 15, 1938, Baltimore) Novelist.

Educated privately, Wolfe entered the University of North Carolina at 15. Having written and acted in several one-act plays there, in 1920 he enrolled in George Pierce Baker's 47 Workshop at Harvard, intending to become a dramatist. Several of his works were produced at Harvard, including *Welcome to Our City* (1923), in which the town of Altamont (Asheville) first appears. There, too, he began the play *Mannerhouse* (published 1948), which was never performed in his lifetime.

In 1923 Wolfe left Harvard for New York, where, except for trips to Europe and elsewhere, he would reside most of his life. Some of his stories, notably "Only the Dead Know Brooklyn," contain observations of city life. Still intending to be a playwright, he taught at New York University, an experience he would describe in his novels. In 1926, while abroad, he began work on what would eventually become *Look Homeward, Angel* (1929), a sprawling novel in which he recounted the growth of its thoroughly autobiographical protagonist, Eugene Gant, in the mountain town of Altamont.

After its publication Wolfe quit teaching to write full-time. OF TIME AND THE RIVER (1935) is perhaps the most turbulent of his books. In his memoir *The Story of a Novel* (1936) he describes his close working relation with his editor at Scribner's, the legendary Maxwell Perkins, to bring the enormous manuscripts of these two works into manageable novelistic proportions.

Wolfe's short-story collection *From Death to Morning* appeared in 1935, but he did not publish another novel before his death at 37 from tuberculosis, though he left a prodigious quantity of manuscript, from which the editor Edward Aswell extracted two more novels, THE WEB AND THE ROCK (1939) and YOU CAN'T GO HOME AGAIN (1940). All four vast, unruly, lyrical, and hyperromantic novels enjoyed great esteem, especially among young people, for decades. A collection of shorter pieces and chapters of an uncompleted novel, *The Hills Beyond*, was published in 1941, his *Letters to His Mother* in 1943, and his *Selected Letters* in 1956. *The Good Child's River,* which Wolfe wrote in the voice of his lover, Aline Bernstein, was published in 1991.

Wolfe, Tom *in full* Thomas Kennerly Wolfe, Jr. (b. March 2, 1930, Richmond, Va.) Novelist, journalist, and social commentator.

After graduating from Washington and Lee University and earning a doctorate in American studies from Yale University, Wolfe wrote for several newspapers, including the *Washington Post*. He later worked as an editor on such magazines as *New York* and *Esquire* (from 1977).

His first book, *The Kandy-Kolored Tangerine-Flake Streamline Baby* (1964), is a collection of essays satirizing American trends and celebrities of the 1960s. *The Electric Kool-Aid Acid Test* (1968) chronicles the antics of Ken Kesey and his Merry Pranksters and the psychedelic drug culture of the 1960s. The two books made Wolfe a leading figure in what was dubbed the New Journalism, which relied on fiction-writing techniques and first-person involvement. His other works, several of them witty and controversial polemics, include *The Pump House Gang* (1968); *Radical Chic & Mau-Mauing the Flak Catchers* (1970), about fashionable leftism; *The Painted Word* (1975), about modern art; *Mauve Gloves & Madmen, Clutter & Vine* (1976); and *From Bauhaus to Our House* (1981), about international architectural styles. *The Right Stuff* (1979, American Book Award; film, 1983) examines the first U.S. astronaut program. *The Bonfire of the Vanities* (1987; film, 1990), a novel of urban greed and corruption that mocks the pieties of the New York liberal establishment, became an extraordinary best-seller. His next full-length novel, *A Man in Full* (1998), about an Atlanta tycoon, was also a major success.

Wolff, Tobias (Jonathan Ansell) (b. June 19, 1945, Birmingham, Ala.) Writer known for his memoirs and short stories.

Wolff's parents divorced when he was a child, and from age 10 until he joined the army he traveled with his mother, who relocated frequently and finally settled in Seattle, where she remarried. He wrote about his childhood, including his relationship with an abusive stepfather, in the memoir *This Boy's Life* (1989; film, 1993). His older brother, the writer Geoffrey Wolff (born 1937), was brought up by their father, of whom he wrote in *The Duke of Deception* (1979). The brothers were reunited in their teens.

Tobias served in the Vietnam War, after which he was educated at Oxford and Stanford universities. His first collection of short stories, *In the Garden of the North American Martyrs* (1981), was followed by the collections *Back in the World* (1985) and *The Night in Question* (1996). His admired memoir *In Pharaoh's Army* (1994) tells of his Vietnam experiences. *The Barracks Thief* (1984) is a novella; *Old School* (2003) is a full-length novel.

Woodward \\'wu̇d-wərd\\, **C(omer) Vann** (b. Nov. 13, 1908, Vanndale, Ark.—d. Dec. 17, 1999, Hamden, Conn.) Historian whose writings focused on the South and the Civil War.

Woodward studied at Emory and Columbia universities and the University of North Carolina (Ph.D., 1937), and he later taught at Johns Hopkins (1947–61) and Yale (1961–77). From his young adulthood he aspired to reform the South, opposing racism and befriending the leading black artists and intellectuals of his day. His most famous work was *The Strange Career of Jim Crow* (1955), an examination of legal segregation that Martin Luther King called "the historical Bible of the civil-rights movement." This and such other works as *Origins of the New South* (1951), *The Burden of Southern History* (1961), *American Counterpoint* (1971), and *Mary Chesnut's Civil War* (1981, Pulitzer Prize) earned him a reputation as the dean of historians of the South.

Woolf, Douglas (b. March 23, 1922, New York City—d. Jan. 18, 1992, Urbana, Ill.) Author of gently comic fiction about people unassimilated into materialistic, technological society.

Woolf's short stories were published in literary periodicals beginning in the 1940s; his first novel, *The Hypocritic Days*, appeared in 1955. Most of his longer works concern cross-country journeys. In his most popular novel, *Fade Out* (1959), an elderly man rejected by his offspring makes a comic odyssey to an Arizona ghost town. *Wall to Wall* (1962), the story of a car salesman's son traveling from Los Angeles to New England, is often considered his finest work. The travels of the protagonist in *On Us* (1977) are interrupted by a meeting with a movie producer. *The Timing Chain* (1985) recounts a car trip from the Rocky Mountains to Boston. The short novels *Ya!* and *John-Juan* were published together in 1971, and some of Wolff's short fiction was published in *Hypocritic Days & Other Tales* (1993).

Woollcott, Alexander (Humphreys) (b. Jan. 19, 1887, Phalanx, N.J.—d. Jan. 23, 1943, New York City) Author, critic, and actor known for his acerbic wit.

After graduating from Hamilton College, Woollcott joined the staff of the *New York Times* as cub reporter and took the post of drama critic in 1914. After a brief stint in the army, reporting for *Stars and Stripes*, he returned to the *Times* and subsequently worked for the *New York Herald* and the *New York World*. He wrote regularly for the *New Yorker*, and from 1929 he also appeared on radio, establishing a nationwide reputation as raconteur, gossip, conversationalist, wit, and man-about-town. As a literary critic Woollcott wielded great influence. He was the author of *Mrs. Fiske, Her Views on Actors, Acting, and the Problems of Production* (1917), *Two Gentlemen and a Lady* (1928), and *While Rome Burns* (1934) and the publisher of two anthologies, *The Woollcott Reader* (1935) and *Woollcott's Second Reader* (1937). Portly, gregarious, and overbearing, he was the self-appointed leader of the Algonquin Round Table literary coterie, and he appeared on stage in the hit play *The Man Who Came to Dinner*, whose central character was based on him.

Wouk \\'wōk\\, **Herman** (b. May 27, 1915, New York City) Novelist known for his epic war novels.

Wouk graduated from Columbia and for several years wrote scripts for radio comedians. During World War II he served in the Pacific aboard the destroyer-minesweeper *Zane*. He would later base his best-known novel, the drama of naval tradition THE CAINE MUTINY (1951, Pulitzer Prize; film, 1954), on that experience.

Wouk's novels, though in no way technically innovative, have been tremendously popular. All are meticulously researched and provide an accurate and detailed portrait of the milieus in which they are set. They are built on a belief in the goodness of man—in the case of MARJORIE MORNINGSTAR (1955; film, 1958), the purity of women—and revolve around moral dilemmas. *Youngblood Hawke* (1962; film, 1964) was a later success. Popular television miniseries were based on his expansive two-volume historical war novel consisting of *The Winds of War* (1971) and *War and Remembrance* (1978). His later novels include *Inside, Outside* (1985), *The Hope* (1993), and *The Glory* (1994).

Wright, Harold Bell (b. May 4, 1872, Rome, N.Y.—d. May 24, 1944, La Jolla, Calif.) First American novelist to become a millionaire from his writing.

Largely self-educated, Wright worked as a landscape painter and later as a traveling minister and as pastor to several congregations in succession, though he had no theological training. His first publication was a collection of mini-sermons given in 1902. His novel *Shepherd of the Hills* (1907; film, 1941) described the lives of the people of the Ozarks. *The Winning of Barbara Worth* (1911; film, 1926) and *Their Yesterdays* (1912) were both best-sellers; the former sold more than a million copies. In 1914 *The Eyes of the World* was the best-selling novel of the year, and in 1916 *When a Man's a Man* outsold all but one title. All display a direct and forceful style and exemplify moral lessons.

Wright, James (Arlington) (b. Dec. 13, 1927, Martin's Ferry, Ohio—d. March 25, 1980, New York City) Poet of the postmodern era who wrote about sorrow, salvation, and self-revelation, often drawing on his native Ohio River valley for images of nature and industry.

Wright studied under John Crowe Ransom at Kenyon College, attended the University of Vienna, and continued his studies under Theodore Roethke at the University of Washington, from which he earned his doctorate in 1959.

His first two books, *The Green Wall* (1957) and *Saint Judas* (1959), were influenced by the poetry of E. A. Robinson, Georg Trakl, and Robert Frost, and displayed an elegant formality. *The Branch Will Not Break* (1963), the watershed of his career, is characterized by free verse, simple diction, and a casual mix of objective and subjective imagery; its style influenced many younger poets. His *Collected Poems* (1971) won the Pulitzer Prize. It was followed by *Shall We Gather at the River* (1968), *Two Citizens* (1973), and *To a Blossoming Pear Tree* (1977); *This Journey* (1982) and *The Shape of Light* (1986) were published posthumously. Wright also translated (often with Robert Bly) the works of Trakl, César Vallejo, Hermann Hesse, and Pablo Neruda.

Richard Wright

Wright, Richard (b. Sept. 4, 1908, near Natchez, Miss.—d. Nov. 28, 1960, Paris, France) Novelist and short-story writer, one of the first American black writers to protest white treatment of blacks.

Wright's father left home when Wright was 5, and he grew up in poverty, often shifted from one relative to another. Though largely self-educated, he published his first story at 16. He worked at a number of jobs before joining the northward migration, first to Memphis and then to Chicago. There, frustrated at being offered only menial employment, he joined the Communist Party in 1932 and became executive secretary of the local John Reed Club of leftist writers and artists. In 1934 he found employment in the Federal Writers' Project. In 1937 he moved to New York, where he became Harlem editor of the communist *Daily Worker,* and later vice president of the League for American Writers.

He first came to the general public's attention with a volume of novellas, UNCLE TOM'S CHILDREN (1938). His fictional scene shifted to Chicago in NATIVE SON (1940), the novel that brought him fame; it relates how the accidental killing of a white girl by its protagonist makes clear and immediate the latter's hitherto vague awareness of the hostility of white society. Early versions of his best novella, *The Man Who Lived Underground* (collected in its final version in *Eight Men*, 1961), appeared in 1942 and 1944; the absurd, isolated subterranean life of its black hero foreshadows the existentialism of Wright's later works.

In 1944 Wright left the Communist Party. The moving autobiography BLACK BOY appeared in 1945. Soon thereafter he settled in Paris as a permanent expatriate. *The Outsider* (1953), acclaimed as the first American existential novel, warned that blacks had awakened in a disintegrating society not ready to include them. Three later novels, including *The Long Dream* (1958), were not well received. Wright's polemical writings of that period include *Black Power* (1954), based on a trip to Africa, and *White Man, Listen!* (1957). The autobiographical *American Hunger* was published posthumously (1977), as was the early novel *Lawd Today* (1963).

Wylie, Elinor *originally* Elinor Morton Hoyt (b. Sept. 7, 1885, Somerville, N.J.—d. Dec. 16, 1928, New York City) Poet and novelist whose aristocratic and traditionalist work reflected changing American attitudes in the aftermath of World War I.

Wylie came from a prominent Philadelphia family, and her peripatetic and occasionally scandalous adult life was spent mostly in New York and England. Her work included four volumes of poetry, beginning with *Nets to Catch the Wind* (1921). Carefully structured and sensuous in mood, her poems show the influence of 16th- and 17th-century English verse. Her four novels, which display gentle fantasy, comedy, and classical formality against thoroughly researched historical settings, include the successful *Jennifer Lorn* (1923) and *The Orphan Angel* (1926), which imagines the life of the poet Shelley if he had been rescued from drowning and taken to America. Her third husband, the poet and critic William Rose Benét, edited her *Collected Poems* (1932), *Collected Prose* (1933), and *Last Poems* (1943) after her death from a stroke at 43.

Elinor Wylie

Yerby \\'yər-bē\\, **Frank (Garvin)** (b. Sept. 5, 1916, Augusta, Ga.—d. Nov. 29, 1991, Madrid, Spain) American-Spanish author of popular historical fiction.

The son of a racially mixed couple, Yerby did graduate work at Fisk University and the University of Chicago and later taught at various colleges. His story "Health Card" won the O. Henry award for best first published short story in 1944. His first novel, *The Foxes of Harrow* (1946; film, 1947), was an immediate success, and he wrote at least 20 more, most of them action-packed historical romances with strong heroes set in the deep South. Their stories unfold in colorful language and include characters of all ethnic backgrounds, enmeshed in complex story lines laced with intrigue and violence. His best novel may be *The Dahomean* (1971), one of the few in which blacks are central characters. Yerby moved permanently to Spain in 1955.

Yezierska \\yi-'zyir-skə\\, **Anzia** (b. 1880?, Plinsk, Poland—d. Nov. 21, 1970, Ontario, Calif.) Novelist who chronicled the Jewish immigrant experience.

Born in poverty in Poland, Yezierska immigrated to the United States at 15 with her family and worked in a sweatshop before winning a scholarship to Columbia University. She married twice and had one child, but gave up the life of a wife and mother to pursue her writing. In 1917–18 she had a romantic relationship with the philosopher John Dewey. Her first collection of short stories, *Hungry Hearts,* appeared in 1920 (film, 1922); Samuel Goldwin bought the movie rights, and Yezierska was hailed as "The Immigrant Cinderella." *Salome of the Tenements* (1923) was her first novel, and *Bread Givers* (1925) was one of the most successful of those that followed. *Red Ribbon on a White Horse* (1950) is her autobiography. Though she continued writing all her life, she died impoverished.

Young, Marguerite (Vivian) (b. 1909, Indianapolis, Ind.—d. Nov. 17, 1995, Indianapolis) Writer best known for *Miss MacIntosh, My Darling*, a mammoth, many-layered novel of illusion and reality.

Raised by her grandmother, Young received her master's degree from the University of Chicago, having published early poems in the journal *Poetry*, and did doctoral work at the University of Iowa. She thereafter taught at several colleges, principally New York's New School for Social Research.

Her first books were the poetry collections *Prismatic Ground* (1937) and *Moderate Fable* (1944). The nonfiction *Angel in the Forest* (1945) examines the foundation of two utopian communities of New Harmony, Ind. *Miss MacIntosh, My Darling* (1965), a project that occupied 18 years of her life, is an exploration of myth and the mythmaking impulse. Its protagonist, Vera Cartwheel, rejects her mother's opium-induced vagueness and searches for her long-lost nursemaid, Miss MacIntosh, who represents common sense and reality, but her journey ends in disillusionment. Young's later works include the story collection *Below the City* (1975) and *Inviting the Muses: Stories, Essays, Reviews* (1994). She worked for some 25 years on the remarkable *Harp Song for a Radical* (1999), which was left unfinished at her death. Ostensibly a biography of the socialist Eugene Debs, its epic sweep ranges over vast expanses of history and geography, and its deliberately excessive style mocks the conventions of historiography. Obscure throughout her life, Young's books have received increasing attention since her death.

Young, Stark (b. Oct. 11, 1881, Como, Miss.—d. Jan 6, 1963, Fairfield, Conn.) Novelist and critic.

Young graduated from the University of Mississippi and earned an M.A. from Columbia, after which he taught at the Universities of Mississippi and Texas and at Amherst College before embarking on a career as a drama critic in New York. In 1922 he became an associate editor of *Theatre Arts Magazine* and joined the editorial board of the *New Republic*. His early novels had modest success, but with *So Red the Rose* (1934; film, 1935) he won both fame and financial success. Late in life he took up painting, and his works were displayed at major museums. He resigned from the *New Republic* in 1947 when his reviews were reduced to one column. His later works include the novel *The Pavilion* (1951) and the translations *Best Plays by Chekhov* (1956).

Zabel \\'zä-bəl\\, **Morton Dauwen** (b. Aug. 10, 1901, Minnesota Lake, Minn.—d. April 28, 1964, Chicago) Educator and writer.

Zabel received his Ph.D. from the University of Chicago (1933) and later taught principally at Loyola (1922–46) and Chicago (from 1947), as well as at South American and Mexican universities. From 1928 he was associate editor of *Poetry* magazine. His many scholarly works include *Craft and Character in Modern Fiction* (1957) and *The Art of Ruth Draper* (1959), and he edited compilations of works of such writers as Henry James, Joseph Conrad, and Charles Dickens. A prize established in his name by the American Academy of Arts and Letters is awarded to poets, fiction writers, and critics.

Zindel \\zin-'del\\, **Paul** (b. May 15, 1936, Staten Island, N.Y.—d. March 27, 2003, New York City) Playwright and novelist whose work features poignant, alienated characters who learn to deal pragmatically with life's difficulties.

Paul Zindel

Zindel attended Wagner College, where he was encouraged in his writing by Edward Albee, and he taught high-school science for 10 years before becoming a full-time writer in 1972. He came to wide public notice with THE EFFECT OF GAMMA RAYS ON MAN-IN-THE-MOON MARIGOLDS (1971, Pulitzer Prize). It was followed by the plays *And Miss Reardon Drinks a Little* (1971), *The Secret Affairs of Mildred Wild* (1973), *Let Me Hear You Whisper* (1970), *The Ladies Should Be in Bed* (1973), *A Destiny with Half Moon Street* (produced 1983, published 1992), and *Amulets Against the Dragon Forces* (1989; based partly on his novel *Confessions of a Teenage Baboon*). In most of his dramas the main tension is between a nonconformist, domineering mother and an impressionable, bewildered young person. Of his novels for adolescents, the best-known is the durably popular *The Pigman* (1968); his later young-people's books include *My Darling, My Hamburger* (1969), *Harry and Hortense at Hormone High* (1984), and *A Begonia for Miss Applebaum* (1989).

Zukofsky \\zü-'kȯf-skē\\, **Louis** (b. Jan. 23, 1904, New York City—d. May 12, 1978, Port Jefferson, N.Y.) Poet, the founder of Objectivist poetry and author of the massive poem *"A."*

The son of Russian-Jewish immigrants, Zukofsky attended Columbia University and taught several years at the Polytechnic Institute of Brooklyn. By the 1930s he had begun the ill-defined Objectivist movement, and poets as radically different as W. C. Williams, T. S. Eliot, and Ezra Pound contributed to the special Objectivist issue of *Poetry* magazine (1931) and to the *"Objectivist" Anthology* (1932) that he edited.

Meanwhile, in 1928 he had embarked on *"A"* (published 1978), the great work of his life, which treats subjects as diverse as history, politics, aesthetics, and science. The poem is organized in a mosaic structure and planned in 24 parts. Over 800 pages long, it begins with the word "A" and ends with "Zion." Zukofsky described himself as a comic poet, and punning is the characteristic medium of his and his wife Celia's *Catullus Fragmenta* (1969), a translation of Catullus's works into an obscure English that attempts to reproduce the sounds of the original Latin. His several volumes of prose include the critical study *Bottom: On Shakespeare* (1963) and *Little: A Fragment For Careenagers* (1967), a short novel about a violin prodigy. *All: The Collected Short Poems, 1923–1964* was published in 1971.

Literary Works

Abe Lincoln in Illinois Drama in 12 scenes by Robert E. SHERWOOD, produced in 1938 and published in 1939. It concerns Lincoln's life and career, from his early, unsuccessful days as a postmaster in New Salem, Ill., through his initial forays into local politics, his relationship with Mary Todd, and his debates with Stephen Douglas, and culminates with his election to the presidency and imminent departure for Washington, D.C., 30 years later.

Absalom, Absalom! Novel by William FAULKNER, published in 1936. The principal narrative, set in 19th-century Mississippi, concerns the efforts of Thomas Sutpen to transcend his lowly origins by establishing and maintaining a slave-driven empire—"Sutpen's Hundred"—on the frontier. Sutpen's consuming notion of racial superiority undermines his closest relationships and proves his undoing. By the novel's end his plantation is in ruins and his only living heir is a mentally deficient great-grandson of mixed blood. Bracketing this mythic story is the struggle of Quentin Compson, a young Mississippian at Harvard decades later (and the grandson of a Sutpen acquaintance), to come to terms with the story's implications for his native region. Criticized by contemporary critics for its turgid style and convoluted, redundant narration, the novel later came to be considered one of the finest in American literature.

Ada(; or Ardor: A Family Chronicle) Novel by Vladimir NABOKOV, written in English and published in 1969. Its prodigious length and the family tree on its frontispiece recall the great 19th-century novels of the author's native Russia, but *Ada* boldly overturns their conventions. For his rich, sweeping saga of the Veen-Durmanov clan, Nabokov invents an incestuous pair of "cousins" (actually siblings, Van and Ada), a hybrid country (Amerussia), a familiar but strange planet (Antiterra), and a dimension of malleable time. The novel follows the lovers from their childhood idylls through impassioned estrangements and reunions to a tenderly shared old age. Its rich narrative style incorporates untranslated foreign phrases, esoteric data, and countless literary allusions.

Adventures of Augie March, The Novel by Saul BELLOW, published in 1953. The picaresque story of a poor Jewish youth from Chicago, it traces Augie's progress through the 20th-century world and his attempts to make sense of it. Augie shuns a settled existence, and, though knocked down, always rises up,

swept along by events that are comic and tragic by turns.

After the Fall Play in two acts by Arthur MILLER, produced and published in 1964. It presents retrospectively a series of encounters over a 25-year span between Quentin, a middle-aged lawyer, and his intimate associates. His first wife, Louise, accuses him of neglect; a friend from his days as a Communist Party member appears now as an informer before congressional investigators; another former "fellow traveler" commits suicide before Quentin has the opportunity to defend him. The second act traces the downward course of his second wife, Maggie (modeled on Miller's former wife, Marilyn Monroe), from popular entertainer to bitter neurotic to suicide. As the play ends, Quentin appears poised to marry Holga, whose struggle against Nazism embodies his own desire to confront evil. Thematic issues of ethical ambiguity and personal integrity help compensate for the somewhat disjointed dramatic structure.

Age of Innocence, The Novel by Edith WHARTON, published in 1920. It is set in upper-class New York society in the late 19th century. Newland Archer, though engaged to the beautiful May Welland, is attracted to Ellen Olenska, a former member of their circle who has been living in Europe but who has left her husband under mysterious circumstances and returned to her family's New York home. May prevails by subtly adhering to the conventions of that world.

Ah, Wilderness! Comedy in four acts by Eugene O'NEILL, published and first performed in 1933. Perhaps the least typical of the author's works, the play is a sentimental tale of youthful indiscretion in a turn-of-the-century New England town. Richard, adolescent son of the local newspaper publisher, Nat Miller, exhibits the wayward tendencies of his dissolute uncle, Sid Davis. Forbidden to court his neighbor Muriel by her father, Richard goes on a bender and falls under the influence of Belle, whom he tries to impress but whose worldly ways frighten him. It is Sid who handles the situation upon the prodigal's drunken return, and with the aid of Richard's warmhearted father and the forgiving Muriel, everything is put to right. The play became a staple of the community-theater repertoire.

Alice Adams Novel by Booth TARKINGTON, published in 1921. The title character, a social climber, is ashamed of her lower-middle-class family. Hoping to attract a wealthy husband, she lies about her background, but is found out and shunned by those she sought to attract. At the novel's end, she knows her chances for happiness and a successful marriage are bleak, but remains unbowed.

All My Sons Drama in three acts by Arthur MILLER, performed and published in 1947. It centers on Joe Keller, a manufacturer of substandard and defective war materials, whose faulty airplane parts cause the death of his son and other fliers during World War II. With its intense exploration of guilt and responsibility, *All My Sons* is considered Miller's first significant play.

All the King's Men Novel by Robert Penn WARREN, published in 1946. It traces the rise and fall of Willie Stark, a character modeled on Huey Long, governor of Louisiana in the late 1920s and early 1930s. Stark, who comes from a poor background, becomes a lawyer and is elected governor. A self-styled man of the people, he soon learns to use such tactics as bribery and intimidation to assure passage of his populist programs, which include rural construction and development projects. His shady methods increase his power but ultimately lead to his assassination.

Ambassadors, The Novel by Henry JAMES, published in 1903. The "eye" of the story, Lambert Strether, is a Massachusetts editor engaged to the widowed Mrs. Newsome. Disturbed by reports concerning her son Chad's love life in Paris, Mrs. Newsome presses Strether to engineer the young man's return. The Chad that Strether finds is, to his mind, an improvement over the former one, though the nature of Chad's relationship with Marie de Vionnet and her daughter remains indeterminate. Strether's "investigations" proceed slowly, and eventually he himself falls under the Vionnets' spell. His discovery of Chad and Marie's affair is considered one of the sublime revelations in American literature. Mrs. Newsome sends in reinforcements who eventually defer to Chad regarding the direction of his future; heeding Strether's advice, he remains in Paris.

American, The Novel by Henry JAMES, published serially in 1876 in the *Atlantic Monthly* and in book form a year later. The guilelessness and forthrightness of Christopher Newman, a self-made millionaire, are in sharp contrast with a family of arrogant and cunning French aristocrats, the Bellegardes, whose daughter, the widowed Claire de Cintré, he seeks to marry. Deemed socially unacceptable by her older brother and mother, he befriends her younger brother, Valentin, who, on his deathbed, tells Newman how to blackmail the family into approving the marriage. Newman ulti-

mately decides not to carry out his threat of blackmail, and the Bellegardes' uncompromising allegiance to social class and family tradition remains unswayed.

American Buffalo Two-act play by David MAMET, produced in 1975 and published in 1976. Don Dubrow, the owner of a junk shop where the action takes place, decides to steal a customer's coin collection when he feels he has been bested in a transaction involving a buffalo nickel. He enlists the help of a young junkie named Bobby, but is convinced by a manipulative friend that Bobby is incompetent. Unable to trust either, Don invites a third person to join him. Bobby becomes a scapegoat as the burglary plot unravels in suspicion, anger, and violence.

American Dream, The One-act drama by Edward ALBEE, published in 1959 (with *The Zoo Story*) and first produced in 1961. Its central figures, Mommy and Daddy, represent banal American life. The clubwoman Mrs. Barker visits and Grandma reminds her of an earlier visit, when she brought an infant. This child did not turn out as Mommy and Daddy expected and so was abused by them until it died. When a handsome but emotionless young man—the American Dream—later arrives, Grandma suggests Mommy and Daddy adopt him, since his emptiness seems to be what they desire. The brief absurdist play established Albee as an acerbic critic of American values.

American Tragedy, An Novel by Theodore DREISER, published in 1925. The complex and compassionate account of the life and death of the young Clyde Griffiths. The novel (based on an actual murder case) begins with Clyde's blighted background, recounts his path to success, and culminates in his apprehension, trial, and execution for murdering his wife, who he saw as an obstacle to his advancement. Called by one influential critic "the worst-written great novel in the world," its questionable grammar and style are transcended by its narrative power. Dreiser's intricate speculations on the extent of Clyde's guilt are countered by his searing indictment of materialism and the American dream of success.

Annabel Lee Lyric poem by Edgar Allan POE, published in the *New York Tribune* on Oct. 9, 1849, two days after his death. Thought to have been written in memory of his young wife and cousin, Virginia, who died in 1847, the poem's theme—the death of a young, beautiful, and dearly beloved woman—is one that occurs frequently in Poe's works.

Anna Christie Four-act play by Eugene O'NEILL, produced in 1921 and published in 1922. The title character, long separated from her bargemaster father, is reunited with him in adulthood. Not realizing that she has become a prostitute, her sentimental father comes to blows with a seaman who has been smitten by her. When Anna reveals her sordid past, both men abandon her, go their separate ways, get drunk, and unwittingly sign on for the same distant voyage. At the play's end, Anna has agreed to wait for their return.

Another Country Novel by James BALDWIN, published in 1962. The suicide of Rufus Scott, a black jazz musician, impels his friends to search for the meaning of his death and, consequently, for a deeper understanding of their own identities. Employing a loose, episodic structure, the book traces the romantic affairs—heterosexual and homosexual as well as inter-racial—among Scott's friends. In its language and structure, it is a departure from Baldwin's earlier work; it was widely noted for his graphic portrayal of bisexuality and interracial relations.

Anthony Adverse Historical novel by Hervey ALLEN, published in 1933. A long, rambling work set in Europe, Africa, and the Americas during the Napoleonic era, it relates the many adventures of its eponymous hero, including slave trading in Africa, owning a plantation in New Orleans, and imprisonment and eventual death in Mexico. It was one of the best-selling American novels up to its time.

archy and mehitabel Collection of humorous stories and verses by Don MARQUIS, originally published from 1916 in his newspaper columns and published in book form in 1927. Archy is a philosophical cockroach who types messages to the author in lowercase letters (being unable to activate the shift mechanism); Mehitabel is a free-spirited alley cat whose motto is "toujours gai." The book consists mostly of free-verse poems on such topics as transmigration of souls, social injustice, life in New York City, and death. Sequels included *archy's life of mehitabel* (1933) and *archy does his part* (1935). *the lives and times of archy and mehitabel* (1940) is a posthumously published compendium of the previous books.

Ariel Collection of poetry by Sylvia PLATH, published posthumously in 1965. Most of the poems were written during the five months prior to Plath's suicide. Though they range in subject from pastoral chores ("The Bee Meeting") to medical trauma ("Tulips"), each con-

tributes to an impression of the inevitability of the author's self-destruction. The collection contains DADDY, one of Plath's best-known poems.

Arrowsmith Novel by Sinclair LEWIS, published in 1925. Disheartened successively by rural practice, the state of public health care, and the elitism of an urban clinic, Martin Arrowsmith, a Midwestern physician, accepts a research position at an institute in New York that leads him, along with his wife, Leora, a nurse, to an epidemic-ravaged island. Leora dies there, and Martin abandons his scientific principles in order to make an experimental serum more widely available. Returning to the institute, he marries a wealthy widow, but comes to find her social demands a distraction. He eventually leaves institutional medicine, as well as his wife, and sets up his own laboratory on a New England farm. Lewis declined a Pulitzer Prize for the work because he had not been awarded one for the earlier *Main Street*.

Art of Fiction, The Long critical essay by Henry JAMES, first published in 1884 in *Longman's Magazine*. Written as a rebuttal to Sir Walter Besant's "Fiction as One of the Fine Arts" (1884), James's manifesto of literary realism decries the popular demand for novels saturated with sentimentality or pessimism, assailing Besant's assertions that plot is more important than characterization, that fiction must have a "conscious moral purpose," and that experience and observation outweigh imagination as creative tools, and noting that "no good novel will ever proceed from a superficial mind."

Ash Wednesday Long poem by T. S. ELIOT, first published complete in 1930. Published after Eliot's confirmation in the Church of England (1927), it expresses the pangs and the strain involved in the acceptance of religious belief and religious discipline. The first section introduces the irony of the modern individual whose intellectual dithering stands in the way of any spiritual renewal. The second section is an allegory of rebirth, based on a prophecy by Ezekiel, with a famous image of devouring leopards. The next two sections discuss spiritual journeys such as that described by Dante. The fifth section plays on the many religious and philosophical connotations of the word "word." The final section concerns the tension between meditation and distraction.

As I Lay Dying Novel by William FAULKNER, published in 1930. Set in Faulkner's Yoknapatawpha County, the story is told through multiple characters' fragmented and intercut narration. Narrators include

Addie Bundren, her husband Anse, their sons Cash, Darl, and Vardaman, their daughter Dewey Dell, and Addie's illegitimate son, Jewel. Addie watches from her deathbed as Cash builds her coffin. Upon her death, the family, under the direction of the small-minded and ineffectual Anse, endeavors for once to respect Addie's wishes and transport her to her hometown for burial. The rest of the novel is an account of the family's journey and of the fates of its individual members.

Aspern Papers, The Novella by Henry JAMES, published in 1888. An unnamed American editor rents a room in Venice in the home of Juliana Bordereau, the elderly mistress of Jeffrey Aspern, a deceased poet, in order to procure the poet's papers. The stingy, domineering Bordereau lives with her timid, middle-aged niece, Tina (named Tita until James revised the text in 1908). The obsessed editor becomes increasingly unscrupulous, assuming an alias, making false romantic overtures to Tina, and attempting burglary. When Bordereau dies, Tina offers him the coveted documents on condition that he marry her. He initially refuses but returns to negotiate, only to find that Tina has burned the papers. The story was inspired by an actual incident involving Claire Clairmont, the mistress of Lord Byron.

Assistant, The Novel by Bernard MALAMUD, published in 1957. Set in Brooklyn, it examines the complex relationship that develops between Morris Bober, a worn-out Jewish grocer, and Frank Alpine, a young Italian-American who first robs Morris and then comes to his aid after wounding him. Frank eventually becomes Morris's assistant, falls in love with his high-minded daughter, Helen, and challenges the old man's expectations of life. Morris pursues various schemes for unburdening himself of the store. Religious differences undermine Frank's amorous intentions, and Morris fires him for petty theft. After Morris's death, Frank comes back to revive the store and converts to Judaism.

Atlas Shrugged Novel by Ayn RAND, published in 1957. Its female protagonist, Dagny Taggart, struggles to manage a transcontinental railroad amid the pressures and restrictions of massive bureaucracy. Her antagonistic reaction to a libertarian group seeking an end to government regulation is later echoed and modified in her encounter with a utopian community, Galt's Gulch, whose members regard self-determination rather than collective responsibility as the highest ideal. The novel contains the most complete presentation of Rand's personal "Objectivist" philosophy in fictional form.

Autobiography of Alice B. Toklas, The Autobiography by Gertrude STEIN, published in 1933; it first appeared in an abridged version in the *Atlantic Monthly*. Written as if it were the autobiography of her lifelong companion, Alice B. Toklas, the work ostensibly contains Toklas's first-person account not of her own life but of Stein's, written from Toklas's viewpoint and replete with Toklas's sensibilities, observations, and mannerisms. It describes the life Toklas and Stein led in Paris and their association with such figures as Picasso, Hemingway, Matisse, and Braque. While Stein exchanges ideas with men of genius, Toklas sits with their wives. The work's droll premise, masterly execution, and witty insights proved Stein capable of writing for a general public.

Autobiography of an Ex-Colored Man, The Novel by James Weldon JOHNSON, published in 1912. The unnamed narrator of this fictional autobiography, born in Georgia, tells of his childhood in Connecticut, where his mulatto mother, aided by monthly checks from his white father, is able to provide a secure and cultured environment. Learning of his black heritage only by accident, he experiences the first of several identity shifts that will eventually find him choosing membership in white society. Throughout the work, Johnson employs characters, locales, incidents, and motifs from his own life, but the narrator is less a conscious self-portrait than a representative of the author's own ambivalence. The novel was originally published anonymously in order to suggest authenticity.

Autobiography of Malcolm X, The Autobiography of the religious leader and activist, published in 1965. It was actually written by Alex HALEY, who, working for *Playboy* magazine, had conducted extensive audiotaped interviews with Malcolm X just before his assassination in 1965. It recounts Malcolm's life from his traumatic childhood, plagued by racism, to his years as a drug dealer and pimp, his conversion to the Nation of Islam while in prison, his subsequent years of militant activism, and his later turn to more orthodox Islam. Though some of its factual claims have been disputed, the book is still regarded as an African-American classic.

Autobiography of Miss Jane Pittman, The Novel by Ernest J. GAINES, published in 1971. Set in rural southern Louisiana, it follows the life of Jane Pittman through 100 years of American history, from the early 1860s to the onset of the civil-rights movement in the 1960s. A child at the end of the Civil War, she survives a massacre by former Confederate soldiers. She serves as a steadying influence on several black men who struggle for economic and political equality. After the death of her husband, Joe, she becomes a committed Christian and a spiritual guide in her community. Spurred by the violent death of a young community leader, she finally confronts a plantation owner who represents the white power structure to which she has always been subservient.

Awakening, The Novella by Kate CHOPIN, published in 1899. Edna Pontellier, the wife of an older businessman in New Orleans, finds herself awakening to the sensuous possibilities of life when she encounters Creole society while at a vacation resort at Grande Isle. There she becomes smitten with a young man, Robert LeGrun. Though he returns her feelings, he eventually leaves her, hoping she will preserve her marriage. Instead she returns to the resort, plunges into the ocean, and swims out far enough to ensure that she will drown. The novel's frank examination of female sexuality and treatment of adulterous love made it controversial in its time; in recent years it has been embraced as a harbinger of American feminist fiction.

Awakening Land, The Trilogy of novels by Conrad RICHTER, published together in 1966. It consists of *The Trees* (1940). *The Fields* (1946), and *The Town* (1950). Set in the Ohio River valley from the late 18th to the mid-19th century, the trilogy offers a realistic portrayal of frontier life as it chronicles the development of the area from wilderness. The changing landscape provides the background for the story of the pioneer Sayward Luckett Wheeler, who grows from girlhood to maturity as a wife and mother and into old age over the trilogy's course.

Awkward Age, The Novel by Henry JAMES, published in 1899. Written mostly in dialogue with limited narrative explanation, it is the story of Nanda Brookenham, a young London society woman whose attempts at marriage are foiled by various members of her mother's social circle. Nanda's manipulative mother, Fernanda, appears to be her rival for the affections of Gustavus Vanderbank, a young government employee, who becomes alienated from both women. Nanda is befriended by the elderly Mr. Longdon, who once courted her grandmother, and by the young Mr. Mitchett, who unhappily marries Little Aggie, a naive young woman steered into the marriage by her devious aunt, the Duchess.

Axel's Castle(: A Study in the Imaginative Literature of 1870–1930) Book of critical essays by Edmund WILSON, published in 1931. Wilson traced the origins of specific trends in contemporary literature, which, he held, was largely concerned with Symbolism and its relationship to naturalism. After an introductory essay on Symbolism, Wilson tracks the development of those trends in the works of W. B. Yeats, Paul Valéry, T. S. Eliot, Marcel Proust, James Joyce, Gertrude Stein, and Arthur Rimbaud and Auguste Villiers de l'Isle-Adam.

Babbitt Novel by Sinclair LEWIS, published in 1922. George F. Babbitt is a prosperous real-estate broker in the Midwestern town of Zenith, a pillar of his community, a civic booster, and a believer in success for its own sake. When his best friend is arrested for shooting his own wife, Babbitt begins to question some of the values he has always upheld. He takes vacations away from his wife, has an adulterous affair, and dabbles with socialism. Since he lacks inner strength, his rebellion is brief; when his wife becomes ill, he returns to her and to his former way of life. The novel's scathing indictment of middle-class American values made "Babbittry" a synonym for an attitude combining conformism, materialism, and anti-intellectualism.

Ballad of the Sad Café, The Novella by Carson MCCULLERS, the title work in a collection published in 1951. The tall, lonely Amelia Evans falls passionately in love with her cousin Lymon, a malevolent dwarf. She opens a café that comes to serve as a much-needed social center for their tiny Southern town. Lymon falls in love with Amelia's estranged husband, Marvin Macy, who has just been released from prison. Lymon and Macy overpower Amelia physically and wreck her beloved café, after which they disappear together.

Bartleby the Scrivener(: A Story of Wall Street) Novella by Herman MELVILLE, published anonymously in 1853 in *Putnam's Monthly Magazine* and subsequently in *The Piazza Tales* in 1856. The narrator, a successful Wall Street lawyer, hires Bartleby to copy legal documents. Bartleby initially works hard, but one day, when asked to proofread, he responds, "I would prefer not to." As time progresses, he increasingly prefers not to do anything asked of him, and he eventually dies of self-neglect, refusing offers of help, while jailed for vagrancy. Melville wrote "Bartleby" at a time when his career seemed to be in ruins, and the much-discussed story reflects his pessimism.

Bear, The Novella by William FAULKNER, early versions of which first appeared as "Lion" in *Harper's* (1935) and "The Bear" in the *Saturday Evening Post* (1942) before it was published in GO DOWN, MOSES. Set in the late 19th century, it is a hunting story told from the perspective of Ike McCaslin, a young man from an old family in Yoknapatawpha County. In its first three parts, Ike trains under the expert tracker Sam Fathers and hunts down the legendary bear Old Ben. The fourth part (omitted in some publications) comprises a long, convoluted dialogue between Ike and his cousin Carothers ("Cass") Edmonds, in which Ike repudiates his inheritance after he discovers incest and miscegenation in the family history. The final part conveys Ike's affinity for nature and his dismay at its gradual destruction.

Beast in the Jungle, The Novella by Henry JAMES that first appeared in *The Better Sort* (1903). It concerns John Marcher, a neurotic egoist obsessed with the lurking feeling that something remarkable is to happen to him. This impending fate has a predatory quality, like "a crouching beast in the jungle." Consumed with anticipation and dread, he is unable to reciprocate the love of his long-suffering companion, May Bartram. She comes to comprehend his fate but is unable to make him understand it before she dies. While visiting her grave one year later, Marcher suddenly realizes that his fate was precisely his inability to comprehend her love for him. Despite its sluggish pace, implausible dialogue, and ornate style, James's novella is a suspenseful story of despair.

Beautiful and Damned, The Novel by F. Scott FITZGERALD, published in 1922. Anthony Patch pursues and wins the beautiful and sought-after Gloria Gilbert. He decides that they can survive on his limited income until he comes into the large fortune he stands to inherit from his grandfather. Through the ensuing years, their lives deteriorate into mindless alcoholic ennui. Anthony's grandfather makes a surprise appearance at one of their wild parties and, in disgust, disinherits him. After his grandfather's death, Anthony institutes a lawsuit that takes years to settle. Though the Patches eventually win, Anthony's spirit is broken, he and Gloria have grown apart, and they care about nothing.

Bell for Adano, A Novel by John HERSEY, published in 1944. It takes place during World War II after the occupation of Sicily by Allied forces. Major Victor Joppolo, an American army officer of Italian descent, is part of the Allied military government ruling the town of Adano. In his attempts to reform the town and bring democracy to its people by treating them with respect and decency—his concern being epitomized by his efforts to replace a bell that the fascists had melted down for ammunition—Joppolo comes into conflict with his hard-nosed commanding officer, who eventually has him transferred for refusal to follow orders.

Bell Jar, The Novel by Sylvia PLATH, published in 1963 under the pseudonym Victoria Lucas. A thinly veiled and painfully introspective autobiography, it details the life of Esther Greenwood, a college woman who, coming of age in a hypocritical world, struggles through a mental breakdown in the 1950s. The novel is noted for its symbolic use of bottles and jars, the colors black and white, and symbols of imprisonment and death. Plath's only novel, it was published a month before she committed suicide.

Bells, The Poem by Edgar Allan POE, published posthumously in the magazine *Sartain's Union* (November 1849). This incantatory poem, a showcase of onomatopoeia, alliteration, repetition, and assonance, uses bell sounds as symbols of childhood, youth, maturity, and death. The first stanza rings with merry sleigh bells, the second resounds with joyous wedding bells, the third is a cacophony of roaring alarm bells, and the last echoes with the sullen, rhythmic tolling of funeral bells.

Beloved Novel by Toni MORRISON, published in 1987. *Beloved* chronicles the life of a black woman named Sethe, following her from her pre–Civil War life as a slave in Kentucky to her life in Cincinnati in 1873. Though she is a free woman, she is held prisoner by memories of the trauma of her life as a slave. During her escape Sethe had given birth to her fourth child. Rather than see her children re-enslaved, she attempts to kill them. Only her infant daughter dies; it is the spirit of this child, called Beloved, who returns to Sethe in her new life.

Ben-Hur(: A Tale of the Christ) Historical novel by Lew WALLACE, published in 1880 and widely translated. The setting is ancient Palestine under the oppressive Roman occupation at the time of the birth of Christ. The Jew Judah Ben-Hur is wrongly accused by his former friend, the Roman Messala, of attempting to kill a Roman official. He is sent to be a slave, and his mother and sister are imprisoned. Years later he returns, wins a chariot race against Messala, and is reunited with his now leprous mother and sister. Both are cured on the day of the Crucifixion, and the family is converted to Christianity.

Benito Cereno Novella by Herman MELVILLE, published in *Putnam's Monthly Magazine* in 1855 and later included in *The Piazza Tales* (1856). Amasa Delano, captain of a seal-hunting ship, encounters off the coast of Chile a slave ship whose human cargo has revolted. Though it takes him some time to unravel the situation, he eventually saves the title character, captain of the slaver, along with his remaining crew, and the leaders of the insurrection are slaughtered.

Berlin Stories, The Collection of two previously published novels by Christopher ISHERWOOD, published in 1946. Set in pre–World War II Germany, the semiautobiographical work consists of *Mr. Norris Changes Trains* (1935; U.S. title, *The Last of Mr. Norris*) and *Goodbye to Berlin* (1939). Merging fact and fiction, it contains ostensibly objective, frequently comic tales of marginal characters who live shabby and tenuous existences as expatriates in Berlin; the threat of political horrors to come serves as subtext. In *Goodbye to Berlin* the character Isherwood uses the phrase "I am a camera with its shutter open" to claim that he is simply a passive recorder of events. The two novels made Isherwood's reputation; they were the basis for the play *I Am a Camera* (1951; film, 1955) and the musical *Cabaret* (1966; film, 1972).

Biglow Papers, The Satirical poetry in Yankee dialect by James Russell LOWELL. The first series of papers was published in the *Boston Courier* in 1846–48 and collected in book form in 1848; the second was published in the *Atlantic Monthly* during the Civil War and collected in 1867. An opponent of the Mexican War, which he regarded as an attempt to extend slavery, Lowell used the first series of poems to express his opposition, using the voice of the rustic poet Hosea Biglow. The Massachusetts wastrel Birdofredum Sawin, one of Lowell's most inspired inventions, reports on the war in several letters; he loses an arm, a leg, and an eye in the fighting. Lowell's radical fires had cooled somewhat by the time he issued the second series, which contains less-effective satire of the wartime South.

Billy Budd, Foretopman Novel by Herman MELVILLE, written in 1891 and left unfinished at his death. Provoked by a false charge, the angelically innocent sailor Billy Budd accidentally kills John Claggert, the satanic master-at-arms. In a time of threatened mutiny, he is sentenced to be hanged, and goes willingly to his fate. *Billy Budd* is particularly noted for its powerful symbolic characterizations and for its sympathetic treatment of the ambivalence of Captain Vere toward Billy's death. First published in 1924, it appeared in its definitive edition only in 1962.

Black Boy Autobiography by Richard WRIGHT, published in 1945. The book vividly describes Wright's often harsh, hardscrabble boyhood and youth in rural Mississippi and in Memphis, Tenn. Because of its use of novelistic techniques, it is sometimes called a fictionalized autobiography or an autobiographical novel. When it was first published, many white critics viewed it primarily as an attack on racist Southern society, but from the 1960s it came to be understood as principally the story of Wright's coming-of-age and of his development as a writer.

Black Cat, The Short story by Edgar Allan POE, first published in the *Saturday Evening Post* in August 1843 and included in *Tales* (1845). Its narrator is an animal lover who descends into alcoholism and begins mistreating his wife and his black cat, Pluto. When Pluto attacks him in self-defense one night, he seizes the cat in a fury, cuts out its eye, and hangs it. That night a fire destroys his house, leaving him in dire poverty. He later adopts a one-eyed black cat that he finds at a lowlife tavern, but after nearly tripping on the cat he attempts to kill it too. When his wife intervenes, he kills her instead and calmly conceals her in a wall. In the end the cat reveals his crime to the police.

Black Elk Speaks (: Being the Life Story of a Holy Man of the Oglala Sioux as Told to John G. Neihardt (Flaming Rainbow)) Autobiography of BLACK ELK. He tells of his boyhood participation in battles with the U.S. Army, of becoming a medicine man, and of joining Buffalo Bill's Wild West Show in 1886. On his return from a European tour, he found his tribe living on the bleak Pine Ridge reservation in South Dakota, starving, diseased, and hopeless, and joined the Ghost Dance movement; the book concludes with a description of the infamous Wounded Knee massacre. His son Ben Black Elk interpreted his words for Neihardt, who published the autobiography in 1932. It became a major source of information about 19th-century Plains Indian culture.

Blithedale Romance, The Minor novel by Nathaniel HAWTHORNE, published in 1852. The novel, about a group of people living in an experimental community, was based largely on Hawthorne's disillusionment with the Brook Farm utopian community near Boston in the 1840s and is often read for insight into the relationships between Emerson, Hawthorne, and Margaret Fuller. It was Hawthorne's only novel to be narrated in the first person. The character of Zenobia, apparently based on Fuller, is considered by some to be his most completely realized female character.

Blue Hotel, The Short story by Stephen CRANE, published serially in *Collier's Weekly* (1898) and later in *The Monster* (1899). Three men—a nervous New Yorker known as the Swede, a rambunctious Westerner named Bill, and the reserved Easterner Mr. Blanc—find shelter from a blizzard at Pat Scully's hotel in Fort Romper, Neb. The Swede becomes increasingly drunk, defensive, and reckless. He beats Scully's son, Johnnie, in a fight after accusing him of cheating at cards, but is himself stabbed and killed after accosting a patron at a bar. The story ends ambiguously months later, when timid Mr. Blanc confesses to Bill that he feels responsible for the Swede's death because he failed to act when he saw that Johnnie was indeed cheating. The story combines symbolic imagery with naturalistic detail in an existential tale of vanities and delusions.

Blues for Mister Charlie Tragedy in three acts by James BALDWIN, produced and published in 1964. A denunciation of racial bigotry and hatred, it was based on a 1955 murder trial in Mississippi. Richard Henry, a black man who returns to the Southern town of his birth to begin a new life, is killed by Lyle Britten, a white bigot, for "not knowing his place." At his trial Britten is acquitted by an all-white jury. Racism scars both black and white members of the community who attempt to intervene. "Mister Charlie" is a slang term for a white man.

Bluest Eye, The First novel by Toni MORRISON, published in 1970. Pecola Breedlove, an adolescent black girl, longs to have "the bluest eye" and thus to be acceptable to her family, schoolmates, and neighbors, all of whom have convinced her that she is ugly. This tragic study of her struggle to achieve white ideals of beauty and her consequent descent into madness was acclaimed as an eloquent indictment of some of the more subtle forms of racism in American society.

Bostonians, The Satirical novel by Henry JAMES, published serially in *Century Illustrated Magazine* in 1885–86 and in book form in 1886. Olive Chancellor, a Boston feminist in the 1870s, thinks she has found a kindred spirit in Verena Tarrant, a beautiful young woman who, though passive and indecisive, is a spellbinding orator for women's rights. Olive vies for Verena's attention and affections with Basil Ransom, a gracious but reactionary Confederate army veteran. At the end Verena marries Basil and departs for the South, leaving Olive grief-stricken. *The Bostonians* was one of the earliest American novels to deal even obliquely with lesbianism. It was based on Alphonse Daudet's novel *Lévangéliste* (1883).

Bride Comes to Yellow Sky, The Short story by Stephen CRANE, published in *The Open Boat* in 1898. Jack Potter, the marshal of Yellow Sky, having returned with his bride, is challenged by drunken, belligerent Scratchy Wilson, a cowboy who represents the Old West. When Jack refuses to fight, responding to the cowpoke's taunts with "I'm married," Scratchy leaves without fighting, bewildered that the old rules have changed.

Bride of the Innisfallen, The Collection of short stories by Eudora WELTY, published in 1955. The seven stories, focused largely on female characters, elaborate on tenuous relationships of the heart in a difficult world and on the importance of place. They are written in a more experimental, allusive style than the rest of Welty's work.

Bridge, The Poem by Hart CRANE, published in 1930. The Brooklyn Bridge was one of the creative feats of humanity that inspired Crane to attempt an epic exploration of the entire American experience from Columbus on. The poem consists of 15 parts, each devoted to a different historical epoch and focus; they are unified by a symphonylike structure influenced by the poetry of T. S. Eliot, though the work ultimately opposes the negativity of Eliot's *Waste Land*. Though the poem has been deemed a failure as a coherent whole, some of the individual lyrics are among the best in American 20th-century poetry.

Bridge of San Luis Rey, The Novella by Thornton WILDER, published in 1927. The plot centers on five travelers in 18th-century Peru who are killed when a bridge across a canyon collapses. A priest interprets the story of each victim in an attempt to explain the workings of divine providence. This was the first novel in which Wilder used historical subject matter as a background for themes of the search for justice, the possibility of altruism, and the role of Christianity in human relationships. For decades the book was widely taught in American high schools.

Bronx Primitive: Portraits in a Childhood   Memoir by Kate SIMON, published in 1982. Simon vividly evokes working-class Jewish immigrant life in the Bronx in the 1920s and her frequently unhappy childhood, during which she was the victim of sexual abuse. *A Wider World* (1986) and *Etchings in an Hourglass* (1990) are later installments in Simon's autobiography.

Brown Girl, Brownstones   First novel by Paule MARSHALL, originally published in 1959. Somewhat autobiographical, this groundbreaking work describes the coming-of-age of Selina Boyce, a Caribbean-American girl in New York City. Though initially admired for its expressive dialogue, the book did not gain widespread recognition until it was reprinted in 1981.

Buried Child   Three-act tragedy by Sam SHEPARD, performed in 1978 and published in 1979. Shepard had his first critical and commercial success with this corrosive study of American family life. Set on an Illinois farm, it centers on the homecoming of Vince and his girlfriend, Shelly. Vince cherishes a romantic, bucolic vision of the home he left six years earlier, but the actual family turns out to be a collection of twisted grotesques. Shepard considered the work part of a family trilogy with *Curse of the Starving Class* (1976) and TRUE WEST (1981), which likewise portray destructive familial relationships.

Bus Stop   Romantic comedy in three acts by William INGE, performed and published in 1955. An expansion of the one-act play *People in the Wind*, *Bus Stop* is set in a small town in Kansas. Passengers on a cross-country bus, stranded overnight by a blizzard, congregate in Grace's restaurant. They include Cherie, a flighty blonde bar singer, the cowboys Bo and Virgil, and a drunken doctor; they are joined by the sheriff, the bus driver, and a waitress. The passengers devise entertainments for themselves, and the men vie for Cherie's attention. When Bo eventually confesses his love to Cherie and tells her she is his first girl, she agrees to go to Montana with him.

Caine Mutiny, The   Novel by Herman WOUK, published in 1951. It grew out of Wouk's experiences aboard a destroyer-minesweeper in the Pacific in World War II. The protagonist is Willie Keith, a rich New Yorker assigned to the USS *Caine*, who gradually matures during the course of the book, but the work is best known for its portrayal of the neurotic Captain Queeg, who becomes obsessed with petty infractions at the expense of the safety of ship and crew. The cynical, intellectual Lieut. Tom Keefer persuades the loyal Lieut. Steve Maryk that Queeg's bizarre behavior is endangering the ship, and Maryk reluctantly relieves Queeg of command. Much of the book describes Maryk's court-martial and its aftermath, when the unstable Queeg eventually breaks down completely.

Call It Sleep   Novel by Henry ROTH, published in 1934. Roth uses stream-of-consciousness techniques to trace the psychological development of a young boy, the son of Yiddish-speaking Jewish immigrants in a New York ghetto, and to explore the boy's perceptions of his family and of the larger world around him. He powerfully evokes the terrors and anxieties the child experiences in his anguished relations with his father and realistically describes the family's squalid urban environment. Rediscovered in the late 1950s, the novel was belatedly recognized as an important proletarian work of the 1930s and a classic of Jewish-American literature.

Call of the Wild, The   Novel by Jack LONDON, published in 1903. London's version of the classic quest story uses a dog as the protagonist. Buck, shipped to the Klondike to be trained as a sled dog, eventually reverts to his wolf origins. He then undertakes a journey of almost mythical dimensions, abandoning the safety of his familiar world to encounter danger, adventure, and fantasy. Transformed into the legendary "Ghost Dog" of the Klondike, he becomes a true hero.

Cane   Experimental novel by Jean TOOMER, published in 1923. This symbolic, poetic work comprises a variety of literary forms, including poems and short stories, and incorporates elements from both Southern black folk culture and the contemporary white avant-garde. Some have associated the title with the Old Testament figure of the exiled Cain. The first of the novel's three sections focuses on the rural Southern past and sexuality; its characters, unable to find success, are constantly frustrated by what life offers them. The second section deals with blacks moving from the agrarian South to the urban North and the spiritual quest of those who abandon their rural roots in search of a new life. In the final section, which synthesizes the earlier ones, Kabnis is a black teacher and writer who struggles with the dilemma of race, his ambivalent feelings about his African heritage and Southern enslavement, and his difficulties in being a creative artist.

Cannery Row Novel by John STEINBECK, published in 1945. Peopled with good-natured bums and warm-hearted prostitutes living on the fringes of Monterey, Calif., the novel celebrates lowlifes who are poor but happy. Like most of Steinbeck's postwar work, *Cannery Row* is sentimental in tone while retaining elements of social criticism.

Cantos, The Major collection of poems by Ezra POUND. Pound wrote the first of his cantos in 1915, and through the decades they gradually became his major poetic occupation. The complete edition (1970) consists of 117 sections, the latest of which are fragmentary. In the early cantos Pound offered personal, lyrical reactions to such writers as Homer, Ovid, Dante, and Rémy de Gourmont, as well as to sundry political figures. In the course of the work he devotes notable attention to economics, American history, Chinese literature and Confucianism, and the poetry of medieval Provence. Bewildering in the variety of their subject matter, they range almost as widely in tone, from pedantry to intense lyricism. The highly idiosyncratic mixture often makes apprehension very difficult. Several of the earliest cantos have been highly praised, and the *Pisan Cantos* (1948), written during Pound's postwar incarceration—first in a prison camp in Pisa for war criminals and later in a hospital for the criminally insane—are among the most admired portions of the complete work.

Cask of Amontillado, The Short story by Edgar Allan POE, first published in *Godey's Lady's Book* in 1846. The narrator is the aristocrat Montresor, who claims to have endured a thousand injuries at the hand of the connoisseur Fortunato. Finally driven by yet another insult to seek revenge, he finds the drunken Fortunato during carnival celebrations and, on the pretext of seeking his judgment of a new cask of amontillado sherry, takes him to his palazzo. While keeping up a conversation heavy with irony, he leads Fortunato into the deepest crypt in the cellar, where he chains him in a small chamber and, brick by brick, walls him in.

Catcher in the Rye Novel by J. D. SALINGER, published in 1951. It details two days in the life of 16-year-old Holden Caulfield after he has been expelled from prep school. Confused and disillusioned, he wanders New York City searching for truth and railing against the "phoniness" of the adult world. He finds an old girlfriend, Sally, but discovers the psychological gulf that has opened between them. Though anxious to avoid his parents, he manages to meet his beloved sister, Phoebe, who tries unsuccessfully to allay his black view of the world. He contacts a former English teacher, but flees after the teacher makes homosexual advances to him. He ends up in a psychiatrist's office, exhausted and emotionally ill. Influential and widely acclaimed, the novel (whose title reflects Holden's misreading of a Robert Burns poem) has struck a powerful chord with generations of young readers.

Catch-22 Satirical novel by Joseph HELLER, published in 1961. The plot centers on Capt. John Yossarian, stationed at an airstrip on a Mediterranean island near the end of World War II, and his desperate attempts to stay alive. He hopes that, by pleading insanity, he will be relieved of his duty flying the dangerous bombing missions ordered by Capt. Cathcart and his superior, Gen. Peckham, but a doctor quotes him the famous catch-22: Though a person would have to be insane to fly such missions, seeking to avoid them proves his sanity and makes him ineligible for discharge on grounds of insanity. (The term has since become a generic term for examples of such paradoxical bureaucratic logic.) Yossarian eventually deserts for Sweden. The novel's memorable characters include Lieut. Milo Minderbender, who devotes himself singlemindedly to the pursuit of profits in the black market. A sequel, *Closing Time* (1994), details the current lives of *Catch-22*'s characters.

Cat on a Hot Tin Roof Play by Tennessee WILLIAMS, published and produced in 1955. Big Daddy, a wealthy Southern planter of humble origins, is about to celebrate his 65th birthday. His two married sons, the brutish Gooper (Brother Man) and the alcoholic Brick, have returned for the occasion, the former with his pregnant wife and five children, the latter with his restless wife Margaret (Maggie, the "cat"). Maggie's affair with Brick's recently deceased best friend, Skipper, and Brick's own homosexual relationship with Skipper are revealed. The greedy Gooper seeks by virtue of his progeny to inherit the plantation; Maggie determines to produce an heir to thwart him.

Cat's Cradle Science-fiction novel by Kurt VONNEGUT, Jr., published in 1963. It features two notable inventions: Bokononism, a religion of lies "that make you brave and kind and healthy and happy," and ice-nine, a type of ice that forms at any temperature up to 114.4 degrees and continues freezing any liquid it contacts in a kind of chain reaction. The story's two principal figures are Bokonon, the religion's founder, and Dr. Felix Hoenikker, inventor of ice-nine. The novel concludes with the inevitable end of the world caused by the release of ice-nine (as transmitted by a frozen body to the ocean).

Celebrated Jumping Frog of Calaveras County, The Short story by Mark TWAIN, first published in the *Saturday Press* in 1865. The narrator visits the long-winded miner Simon Wheeler, hoping to learn the whereabouts of the Rev. Leonidas Smiley. Wheeler instead relates an elaborate tall tale of a different man named Jim Smiley, a compulsive and imaginative gambler who once spent three months training a frog to jump and then won money by betting on it, and who was eventually duped by a quick-thinking stranger who poured lead shot down the frog's throat.

Celestial Railroad, The Allegorical short story by Nathaniel HAWTHORNE, published in 1843 and included in MOSSES FROM AN OLD MANSE. Following the path of Christian in John Bunyan's *Pilgrim's Progress*, the narrator travels from the City of Destruction to the Celestial City—not on foot like the original pilgrim but as a passenger on the Celestial Railroad. Mr. Smooth-it-away, a friendly fellow traveler, comments contemptuously about the arduous trip the old-fashioned pilgrims had to undergo. At journey's end he leaves the other passengers and divulges his true identity by breathing fire and brimstone. The narrator awakens and realizes that it has all been a dream.

Chambered Nautilus, The Poem by Oliver Wendell HOLMES, first published in his "Breakfast-Table" column in the *Atlantic Monthly* in February 1858. The nautilus, a sea creature that constructs its shell in an ever-widening coil of chambers, is presented as a metaphor for the striving individual who builds diligently on his experience to achieve ever greater things.

Charlotte's Web Children's novel by E. B. WHITE, published in 1952, with illustrations by Garth Williams. The story takes place on a farm in Maine (resembling White's own farm), where the pig Wilbur is saved from slaughter by his devoted friend Charlotte, a spider, who advertises Wilbur's finer qualities by writing adjectives in her web. It became one of the most universally loved classics of children's literature.

Chicago Poem by Carl SANDBURG, first published in *Poetry* magazine in 1914 and later in *Chicago Poems* (1916). An ode to the city where he lived, "Chicago" is perhaps his best-known poem. Sandburg addresses the city directly, notably in the terse epithets of the opening and closing lines, where it is personified with the qualities of its leading industries. Reminiscent of the poetry of Whitman, it affirms and celebrates ordinary life.

Children's Hour, The Drama in three acts by Lillian HELLMAN, performed and published in 1934. Mary Tilford, a student at a New England boarding school, tells her rich, indulgent grandmother that she has run away from school because she head the headmistresses, Karen Wright and Martha Dobie, to be lesbians, a lie she makes up after a mild altercation with the women. Though Karen's fiancé, Dr. Joe Cardin, exposes Mary as a liar, the school is forced to close. After losing a libel suit, Karen realizes that Joe's trust in her is altered and ends their relationship. Martha confesses her self-doubt about her sexuality to Karen and commits suicide. The story was based on an actual case in 19th-century Edinburgh, detailed in William Roug's *Bad Companions* (1931).

Civil Disobedience Essay by Henry David THOREAU, originally delivered at the Concord Lyceum in 1848, then published in the only issue of *Aesthetic Papers* in 1849. A defense of the private, individual conscience against the expedient majority, it articulates Thoreau's defiantly anarchistic views on government. To Thoreau, moral law is superior to civil law, even if a penalty ensues; "under a government which imprisons any unjustly, the true place for a just man is also a prison." The essay, which greatly influenced Mohandas Gandhi and Martin Luther King, remains an important treatise on American individualism.

Clean, Well-Lighted Place, A Short story by Ernest HEMINGWAY, first published in *Scribner's Magazine* in 1933 and later that year in *Winner Take Nothing*. Late one night two waiters in a café wait for their last customer, an old man who has recently attempted suicide, to leave. The younger waiter, eager to get home to his wife, turns the old man out, but the older one is sympathetic to the human need for a clean, well-lighted place, an outpost in the darkness. A powerful existential statement about the insufficiency of religion as a source of comfort, the story contains an often-cited version of the Lord's Prayer in which the Spanish word *nada* ("nothing") is substituted for most of the prayer's nouns.

Clotel(; or, The President's Daughter: A Narrative of Slave Life in the United States) Novel by William Wells BROWN, published in England in 1853 and in the United States (as *Clotelle: A Tale of Southern*

States) in 1864. It is a melodramatic tale of three generations of black women who struggle with the constrictions of slavery, miscegenation, and concubinage (Thomas Jefferson is the owner and father of its main characters). Though criticized for its cluttered narrative and stiff characters, it provides insight into the antebellum slave culture. Brown revised it three times for its American publication—serially and in book form—each time changing the plot, the title, and the characters' names. Though it was apparently the first novel written by a black American, its U.S. publication followed Harriet Wilson's *Our Nig*.

Cocktail Party, The   Verse drama in three acts by T. S. ELIOT, produced in 1949 and published in 1950. The marital problems of Edward and Lavinia Chamberlayne are of special interest to an unidentified guest at their dismal cocktail party. The guest is later identified as Sir Henry Harcourt-Reilly, a prescient psychiatrist who helps heal the marriage. Harcourt-Reilly also counsels Celia Coplestone, Edward's mistress and the main moral figure of the piece, to work out her salvation. Based on Euripides' *Alcestis*, the drama is a morality play presented as a comedy of manners. Eliot's most commercially successful play, it was more conventional and less poetic than his earlier dramas.

Color Purple, The   Epistolary novel by Alice WALKER, published in 1982. Celie, an uneducated black woman, is repeatedly raped by her stepfather as a teenager; her mother gives away the two children she bears, and Celie marries a brutal man with children of his own. Celie's sister, Nettie, moves into the house but, spurning the advances of Celie's husband, is thrown out. Through Celie she becomes attached to a missionary couple—by coincidence the same people who have adopted Celie's children—and they move to Africa, where Nettie will remain for 30 years. The voluminous correspondence Nettie sends to Celie is hidden from Celie by her husband and only found by her years later. When Shug Avery, a female blues singer, moves into Celie's house, Celie and Shug fall in love, and the two leave together for Memphis. Shug eventually leaves her for a young man. In time Celie inherits her father's property, Nettie returns from Africa with Celie's children, and Shug returns as well. The book was praised for the depth of its female characters and its eloquent use of black vernacular.

Come Back, Little Sheba   Drama in two acts by William INGE, published in 1949 and performed in 1950. It centers on the frustrated lives of Doc and Lola. Trapped in a barren marriage for 20 years, Doc drowns his disappointment in alcohol and fantasizes about Marie, their young boarder. Lola sublimates her pain over her empty life by pining for Sheba, her lost dog. When in a drunken outburst Doc wrecks their home and nearly kills Lola, the couple are forced to realize their mutual dependence.

Company She Keeps, The   First novel by Mary MCCARTHY, published in 1942; its chapters originally appeared earlier as six separate short stories. The story of Margaret Sargent, "a princess among the trolls" at a women's college, it describes the failure of a marriage, random love affairs, and a passing flirtation with Trotskyism. Margaret's search for personal identity, her need for honesty, and the necessity of distinguishing appearance from reality are the real themes of the stories, thinly disguised accounts of the author's own years as a young New Yorker.

Confessions of Nat Turner, The   Novel by William STYRON, published in 1967. A fictional account of the Virginia slave revolt of 1831, it is narrated by the rebellion's leader. Styron based his novel on a pamphlet of the same title published in Virginia shortly after the revolt, but took many liberties in developing Turner's character. His Turner is a man of moral depth and farseeing vision whose quest for physical and spiritual freedom is hindered by his bitterness, self-denial, and sexual repression. The book generated great controversy, primarily among black critics who objected (notably in the 1968 book *William Styron's Nat Turner: Ten Black Writers Respond*) to the white author's attempt to speak in a slave's voice, accusing Styron of falsifying historical truth and misrepresenting Turner. Styron's defense was supported by several eminent historians.

Confidence-Man(: His Masquerade), The   Satirical allegory by Herman MELVILLE, published in 1857. Set on a Mississippi steamboat, it is a series of vignettes on various passengers—some dupes, some tricksters—who represent a gullible American public that can be deceived by charlatans and the lure of easy money. The last of Melville's novels published during his lifetime, it reveals his pessimistic view of American greed, self-delusion, and lack of charity.

Conjure Woman, The   First of Charles W. CHESNUTT's short-story collections; the seven stories began appearing in magazines in 1887 and were first collected in

1899. The narrator is a white Northerner living in the South who passes along the stories told him by the ex-slave Julius McAdoo. Unusual for dialect tales of the period, they provide a realistic picture of the pre–Civil War South, including descriptions of penurious, brutish masters. Conjuration—magic effected by hoo-doo practitioners—helps slaves overcome their difficulties. The relationships between the patronizing narrator, his wife (who sometimes glimpses the stories' deeper meanings), and the crafty and manipulative Uncle Julius develop over the course of the book.

Connecticut Yankee in King Arthur's Court, A Satirical novel by Mark TWAIN, published in 1889. Hank Morgan, a gun-factory mechanic, is knocked unconscious and awakens in England in 528. Captured and taken to Camelot, he is put on exhibit before King Arthur's knights. Condemned to death, he remembers having read of an eclipse on the day of his execution and amazes the court by predicting it. Accepted as a sorcerer like Merlin, he is made minister to the ineffectual king. Seeking to impart democratic principles and mechanical knowledge, he strings telephone wire, starts schools, trains mechanics, and teaches journalism, but when he tries to better the peasants' lot he meets broad opposition. Traveling with Arthur in disguise among the miserable common folk, he is captured and sold as a slave, and only rescued at the last second by 500 knights on bicycles. After a brief absence, he returns to find the kingdom engulfed in civil war, Arthur killed, and his innovations abandoned. When he is wounded, Merlin, pretending to nurse him, puts him to sleep until the 19th century. The story celebrates homespun ingenuity and democratic values as against the superstitious ineptitude of a feudal monarchy.

Contending Forces(: A Romance Illustrative of Negro Life North and South) Novel by Pauline HOPKINS, published in 1900. The complicated plot follows a mixed-race family from early-19th-century slavery in the West Indies and the South to early-20th-century Massachusetts. It centers on Will and his sister Dora; their marriages to ideological opposites suggest Hopkins's hopes for reconciling the contrary philosophies of Booker T. Washington and W. E. B. Du Bois. *Contending Forces* is notable as one of the earliest novels by a black woman.

Country of the Pointed Firs, The Collection of sketches by Sarah Orne JEWETT, published in 1896. Highly regarded for their sympathetic yet unsentimental portrayal of life in the fictional Maine coastal village of Dunnet Landing, the sketches are narrated by a nameless summer visitor who relates the life stories of various inhabitants, capturing the language, customs, mannerisms, and humor peculiar to Down-Easters. The villagers include the narrator's landlady, Mrs. Almira Todd; a former seaman, Capt. Littlepage, who scorns modern ways; Mrs. Todd's gracious mother, Mrs. Blackett; Mrs. Todd's brother, William; and an old widower and former fisherman, Elijah Tilley. The book evokes both the isolation and the sense of community of this small, dying town, whose inhabitants live chiefly to preserve memory and affirm and maintain the values of the past.

Crack-Up, The Essay by F. Scott FITZGERALD, published serially in *Esquire* magazine in 1936. A confessional piece, it documents Fitzgerald's spiritual and physical deterioration in the mid-1930s. After Fitzgerald's death Edmund Wilson published the compilation *The Crack-Up* (1945), which includes selected correspondence, poems, and critical appreciations of Fitzgerald by a number of literary luminaries.

Crimes of the Heart Drama in three acts by Beth HENLEY, produced in 1979 and published in 1982. Set in a small Mississippi town, it examines the lives of three quirky sisters who have gathered at the home of the youngest. During the course of the play the sisters unearth grudges, criticize each other, reminisce about their family life, and attempt to understand their mother's suicide years earlier.

Crossing Brooklyn Ferry Poem by Walt WHITMAN, originally published as "Sun-Down Poem" in the second edition of *Leaves of Grass* in 1856. It is a sensitive, detailed record of the poet's thoughts and observations about the continuity of nature and of brotherhood while aboard the Brooklyn–Manhattan ferry. His panoramic description of the harbor includes rich images of sunlight on the water, the flight of seagulls, and the commerce of ships. Through repetition, exclamation, and apostrophe, he conveys his joyful belief in world solidarity.

Crucible, The Four-act play by Arthur MILLER, performed and published in 1953. Set in 1692 during the Salem, Mass., it opens with Rev. Parris ministering to his daughter Betty, who has been mysteriously stricken dumb. Parris has seen his daughter, his niece Abigail Williams, and other girls dancing in the woods with

Tituba, his West Indian housemaid. Abigail has recently been dismissed from her job at John and Elizabeth Proctor's because Elizabeth had discovered her adulterous relationship with John. Betty, having regained her voice, begins to hysterically name the names of other local "witches." The Proctors soon begin to be implicated as well. To prevent further damage, John is forced to admit his adultery. Eventually he signs a confession of witchcraft, but snatches it back, unwilling to let it be announced in public, and is taken to be hanged with others of the witches. The play comments by analogy on the anticommunist "witch hunt" of Sen. Joseph McCarthy and others, under way when the play was written.

Custom of the Country, The   Novel of manners by Edith WHARTON, published in 1913. It tells the story of Undine Spragg, a young Midwestern woman with social aspirations who convinces her nouveau-riche parents to resettle in New York. There she captures and marries a young man from the city's high society. Chiefly because of her greed and great ambition, this and each subsequent relationship she engineers prove unsatisfactory.

Daddy   Poem by Sylvia PLATH, published posthumously in 1965 in the collection ARIEL. One of Plath's most famous poems, it was completed during a brief prolific period of writing before her suicide in February 1963. In images that progress from domestic to demonic, it confronts a woman's conflicting feelings about her father's death when she was a child (and perhaps also the recent departure of Plath's husband), bizarrely imagining him as a Nazi (on the basis of his German birth).

Daisy Miller   Novel by Henry JAMES, published in *Cornhill Magazine* in 1878 and in book form in 1879. Its title character is an American girl traveling in Europe with her mother. There she is courted by Frederick Forsyth Winterbourne, an American living abroad. In her innocence, Daisy is compromised by her friendship with an Italian man. Her behavior shocks Winterbourne and the other Americans living in Italy, and they shun her. Only after she dies does Winterbourne recognize that her actions reflected her spontaneous, genuine, and unaffected nature and that his suspicions were unwarranted. As in other works by James, the contrast between American innocence and European sophistication are used to examine social conventions.

Day of the Locust, The   Novel by Nathanael WEST, published in 1939. Tod Hackett, a set designer, becomes involved in the lives of several people who have been warped by their proximity to the artificial world of Hollywood. His completion of the painting "The Burning of Los Angeles" coincides with the explosion of the other characters' unfulfilled dreams in a conflagration of riot and murder. A story of the savagery lurking beneath the Hollywood dream, it is one of the most striking examples of the "Hollywood novel."

Dead Lecturer, The   Collection of verse by Amiri BARAKA, published in 1964 under the name LeRoi Jones. Notable for its strong imagery and lyrical treatment of violence, it marked a break from the style and literary philosophy of the Beats, with whom Baraka had been associated. In "Rhythm & Blues" he uses the structures of jazz and blues to forge a new, distinctly black voice. Poems such as "Black Dada Nihilismus" and "An Agony. As Now." reveal his anger and despair at being trapped in a white, middle-class society.

Deal in Wheat, A   Short story by Frank NORRIS, first published serially in 1902 and reprinted in *A Deal in Wheat and Other Stories of the New and Old West* (1903). Employing the techniques of naturalism, the five-part story examines the business of wheat speculation at the Chicago Board of Trade. Its first episode features Sam Lewiston, who loses his Kansas farm as a result of low wheat prices. The middle three episodes detail the economic warfare of two wealthy speculators, Mr. Hornung of the bull market and Mr. Truslow of the bear market. In the last episode, Lewiston is denied free bread in Chicago because of high wheat prices.

Death Comes for the Archbishop   Novel by Willa CATHER, published in 1927. Based on the lives of Bishop Jean-Baptiste L'Amy and his vicar, Father Joseph Machebeut, the novel is considered emblematic of the author's moral and spiritual concerns. It traces the friendship and adventures of Bishop Jean Latour and Father Joseph Vaillant as they organize the new Catholic diocese of New Mexico. Latour is patrician, intellectual, and introverted; Vaillant, practical, outgoing, and sanguine. Friends since their childhood in France, the clerics triumph over corrupt Spanish priests, natural adversity, and the indifference of the Hopi and Navajo to establish their church and build a cathedral in the wilderness. The greatly admired novel explores Latour's inner conflicts and his relationship with the land, which through the author's powerful description becomes an imposing, unyielding character in its own right.

Death in the Family, A Novel by James AGEE about a family's reactions to the accidental death of the father. Published in 1957 shortly after Agee's own death, the novel was praised as one of the best examples of American autobiographical fiction. Jay Follet is killed in an automobile accident. His wife, brother, and little son Rufus narrate a story that explores conflicts both among members of the family and in society. The differences between black and white, rich and poor, country life and city life, and, ultimately, life and death are richly depicted. Agee used contrasting narratives as a structural device to link the past and present; italicized passages describing the family's life before the fatal accident, sometimes in lushly lyrical prose, are incorporated into the primary narrative of the crash and its immediate effects.

Death of a Salesman Play in "two acts and a requiem" by Arthur MILLER, written in 1948 and produced in 1949. After many years on the road as a traveling salesman, Willy Loman realizes he has been a failure as a father and husband. His sons, Happy and Biff, are not successful by Willy's standard or any other. His career fading, Willy escapes into reminiscences of an idealized past. In the climactic scene, Biff prepares to leave home, starts arguing with Willy, confesses that he has spent three months in jail, and mocks his father's lifelong salesman's belief in "a smile and a shoeshine." Willy, bitter and broken, commits suicide.

Death of the Hired Man, The Narrative poem by Robert FROST, published in *North of Boston* in 1914. Written in blank verse, it is a conversation between the farmer Warren and his wife Mary about their former farmhand Silas, an elderly man who has come "home" to their farm to die. Silas's plight is poignantly presented, and the characterizations of home as "where, when you have to go there, / They have to take you in" and "Something you somehow haven't to deserve" are well known.

Deerslayer(; or, The First War-Path), The The last of the five novels constituting THE LEATHERSTOCKING TALES, by James Fenimore COOPER, published in two volumes in 1841. Cooper here returns to Natty Bumppo's youth at Lake Oswego, N.Y. (called Glimmerglass), in the 1740s, at the time of the French and Indian War. Young Bumppo (known as "Deerslayer" among the Delaware Indians with whom he lives) and the giant Hurry Harry help the trapper Thomas Hutter resist an attack by the Iroquois, who are allied with the French. The Iroquois capture Hutter and Hurry Harry; Bumppo and the Mohican chief Chingachgook secure their release. In an attempt to rescue Chingachgook's bride, Bumppo himself is captured. Hutter is killed; his daughter, Judith, confesses her love to Bumppo and manages to delay his execution until Chingachgook arrives with a troop of British soldiers.

Delicate Balance, A Drama in three acts by Edward ALBEE, published and produced in 1966. Set in an upper-middle-class suburban living room, it tells the relatively simple story of a frightened couple who ask their friends for refuge, through which Albee examines illusion and loss in American families and reveals his concern with the hidden terrors of everyday life. Though the play was criticized for repeating the structure and thematic content of his *Who's Afraid of Virginia Woolf*, it stands as a dark comic portrait of modern angst.

Deliverance Novel by James DICKEY, published in 1970. Four men set out on a whitewater canoe voyage in the Georgia wilderness; an encounter with savage backwoodsmen results in a death, and the men must escape down the river, tracked by a killer bent on vengeance. Ed, the hero, survives and returns to his suburban home improved for having his mettle tested. The "maleness" of the novel, which embodies Dickey's enthusiasm for the outdoors and hunting, accounted for much of its huge popular success.

Delta Wedding Novel by Eudora WELTY, published in 1946. Welty's first full-length novel, it presents a comprehensive and insightful portrait of a Southern plantation family in 1923. Most of the Fairchilds have been sheltered from any contact with the world outside the Mississippi Delta. Though they quarrel among themselves, they also unite against any threats to the status of the family, honoring it as a sacred and unchanging entity. Only Ellen Fairchild, who has married into the clan, has a more worldly perspective; her clear-sightedness allows her to work toward family harmony without being defeated by the internal bickering.

Democratic Vistas Prose pamphlet by Walt WHITMAN, published in 1871. It comprises three essays that outline Whitman's ideas about the role of democracy in establishing a new cultural foundation for America. Writing after the Civil War, he suggested that Americans had lost some notion of heroism and honor, and particularly criticized society's materialism and preoccupation with business. The antidote he prescribed was a return to Jeffersonian-Jacksonian democracy and the cultivation of spiritual fellowship. Often criticized for its optimistic belief in progress and its naive dismissal of history as a factor in human development, it remains an important supplement to Whitman's poetry as well as an expression of his philosophy of government.

Désirée's Baby Short story by Kate CHOPIN, published in *A Night in Acadie* in 1897. The widely acclaimed story, set in antebellum New Orleans, deals with slavery, the Southern social system, Creole culture, and the ambiguity of racial identity. Désirée and her husband Armand are happily married until Désirée gives birth to a child who is obviously of mixed racial ancestry. Armand forces her and the child into exile and to a tragic end and becomes increasingly brutal toward his slaves. Only when it is too late does he discover that it is he rather than Désirée who is part black.

Desire Under the Elms Tragedy in three parts by Eugene O'NEILL, produced in 1924 and published in 1925. Ephraim Cabot abandons his farm and his three sons, who hate him. The youngest son, Eben, buys out his brothers, who head out for California. Ephraim soon returns with his young new wife, Abbie. Abbie becomes pregnant by Eben; she lets Ephraim believe the child is his, but later kills the infant when she sees it as an obstacle between herself and Eben. Eben, enraged, turns her over to the sheriff, but not before he realizes his love for her and confesses his complicity. One of O'Neill's most admired works, the play, with its Freudian treatment of sexual themes, evokes his own family conflicts. The last of O'Neill's naturalistic plays and the first in which he recreated the starkness of Greek tragedy, it draws from Euripides' *Hippolytus* and Racine's *Phèdre*, in both of which a father's new wife falls in love with her stepson. Though it is now considered a classic, its subject matter scandalized some early audiences, and the first Los Angeles cast was arrested for obscenity.

Devil and Daniel Webster, The Short story by Stephen Vincent BENÉT, published in 1937. Jabez Stone, a New Hampshire farmer, sells his soul to the Devil (Mr. Scratch) in return for a decade of material wealth. When the Devil comes to claim Stone's soul, Jabez calls on Daniel Webster to argue his case at midnight before a jury of historic American villains. The

Faust legend, gentle satire of New England eccentricities, patriotism, and faith in humanity's higher aspirations are all elements of this tall tale. Benét's prose style, colloquial yet flexible, was central to the story's success. It has been set to music by Douglas Moore (in 1939) and others.

Devil's Dictionary, The Satiric lexicon by Ambrose BIERCE, first compiled as *The Cynic's Word Book* in 1906 and reissued under his preferred title five years later. The barbed definitions that Bierce began publishing in the *Wasp*, the San Francisco weekly he edited (1881–86), brought this 19th-century stock form to a new level of artistry. Employing a terse, aphoristic style, he lampooned social, professional, and religious convention, as in his definitions for *bore* ("A person who talks when you wish him to listen"), *architect* ("One who drafts a plan of your house, and plans a draft of your money"), and *saint* ("A dead sinner revised and edited"), often supplying "authenticating" citations from spurious scholarly sources.

Dharma Bums, The Autobiographical novel by Jack KEROUAC, published in 1958. Its narrator, Raymond Smith, suffering spiritually amid the emptiness of middle-class American life, is based on Kerouac himself, and the poet-woodsman-Buddhist Japhy Ryder, whom Smith immediately recognizes as a spiritual model, is a thinly disguised portrait of Gary Snyder. Several other characters are also drawn from actual poets and writers. The novel describes the growth of the men's friendship and Smith's groping toward personal understanding.

Diamond as Big as the Ritz, The Allegorical short story by F. Scott FITZGERALD, published in 1922 in *Tales of the Jazz Age*. John Unger, a student at a Massachusetts prep school, befriends Percy Washington, a new classmate who boasts that his father is "the richest man in the world" and invites John to visit the family home in the Montana Rockies. The mansion is built upon a secret diamond mine that contains a single diamond one cubic mile in size. After government aircraft locate the diamond mine, military climbers begin to scale the mountain. Rather than allow his private domain to be invaded and appropriated, Percy's father blows up the diamond mountain, killing himself and his wife, the invaders, and Percy, as John and the Washington sisters watch helplessly.

Dodsworth Novel by Sinclair LEWIS, published in 1929. The protagonist, Sam Dodsworth, is an automobile manufacturer who sells his company and takes an extended European vacation with his wife, Fran. *Dodsworth* recounts their reactions to Europeans and European values, their various relationships with others, their estrangement, and their brief reconciliation.

Dream Songs, The Poetic masterwork of John BERRYMAN, published in 1969, a compilation of the earlier *77 Dream Songs* (1964) and *His Toy, His Dream, His Rest* (1968). The entire sequence of 385 verses, consisting of three six-line stanzas each, is the self-narrated, confessional story of the antihero Henry, Berryman's poetic persona.

Dr. Heidegger's Experiment Story by Nathaniel HAWTHORNE, published in *Twice-Told Tales* (1837). Elderly Dr. Heidegger and four contemporaries participate in his scientific experiment on aging. Dr. Heidegger applies water from the Fountain of Youth to a faded rose, which regains its freshness and beauty. After drinking the fabled water, each of the three male participants gradually revert to young manhood and woo the sole female subject, whose youthful beauty has been revived. When the vial of water is spilled accidentally, the rose and the experimenters age and wither. The experiment has taught Dr. Heidegger not to desire youth's transient headiness, but his four friends resolve to search for the Fountain of Youth.

Driving Miss Daisy One-act play by Alfred Uhry, produced and published in 1987. It is the story of a friendship that develops over 25 years, including the years of the civil-rights movement, between Daisy Werthan, an elderly Jewish widow living in Atlanta, and Hoke Coleburn, the black chauffeur her son hires for her. It was hailed for its quiet, unsentimental examination of its elderly characters and for its balanced depiction of gradually changing political sensibilities in the South.

Drum-Taps Collection of free-verse poems by Walt WHITMAN, published in May 1865. The mood of the poetry moves from excitement at the falling-in and arming of young soldiers at the beginning of the Civil War to disquietude at the troubled realization of its true significance. Disillusionment following the Battle of Bull Run is reflected in "Beat! Beat! Drums!" while deep empathy with the wounded informs "Vigil Strange I Kept on the Field One Night." *Sequel to Drum-Taps*, published that fall, includes "Pioneers! O Pioneers!" and Whitman's poems on the death of Lincoln, O CAPTAIN! MY CAPTAIN! and WHEN LILACS LAST IN THE DOORYARD BLOOM'D. Both collections were incorporated into the fourth (1867) edition of LEAVES OF GRASS.

Dust Tracks on a Road Autobiography of Zora Neale HURSTON, published in 1942. It opens with the author's childhood in Eatonville, Fla., the site of the first organized effort at self-government by black Americans. It follows her through an expanding world of experience and intellectual growth to Howard University, where the writer Charles S. Johnson discovers her work. Her most notable patrons thereafter are the white writer Fannie Hurst, for whom she works, and the anthropologist Franz Boas, who arranges a fellowship for her research of black folklore. Hurston maintains a sunny, invincible attitude throughout. Many black critics condemned her failure to address issues of racism and segregation and accused her of playing up to whites, not realizing that the book's editors had excised her critical comments on race relations and foreign policy.

Dutchman One-act drama by Amiri BARAKA, produced and published in 1964 under his original name, LeRoi Jones. Set in a New York City subway car, it involves Clay, a young, middle-class black man who is approached seductively by Lula, a white fellow passenger. Lula provokes Clay to anger and finally murders him. The stylized encounter illustrates black–white hatred and the political and psychological conflicts facing black American men in the 1960s. The play won the Obie Award for best off-Broadway play of 1964 and was made into a film in 1967.

East of Eden Novel by John STEINBECK, published in 1952. Spanning the period between the Civil War and World War I, it highlights the conflicts of two generations of brothers: the kind, gentle Adam Trask and his wild brother Charles, and Adam's twin sons, the fair-haired, winning, yet intractable Aron and the dark, clever Caleb. The twins' mother, Cathy Ames, is an evil, manipulative ex-prostitute who abandons her family to return to her former profession. Aron and Caleb vie for their father's approval; when Caleb reveals the truth about their mother to Aron, Aron joins the army and is killed in France. A symbolic recreation of the story of Cain and Abel woven into a history of California's Salinas Valley, the novel was an attempt by Steinbeck to reclaim his standing as a major writer, but his broad depictions of good and evil at the expense of subtlety in characterization and plot foiled his hopes, and the novel was not a critical success.

Education of Henry Adams, The Autobiographical work by Henry ADAMS, privately printed in 1906 and published in 1918. Considered perhaps the most distinguished of all American autobiographies, it incorporates a critical and philosophical evaluation of Adams's era. Adams marks the destruction of the human values that supported the achievements of his forebears and fears a future age driven by corruption and greed. The chapter "The Dynamo and the Virgin" contrasts the Virgin Mary, the unifying force acting on the European Middle Ages, with the dynamo, as representative of the forces of technology and industry acting on civilization in the early 20th century. MONT SAINT MICHEL AND CHARTRES can be considered the autobiography's companion piece insofar as its subject is human history.

Effect of Gamma Rays on Man-in-the-Moon Marigolds, The Naturalistic drama in two acts by Paul ZINDEL, produced in 1965 and published in 1971. It centers on Beatrice Hunsdorfer, an impractical, embittered widow living with her two awkward teenage daughters in a ramshackle house where she makes a living by nursing an elderly invalid. Alternately charming and abrasive, Beatrice is generally selfish like her elder daughter, Ruth, who suffers from convulsions brought on by a childhood trauma. The younger daughter, Tillie, is an eccentric outcast who earns respect with a prize-winning science project.

Elmer Gantry Novel by Sinclair LEWIS, published in 1927. The title character starts out as a greedy, shallow, philandering Baptist minister, turns to evangelism, and eventually becomes the leader of a large Methodist congregation. Throughout the novel he encounters fellow religious hypocrites, including Mrs. Evans Riddle, Judson Roberts, and Sharon Falconer, with whom he carries on an affair. Though he is often exposed as a fraud, Gantry is never fully discredited. The novel's indictment of fundamentalist religion caused an uproar when it first appeared.

Emperor Jones, The Drama in eight scenes by Eugene O'NEILL, produced in 1920 and published in 1921. Based loosely on an event in Haitian history, it tells of a former Pullman porter, Brutus Jones, who has escaped from prison to a Caribbean island. With help from a Cockney adventurer, Jones persuades the superstitious natives that he is a magician, and they crown him emperor. He abuses and exploits his subjects while boasting of his powers, insisting that only a silver bullet can kill him. Warned of an uprising, he flees into the jungle. There he is forced to confront his internal demons. Images of his victims assail him, while other scenes depict bizarre racial memories, including the capture and sale at auction of his African ancestors. Terrified, Jones fires all his ammunition at his ghostly tormentors. In the final scene, the rebels find Jones and shoot him. The play, while not considered one of O'Neill's finest, marked his first foray into Expressionist writing, caused a sensation, and remains a staple of small theater groups.

Encantadas, The Ten fictional sketches by Herman MELVILLE, published in 1854 in *Putnam's Monthly Magazine* as "The Encantadas, or Enchanted Isles," under the pseudonym Salvator R. Tarnmoor. Seven of them describe the Galápagos Islands (thought by sailors to be enchanted), which Melville had seen as a sailor and read about in Darwin's *Voyage of the Beagle*. The other three pieces are sketches of people who resided for a time in the Encantadas, mostly renegades and castaways.

Ethan Frome Tragic novel by Edith WHARTON, published in 1911. The main characters are Ethan Frome, his wife Zeena, and her young cousin Mattie Silver. Frome and Zeena marry after she nurses his mother in her last illness. Though Frome seems ambitious and intelligent, Zeena holds him back. When Mattie comes to stay on their New England farm, Frome falls in love with her, but the social conventions of the day doom their love and hopes. The story forcefully conveys Wharton's abhorrence of society's unbending standards of loyalty. Her use of hard-edged irony and flashback technique set it apart from the work of her contemporaries. Written while she was living in France but before her 1913 divorce, it became one of her most popular works.

Evangeline(, A Tale of Acadie) Long narrative poem by Henry Wadsworth LONGFELLOW, published in 1847. It tells the tale of two lovers, Evangeline and Gabriel, separated when British soldiers expel the Acadians (French colonists) from what is now Nova Scotia. They are reunited years later as Gabriel is dying; after Evangeline's own death, they are buried together. Written in classical hexameters, the poem intentionally echoes such epics as Homer's *Odyssey*. Though often considered sentimental, *Evangeline* is respected for its evocation of its era and of the vast and pristine North American landscape.

Everything That Rises Must Converge Collection of nine short stories by Flannery O'CONNOR, published posthumously in 1965. In the title story, a tragicomedy about social pride, racial bigotry, generational conflict, false liberalism, and filial dependence, Julian Chestny is hypocritically disdainful of his mother's prejudices; his smug selfishness is replaced with childish fear when she suffers a fatal stroke after being struck by a black woman she has insulted out of oblivious ignorance rather than malice. In "The Comforts of Home" an intellectual son, driven by the voice of his dead father, accidentally kills his sentimental mother in an attempt to murder a prostitute. In these and such other much-admired stories as "Revelation," "The Lame Shall Enter First," and "A View of the Woods," the flawed characters are fully revealed in apocalyptic moments of conflict and violence, presented with comic detachment.

Fall of the House of Usher, The Story of supernatural horror by Edgar Allan POE, published in 1839 in *Burton's Gentleman's Magazine* and issued in *Tales* (1845). One of Poe's most terrifying tales, it is narrated by a man who has been invited to visit his childhood friend Roderick Usher. Usher gradually reveals that his twin sister Madeline has been placed in the family vault not quite dead. When she reappears in her blood-stained shroud, the visitor flees as the entire house splits and sinks into a lake.

Family Moskat, The Novel by Isaac Bashevis SINGER, first serialized in the Yiddish daily *Forverts* (1945–48) and in English translation in 1950. Panoramic in sweep, it follows many characters and story lines in depicting Jewish life in Warsaw from 1911 to the late 1930s. Singer examines Hasidism, Orthodoxy, the rise of secularism, the breakdown of 19th-century traditions, assimilation, Marxism, and Zionism.

Farewell to Arms, A Novel by Ernest HEMINGWAY, published in 1929. While serving with the Italian ambulance service during World War I, the American lieutenant Frederick Henry falls in love with the English nurse Catherine Barkley, who tends him after he is wounded. She becomes pregnant but refuses to marry him, and he returns to his post. He deserts during the Italians' retreat after the Battle of Caporetto, and the reunited couple flee to Switzerland. There Catherine and her baby die during childbirth, leaving Henry desolate. Like his early short stories and his novel *The Sun Also Rises*, the work is full of the disillusionment of the Lost Generation expatriates.

Fences Play in two acts by August WILSON, performed in 1985 and published in 1986. Set in 1957, it forms part of Wilson's decade-by-decade depiction of African-American life. The protagonist, Troy Maxson, was an outstanding baseball player at a time when the major leagues were closed to black players; he bitterly resents his lost opportunities. An ex-convict as well, he is now a garbage collector. He is married to Rose and is the father of teenaged Cory. Emotional and hard-drinking, Troy ranges from tyrannical fury to delicacy as his preconceived ideas are challenged.

Financier, The Novel by Theodore DREISER, published in 1912. Frank Algernon Cowperwood, driven, vital, and unscrupulous, sees himself bound for greatness. The novel describes his career as a broker, his advantageous but ultimately doomed marriage, his deals with corrupt politicians, and his relationship with his mistress, whose father eventually uses political influence to ruin him and send him to prison. Released from prison, he recoups his fortune during the panic of 1873 and moves to Chicago. *The Financier* is the first book in an epic trilogy based on the life of the transportation magnate Charles T. Yerkes. Its remaining two novels, *The Titan* (1914) and *The Stoic* (1947; completed by Dreiser's wife), follow Cowperwood to Chicago and London through a series of shady deals, love affairs, and intrigues until, after his death, his empire collapses and his life is seen as meaningless.

Fire Next Time, The Nonfiction book, published in 1963, comprising two previously published essays in letter form by James BALDWIN. Together they constitute a powerful warning that violence would result if white America did not change its attitudes and policies toward black Americans and alter the conditions under which they were forced to live. The first, "My Dungeon Shook: Letter to My Nephew on the One Hundredth Anniversary of the Emancipation," attacks the idea that blacks are inferior to whites and emphasizes the intrinsic dignity of black people. The second, "Down at the Cross: Letter from a Region in My Mind," recounts Baldwin's coming-of-age in Harlem, appraises the Black Muslim movement, and states his personal beliefs.

Fixer, The Novel by Bernard MALAMUD, published in 1966. Set in Czarist Russia in the early 20th century, it is the story of a Jewish handyman, Yakov Bok, who discovers that there is no rational reason for human cruelty and that freedom requires constant vigilance. Bok says of himself that he fixes what's broken—except in the heart. His tinkering includes altruistic acts, but his generosity is repaid with misfortune and vilification. Most of the novel takes place while Bok is imprisoned awaiting trial for a murder he did not commit. As in Malamud's other works, the condition of the Jews serves as a metaphor for that of humanity. It is often considered Malamud's finest novel.

Flowering Judas Short story by Katherine Anne PORTER, published in *Hound and Horn* magazine in 1930. The title story of Porter's first and most popular collection (1930), it is set in 1920 during the Mexican Revolution. Laura, a beautiful young American teacher of Indian children and a clandestine worker for the revolutionary cause, must rationalize her actions as she faces the loss of her ideals.

Fool for Love One-act play by Sam SHEPARD, produced in San Francisco and published in 1983. It is a bizarre tragedy about the tumultuous, incestuous love between a rodeo performer and his half-sister. The father they have in common, a character called Old Man, acts as narrator and chorus.

For the Union Dead Title poem of a collection by Robert LOWELL, published in 1964. The poem, first published in *Life Studies* (1960) under a different title, commemorates Col. Robert Gould Shaw, the white Bostonian who commanded a battalion of black Union troops during the Civil War, and alludes to three significant incidents: Shaw's death and anonymous burial; the dedication of a memorial to Shaw and other Union soldiers in Boston in the 1890s; and the violent resistance to school integration in the 1960s.

For Whom the Bell Tolls Novel by Ernest HEMINGWAY, published in 1940. Set in the Spanish Civil War in 1937, it follows the American teacher Robert Jordan, who, having joined the antifascist Loyalist army, is sent to make contact with a guerrilla band and blow up a bridge to advance a Loyalist offensive. At the guerrilla camp, he falls in love with Maria and befriends the shrewd but cowardly guerrilla leader Pablo and Pablo's courageous wife Pilar. He succeeds in destroying the bridge; Pablo, Pilar, Maria, and two other guerrillas escape, but Jordan is injured. Proclaiming his love to Maria once more, he awaits the fascist troops and certain death. The title quotes John Donne—"no man is an Iland, intire of it selfe; every man is a peece of the Continent. . . . And therefore never send to know for whom the bell tolls; it tolls for thee"—to express socialist solidarity.

Fountainhead, The Novel by Ayn RAND, published in 1943. An exposition of the author's anticommunist philosophy of Objectivism, it tells of the struggle of the brilliant architect Howard Roark (said to be based on Frank Lloyd Wright) as he confronts conformist mediocrity. Though expelled from architectural school for his nonconformist ideas, Roark pursues his vision undaunted. In Rand's world, suppression of individual creativity is the greatest evil.

Four Quartets Series of four poems by T.S. ELIOT, published individually from 1936 to 1942 and in book form in 1943. Each has five "movements," is written in strong-stress meter, and is titled with a place-name— "Burnt Norton" (1936), "East Coker" (1940), "The Dry Salvages" (1941), and "Little Gidding" (1942). The work addresses the connections of the personal and historical present and past, spiritual renewal, and the very nature of experience; Eliot's insights into the cyclical nature of life are revealed through themes and images deftly woven throughout. It is considered his clearest exposition of his Christian beliefs and, by many, his masterpiece. "Burnt Norton," named for a Cotswold Hills country house Eliot visited in 1934, is set in its rose garden and addresses the pervasive theme of cyclical patterns in time. "East Coker," named after the hamlet where Eliot's ancestors lived before immigrating to America in the 1660s, examines the nature of history and spiritual renewal. Bleak in tone, with images of deserted streets, subterranean shelters, and hospitals, it closes with the determination that "For us, there is only the trying. The rest is not our business." "The Dry Salvages," named for a formation of rocks off Cape Ann, Mass., which Eliot visited as a child, is concerned with experience and the human response to Christian doctrines, particularly the Incarnation. "Little Gidding" is named for the Huntingdonshire village where Nicholas Ferrar established an Anglican community in the 17th century; the poem, set in winter at its chapel and in London during World War II, addresses spiritual renewal.

Four Saints in Three Acts Opera consisting of a prologue and four acts, with libretto by Gertrude STEIN (1927) and music by Virgil Thomson (1934). Thomson divided Stein's libretto into scenes and acts, and added two figures representing the laity to the cast of characters. The plotless opera (whose music is so light it resembles a musical), set in 16th-century Spain, treats the Spaniards St. Theresa of Ávila, St. Ignatius of Loyola, and two fictional figures, St. Settlement and St. Chavez.

Franny and Zooey Volume containing two interrelated stories by J. D. SALINGER, published in 1961. The stories, originally published in the *New Yorker*, focus on Franny and Zooey Glass, two members of the fictional family that is the subject of most of Salinger's short fiction. Franny, an intellectually precocious late adolescent, tries to attain spiritual purification by obsessively repeating the "Jesus prayer" as an antidote to the perceived superficiality and corruptness of life, but eventually suffers a nervous breakdown. In the second story, her closest brother, Zooey, tries to heal her by pointing out that love is the answer to her cynicism and despair.

From Here to Eternity Novel by James JONES, published in 1951. Set in Hawaii just before the attack on Pearl Harbor, it details peacetime army life as seen through the eyes of Private Robert E. Lee Prewitt, who hopes to become a career military man, and Sgt. Milton Warden, who embarks on an affair with his senior officer's wife. The novel shocked audiences of its time with its vulgar language and frank portrayal of sex, but it was universally acclaimed for its sensitive and accurate picture of the army's paradoxical brutality and decency. Its sequels are *The Thin Red Line* (1962) and *Whistle* (1978).

Furnished Room, The Short story by O. HENRY, published serially in 1904 and collected in *The Four Million* (1906). Set in New York City, it is a melodramatic tale about a young man who, after a futile search for his missing girlfriend, commits suicide in his rented room, not knowing that it is the same room in which his girlfriend had killed herself a week earlier.

Giant Novel about two generations of wealthy Texans by Edna FERBER, published in 1952. Leslie Lynnton, a patrician Virginian, marries Bick Benedict, a Texas cattle baron. The reader experiences Texas from Leslie's point of view, as she attempts to understand and adapt to the Texans' customs and expansive way of life. The work offers a vivid description of the crudeness of the newly rich oilmen and cattle barons and their exploitation of the impoverished Mexicans who work for them.

Giants in the Earth(: A Saga of the Prairie) Novel by O. E. ROLVAAG, first published in Norway in two volumes (1924, 1925) and published in English in 1927. It chronicles the struggles of Norwegian immigrant settlers in the Dakota territory in the 1870s. Its indomitable protagonist, Per Hansa, his wife Beret, their children, and three other families build makeshift sod huts at Spring Creek. Surviving the winters' fierce blizzards, they see their crops destroyed by locusts in

summer. They nonetheless persist; new settlers arrive, and the community grows. Beret, who cannot adapt to prairie life, almost dies giving birth to a son, whom Per names Peder Victorious. Cheered when a traveling minister baptizes Peder, Beret eventually becomes obsessively religious. When another settler lies dying, she sends Per to find a minister, but he is caught in a fierce snowstorm and dies. The novel had two sequels, *Peder Victorious* (1928) and *Their Fathers' God* (1931).

Gift, The Novel by Vladimir NABOKOV. Originally published serially in Russian (in expurgated form) as *Dar* in 1937–38, it was published complete in English in 1952. Set in post–World War I Berlin (where Nabokov himself had settled) and brimming with satiric detail about the Russian émigré community, it tells of Fyodor's maturation as a gifted young writer and of his love affair with Zina, a fellow émigré.

Gift of the Magi, The Short story by O. HENRY, published in the *New York Sunday World* in 1905 and collected in *The Four Million* (1906). Based on Maupassant's "The Necklace," it concerns James and Della Dillingham Young, a young couple who, despite their poverty, individually resolve to give each other an elegant gift on Christmas Eve. Della sells her beautiful long hair to buy a platinum fob chain for Jim's antique gold watch, while Jim pawns his treasured watch to purchase jeweled tortoiseshell combs for Della's precious tresses.

Giles Goat-Boy(: or, The Revised New Syllabus) Satiric allegorical novel by John BARTH, published in 1966. Its protagonist, Billy Bockfuss (also called George Giles, the goat-boy), was raised with herds of goats on a university farm after being found as a baby in the bowels of the giant West Campus Automatic Computer (WESCAC). The WESCAC plans to create a being called GILES (Grand-Tutorial Ideal, Laboratory Eugenical Specimen) that would possess superhuman abilities. Billy's foster father, who tends the herd, suspects Billy of being GILES but tries to groom him to be humanity's savior and to end WESCAC's domination over humans.

Gimpel the Fool Short story by Isaac Bashevis SINGER, published in 1945 in Yiddish, and in English in the collection *Gimpel the Fool* (1957). Set in a bygone era in an Eastern European shtetl, the tale concerns Gimpel, a gullible man who responds to a lifetime of betrayal, heckling, and deception with childlike acceptance and complete faith.

Giovanni's Room Novel by James BALDWIN, published in 1956. After a single homosexual experience in adolescence, David represses his unacceptable impulses. In Paris he has an affair with Hella Lincoln and, determined to live a respectable life, proposes marriage. While Hella is in Spain considering his proposal, he has an affair with Giovanni, an Italian bartender, but still unable to reconcile homosexuality with the life he desires, eventually rejects him. He and Hella vacation in the south of France; she finds him in a gay bar and, realizing what his relationship with Giovanni had been, abandons him. At the novel's end he remains agonizing over his sexuality.

Glass Menagerie, The Drama by Tennessee WILLIAMS, produced in 1944 and published in 1945. Amanda Wingfield lives in a St. Louis tenement, clinging to a myth of her early years as a Southern belle. Her daughter Laura, who wears a leg brace, is painfully shy and seeks solace in her collection of small glass animals. Laura's brother, Tom, is desperate to escape his stifling home life and his warehouse job. Amanda encourages him to bring "gentlemen callers" home to his sister. When he brings Jim O'Connor for dinner, Amanda believes her prayers have been answered. Laura blossoms during Jim's visit, flattered by his attention, but after kissing her he confesses that he is engaged. She retreats into her shell and Amanda blames Tom, who leaves home for good after a final fight with his mother. The play launched Williams's career and is still considered by some to be his finest work.

Glengarry Glen Ross Play in two acts by David MAMET, produced in 1983 and published in 1984. It concerns a group of ruthless real-estate salesmen who compete to sell lots in Florida developments known as Glengarry Highlands and Glen Ross Farms. Built on the strength of its explosive and often profane dialogue, it depicts the real-estate industry—and by extension much of American business—as seedy and unscrupulous.

Go Down, Moses Collection of seven stories by William FAULKNER, first published together in 1942 as *Go Down, Moses, and Other Stories*. Set in Yoknapatawpha County, it contains some of his best writing. Though the stories were originally published separately, the book is best read as a novel of interconnecting generations, races, and dreams. The tone of this sprawling tale of the McCaslin clan ranges from the farcical to the profound. "Was," considered a comic masterpiece, opens with a raucous fox chase that suggests the story's theme and action: the twins Buck and Buddy chase their slave and half-brother, Turl; Turl chases his girlfriend Tennie, slave of Hubert and his sister Sibbey Beauchamp; and Sibbey, the only white woman in the countryside, pursues Buck. A poker game decides the fate of the couples and ownership of the slaves. "The Fire and the Hearth" establishes the dignity of Lucas Beauchamp, son of Turl and Tennie. "Pantaloon in Black," the story of a black man lynched for killing a deceitful white, stands somewhat apart. "The Old People" and THE BEAR feature Ike McCaslin's confrontations with nature. In "Delta Autumn," Ike, at 79, is forced to confront his role in perpetuating the exploitation of his own black relatives. "Go Down, Moses" focuses on the entire community.

God's Trombones(: Seven Negro Sermons in Verse) Volume of poetry by James Weldon JOHNSON, published in 1927. Representing what Johnson called an "art-governed expression" of the traditional black preaching style, it consists of the introductory prayer "Listen, Lord—A Prayer" and seven verse sermons: "The Creation," "The Prodigal Son," "Go Down Death—A Funeral Sermon," "Noah Built the Ark," "The Crucifixion," "Let My People Go," and "The Judgment Day." Though an agnostic, Johnson drew heavily from the oral tradition and biblical poetry of his Christian upbringing, conveying the raw power of fire-and-brimstone oratory while avoiding the hackneyed devices of dialectal transcription that had marred previous literature in the black idiom.

Gold Bug, The Mystery story by Edgar Allan POE, published in 1843 in the Philadelphia *Dollar Magazine* and later in *Tales* (1845). William Legrand has sequestered himself on South Carolina's Sullivan's Island, after a series of economic setbacks. With his servant Jupiter he finds a golden beetle. The parchment in which he captured it is later revealed to be inscribed with cryptic writing and an emblem similar to the death's-head marking on the insect. He deciphers the message and follows its strange instructions, which lead him to the buried treasure of Captain Kidd.

Golden Apples, The Short-story collection by Eudora WELTY, published in 1949. Symbolism from Greek mythology unifies the stories, all of which are set in the Mississippi Delta town of Morgana over a 40-year period. The hero of "Moon Lake" and the guitarist in

"Music from Spain" are Perseus figures; King MacLain in "Shower of Gold," is a sexually adventurous Zeus figure.

Golden Bowl, The Novel by Henry JAMES, published in 1904. The wealthy American widower Adam Verver and his daughter Maggie live in Europe, where they collect art and relish each other's company. Through the efforts of the manipulative Fanny Assingham, Maggie becomes engaged to Amerigo, an Italian prince in reduced circumstances, but remains blind to his rekindled affair with her longtime friend Charlotte Stant. Maggie and Amerigo marry, and later, after Charlotte and Adam have also wed, both spouses learn of the ongoing affair, though neither seeks a confrontation. Not until Maggie buys a gilded crystal bowl as a present for Adam does truth crack the veneer of propriety.

Golden Boy Drama in three acts by Clifford ODETS, produced and published in 1937. Joe Bonaparte, a gifted young musician, becomes corrupted by money and brutality when he chooses to become a prizefighter rather than a classical violinist.

Gone with the Wind Novel by Margaret MITCHELL, published in 1936. A sweeping, romantic story about the Civil War from the Southern point of view, it is the story of Scarlett O'Hara, a selfish, headstrong, and resourceful Southern belle who survives the hardships of the war, including the burning of Atlanta, and afterwards manages to establish a successful business by capitalizing on the struggle to rebuild the South. Throughout the book she is motivated by her unfulfilled love for Ashley Wilkes, an honorable and happily married man. Her yearning prevents her from finding happiness with other men, notably the dashing Rhett Butler.

Good Earth, The Novel by Pearl BUCK, published in 1931. It follows the life of Wang Lun, from his beginnings as an impoverished peasant to his eventual position as a prosperous landowner. He is aided immeasurably by his wife, O-Lan, with whom he shares a devotion to the land, duty, and survival.

Good Man Is Hard to Find, A First volume of short stories by Flannery O'CONNOR, published in 1955. Like much of her work, it presents vivid, hidebound characters seemingly hounded by a redemption that they often successfully elude. Several of the stories are considered masterpieces. These include "The Artificial Nigger," in which the sight of a lawn figurine of a black jockey causes a bigoted grandfather to realize a truth

about injustice; "Good Country People," in which a young woman's sense of moral superiority leads to her downfall at the hands of a bible salesman; and the title story, in which a demonic escaped convict called the Misfit becomes an instrument of revelation for the matriarch of the family he murders.

Go Tell It on the Mountain First novel by James BALDWIN, published in 1953. This semiautobiographical work, the most highly regarded of Baldwin's novels, evokes the Harlem of his youth in both its raffish and religious aspects. The framing story concerns 14-year-old John Grimes, who experiences a spiritual awakening one Saturday night; through John, Baldwin reaches back into the torn lives of John's parents. The novel's language is rich, and filled with biblical allusions. When accused of not adequately addressing the issue of black-white relations, Baldwin replied that he was attempting to break out of the "cage" of black writing.

Grapes of Wrath, The Novel by John STEINBECK, published in 1939. The narrative, interrupted by prose-poem interludes, chronicles the struggles of the Joad family's life on a failing Oklahoma farm during the Dust Bowl years, their difficult journey to California, and their disillusionment once they arrive there and become migrant farmworkers. The Joads' insularity—Ma's obsession with family togetherness, her son Tom's self-centeredness, and her daughter Rose of Sharon's materialism—ultimately gives way to a sense of universal community. The work did much to publicize the injustices of migrant labor.

Graustark(: The Story of a Love Behind a Throne) Romantic quasi-historical novel by George Barr MCCUTCHEON, first published in 1901. Modeled on Anthony Hope's novel *The Prisoner of Zenda* (1894), it is set in the mythical Central European kingdom of Graustark and is suffused with derring-do, court intrigues, and passionate romance. McCutcheon's later novels include *Beverly of Graustark* (1904) and *The Prince of Graustark* (1914). The word Graustark has since been used to refer to an imaginary land of high romance or a highly romantic piece of writing.

Gravity's Rainbow Novel by Thomas PYNCHON, published in 1973. The sprawling narrative, told in brilliantly allusive prose, comprises numerous threads having to do either directly or tangentially with the secret development and deployment of a rocket by the Nazis near the end of World War II. Lieut. Tyrone

Slothrop is an American working for Allied Intelligence in London. Agents of the Firm, a clandestine military organization, are investigating an apparent connection between Slothrop's erections and the targeting of incoming V-2 rockets. As a child, Slothrop was the subject of experiments conducted by a Harvard professor who is now a Nazi rocket scientist. Slothrop's quest for the truth behind these implications leads him on a nightmarish journey of either historic discovery or profound paranoia, depending on his own and the reader's interpretation.

Great Gatsby, The   Novel by F. Scott FITZGERALD, published in 1925. The narrator, Nick Carraway, is a young Princeton man who works as a bond broker in Manhattan. His neighbor at West Egg, Long Island, is Jay Gatsby, a Midwesterner of considerable self-made wealth whose mysterious origin turns out to be bootlegging. For many years Gatsby has been in love with Nick's cousin Daisy, who is married to the wealthy but coarse Tom Buchanan. Daisy and Gatsby begin an affair. Tom's own mistress, Myrtle, is the wife of a garbageman. When a distraught Myrtle is hit and killed by Daisy's car on the highway, Daisy drives away from the scene. The jealous Tom tells Myrtle's husband that it was Gatsby who killed Myrtle, and the husband shoots Gatsby and then himself. With its sharp depiction of the consequences of the "American dream" and of a man betrayed by the ambitions nurtured by a meretricious society, *The Great Gatsby* is widely regarded as one of the greatest English-language novels of the 20th century.

Great God Brown, The   Drama in four acts and a prologue by Eugene O'NEILL, produced and published in 1926. An example of O'Neill's pioneering experiments with Expressionistic theater, it makes use of multiple masks to illustrate the private and public personas of the characters and the changing tenor of their interior lives. Billy Brown, a mediocre architect, and Dion Anthony, a talented but dissolute artist, are both in love with Margaret, who chooses Dion because she is in love with the sensual, cynical mask he presents to the world. When he removes his mask to reveal his spiritual, artistic side, she is repelled. Frustrated at his inability to realize his artistic promise, he sinks deeper into his self-destructive habits and soon dies. Billy steals Dion's mask, takes on his persona, and marries Margaret, who believes him to be Dion. He is eventually accused of the murder of his "old" self and is shot by the police. Margaret continues to worship Dion's mask.

Group, The   Novel by Mary MCCARTHY, published in 1963. It chronicles the lives of eight Vassar College friends from their graduation in 1933 to the funeral of Kay Strong, the story's principal character, in 1940. The women all believe that their superior education has given them control over their lives and the ability to break down existing taboos and limitations, and all believe in progress, modernity, marrying well, and accumulating wealth and possessions. The novel recounts their discovery, as they encounter the realities of sex, marriage, motherhood, and careers, that both bohemia and high society have their hypocrisies and that resistance to change is universal.

Hairy Ape, The   Drama in eight scenes by Eugene O'NEILL, produced in 1922 and published in 1923. Yank Smith, a brutish stoker on a transatlantic liner, bullies and despises everyone around him, considering himself superior. Devastated when a millionaire's daughter is repelled by his simian ways, he vows to get even with her. Ashore in New York, he schemes to destroy the factory owned by her father, but his plans fail. He wanders into a zoo; there, alienated from humanity, he releases an ape, for whom he feels some kinship, and it kills him. The play is considered one of the prime achievements of Expressionistic drama.

Hamlet, The   Novel by William FAULKNER, published in 1940. In three loosely connected sections, it depicts the early years (in the late 19th century) of the crude and contemptible Flem Snopes and his grotesque clan. It is the first volume of a trilogy that includes *The Town* (1957) and *The Mansion* (1959); by the trilogy's end, the Snopeses have supplanted the dispirited gentry class (represented by the Sartoris family) of Frenchman's Bend, Miss.

Hans Brinker; or, The Silver Skates   Novel by Mary Mapes DODGE, published in 1865. Set in the Netherlands, the novel, a perennial children's classic, concerns the fortunes of the impoverished Brinker family. The good deeds of the Brinker children, Hans and Gretel, help restore their father's health and bring about their own good fortune. The plot is secondary to informative details about Dutch family life and to considerable history and geography of the country, which Dodge had never visited.

Harlem   Poem (also known as "A Dream Deferred") by Langston HUGHES, published in 1951 as part of *Montage of a Dream Deferred*, an extended poem cycle about Harlem life. The 11-line poem speculates about the consequences of white society's withholding of equal opportunity, and concludes by suggesting that a dream deferred may explode.

Heart Is a Lonely Hunter, The Novel by Carson MCCULLERS, published in 1940. It focuses on John Singer, a deaf-mute in a Georgia mill town during the 1930s, and his effect on those who confide in him. When his mute Greek companion of 10 years goes insane, Singer is left alone and isolated. He takes a room with the Kelly family; there he is visited by the town's misfits, who turn to him for understanding but have no knowledge of his inner life. When he discovers that his Greek friend has died, he realizes there is no one with whom he can communicate and shoots himself. With its intense evocation of moral isolation and its sensitive glimpses into the psyches of the lonely, it is considered McCullers's finest work.

Henderson the Rain King Seriocomic novel by Saul BELLOW, published in 1959. It examines the midlife crisis of Eugene Henderson, a larger-than-life 55-year-old who has accumulated money, position, and a large family but nonetheless feels unfulfilled. He makes a spiritual journey to Africa, where he draws emotional sustenance from experiences with its tribes. Deciding that his true destiny is as a healer, he returns home, planning to enter medical school.

Herzog Novel by Saul BELLOW, published in 1964. Moses Herzog, like many of Bellow's heroes, is a Jewish intellectual who confronts a world peopled by sanguine, incorrigible realists. Much of the action, including a series of flashbacks, many of which involve Herzog's sexual and marital past, takes place within the hero's disturbed consciousness. The book was highly praised for its combination of erudition and street smarts, its lively, Yiddish-influenced prose, and its narrative drive, though some critics felt Herzog's wives and lovers were not fully realized.

Hiawatha, The Song of Long narrative poem by Henry Wadsworth LONGFELLOW, published in 1855. Longfellow's Hiawatha is an Ojibwa Indian, raised by Nokomis, his wrinkled and wise grandmother, "daughter of the Moon." Hiawatha desires to avenge the wrong done by his father, the West Wind, to his mother, Wenonah, but father and son eventually reconcile. Hiawatha becomes his people's leader and marries Minnehaha, of the formerly hostile Dakota tribe, and an era of peace and enlightenment ensues. Later, disease and famine afflict the tribe and Minnehaha dies;

before Hiawatha takes leave of the tribe to go to the Isles of the Blessed, he tells his people to heed those who will come with a new religion. The poem is especially notable for its relentless trochaic meter, which Longfellow adapted from the Finnish epic *Kalevala*. He perpetuated Henry Rowe Schoolcraft's error in placing Hiawatha among the forest tribes of the northern Midwest rather than among the eastern Onondagas.

Hills Like White Elephants Short story by Ernest HEMINGWAY, published in 1927 in the periodical *transition* and later that year in *Men Without Women*. The themes of this sparsely written vignette about an American couple waiting for a train in Spain are almost entirely implicit. Largely devoid of plot, the story is notable for its use of irony, symbolism, and repetition.

Hiroshima Report by John HERSEY on the atomic-bomb blast over Hiroshima, Japan, on August 6, 1945, and its aftermath. First published in the *New Yorker* as the entire editorial content of its issue of August 31, 1946, the account—which mingles fact and fiction—is objective rather than sensational, focusing on six survivors of the atomic blast and on the horrors they witnessed and endured. It gave many Americans their first vivid account of the consequences of the explosion.

History of New York (from the Beginning of the World to the End of the Dutch Dynasty, by Diedrich Knickerbocker), A Satirical history by Washington IRVING, published in 1809. Originally intended as a burlesque of historical methodology and heroic styles of epic poetry, the work became more serious as the author proceeded. Diedrich Knickerbocker, the putative narrator, begins with a mock-pedantic cosmogony and proceeds to a history of New Netherlands, often ignoring or altering facts. Descriptions of early New Amsterdam landmarks and old Dutch-American legends are included, as are the discovery of America, Henry Hudson's voyage, and the founding of New Amsterdam. Its portrait of the over-educated, belligerent governor William the Testy (Willem Kieft) is actually a Federalist satire of Thomas Jefferson. It concludes with the rule of Peter the headstrong (Peter Stuyvesant) and the fall of New Amsterdam to the British in 1664.

Homage to Mistress Bradstreet Long poem by John BERRYMAN, written in 1948–53 and published in 1956. Noted for its intensity, it is a tribute to the colonial poet Anne Bradstreet that reveals much about the author. The poem examines the tension between Bradstreet's personal and artistic life, concluding in a spirit of fatalism. It shows throughout a loving and intimate grasp of the details of American history, while examining creative repression, religious apostasy, and the temptation to adultery.

Home to Harlem First novel by Claude MCKAY, published in 1928. Jake Brown deserts the army during World War I and lives in London until a race riot inspires him to return to Harlem. On his first night home he meets the prostitute Felice, for whom he spends much of the rest of the novel searching. Amid his adventures in Harlem, a gallery of rough, lusty, heavy-drinking characters appear to vivid effect. While working as a dining-car waiter he encounters another point of view in Ray, a pessimistic, college-educated Haitian immigrant who advocates behavior based on racial pride. In *Home to Harlem* and its sequel, *Banjo*, McKay attempted to capture the vitality of the black vagabonds of urban America and Europe.

Hoosier School-Master, The Regional novel by Edward EGGLESTON, serialized in *Hearth and Home* in 1871 and published in book form the same year. Based partly on the experiences of the author's brother, it relates episodes in the lives of inhabitants of a backwoods Indiana town and the experiences of the young man hired to be its school's only teacher. The novel is primarily of interest for its naturalism, its description of its Indiana setting, and its extensive use of Hoosier dialect.

House of Mirth, The Novel by Edith WHARTON, published in 1905. It concerns the tragic fate of the beautiful and well-connected but penniless Lily Bart, who at 29 lacks a husband to secure her position in society. Maneuvering to correct this situation, she encounters both Simon Rosedale, a rich man outside her class, and Lawrence Selden, who is personally appealing and socially acceptable but not wealthy. She becomes indebted to an unscrupulous man, has her reputation sullied by a promiscuous acquaintance, and slides into genteel poverty. Unable or unwilling to marry either Rosedale or Selden, she finally despairs and takes an overdose of sleeping pills.

House of the Seven Gables, The Romance by Nathaniel HAWTHORNE, published in 1851. Set in mid-19th-century Salem, Mass., the work is a somber study in hereditary sin based on the legend of a curse pronounced on Hawthorne's own family by a woman condemned to death during the infamous Salem witchcraft

trials. The Pyncheon family's greed and arrogant pride through the generations is mirrored in the gloomy decay of their seven-gabled mansion, in which the family's enfeebled and impoverished relations live. At the book's end the descendant of a family long ago defrauded by the Pyncheons lifts his ancestors' curse on the mansion and marries a niece of the family.

Howl Poem in three sections by Allen GINSBERG, published in *Howl and Other Poems* in 1956. A denunciation of the failings of American society, *Howl* combines lamentation, jeremiad, and vision. Its long opening sentence begins "I saw the best minds of my generation destroyed by madness, starving/hysterical naked, / dragging themselves through the negro streets at dawn looking for an / angry fix." It was praised for its incantatory rhythms and raw emotion; critics noted the influences of William Carlos Williams (who introduced the 1959 edition), Walt Whitman, and William S. Burroughs. It also was an unabashed celebration and critique of the masculine. Its frank references to heterosexual and especially homosexual coupling landed its publisher, Lawrence Ferlinghetti, in court on obscenity charges; he was acquitted in 1957 in a landmark decision. *Howl* is considered the foremost poetic expression of the Beat movement.

Huckleberry Finn, The Adventures of Novel by Mark TWAIN, published in 1884. Huckleberry Finn, the young narrator, runs away from his appalling father and, with his companion, the runaway slave Jim, makes a long and frequently interrupted voyage down the Mississippi River on a raft. During the journey Huck encounters a variety of characters—notably the two con men who call themselves the King and the Duke—and types representing almost every class living on or along the river. A thread of cruelty runs through adventure after adventure, showing itself both in individuals' acts and in unthinking acceptance of such social institutions as slavery, and Huck's natural goodness—which leads to his gradually overcoming his own racial prejudices and learning to love and respect Jim—is continually contrasted with the effects of a corrupt society. Idyllic descriptions of the great river abound, and Huck's good nature and unconscious humor permeate the whole.

Hugh Selwyn Mauberley Long dramatic poem by Ezra POUND, published in 1920. The opening section's subject is the gaudiness, corruption, and deterioration of culture in modern commercial society. The second section introduces the fictional Mauberley, who represents the worst failings of contemporary artists and serves as a springboard for Pound's plea that form and style be reinstated as the bearers of authentic meaning. Pound referred to *Mauberley* as an attempt "to condense a James novel."

Human Comedy, The Sentimental novel by William SAROYAN, published in 1943. Its narrator, 14-year-old Homer Macauley, lives with his widowed mother, his sister Bess, and his little brother Ulysses in a small California town; his older brother has left home to fight in World War II. While family relationships and domestic situations occupy the foreground, the events of the outside world, including the war, are never absent.

Humboldt's Gift Novel by Saul BELLOW, published in 1975. Charlie Citrine, an intellectual, middle-aged author of award-winning biographies and plays, contemplates two significant figures in his life: Von Humboldt Fleisher, a dead poet who had been his mentor, and Rinaldo Cantabile, a vigorous minor mafioso, formerly the bane of Humboldt's existence. Humboldt taught Charlie that art is powerful and that one should be true to one's creative spirit. Rinaldo, Charlie's self-appointed financial adviser, has always urged Charlie to use his art to turn a profit. By the novel's end, Charlie has managed to set his own course. Bellow described the novel, whose title character he modeled on the self-destructive poet Delmore Schwartz, as a "comic book about death."

Iceman Cometh, The Tragedy in four acts by Eugene O'NEILL, written in 1939 and produced and published in 1946. Sometimes considered O'Neill's finest work, it exposes the need for illusion as an antidote to despair. O'Neill mined the tragedies of his own life for this depiction of a ragged collection of alcoholics in a run-down New York tavern-hotel run by Harry Hope. The saloon regulars numb themselves with whiskey and make grandiose plans but do nothing, awaiting the arrival of big-spending Theodore Hickman ("Hickey"). This year a changed Hickey pressures his cronies to pursue their much-discussed plans, hoping that real failure will make them face reality. He then confesses that he killed his long-suffering wife hours before arriving at Harry's, and is taken away by the police. The others slip back into an alcoholic haze, still clinging to their dreams.

If He Hollers Let Him Go First novel by Chester HIMES, published in 1945, often considered his most powerful work. Bob Jones, a sensitive black man, is driven to the brink by the humiliation he endures from racism at the defense plant he works at during World War II. Dishonesty and violence mark his relationship with his demanding fiancée; a greater threat is a white female coworker who insults, then entices him.

Innocents Abroad(; or, The New Pilgrims' Progress), The Humorous travel narrative by Mark TWAIN, published in 1869. Twain's 1867 steamship voyage to Europe, Egypt, and the Holy Land, recorded in letters to newspapers at home, provided material for the account. Twain is refreshingly honest and vivid in describing foreign scenes and his reactions to them, and sharply satirizes tourists who learn what they should see and feel by reading guidebooks. Serious passages—history, statistics, description, explanation, argumentation—alternate with humorous ones. The humor is sometimes in the vein of the Southwestern yarn-spinners Twain encountered as a young man, and sometimes resembles that of his contemporaries Artemus Ward and Josh Billings in its use of burlesque, parody, and other verbal devices.

Intruder in the Dust Novel by William FAULKNER, published in 1948. Set in the fictional Yoknapatawpha county, it combines a murder mystery with an exploration of Southern race relations. Chick Mallison, a 16-year-old white boy, feels he must repay a debt of honor to Lucas Beauchamp, an elderly black man who has helped him but spurns his offers of payment. When Beauchamp is arrested for the murder of a white man, Chick searches for the real killer to save him from being lynched.

Invisible Man Novel by Ralph ELLISON, published in 1952. The narrator, a nameless young black man, moves through a 20th-century America where reality is surreal and where he can survive only through pretense. Because the people he encounters "see only my surroundings, themselves, or figments of their imagination," he is effectively invisible. He leaves the racist South for New York City, but his encounters continue to disgust him. Ultimately, he retreats to a hole in the ground, which he furnishes and makes his home.

Invitation to a Beheading Anti-utopian novel by Vladimir NABOKOV, published serially in Russian from 1935 to 1936 and in book form in 1938. Set in a mythical totalitarian country, it presents the thoughts of Cincinnatus, a former teacher convicted of "gnostic turpitude" for being different from his mediocre fellow countrymen. He sees the world around him as delusional and himself as the only "real" person in the universe. Sentenced to be executed at an unknown date, he sits in his cell and records in his diary his thoughts and intuitions about an ideal world he considers his "true" home. As the ax falls, he—or his spirit—rises toward other beings like himself.

Iron Heel, The Novel by Jack LONDON, published in 1908. The United States falls to the cruel fascist dictatorship of the Iron Heel, a group of monopoly capitalists. Fearing the popularity of socialism, the plutocrats conspire to eliminate democracy and terrorize the citizenry with their secret police and military. They instigate a German attack on Hawaii on Dec. 4, 1912, and, as socialist revolutions topple capitalist governments around the world, have 52 socialist members of the U.S. Congress imprisoned for treason. Elements of London's vision of fascism, civil war, and oppression proved prophetic.

I Sing the Body Electric Poem by Walt WHITMAN. The poem was originally published without a title in *Leaves of Grass* (1855 edition), and later appeared as "Poem of the Body." It acquired its present title in 1867. A paean to the human form in all its manifestations of soundness, the vigors of male and female, youth and age are equally celebrated and ultimately equated with the soul.

Israel Potter(: His Fifty Years of Exile) Novel by Herman MELVILLE, published serially in 1854–55 in *Putnam's Monthly Magazine* and in book form in 1855. Melville used a biography of Israel Potter as the basis for this short picaresque novel. Potter lived a life of adventure, serving bravely as a regular soldier in the Revolution, and later serving under John Paul Jones in the new American navy and as a secret courier for Benjamin Franklin. In exile in Europe, he lived in poverty; on his return to the United States, his request for a pension was denied, and he died forgotten and destitute. Melville embellished the facts of Potter's life, satirizing his encounters with Franklin and adding a vignette about Ethan Allen.

It Can't Happen Here Novel by Sinclair LEWIS, published in 1935. During the 1936 presidential election, Doremus Jessup, a newspaper editor, observes with dismay that many of the people he knows support the candidacy of a fascist, Berzelius Windrip. When Windrip wins the election, he forcibly gains control of Congress and the Supreme Court, and, with the aid of

his personal paramilitary storm troopers, turns the country into a totalitarian state. Jessup opposes him, is captured, and escapes to Canada.

Jennie Gerhardt Novel by Theodore DREISER, published in 1911. The unhappy story of a working-class woman who accepts all the adversity life visits on her and becomes the mistress of two wealthy and powerful men in order to help her impoverished family, it was more successful than the more controversial SISTER CARRIE, but is less highly regarded today, as most modern readers find the title character unrealistically saintly.

Joe Turner's Come and Gone Play in two acts by August WILSON, performed in 1986 and published in 1988. Set in 1911, it belongs to Wilson's series of plays depicting the lives of blacks in each decade of the century. The setting is a Pittsburgh boardinghouse whose inhabitants are all from the rural South, new to the industrial North, separated from their families and from their heritage. Each is engaged in a search for identity and equilibrium; all maintain links with African traditions as they try to find their places in post–Civil War society.

John Brown's Body Epic book-length poem in eight sections by Stephen Vincent BENÉT, published in 1928. The scrupulously researched narrative begins just before John Brown's raid on Harpers Ferry and ends after the assassination of Abraham Lincoln. Benét's tone is one of reconciliation. From his viewpoint there are few villains and many heroes; the North and the South are afforded equal respect. Along with such historical figures as Lincoln and Robert E. Lee, Benét presents Americans of many backgrounds, occupations, and opinions, from Southern aristocrats and their slaves to farmboy soldiers from Pennsylvania and Illinois.

JR Novel by William GADDIS, published in 1975. Written almost entirely in dialogue, with the speakers rarely identified, it offers a comic, sharply satiric look at American education, the power of capitalism, and the corrupting influence of money in American society through the escapades of an 11-year-old boy whose money-making scheme earns him a Wall Street empire.

Jungle, The Novel by Upton SINCLAIR, published privately by Sinclair in 1906 after commercial publishers refused the manuscript. The most famous, influential, and enduring of all muckraking novels, *The Jungle* was an exposé of conditions in the Chicago stockyards, where Sinclair was sent by the socialist weekly *Appeal to Reason* to investigate working conditions in the meatpacking industry. Though his chief goal was to expose abusive labor conditions, the public was most horrified by his descriptions of the appalling filth of the processing plants and the actual ingredients of processed meats. The novel provided the final impetus for passage of the U.S. Pure Food and Drug Act and led to improved working conditions in the slaughterhouses.

Jurgen(: A Comedy of Justice) Novel by James Branch CABELL, published in 1919. One of a series of novels about the mythical medieval kingdom of Poictesme, it chronicles the adventures of the pawn-broker Jurgen, who, motivated by guilt and gossip, sets off reluctantly in search of Dame Lisa, his nagging wife, who has been abducted by the Devil. Encountering Dorothy, the love of his youth, he relives one day with her through the power granted him by the earth goddess. He goes on to erotic experiences with such legendary women as Guinevere before his ultimate reunion with his wife. The New York Society for the Prevention of Vice declared *Jurgen* obscene and banned all displays and sales, and Cabell achieved considerable notoriety during the two years it could not be sold legally.

Kaddish Long poem in five parts by Allen GINSBERG, published in 1961 in *Kaddish and Other Poems: 1958–1960*. Taking its name from the Jewish hymn of mourning, *Kaddish* is an emotionally driven, personal eulogy, composed under the influence of hallucinogenic drugs, for Ginsberg's mother, Naomi, who died insane in 1956.

King, Queen, Knave Novel by Vladimir NABOKOV, first published in Russian in 1928. Franz, an unsophisticated young man, works in the department store of his rich uncle Dreyer. Out of boredom Martha, Dreyer's young wife, seduces Franz, and the lovers subsequently plot to drown Dreyer and marry each other. Martha changes her mind abruptly when she learns that an invention by Dreyer stands to increase his wealth, but she dies suddenly from pneumonia and her husband never discovers her duplicity. With this novel, Nabokov began his career-long obsession with games (the image of a deck of playing cards is used throughout), wordplay in several languages, and multiple surreal images and characterizations.

Last Leaf, The Short story by O. HENRY, published in 1907 in *The Trimmed Lamp and Other Stories*. Johnsy, a poor young woman seriously ill with pneumonia, believes that she will die when the ivy vine on the wall outside her window loses all its leaves. Her neighbor Behrman, an artist, tricks her by painting a leaf on the wall. Johnsy recovers, but Behrman, who caught pneumonia while painting the leaf, dies.

Last of the Mohicans(: A Narrative of 1757), The The second and most popular of THE LEATHERSTOCKING TALES by James Fenimore COOPER, first published in two volumes in 1826. Its protagonist, Natty Bumppo (or Hawkeye, as he is known in this novel), is in middle life and at the height of his powers. The story, set during the French and Indian War, tells of brutal battles with the Iroquois and their French allies, cruel captures, narrow escapes, and revenge, as Hawkeye and his Mohican friends Uncas and Chingachgook help the daughters of a British commander rejoin their father.

Last Tycoon, The Unfinished novel by F. Scott FITZGERALD, published posthumously in 1941. As edited by Edmund Wilson, it contains six completed chapters, an abridged conclusion, and some of Fitzgerald's notes. The work is an indictment of the Hollywood film industry, in which Fitzgerald had a disappointing career as a screenwriter. Monroe Stahr is a studio executive who has worked obsessively to produce high-quality films without regard for their financial prospects, taking a personal interest in every aspect of the studio. Almost burned out at 35, he loses control of the studio and his life over the course of the novel.

Leatherstocking Tales, The Series of five novels by James Fenimore COOPER, published between 1823 and 1841. A saga of 18th-century life among Indians and white pioneers on the New York State frontier, the novels focus on the adventures of Natty Bumppo, who takes on various names, including Leatherstocking, throughout the series. The books cover his life from youth to old age, though they were not written or published in chronological order. The individual novels are THE PIONEERS (1823), THE LAST OF THE MOHICANS (1826), THE PRAIRIE (1827), THE PATHFINDER (1840), and THE DEERSLAYER (1841). Leatherstocking dies in *The Prairie*, and Cooper intended him to rest in peace, but many years later he resuscitated the character and portrayed his early maturity in *The Pathfinder* and his youth in *The Deerslayer*.

Leaves of Grass Collection of poetry by Walt WHITMAN, first presented as a group of 12 poems published anonymously in 1855. The initial publication, which contained SONG OF MYSELF and I SING THE BODY ELECTRIC, was followed by five revised and three reissued editions during the author's lifetime. Poems not published in his lifetime were added in 1897; the collection thus eventually included virtually his entire poetic output. The poems' unconventional language and subjects exerted strong influence on American and foreign literature but also led to the book's suppression on charges of indecency. In a preface (deleted from later editions), Whitman maintained that a poet's style should be simple and natural, without orthodox meter or rhyme, like an animal or tree in harmony with its environment. Among the 122 new poems in the third edition (1860–61) were the "Calamus" poems, which record an intense homosexual love affair. The Civil War poems of DRUM-TAPS (1865) and *Sequel to Drum-Taps* (1865), were included in the fourth edition (1867). The seventh edition (1881–82) grouped the poems in their final order, and the eighth edition (1889) incorporated his *November Boughs* (1888).

Left Hand of Darkness, The Science-fiction novel by Ursula K. LE GUIN, published in 1969. The planet of Gethen, or Winter, is inhabited by a race of androgynous humans who may change sexual roles during monthly estrus periods, so that at different times any individual may be either a mother or a father. The plot—interspersed with anthropological comments on the Gethenians as well as extracts from their folklore and philosophy—follows the exploits of Genly Ai, the first ambassador to Gethen from the Ekumen (the league of known worlds), who with the aid of Estraven, a sympathetic Gethenian, attempts to bring the peoples of Gethen into the Ekumen. Le Guin used the novel to express her Taoist view of the complementary nature of all relationships.

Legend of Sleepy Hollow, The Short story by Washington IRVING, first published in THE SKETCH BOOK in 1819–20. Ichabod Crane is a Yankee schoolteacher in the Hudson River town of Sleepy Hollow. A credulous believer in ghosts, he is impressed by the tale of a spectral headless horseman said to haunt the area. He courts Katrina Van Tassel, mostly because she is expected to receive a large inheritance. Abraham Van Brunt (also called Brom Bones), his jealous rival, often plays tricks on him. As Crane rides home at night from a party at Katrina's home, he is frightened by a headless horseman that pursues him and hurls a round object, apparently his head, which later turns out to have been a pumpkin. Crane is never seen in Sleepy Hollow again.

Letters from the Earth Miscellany of fiction, essays, and notes by Mark TWAIN, published posthumously in 1962. Written over a period of 40 years, the pieces are characterized by a sense of ironic pessimism. The title piece comprises letters written by Satan to his fellow fallen angels about the shameless pride and foolishness of humans. "Papers of the Adam Family," a first-person family history of Adam and Eve, traces the first failed attempts at civilization. Other pieces include "A Cat-Tale," an amusing, alliterative bedtime story; "Fenimore Cooper's Literary Offenses," a humorous critique; and "The Damned Human Race," a collection of bitter satirical bits.

Let Us Now Praise Famous Men Nonfictional examination of the daily lives of Depression-era tenant farmers, with text by James AGEE and black-and-white portraits by the photographer Walker Evans, published in 1941. Agee and Evans went to Alabama to report on the lives of tenant farmers in 1936 at the request of *Fortune* magazine. The project evolved over five years into a visually stunning, multilayered work that conveyed in the first person Agee's responses to his subjects as an involved observer, as well as his difficulties in chronicling their lives in this manner.

Life on the Mississippi Mark TWAIN's memoir of the steamboat era on the Mississippi, published in 1883. It begins with a brief history of the river, starting with its discovery by Hernando de Soto in 1541. Chapters 4–22 describe Twain's career (from 1857 until the start of the Civil War) as a Mississippi steamboat pilot, the fulfillment of a childhood dream. The second half tells of Twain's return, in 1882, to travel the river from St. Louis to New Orleans. By then the competition from railroads had made steamboats passé, in spite of improvements in navigation and boat construction. Twain sees new, large cities on the river and records his observations on greed, gullibility, tragedy, and bad architecture.

Life Studies Collection of poetry and prose by Robert LOWELL, published in 1959. A major turning point in Lowell's writing, it helped initiate the 1960s trend to confessional poetry. The first of its four sections, "91 Revere Street," is a prose autobiographical sketch of Lowell's youth amid stormy domestic tensions. The other sections include a series of poems in traditional forms; a group of poems about Ford Madox Ford, George Santayana, Delmore Schwartz, and Hart

Crane; and "Life Studies," 15 confessional poems that include the well-known SKUNK HOUR and "Waking in Blue."

Ligeia Short story by Edgar Allan POE, published in *American Museum* in September 1838 and later in *Tales of the Grotesque and Arabesque* (1840). Its aristocratic narrator describes the beauty and intelligence of his late wife, the dark-haired Ligeia, and how she died convinced that a strong will could stave off death. Distraught, he enters into an unhappy marriage with the fair-haired Lady Rowena Trevanion. He takes to using opium; Rowena falls ill and dies. Sitting with the corpse, he watches in amazement as it rises and sheds the burial shroud, revealing the reborn Ligeia.

Light in August Novel by William FAULKNER, published in 1932, the seventh in the series set in the fictional Yoknapatawpha County, Miss. Its central figure is the orphan Joe Christmas, whose mixed blood condemns him to life as an outsider, hated or pitied. He is frequently whipped by Simon McEachern, the puritanical farmer who raises him. After savagely beating his tormentor, Joe leaves home at 18. He wanders for 15 years, eventually moving in with Joanna Burden, a white woman devoted to helping blacks. Her evangelism comes to remind Joe of Simon's, and he murders her. Betrayed by his companion Lucas Burch, Joe is hunted down, castrated, and killed.

Little Foxes, The Drama in three acts by Lillian HELLMAN, produced and published in 1939. Set at the beginning of the century, it concerns the manipulative Regina Giddens and her two brothers, Ben and Oscar Hubbard, who want to borrow money from her rich, terminally ill husband Horace so that they can open the town's first cotton mill. When Horace discovers that they have arranged the theft of $80,000 in bonds, instead of prosecuting his brothers-in-law, he informs Regina that he will draw up a new will leaving her only $80,000. The threatened disinheritance causes her to reveal all the loathing and disgust she feels for him. When he suffers an attack, she withholds his medication and watches him die. *Another Part of the Forest* (1947) portrays the Hubbard family 20 years earlier.

Little Orphant Annie Poem by James Whitcomb RILEY, first published under the pseudonym "Benj. F. Johnson, of Boone" in the popular collection *The Old Swimmin' Hole and 'Leven More Poems* (1883). The sentimental and cheerfully philosophical poem, written in the Hoosier dialect of Riley's native Indiana, concerns an orphaned girl who tells scary stories about "the Gobble-un" to the children in whose house she lives.

Little Women(, or Meg, Joe, Beth, and Amy) Novel for young people by Louisa May ALCOTT, published in two parts in 1868 and 1869. Meg, Jo, Beth, and Amy March are raised in genteel poverty by their loving mother in a quiet Massachusetts town while their father serves as an army chaplain during the Civil War. They befriend Laurie, the lonely grandson of a rich old man next door. The vital force of the family is Jo, a headstrong tomboy. Beautiful, mature Meg marries Laurie's tutor John Brooke and starts her own family; quiet, sickly Beth dies from scarlet fever; artistic Amy marries Laurie after he is turned down by Jo; and Jo marries Professor Bhaer, whom she meets while living in a boardinghouse. The autobiographical novel had two sequels, *Little Men: Life at Plumfield with Jo's Boys* (1871) and *Jo's Boys and How They Turned Out* (1886), and initiated a genre of family stories for the young.

Lolita Novel by Vladimir NABOKOV, published in 1955. Presented as the posthumously published memoirs of its narrator, the cosmopolitan Humbert Humbert, it chronicles Humbert's obsessive lust for 12-year-old Dolores (Lolita) Haze, in whose house he becomes a lodger and whose mother he weds in order to remain near Lolita. After the mother's sudden death, Humbert takes Lolita on a journey across the U.S., sleeping in motels and cabins, and the two become lovers. They soon discover that they are being silently pursued by an unknown man. The restless and distressed Lolita eventually leaves Humbert for their shadowy pursuer, who is revealed as the writer Clare Quilty; Humbert eventually tracks him down and murders him, after Lolita has gone on to marry another man. The novel examines love in the light of lechery, but also contrasts America and Europe and (at a deeper level) art and life. Brilliantly written, with extravagant wordplay and allusions, it became one of the most admired novels of the 20th century. Its American publication in 1958 created a cultural and literary sensation, and many attempts were made to ban the book.

Long Day's Journey into Night Drama in four acts by Eugene O'NEILL, written 1939–41 and produced and published posthumously in 1956. Considered an American masterpiece, O'Neill's autobiographical play is a shattering depiction of a day in the life of a couple and their two sons. James Tyrone, a semiretired actor, is vain and miserly; his wife Mary retreats into a morphine haze. Jamie, their older son, is a bitter alcoholic. James refuses to acknowledge the illness of his consumptive younger son, Edmund. As Mary sinks into hallucination and madness, father and sons confront each other in searing scenes that reveal their hidden motives and interdependence. *A Moon for the Misbegotten* (1952) was a sequel, charting Jamie's subsequent life.

Look Homeward, Angel(: A Story of the Buried Life) Novel by Thomas WOLFE, published in 1929. A thinly veiled autobiography, it traces the unhappy early years of its introspective protagonist, Eugene Gant, before he sets off for graduate study at Harvard. Wolfe employed a remarkable variety of literary styles in the novel, reflecting Gant's shifting feelings and attitudes: evocative description, acutely realistic dialogue, satire, fantasy, and many meandering passages in which the author becomes intoxicated with his own prose. OF TIME AND THE RIVER continued Gant's story.

Lost Lady, A Novel by Willa CATHER, published in 1923. As seen through the adoring eyes of young Niel Herbert, Marian Forrester, the gracious wife of an industrial magnate and Western pioneer, is the personification of ladylike propriety. She is less perfect in reality than she seems, and her husband's death leads her to drink too much and to look to other men for emotional and financial support. By the time Niel leaves home to start his adult life in Boston, he feels only a "weary contempt" for her. He learns much later that she managed to marry a suitable, wealthy man. The novel depicts the decline of the pioneer spirit and the aridity of small-town life.

Lottery, The Short story by Shirley JACKSON, published in the *New Yorker* in 1948 and included in 1949 in *The Lottery; or, The Adventures of James Harris*. It takes place on the day of a small New England town's annual lottery. Mr. Summers and Mr. Graves conduct the lottery drawing, a festive event that, according to nostalgic Old Man Warner, has lost some of its traditional luster. Tessie Hutchinson is announced as the winner; she begins to protest as the community surrounds her and stones her to death. The unemotional narrative voice underlines the horror of the final act. The much-debated story is often seen as a powerful allegory of barbarism and social sacrifice.

Love Song of J. Alfred Prufrock, The Poetic monologue by T. S. ELIOT, published in *Poetry* magazine in 1915 and in *Prufrock and Other Observations* in 1917. It consists of the musings of a weary middle-aged man haunted by the feeling that he has lost both youth and happiness, having "measured out my life with coffee spoons." Eliot's first major publication and the first masterpiece of modernism in English, "Prufrock" experiments with poetic form, meter, rhyme, and voice in a radical departure from the restrictions of established forms and diction.

Luck of Roaring Camp, The Short story by Bret HARTE, published in 1868 in Harte's *Overland Monthly*. "The Luck" is a baby boy born to Cherokee Sal, a prostitute who dies in childbirth at Roaring Camp, a California gold-rush settlement. The men of the camp decide to raise the child themselves, and his presence inspires them to stop fighting and gambling and to clean up the camp. When they discover gold, they attribute their fortune to the child, but tragedy strikes when a flood sweeps the camp, killing the Luck and his protector.

Magic Barrel, The Collection of 13 short stories by Bernard MALAMUD, published in 1958. It was his first published collection. Most of the stories concern impoverished New York Jews. Their settings are often bleak, their prose reflects the rhythm and style of Yiddish folktales, and their ironic and humorous plots likewise show the influence of Hasidic tales. The title story, first published in 1954, is considered one of Malamud's finest.

Magician of Lublin, The Novel by Isaac Bashevis SINGER, published serially in the Yiddish daily *Forverts* in 1959 and in English translation in 1960. Yasha Mazur is an itinerant professional conjurer, tightrope walker, and hypnotist in late-19th-century Poland. He loves five women, including his barren and pious wife. To support himself, his assorted women, and his plans to escape to Italy, he attempts a robbery and fails, after which he has a crisis of conscience and returns to his wife, becoming a recluse. People begin to refer to him as Jacob the Penitent and treat him as a holy man.

Magnificent Ambersons, The Novel by Booth TARKINGTON, published in 1918. It was the second volume in the trilogy *Growth*, which included *The Turmoil* (1915) and *The Midlander* (1923; later retitled *National Avenue*). It traces the growth of the United States through the decline of the once-powerful and socially prominent Amberson family. Their fall is contrasted with the rise of the industrial tycoons and land developers, whose power comes not through family connections but through financial dealings and modern manufacturing.

Maine Woods, The Collection of three autobiographical narratives by Henry David THOREAU, edited by his frequent touring companion Ellery Channing and issued posthumously in 1864. Each of the essays—"Ktaadn and the Maine Woods," "Chesuncook," and "The Allegash and East Branch"—recounts an excursion in Maine, describing Thoreau's guides and including detailed studies of each area's flora, fauna, and history.

Main Street Novel by Sinclair LEWIS, published in 1920. Carol Kennicott, a young woman married to a Midwestern doctor who settles in the Minnesota town of Gopher Prairie (modeled on Lewis's hometown of Sauk Center), tries to bring culture to the small town, but is rebuffed. The book's power derives from Lewis's careful rendering of local speech, customs, and social amenities. The satire is double-edged—directed against both the townspeople and the superficial intellectualism of those who despise them.

Making of Americans(: Being a History of a Family's Progress), The Novel by Gertrude STEIN, completed in 1911. It was not published in book form until 1925 because of its length and experimental style: it lacks plot, dialogue, and action. The work is ostensibly a history of three generations of Stein's forebears; by generalizing from her own family, she claimed that the book was the history of all Americans. By achieving prose equivalents of the great similarity she discerns among the various personalities described, Stein produced what many readers have deemed a repetitious, prolix compilation of vignettes.

Maltese Falcon, The Mystery novel by Dashiell HAMMETT, originally serialized in *Black Mask* in 1929 and published in book form the next year. The novel, generally considered Hammett's best, creates sustained tension through its vivid scenes and the pace and spareness of his style. Its colorful cast of characters includes the gritty detective Sam Spade, the deceptive beauty Brigid O'Shaughnessy, the effeminate Joel Cairo, the fat and jovial but sinister Casper Gutman, and Gutman's "gunsel" Wilmer, eager to be feared. All seek the Maltese falcon, a 16th-century artifact.

Manchild in the Promised Land Autobiographical novel by Claude Brown, published in 1965. The hero, Sonny, narrates the story of his escape from the addiction and violence that defined his childhood in Harlem. Sent to the Wiltwyck School for Boys at 9, he is encouraged to pursue an education, but once back home he returns to stealing and selling drugs. After more time in reform school, he escapes the neighborhood and immerses himself in African and African-American culture. The most vivid passages detail Sonny's return visit to Harlem, where he discovers his younger brother mired in a life of crime and both an old friend and a former sweetheart destroyed by heroin. Brown's realistic depiction of desperate inner-city poverty shocked millions of readers unfamiliar with ghetto life.

Mansion, The Novel by William FAULKNER, published in 1959 as the third volume of his Snopes trilogy. The rapacious Snopes family meets its final dissolution in *The Mansion*. Whereas *The Hamlet* (1940) and *The Town* (1957) described the ruthless Flem Snopes's ascent to power in Jefferson, Miss., *The Mansion* focuses on his stepdaughter Linda—widowed and deafened while fighting alongside her husband for the Loyalists in the Spanish Civil War—and her return to Jefferson.

Man That Corrupted Hadleyburg, The Short story by Mark TWAIN, first published in *Harper's* magazine in 1899 and collected in *The Man That Corrupted Hadleyburg* in 1900. It relates the downfall of the citizens of a town—which boasts of its honesty with the motto "Lead us not into temptation"—when a mysterious stranger exposes their underlying greed and hypocrisy. The story reflects Twain's disillusionment and pessimism after a period of financial reversals and sadness over the death of his daughter.

Man with the Golden Arm, The Novel by Nelson ALGREN, published in 1949. Set on Chicago's West Side, it evokes the gritty street life of petty criminals and hustlers. The hero, Frankie Machine, is a shrewd poker dealer whose once "golden" arm begins shaking as he increasingly relies on morphine to overcome the pain of a war injury and to numb the guilt he feels for a drunken spree that put his wife Sophie in a wheelchair. Much of the psychological action centers on Sophie's attempts to manipulate her husband. After killing his drug dealer, Frankie hangs himself in a seedy hotel.

Ma Rainey's Black Bottom Drama in two acts by August WILSON, performed in 1984 and published in 1985. Set in a recording studio in Chicago in 1927, it features the historical blues singer Ma Rainey and the members of her band, and comments on the violence perpetrated by blacks against other blacks in their frustration over exclusion from white society. The play is part of a series portraying the lives of African-Americans decade by decade.

Marble Faun(; or, the Romance of Monte Beni), The Novel by Nathaniel HAWTHORNE, published in 1860. A statue of a faun by Praxiteles that Hawthorne saw in Florence provided him with a symbol of the fall of man from amoral innocence to the knowledge of good and evil. The faun of the novel is Donatello, a passionate young Italian who meets three American artists, Miriam, Kenyon, and Hilda, who are spending time in Rome. When Donatello kills a man who has been shadowing Miriam, the act precipitates his moral maturation; he eventually turns himself over to the police. Miriam and Hilda are also tainted by guilt.

Mardi (and a Voyage Thither) Third novel by Herman MELVILLE, originally published in two volumes in 1849. The action involves two whaling-ship deserters—the American Taji and the Norwegian Jarl—who meet up with a variety of characters, including Yillah, a blonde Pacific Islander who symbolizes Absolute Truth. The novel uses allegory to comment on contemporary ideas—about nations, politics, institutions, literature, and religion. Uneven and disjointed, it was a dismal failure when first published.

Marjorie Morningstar Novel by Herman WOUK, published in 1955. The title character rebels against the confining middle-class values of her industrious Jewish family. When her dream of being an actress ends in failure, she ultimately marries a conventional man with whom she finds sufficient contentment as a suburban wife and mother, thus finally coming to accept her parents' values.

Martin Eden Semiautobiographical novel by Jack LONDON, published in 1909. Martin Eden becomes a writer, hoping to acquire the respectability sought by his society sweetheart, but she spurns him when his writing is rejected by several magazines and he is falsely accused of being a socialist. After he achieves fame she tries to win him back, but he realizes her love is false. Financially successful but robbed of connection to his own class and aware that his quest for bour-

geois respectability was hollow, he travels to the South Seas, where he jumps ship and drowns.

Masque of the Red Death, The Allegorical short story by Edgar Allan POE, first published in *Graham's Magazine* in April 1842. In a medieval land ravaged by the Red Death, a lethal plague, Prince Prospero retreats to his castle with 1,000 knights and ladies and welds the doors and windows shut, confident that he and his guests will escape death. He gives a masquerade ball, and at midnight the grotesquely costumed courtiers find a fearful figure among them, costumed in shrouds and dried blood as the Red Death. Prospero orders its execution, then raises his sword to stab it himself, but falls dead. When others try unsuccessfully to seize it, they realize that it is the Red Death itself, and one by one they expire.

Matchmaker, The Comedy in four acts by Thornton WILDER, produced in 1954 and published in 1955. The wealthy merchant and widower Horace Vandergelder hopes to marry the milliner Irene Molloy. He turns to his late wife's friend Dolly Levi for help, but Dolly wants Horace herself. A series of comic misadventures follow. In 1964 the play was adapted as the hit musical *Hello, Dolly!* (film, 1969). Though more traditional stylistically than Wilder's earlier plays, it employs the nontraditional device of having the characters address the audience directly.

McTeague Novel by Frank NORRIS, published in 1899. The dentist McTeague marries Trina, whose acquisitiveness is revealed when she wins a lottery. Initially free of the destructive avarice that defines Trina and his friend and rival Schouler, McTeague is a bovine "natural man," brutalized by the more rapacious urban characters. His marriage disintegrates as Trina becomes more and more miserly with her fortune and Schouler exposes his lack of a professional license, and he starts drinking heavily. McTeague eventually leaves Trina, taking some of her money; returning for more, he ends up killing Trina. Apprehended by Schouler while crossing Death Valley, he strangles him, but not before Schouler has handcuffed them together, condemning McTeague to die chained to the his enemy's body. The work, in which Norris sought to describe the influence of heredity and environment on human life, was considered the first great portrait in American literature of an acquisitive society.

Member of the Wedding, The Novel by Carson MCCULLERS, published in 1946. Frankie Addams, a 12-

year-old Georgia tomboy, imagines she will be taken by her brother and his bride on their honeymoon. She finds refuge in the company of two equally isolated characters, her ailing 6-year-old cousin John Henry and her father's black housekeeper, Berenice, who serves as both mother figure and oracle. Much of the novel consists of kitchen-table conversations among these three. The threesome is broken by John Henry's death and Berenice's own wedding.

Memoirs of Hecate County Collection of six loosely connected short stories by Edmund WILSON, first published in 1946. Some of the stories are narrated by an upper-middle-class intellectual recollecting his past sexual relationships and friendships in Manhattan and in insular, suburban Hecate County. Each story portrays a different aspect of socially dysfunctional America, including the vapid ritual of the cocktail hour, bogus artists, and the erosion of intellectual rigor by popular culture. Because of the frankly sexual nature of the story "The Princess with the Golden Hair," the book was suppressed on obscenity charges until 1959, when Wilson published a revised edition.

Mending Wall Poem by Robert FROST, published in *North of Boston* (1914). Written in blank verse, it depicts a pair of neighboring farmers working together on the annual spring chore of rebuilding their common wall. The wall serves as the symbolic fulcrum of their friendly antagonism, balancing their contrasting philosophies about brotherhood, which are represented by the sentiments "Good fences make good neighbors" and "Something there is that doesn't love a wall."

Miniver Cheevy Poem by Edwin Arlington ROBINSON, published in *The Town Down the River* (1910). Set in Tilbury Town, the imaginary New England town where he frequently set his poetry, it portrays the melancholy Miniver Cheevy, who, with exaggerated romantic sadness and little insight into his own deficiencies, broods over his misfortune in not having been born in a more colorful era.

Miss Lonelyhearts Novel by Nathanael WEST, published in 1933. A male newspaper columnist takes the nom de plume "Miss Lonelyhearts" and attempts to give advice to the lovelorn, but feels powerless to truly help his generally hopeless correspondents. His boss, Willie Shrike, relentlessly mocks him for taking his job seriously. When Lonelyhearts tries to become personally involved with one of his correspondents, he is killed.

Moby-Dick(; or, The Whale) Novel by Herman MELVILLE, originally published in London in 1851. The narrator (who asks to be called "Ishmael") tells of the last voyage of the whaler *Pequod*, on which Captain Ahab obsessively pursues the white whale Moby-Dick, which has deprived Ahab of his leg. The other characters include the Polynesian harpooner Queequeg, chief mate Starbuck, second mate Stubb, third mate Flask, and the black cabin boy Pip. The ship virtually circles the globe in search of its prey. When Moby-Dick is finally harpooned, Ahab is caught in the line and ends up lashed to the side of the whale as it smashes the ship to splinters; only Ishmael is left alive. On a narrative level, the work is intense and superbly authentic. Its theme and the central figure of Ahab resonate on deeper levels as well, calling to mind Job's search for justice and Oedipus's search for truth. The equivocal defeats and triumphs of the human spirit and its fusion of creative and murderous urges are of central importance. The novel is regarded as its author's masterpiece and one of the greatest of all American novels, though it did not attain that status until after Melville's death.

Mont-Saint-Michel and Chartres(: A Study of Thirteenth-Century Unity) Extended essay by Henry ADAMS, printed privately in 1904 and commercially in 1913. It is best considered a companion to the great autobiography *The Education of Henry Adams* (1918). Adams here describes the medieval worldview as reflected in its cathedrals, which he believed expressed "an emotion, the deepest man ever felt—the struggle of his own littleness to grasp the infinite." Drawn to the ideological unity expressed in Roman Catholicism and symbolized by the Virgin Mary, he contrasted this coherence with the uncertainties of the 20th century.

Moon for the Misbegotten, A Drama in four acts by Eugene O'NEILL, written in 1943, published in 1952, and first performed posthumously in 1957. This sequel to LONG DAY'S JOURNEY INTO NIGHT is set on the Tyrones' Connecticut farm, which has been leased to the bullying widower Phil Hogan. Hogan's daughter Josie loves Jamie Tyrone, Jr., an alcoholic actor who has come back to the farm after his mother's death. To secure his hold on the farm, Hogan convinces Josie that Jamie intends to sell it; he encourages Josie to seduce Jamie and force a marriage proposal. Jamie spurns her advances, reassures her that he is not going to sell the farm, and confesses that he had been too drunk to attend his mother's funeral. They part when Josie realizes that Jamie lives in misery and longs for deliverance in death.

Mosses from an Old Manse Collection of short stories by Nathaniel HAWTHORNE, published in two volumes in 1846. Written while Hawthorne lived at the Old Manse in Concord, Mass., home of R. W. Emerson's ancestors, the 25 tales and sketches include some of his finest short works. Many of the Romantic themes found in his longer fiction find expression here, including the conflict between superficial purity and true spiritual goodness in the gothic tales RAPPACCINI'S DAUGHTER and "The Birthmark," and between Puritan religion and the supernatural in YOUNG GOODMAN BROWN. Also noteworthy are the title essay describing the parsonage and the historical tale ROGER MALVIN'S BURIAL.

Mourning Becomes Electra Trilogy of plays by Eugene O'NEILL, consisting of *Homecoming*, *The Hunted*, and *The Haunted*, produced and published in 1931. Set in the New England of the post–Civil War period and modeled on the *Oresteia* trilogy of Aeschylus, its principal characters are Gen. Ezra Mannon, his wife Christine, his daughter Lavinia and son Orin, Christine's lover (and Ezra's nephew) Capt. Adam Brant, and Lavinia's suitor Peter Niles. It represents O'Neill's most complete use of Greek forms, themes, and characters.

Moviegoer, The Novel by Walker PERCY, published in 1961. A philosophical exploration of the problem of personal identity, the story is narrated by Binx Bolling, a successful but alienated businessman who undertakes a search for meaning in his life, first through an obsession with the movies and later through an affair.

Mr. Flood's Party Rhymed narrative poem by Edward Arlington ROBINSON, published in his *Collected Poems* (1921). Lonely, isolated Eben Flood climbs a hill above the town one moonlit night and walks down an empty road. Frequently drinking from a jug of liquor, "secure, with only two moons listening," he salutes the harvest moon, the bird on the wing, and old times.

Mr. Sammler's Planet Novel by Saul BELLOW, published in 1970. The setting is New York City during the politically tumultuous late 1960s. Sammler, an elderly Polish-Jewish survivor of the Holocaust, is an intellectual who has been injured both physically and psychologically, blind in one eye and suffering from a sense of emotional and intellectual alienation. With his intact eye, he views the world, its people, and their insanities; with his blind eye, he internalizes current events, using his historical and philosophical training to analyze and synthesize.

MS. Found in a Bottle Short story by Edgar Allan POE, published in the Baltimore *Saturday Visiter* (October 1833) as the winner of a contest, and later in *Tales of the Grotesque and Arabesque* (1840). Its narrator, whose journal entries initially reveal him to be a staunch rationalist, begins to accept supernaturalism when a hurricane throws him from his sinking boat onto a large, mystical ship. The crew, made up of extremely aged foreigners who busy themselves with ancient nautical instruments, are oblivious to him, and he walks unnoticed among them. At the end the ship vanishes into a whirlpool in icy, uncharted waters. The story was one of Poe's first notable works.

Mule Bone(: A Comedy of Negro Life in Three Acts) Play about African-American rural life written collaboratively in 1931 by Zora Neale HURSTON and Langston HUGHES; unfinished and unproduced during the authors' lifetimes, it was first published in 1990. It features examples of oral tradition and folklore that Hurston, an anthropologist, had collected in Southern black communities, including "mule-talking," a type of verbal one-upmanship.

Murder in the Cathedral Poetic drama in two parts, with a prose sermon interlude, by T. S. ELIOT, performed at Canterbury Cathedral in 1935 and published the same year. Set in December 1170, it is a modern miracle play on the martyrdom of St. Thomas Becket, archbishop of Canterbury. Its most striking feature is the use of a chorus in the classical Greek manner. The poor women of Canterbury who make up the chorus nervously await Thomas's return from his seven-year exile, fretting over his volatile relationship with King Henry II. Once Thomas arrives, he is confronted with four temptations—worldly pleasures, lasting power as chancellor, recognition as a leader of the barons against the king, and eternal glory as a martyr—all of which he resists. After he delivers his Christmas-morning sermon, four knights accost him and order him to leave the kingdom; when he refuses, they return to slay him in the cathedral. It was Eliot's most successful play.

Murders in the Rue Morgue, The Short story by Edgar Allan POE, first published in *Graham's* magazine in 1841. It opens with the discovery of the grisly murder of an old woman and her daughter. The police are baffled by the fact that the murderer has managed to escape even though the women's apartment appears to have been completely sealed from the inside. The genteel but impoverished C. Auguste Dupin and his friend, the story's narrator, offer their services and, through their brilliant interpretation of clues, identify the murderer—an escaped orangutan. In its presentation of an amateur detective who uses "ratiocination" to solve a mystery, it shaped a new genre of fiction and is considered the first work of detective fiction.

Mutiny on the Bounty   Historical novel by Charles Nordhoff and James Norman Hall, published in 1932. The vivid narrative is based on the actual 1789 mutiny against Capt. William Bligh of HMS *Bounty*. Narrated by Roger Byam, a former midshipman and linguist aboard the vessel, it describes how Fletcher Christian and 15 others revolted against the petty, tyrannical Bligh, setting him and a number of loyal men adrift in a small craft in the South Seas. Nordhoff wrote the Polynesian chapters, Hall the British chapters, though each assisted the other. They collaborated on two sequels, *Men Against the Sea* (1934) and *Pitcairn's Island* (1934), which respectively addressed the fate of Bligh's boat and the *Bounty*'s mutinous crew.

My Ántonia   Novel by Willa CATHER, published in 1918. It recounts the history of Ántonia Shimerda, the daughter of Bohemian immigrants who settled on the Nebraska frontier, through the eyes of her lifelong friend, Jim Burden, and contains a number of poetic passages about the disappearing frontier and the spirit and courage of frontier people. Cather's best-known work, it is considered by many her finest achievement.

My Kinsman, Major Molineux   Short story by Nathaniel HAWTHORNE, first published in 1832 in the annual Christmas gift book *The Token*, and collected in *The Snow-Image, and Other Twice-Told Tales* (1851). The setting is New England before the American Revolution. Young Robin Molineux seeks out his kinsman, a major in the British army, hoping to gain access to power, but he finds that the major is scorned and he is advised to make his own way in the world. On one level, the story's theme is the loss of innocence; on another, it may be interpreted as a political allegory of nascent democratic self-government.

Naked and the Dead, The   Novel by Norman MAILER, published in 1948. It concerns a platoon of 13 American soldiers stationed on the Japanese-held Pacific island of Anopopei. With almost journalistic detail, Mailer records the lives of men at war, characterizing the soldiers individually in flashbacks that illuminate their past. The book was hailed as one of the finest American novels to come out of World War II.

Naked Lunch   Novel by William S. BURROUGHS, published in Paris in 1959 and in the United States in 1962. The tale of a junkie's sexual and drug escapades, it was ahead of its time in its nonlinear development, in which scenes are juxtaposed as if in a scrapbook. The story, which incorporates elements of science fiction and crime fiction, seems to satirize American society in its entirety. When first published in America, it provoked controversy and led to an obscenity trial. It is considered Burroughs's best work.

Native Son   Novel by Richard WRIGHT, published in 1940. It addresses white American society's responsibility for the repression of blacks through the story of Bigger Thomas, a black man imprisoned for two murders, the accidental smothering of his white employer's daughter and the deliberate killing of his girlfriend to silence her. In his cell Thomas confronts his growing sense of injustice and concludes that violence is the only alternative to submission to white society.

Natural, The   First novel by Bernard MALAMUD, published in 1952. The promising baseball career of Roy Hobbs, with his bat "Wonderboy," is cut short when he is shot by a mysterious woman. He turns up some 15 years later to play left field for the New York Knights, whose fortunes suddenly and miraculously improve. Off the playing field, Roy is torn between the dangerous affection of Memo Paris, the niece of the team's manager, Pop Fisher, and Iris Lemon, whose love is genuine. After rejecting Iris for Memo, Hobbs agrees to throw a playoff game. During the game he regrets his decision and decides to play honestly, but Wonderboy is split asunder and Hobbs strikes out, losing the game. The story is counted among the finest of all baseball novels.

Nature   Book-length essay by Ralph Waldo EMERSON, published anonymously in 1836. In it Emerson reevaluates traditional views of God and Nature, asserting that humans can transcend the materialistic world of sense experience and facts to become conscious of the all-pervading spirit of the universe and the potentialities of human freedom. Though these concepts were not original, Emerson's polished style and breadth of vision lent them a particular vividness. A formulation of Emerson's essential philosophy, the essay helped initiate Transcendentalism.

Negro Speaks of Rivers, The Poem in free verse by Langston HUGHES, published in the June 1921 issue of *Crisis*. Hughes's first acclaimed poem, it is a panegyric, written in a style derived from Walt Whitman and Carl Sandburg as well as from black spirituals, to people of black African origin throughout history.

Night of the Iguana, The Three-act drama by Tennessee WILLIAMS, produced and published in 1961. Williams abandoned his usual Southern settings and themes in this tale of tourists at a seedy Mexican hotel. Though its first act is noted for its detailed evocation of a dank jungle, some critics found the plot and the characters—among them a defrocked priest, a lusty widow, and a dying poet—overblown.

Notes Towards the Definition of Culture Critical treatise by T. S. ELIOT, published as a series of articles in *New England Weekly* in 1943 and in book form in 1948. Eliot presents culture as an organic, shared system of beliefs that cannot be planned or artificially induced. Its chief means of transmission, he holds, is the family. The book has been viewed as a critique of postwar Europe and a defense of conservatism and Christianity.

O Captain! My Captain! Three-stanza poem by Walt WHITMAN, published in *Sequel to Drum-Taps* in 1865. An elegy on the death of Abraham Lincoln, it portrays him as the captain of a sea-worn ship (the Union), triumphant after the Civil War. While "The ship is anchor'd safe and sound, its voyage closed and done," the Captain lies on the deck, "Fallen cold and dead." From 1867 the poem was included in *Leaves of Grass*. Highly popular, despite its sentimentality, it displays regular form, meter, and rhyme.

Occurrence at Owl Creek Bridge, An Short story by Ambrose BIERCE, published in 1891 in *Tales of Soldiers and Civilians*. A Southern planter is being hanged on a bridge by Union soldiers. As the noose is tightened, he falls into the river and escapes as the soldiers fire at him. Making his way home, he runs toward the waiting arms of his wife just as his neck breaks in the noose, revealing the escape as only a final desperate fantasy.

Octopus(: A Story of California), The Novel by Frank NORRIS, published in 1901. It examines the struggle of California wheat farmers in the San Joaquin valley against the powerful Pacific and Southwestern Railroad monopoly. A leading example of American naturalism, the novel dramatizes the issues of environmental determinism and social justice. It was the first volume of *The Epic of the Wheat*, Norris's unfinished trilogy about the production, distribution, and consumption of American wheat.

Of Mice and Men Novella by John STEINBECK, published in 1937. The tragic story, given poignancy by its objective narration, is about the complex bond between two migrant laborers. George Milton and Lennie Small are itinerant ranch hands who dream of one day owning a small farm. George looks after Lennie, who is large and simpleminded, calming him and helping to rein in his immense physical strength. When Lennie accidentally kills the ranch owner's flirtatious daughter-in-law, George shoots his friend rather than allow him to be captured by a lynch mob. The book, which Steinbeck adapted into a play (produced 1937), earned him national renown.

Of Time and the River(: A Legend of Man's Hunger in His Youth) Novel by Thomas WOLFE. Begun in 1931, it underwent wholesale editing by Wolfe and his editor, Maxwell Perkins, before being published in 1935 as a sequel to LOOK HOMEWARD, ANGEL (1929). It chronicles the maturing of the autobiographical Eugene Gant as he leaves his Southern home for the wider world of Harvard University, New York City, and Europe.

Old Forest, The Title story of *The Old Forest and Other Stories* (1985) by Peter TAYLOR, a collection of 14 pieces representative of 50 years of his fiction, most of which concerns upper-middle-class Southerners whose privileged, semiagrarian way of life is vanishing as the South becomes industrialized and urbanized. The action is recalled by Nat Ramsey after 50 years; he remembers a snowbound day in 1937, a week before his marriage to the debutante Caroline Braxley, when he took Lee Ann Deehart, a girl of "unknown origins," for an innocent ride in his car. The car was involved in an accident, and Lee Ann ran away, disappearing into the old forest. The Braxleys refused to let the wedding take place until Lee Ann was located and any hint of scandal dissipated.

Old Man and the Sea, The Novella by Ernest HEMINGWAY, published in 1952. Written in Hemingway's characteristically spare prose, it concerns an old Cuban fisherman named Santiago who catches a magnificent fish after weeks of catching nothing. After three days of playing the fish, he finally manages to reel it in and lash it to his boat, only to have sharks eat it as he returns to the harbor. The other fishermen marvel at the size of the skeleton; Santiago is spent but triumphant. Completed after a 10-year literary drought, it would be Hemingway's last major work of fiction.

Omoo(: A Narrative of Adventures in the South Seas) Novel by Herman MELVILLE, published in 1847 as a sequel to TYPEE. Based on his own experiences in the South Pacific, this episodic novel, more comical than *Typee*, tells of the narrator's participation in a mutiny on a whaler and his subsequent wanderings in Tahiti with the ship's former doctor.

One of Ours Novel by Willa CATHER, published in 1922. The story of a Nebraska farmboy who dies fighting in France in World War I, it was based on letters written by a cousin of Cather's who had died in the war. It took her four years to write and became a best-seller.

On the Road Novel by Jack KEROUAC, published in 1957. It describes a series of five frenetic trips back and forth across the United States over the course of five years by Sal Paradise (Kerouac's fictional self) and his wildly adventurous companion, the reform-school graduate Dean Moriarty (a version of Kerouac's friend Neal Cassady). In love with life, beauty, jazz, sex, drugs, speed, and mysticism, the two pursue their amorous escapades and their search for sensation, thumbing their noses at middle class conformity and the pursuit of security. Kerouac wrote his early version of the book in 1947; he wrote a new version in 1951, typing on a continuous roll of paper over a period of three weeks. Though not published for another six years, it became one of the first novels associated with the Beat movement; enormously popular among young people, it won Kerouac a huge cult following.

Open Boat, The Short story by Stephen CRANE, published in *The Open Boat and Other Tales of Adventure* in 1898. It recounts the efforts of four survivors of a shipwreck—a newspaper correspondent, the ship's cook, the captain, and the oiler—to remain afloat in a dinghy on the rough seas. The narrative, told from a shifting point of view, reveals nature's indifference.

O Pioneers! Regional novel by Willa CATHER, published in 1913. It is known for its vivid portrayal of the hardships of prairie life and of the struggle of immigrant pioneer women. Partly based on Cather's Nebraska childhood, it reflects her belief in the primacy of spiritual and moral values over the purely material. Its heroine, Alexandra Bergson, exemplifies the courage and purpose Cather felt were necessary to subdue the wild land. The title is taken from Walt Whitman's "Pioneers! O Pioneers!" which, like the novel, celebrates frontier virtues of inner strength and spirit.

Our Town Drama in three acts by Thornton WILDER, produced and published in 1938. Set in Grover's Corners, N.H. (approximately the site of the MacDowell Colony, where it was written), it features a narrator, the Stage Manager, who sits at the side of the unadorned stage and explains the action. The other characters reveal themselves to the audience through flashbacks, dialogue, and direct monologues. George Gibbs, a doctor's son, and Emily Webb, a newspaper editor's daughter, court and marry; Emily dies in childbirth, and she and other inhabitants of the graveyard describe their peace. Considered enormously innovative for its lack of props and scenery and revered for its sentimental yet realistic depiction of rural America, *Our Town* soon became a staple of the American theater.

Outcasts of Poker Flat, The Short story by Bret HARTE, first published in the *Overland Monthly* in 1869 and later published in *The Luck of Roaring Camp* (1870). When the despised exiles of a California mining camp in 1850 are caught in a blizzard, they show they are capable of acting unselfishly to help others in danger. A minor classic of American literature, the tale is one of the best examples of Harte's local-color fiction.

Out of the Cradle Endlessly Rocking Poem by Walt WHITMAN, first published as "A Word out of the Sea" in the 1860 edition of *Leaves of Grass*. A long poem, one of the most powerful in the collection, it is written in lyrical free verse. A boy stands by the seashore at night listening to the song of a mockingbird mourning its mate; at the same time he listens to the death song of the sea and realizes that "my own songs awaked from that hour." The lonely mockingbird, singing to relieve his solitude, is a metaphor for the poet, while the sea is a symbol of the spiritual world to which poetry is witness.

Ox-Bow Incident, The Novel by Walter van Tilburg CLARK, published in 1940. Set in Nevada in 1885, it depicts the brutal lynching of three characters falsely accused of murder and theft. The lynch mob's strong-willed leader, Major Tetley, easily takes advantage of the townspeople's suppressed resentment and boredom. This psychological study of corrupt leadership and mob rule was read as a parable of fascism when it first appeared.

Painted Bird, The Novel by Jerzy KOSINSKI, published in 1965 and revised in 1976. A dark-haired Polish child who is taken for either a Gypsy or a Jew loses his parents in the mayhem of World War II and wanders through the countryside, at the mercy of the brutal, thickheaded peasants he meets in the villages. He learns how to stay alive at any cost, turning survival into a moral imperative. Full of graphic depictions of rape, torture, and bestiality, the novel portrays evil in many manifestations and represents human isolation as inevitable. The boy's ordeals parallel what Kosinski claimed were his own wartime experiences.

Pale Fire Novel in English by Vladimir NABOKOV, published in 1962. A unique tour de force, it consists of a long poem by the great American poet John Shade, followed by a lengthy commentary on it by Charles Kinbote, an insane pedant who imagines himself the deposed king of the country of Zembla. Having managed to acquire the house next to Shade's near the college where they both teach, Kinbote descries in Shade's poem, which he has stolen after Shade's death, an elaborate coded account of Kinbote's life and the coming assassination attempt against him. A brilliant parody of literary scholarship, based partly on Shakespeare's *Timon of Athens*, *Pale Fire* is also an experimental synthesis of Nabokov's talents for both poetry and prose, extending and completing his mastery of unorthodox structure.

Pale Horse, Pale Rider Collection of three novellas by Katherine Anne PORTER, published in 1939. The title story concerns an affair between a newspaperwoman and a soldier during the influenza epidemic of 1918–19. The other two novellas are "Noon Wine" and "Old Mortality." For their stylistic grace and sense of life's ambiguity, these stories are considered some of Porter's best.

Paterson Long poem by William Carlos WILLIAMS, published in five consecutive parts, each a separate book, between 1946 and 1958; fragments of a sixth volume appeared posthumously in 1963. According to Williams, "a man in himself is a city," and Paterson is both an industrial city in New Jersey and a character of that name. Written principally in Williams's "variable-foot" free verse, *Paterson* has a mosaic structure, with occasional passages of prose, including letters and a diary, integrated into the poem.

Pathfinder(: or, The Inland Sea), The Novel by James Fenimore COOPER, published in two volumes in 1840. Chronologically the third of THE LEATHERSTOCKING TALES, it was the fourth of the five to be published.

Natty Bumppo (the Pathfinder), now 40, comes to the aid of a British colonial garrison under attack during the French and Indian War. He dearly loves Mabel Dunham, daughter of a sergeant. She refuses his offer of marriage, being in love with his friend Jasper Western, who is under suspicion of being a traitor, largely because of his fluency in French. The actual traitor, Lieut. Davy Muir, is eventually killed. At the novel's end Mabel and Jasper are married. The story also includes an Indian heroine, Dew-of-June.

Patriotic Gore(: Studies in the Literature of the American Civil War) Collection of 16 essays by Edmund WILSON, published in 1962. They reveal contemporaneous attitudes toward the Civil War and the effects of the postwar Reconstruction period. Among their subjects are Oliver Wendell Holmes, Jr., diaries of Southern women from various social strata, fiction such as Harriet Beecher Stowe's *Poganuc People* and George W. Cable's *Old Creole Days*, and memoirs by Grant and Sherman and their Confederate counterparts, Robert E. Lee and John Mosby.

Paul Revere's Ride Poem by Henry Wadsworth LONGFELLOW, published in 1861 and later in *Tales of a Wayside Inn* (1863). Written in anapestic tetrameter meant to suggest the galloping of a horse, this popular folk ballad about the American Revolutionary hero is narrated by the landlord of an inn who remembers Revere's famous "midnight ride" to warn the Americans about the impending British invasion. Though historically inaccurate, the poem created an American legend.

Paul's Case Short story by Willa CATHER, published in *The Troll Garden* in 1905. Paul, a sensitive high-school student who despises his middle-class family and home and sees the art world as a glamorous alternative, frequents art galleries, concert halls, and theaters until his father pulls him out of school and sends him to work in an office. After stealing money from the firm, he runs away to New York, where he buys elegant clothes and rents a luxurious room in the Waldorf Hotel. When he learns that his father is coming to find him, he realizes that his idyllic life is over and commits suicide.

Pearl, The Novella by John STEINBECK, published in 1947. Kino, a Mexican Indian pearl diver, finds a valuable pearl. He is soon beset by the greedy people of his village; disaster and bereavement follow, and Kino eventually throws the pearl back into the ocean. Steinbeck's retelling of a Mexican folk tale inverts the biblical parable of the Pearl of Great Price.

Penrod Comic novel by Booth TARKINGTON, published in 1914. Penrod Schofield, a 12-year-old boy from a small Midwestern city, rebels against his parents and teachers and experiences the baffling ups and downs of preadolescence. Tarkington writes with charm and humor about Penrod's escapades, while expertly conveying the speech and behavior of young boys. *Penrod and Sam* (1916) and *Penrod Jashber* (1929) are its sequels.

Personae(: The Collected Poems of Ezra Pound) Anthology of short verse by Ezra POUND, published in 1926. It contains many of his shorter poems, including selections from the earlier collections *A lume spento* (1908), *A Quinzaine for This Yule* (1908), *Personae* (1909), *Exultations* (1909), *Canzoni* (1911), *Ripostes* (1912), and *Lustra* (1916), but emphasizes his later verse.

Petrified Forest, The Drama in two acts by Robert E. SHERWOOD, published and produced in 1935. A melodramatic Depression-era tale of frustrated lives and spiritual emptiness, it is set in a gas station and lunchroom along an Arizona highway. Gabby, the owner's daughter, is unhappy with her desert life and longs to go to Paris to paint. She falls in love with Alan Squier, a failed author who stops at the restaurant on his way to California and proposes elopement. Everything changes when the escaped criminal Duke Mantee arrives and holds them hostage. Though flawed by didacticism and romantic clichés, the play offers insight into the search for values in a decadent civilization.

Piano Lesson, The Drama in two acts by August WILSON, produced in 1987 and published in 1990. It forms part of Wilson's decade-by-decade cycle about the life of African-Americans. The setting is Pittsburgh in 1936, at the house of a family that has migrated from Mississippi. The conflict centers around a piano that was once traded by the family's white master for two of the family's ancestors. Boy Willie and Berniece, the siblings who inherit the piano (into which the family history has been carved), argue about whether to sell it. Berniece's climactic refusal to allow Boy Willie to move the piano exorcises both the literal and figurative ghosts of the white slave owner who has been haunting the family.

Piazza Tales, The Collection of sketches and short fiction by Herman MELVILLE, published in 1856. The sketch "The Piazza" describes Melville's farmhouse, "Arrowhead," in Pittsfield, Mass. The collection's other tales, including BARTLEBY THE SCRIVENER and BENITO CERENO, were supposedly narrated on the house's piazza.

Picnic Drama in three acts by William INGE, produced and published in 1953. The lives of a group of lonely women in a small Kansas town are disrupted by the appearance of a virile, charming drifter. Inge slightly rewrote the ending in a 1962 version called *Summer Brave*. The popular play captured the frustrations and limitations of Midwestern life.

Pictures from Brueghel(, and Other Poems) Collection of poetry by William Carlos WILLIAMS, published in 1962. Williams here transcends the objectivist style of his earlier work, treating poetry as a medium for ideas as well as a means of depicting the physical world. Seeking a rhythm suited to American speech, he experimented with a version of free verse he termed *versos sueltos* ("loose verses"), which employs the triadic stanza and a "variable foot" measure.

Pierre; or, The Ambiguities Novel by Herman MELVILLE, published in 1852. An intensely personal work, *Pierre* reveals the somber mythology of Melville's private life. When Pierre Glendinning, a well-to-do young man, discovers that he has an illegitimate half-sister, he tries to provide for her by taking her to live in New York City, where they live in poverty as he attempts to make a living as a writer. Partly through their relationship, which becomes incestuous, he ultimately destroys both their lives as well as that of his fiancée. The novel, rooted in Melville's relationships with his own family, was a resounding critical failure.

Pigeon Feathers (and Other Stories) Collection of short fiction by John UPDIKE, published in 1962. The well-known title story concerns 14-year-old David Kern's religious doubts, his fear of death, and his triumphant return to faith, the unexpected gift he receives while shooting pigeons in a barn. In such other early stories as "Flight" and "Friends from Philadelphia," Updike attempts to capture overlooked or unexpected moments and instances of beauty in everyday life.

Pilot(: A Tale of the Sea), The Novel by James Fenimore COOPER, published in two volumes in 1823. It features a mysterious and almost superhuman American sea pilot (based on John Paul Jones) who fights battles off the coast of England against the British and American loyalists. One of the book's themes is the ambiguous nature of loyalty. Though often complicated by nautical terminology and intrusive philosophical dialogue, the novel is noted for its spiritual and moral dimensions. Admired for its authentic portrayal of a seafaring life, it launched a whole genre of maritime fiction.

Pioneers(; or, The Sources of the Susquehanna), The One of THE LEATHERSTOCKING TALES by James Fenimore COOPER, first published in two volumes in 1823. The first of the *Leatherstocking Tales* to be published, it was the penultimate volume in terms of narrative chronology. Natty Bumppo (Leatherstocking) is an old man, as is his Indian friend Chingachgook; together they have seen the frontier change from wilderness to settlement, and they know their way of life is about to vanish. The first and finest detailed portrait of frontier life in American literature, the book has been called the first truly original American novel.

Pit and the Pendulum, The Gothic horror story by Edgar Allan POE, first published in 1843 in *The Gift,* an annual giftbook. Like many of his stories, it is a dramatic monologue. Sentenced to death by the Spanish Inquisition, the imprisoned narrator finds himself in absolute darkness, in danger of falling down a pit in the center of the cell to his death. After narrowly escaping the razor-edged blade of a swinging pendulum, he is forced toward the pit as the hot metal dungeon walls begin to close in. Just as he begins to slip, the walls recede and he is rescued. The story helped secure Poe's reputation as a master of lurid gothic suspense.

Pnin Novel written in English by Vladimir NABOKOV, published in 1957. It is a comic and tender portrait of a defenseless intellectual—Timofey Pnin, an older, exiled Russian professor of entomology at Waindell College in upstate New York—trying to deal with the complexities of American life. It is one of Nabokov's best-loved, if not major, works. Pnin turns up again as a minor character in PALE FIRE.

Poetry Poem by Marianne MOORE, first published in 1921. Moore's original poem ran to 30 lines; she cut it to 13 lines in 1924, replaced most of the excised lines in 1935, and again cut it drastically in 1967. Most critics prefer the 1935 poem published in *Selected Poems* (1935). Beginning with the famous line "I, too, dislike it," Moore examines her ambivalent feelings toward poetry, which, she feels, is not important in itself but can be "useful" if written properly. A "useful" poem, she believes, is one that has successfully merged the world of the imagination with that of the senses; a poet's subject, she holds, should arise from firsthand experience.

Ponder Heart, The Comic novella by Eudora WELTY, published in 1954. Miss Edna Earle Ponder, one of the last members of a once-prominent family, and manager of the Beulah Hotel in Clay, Miss., tells a traveling salesman the history of her family and fellow townsfolk. The novel, cast as a monologue, is rich with colloquial speech and descriptive imagery.

Poor Richard's Almanac Almanac edited by Benjamin FRANKLIN under the pseudonym Richard Saunders, 1732–57. Poor Richard, initially a dim-witted astronomer, metamorphosed over the years into a quiet country dweller who was a rich source of prudent and witty aphorisms on the value of thrift, hard work, and the simple life, as epitomized by the famous "Early to bed and early to rise, makes a man healthy, wealthy, and wise." His character, delineated mainly by his comments in the almanac's margins, made him worthy of his own novel, though Franklin never wrote one. Some of the epigrams have been traced to earlier sources.

Porgy Novel by DuBose HEYWARD, published in 1925. Based partially on Heyward's experiences working on the wharves in Charleston, S.C., *Porgy* records the tragic story of a crippled black beggar and his mistress, Bess. Narrated in a simple, straightforward style, the authentic rendering of black life on Catfish Row led many readers to assume mistakenly that Heyward himself was black. He and his wife, Dorothy, dramatized the book in 1927. It became the basis for the famous "folk opera" *Porgy and Bess*, with music by George Gershwin and libretto by Ira Gershwin and Heyward.

Portnoy's Complaint Novel by Philip ROTH, published in 1969. A minor classic of Jewish-American literature, this comic novel is structured as a confession to a psychiatrist by Alexander Portnoy, who relates the often obscene details of his adolescent obsession with masturbation and his subjection to his possessive mother, Sophie. Portnoy's "complaint" refers to the damage done to him by the culture that has shaped him; though he is successful, his achievements are marred by his nagging guilt.

Portrait of a Lady, The Novel by Henry JAMES, published in three volumes in 1881. The masterpiece of the first phase of James's career, it is a study of Isabel Archer, a young American woman of great promise who travels to Europe and becomes a victim of her own provincialism. It offers a shrewd appraisal of the American character and the national myth of freedom and equality hedged with historical blindness and pride.

Prairie, The Novel by James Fenimore COOPER, published in two volumes in 1827. The third of the five LEATHERSTOCKING TALES to be published, it is chronologically the last in the series, Natty Bumppo, now an octogenarian, travels with a party of settlers across the still-unsettled prairie of the Great Plains, but ultimately rejects life with the settlers and goes to live out his final days in a Pawnee village, away from the encroaching civilization he distrusts. The novel extols the vanishing American wilderness, disappearing as the West becomes increasingly settled.

Praisesong for the Widow Novel by Paule MARSHALL, published in 1983. The recently widowed Avey Johnson, a wealthy, middle-aged black woman, undergoes a spiritual rebirth and finds a vital connection to her past while visiting a Caribbean island. In her well-received novel, compared by some critics to those of Toni Morrison, Marshall portrays the special anguish of those blacks who, in their drive for material success, have lost touch with their heritage.

Premature Burial, The Short story by Edgar Allan POE, first published in Philadelphia's *Dollar Newspaper* in July 1844. A frequent victim of catalepsy, the narrator has obsessive fears and horrible nightmares that he will be buried alive while comatose. As a precaution, he supplies his tomb with escape routes and provisions. Once, on awakening, he feels trapped in a coffin not of his making; after realizing that he has fallen asleep in a ship's narrow berth, he conquers his morbid fears and ceases to suffer from catalepsy.

Prince and the Pauper, The Novel by Mark TWAIN, published in 1881. The story is set in the 16th century. When the young Prince Edward Tudor of Wales meets the street urchin Tom Canty and discovers that he is his physical twin, the two decide to exchange clothes. In the ensuing mix-up, each is mistaken for the other and both are believed to have gone mad. Edward learns about the dismal lives of commoners, while Tom learns to play the role of a prince and then a king. The novel succeeds as a critique of legal and moral injustices, and Twain's satire of social conventions concludes that appearances often hide a person's true value.

Princess Casamassima, The Novel by Henry JAMES, published in three volumes in 1886. It examines the anarchist violence of the late 19th century through the struggle of Hyacinth Robinson, a man who toys with revolution and is destroyed by it. In the character of the Princess Casamassima, who has rejected the empty social life of her husband to become involved with reformers and proletarian groups in London, James offers a notable portrait of an upper-class reformer.

Professor's House, The Novel by Willa CATHER, published in 1925. Professor Godfrey St. Peter has completed his significant academic work (on Spanish explorers in North America), his daughters have married, and his favorite student has died in World War I. Though his wife has moved into a new house, he prefers to work in his study in the garret of their old house, and there he is almost asphyxiated by a gas leak from a defective stove. He is ready to let go of life when he is saved by Augusta, an old sewing woman who shares the garret. Through her patience and friendship, he learns to accept life on its own terms.

Prophet, The Book of 26 poetic essays by Khalil GIBRAN, published in 1923. The book employs a narrative frame: The Prophet, about to board a ship that will take him back to his homeland after 12 years in a foreign city, is stopped by a group of the city's inhabitants, who ask him to speak to them about the mysteries of life. The essays address such topics as love, marriage, beauty, reason and passion, and death. Though many critics thought Gibran's poetry mediocre, his book of popular mysticism was translated into more than a dozen languages and achieved cult status among American youth for several generations.

Pudd'nhead Wilson(, and the Comedy of Those Extraordinary Twins), The Tragedy of Novel by Mark TWAIN, originally published as *Pudd'nhead Wilson, A Tale* (1894). Roxana, a light-skinned mixed-race slave in the antebellum South, switches her baby with her white owner's baby. Her natural son, Tom Driscoll, grows up in a privileged household to become a criminal who finances his gambling debts by selling her to a slave trader and later murders his putative uncle. Meanwhile, Roxy raises Valet de Chambre as a slave. David ("Pudd'nhead") Wilson, an eccentric lawyer, determines the true identities of Tom and Valet; as a result Roxy is exposed, Wilson is elected mayor, Tom is sold into slavery, and Valet, unfitted for his newly won freedom, becomes an illiterate, uncouth landholder. The novel is noted for its grim humor.

Purloined Letter, The Short story by Edgar Allan POE, first published in an unauthorized version in 1844, published in an enlarged version in the annual *The Gift* in 1845, and collected that year in *Tales*. The Paris police prefect approaches the amateur detective C. Auguste Dupin with a puzzle: a cabinet minister has stolen a letter from a woman of royalty whom he is now blackmailing. Despite a painstaking search of the minister's rooms, the police find nothing. When the prefect later mentions a large reward for the letter, Dupin casually produces it. He later explains to his assistant that by analyzing the minister's personality and behavior, he concluded that the letter would be hidden in plain sight. The tale, an early prototype of detective fiction, has been the subject of scholarly debate, notably between the philosopher Jacques Derrida, who upheld it as a model of ambiguous narrative, and the psychoanalyst Jacques Lacan, who saw it as a sexual allegory.

Q.E.D. Novella by Gertrude STEIN, written in 1903 and published posthumously in 1950 in the three-part novel *Things as They Are*. It is the story of an ill-fated relationship between Adele, an exuberant young woman based on Stein herself, and Helen, who seduces her. Helen eventually rejects Adele for Mabel, a wealthy, manipulative woman who dominates Helen through her money and passionate nature.

Quaker Graveyard in Nantucket, The Poem by Robert LOWELL, published in 1946 in *Lord Weary's Castle*. An elegy for a cousin who died at sea during World War II, the seven-part poem echoes Melville and Thoreau in its exploration of innocence, corruption, sin, and redemption.

Rabbit, Run Novel by John UPDIKE, published in 1960, the first part of a noted tetralogy whose novels are set in successive decades. Its hero is Harry ("Rabbit") Angstrom, a 26-year-old former high-school athletic star who, disillusioned with his present life, flees from his wife Janice and their infant child in a futile search for grace and order. He meets a young woman, who becomes pregnant by him. Janice, drunk, accidentally drowns their own child in the bathtub. In *Rabbit Redux* (1971), Rabbit is working for his wife's father at Springer Motors. A fellow salesman, Charlie Stavros, begins an affair with Janice which results in her moving in with him. Rabbit takes up with two young radicals, one of whom is accidentally killed by a neighbor. In *Rabbit Is Rich* (1981, Pulitzer Prize), the funniest of the novels, Rabbit has relaxed into his new affluence as part-owner of the dealership. He searches for his illegitimate daughter; his son, Nelson, impregnates his girlfriend. A Caribbean vacation with friends leads to a night of spouse-swapping. *Rabbit at Rest* (1990, Pulitzer Prize) sees Nelson running the business and ends with Rabbit's death while playing basketball. Thoroughly unimpressive but rather likable in spite of it, Rabbit seems to represent Updike's view of the broad American middle class.

Ragged Dick (; or, Street Life in New York with the Bootblacks) Book for young people by Horatio ALGER, Jr., published serially in 1867 and in book form in 1868. The immensely popular though formulaic story chronicles the successful rise of the title character from rags to respectability. Like most of Alger's novels, it served a second purpose as a guide to proper behavior for city youth. The story was Alger's first huge success.

Raisin in the Sun, A Drama in three acts by Lorraine HANSBERRY, published and produced in 1959. Titled after a line in Langston Hughes's "Harlem"—"What happens to a dream deferred? Does it dry up / like a raisin in the sun?"—Hansberry's penetrating psychological study of a working-class black family on Chicago's South Side in the late 1940s drew on her own family's experiences. Walter Lee Younger, a chauffeur, hopes to use his father's life-insurance money to open a liquor store with two partners. His mother, with the support of Walter's pragmatic wife Ruth and independent sister Beneatha, instead uses part of it as a down payment on a house in a white neighborhood, and gives the remaining money, including Beneatha's share, to Walter. After a partner absconds with the money, Walter despondently contacts Karl Lindner, a white man who had tried to buy out the Youngers so as to avoid racial integration, intending to accept his offer, but finally rejects the proposal.

Ransom of Red Chief, The Short story by O. HENRY, published in *Whirligigs* in 1910. Two kidnappers make off with the young son of a prominent man only to find that the child is more trouble than he is worth; in the end, they agree to pay the boy's father to take him back. Told in the first person in a humorous, energetic style, the highly popular story reflects the influences of Mark Twain and Ambrose Bierce.

Rappaccini's Daughter Allegorical short story by Nathaniel HAWTHORNE, first published in *United States*

Magazine and Democratic Review (December 1844) and collected in MOSSES FROM AN OLD MANSE. Rappaccini, a scholar-scientist in Padua, has created an Eden of poisonous plants in his lush garden. His lovely daughter Beatrice, nurtured on her father's plants, is imbued with their poison; though her heart is pure, her touch is enough to wither ordinary flowers and her fragrant breath kills butterflies. Giovanni, a student next door, falls in love with Beatrice and becomes contaminated by the garden's poisonous aura. Rappaccini's competitor gives Giovanni an antidote that cures him, but when Giovanni gives it to Beatrice it kills her.

Raven, The Best-known poem by Edgar Allan POE, published in 1845 and collected in *The Raven and Other Poems* the same year. Poe achieved instant national fame with this melancholy evocation of lost love. On a stormy December midnight, a grieving student is visited by a raven who speaks but one word, "Nevermore." As the student laments his lost love Lenore, the raven's insistent repetition of the word becomes an increasingly harrowing response to the student's own fears and longing. The rhyme pattern of the 18 six-line stanzas, *abcbbb*, enhances the gloom of the lyric; the *b* rhymes are, or rhyme with, "Lenore" and "Nevermore." Poe's 1846 essay "The Philosophy of Composition" describes his careful crafting of the poem.

Raven cycle Collection of oral trickster-transformer tales popular mainly among the Indians of the Northwest Pacific Coast from Alaska to northwestern Washington. The tales feature Raven, an alternately clever and stupid bird-human whose voracious appetites give rise to violent and amorous adventures. The cycle begins with a boy's birth and relates his early adventures, including his seduction of his aunt (some versions substitute the daughter of the Sky Chief) and his flight to the sky to escape the ensuing flood. Raven, his child, falls to earth, where he is adopted by a chief; as an adult he transforms the earth from a dark and arid land inhabited by a variety of ferocious monsters into a land of rivers, lakes, and mountains inhabited by animals and human beings. In Raven's later travels, he changes aspects of the physical environment into their present form, often through deception.

Real Life of Sebastian Knight, The Novel by Vladimir NABOKOV, published in 1941. A satire of literary biography and scholarship, it purports to be the true biography of a great writer, the late and neglected Sebastian Knight, written by his half-brother, V., in response to another biographer's belittling analysis of Sebastian. Before long, it turns into a mystery story, as V. searches for the true facts about Sebastian among Sebastian's acquaintances. Himself a mediocre writer, V. eventually suffers a crisis of identity, and his search for the real Sebastian becomes a search for himself. The novel was Nabokov's first prose narrative in English.

Recognitions, The Long first novel by William GADDIS, published in 1955. Wyatt is an artist who prefers copying to creating originals; his forgeries fool art appraisers and art scholars alike. Through art, Gaddis attacks fakes and counterfeits on all levels of society. Though many critics initially disparaged the work for its difficulty, it is now considered by some to be one of the greatest American novels of the mid to late 20th century.

Red Badge of Courage, The Civil War novel by Stephen CRANE, published in 1895. Henry Fleming is eager to demonstrate his patriotism in a glorious battle, but when the slaughter starts he flees the battlefield. He receives his spurious "red badge of courage" when he is slightly wounded by being struck on the head by a deserter. After witnessing a friend's gruesome death he becomes enraged at war's injustice. The courage of common soldiers and the agonies of death cure him of his romantic notions; he returns to his regiment and continues to fight on with true courage and without illusions. The book has been called the first modern war novel because, uniquely for its time, it describes war from the point of view of an ordinary soldier. Though Crane had had no experience of war, his perceptive depiction of warfare and of the soldier's psychological turmoil earned the novel recognition as his masterwork.

Redburn(: His First Voyage) Novel by Herman MELVILLE, published in 1849. A hastily written adventure about Wellingborough Redburn, a genteel but impoverished boy from New York City who endures a rough initiation into life as a sailor, it was based on a trip Melville took to Liverpool in 1839.

Red Pony, The Novel consisting of four related stories by John STEINBECK, published in 1937 and expanded in 1945. In the well-known "The Gift," young Jody Tiflin is given a red pony by his rancher father. He names it Gabilan and raises it under the guidance of the ranch hand Billy Buck. Caught in an unexpected rain, Gabilan catches a cold and dies, despite Billy Buck's ministrations; Jody watches the buzzards alight on Gabilan's body and, distraught, kills one. In the remaining stories—"The Great Mountains," "The Promise," and "The Leader of the People"—Jody develops empathy and learns from his grandfather about "westering," the migration of people to new places and the urge for new experiences.

Reflections in a Golden Eye Novel by Carson MCCULLERS, published in 1941. Set in the 1930s on a Southern army base, it concerns the relationships between self-destructive misfits, whose lives end in tragedy and murder. They include Capt. Penderton, a sadomasochistic latent homosexual; his wife, who is having an affair with Maj. Langdon; the major's wife, who responds to the trauma of her son's death with self-mutilation; Anacleto, a homosexual servant who is befriended by the major's wife; and a voyeuristic army private.

Remembrance Rock Novel by Carl SANDBURG, published in 1948. Sandburg's only novel, the work is a massive chronicle that uses historical facts and both historical and fictional characters to depict American history from 1607 to 1945 in a mythic, passionate tribute to the American people.

Renascence Poem by Edna St. Vincent MILLAY, published in the anthology *The Lyric Year* (1912) and later in her first published collection, *Renascence and Other Poems* (1917). Written when Millay was 20, the 214-line poem, composed in octosyllabic couplets, reflects in simple, direct language the poet's feelings of wonder at the magnitude of the universe and the concepts of God and death.

Richard Cory Best-known poem by Edwin Arlington ROBINSON, published in *The Children of the Night* (1897). The villagers of Robinson's familiar fictional village Tilbury Town, represented by the collective "we," admire and envy Richard Cory, a mysterious fellow villager, for his wealth, education, and manners. Their ignorance of his troubled soul is underscored by the abrupt ending, which reports his suicide.

Rip Van Winkle Short story by Washington IRVING, published in THE SKETCH BOOK in 1819–20. Though set in the Dutch culture of pre–Revolutionary War New York state, it is based on a German folktale. Rip Van Winkle is an amiable farmer who wanders into the Catskill Mountains, where he comes upon a group of dwarfs playing ninepins. He accepts their offer of a drink of liquor and promptly falls asleep. When he awakens 20 years later, he is an old man with a long white beard. When he descends into town, he finds that his wife is dead, his children are grown, and George Washington's portrait has replaced George III's. The old man entertains the townspeople with tales of the old days and his fateful encounter.

Rise of Silas Lapham, The Best-known novel of William Dean HOWELLS, published in 1885. It recounts the moral dilemma of Col. Silas Lapham, a newly wealthy, self-made businessman who has climbed over his former partner on the ladder to success. After Lapham moves from Vermont to Boston, his family befriends the Coreys, a Brahmin family in financial difficulties. Tom Corey, the son, appears to return the love of the Laphams' daughter Irene, but really loves her older sister Penelope. Lapham moves awkwardly in Boston's highly stratified society; at a party he gets drunk and reveals his common origins. Business reversals cause him to contemplate selling a worthless property to an English syndicate, but although resulting money would enable him to continue to rise in society, he at last refuses to sell and bankruptcy results. Though Silas has fallen socially, he has risen morally. Penelope elopes to Mexico with Tom, thus escaping Boston's tedious social strictures.

Road Not Taken, The Poem by Robert FROST, published in the *Atlantic Monthly* in 1915, and used as the opening poem of *Mountain Interval* in 1916. One of Frost's best-known poems, it presents a narrator recalling a journey through a woods, where he must choose which of two diverging roads to travel. The work's meaning has long been disputed; Frost himself claimed it was a parody of the Georgian poet Edward Thomas.

Roderick Hudson First novel by Henry JAMES, serialized in the *Atlantic Monthly* in 1875 and published in book form in 1876. The story, which concerns the conflict between art and the passions, tells of an American sculptor in Italy, who, faltering in both his artistic ambitions and his personal relationships, travels to Switzerland and dies there.

Roger Malvin's Burial Short story by Nathaniel HAWTHORNE, first published in 1832 in the *Token* and collected in MOSSES FROM AN OLD MANSE. Roger Malvin and Reuben Bourne make their way home after a skirmish with Indians. Badly wounded, Roger urges Reuben to leave him and Reuben agrees, swearing that he will either send help or return to give Roger a decent burial. He never fulfills his oath, and for years he lives as if under a curse. His guilt is finally expiated through a tragic sacrifice. The story, though based on fact, is primarily concerned with the theme of real or obsessive guilt, to which Hawthorne returned in much of his fiction.

Rootabaga Stories Collection of children's stories by Carl SANDBURG, published in 1922. These fanciful tales, which feature such silly characters as Hot Dog the Tiger, Gimme the Ax, White Horse Girl, Blue Wind Boy, and Jason Squiff the Cistern Cleaner, reflect Sandburg's interest in folk ballads and nonsense verse. He modeled his expansive fictional land on the Midwest. Succeeding books in the same vein include *Rootabaga Pigeons* (1923), *Rootabaga Country* (1929), and *Potato Face* (1930).

Roots(: The Saga of an American Family) Book combining history and fiction, by Alex HALEY, published in 1976. Inspired by stories recounted by his grandmother in Henning, Tenn., Haley spent 12 years tracing the saga of seven generations of his family, beginning with Kunta Kinte, his Gambian ancestor who was brought to America in 1767. Through oral tradition, Kunta Kinte's descendants kept alive the tales of their forebears through each generation. A runaway best-seller, *Roots* was adapted for television in 1977 and became one of the most widely viewed programs of all time. Its success precipitated a nationwide resurgence of interest in genealogy, particularly among blacks who had regarded their heritage as untraceable. Later investigations cast serious doubts on the accuracy of Haley's story, and he was forced to settle a major plagiarism suit. Nevertheless, *Roots* retains its emotional impact and its significance for black literature.

Roughing It Semiautobiographical novel by Mark TWAIN, published in 1872. A humorous travel book based on Twain's stagecoach journey through the West and his adventures in the Pacific islands, it is full of colorful caricatures of outlandish locals and detailed sketches of frontier life. The narrator, a polite greenhorn from the East, is initiated into rough-and-tumble frontier society and works his way through Nevada, California, and the islands as a prospector, journalist, and lecturer.

Sacred Wood, The Book of critical essays by T. S. ELIOT, published in 1920. Its best-known essay, "Tradition and the Individual Talent," puts forth Eliot's theory of European literary tradition from Homer to the present and of the relationship of the individual poet to that tradition. In another notable essay, "Hamlet and

His Problems," Eliot propounds the theory of the "objective correlative," the use of an external object, event, or situation to evoke emotion in the reader.

Sanctuary Novel by William FAULKNER, published in 1931. A vision of a decayed South set in the author's fictional Yoknapatawpha County, Miss., it pits the idealistic lawyer Horace Benbow against a cast of amoral fiends. Faulkner's dismayed publisher asked him to rewrite it in proof, and he did, refining it without softening its horror. Its seething violence and despair were characteristic of Faulkner, though elsewhere less brutally displayed; its depictions of degraded sexuality generated both controversy and spectacular sales, making it his only popular success during his lifetime.

Sandbox, The One-act play by Edward ALBEE, published in 1959 (with *The Death of Bessie Smith*) and produced in 1960. It is a trenchant satire on false values and the lack of love and empathy in the American family. For his expanded play *The American Dream* (1961), Albee reused the characters from *The Sandbox*—Mommy, Daddy, and Grandma—as well as some of its dramatic material.

Sapphira and the Slave Girl Novel by Willa CATHER, published in 1940. It is set in Virginia in the mid-1800s, on the estate of a declining slaveholding family. The family's matriarch, the strong-willed invalid Sapphira Colbert, attempts to sell Nancy Till, a mixed-race slave girl. Her plot is foiled by her husband Henry and their widowed daughter Rachel Blake. Despite her subtle cruelty toward Nancy, Sapphira has earned the respect of many of her slaves. Henry is a pious miller whose simple upbringing and passivity contrast with his wife's aristocratic and manipulative nature. His nephew Martin, a suave and lecherous ex-soldier, tries to seduce Nancy. Rachel, who helps Nancy flee to Canada, remains at odds with Sapphira over slavery until the death of Rachel's daughter reconciles the pair. Cather appears in the epilogue as a child who notes Nancy's triumphant return 25 years later.

Sartoris Novel by William FAULKNER, published in 1929, a shorter version of a novel that would eventually be published complete in 1973 under the original title, *Flags in the Dust*. Members of the Sartoris family revel in a mythical family history of clan heroism and nobility that is belied by their current desperation and recklessness. Many of Faulkner's later themes (innate brutality, racial tension, the contrast between a romanticized Southern past and a tawdry present) are present in *Sartoris,* which also introduces characters who will feature prominently in later novels, including the crass Snopes family and the lawyer Horace Benbow. Faulkner's third novel, disproportioned and sometimes emotionally overwrought, was the last of his apprentice works and the first set in his fictional Yoknapatawpha County, Miss.

Scarlet Letter, The Novel by Nathaniel HAWTHORNE, published in 1850. Hester Prynne, wife of an older man who has been absent in England for two years, becomes the mother of an illegitimate child in Puritan New England, and is forced to wear the scarlet letter *A* on her chest as punishment for her adultery. She refuses to name the father, despite the exhortations of the community's saintly young minister, Arthur Dimmesdale, who is in fact the father. Hester's husband arrives and, concealing his identity under the name Roger Chillingworth, attempts to learn the identity of Hester's lover. His attention is soon drawn to Dimmesdale, whom he set about tormenting relentlessly. In the end Chillingworth is morally degraded by his monomaniacal pursuit of revenge, and Dimmesdale, broken by his guilt, publicly confesses his adultery before dying in Hester's arms. Only the forthright and deeply sympathetic Hester can face the future bravely, as she plans to take her daughter Pearl to Europe to begin a new life. Dark and compelling in its symbolism, *The Scarlet Letter* is regarded as one of the supreme masterpieces of American literature.

Sea of Grass, The Novel by Conrad RICHTER, published in 1936. Set in New Mexico in the late 19th century, it concerns the often violent clashes between the pioneering ranchers, whose cattle ranged freely through the vast sea of grass, and the farmers, or "nesters," who built fences and plowed the sod. Against this background is set the triangle of rancher Col. Jim Brewton, his unstable Eastern wife Lutie, and the ambitious Brice Chamberlain. Richter casts the story in Homeric terms, with the children caught up in the conflicts of their parents.

Sea-Wolf, The Novel by Jack LONDON, published in 1904. Combining elements of naturalism and romantic adventure, this highly popular novel follows Humphrey Van Weyden, a refined castaway who is put to work on the motley schooner *Ghost.* The ship is run by the brutal Wolf Larsen, intelligent and strong but also antisocial and self-destructive. Hardened by his arduous experiences at sea, Humphrey develops strength of both body and will, protecting another castaway, Maud Brewster, and facing down the increasingly deranged Larsen.

Secret Garden, The Novel for children by Frances Hodgson BURNETT, published in 1911. Mary Lennox, a sickly and unpleasant orphan, is sent to England to live with a reclusive uncle she has never met. His housekeeper takes Mary in hand, turning her into a healthy, delightful child. Exploring the estate, Mary discovers a secret garden that had been abandoned 10 years earlier, after the death of her uncle's wife. She brings the garden back to life and works a similar transformation on her guardian's spoiled, semi-invalid son. The book is a classic of children's literature.

Seize the Day Novella by Saul BELLOW, published in 1956. It examines one day in the unhappy life of Tommy Wilhelm, who has fallen from marginal middle-management respectability to unemployment, divorce, and despair. Like many of Bellow's novels, it exhibits an ambivalent attitude toward worldly success as it chronicles its sensitive, gullible protagonist's quest for meaning in a chaotic and hostile world.

Self-Reliance Best-known essay of Ralph Waldo EMERSON, published in his *Essays* in 1841. Developed from his journals and from a series of lectures he gave in 1836–37, it exhorts the reader to consistently obey "the aboriginal self," or inner law, regardless of institutional rules, popular opinion, tradition, or other social regulators. Its doctrine of self-sufficiency and self-reliance arose naturally from his view that the individual need only look inward for spiritual guidance, previously the province of established churches.

Separate Peace, A Novel by John KNOWLES, published in 1959. Looking back on his youth, the adult Gene Forrester reflects on his days at a New Hampshire boarding school, the Devon School, in 1942, where, though an excellent student, he envied the athleticism and vitality of his friend Phineas (Finny). Virtually unconsciously, he causes Finny to break his leg, sabotaging his athletic career. When the incident is later examined in a mock trial, Finny runs away in dismay on realizing Gene's role in the accident, reinjures himself, and dies during consequent surgery.

Seventeen Humorous novel by Booth TARKINGTON, published in 1916. It recalls the events of one summer in the life of Willie Baxter, his family, and his friends in a Midwestern town. Seventeen-year-old Willie develops a crush on Lola Pratt, a flirtatious, baby-talking visitor, and the novel presents an accurate picture of the emotional ups and downs of the self-absorbed, love-struck teenager.

Shadows on the Rock Novel by Willa CATHER, published in 1931. It is a detailed study of the lives of French colonists in the late 17th century on the "rock"—that is, the city of Quebec. Euclide Auclair is a widowed apothecary who initially desires to return to France but later accepts his frontier surroundings. Much of the story is presented from the perspective of Auclair's daughter, Cécile, who eventually marries the woodsman and fur trader Pierre Charron. Like many of Cather's novels, it evokes the pioneer spirit and emphasizes the importance of religious tradition.

Sheltering Sky, The First novel by Paul BOWLES, published in 1948. Port and Kit Moresby, an American couple of independent means, have been traveling aimlessly for 12 years. By the time they reach Morocco they are disaffected and alienated, and they take up with a series of unreliable, rootless wanderers. On a trip to the desert interior Port contracts typhoid fever—out of apathy he has neglected to be vaccinated—and dies. Kit becomes the prisoner of an Arab and joins his household as his lover, but their liaison soon falls apart. She is found and returned to Oran. Teetering on the brink of insanity, she finds an opportunity to disappear into the crowded bazaar. Bowles's cool, detached prose contrasts with the increasingly violent and irrational events of the novel, long considered a model of existential fiction.

Ship of Fools Novel by Katherine Anne PORTER, published in 1962. She used as a framework Sebastian Brant's famous Renaissance satire *Das Narrenschiff* (1494; *The Ship of Fools*), in which the world is likened to a ship whose passengers, fools and deranged people all, are sailing toward eternity. Porter's novel is set in 1931 aboard a German passenger ship returning to Bremerhaven, Germany, from Veracruz, Mexico. It carries a microcosm of nationalities, including Germans, Americans, Spaniards, Gypsies, and Mexicans. Jews, anti-Semites, political reactionaries, revolutionaries, and neutrals coexist aboard ship; jealousy, cruelty, and duplicity pervade their lives.

Short Happy Life of Francis Macomber, The Short story by Ernest HEMINGWAY, first published in *Cosmopolitan* in 1936 and collected in *The Fifth Column and the First Forty-Nine Stories* (1938). Francis Macomber and his wife Margot are on safari with their English guide. Macomber wounds a lion and runs away in fear. The guide is horrified at his bad sportsmanship; his wife ridicules him, then secretly seduces the guide. The next day, Macomber redeems himself by killing a buffalo cleanly and bravely, and achieves a feeling of happiness he has never known. He stands his ground as another, wounded buffalo charges him; from the car, Margot shoots at it, instead killing her husband at his moment of triumph. The story explores such recurrent Hemingway themes as grace under pressure and adherence to a manly code of behavior.

Show Boat Popular sentimental novel by Edna FERBER, published in 1926. Spanning the period from the 1880s to the 1920s, it chronicles three generations of the Hawks, a theatrical family who live and perform on a Mississippi River steamboat, the *Cotton Blossom*. It insistently addresses issues of race, including miscegenation. The basis of a historic Broadway musical, it has been produced several times for film and television.

Sign in Sidney Brustein's Window, The Drama in three acts by Lorraine HANSBERRY, produced in 1964 and published in 1965. Sidney Brustein is a disillusioned white intellectual. Alton Scales, a black activist who loves Sidney's sister-in-law, Gloria, persuades Sidney to support the candidacy of Wally O'Hara, a local reform politician. Sidney does so but eventually learns of O'Hara's corruption. Sidney's wife, Iris, is an aspiring actress who leaves him to act in television commercials. When Alton learns that Gloria is a prostitute and not a model, he leaves her and Gloria kills herself. Her suicide effects a reconciliation between Sidney and Iris.

Silent Spring Nonfiction work by Rachel CARSON, published in 1962. Carson's meticulous research showed how the standard use of insecticides was killing off not only their intended victims but other creatures up the food chain, and how resistant populations of the pests soon developed, when their natural predators, killed either directly or indirectly by the poisons, were no longer present to control them. Saddened by the environmental damage already done, she urged humility and caution to avoid further upsetting the balance of nature. Carson's superb prose and already solidly established reputation helped ensure the book's immediate effect and subsequent wide influence. Its publication sparked the outcry that eventually led to a ban on DDT, legislation to protect the purity of the water and air, and the launching of the environmental movement.

Sister Carrie First novel by Theodore DREISER, published in 1900 but suppressed until 1912. It tells of a small-town girl who comes to the big city filled with vague ambitions. She is used by men and uses them in turn to become a successful Broadway actress. George Hurstwood, the married man who has run away with her, loses his grip on life and descends into beggary and suicide; his emotional disintegration is a much-praised triumph of psychological analysis. The first masterpiece of the American naturalistic movement and a model for subsequent realist writers, *Sister Carrie* presents the vagaries of urban life with gritty bluntness; it was remarkable in its time in that its ingenuous heroine went unpunished for her transgressions against conventional sexual morality. Its strengths include a brooding but compassionate view of humanity, a memorable cast of characters, and a compelling plot.

Sketch Book (of Geoffrey Crayon, Gent.), The Short-story collection by Washington IRVING, first published in 1819–20 in seven separate parts. Most of its 30-odd pieces concern Irving's impressions of England, but six chapters deal with American subjects. Of these, THE LEGEND OF SLEEPY HOLLOW and RIP VAN WINKLE have been called the first American short stories, though both are actually versions of German folktales. In addition to stories based on folklore, the collection contains travel sketches, literary essays, and miscellany. *The Sketch Book* was the first American work to gain international literary acclaim and popularity, and its unprecedented success allowed Irving to devote himself professionally to a writing career.

Skin of Our Teeth, The Comedy in three acts by Thornton WILDER, performed and published in 1942. From their New Jersey living room, George and Maggie Antrobus (from the Greek *anthropos*, "human")— with their promiscuous daughter Gladys, their hostile and destructive son Henry (who represents the biblical Cain), and their maid Sabina (who represents Lilith, the eternal temptress)—endure the trials of humanity through the ages, from icy destruction to flood and war. Wilder's experimental tour de force employs bizarre anachronisms and audience-involvement techniques to argue that human experience is much the same whatever the time or place.

Skunk Hour Poem by Robert LOWELL, published in LIFE STUDIES (1959). Modeled on Elizabeth BISHOP's "The Armadillo" (the two poets dedicated their respective poems to each other), it is one in a series of confessional poems that characterized Lowell's verse from the 1950s. In the first four stanzas, the narrator describes residents of his coastal resort town in Maine; in the final four, he focuses on his inner turmoil. His anguished reverie gives way to a description of other inhabitants of the town, a bold family of hungry skunks engaged in a single-minded and confident search for food.

Slaughterhouse-Five(; or, The Children's Crusade: A Duty-Dance with Death) Novel by Kurt VONNEGUT, Jr., published in 1969. While serving in the army during World War II, Billy Pilgrim becomes "unstuck in time," and from then on lives concurrently on earth and on the distant planet Tralfamadore. On earth he preaches the fatalistic philosophy of the Tralfamadorians, who know the future of all things, including the inevitable demise of the universe. They are resigned to fate, unfailingly responding to events with their catchphrase "So it goes." Vonnegut blends science fiction with historical fact, incorporating elements of his own experience as a prisoner of war in Dresden during the Allied firebombing of that city.

Slave, The One-act play by Amiri BARAKA, performed and published in 1964. It is the story of a visit by Walker Vessles, who is black, to the home of Grace, his white ex-wife, and Easley, her white husband. While pointing up the black man's low status in American society, Baraka also stresses that he is so victimized and enslaved by his own hatred that he is unable to effect social change.

slave narrative Literary genre consisting of slave memoirs of daily plantation life. The narratives contain humorous anecdotes of the deception and pretenses that slaves engaged in, expressions of religious fervor and superstition, and, above all, a pervasive longing for freedom, dignity, and self-respect. *A Narrative of the Uncommon Sufferings and Surprising Deliverance of Briton Hammon, a Negro Man*, often considered the first slave narrative, was published in Boston in 1760. (*Adam Negro's Tryall*, published in 1703, was about, not by, Adam.) Other early examples include *A Narrative of the Lord's Wonderful Dealings with J. Murrant, a Black* (1784) and *The Interesting Narrative of Olaudah Equiano, or Gustavus Vassa, the African* (1789). Encouraged by abolitionists, publications multiplied during the years 1830–60, which became the major period of slave narratives. Many were based on oral accounts. Though some, such as *Scenes in the Life of Harriet Tubman* (1869), are factual autobiographies, many others were influenced or sensationalized through a desire to arouse sympathy for the abolitionist cause; the reworkings and interpolations in such works are usually obvious. Such narratives as Mattie Griffith's *Autobiography of a Female Slave* (1856) and Richard Hildreth's *The Slave, or Memoirs of Archy Moore* are entirely fictitious. The genre reached its height with the classic *Narrative of the Life of Frederick Douglass, an American Slave* (1845). In the early 20th century folklorists and anthropologists compiled documentary narratives based on recorded interviews with former black slaves; notable compilations include Charles S. Johnson's *Shadow of the Plantation* (1934) and B. A. Botkin's *Lay My Burden Down* (1945), an extract from 17 volumes of narratives collected by interviewers for the WPA Federal Writers' Project. In the later 20th century the growth of black cultural consciousness stimulated renewed interest in the narratives.

Snow-Bound(: A Winter Idyll) Poem by John Greenleaf WHITTIER, published in 1866. This nostalgic pastoral poem recalls the New England rural home of Whittier's youth, where, despite the pummeling of winter's winds and snow, he and his family remained secure and comfortable inside the house.

Snows of Kilimanjaro, The Short story by Ernest HEMINGWAY, first published in *Esquire* magazine in 1936 and later collected in *The Fifth Column and the First Forty-Nine Stories* (1938). The stream-of-consciousness narrative relates the feelings of Harry, a novelist dying of gangrene poisoning while on an African safari. Hemingway considered it his finest story.

So Big Novel by Edna FERBER, published in 1924. Set in turn-of-the-century Chicago, it tells the story of Selina Peake DeJong, a gambler's daughter with a love of life and a nurturing spirit, through her marriage and widowhood as she struggles to support herself and her son, Dirk, eventually becoming a truck farmer. It was chosen for the 1925 Pulitzer Prize over *The Great Gatsby*.

Soldier's Play, A Drama in two acts by Charles FULLER, produced and published in 1981. Set on an army base in Louisiana during World War II, it deals with the open and covert conflicts between whites and blacks. The black sergeant of an all-black company is murdered; by interviewing witnesses, the investigator discovers that the sergeant was a tyrannical sadist who hated everyone, black and white. He eventually discovers that the murder was committed not by white soldiers, town bigots, or the Ku Klux Klan but by a young black soldier whom the sergeant had goaded unmercifully.

Song of Myself Poem of 52 sections and some 1,300 lines by Walt Whitman. First published untitled in the collection LEAVES OF GRASS in 1855, the expansive, exuberant, incantatory poem was given its current title in 1881. Many sections, compelling in their unrelenting rhythm, are catalogs of individuals, locations, and actions that move the poet. Considered Whitman's most important work, and certainly his best-known, the poem, which departed from traditional rhyme, meter, and form, employing repetition and exclamation and introducing frank sexual imagery, revolutionized American verse.

Song of Solomon Novel by Toni MORRISON, published in 1977. Morrison's third novel features a male protagonist, Macon "Milkman" Dead, who, over the course of the book, comes to know himself and to overcome his alienation from his family and his roots. Based partly on a folktale about slaves who escaped back to Africa by flying out of the fields, the story, told in rich language, employs magical realism and multiple viewpoints and builds through the power of accretion rather than linear plot development.

Song of the Lark Novel by Willa CATHER, published in 1915. The story of Thea Kronborg, who overcomes many hardships to become a leading Wagnerian soprano at the Metropolitan Opera, is one of several works in which Cather displayed her lyrical powers and in which she presents a protagonist who, by virtue of talent and determination, is able to rise above small-town provincialism.

Sophie's Choice Novel by William STYRON, published in 1979. Set in the late 1940s, it is narrated by Stingo, a young Southern writer who is the author's thinly veiled alter ego. In a boardinghouse in Brooklyn, he becomes friends with a pair of tormented lovers: Nathan Landau, a brilliant but unstable Jew, and Sophie Zawistowska, a beautiful but guilt-ridden Polish refugee. On a journey to the South, accompanied by Sophie, Stingo learns that, while at Auschwitz, Sophie was forced to choose which of her two children would survive and which would die. Sophie leaves unexpectedly and Stingo trails her to the boardinghouse, where he discovers that she and Nathan have committed suicide.

Sot-Weed Factor, The Picaresque novel by John BARTH, originally published in 1960 and revised in 1967. A parody of the historical novel, it is based on and takes its title from a satirical poem published in 1708 by Ebenezer Cooke, the protagonist of Barth's work. The novel's black humor derives from its purposeful misuse of conventional literary devices.

Souls of Black Folk, The Collection of essays by W. E. B. DU BOIS, published in 1903. In this epochal work, Du Bois expressed his opposition to Booker T. Washington, polarizing the black intellectual community and setting himself up as the leader of its radical faction. Here he claims that Washington's rejection of higher education for blacks essentially accepted the white allegation of inferiority and failed to acknowledge all that African-Americans had to offer their country. Some of the essays are historical, looking at black life and circumstances during and after Reconstruction, and some are personal reflections. The collection remains Du Bois's best-known work.

Sound and the Fury, The First major novel of William FAULKNER, published in 1929. Set in Faulkner's fictional Yoknapatawpha County, Miss., in the early 20th century, the novel describes the decay and fall of the aristocratic Compson family, and, implicitly, of an entire social order, from four different points of view. The first three sections are presented from the perspectives of the three Compson sons: Benjy, an "idiot"; Quentin, a suicidal Harvard freshman; and Jason, the eldest. Each section focuses primarily on a sister who has married and left home. The fourth section comments on the other three as the Compsons' black servants, whose chief virtue is their endurance, reveal the family's moral decline. In this novel Faulkner for the first time incorporated such challenging stylistic techniques as interior monologues and stream-of-consciousness narrative.

Speak, Memory Autobiographical memoir of the early life and European years of Vladimir NABOKOV. Fifteen chapters were published individually (1948–50), mainly in the *New Yorker*. A later edition (1966) contains family photographs and incorporates recollections and revisions by his sisters and cousins. The first 12 chapters describe Nabokov's happy childhood in an aristocratic family in St. Petersburg; the remaining three chapters cover his years as a student at Cambridge and as an intellectual and fledgling writer in the Russian émigré communities of Berlin and Paris.

Spinoza of Market Street, The Title story of a short-story collection by Isaac Bashevis SINGER, first published in Yiddish in 1944; the collection was published in English in 1961. The story is set in Warsaw on the brink of World War I. Dr. Nahum Fischelson lives a meager, isolated existence alone in an attic room overlooking teeming Market Street, explicating the works of Benedict de Spinoza, descending to the street only once a week to buy food. Black Dobbe, the ugly, illiterate woman in the room next to his, goes to his room to have him read a letter; when she discovers him unconscious and ill, she nurses him back to health. To their neighbors' amusement, the two are married, and Fischelson discovers he has the ardor and vigor of a young man. As he gazes at the stars, he silently asks Spinoza to forgive him his happiness and his acceptance of the world of passion and joy.

Spoils of Poynton, The Novella by Henry JAMES, first published as a serial (titled *The Old Things*) in the *Atlantic Monthly* in 1896 and published as a book in 1897. Poynton Park is the home of old Mrs. Gereth, an antique collector with impeccable taste who has filled her lodgings with splendid art objects and furniture. The possessive Mrs. Gereth wants her weak-willed son to marry a pleasant young woman who shares her refined tastes. Instead he becomes engaged to a vulgar, greedy woman, and the treasures of Poynton become the prize over which mother and fiancée battle. In the end Poynton and its spoils, which have destroyed all the novel's relationships, are immolated in a fire of undetermined origin.

Spoon River Anthology Poetry collection, the major work of Edgar Lee MASTERS, published in 1915. It is a collection of 245 free-verse epitaphs in the form of monologues spoken from beyond the grave by former residents of the dreary, confining small town of Spoon River, much like the towns Masters himself had known during his Illinois boyhood. The speakers tell of their hopes and ambitions, and of their bitter, unrealized lives. The realistic poems contradicted the popular view of small towns as repositories of moral virtue and respectability.

Spring and All Volume of poems and prose by William Carlos WILLIAMS, published in 1923 in Paris in an edition of 300 copies. In it Williams tried to articulate his beliefs about the role and form of art in the present day. It includes some of his best-known poems; the poetry is straightforward and concerned with the matter of daily life. In "By the Road to the Contagious Hospital," the poet observes fragile signs of spring emerging from a blighted landscape; the theme of awakening life recurs in many of the other 26 poems. Despite the harsh social criticism of "The Crowd at the Ball Game" and "The Pure Products of America," the dominant mood is hopeful, and the images, such as those in "The Red Wheelbarrow," are vivid and sensuous. Its prose portions were, according to the author, "a mixture of philosophy and nonsense" in a format that parodied contemporary experimentation with typography.

Stopping by Woods on a Snowy Evening Poem by Robert FROST, published in *New Hampshire* (1923). One of Frost's most frequently explicated works, it describes a solitary traveler in a carriage who is both driven by the business at hand and transfixed by a wintry woodland scene. Composed of four iambic tetrameter quatrains, it derives its incantatory tone from an interlocking rhyme scheme of *aaba bbcb ccdc dddd*.

Story of a Bad Boy, The Classic novel for young people by Thomas Bailey ALDRICH, published serially in *Our Young Folks* (1869) and in book form in 1870. An autobiographical book about a happy boyhood, it was the first full-length work in which the protagonist was a realistic boy instead of a priggish paragon.

Strange Interlude Drama in two parts and nine acts by Eugene O'NEILL, produced and published in 1928. Its complicated plot involves a woman in her roles as daughter, wife, mistress, mother, and friend. Its length was an innovation; in its original production it began in the late afternoon, paused for a dinner intermission, and resumed at the hour when most plays begin. Its innovative stage techniques included stream-of-consciousness soliloquies and asides.

Street, The Naturalistic novel by Ann PETRY, published in 1946. Set in Long Island, suburban Connecticut, and Harlem, it is the story of intelligent, ambitious Lutie Johnson, who strives to make a better life for herself and her son despite a constant struggle with sexual brutality and racism. It was one of the first novels by a black woman to receive widespread critical acclaim.

Streetcar Named Desire, A Play in three acts by Tennessee WILLIAMS, first produced and published in 1947. One of the most admired plays of its time, it concerns the mental and moral disintegration and ultimate ruin of Blanche DuBois, a former Southern belle. Mourning the loss of the family's estate through bankruptcy, she moves in with her sister, Stella, and Stella's brutish husband Stanley Kowalski. Her neurotic, genteel pretensions are no match for the harsh realities epitomized by Stanley, who, enraged by Blanche's affectations of superiority, reveals gossip he has heard to the effect that she has been picking up men for promiscuous sex. Finally he rapes her; when Blanche tells Stella the story, Stella has her committed to a mental institution.

Street Scene Play in three acts by Elmer RICE, produced and published in 1929. Set in a New York slum, it offers a realistic portrayal of tenement life. The story focuses particularly on the tragedy of one family, the Maurrants, who are destroyed when the husband kills his wife and her lover. A musical adaptation, with lyrics by Langston Hughes and music by Kurt Weill, was produced in 1947.

Stuart Little Children's novel by E. B. WHITE, published in 1945. Stuart is a mouse born into a human family in New York City. Confident and courageous, he undertakes such daring escapades as racing a toy boat in a Central Park pond, retrieving his mother's ring from a drain, and crawling inside a piano to fix the keys. He ultimately embarks on a quest to find his beloved Margalo, a little bird who is frightened away by the ferocious family cat, Snowbell.

Studs Lonigan Trilogy of novels by James T. FARRELL consisting of *Young Lonigan: A Boyhood in Chicago Streets* (1932), *The Young Manhood of Studs Lonigan* (1934), and *Judgment Day* (1935). As a boy, William Lonigan (always referred to as "Studs") makes a slight effort to rise above his squalid urban environment, but the combination of his own personality, unwholesome neighborhood friends, a small-minded family, and his schooling and religious training all condemn him to a life of futility and dissipation.

Suddenly Last Summer Drama in two acts by Tennessee WILLIAMS, published in 1958 and produced the same year under the title *Garden District*. The story of Sebastian, a self-involved, sadistic homosexual, and his domineering mother, it is a lurid Southern Gothic story whose subject matter includes pederasty and lobotomy. On a Caribbean vacation, Sebastian is eventually murdered and eaten by the street boys on whom he had preyed.

Sula Novel by Toni MORRISON, published in 1973. Following the lives of Sula and her friend Nel from childhood to maturity and death, it examines the stunted, inward-looking community of Medallion, Ohio, whose inhabitants' rage and disordered lives are seen as a reaction to their stifled hopes.

Sun Also Rises, The Novel by Ernest HEMINGWAY, published in 1926. Set in the 1920s, it deals with a group of aimless expatriates in France and Spain. They are members of the cynical and disillusioned Lost Generation; many suffer psychological and physical wounds as a result of World War I. Lady Brett Ashley drifts through a series of affairs despite her love for Jake Barnes, who has been rendered impotent by a war wound. Friendship, stoicism, and grace under pressure are offered as the values that matter in an otherwise amoral and often senseless world.

Sweeney Agonistes(: Fragments of an Aristophanic Melodrama) Poetic drama in two scenes by T. S. ELIOT. The play was published in two parts in the *New Criterion* as "Fragment of a Prologue" (1926) and "Fragment of an Agon" (1927), and together in book form in 1932. Cast in a music-hall format, complete with songs, *Sweeney Agonistes* comments on the meaninglessness of contemporary life and the pettiness and sinfulness of humanity.

Sweet Bird of Youth Drama in three acts by Tennessee WILLIAMS, published and produced in 1959 as an expanded version of his one-act play *The Enemy: Time* (1959). An aging movie star, traveling incognito as the Princess Kosmonopolis, and her kept lover, Chance Wayne, return to Chance's Southern hometown to avoid the negative reception she assumes her latest movie will receive. Chance is also a failure, having wasted his youth in the pursuit of fame. When the actress learns that her movie is in fact a success, she makes plans to leave and asks Chance to go with her. Chance has learned that on a previous visit home he infected a local politician's daughter with a venereal disease. He decides to stay and face his punishment, which he knows will be castration.

Swimmer, The Short story by John CHEEVER, published in the *New Yorker* in 1964 and collected in *The Brigadier and the Golf Widow* the same year. A masterly blend of fantasy and reality, it tells of a middle-aged man who, leaving a suburban pool party, decides to swim his way home through the backyard pools of the county. As he progresses, summer turns to fall and unsettling intimations proliferate. The truth he has avoided facing—that his life is in ruins—slowly emerges, and he finally arrives to find his house locked and empty.

Tales of the Jazz Age Second collection of short works by F. Scott FITZGERALD, published in 1922. Though the title alludes to the flapper era of the 1920s, all but two pieces were written before 1920. Best

known is the story THE DIAMOND AS BIG AS THE RITZ; the other works include the novella *May Day*, several sketches Fitzgerald had written in college, and two minor short plays. The collection was published to coincide with release of Fitzgerald's novel *The Beautiful and Damned*.

tall tale Narrative that depicts the extravagantly exaggerated wild adventures of folk heroes. The tall tale is essentially an oral form of entertainment; the audience appreciates the imaginative invention rather than the literal meaning of the tales. Tall tales often explain the origins of lakes, mountains, and canyons; they are spun around real and fictional heroes such as the giant lumberjack Paul Bunyan, the rowdy Mississippi River keelboatman Mike Fink, and the backwoods Tennessee marksman Davy Crockett. Other tall tales attribute superhuman exploits to Western cowboy heroes such as Buffalo Bill and Annie Oakley. Native to the Northeast are the tales of Capt. Stormalong, whose hurricane-driven ship is credited with digging the Panama Canal, and Johnny Appleseed, who planted apple orchards from the East Coast to the Western frontier. Washington Irving and Mark Twain both made literary use of the tale.

Tamerlane Dramatic monologue by Edgar Allan POE, published in *Tamerlane and Other Poems* (1827) and later revised. On his deathbed the great conqueror Tamerlane makes his confession to a friar. He tells of his return to his native village and his dismay upon discovering that his beautiful childhood sweetheart is now dead. Like much of Poe's early verse, "Tamerlane" shows the influence of the Romantic poets, in particular Lord Byron.

Tanglewood Tales for Girls and Boys Collection of children's stories by Nathaniel HAWTHORNE, published in 1853. Written as a sequel to *A Wonder-Book for Girls and Boys* (1851), it is more serious than its light-hearted predecessor. It includes six ancient Greek tales: "The Minotaur," "The Pygmies," "The Dragon's Teeth," "Circe's Palace," "The Pomegranate Seeds," and "The Golden Fleece." Hawthorne altered such incidents as Ariadne's seduction and Proserpine's abduction, regarding the original versions as inappropriate for his readership.

Tell-Tale Heart, The Short story by Edgar Allan POE, published in *The Pioneer* in 1843. The narrator, a homicidal madman, relates with relish his murder and dismembering of an old man, having been driven to the act by what he believed to be the old man's maddeningly loud heartbeats. The police arrive, summoned by a neighbor. While talking to them, the narrator begins to hear again what he believes to be the man's beating heart, and hysterically confesses his crime. Poe's revelation of the narrator's dementia is a classic study in psychopathology; the tale influenced later stream-of-consciousness fiction and helped secure Poe's reputation as master of the macabre.

Tender Buttons (: Objects, Food, Rooms) Book of poems by Gertrude STEIN, first published in 1914. Heavily influenced by Cubism, the poetry—dense, obscure, and devoid of conventional logic, syntax, or grammar—was considered by many to have taken abstraction and fragmentation past the limits of comprehensibility. Avoiding conventional means of conveying meaning and impressions, Stein juggles the sequence of the sounds of words to create verbal still-lifes.

Tender Is the Night Semiautobiographical novel by F. Scott FITZGERALD, published in 1934. Dick Diver, a psychiatrist, marries one of his patients, Nicole. At first a charming success, he disintegrates into drunkenness, failure, and anonymity as Nicole recovers her strength and independence. Fitzgerald's portrayal of the Divers' life of lassitude reflects his years spent among the American expatriate community in France; that of Nicole's increasing mental instability was based on his observations of his wife Zelda's nervous breakdowns. Though Diver was principally based on Fitzgerald's friend Gerald Murphy, the character reflects much of Fitzgerald as well. A revised version (1948) abandons the original edition's flashbacks and relates the story in chronological order.

Thanatopsis Poem by William Cullen BRYANT, published in the *North American Review* in 1817 and revised for *Poems* (1821). Written when Bryant was 17, it remains his best-known work. In its musings on a magnificent, omnipresent Nature, the poem (whose Greek title means "view of death") shows the influence of deism; it in turn influenced the Transcendentalist ideas of Emerson and Thoreau. Its colloquial voice and celebration of nature were considered poetic innovations; it brought Bryant early fame and established him as a major nature poet.

Their Eyes Were Watching God Novel by Zora Neale HURSTON, published in 1937. In lyrical prose influenced by the black folktales she heard while assembling her folklore anthology *Mules and Men*

(1935), she tells the story of Janie Crawford, her three marriages, her increasing self-reliance, and her identity as a black woman. While her first two husbands are domineering, her third, Tea Cake, is easygoing and reluctantly willing to accept Janie as an equal. Hurston manages to characterize these three very different men without resorting to caricature (in the first two instances) or idealization (in the third), and Janie is one of few fictional heroines of the period who is not punished for her sensual nature. The novel is considered Hurston's finest work.

them Novel by Joyce Carol OATES, published in 1969. Violent and explosive in both incident and tone, it chronicles the efforts of the Wendell family to break away from their destructive, crime-ridden background in urban Detroit. Critics praised it for its detailed social observation and its bitter indictment of American society.

Theophilus North Novel by Thornton WILDER, published in 1973. The last of Wilder's works to be published during his lifetime, it has striking parallels to his own life experiences and may be considered a fictionalized memoir of his idealized artistic and philosophical life. It is structured as a first-person reminiscence of life among the rich at Newport, R.I., and is narrated by the elderly North from a distance of 50 years.

Thin Man, The Novel by Dashiell HAMMETT, published in 1934. Hammett's portrayal of sophisticated New York café society during Prohibition and his witty protagonists Nick and Nora Charles made this the most popular of his works, if not the most critically successful. Nick is a detective who has given up his profession to manage his wife Nora's fortune, which allows the couple to lead an easy life of nonstop parties and cocktails. The murder of a former client's secretary draws him back in, urged on by Nora, who loves a mystery. The couple's playful banter, rather than the crime, forms the actual center of the book.

This Side of Paradise First novel by F. Scott FITZGERALD, published in 1920. It is the story of Amory Blaine, a handsome, spoiled young man who attends Princeton, becomes involved in literary activities, and has several ill-fated romances. Immature though it seems today, the work when first published was considered a revelation of the new morality of the young in the early Jazz Age, and it made Fitzgerald famous. Already evident is his later theme of love distorted by social climbing and greed.

To a Waterfowl Lyric poem by William Cullen BRY-ANT, published in 1818 and collected in *Poems* (1821). Written in alternately rhymed quatrains, it portrays a poet who is comforted at the end of a difficult day filled with uncertainty and self-doubt by the sight of a solitary waterfowl on the horizon, and realizes that everything in nature is guided by a protective divine providence.

Tobacco Road Novel by Erskine CALDWELL, published in 1932. The Georgia sharecropper Jeeter Lester and his family are trapped by the bleak economic conditions of the Depression and by their own limited intelligence and destructive sexuality. The tragic ending is almost foreordained by the characters' inability to change their lives. Highly controversial in its time, *Tobacco Road* was one of the era's best examples of literary naturalism; it was adapted as an enormously successful play in 1933.

To Build a Fire Short story by Jack LONDON, published in *Century Magazine* in 1908 and later in *Lost Face* (1910). An earlier draft had been published in 1902 in *Youth's Companion*. Set in the Klondike in winter, it concerns a man who, despite warnings, attempts to travel a great distance in the extreme cold. Though even his dog senses the folly of the journey, the man stubbornly continues to believe in his own infallibility. His doom is sealed when, after getting his feet wet, he is unable to build the crucial fire that might save his life. London relates his small masterpiece in stark, unadorned prose.

To Kill a Mockingbird Novel by Harper LEE, published in 1960. In a small and quiet Alabama town in the 1930s, 6-year-old "Scout" Finch observes the reactions of the townspeople to the trial of Tom Robinson, a black man whom her father, the lawyer Atticus Finch, is defending against charges of raping a white girl. His stalwart championing of Robinson's innocence earns him the town's hatred; the innocent Robinson is convicted, and he is shot to death when he tries to escape. Scout and her brother are set upon on Halloween night while in their costumes by the father of the lying girl; they are rescued by their strange and hitherto ostracized neighbor, Boo Radley.

Tom Sawyer, The Adventures of Novel by Mark TWAIN, published in 1876. In a small Mississippi River town in the 1830s, Tom and his friend Huckleberry Finn witness a murder and flee out of fear of the murderer, Injun Joe. The townspeople think them dead, and the two

return in time to hear their own funeral eulogies. Though they have sworn never to reveal what they know, Tom is unable to let an innocent man, Muff Potter, be convicted, and tells the true story. He and his girlfriend get lost in the cave where Injun Joe is hiding, but escape, and Tom and Huck find Injun Joe's buried treasure. Like Thomas Bailey Aldrich's *Story of a Bad Boy, Tom Sawyer* (and later the more ambitious *Huckleberry Finn*) gave the reading public a mischievous but goodhearted hero rather than the "model boy" of didactic fiction. It is perhaps the best of Twain's books for a juvenile audience.

Tortilla Flat Novel by John STEINBECK, published in 1935. The first of Steinbeck's novels to be set on California's Monterey Peninsula, this episodic, humorous tale of the adventures of a group of pleasure-loving Mexican-Americans contains some of his most interesting characters. The men drink, steal, chase women, make music, and dance until they are eventually undone by a climactic fire.

To the Finland Station Critical and historical study by Edmund WILSON, published in 1940, though much of it had previously appeared in the *New Republic*. It discusses European socialism, anarchism, and various theories of revolution from their origins to their implementation and presents the ideas and writings of political theorists representing all aspects of socialist, anarchist, and communist thought, including Jules Michelet, Henri de Saint-Simon, Robert Owen, Mikhail Bakunin, Anatole France, Karl Marx, Friedrich Engels, Leon Trotsky, and Vladimir Ilich Lenin—who arrived at Petrograd's (St. Petersburg's) Finland Station in 1917 to lead the Bolshevik revolution.

Town, The Novel by William FAULKNER, published in 1957. It relates through three narrators of varying reliability the story of Flem Snopes's rise to prominence in the fictional Yoknapatawpha County. Flem's coldly calculated vengeance on his wife, Eula, and her lover culminates in Eula's suicide and Flem's rise to power in Jefferson, the county seat. Because he longs for respect as well as money, he turns against the clan of shiftless Snopes cousins who have followed him to town and forces them to leave Jefferson. In his hunger for social validation, he denies his own origins, and the book ends with a hint that the cousins' revenge will follow. The second work in the Snopes trilogy, it was preceded by THE HAMLET (1940) and followed by THE MANSION (1959).

Tragic Muse, The Novel by Henry JAMES, published serially in the *Atlantic Monthly* (1889–90) and in book form in 1890. Set in London and Paris in the 1880s, it reflects on the conflicting demands of art and the workaday world in the story of Nicholas Dormer, an Englishman who gives up a career in Parliament and marriage to a beautiful, wealthy woman to become a portrait painter. He is encouraged by his actress friend and "tragic muse" Miriam Rooth. Though by the end of the novel he has still not achieved his goal, it is implied that he made the right decision in choosing to live at a higher level of consciousness, regardless of material success. Written when James himself was suffering setbacks as a playwright, the novel reflects many of his concerns.

Troll Garden, The First short-story collection by Willa CATHER, published in 1905. The stories are linked thematically by their depiction of characters who seek a realm of beauty and imagination but are constantly assaulted by the vulgar and brutal outside world. In "The Sculptor's Funeral," residents of a prairie village react to the burial of a famous sculptor brought home to be buried there. PAUL'S CASE is the book's climactic story.

Tropic of Cancer Autobiographical novel by Henry MILLER, published in France in 1934; censorship prevented U.S. publication until 1961. A monologue about Miller's picaresque life as an impoverished expatriate in France in the early 1930s, it is made up of anecdotes, philosophizing, and rambling celebrations of life. Despite his poverty, he extols his manner of living (largely off the resources of his friends), unfettered by moral and social conventions. In exuberant and sometimes preposterous passages of unusual sexual frankness, he chronicles numerous encounters with women, including his mysterious wife Mona, as he pursues a fascination with female sexuality. The first volume of an autobiographical trilogy, it was followed by *Black Spring* (1936) and *Tropic of Capricorn* (1939).

True West Drama in two acts by Sam SHEPARD, produced in 1980 and published in 1981. Two brothers—Lee, a drifter and petty thief, and Austin, a successful screenwriter—struggle for power while they collaborate on a screenplay in their mother's Southern California home. This savage and blackly humorous version of the Cain and Abel story also satirizes the exploitation of the romanticized West of American mythology.

Tunnel, The Novel by William GASS, published in 1995. The tale of a professor of history specializing

in, and sympathetic to, Nazi Germany, it features thousand-word sentences, typographical tricks, and dirty limericks. Gass began work on it in the 1960s and published sections in literary journals and magazines during the 30 years it took to complete. He has referred to it as an attempt to write an "anti-narrative" about "fascism of the heart." The subject of intense attention when it appeared, it generated extremely mixed reviews.

Turn of the Screw, The Novella by Henry JAMES, published serially in *Collier's Weekly* in 1898 and in book form later that year. One of the world's most famous ghost stories, it is told mostly through the journal of a governess and depicts her struggle to save her two young charges from the demonic influence of the eerie apparitions of two former servants in the household. It inspired debate over the question of the "reality" of the ghosts and of James's intentions. James himself called the tale a "fable" and said that he did not specify details of the ghosts' evil deeds because he wanted readers to supply their own vision of terror.

Twice-Told Tales Collection of previously published short stories by Nathaniel HAWTHORNE, issued in 1837 and revised and expanded in 1842. Stories such as "The Gray Champion," "The May-pole of Marymount," "The Gentle Boy," and "Endicott and the Red Cross" reflect Hawthorne's moral insight and his lifelong interest in the history of Puritan New England. Among the other stories, "The Minister's Black Veil" and "Wakefield" are psychological explorations of sin and guilt, "Howe's Masquerade" is a ghostly legend set in Boston just before the American Revolution, and DR. HEIDEGGER'S EXPERIMENT examines humanity's fascination with youth.

Two Years Before the Mast Autobiographical narrative by Richard Henry DANA, published in 1840. Based on the well-born Dana's experiences as a common sailor aboard the brig *Pilgrim,* it proved very popular and eventually attained the status of a classic. In describing the mistreatment of sailors, Dana hoped to spur changes that would better their lot. The *Pilgrim* traveled from Boston to California via Cape Horn; Dana's vivid descriptions of California are said to have influenced President James K. Polk's decision to embark on the Mexican War, through which California became U.S. territory. The narrative marked the beginning of a new tradition of blending the techniques of literature and journalism.

Typee(: A Peep at Polynesian Life) First novel by Herman MELVILLE, published in 1846 as *Narrative of a Four Months' Residence Among the Natives of a Valley of the Marquesas Islands*. It is based on Melville's month-long adventure as a guest-captive of the Typee people of the Marquesas Islands in present-day French Polynesia, following his desertion from the whaler *Acushnet* with a shipmate in 1842. Tom (or Tommo) spends four months with his companion Toby as a prisoner of the Typees. His opportunities for escape are limited by his disease-swollen leg and by his personal jailer-servant, the devoted Kory-Kory. He befriends several natives, notably the beautiful Fayaway. Though intrigued by the Typees' social and religious customs, he is disgusted by their indolence and cannibalism; ultimately he chooses civilization over island life.

Ulalume Poem by Edgar Allan POE, published in *American Review* in December 1847. With the nighttime stars as his guide, the narrator wanders through an eerie woodland. His dreamy walk brings him to a tomb, which he recognizes with anguish as that of his lover, Ulalume. He had buried her there exactly one year before. Regarded by Poe as a ballad, it originally comprised 10 stanzas but is often printed without the final stanza.

Uncle Remus: His Songs and His Sayings Collection of dialect stories and verse by Joel Chandler HARRIS, published in 1880. Uncle Remus, a kindly old black man, tells stories to the young son of a plantation owner. The stories feature animals (especially notable is the trickster Brer Rabbit) and are adapted from actual black folktales, many of which have African antecedents. Their warmth and humor, expressed in an accurate rendition of Southern black dialect, won them instant and enduring popularity, though the characterization of Uncle Remus himself would later be found demeaning by blacks. Harris went on to publish a series of further collections featuring Uncle Remus and his beloved characters.

Uncle Tom's Cabin(; or, Life Among the Lowly) Novel by Harriet Beecher STOWE, published in serialized form in 1851–52 and in book form in 1852. While being transported by boat to a slave auction in New Orleans, the saintly, dignified slave Uncle Tom saves the life of Little Eva St. Clare, whose grateful father purchases Tom. Little Eva and Tom become great friends. Eva's health, always frail, declines rapidly, and on her deathbed she asks her father to free all his slaves. Mr. St. Clare makes plans to do so but is killed before he can, and Tom's new owner, the brutal Simon Legree, has Tom whipped to death after he refuses to divulge the whereabouts of some runaway slaves. The novel, which sold in enormous numbers, is often cited as a cause of the Civil War. A dramatic adaptation played to capacity audiences for years and was a staple of touring companies into the 20th century.

Uncle Tom's Children Collection of four novellas by Richard WRIGHT, published in 1938. The stories are "Big Boy Leaves Home," "Down by the Riverside," "Long Black Song," and "Fire and Cloud." Thematically and stylistically, they form a consistent whole; each treats an aspect of black life in the Deep South and explores black resistance to racism and oppression. An enlarged edition (1940) added an essay, "The Ethics of Living Jim Crow," and a polemical short story, "Bright and Morning Star," but critics claimed that the additions harmed the work's literary integrity.

Up from Slavery Autobiography of Booker T. WASHINGTON, published in 1901. It traces Washington's life from slavery on a Virginia plantation to a position of fame as an educator and spokesperson for African-Americans. Its emphasis on vocational (as opposed to higher) education and separation of the races drew opposition from many blacks, notably W. E. B. Du Bois, who accused Washington of colluding with the myth of black inferiority. For his part, Washington believed his compromise would allow blacks to achieve economic security, after which they could win equality. In his conclusion he remarks that he has never sought fame, and that the greatest surprise of his life was the news that Harvard intended to grant him an honorary degree.

U.S.A. Trilogy of novels by John DOS PASSOS. *The 42nd Parallel* (1930) covers U.S. history from 1900 to World War I; *1919* (1932) deals with the war and the critical year of the Treaty of Versailles; *The Big Money* (1936) moves from the boom of the 1920s to the bust of the '30s. Dos Passos reinforces the histories of his fictional characters with interpolated montages of newspaper headlines and popular songs. He also includes biographies of establishment figures such as Henry Ford and Thomas Edison and of voices for social change such as Eugene Debs and Thorstein Veblen.

V. Novel by Thomas PYNCHON, published in 1963. Benny Profane, recently discharged from the navy, joins an organization that hunts for blind alligators that have grown up in the New York sewers. He repeatedly crosses paths with Herbert Stencil, who is searching for the mysterious and elusive V., a woman who surfaces in various incarnations and guises at crucial moments in the history of late-19th- and early-20th-century Europe. The complex, erudite, and frequently whimsical narrative negotiates a mazelike network of interlocking lives and events that suggest the products of a raving paranoid mind.

Varieties of Religious Experience, The Series of lectures by William JAMES, published in 1902. James was invited to give the Gifford Lectures on natural religion at the University of Edinburgh; as a psychologist, he proposed to focus on the "religious propensities of man." He examined religion as it was felt and experienced by the individual on a daily basis rather than as a set of doctrines and tenets established formally by a religious institution. The varieties of religious experience, he concluded, were evidence of the existence of specific consciousness-like energies with which people could make contact in times of trouble. The book is regarded as one of the century's greatest works of nonfiction.

Violent Bear It Away, The Novel by Flannery o'CONNOR, published in 1960. Young Francis Marion Tarwater has been reared by his fanatical, tyrannical granduncle Mason to be a prophet. When Mason dies, Tarwater rejects his mission and consequently suffers tortures of doubt and indecision. Though for a time he weighs the value of humanistic rationalism, as exemplified by his uncle George Rayber, he unexpectedly experiences a vision and comes to accept his calling. The novel, which lacks the humor of the earlier *Wise Blood* and was not a critical success, presents O'Connor's original version of Christianity.

Virginian(: A Horseman of the Plains), The Western by Owen WISTER, published in 1902. A chivalrous and courageous but mysterious cowboy known only as "the Virginian" works as foreman of a cattle ranch in the Wyoming territory during the late 1870s and 1880s. The gunplay and violence inherent in his frontier code of behavior threaten his relationship with a pretty schoolteacher from the East. The novel's climactic gun duel was the first "showdown" in fiction, and the book introduced the now-classic phrase "When you call me that, *smile.*" Its great popularity contributed to enshrining the American cowboy as an icon of American popular culture and a folk ideal.

Vision of Sir Launfal, The Long verse parable by James Russell LOWELL, published in 1848. Influenced by Tennyson and Malory, Lowell offers his version of the Grail story in this tale of a knight who decides not to search for the Holy Grail after he learns, during the course of a long dream, that the Grail's real meaning is charity. The poem is written in iambic tetrameter and is divided into two parts, each with a prelude. Though set in the Middle Ages, it contains moving descriptions of the American landscape.

Waiting for Lefty One-act play by Clifford ODETS, published and produced in 1935. One of the first examples of proletarian drama, it takes place during the Depression, in a meeting hall of the taxi drivers' union. The union members are waiting for their representative, Lefty, to arrive so that they can vote on a strike. In a series of six vignettes, various drivers make a plea to strike, relating the stories of their lives as justification for their decision. Odets placed actors representing union members in the audience to increase audience involvement.

Walden(; or, Life in the Woods) Series of 18 essays by Henry David THOREAU, published in 1854. An important contribution to New England Transcendentalism, the book was Thoreau's record of simple living on the northern shore of Walden Pond in Concord, Mass. (1845–47). It is viewed not only as a philosophical treatise on labor, leisure, self-reliance, and individualism but also as an influential piece of nature writing. Though relatively neglected during Thoreau's lifetime, it achieved tremendous popularity in the 20th century, when it came to be regarded as his masterwork.

Walk on the Wild Side, A Novel by Nelson ALGREN, published in 1956. It reworks *Somebody in Boots* (1935). Dove Linkhorn (Cass McKay from the earlier book), a drifter in Depression-era New Orleans, gets involved with prostitutes, pimps, and con men and eventually ends up isolated and hopeless after he has been blinded by a man whose girlfriend he tried to steal. Written with black humor in Algren's characteristic tough-guy style, the novel has been called an erotic epic of bohemianism.

Wall, The Novel by John HERSEY, published in 1950. Based on historical fact but using fictional characters and fictional diary entries, it presents the background of the valiant but doomed uprising of Jews in the Warsaw Ghetto against the Nazis, achieving a powerful representation of the tragedy of the Holocaust.

Wapshot Chronicle, The Novel by John CHEEVER, published in 1957. Based in part on Cheever's adolescence in New England, it takes place in a small Massachusetts fishing village and relates the breakdown of both the Wapshot family and the town. Part One focuses on Leander, a gentle ferryboat operator harried by a tyrannical wife and an eccentric sister; he eventually swims out to sea and never returns. Part Two chronicles the disastrous lives of Leander's sons, Coverly and Moses. Told in a comic rather than a tragic vein, the novel uses experimental prose techniques to convey a nostalgic vision of a lost world. A sequel, *The Wapshot Scandal*, was published in 1964.

Washington Square Short novel by Henry JAMES, published in 1880. Its protagonist is Catherine Sloper, a plain, rather stolid young woman who is a disappointment to her father. She is courted by Morris Townsend, who is interested only in her potential inheritance. When her father threatens to disinherit her if she marries him, Townsend abandons her. Many years later, after her father's death, Townsend reappears and tries to renew his suit; Catherine rejects him and lives on as a confirmed spinster in her Washington Square house.

Waste Land, The Long poem by T.S. ELIOT. It was first published in 1922 in the *Criterion* in London and the *Dial* in New York, and finally in book form with Eliot's footnotes. The five-part, 433-line poem is dedicated to Ezra Pound, who helped condense it to nearly half its original size. In a series of fragmentary vignettes, loosely linked by the legend of the search for the Grail and symbols supplied by that myth, it portrays a sterile world of panicky fears and barren lusts, and of human beings waiting for some sign or promise of redemption. It ends with hope of rebirth but no certainty of it. Initially met with controversy, its complex and erudite style alternately denounced for its obscurity and praised for its modernism, the poem became one of the most influential works of the 20th century.

Watch on the Rhine Drama in three acts by Lillian HELLMAN, published and produced in 1941. It is set in 1940 in the Washington, D.C., home of the wealthy widow Fanny Farrelly, who is expecting the arrival of her daughter Sara with her German husband Kurt and their three children. A leader in the anti-Nazi resistance movement, Kurt has been forced to flee Europe. Count Teck de Brancovis, a Romanian houseguest in the Farrelly home and a Nazi supporter, discovers Kurt's identity and threatens to expose him to the German embassy. The play gradually evolves from a comedy of manners into a tense thriller. Performed just eight months before the United States entered World War II, it exposed the dangers of fascism in America, asserting that tyranny can also be battled on the home front.

Web and the Rock, The Novel by Thomas WOLFE, published posthumously in 1939 after being reworked by Edward Aswell from a larger manuscript. Like Wolfe's other novels, it is an autobiographical account of a successful young writer from North Carolina living in New York City. George Webber bears many similarities to Eugene Gant, the soul-searching protagonist of LOOK HOMEWARD, ANGEL (1929) and OF TIME AND THE RIVER (1935). Esther Jack, who first appeared in *Of Time and the River,* is an urban sophisticate who becomes Webber's lover and muse. Though criticized for its inconsistent style, the novel was praised for its poetry and passion. Its sequel is YOU CAN'T GO HOME AGAIN (1940).

Week on the Concord and Merrimack Rivers, A Autobiographical narrative by Henry David THOREAU, published in 1849. A philosophical treatise couched as a travel adventure, it chronicles a boating trip he took with his brother John to New Hampshire's White Mountains in 1839. Comprising both prose and poetry, it includes romantic descriptions of the natural environment and thoughtful digressions on philosophy, literature, and history. It was written mainly during Thoreau's years by Walden Pond (1845–47); like WALDEN, it achieved fame only after the author's death.

What Maisie Knew Novel by Henry JAMES, published in 1897. Set mostly in England, it is related from the perspective of the preadolescent Maisie, who spends six months of the year with each of her divorced parents. The only emotional constant in Maisie's life is Mrs. Wix, a motherly old governess. Maisie's parents marry other partners, but neither marriage succeeds. Her new stepparents are attracted to each other, divorce Maisie's parents, and marry. Maisie chooses to live with Mrs. Wix, on whose unconditional love she can depend.

When Lilacs Last in the Dooryard Bloom'd Elegy in free verse by Walt WHITMAN, first published in *Sequel to Drum-Taps* (1865) and later included in the 1867 edition of LEAVES OF GRASS. One of Whitman's greatest poems, it expresses revulsion at the assassination of the country's first "great martyr chief," Abraham Lincoln, and implicitly condemns the brutality and waste of war. It is notable for its use of pathetic fallacy in attributing grief to nature.

White Fang Novel by Jack LONDON, published in 1906. Intended as a companion piece to THE CALL OF THE WILD, in which a domesticated dog reverts to a wild state, it is the story of a wolf dog that is rescued from its brutal owner and gradually becomes domesticated through the patience and kindness of its new owner, Weedon Scott, whose father White Fang eventually defends from an attack by an escaped convict.

White-Jacket(: The World in a Man-of-War) Novel by Herman MELVILLE, published in 1850. Based on his experiences in 1834–44 as an ordinary seaman aboard the frigate *United States*, the novel depicts life aboard the frigate *Neversink*, including the tyrannies to which ship's officers subject ordinary seamen and the appalling conditions under which the seamen live. The critically acclaimed novel was noted for its stand against the use of flogging as corporal punishment aboard naval vessels; members of Congress received copies of the book during the Congressional debate on the issue, and flogging was abolished that year.

Who's Afraid of Virginia Woolf? Play in three acts by Edward ALBEE, published and produced in 1962. It takes place in the living room of a middle-aged couple, George and Martha, who have come home from a faculty party drunk and quarrelsome. When Nick, a young biology professor, and his fey wife Honey stop by for a nightcap, they are enlisted as fellow fighters, and the battle begins. Malicious games, insults, humiliations, betrayals, painful confrontations, and savage witticisms ensue. The secrets of both couples are laid bare and illusions are viciously exposed. When, in a climactic moment, George decides to "kill" the son they have invented to compensate for their childlessness, George and Martha finally face the truth and, in a quiet ending to a noisy play, stand together against the world, sharing their sorrow.

Why I Live at the P.O. Short story by Eudora WELTY, published in the *Atlantic Monthly* and collected in *A Curtain of Green* in 1941. Sister, a young woman in a small Mississippi town, sets up housekeeping in the post office to escape from her eccentric family. As her story of betrayal and injustice unfolds, it gradually emerges that her view of the world is as strange as that of the various members of her family. While the narrow-minded and hostile characters are portrayed as cartoonish grotesques, Welty's exact depiction of small-town Southern life lends an air of uncomfortable realism, and her perfectly nuanced dramatic monologue gives the story the wickedly funny air that has made it a classic of the Southern Gothic.

Wide Net, The Short-story collection by Eudora WELTY, published in 1943. In the title story, a man quarrels with his pregnant wife, leaves the house, and descends into a mysterious underwater kingdom where he meets the King of the Snakes, who forces him to confront the darker mysteries of nature; he returns to his wife a wiser man. In its blend of domestic realism, mythology, and ancient fertility tales, the story is characteristic of the entire collection.

Wieland(, or The Transformation) Gothic novel by Charles Brockden BROWN, published in 1798. Wieland's father has died by spontaneous combustion, apparently for violating a vow to God. The younger Wieland misguidedly assumes that a ventriloquist's utterances are supernatural in origin; driven insane, he acts upon the prompting of this "inner voice" and murders his wife and children, and is eventually driven to kill himself.

Winesburg, Ohio Collection of interrelated stories by Sherwood ANDERSON, published in 1919. George Willard, a young reporter, feels hemmed in by life in the small town of Winesburg. In 23 sketches, various residents of Winesburg confide in him, revealing their own thwarted ambitions and desires. While Anderson's contemporary, Booth Tarkington, told cheerful tales of the Midwest, Anderson here exposed its isolation and loneliness. Considered his best work, the book was admired by such writers as Ernest Hemingway, Hart Crane, and E. M. Forster.

Wings of the Dove, The Novel by Henry JAMES, published in 1902. It explores James's favorite theme of the cultural clash between naive Americans and sophisticated, often decadent Europeans. Kate Croy is a Londoner who encourages her secret fiancé, Merton Densher, to woo and marry Milly Theale, a wealthy young American dying of a mysterious malady. Kate reasons that although Milly will die soon, she will at least be happily in love; Merton will inherit her fortune, and Kate and Merton can then marry. Milly dies soon after learning of Merton's and Kate's motives, leaving Merton a legacy that he is too guilt-ridden to accept. Kate is unwilling to forgo the inheritance, and she and Merton part forever, their relationship destroyed by Milly's gift.

Wise Blood First novel by Flannery O'CONNOR, published in 1952. Hazel Motes is a discharged serviceman who abandons his fundamentalist faith to become a preacher of anti-religion in a Tennessee city, establishing his churchless "Church Without Christ." A ludicrous and ultimately tragic hero, he meets a collection of equally grotesque characters. One of his young followers, Enoch Emery, worships a museum mummy; Hoover Shoats is a competing evangelist who creates the "Holy Church of Christ Without Christ"; Asa Hawks is an itinerant preacher who pretends to have blinded himself to show his faith in redemption. The novel is noted for its superb Southern dialect, hilarious characterizations and incidents, and ironic symbolism.

Women of Brewster Place, The Novel by Gloria NAYLOR, published in 1982. It chronicles the lives of seven black women who live in decaying rented houses on a walled-off urban street. Mattie Michael, the middle-aged matriarch, is a source of comfort and strength. Etta Mae Johnson is a restless free spirit who repeatedly attaches herself to disappointing men. Kiswana Browne embraces racial pride and disparages but later accepts her mother's middle-class values. Mattie saves Ciel Turner from self-destruction after a series of personal disasters. Kiswana helps the unwed Cora Lee realize that her many children should not be treated like dolls. Lorraine seeks social acceptance, unlike her outspoken lesbian lover, Theresa. Deranged by a gang rape, Lorraine murders one of her only supporters, Ben, Brewster Place's kind janitor. At the novel's end the women angrily demolish the wall that separates them from the rest of the city.

Wonderful "One-Hoss Shay," The Deacon's Masterpiece, or The Poem by Oliver Wendell HOLMES, published in his "Breakfast-Table" column in the *Atlantic Monthly* in September 1858. It concerns a "one-hoss shay" (one-horse chaise) constructed with all parts of equal strength by a New England deacon. Extraordinarily durable and meant to last forever, the vehicle spontaneously turns to dust exactly 100 years after it was built. The poem has often been interpreted as a satire on the breakdown of Calvinism in America.

Wound and the Bow, The Book of literary criticism by Edmund WILSON, published in 1941. Employing psychological and historical analysis, Wilson examines the childhood psychological traumas experienced by such writers as Charles Dickens, Ernest Hemingway, James Joyce, Rudyard Kipling, and Edith Wharton, and the effects of those experiences on their writing.

Wrinkle in Time, A Children's novel by Madeleine L'ENGLE, published in 1962. Combining theology, fantasy, and science, it is the story of young Meg Murry's search, with her friend Calvin O'Keefe and her brother Charles Wallace, to find her lost father, a scientist studying time travel. Assisted by the eccentrics Mrs. Whatsit, Mrs. Who, and Mrs. Which, the children travel to the planet Camazotz, where they encounter a rigidly conformist society controlled by an evil disembodied brain. Unlike in most tales of good versus evil, the protagonists triumph not through strength or righteousness but through the power of redemptive love. *A Wind in the Door* (1973), *A Swiftly Tilting Planet* (1978), and *Many Waters* (1986) are sequels.

Yearling, The Novel by Marjorie Kinnan RAWLINGS, published in 1938. In the backwoods of northern Florida, 12-year-old Jody Baxter adopts a fawn, Flag, who grows up to be a pest, eating the family's crops. Jody's father forces Jody to shoot Flag, and the tragedy propels the boy into greater maturity and a stronger apprehension of his parents' hardscrabble life.

Yellow Wallpaper, The Novella by Charlotte Perkins GILMAN, published in *New England Magazine* in May 1892 and in book form in 1899. It describes the experience of a young wife and mother who, apparently suffering from postpartum depression, undergoes a "rest cure" involving strict bed rest and a complete absence of mental stimulation, which leads to her gradual emotional and intellectual deterioration. Initially interpreted as a gothic horror tale, the tale was a fictionalized autobiographical account.

Yet Do I Marvel Sonnet by Countee CULLEN, published in *Color* in 1925. Reminiscent of the sonnets of Wordsworth and Blake, it is concerned with racial identity and injustice. The poet states "I do not doubt God is good, well-meaning, kind," but while accepting God's wisdom in most puzzling matters of life and death, he is confounded by the contradiction of his own plight in a racist society: "Yet do I marvel at this curious thing: / To make a poet black, and bid him sing!"

You Can't Go Home Again Novel by Thomas WOLFE, published posthumously in 1940 after heavy editing by Edward Aswell. Largely autobiographical, it reflects details of Wolfe's life in the 1930s. It continues the story of George Webber (begun in THE WEB AND THE ROCK), a thoughtful author in search of meaning in his personal life and in American society. Leaving New York City, Webber is dismayed at the social decay he finds on his travels to England, Germany, and his small hometown in the Carolinas, but remains optimistic about the American future.

Young Goodman Brown Allegorical short story by Nathaniel HAWTHORNE, published in 1835 in *New England Magazine* and collected in MOSSES FROM AN OLD MANSE. It concerns a young Puritan who ventures into the forest to meet with a stranger. It soon becomes clear that he is approaching a witches' Sabbath; he views with horror prominent members of his community participating in the ceremonies. Ultimately Brown sees his wife, Faith, and cries out to her to "resist," only to find himself alone among the trees. He returns home, having lost forever his faith in goodness and piety.

Zoo Story, The One-act play by Edward ALBEE, produced and published in 1959. Peter, a publishing executive, is reading in New York's Central Park when he is approached by a stranger named Jerry. Announcing "I've been to the zoo!" Jerry proceeds to probe deep into Peter's life. He relates details from his own life, particularly details of his stay in a rooming house with a bizarre landlady and her repulsive dog, and his unsuccessful attempt to poison the dog. As Peter grows increasingly agitated, Jerry becomes abusive, tosses Peter a knife, provokes him into a fight, and impales himself on the knife.

Groups, Movements, and Periodicals

Accent(: A Quarterly of New Literature) Literary magazine published from 1940 to 1960 at the University of Illinois. Founded by Kerker Quinn and Charles Shattuck, it evolved from the earlier journal *Direction,* which Quinn had put out in his undergraduate days. *Accent* published some of the best examples of contemporary writing by both new and established authors, including Wallace Stevens, Thomas Mann, Bertolt Brecht, James T. Farrell, Katherine Anne Porter, Richard Wright, Eudora Welty, and William Gass.

Algonquin Round Table Informal group of American literary men and women who met daily for lunch on weekdays at a large round table in New York's Algonquin Hotel during the 1920s and '30s. The Round Table began in 1919 with the *Vanity Fair* writers Dorothy PARKER, Robert BENCHLEY, and Robert E. SHERWOOD, and within a few years its participants included many of New York's best-known writers, journalists, and artists. Among them were Alexander WOOLLCOTT, George S. KAUFMAN, Franklin P. ADAMS, Marc CONNELLY, Harold ROSS, Edna FERBER, Harold Ross, Heywood Broun, Harpo Marx, and Russel Crouse. It became celebrated for its members' lively, witty conversation and urbane sophistication. After 1925, many of its members were closely associated with Ross's new *New Yorker* magazine, whose editorial offices he established on the same block. The Round Table continued only in diminished form after the onset of the Great Depression in 1929.

American Academy of Arts and Letters *originally* National Institute of Arts and Letters, *later (1904–92)* American Academy and Institute of Arts and Letters. Organization founded in 1898 whose stated purpose is to "foster, assist and sustain an interest" in literature, art, and music. The New York-based academy was the inspiration of H. Holbrook Curtis, a physician, and Simeon E. Baldwin, a judge. After organizing the original 250 members, they decided (perhaps with an eye to the Académie Française's 40 "Immortals") that they had not been exclusive enough; they renamed the 250-member body the Institute and from among its members were elected the Academy, an elite membership of 50. The first seven members, elected in 1904, were the writers William Dean Howells, Mark Twain, Edmund C. Stedman, and John Hay, the sculptor Augustus Saint-Gaudens, the painter John LaFarge, and the composer Edward MacDowell. The first female member was Julia Ward Howe, elected to the institute in 1907 and to the academy in 1908; she was followed by Edith Wharton in 1926. In 1993 the organization reverted to a single form of membership for all 250 members. Membership in the academy is for life. Committees award any of several annual monetary gifts to selected struggling artists.

American Mercury Monthly literary magazine known for its often satiric commentary on American life, politics, and customs. It was founded in 1924 by H. L. MENCKEN and George Jean NATHAN, the coeditors of the SMART SET. Under Mencken's editorship (1924–34) it quickly gained a reputation for his vitriolic articles directed at the American public (the "booboisie") and for Nathan's excellent theatrical criticism. Its fiction and other articles were the work of the most distinguished American authors and often the sharpest satiric minds of the day. In the 1950s the magazine developed a militant anticommunist stand and a strident right-wing tone, and came to bear little relation to the original magazine. It ceased publication in 1980.

American Poetry Review, The Literary periodical founded in 1972 in Philadelphia by Stephen Berg and Stephen Parker. Issued bimonthly in a newspaper tabloid format, it sought a mass-market readership for its high-quality contributors and content. The *APR* offers an eclectic collection of serious poetry and prose by outstanding English-language writers and critics, as well as works in translation from around the world. Contributors have included Isaac Bashevis Singer, Vladimir Nabokov, Roland Barthes, Richard Wilbur, Allen Ginsberg, William Stafford, Czeslaw Milosz, Octavio Paz, Denise Levertov, Adrienne Rich, May Swenson, John Updike, Elie Wiesel, David Ignatow, Marge Piercy, Ntozake Shange, and Tess Gallagher.

American Renaissance *or* **New England Renaissance** Period from the 1830s until the end of the Civil War in which American literature, in the wake of the Romantic movement, came of age as an expression of a national spirit. The literary scene of the period was dominated by a group of New England writers, the "Brahmins," notably H. W. LONGFELLOW, O. W. HOLMES, and J. R. LOWELL. They were aristocrats, steeped in foreign culture, active as professors at Harvard College, and interested in creating an American literature based on foreign models. Longfellow adapted European methods of storytelling and versifying to narrative poems dealing with American history; Holmes, in his occasional poems and his "Breakfast-Table" series (1858–91), brought touches of urbanity and jocosity to polite literature; and Lowell put much of his homeland's outlook and values into verse, especially in his satirical BIGLOW PAPERS (1848–67). One of the most important influences in the period was that of TRANSCENDENTALISM. Centered in the village of Concord, Mass., it included among its members R. W. EMERSON, H. D. THOREAU, Bronson ALCOTT, George RIPLEY, and Margaret FULLER. The Transcendentalists advocated reforms in church, state, and society, fostering the rise of Free Religion and the abolition movement and the formation of such utopian communities as Brook Farm. The movement contributed to the founding of a new national culture based on native elements. The abolition movement was bolstered by such other New England writers as J. G. WHITTIER and H. B. STOWE. Apart from the Transcendentalists, there emerged during this period great imaginative writers—Nathaniel HAWTHORNE, Herman MELVILLE, and Walt WHITMAN—whose novels and poetry left a permanent imprint on American literature. Contemporary with these writers but outside the New England circle was Edgar Allan POE, who later in the century had a strong impact on European literature.

Atlantic Monthly, The Monthly journal of literature and opinion, founded in 1857 by Moses Dresser Phillips and published in Boston. One of the oldest and most respected of American reviews, it has long been noted for the quality of its contents. Early figures in its long line of distinguished editors and authors included J. R. LOWELL, R. W. EMERSON, H. W. LONGFELLOW, and O. W. HOLMES. In the early 1920s, it expanded its scope to political affairs, featuring articles by such figures as Theodore Roosevelt, Woodrow Wilson, and Booker T. Washington. The high quality of its literature and its literary criticism have preserved the magazine's reputation as a lively literary periodical with a moderate worldview.

Beat movement Social and literary movement that originated in the 1950s and was centered in the bohemian artists' communities of San Francisco, New York, and Los Angeles. Its adherents, self-styled as "beat" (originally meaning "weary," but later also connoting its musical sense, a "beatific" spirituality, and other meanings) and derisively called "beatniks," expressed their alienation from conventional (or "square") society by adopting an almost uniform style of seedy dress, "cool" (detached and ironic) manners, and "hip" vocabulary borrowed from jazz musicians.

They advocated personal release, purification, and illumination through the heightened sensory awareness that might be induced by drugs, jazz, sex, or the disciplines of Zen Buddhism. Beat poets—including Gregory CORSO, Lawrence FERLINGHETTI, Allen GINSBERG, Gary SNYDER, and Philip WHALEN—sought to liberate poetry from academic preciosity and bring it "back to the streets." Their verse, while frequently chaotic and liberally sprinkled with obscenities, could also—as in Ginsberg's HOWL (1956)—be ruggedly powerful and moving. Ginsberg and other major figures of the movement, such as the novelist Jack KEROUAC, advocated a type of free, unstructured composition in which the writer put down thoughts and feelings without plan or revision—to convey the immediacy of experience—an approach that led to the production of much undisciplined and incoherent verbiage from their imitators. By the 1960s the movement had paved the way for acceptance of such unorthodox and previously ignored writers as the BLACK MOUNTAIN POETS and the novelist William BURROUGHS, one of the original Beats.

black aesthetic movement *or* **black arts movement** Period of artistic and literary development among African-Americans in the 1960s and early 1970s. Based on the cultural politics of black nationalism, the movement sought to create a populist art form to promote the idea of black separatism. Many adherents viewed the artist as an activist responsible for the formation of racially separate publishing houses, theater troupes, and study groups. The movement's literature, generally written in black vernacular and confrontational in tone, addressed interracial tensions, sociopolitical awareness, and the relevance of African history and culture to American blacks. Its leading theorists included LeRoi Jones and Larry Neal, editors of the anthology *Black Fire* (1968); Hoyt W. Fuller, editor of the journal *Negro Digest* (which became *Black World* in 1970); Addison Gayle, editor of the anthology *The Black Aesthetic* (1971); Houston A. BAKER; and Henry Louis GATES. Jones, later known as Amiri BARAKA, wrote the acclaimed play *Dutchman* (1964) and founded the Black Arts Repertory Theater in Harlem (1965). Haki R. MADHUBUTI (known as Don L. Lee until 1973) became one of the movement's most popular writers with *Think Black* (1967) and *Black Pride* (1968). Characterized by an acute self-awareness, the movement produced notable autobiographies by MALCOLM X, Eldridge Cleaver (*Soul on Ice,* 1968), and Angela Davis. Other important writers were Ishmael

REED, Toni MORRISON, Ntozake SHANGE, Sonia SAN-CHEZ, Alice WALKER, and June JORDAN.

Black Mountain poets Loosely associated group of poets that formed an important part of the American avant-garde in the 1950s. Their innovative yet disciplined poetry appeared in the *Black Mountain Review* (1954–57), a leading forum of experimental verse. The group grew up around the poets Robert CREELEY, Robert DUNCAN, and Charles OLSON at North Carolina's Black Mountain College, an experimental college focused on the arts whose brief but notable life lasted from 1933 to 1956. The Black Mountain poets, turning away from the poetic tradition espoused by T. S. Eliot, emulated the freer style of William Carlos WILLIAMS. Olson's essay *Projective Verse* (1950), stating his view of the creative process as a transferral of the poet's energy through the poem to the reader, became their manifesto. Their poetry was noted for its reliance on colloquial language. Much of the group's early work was published in the journal *Origin* (1951–56). Dissatisfied with *Origin*'s lack of critical material, Creeley and Olson established the *Black Mountain Review*. It featured the work of Williams, Duncan, and such other important figures as Paul Blackburn, Denise LEVERTOV, and Gary SNYDER.

black theater Dramatic movement encompassing plays written by, for, and about African-Americans. The minstrel shows of the mid-19th century are believed by some to be the roots of black theater. Though they were initially written and acted (in blackface) by whites and performed for white audiences, blacks began to perform in minstrel shows after the Civil War. By the turn of the century blacks were producing their own musicals, many of them written, produced, and acted entirely by blacks. The first known play by an African-American was James Brown's *King Shotaway* (1823). William Wells BROWN's *Escape; or, A Leap for Freedom* (1858) was the first black play published, but the first real success by a black dramatist was Angelina Weld GRIMKÉ's *Rachel* (1916). Black theater flourished during the HARLEM RENAISSANCE of the 1920s and '30s, when experimental groups and black theater companies emerged in Chicago, New York, and Washington, D.C. Garland Anderson's *Appearances* (1925) was the first play of black authorship produced on Broadway; the first black Broadway hit was Langston HUGHES's *Mulatto* (1935). Black community theaters began to appear in the late 1930s,

and by 1940 black theater was firmly grounded in the American Negro Theater and the Negro Playwrights' Company. After World War II black theater grew more progressive, radical, and militant, seeking to establish a mythology and symbolism apart from white culture. Such successful black plays of the 1950s as Lorraine HANSBERRY's *A Raisin in the Sun* (1959) portrayed the difficulty blacks had in maintaining an identity in a society that degraded them. The 1960s saw the emergence of an angrier and more defiant black theater. LeRoi Jones (later Amiri BARAKA), its strongest proponent, established the Black Arts Repertory Theatre in Harlem in 1965 and inspired Ed BULLINS and others seeking to create a strong "black aesthetic." Another playwright of this era was Ntozake SHANGE. In the 1970s several black musicals were widely produced. In the early 1980s Charles FULLER's *A Soldier's Play* won a Pulitzer Prize, an award later given also to the prolific August WILSON.

Brook Farm (Institute of Agriculture and Education) Utopian experiment in communal living that lasted from 1841 to 1847. The 175-acre farm was located in West Roxbury, Mass., near Boston. It was organized and virtually directed by George RIPLEY, editor of the DIAL and a leader in the Transcendental Club, an informal gathering of Boston-area intellectuals. Among the original shareholders were Charles A. Dana and Nathaniel HAWTHORNE. Ralph Waldo EMERSON, Bronson ALCOTT, Margaret FULLER, Elizabeth PEABODY, Orestes A. BROWNSON, and Horace GREELEY were among its interested visitors. The project initially seemed to prosper, its school becoming especially noted for its progressive philosophy, but disaster struck when all available funds were sunk into construction of a large central building, which burned to the ground as its completion was being celebrated. Though the colony struggled on, it gradually failed; the land and buildings were sold in 1849. Hawthorne's BLITHEDALE ROMANCE (1852) is a fictional treatment of some aspects of the experiment.

Chicago literary renaissance Flourishing of literary activity in Chicago during the period from about 1912 to 1925. Its leading writers—Theodore DREISER, Sherwood ANDERSON, Edgar Lee MASTERS, and Carl SAND-BURG—realistically depicted the contemporary urban environment, condemning the loss of traditional rural values in the increasingly industrialized and materialistic American society, and mourned the failure of the romantic promise that hard work would automatically bring material and spiritual rewards. Most of the Chicago renaissance writers were originally from small Midwestern towns and were deeply affected by the regional writing of the 1890s. The renaissance also encompassed the revitalization of journalism as a literary medium; writers such as Floyd DELL, Anderson, Dreiser, and Sandburg all were associated at one time with Chicago newspapers. Chicago's Little Theatre, established in 1912 by Maurice Browne, became an important outlet for young playwrights. The Little Room, a literary group that included both artists and patrons, encouraged literary activity; Hamlin GARLAND, already famous for novels on the bleakness of rural Midwestern life, was briefly a member. THE DIAL, established in 1880, grew to be a respected literary journal. Henry Blake Fuller and Robert Herrick, practitioners of genteel fiction, wrote several novels that foreshadowed the later realistic works of Dreiser and Anderson. The appearance of Masters's SPOON RIVER ANTHOLOGY (1915), Sandburg's *Chicago Poems* (1916), and Anderson's WINESBURG, OHIO (1919) marked the height of the renaissance. Two literary magazines—POETRY, founded in 1912 by Harriet MONROE, and THE LITTLE REVIEW (1914–29)—published exciting new verse by such local poets as Vachel LINDSAY, Masters, and Sandburg. Dell, associated with the *Chicago Evening Post*'s weekly *Friday Literary Review* (1909–11), was the center of a vital literary circle that included Dreiser, Anderson, Monroe, and Margaret ANDERSON.

Contact Avant-garde literary magazine founded in 1920 by Robert MCALMON, aided by William Carlos WILLIAMS, which led to McAlmon's Contact Editions publishing enterprise. *Contact* began in New York as a mimeographed magazine and relocated to Paris in 1921 following McAlmon's marriage to the English author Bryher. Four issues were published in 1920–21 and a fifth in 1923; contributors included Ezra Pound, Marianne Moore, H.D., Wallace Stevens, Kay Boyle, and Glenway Wescott. In 1922 McAlmon published his story collection *A Hasty Bunch*, and his contacts with fellow expatriate writers and a gift of money from his father-in-law soon led him to establish Contact Editions, which began publishing books in 1923. Over the years he issued such works as Williams's SPRING AND ALL, Ernest Hemingway's first book, Gertrude Stein's THE MAKING OF AMERICANS, and the *Contact Collection*

of Contemporary Writers, which included works by James Joyce and Ford Madox Ford. Nathanael West's *Dream Life of Balso Snell* (1931) was the last Contact book. Williams and West revived *Contact* magazine for three issues in 1932.

Crisis, The(: A Record of the Darker Races) Monthly magazine published by the National Association for the Advancement of Colored People (NAACP). It was founded in 1910 and, for its first 24 years, edited by W. E. B. DU BOIS. By the end of its first decade, it had achieved a monthly circulation of 100,000 copies. In its pages Du Bois displayed the evolution of his thought from his early, hopeful insistence on racial justice to his resigned call for black separatism. *The Crisis* was an important medium for the young black writers of the HARLEM RENAISSANCE, especially from 1919 to 1926, when Jessie Redmon FAUSET was its literary editor. The writers she discovered or encouraged included Arna BONTEMPS, Langston HUGHES, Countee CULLEN, and Jean TOOMER. After Fauset's departure *The Crisis* was unable to sustain its high literary standards, and literature has constituted only a small part of its content since the 1930s.

Dial, The Quarterly journal published between July 1840 and April 1844, associated with the TRANSCENDENTALISM movement. Edited first by Margaret FULLER and later by Ralph Waldo EMERSON, it printed poems and essays by Emerson, Fuller, Henry David THOREAU, and Bronson ALCOTT, among others. Though it often suffered from undeveloped material and a lack of consensus about its purpose, it was an important vehicle for Transcendental philosophy.

Dial, The Literary magazine founded in Chicago by Francis F. Browne and published from 1880 to 1929, from 1918 in New York City. Intended as a forum in which to carry on the tradition of the Transcendentalist journal of the same name, it became famous for introducing some of the best new writing and artwork of the early 20th century. In its heyday it published works by Thomas Mann, T. S. Eliot, Sherwood Anderson, D. H. Lawrence, Djuna Barnes, and E. E. Cummings, among others, as well as line drawings by Henri de Toulouse-Lautrec, Pablo Picasso, and Marc Chagall. The prestigious succession of its editors included Conrad AIKEN, Van Wyck BROOKS, Scofield Thayer, and Marianne MOORE.

Double Dealer, The Literary magazine (subtitled *A National Magazine from the South* from 1921) founded in New Orleans and published from January 1921 until May 1926. It was named after William Congreve's play of 1693. Supported by H. L. MENCKEN and Sherwood ANDERSON, it helped launch the careers of Hart Crane, Thornton Wilder, Jean Toomer, and Kenneth Fearing, and was the first journal to publish the fiction of Ernest Hemingway (May 1922) and the second to publish William Faulkner's verse (June 1922). Among its other writers were Robert Penn Warren, Edmund Wilson, Amy Lowell, John Crowe Ransom, Hilda Doolittle, Mary Austin, Ben Hecht, and Joseph Campbell.

Epoch Literary journal founded in 1947 by Baxter Hathaway at Cornell University. Its first issue contained works by E. E. Cummings and John Ciardi; subsequent issues have included writings by Ray Bradbury, Leslie Fiedler, Philip Roth, Anne Sexton, May Swenson, Richard Fariña, Hayden Carruth, Joyce Carol Oates, William Kennedy, David Ignatow, and Diane Ackerman. *Epoch* was the first journal in which the works of Thomas Pynchon and Don DeLillo appeared. Since 1956 it has published two or three times yearly. Most later issues have been devoted in large measure to special topics.

Esquire Monthly magazine, founded in 1933 by Arnold Gingrich. It began production as an oversized magazine for men, featuring drawings of scantily clad young women. It later abandoned titillation, cultivating an image of refined taste. In 1943 the postmaster general attempted to withdraw *Esquire*'s second-class mailing privileges (generally essential to a magazine's survival), claiming it did not make a "special contribution to the public welfare"; its publisher eventually prevailed in the U.S. Supreme Court. Publishing the work of such writers as Thomas Wolfe, Ernest Hemingway, William Faulkner, John Steinbeck, Truman Capote, and Norman Mailer, the magazine's risqué image gradually receded, and it came to fill a void between literary and opinion periodicals in the American market. Since the early 1970s it has ceased to be a significant literary venue.

Evergreen Review Literary magazine published from 1957 to 1973. It was founded and edited by Barney Rosset, founder of Grove Press, who developed the progressive periodical into a forum for radical expression of ideas on topics from sex to politics. It was known for publishing erotic—some said pornographic—material. Noteworthy contributors included Che Guevara, Vladimir Nabokov, Jack Kerouac, Allen Ginsberg, Samuel Beckett, Henry Miller, and E. E. Cummings.

Fire!! Magazine of the HARLEM RENAISSANCE of which only a single issue (November 1926) was published. The idea for an experimental, apolitical black literary journal was conceived in Washington, D.C., by Langston HUGHES and Richard Bruce NUGENT. With an editorial board comprising Zora Neale HURSTON, Gwendolyn BENNETT, John Davis, and Aaron Douglas, they selected Wallace Henry THURMAN as editor, and he solicited art, poetry, fiction, drama, and essays from such writers as Countee Cullen and Arna Bontemps. The magazine received minimal notice in the white press and provoked heated contention among black critics. Financial viability quickly proved unattainable, and several hundred undistributed copies met with an ironic fate when the building where they were stored burned to the ground.

Forverts *or* **Jewish Daily Forward** Yiddish-language newspaper founded in 1897 and published in New York City. It was established by Abraham CAHAN and the Jewish Socialist Press Federation as a civic aid and a unifying device for Jewish immigrants from Europe. Under Cahan's guidance from 1903 to 1951, the paper combined conventional news coverage with a commitment to democratic socialism and Jewish trade unionism. It carried socialist-oriented columns on government and politics and covered subjects intended to familiarize readers with American culture. It also published short stories and novels in serial form, most notably those of Isaac Bashevis SINGER and I. J. SINGER. At the height of its influence, *Forverts* had a daily circulation of 200,000 in several regional editions, but by the end of the 20th century it had seen a large reduction in its readership. In 1984 it changed from a daily to a weekly; from 1990 an English-language version, *Forward,* has also appeared.

Fugitive Any of a group of young poets and critics formed shortly after World War I at Vanderbilt University. From 1922 to 1925 the group, led by John Crowe RANSOM, published a bimonthly magazine, the *Fugitive*, edited by Allen TATE. Its other important members included Donald DAVIDSON, Robert Penn WARREN, and John Gould FLETCHER. Selections from the magazine were subsequently collected in the *Fugitive Anthology* (1928). Acutely aware of their Southern heritage, the Fugitives advocated a form of literary regionalism.

Many went on to become leaders in the Agrarian movement of the 1930s, which sought to resist the inroads of industrialism through a return to the agricultural economy of the Old South; their conservative views were published as the noted symposium *I'll Take My Stand: The South and the Agrarian Tradition* (1930).

Godey's Lady's Book Monthly magazine for women of the 19th century. Founded by Louis Antoine Godey in Philadelphia in 1830, it became an important arbiter of fashion and etiquette. It was edited by Godey himself until 1836, when he entrusted it to Sarah Josepha HALE. In the course of Hale's 40 years as editor (until 1877), it became the country's most popular women's magazine, and it distinguished itself by publishing works by such writers as R. W. Emerson, H. W. Longfellow, E. A. Poe, Nathaniel Hawthorne, and H. B. Stowe. In 1892 it was moved to New York City and renamed *Godey's Magazine*; it ceased publication in 1898.

Group Theatre Company of stage craftsmen founded in 1931 in New York City by Harold CLURMAN, Cheryl Crawford, and Lee Strasberg, to present American plays of social significance. The company embraced the Stanislavsky method and engaged such directors as Elia Kazan and Stella Adler. The characteristic Group production was a social-protest play with a leftist viewpoint. Its first trial production of Sergey Tretyakov's *Roar China* was followed by such plays as Paul GREEN's *House of Connelly* (1931) and John Howard LAWSON's *Success Story* (1932). Financial and artistic success came two years later with Sidney Kingsley's *Men in White*, which received a Pulitzer Prize. The famous 1935 production of WAITING FOR LEFTY, written by one of its actors, Clifford ODETS, used flashback techniques and "plants" in the audience. The Group also staged Odets's *Awake and Sing!*, *Till the Day I Die*, *Paradise Lost*, and GOLDEN BOY. Other productions included Paul Green's *Johnny Johnson*, Irwin Shaw's *Bury the Dead*, Robert Ardrey's *Thunder Rock*, and William Saroyan's *My Heart's in the Highlands*. It disbanded in 1941.

hard-boiled fiction Tough, unsentimental style of crime writing that brought a new tone of earthy realism or naturalism to the field of detective fiction. It is characterized by impersonal, matter-of-fact presentation of naturalistic or violent themes or incidents, by a generally unemotional or stoic tone, and often by a total absence of explicit or implied moral judgments. Hard-boiled fiction uses graphic sex and violence, vivid but often sordid urban backgrounds, and fast-paced, slangy dialogue. The genre was popularized by Dashiell HAMMETT, whose story "Fly Paper" appeared in the pulp magazine *Black Mask* in 1929. Combining his own experiences with the realistic influence of writers such as Ernest Hemingway and John Dos Passos, Hammett developed a distinctly American type of detective fiction that differed greatly from the more genteel English mystery story. His innovations were incorporated in James M. CAIN's hard-boiled melodramas *The Postman Always Rings Twice* (1934) and *Double Indemnity* (1936). Successors included Raymond CHANDLER's *The Big Sleep* (1939) and *Farewell, My Lovely* (1940) and Jim THOMPSON's *The Killer Inside Me* (1952) and *Pop. 1280* (1964). Other writers of the hard-boiled school included George Harmon Coxe, author of *Murder with Pictures* (1935) and *Eye Witness* (1950), and W. R. Burnett, who wrote *Little Caesar* (1929) and *The Asphalt Jungle* (1949). Hard-boiled fiction ultimately degenerated into the extreme sensationalism and undisguised sadism of the so-called "guts-gore-and-gals-school," as found in the works of Mickey SPILLANE, writer of such phenomenal best-sellers as *I, the Jury* (1947).

Harlem Renaissance *or* **New Negro Movement** Period of outstanding literary vigor and creativity centered in New York's black ghetto of Harlem in the 1920s. The Harlem Renaissance, which coincided with a similar renaissance in the visual arts and with the great creative and commercial growth of jazz, altered the character of literature created by many African-American writers, which moved from quaint dialect works and conventional imitations of white writers to sophisticated explorations of black life and culture that revealed and stimulated a new confidence and racial pride. One of its leading figures and chief interpreters was Alain LOCKE, who compiled the influential anthology *The New Negro* (1925). James Weldon JOHNSON, author of AUTOBIOGRAPHY OF AN EX-COLOURED MAN (1912) and GOD'S TROMBONES (1927), acted as mentor to many of the young black writers who formed the core of the Harlem group. The Jamaican immigrant Claude MCKAY produced the poetry collection *Harlem Shadows* (1922) and the best-selling HOME TO HARLEM (1928). Countee CULLEN helped bring Harlem poets to public notice through his anthology *Caroling Dusk*

(1927). Langston HUGHES published his first verse collection, *The Weary Blues,* in 1926 and his novel *Not Without Laughter* in 1930; he collaborated on the play *Mule Bone* (1931) with Zora Neale HURSTON. Wallace THURMAN and William Jourden Rapp collaborated on the popular play *Harlem* in 1929. Thurman's satirical novel *The Blacker the Berry* (1929) ridiculed elements of the movement. Arna BONTEMPS's novel *God Sends Sunday* (1931) is considered the final work of the Harlem Renaissance. The movement was accelerated by philanthropic grants and scholarships and was supported by such white writers as Carl VAN VECHTEN.

Harper's Magazine Monthly magazine published in New York City, one of the oldest and most prestigious literary and opinion journals in the United States. It was founded in 1850 as *Harper's New Monthly* by the printing and publishing firm of the Harper brothers (which in 1857 would found *Harper's Weekly*, and in 1867 *Harper's Bazaar*). The first American magazine to use woodcut illustrations extensively, it was a leader in publishing the writings of the most illustrious British and American authors, and by 1865 it had become the country's most successful periodical. In the late 1920s it changed its editorial format to that of a forum on public affairs, balanced with short stories. From the late 1960s, the magazine was threatened by economic problems; its certain closing in 1980 was averted by grants from the philanthropic MacArthur Foundation. Since 1976 *Harper's* has been edited almost continuously by Lewis Lapham.

Hartford wits *or* **Connecticut wits** Group of Federalist poets centered in Hartford, Conn., who collaborated to produce a considerable body of political satire just after the American Revolution. Employing burlesque verse modeled on Samuel Butler's *Hudibras* and Alexander Pope's *Dunciad*, the wits advocated a strong, conservative central government and attacked such proponents of democratic liberalism as Thomas Jefferson. The group's leaders, all graduates of Yale College, were John TRUMBULL, Timothy DWIGHT, and Joel BARLOW; Barlow later turned apostate and espoused Jeffersonian democracy. The works they produced were generally more notable for patriotic fervor than for literary excellence. Their most important effort was the satirical mock epic *The Anarchiad: A Poem on the Restoration of Chaos and Substantial Night* (1786–87), which attacked states slow to ratify the Constitution.

Home Journal Weekly magazine founded in 1846 by Nathaniel P. WILLIS and George P. Morris. It was one of the earliest general-circulation magazines in the United States. Intended for readers in high society, it represented an attempt to provide both society news and intellectual stimulation. In its early years it published works by such authors as Washington Irving, James Fenimore Cooper, and Edgar Allan Poe; among the transatlantic authors it introduced were Thomas de Quincey, Honoré de Balzac, Thomas Carlyle, and Victor Hugo. In 1901 its name was changed to *Town and Country*, and it became strongly focused on the lives of the wealthy.

Hound and Horn Quarterly magazine of the arts cofounded and edited by Lincoln KIRSTEIN, published from 1927 to 1934. Initially published at Harvard University, it became a widely inclusive American arts review by its third issue (1928), and it moved to New York City in 1930. Its philosophical perspective fluctuated dramatically, from humanism to Southern Agrarianism to Marxism, but it continued to publish works by leading poets, writers, and critics, including its staff editors R. P. BLACKMUR and Yvor WINTERS.

Imagism Movement of American and English poets whose verse was characterized by concrete language and figures of speech, modern subject matter, metrical freedom, and avoidance of romantic or mystical themes. It was a successor to the French Symbolist movement. Its credo, formulated about 1912 by Ezra POUND in conjunction with Hilda DOOLITTLE, Richard Aldington, and F. S. Flint, was inspired by the critical views of T. E. Hulme. The Imagists wrote succinct verse of dry clarity and hard outline in which an exact visual image made a total poetic statement. In 1914 Pound turned to Vorticism, and Amy LOWELL largely assumed spiritual leadership of the group. Others who wrote Imagist poetry were John Gould FLETCHER and Harriet MONROE, and Imagism influenced the poetry of D. H. Lawrence, Conrad Aiken, Wallace Stevens, Marianne Moore, and T. S. Eliot. Four anthologies—*Des Imagistes* (1914) and *Some Imagists* (1915, 1916, 1917)—and the magazines POETRY (from 1912) and the *Egoist* (from 1914) published the work of a dozen Imagist poets.

kayak Literary magazine founded in San Francisco in 1964 by the poet George Hitchcock as a forum for surrealist, Imagist, and political poems. It was known for its irreverence and its openness to experimentation, including found poems (verses made from other printed matter, such as flyers or discarded letters). The nature of poetry itself was addressed in a number of its poems and essays. Its headquarters moved to Santa Cruz in 1970; the last issue was produced in 1984. Regular contributors included W. S. Merwin, Wendell Berry, Robert Bly, James Tate, David Ignatow, Margaret Atwood, Raymond Carver, Carolyn Kizer, Charles Simic, and Sharon Olds.

Kenyon Review, The Intellectual serial founded in 1939 as a quarterly magazine of literary criticism by faculty members of Kenyon College. Under its founding editor, John Crowe RANSOM, it soon became one of the most influential magazines of its kind in the country. Until 1958 it was closely identified with the NEW CRITICISM. It attracted such poets as Allen Tate, Robert Penn Warren, Mark Van Doren, Marianne Moore, Stephen Spender, Wallace Stevens, John Berryman, and Dylan Thomas, and it published criticism by William Empson, Yvor Winters, I. A. Richards, and Cleanth Brooks. From 1960, under the editorship of Robie Macauley, it began to publish more fiction, though the emphasis remained on criticism. It ceased publication in 1970 but was revived in 1979. It currently appears three times a year.

Knickerbocker school Group of writers active in and around New York City during the first half of the 19th century. Taking its name from Diedrich Knickerbocker, putative author of Washington IRVING's satirical HISTORY OF NEW YORK (1809), the group sought to promote a genuinely American national culture and to establish New York as its literary center. Its most important members were Irving, James Kirke PAULDING, James Fenimore COOPER, and William Cullen BRYANT. The *Knickerbocker Magazine* (1833–65), a literary monthly edited by Lewis G. and Willis G. Clark, was the group's principal outlet.

Kulchur Review of contemporary arts, published from spring 1960 to winter 1965–66, and edited by Marc Schleifer and Lita Hornick. Named for Ezra POUND's brilliant but fragmentary *Guide to Kulchur*, the journal was important for its role as the representative of New York's avant-garde arts community. Unlike other avant-garde magazines of its time, *Kulchur* published criticism rather than fiction, on a broad range of subjects including poetry, painting and sculpture, experimental film and theater, dance, jazz and contemporary classical music, sex, and politics.

Ladies' Home Journal Monthly magazine, one of the oldest in the country and long the trendsetter among women's magazines. It was founded in 1883 as a women's supplement to the *Tribune and Farmer* (1879–85) of Cyrus H. K. Curtis. It began independent publication in 1884 with a pious and demure editorial posture and a sentimental literary diet. Under the highly innovative editorship of Edward W. BOK (from 1889 to 1919), it attracted such well-regarded writers as William Dean Howells, Mark Twain, Bret Harte, Rudyard Kipling, Hamlin Garland, Arthur Conan Doyle, and Sarah Orne Jewett.

Little Review, The Avant-garde literary magazine founded in Chicago by Margaret ANDERSON, published from 1914 to 1929, the most influential arts magazine of its time. Its contributors included T. S. Eliot, Wyndham Lewis, Gertrude Stein, W. C. Williams, Ezra Pound, and Wallace Stevens; it is best known for serializing James Joyce's *Ulysses*. Its first issue featured work by Vachel Lindsay and essays on feminism, Nietzsche, and psychoanalysis. Anderson's forthright support for anarchism and the abolition of private property (May 1914) cost her her few financial backers, but she and her coeditor, Jane Heap, moved to New York's Greenwich Village and continued publication. The serialization of *Ulysses* began in March 1918; over the next three years the U.S. Post Office burned the press runs of four issues for obscenity. Financially strapped and demoralized by the tepid response to *Ulysses*, Anderson and Heap switched from monthly to quarterly publication in 1921. In 1922 Anderson turned over the editorship to Heap, who in 1927 relocated the magazine (by now irregularly published) to Paris.

little theater Any of the theaters founded as part of an early-20th-century movement to free dramatic forms and methods of production from the limitations of large commercial theaters by establishing small experimental drama centers. The movement was inspired by the vital European theater of the late 19th century, including the revolutionary theories of the director Max Reinhardt, the designing concepts of Adolphe Appia and Edward Gordon Craig, and the staging experiments at Paris's Théâtre-Libre, Berlin's Freie Bühne, and the Moscow Art Theater. Community playhouses such as Boston's Toy Theatre, Chicago's Little Theatre, and New York's Little Theatre, all founded in 1912, were centers of experimental activity. Such theaters provided valuable early opportunities for such playwrights as Eugene

O'Neill, George S. Kaufman, Elmer Rice, Maxwell Anderson, and Robert E. Sherwood.

Living Newspaper Dramatizations of current events, social problems, and controversial issues, with suggestions for improvement. The technique was used for propaganda in the Soviet Union after the Revolution of 1917, and it became part of the Epic Theater tradition initiated by Erwin Piscator and Bertolt Brecht in Germany in the 1920s. In the United States it began in 1935 as part of the WPA FEDERAL THEATRE PROJECT. One of its major supporters was the dramatist Elmer RICE. Outstanding productions included three works by Arthur Arent: *1935,* about the justice system; *Triple-A Plowed Under*, about the Supreme Court's invalidation of the Agricultural Adjustment Administration; and *One-Third of a Nation*, about the plight of the poor. Its alleged communist leanings contributed to the decision to disband it in 1939.

Living Theatre, The Theatrical repertory company known for its innovative production of experimental drama, often on radical themes. It was formed in New York in 1947 by Julian Beck and Judith Malina. The group struggled during the 1950s, producing plays by Gertrude Stein, Luigi Pirandello, Alfred Jarry, T. S. Eliot, Jean Cocteau, August Strindberg, and others. Its first big success came with *The Connection* (1959), Jack GELBER's drama about drug addiction. Kenneth Brown's *The Brig* (1963) likewise caused a sensation. The troupe tangled with the government over their political views and failure to pay income taxes; Beck and Malina were jailed briefly, and their theater was closed. In 1964 the company took up "voluntary exile" in Europe. Influenced by Asian mysticism, Gestalt psychology, and the desire to abolish the distinction between art and life, it became more shocking and confrontational. It gained its greatest notoriety with such extraordinary productions as *Frankenstein* (1965) and *Paradise Now* (1968), which was intended to spark immediate revolution. In the 1970s the troupe performed specially written plays free of charge in such venues as steel mills and Brazilian slums.

local color Writing marked by the presentation of the features and peculiarities of a particular locality and its inhabitants. In its most characteristic form, it made its appearance just after the Civil War. The frontier novels of James Fenimore COOPER have been cited as precursors of the local-color story, as have the New York Dutch tales of Washington IRVING and the works of Augustus Baldwin LONGSTREET and Johnson J. HOOPER. Bret HARTE's THE LUCK OF ROARING CAMP, with its use of miners' dialect and its western setting, is an early local-color story. Numerous authors, including Mark Twain, Harriet Beecher Stowe, George W. Cable, Kate Chopin, O. Henry, and Zona Gale, first achieved success with vivid descriptions of their own localities.

Lost Generation In general, the post–World War I generation, but specifically a group of American writers who came of age during the war and established their literary reputations in the 1920s. The term stems from Gertrude Stein's remark to Ernest HEMINGWAY, "You are all a lost generation," which Hemingway used as an epigraph to *The Sun Also Rises* (1926). The generation was "lost" because its inherited values could no longer operate in the postwar world and because of its alienation from America, which seemed hopelessly provincial and emotionally barren. The term embraces Hemingway, F. Scott FITZGERALD, John DOS PASSOS, E. E. CUMMINGS, Archibald MACLEISH, and Hart CRANE, among others. The last representative works of the era were Fitzgerald's TENDER IS THE NIGHT (1934) and Dos Passos's *The Big Money* (1936).

Midwestern Regionalism Literary movement of the late 19th century characterized by the realistic depiction of Midwestern small-town and rural life. It represents an early stage in the development of American realistic writing. E. W. HOWE's *Story of a Country Town* (1883) and Joseph KIRKLAND's *Zury* (1887) and *The McVeys* (1888) foreshadowed the stories and novels of Hamlin GARLAND, the foremost representative of Midwestern Regionalism. Chicago was the focal point of Midwestern realist activity; Garland lived there briefly, as did Theodore DREISER, Edgar Lee MASTERS, and Sherwood ANDERSON.

muckrakers Group of writers identified with pre–World War I reform and exposé literature. The movement emerged from the yellow journalism of the 1890s and became associated with certain popular magazines, notably *McClure's Magazine*. President Theodore Roosevelt coined the term as a pejorative, in reference to the passage from John Bunyan's *Pilgrim's Progress* about the man with the muckrake who "could look no way but downwards," but it soon took on favorable connotations of social concern and exposure of injustice. The most prominent of the muckrakers were Ida M. TARBELL, Upton SINCLAIR, Lincoln STEFFENS, Samuel Hopkins ADAMS, and Ray Stannard BAKER.

New Criticism Type of literary criticism that developed after World War I. It focused intensively on the language, imagery, and emotional or intellectual tensions in literary works in an attempt to explain their total formal aesthetic organization. New Critics separated the work from the context of its creation and opposed bringing historical or biographical data to bear on interpretation. With regard to poetry, the New Critics set out to define and formalize the qualities of poetic thought and language, with special emphasis on the connotative and associative values of words and on the multiple functions of figurative language; for both poetry and prose they practiced analytic (or "close") reading. Seminal works in the tradition were I. A. Richards's *Principles of Literary Criticism* (1924), William Empson's *Seven Types of Ambiguity* (1930), R. P. BLACKMUR's *The Double Agent* (1935), and John Crowe RANSOM's *The New Criticism* (1941), which loosely organized the principles of this basically linguistic approach to literature. Other important figures associated with the movement include Robert Penn WARREN, Allen TATE, and Cleanth BROOKS.

New Humanism Critical movement (1910–30) based on the literary and social theories of the English Victorian poet and critic Matthew Arnold, who sought to recapture the moral quality of past civilizations. Reacting against the scientifically oriented philosophies of literary realism and naturalism, the New Humanists, who included Paul Elmer MORE, Irving BABBITT, Norman Foerster, and Robert Shafer, argued that human beings were unique among nature's creatures, that the essence of experience is fundamentally moral and ethical, and that the will, though subject to genetic laws and shaped by the environment, is essentially free. By the 1930s they were regarded as cultural elitists and social and aesthetic conservatives, and their influence became negligible.

New Yorker, The Weekly magazine famed for its varied literary fare and humor. Harold Ross founded it in 1925, initially relying heavily on contributions from his ALGONQUIN ROUND TABLE companions; he remained editor until his death in 1951. Initially it focused on New York's amusements and social and cultural life, but it gradually came to cover literature, current affairs, and other topics. Aimed at a sophisticated, liberal audience, it became renowned for its short fiction, essays, foreign reporting, and probing biographical "profiles," as well as for its cartoons and its detailed reviews of new works in all artistic fields. Famous contributors have included Robert Benchley, E. B. White, S. J. Perelman, Dorothy Parker, Ogden Nash, John O'Hara, Edmund Wilson, John Hersey, J. D. Salinger, Rebecca West, John Cheever, and John Updike. Its great cartoonists have included James Thurber, Charles Addams, and Rea Irvin, who created its trademark dandy with top hat and lorgnette. Ross was succeeded as editor by William Shawn (1952–87), under whom the magazine acquired an increasingly serious cast. In 1985 it was sold to Samuel I. Newhouse, Jr. Shawn was followed by Robert Gottlieb (1987–92), Tina Brown (1992–98), and David Remnick (from 1998).

New York Intellectuals Group of literary critics active from the late 1930s through the 1970s. The moniker was not coined until 1968, by Irving Howe in his essay of the same name. Characterized by their rejection of bourgeois culture, their adherence to democratic socialism, and their espousal of modernism in literature, they were famous for their book reviews and essays in such journals as the *Nation*, *Commentary*, and *Dissent*. Lionel Trilling, Philip Rahv, Alfred Kazin, Mary McCarthy, Clement Greenberg, Irving Kristol, and Dwight Macdonald were representative figures.

North American Review, The Magazine that became one of the country's leading literary journals of the 19th and 20th centuries. Founded in Boston in 1815 as the *North American Review and Miscellaneous Journal* (a title it kept until 1821), it followed the model of established English and Scottish literary journals. The work of Goethe and Schiller first became known to American readers in its pages. It later moved to New York City and became a national periodical, providing an impartial forum for the discussion of current public affairs. Noted for its outstanding writing on social and political issues, it featured work by Henry George, David Dudley Field, Wendell Phillips, Walt Whitman, William Gladstone, O. W. Holmes, Henry James, Joseph Conrad, and H. G. Wells. In 1935 it was sold to Joseph Hilton Smyth; it ceased publication in 1940. Resurrected in Iowa in 1964, it remains in print today.

Opportunity(: A Journal of Negro Life) Magazine associated with the HARLEM RENAISSANCE and published from 1923 to 1949. The editor, Charles S. JOHNSON, aimed to give voice to black culture, hitherto neglected by mainstream publishing. He sponsored three literary contests to encourage young writers to submit their work; the 1925 winners included Zora Neale Hurston,

Langston Hughes, and Countee Cullen. *Ebony and Topaz, A Collectanea* (1927) was an anthology of the best works published in the magazine to that date.

Origin(: A Quarterly for the Creative) Literary magazine largely devoted to poetry, edited and published by the poet Cid Corman as a 64-page quarterly in several intermittent series. The first series (1951–57) included works by Wallace Stevens and William Carlos Williams, but its primary focus was on such younger poets as Denise Levertov, Robert Duncan, Robert Creeley, and Charles Olson. Its second series (1961–64) included works by Louis Zukofsky, Gary Snyder, and Michael McClure; its third series (1966–71) published Douglas Woolf's short novel *John-Juan*. It also published translations of troubadour poetry, Chinese and Japanese poetry, and 20th-century European and Latin American poetry. *The Gist of Origin* (1975) contains selected works from the magazine.

Others(: A Magazine of New Verse) Literary magazine founded by Alfred Kreymborg and published monthly from 1915 to 1919. Created in response to the conservatism of POETRY, *Others* featured experimental works. Despite hostility from the mainstream press, it generated three anthologies and a short-lived theater troupe. Its issues were devoted to such themes as women writers, Chicago writers, and Latin American writers. Contributors included T. S. Eliot, Mina Loy, Amy Lowell, Wallace Stevens, Marianne Moore, Ezra Pound, Hilda Doolittle, Carl Sandburg, Conrad Aiken, and Sherwood Anderson.

Overland Monthly Literary magazine published in San Francisco from 1868 to 1875 and from 1883 to 1935. Its first editor (1868–70) was Bret HARTE, who was attempting to establish Western literature as a legitimate genre; Harte's THE LUCK OF ROARING CAMP and THE OUTCASTS OF POKER FLAT first appeared in its pages and solidified his reputation. It also published the early work of Ambrose Bierce, Mark Twain, and Jack London. By 1912 its circulation had reached 75,000.

Partisan Review Literary review founded by William Phillips and Philip RAHV in 1933 as a vehicle for the communist John Reed Club. It was published irregularly from 1934 to 1962 and quarterly thereafter. During its first years it sought to champion intellectual and political freedom and solicited contributions from revolutionary writers. Its radicalism later moderated, and it became more oriented toward literature and art criti-

cism. Contributors have included W. H. Auden, Saul Bellow, Robert Lowell, Mary McCarthy, and Susan Sontag.

Poetry(: A Magazine of Verse) Poetry magazine founded in Chicago in 1912 by Harriet MONROE, who also served for many years as its editor. Because its inception coincided with the Midwestern cultural ferment later known as the CHICAGO LITERARY RENAISSANCE, it is often thought of particularly as the vehicle for the raw, original, local-color poetry of Carl Sandburg, Edgar Lee Masters, Vachel Lindsay, and Sherwood Anderson, but it also championed new formalistic movements in verse. Its early literary eminence owed much to Ezra POUND, its European correspondent. Imagism, impressionism, and vers libre were expounded in its pages. It published T. S. Eliot's LOVE SONG OF J. ALFRED PRUFROCK (1915), as well as experimental poems by Wallace Stevens, Marianne Moore, D. H. Lawrence, and William Carlos Williams. It remains one of the most prestigious publishing venues for poets.

Prairie Schooner Quarterly literary magazine founded in 1927 by Lowry Charles Wimberly and associated with the University of Nebraska. At first it published only literature and criticism relevant to the Midwest, but it later adopted a broader perspective, publishing authors such as Randall Jarrell, Robert Penn Warren, and Tillie Olsen. It was responsible for establishing Willa Cather's reputation. Renowned for its short fiction and poetry, it remains in print today.

Provincetown Players Theatrical organization that began performing in 1915 in Provincetown, Mass. It was founded by a nontheatrical group of writers and artists whose common aim was the production of new and experimental plays. Its chief founders were George Cram COOK and Susan GLASPELL; other original members included Mary Heaton Vorse, Hutchins Hapgood, Wilbur Steele, and Robert Edmond Jones. The group, which took up residence in New York City's Greenwich Village in 1916, is best known for providing the venue for the early works of Eugene O'NEILL; other dramatists discovered and produced by the group include Floyd DELL, Edna St. Vincent MILLAY, Paul GREEN, and Djuna BARNES. It flourished as a noncommercial theater until its demise in 1929.

Salmagundi(; or, The Whim-Whams and Opinions of Launcelot Langstaff, Esq., and Others) Popular pamphlets containing humorous and satiric essays and poems, published 1807–8 and 1819–20. The original publishers—William Irving, James Kirke PAUL-DING, and Washington IRVING—wrote under such pseudonyms as Anthony Evergreen, Jeremy Cockloft the Younger, Will Wizard, Pindar Cockloft, Esq., and Mustapha Rub-a-Dub Keli Khan (putatively a Tripolitan prisoner of war observing American society from his New York cell). The pamphlets consisted of light verse, droll commentary, and caricatures of New York tastemakers and society, along with essays on politics, public mores, women's fashions, music, and theater. The best of the American satirical magazines published to its time, it was an immediate success. Paulding published the second series by himself, but without the heterogeneous mixture that constitutes an authentic salmagundi it was unsuccessful.

Saturday Club Social club of New England literati. It was founded in 1855 and met monthly at the Parker House, a Boston hotel. Notable members included O. W. HOLMES, R. W. EMERSON, H. W. LONGFELLOW, J. R. LOWELL, R. H. DANA, J. G. WHITTIER, W. D. HOWELLS, Nathaniel HAWTHORNE, and Henry JAMES. It was also sometimes called the Magazine Club or the Atlantic Club.

Saturday Review, The Literary periodical founded in New York in 1924 as the *Saturday Review of Literature* (until 1952). Its founder, Henry Seidel Canby, served as its editor until 1936. It was originally devoted to the work of new writers, including many foreign writers in translation, as well as to that of earlier writers such as Whitman and Emerson. Its early contributors included Mary Austin, Edgar Lee Masters, and G. K. Chesterton. Its scope expanded under Norman COUSINS, its editor for 30 years (1942–72). It ceased publication in 1986.

Sewanee Review, The Quarterly periodical of general culture with an emphasis on literature, founded at the University of the South in 1892. In the early 1940s, under the editorship of Andrew Lytle and Allen TATE, it began publishing fiction and increased its emphasis on criticism, becoming particularly associated with the NEW CRITICISM, though it published other views as well. Contributors have included Cleanth Brooks, T. S. Eliot, Robert Lowell, Wallace Stevens, Katherine Anne Porter, Robert Penn Warren, Malcolm Cowley, W. H. Auden, Dylan Thomas, and Louise Bogan. Since 1973 it has been edited by George Core.

Smart Set, The Literary magazine founded by William D'Alton Mann and published monthly in New York City, 1900–30. Most notable among its editors were S. S. VAN DINE and the team of H. L. MENCKEN and George Jean NATHAN. A consciously fashionable magazine that featured novellas, short stories in English and French, essays, poems, plays, criticism, and humorous sketches, it published the early works of O. Henry, Eugene O'Neill, and F. Scott Fitzgerald, and introduced the nation to the writings of Gabriele D'Annunzio, Ford Madox Ford, James Joyce, and D. H. Lawrence. Other notable contributors included Frank Norris, Theodore Dreiser, Willa Cather, Ezra Pound, Sherwood Anderson, Sinclair Lewis, James Branch Cabell, and W. Somerset Maugham.

Southern Gothic Style of writing practiced by many 20th-century Southern writers, characterized by grotesque, macabre, or fantastic incidents, generally in a Southern setting. William FAULKNER, Tennessee WILLIAMS, Truman CAPOTE, Carson MCCULLERS, Flannery O'CONNOR, and James PURDY are among the best-known Southern Gothic writers.

Theatre Guild Theatrical society founded in New York City in 1918 by Lawrence Langner for the production of high-quality, noncommercial plays. It departed from the usual theater practice in that its board of directors shared the responsibility for choice of plays, management, and production. Following the world premiere of G. B. Shaw's *Heartbreak House* (1920), it became Shaw's American agent, producing 15 of his plays, including the premieres of *Back to Methuselah* and *Saint Joan*. Eugene O'NEILL's long association with the guild began with its production of *Marco Millions* in 1928. It also produced works by Sidney Coe Howard, William Saroyan, Maxwell Anderson, and Robert E. Sherwood—all Pulitzer Prize winners. It produced George Gershwin and DuBose Heyward's *Porgy and Bess* and first brought together the team of Richard Rodgers and Oscar Hammerstein II for the musical *Oklahoma!* The "Theatre Guild of the Air" (1945–63) successfully produced plays for radio and television.

Transcendentalism Movement of writers and philosophers in 19th-century New England, centered in Boston and Concord, Mass. It was characterized by an idealistic system of thought based on a belief in the essential unity of all creation, the innate goodness of humankind, and the supremacy of insight over logic and experience for the revelation of the deepest truths.

Transcendentalist literature represented the first flowering of the American artistic genius and was central to the AMERICAN RENAISSANCE. The movement drew on German transcendentalism, especially as interpreted by Samuel Taylor Coleridge and Thomas Carlyle; other influences were Platonism and Neoplatonism, Indian and Chinese religious writings, and the works of such mystics as Jakob Böhme and Emanuel Swedenborg. It attracted such diverse and highly individualistic figures as Ralph Waldo EMERSON, Henry David THOREAU, Margaret FULLER, Orestes BROWNSON, Elizabeth PEABODY, George RIPLEY, Bronson ALCOTT, Jones VERY, James Freeman Clarke, Ellery Channing, and W. H. Channing. THE DIAL published some of the best writings by minor Transcendentalists.

western Genre of fiction, motion pictures, and television and radio shows, set in the American West, usually in the period from the 1850s to 1900. Though basically an American creation, the western has its counterparts in the gaucho literature of Argentina and even in tales of the settlement of the Australian outback. The conflict between white pioneers and Indians and between cattle ranchers and fence-building farmers form two basic themes. Cowboys, the town sheriff, and the U.S. marshal are staple figures. Actual historical figures such as Wild Bill Hickok, Wyatt Earp, Billy the Kid, Jesse James, Sitting Bull, and Geronimo have figured prominently. Historically, the western had its beginnings in the first adventure narratives, accounts of the western plainsmen, scouts, buffalo hunters, and trappers. Perhaps the earliest and finest work in the genre was James Fenimore COOPER's *The Prairie* (1827). E. Z. C. JUDSON (Ned Buntline) wrote hundreds of western novels and was responsible for transforming Buffalo Bill into an archetype. Owen WISTER wrote the first true western that won critical praise, THE VIRGINIAN (1902). Other western classics are Walter van Tilburg CLARK's THE OX-BOW INCIDENT (1940), A. B. GUTHRIE's *The Big Sky* (1947) and *The Way West* (1949), and Larry MCMURTRY's *Lonesome Dove* (1985).By far the best-known and one of the most prolific writers of westerns was Zane GREY, an Ohio dentist who became famous with the classic *Riders of the Purple Sage* (1912). Frederick Faust (writing principally as Max BRAND) wrote dozens of formulaic westerns, and Louis L'AMOUR enjoyed great success with scores of best-sellers. Authors of finer works in the genre include A. H. Lewis, Stephen CRANE, and Conrad

RICHTER. Many western novels and short stories first appeared in pulp magazines, such as *Ace-High Western Stories* and *Double Action Western*.

WPA Federal Theatre Project National theater project funded by the U.S. government as part of the Works Progress Administration (WPA). Its purpose was to create jobs for unemployed theatrical people in the Great Depression years of 1935–39. Overseen by Hallie Flanagan, it employed some 10,000 professionals in all facets of the theater and mounted some 1,000 productions in 40 states, many free to the public. Its productions included classical and modern drama, children's plays, puppet shows, musicals, and the documentary theater known as LIVING NEWSPAPER. It produced plays by young and unknown playwrights, promoted black theater, and made radio broadcasts of dramatic works. Participants included John Houseman, Elmer RICE, and Orson Welles. Its productions included Sinclair LEWIS's *It Can't Happen Here* (1936) and the *Swing Mikado* (1938); Welles directed a notorious "Voodoo" *Macbeth* (1936) and *The Cradle Will Rock* (1937). It was terminated by congressional action following a series of controversial investigations by the House Committee on Un-American Activities and Subcommittee on Appropriations into its leftist leanings.

WPA Federal Writers' Project Project established in 1935 by the Works Progress Administration (WPA) to provided jobs for unemployed writers, editors, and research workers. Directed by Henry G. Alsberg, it operated in all states and at its height employed 6,600 individuals. The American Guide series, its most important achievement, included remarkable historical guidebooks to every state and territory (except Hawaii), as well as to several major cities, highways, and scores of towns, villages, and counties. The project also produced ethnic studies, folklore collections, local histories, and nature studies for a total of more than 1,000 books and pamphlets. The project's personnel came from the relief rolls and included such already prominent authors as Conrad AIKEN, Max BODENHEIM, and Claude MCKAY and such future luminaries as Richard WRIGHT, Ralph ELLISON, Nelson ALGREN, Frank YERBY, Saul BELLOW, Loren EISELEY, and Weldon Kees. Congress ended federal sponsorship in 1939 but allowed it to continue under state sponsorship until 1943.

Yale school Group of English professors at Yale University who became known in the 1970s and '80s for their deconstructionist theories. Its skeptical, relativistic brand of deconstruction expanded on the groundwork laid by Jacques Derrida and helped popularize deconstructionism. Paul de Man and J. Hillis MILLER, the school's most prominent members, contributed essays to the collection *Deconstructionism and Criticism* (1979), which analyzed Shelley's poem *The Triumph of Life*. De Man's theories involve a system of rhetorical figures; Miller focuses on textual opposites and difference. Other prominent American deconstructionists include Barbara Johnson and Jonathan Culler. Geoffrey H. HARTMAN and Harold BLOOM are Yale faculty who have frequently criticized the group's theories.